THE COLONIAL POLICY

OF

LORD JOHN RUSSELL'S ADMINISTRATION

TWO VOLUMES IN ONE

THE

COLONIAL POLICY

OF

LORD JOHN RUSSELL'S ADMINISTRATION

BY

EARL GREY

TWO VOLUMES IN ONE

[1853]

Augustus M. Kelley · Publishers

NEW YORK 1970

First Edition 1853

(London: Richard Bentley, *New Burlington Street*,
1853)

Reprinted 1970 by
AUGUSTUS M. KELLEY · PUBLISHERS
REPRINTS OF ECONOMIC CLASSICS
New York   New York   10001

.   .   .   .

I S B N   0 678 00660 1
L C N   79 118121

.   .   .   .

PRINTED IN THE UNITED STATES OF AMERICA
by SENTRY PRESS, NEW YORK, N. Y. 10019

COLONIAL POLICY.

VOL. I.

THE

COLONIAL POLICY

OF

LORD JOHN RUSSELL'S ADMINISTRATION.

BY EARL GREY.

IN TWO VOLUMES.

VOL. I.

LONDON:

RICHARD BENTLEY, NEW BURLINGTON STREET,

Publisher in Ordinary to Her Majesty.

1853.

PREFACE.

—◆—

It is the object of the following Letters to give
some account of the Colonial Policy of the Administration in which I held the office of Secretary
of State for the Colonial Department. I have not
attempted more than a very slight sketch of the
transactions to which these pages relate, yet much
more time and labour have been occupied in writing them than I anticipated when they were begun,
chiefly, from my having found it necessary to examine minutely the voluminous papers laid before
Parliament, from which the materials have been
principally drawn. The completion of the task which
I ventured to undertake has also been delayed by
various interruptions from other avocations, so that

these pages will be published some months later
than they were intended to appear.

I am sensible that this must somewhat detract
from any value they may possess; for the progress
of events is so rapid in the times in which we live,
that even the delay of a few months has made more
than one material change in the aspect of affairs,
and my remarks will consequently be found in
these cases to have reference to a state of things
which has since been altered. Instead of attempting to correct what I had written, so as to make
it correspond with more recent information, I have
thought it better to affix to each of these Letters
the date at which it was finished, and in reading
them I would request that these dates may be
borne in mind.

I have spoken of the Colonial Policy described
in the following Letters as that of the Administration of which I was a member, because I conceive
it to have been so both constitutionally and in
fact; but I am far from desiring by this to
diminish my own responsibility. Though the Secretary of State entrusted with the Department of
the Colonies receives much assistance from his Colleagues, and though the most important measures
which it is his duty to carry into effect ought to

be decided upon with their advice and concurrence, still the main responsibility for all errors that are committed properly rests with him.

Nor does any portion of this responsibility fall upon those by whose assistance the business of the Department is conducted. It has often been asserted that there is some mysterious influence within the walls of the Colonial Office, which under every different Secretary of State prevents what is right from being done, and causes disappointment and discontent to the Colonists, and persons connected with the Colonies, who have business to transact with the Department. Nothing can be more unfounded than such a notion. Those who have observed with attention the administration of Colonial affairs for the last five-and-twenty years will, I am persuaded, agree with me in thinking that it is much more justly chargeable with want of steadiness and consistency, from the inevitable differences in the views of successive Secretaries of State, than with an obstinate adherence under them all, to the same erroneous system. No doubt there are many demands urgently pressed upon the Department which have been successively rejected by different Secretaries of State; but this only shows that these demands are so unreasonable that

they are alike rejected by men of the most opposite political views, when they are required to decide
upon them with full information and with official
responsibility.

I am glad to have this opportunity of saying,
that while I shall always feel most deeply indebted
to the gentlemen holding permanent situations in
the Colonial Office, for the exceedingly able and
willing assistance I received from them in conducting its business while I presided over it, I
can assert, in the most positive manner, that never
upon any occasion was there on their part the
slightest attempt improperly to influence my decision upon questions brought before me, or to
withhold the best aid they could afford, in the execution of measures which may have been decided
upon contrary to their opinion. Having mentioned
the permanent members of the Colonial Office, I
cannot deny myself the satisfaction of expressing
my regard and esteem for those who were my Parliamentary Under-Secretaries. I should indeed be
most ungrateful if I could ever forget how much I
owe to Mr. Hawes for his unwearied assiduity, and
the friendly zeal with which he shared with me, not
only the ordinary labours of the Department, but
the cares and anxieties of five most toilsome and

harassing Sessions of Parliament, during which I consulted him unreservedly upon every question that arose, and derived the greatest benefit from his advice and assistance. With Mr. Peel my official connection was very much shorter, having lasted only about four months; but this was quite long enough for me to form a very high opinion of his abilities, and to feel much indebted to him for the anxiety he displayed to give his best assistance in conducting the business of the Department, and in preparing to meet the anticipated difficulties of the Parliamentary campaign, which was so speedily cut short by the breaking up of the Administration.

I have nothing further to add in the way of Preface, except to call attention to what I have said in the concluding Letter of the series, as to the information I have thought it right to make use of. If I had felt justified in availing myself of information of a more confidential character, it would not have been difficult to make my account of some of the transactions referred to more complete than it is, and probably more interesting to the reader. It was however obviously my duty to abstain from disclosing information not already public, of which I had come into possession in the discharge of my duties as a Servant of the Crown;

and I trust that whatever may be the other faults of these Letters (and I am painfully sensible that they have many), they are at least free from that which would justly have been regarded as an unpardonable one—a departure from the reserve imposed upon me by the office I had the honour to fill.

DECEMBER 28, 1852.

CONTENTS.

VOLUME I

APPENDIX.

CONTENTS.

VOLUME II

CONTENTS.

APPENDIX.

THE COLONIAL POLICY

OF

LORD JOHN RUSSELL'S ADMINISTRATION.

———◆———

LETTER I.

COLONIAL POLICY.—PRELIMINARY REMARKS.—EFFECT
OF FREE TRADE ON THE COLONIES.

MY DEAR LORD JOHN,

The affairs of the Colonies have of late years been
very largely discussed. The books, the pamphlets,
and the speeches of which they have been the subject,
have been almost innumerable; but of these even the
few to which I should be the last to deny the praise
of ability and fairness, advocate views which seem to me
either incorrect or incomplete; while, as the rest have
for the most part been designed to serve party or personal objects, they have been little calculated to assist
the Public in forming a sound opinion on the questions
to which they relate. No small proportion of what
has been spoken or written about the Colonies for
the last few years, has had for its aim to decry and to
misrepresent the policy pursued towards them by the

Administration of which you were at the head; and as so large a share of the responsibility for the measures of that Government devolves upon myself, it is natural that I should wish the Public to have the means of knowing the real character and scope of those measures, and the grounds upon which they were adopted. Nor is this unimportant on grounds far higher than what concerns any individual : the national interest is deeply involved in having the course of Colonial administration correctly understood. In Parliament, or at least in the House of Lords, the debates which have taken place on Colonial affairs have been entirely confined to particular questions, affecting individual Colonies, and have never afforded me an opportunity of stating my views as to our general system of Colonial Policy, which, to be properly understood, requires to be considered as a whole; perhaps, also, the subject is too extensive for Parliamentary discussion. I propose therefore to endeavour in these pages to supply a deficiency which I conceive to exist, by laying before the Public a connected view of the Colonial policy which was pursued while I was entrusted with the task of conducting it, as a member of your Administration.

It has appeared to me that I shall be able to do this most conveniently in the form of a series of Letters, which I address to you, because you were acquainted, while they were in progress, with the transactions to which I shall have to advert, and will therefore be able to judge of the accuracy of my statements.

You cannot but take an interest in the subject, since all the most important of the measures of which I shall have to speak were, of course, adopted with your knowledge and assent; and I am happy to think that there has never been the slightest difference of opinion between us, as to the principles which ought to form the guide of our policy.

It is my intention to avoid, as far as possible, any notice of the various attacks made upon our measures, and of the misrepresentations to which we have been exposed. I shall do so, because it is my wish to give to these Letters a tone as little controversial as is consistent with the object I have in view, and also because the objections which have been made to our policy have been so multifarious and so contradictory, that an attempt to answer them all would be intolerably tedious. Hence, without adverting to the various speeches and pamphlets by which our Colonial administration has been assailed, I shall endeavour to give a general sketch of our policy, of the views on which it was founded, and of its results; leaving it to those who take an interest in the subject to draw their own conclusions, and noticing objections which have been made to our policy only when necessary for its elucidation. I fear that, even adopting this plan, it will be difficult to compress within a moderate compass a statement, however succinct, of what has been done in the numerous Colonies of the British Empire, with an explanation of the grounds on which we have acted; and that much which is not unimportant will

have to be omitted.   The ample information laid before Parliament, to which I shall take care to refer,
will however enable those who desire it, to obtain a
more perfect knowledge of the transactions to which
I shall advert.

Before I proceed to give an account of what has been
done in particular Colonies, it will be convenient that
I should state, somewhat fully, the general principles
which have in all cases been the guide of our policy,
and that I should call your attention to the manner in
which the peculiar circumstances of the times have affected the administration of Colonial affairs.   To begin
with the last, I have to remark that in these affairs
much of the opposition we have met with, and the
principal difficulties we have encountered, have arisen,
directly or indirectly, from our having thought it our
duty to maintain the policy of free trade, and to extend
its application to the produce of the Colonies.   That
these difficulties must be expected from this policy I
was quite aware when your Government was formed ;
but the greatest service that I believed we were called
upon as a Government to render to the country was
that of completing the work, which had been happily
begun, of removing restrictions from industry, and
securely establishing a system of free trade throughout the empire.   So far back as when I first entered
upon public life,—now more than twenty-five years
ago,—it was my conviction that, next to the removal
of the religious disabilities which then threatened the
disruption of the Empire, and to the accomplishment

of such a reform of the House of Commons as was requisite to make it a fitting instrument for effecting every other public improvement, the political object of the greatest importance to the public good was to relieve industry and commerce from the shackles with which they had been encumbered by measures adopted for their advancement under the erroneous theory of " Protection." Hence, beginning with the year 1827, when I voted with a very small minority against the principle of the sliding scale, in the Bill for the amendment of the Corn Laws brought forward by Mr. Canning, I had, both by votes and speeches, supported every proposal submitted to the House of Parliament of which I was a Member, which I considered to be calculated to advance the object of giving greater freedom to industry. I believed that the Colonial trade ought to form no exception to the general rule, but should be placed on the same footing as other branches of our commerce. I considered it to be no less for the real and permanent interest of the Colonies themselves, than for that of the Mother-country, that industry should cease to be diverted from its natural channels, and a useless burden to be imposed on the consumer by differential duties, levied for the purpose of favouring Colonial produce in our markets, and our produce in the markets of the Colonies.

Entertaining these opinions, I should not have accepted your proposal to form part of your Administration, if I had not felt satisfied that its measures would

be directed to the completion of the work of commercial reform, and had I not expected that, notwithstanding the difficulties I anticipated, we should be
supported in this policy by Parliament.

In that expectation I have not been disappointed.
By the measures which we have succeeded in carrying, for the alteration of the duties on sugar, coffee,
and timber, for the repeal of the Navigation Laws,
and for giving power to the local Legislatures to
abolish differential duties in the Colonies, provision
has been made for placing the Colonial trade on a
footing free from serious objection; while the accomplishment, at no very distant period, of the further
improvements it still requires has obviously been
ensured.

These measures, necessary and beneficial as I am
convinced they will ultimately be admitted to have
been, amounted however to nothing less than a revolution in an established system of policy, which could
not fail to shock many long received opinions, and to
bring about a great change in the relations hitherto
subsisting between this country and the Colonies.
For more than two centuries, the great object of
all European nations, in seeking to obtain possession
of Colonies, was the gain supposed to accrue from
the monopoly of their commerce, which it was the
practice for the parent State to maintain, while, on
the other hand, it gave to their produce a preference
in its own markets. This policy began to be relaxed
by Parliament immediately after the American Revo-

lution (of which calamity it was, in truth, the chief cause); but, although the views on which it is founded had been considerably modified, the principle of placing the trade with the Colonies on a different footing from that with other countries had been maintained up to the year 1846, and was generally regarded as one of unquestionable propriety and wisdom. So much was this the case, that in the beginning of Sir Robert Peel's commercial reforms, the tariff of 1842, as originally submitted to the House of Commons, contained provisions by which various new protected interests would have been created in the Colonies, and a large revenue would have been sacrificed by the Mother-country, without any real benefit accruing to them. Amongst other articles proposed to be dealt with were tea and tobacco, on which it was intended to reduce one half the amount of duty to which they would otherwise be liable when they were the produce of British possessions. It so happens that I was myself the person by whom the attention of the House of Commons (of which I was then a Member) was called to the inexpediency of this mode of dealing with the customs-duties; and I moved a resolution against the establishment of any new protecting duties in favour of Colonial produce*, arguing that, in order to derive a revenue from duties on imports without imposing an undue burden on the consumer, and without diverting ‚industry from its natural and therefore most productive channels, duties

* See Hansard, 3rd series, vol. lxxiii. p. 512.

ought not to be levied on the importation of any articles which would meet in our market articles of the same kind produced in the Colonies, and not subject to an equal amount of taxation.

This principle, which is equally applicable to articles produced at home and to those obtained from the Colonies,* is now recognized as sound by the

---

* It is obvious that, if any article of consumption is subject to a duty when imported from a foreign country, and is either free from duty or pays a lower duty when produced at home or imported from a Colony, the result, whether intended or not, is to give that artificial encouragement to a particular branch of industry which is known by the name of Protection. For this reason, by our present law, beet-root sugar produced at home is subject to an excise-duty equal to that on sugar imported from the Colonies, and which in two years more will also be charged on foreign sugar. Hence, it was a fallacy to contend, as was done in 1842 and in 1843, (if I remember right, the argument, which had much effect at the time, was first used by Mr. Gladstone,) that imports from the Colonies ought to be relieved from duty because they should be considered as "an integral part of the Empire." Though an integral part of the Empire, it is, from the nature of things, impossible that they should be under the same fiscal system as ourselves ; and unless they could be so—that is, unless they paid all the same taxes that we do, and these taxes included excise-duties on all articles on which we raise a revenue, and which they produce—no special exemption from duty could be given to Colonial produce in our ports without incurring all the objectionable consequences of a system of protection. In the United States, free commercial intercourse between the several States of the Union would have led to the utmost confusion, if the power of levying customs-duties had not been given exclusively to Congress, excise-duties not being made use of as a mode of raising revenue. It does not appear to me at all inconsistent with the idea of the unity of the British Empire, that no attempt has been made to unite its several members, divided as they are from each other by the diameter of the globe, in one fiscal system.

majority of intelligent and educated men; but this was far from being the case until very recently, and it was so much otherwise at the time of which I am speaking, that, although in the resolution I moved I abstained from proposing to abolish existing protecting duties in favour of the Colonies, and only sought to lay down the rule that no new ones should be created, the motion was rejected, obtaining the support of a minority far below the usual strength of the Opposition; and in the tariff of 1842 the erroneous principle I had endeavoured to condemn was adhered to, the Government only abandoning its application in those cases in which it would have seriously affected the revenue. I refer to this circumstance, because it shows how strong was the hold on men's minds of the old opinions respecting the Colonial trade, and how great was the shock given to these opinions, when the policy of placing our trade with the Colonies on the same footing as that with foreign countries was first systematically adopted in Sir Robert Peel's Act for the repeal of the former Corn Law, and in the measures which followed it. This accounts for the great bitterness of the political discontent and opposition to your Government excited by these measures. It is notorious that distress is usually the parent of political discontent, even when that distress cannot be referred by the sufferers themselves to the conduct of the Government; much more so, when they believe their difficulties to have been occasioned by its measures. But the abandonment of long established commercial and fiscal regulations, however vicious in policy, generally occasions temporary loss and inconvenience to those engaged in the branches of trade and industry affected by such changes; and if they do not occasion actual loss, these changes invariably excite the apprehension of it, which is nearly as bad. Hence reforms of this description are always found to create many enemies to the Government by which they are accomplished; and in the application of the principles of free trade to Colonial produce, the hostility thus excited was aggravated by its being thought, however unreasonably, that these measures involved an act of injustice, as invading what had long been regarded as a right on the part of the Colonists.

Nor is this all; the abandonment of the ancient commercial system of this country towards the Colonies brought a still larger question under discussion. Not only those who still adhered to the opinion that the former policy with respect to colonial commerce was the right one, but many of the most eager advocates of the principles of free trade, concurred in arguing that, if the Colonies were no longer to be regarded as valuable on account of the commercial advantages to be derived from their possession, the country had no interest in keeping these dependencies, and that it would be better to abandon them; thus getting rid of the heavy charge on the country, especially in providing the requisite amount of naval and military force for their protection. In like manner, the Colonists began to inquire whether, if they were no longer to enjoy their former commercial privileges in the markets of the Mother-country, they derived any real benefit from a continuance of the connection. It is obvious that questions of this kind could not be raised without creating great difficulties in the administration of Colonial affairs, and the more so, because it is impossible to deny that the view of the subject to which I have adverted is at least plausible ; and when the old doctrine, that the great value of Colonies arises from the commercial monopoly which the Mother-country can claim with respect to their trade is abandoned, some other explanation may fairly be asked of the grounds on which we should nevertheless continue to support the charges inseparable from the maintenance of our Colonial empire.

Although it would be impossible, within the limits to which I must confine myself, fully to discuss in this Letter so large a subject, it is requisite, for the clearness of what is to follow, that I should state generally why, and on what terms, I think that the connection between this country and the Colonies ought to be preserved, and also that I should explain how these views have been applied in practice. I consider, then, that the British Colonial Empire ought to be maintained, principally because I do not consider that the Nation would be justified in throwing off the responsibility it has incurred by the acquisition of this dominion, and because I believe that much of the power and influence of this Country depends upon its having large Colonial possessions in different parts of the world.

The possession of a number of steady and faithful allies, in various quarters of the globe, will surely be admitted to add greatly to the strength of any nation ; while no alliance between independent states can be so close and intimate as the connection which unites the Colonies to the United Kingdom as parts of the Great British Empire. Nor ought it to be forgotten, that the power of a nation does not depend merely on the amount of physical force it can command, but rests, in no small degree, upon opinion and moral influence : in this respect British power would be diminished by the loss of our Colonies, to a degree which it would be difficult to estimate. Hence, if it is an advantage, not for the sake of domineering over other countries but with a view to our own security, to form part of a powerful nation rather than of a weak one (and, considering the many examples we have seen of the injustice to which weak ones are compelled to submit, this can hardly admit of a question), it seems to follow, that the tie which binds together all the different and distant portions of the British Empire, so that their united strength may be wielded for their common protection, must be regarded as an object of extreme importance to the interests of the Mother-country and her dependencies. To the latter it is no doubt of far greater importance than to the former, because, while still forming comparatively small and weak communities, they enjoy, in return for their allegiance to the British Crown, all the security and consideration which belong to them as members of one of the most powerful States in the world. No foreign Power ventures to attack or interfere with the smallest of them, while every Colonist carries with him, to the remotest quarters of the globe which he may visit in trading or other pursuits, that protection which the character of a British subject everywhere confers, and can depend, in any difficulties, or under any oppression to which he may be exposed, on the assistance of Her Majesty's diplomatic and consular servants, supported, if necessary, by the whole power of the Empire.

But I should regard it as a very unworthy mode of considering this subject, if it were to be looked at with a view only to the interests of this Country, as that word is usually understood. I conceive that, by the acquisition of its Colonial dominions, the Nation has incurred a responsibility of the highest kind, which it is not at liberty to throw off. The authority of the British Crown is at this moment the most powerful instrument, under Providence, of maintaining peace and order in many extensive regions of the earth, and thereby assists in diffusing amongst millions of the human race, the blessings of Christianity and civilization. Supposing it were clear (which I am far from admitting) that a reduction of our national expenditure (otherwise impracticable), to the extent of a few hundred thousands a year, could be effected by withdrawing our authority and protection from our nume-

rous Colonies, should we be justified, for the sake of
such a saving, in taking this step, and thus abandoning
the duty which seems to have been cast upon us?

It is to be remembered, that if we adopted this policy
we must be prepared for very serious consequences,
which would undoubtedly result from it. Some few
only of these I will mention. No one acquainted with
the actual state of society in the West India islands,
and the feelings prevalent among the different classes
of their inhabitants, can doubt that, if they were
left, unaided by us, to settle amongst themselves in
whose hands power should be placed, a fearful war of
colour would probably soon break out, by which the
germs of improvement now existing there would be
destroyed, and civilization would be thrown back for
centuries. In Ceylon a similar result would follow; its
native races are utterly incapable of governing themselves, and yet they certainly would not submit to be
ruled by the mere handful of Europeans who have
settled among them, if this small body were unsupported by British power. The great wealth which
within the last few years has been created in this
island would be destroyed, and the most hopeless
anarchy would take place of that security which now
exists, and under the shelter of which such promising
signs of improvement are beginning to appear. Even
in New Zealand, although I have little doubt that the
Colonists of European descent would be found capable
of establishing a government, under which they might
eventually rise to prosperity, yet we could scarcely

hope to see this effected without a series of contests with the native inhabitants, in which the latter would in the end be destroyed, but not until they had inflicted and suffered an almost equal amount of misery. On the West Coast of Africa there is at this moment a far more encouraging prospect than at any previous time ; the efforts which have been so long made to improve the negro race seem to be at length beginning to produce important results, and a great change for the better may be looked for. But if we take up a new policy, and abandon our positions on the African coast, the Slave Trade will again revive in the extensive territory within reach of our settlements, where it has now been extirpated, and has given place to a legitimate commerce, which is daily becoming more important.

To say nothing of higher motives, and of the duty which I conceive to be no less obligatory upon nations than upon individuals, of using the power and the advantages entrusted to them by Providence to advance the welfare of mankind, I would ask whether, even in mere money, there would not be something to set off against the saving of expense from the abandonment of our Colonies ? On the other side of the account we have to put the destruction of British property which would thus be occasioned, and the annihilation of lucrative branches of our commerce, by allowing anarchy and bloodshed to arrest the peaceful industry which now creates the means of paying for the British goods consumed daily in larger quantities, by the numerous and various populations now emerging from barbarism under our protection.

It is true there are several of our Colonies to which the last observations do not directly apply; but the policy of abandoning a part of our Colonial Empire could scarcely be adopted, without giving so great a shock to the feeling of confidence and security in the remainder, as greatly to increase the difficulty of maintaining it; and I must add, that it appears to me very doubtful whether even the Colonies most capable of governing themselves, and which have no uncivilized tribes to deal with, from whom any danger could be apprehended, would not for some time have much difficulty in maintaining their present state of tranquillity and security, both externally and internally, if their connection with the Mother-country were suddenly dissolved.

In New South Wales, for instance, the interference of the Home Government in the internal administration of the Colony is exceedingly slight; but, slight as it is, it may be questioned whether, without it, the conflict of interests and opinions between different classes of the inhabitants and between different districts would not be likely to lead to very dangerous struggles; while in their relations with each other it would be still more likely that the different Australian Colonies would be involved in difficulties, if they ceased to be all placed under the supreme authority of the Imperial Government.

I have thought it necessary to state thus strongly my

dissent from the views of those who wish to dismember the British Empire by abandoning the Colonies, because it is impossible not to observe that this policy— unworthy of a great Nation, and unwise as I consider it to be—is not only openly advocated by one active party in the country, but is also hardly less effectually supported by persons occupying an important position in Parliament, and who, while they hesitate to avow their adherence to it, hold language which obviously leads in the same direction, and advocate measures the adoption of which would inevitably bring about this result.

If the reasons which I have just stated for maintaining the connection between this Country and the British Colonies are admitted to be sound, it will follow as a necessary inference, that two very plain rules as to the terms on which that connection should be continued may be laid down. In the first place, I think it will clearly follow that this Country has no interest whatever in exercising any greater influence in the internal affairs of the Colonies, than is indispensable either for the purpose of preventing any one Colony from adopting measures injurious to another, or to the Empire at large ; or else for the promotion of the internal good government of the Colonies, by assisting the inhabitants to govern themselves when sufficiently civilized to do so with advantage, and by providing a just and impartial administration for those of which the population is too ignorant and unenlightened to manage its own affairs. While it was our policy to maintain a monopoly of the trade of the Colonies, it was necessary for the Home Government to exercise a considerable control over their internal administration, because otherwise this monopoly would certainly have been evaded; and accordingly it will be found, on looking back at the earlier history of our Colonies, (especially those which now constitute the United States,) that the interference of the servants of the Crown in their internal affairs, and the differences which that interference occasioned, arose almost entirely from the endeavour to uphold the commercial system then in force. The abandonment of that system has removed the necessity for this interference. Secondly, I think it will follow, that when this Country no longer attempts either to levy a commercial tribute from the Colonies by a system of restriction, nor to interfere needlessly in their internal affairs, it has a right to expect that they should take upon themselves a larger proportion than heretofore of the expenses incurred for their advantage.

In subsequent Letters I shall endeavour to show, with reference to the transactions of the several Colonies, that these rules were strictly adhered to while I held the office of Secretary of State; but before I do this, it will be convenient that I should offer some further general remarks upon the rules themselves, and the manner in which they have been acted upon. And first I would observe, with regard to the vague declamation on the absurdity of attempting to govern the Colonies from Downing-street, of which we have heard so much, that it would undoubtedly be in the highest degree absurd to attempt to govern from Downing-street, if this is to be understood in the sense of directing from thence all the measures of the local Authorities; but I am not aware that such an attempt has at any period of our history been thought of. On the other hand, it is obvious that, if the Colonies are not to become independent States, some kind of authority must be exercised by the Government at home. It will conduce to a clearer understanding of the subject, to consider by what means any control over its dependencies is now practically maintained by the Mother-country, and to what extent that control ought to be carried.

The authority of the Home Government over the Colonies is exercised mainly in two ways; first by the appointment of Governors, and secondly by sanctioning or disallowing the measures of the local Governments, of which these officers are at the head. It is also exercised sometimes, but much more rarely, by prescribing measures for their adoption. With regard to the selection of Governors, though I am aware that a contrary opinion has sometimes been expressed, it appears to me clear that, if we are to have Colonies at all, the appointment of their Governors must necessarily be retained by the Crown, since I do not perceive by what other means any real authority or control could be exercised over the executive government of the Colonies by the advisers of the Crown. But though the Governors of Colonies ought in my opinion always to be named by the Crown, (and, looking to the consequences of Presidential elections in the United States, I believe that the advantage to the Colonies of having persons entirely uncon- nected with local parties, thus appointed to these si- tuations, cannot easily be over-rated), the nature and extent of the powers entrusted to the Governors, and consequently the character of the Colonial Govern- ments, must differ widely in different cases. In the Settlements on the west coast of Africa, the Governors substantially exercise both executive and legislative authority, limited only by an appeal to the Home Government. In Canada, a representative Assembly has not only the chief power of legislation, but also virtually a large share of executive authority, since the members of the Executive Council are required to possess its confidence. Between these two extremes there are many intermediate degrees, of more or less power being exercised by the Governors of different Colonies.

The degree of control to be exercised over the local Authorities by the Secretary of State, as the organ of the Home Government, ought obviously to depend very much on the greater or less amount of power with which the Governors of different Colonies are invested. In a colony like Canada, where representa- tive institutions have attained their full development, and the Governor is aided in his administrative duties by Ministers who are required to possess the confi- dence of the Legislature, exceedingly little interference on the part of the Government at home seems to be required. In Colonies where this system of government is in successful operation, the Home Government should, in my opinion, attempt little (except in those rare cases where Imperial interests or the honour of the Crown are affected by local measures or proceedings), beyond advising the Colonial Authorities, and checking, so as to give an opportunity for further reflection, any ill-considered and hasty measures they may be inclined to adopt. Practically I believe that the influence which can thus be exercised through a judicious Governor is very considerable, and may be of great service to the Colonies. In the strife of parties which prevails in all free governments, the existence of an impartial authority serves to check the too great violence with which political contests are sometimes carried on, and the experience and position of a Minister of the Crown in this country enable him frequently to offer useful advice to the Colonial Legislatures. There are other Colonies in which representative institutions exist, but in a form suited to a less advanced stage of society, and where the Governor consequently is called upon to exercise considerably more power than under the system to which I have just adverted; and there are other Colonies again in which no such institutions yet exist.

In proportion as Governors are more independent of any local control, it becomes necessary that some should be exercised over them from home; and in those Colonies where they are unchecked by any

kind of representative institutions, it is the duty
of the Secretary of State to maintain a vigilant
superintendence over their proceedings. Although
he ought, as I conceive, to abstain from any med-
dling interference in the details of their administration, and to support their authority so long as
they appear to deserve his confidence,—and rather
to advise their recall when they cease to do so,
than to fetter their discretion by detailed instructions,
—he is yet bound to attend to complaints which may
be made against their measures, and to prescribe
for their guidance the general line of policy to be
pursued.

These rules, as to the degree of interference to be
exercised by the Secretary of State, are equally applicable to the legislative and executive measures of
the local Authorities in the Colonies ; but while I am
of opinion that the authority of the Crown, of which
the Secretary of State is the depositary, should be
used in all cases with great caution, and in Colonies
possessing representative institutions with extreme
forbearance, I cannot concur with those who would
prohibit all interference on the part of the Home
Government in the internal affairs of the Colonies. It
seems to have been overlooked, by those who insist
that such interference must always be improper, and
who would adopt without any qualification the rule
that the Colonies should be left to govern themselves,
that this would in some cases imply leaving a dominant party, perhaps even a dominant minority, to

govern the rest of the community without check or control.

To permit the government of a distant Colony to be so carried on, notwithstanding the oppression or corruption which might be known to exist, would in general be for the ease and advantage of the Ministers of the day, but would not be consistent with any but a very low view of the duties belonging to the responsible advisers of the Sovereign of this great Empire. In point of fact, it has not unfrequently happened, that the absence of difficulty in some parts of our Colonial administration has arisen, not from its merits, but from its faults. For instance, so long as the Home Government took no thought of the condition of the Negro population of the West Indies, it met with no opposition from the Assemblies of Jamaica and the other West Indian Colonies; but when, urged on by public opinion in this Country and by the House of Commons, the Government undertook to give effect first to the resolutions of 1823, for the amelioration of the condition of the slaves, and ultimately to the Act of Emancipation, it found itself placed in a position of antagonism to the dominant class in these Colonies, the difficulties arising from which are not yet by any means at an end. Yet it was clearly the duty of the Imperial Government not to leave the population of these Colonies to the unrestricted disposal of the local Governments, and in this respect at least the discontent engendered by the interference of the Home Government was the discontent of the dominant few (who can alone make themselves heard in this Country) at interference exercised for the protection of the helpless and ignorant many. Even now, in the former Slave Colonies which possess representative institutions, the body of the population does not practically exercise such an influence in the Assemblies as to exempt the advisers of the Crown from the duty of keeping a watchful eye upon the proceedings of the Legislatures, for the purpose of checking any attempts which might be made to pass laws bearing unfairly on the labouring classes.

But even where the interference of the Home Government is not necessary for the protection of a part of the population, too ignorant or too weak to protect itself, there is another consideration, which may require the exercise of some control over the proceedings of the local Governments with regard to the internal affairs of the Colonies. Every act of these Governments, whether legislative or executive, is done in the name and by the authority of the Sovereign; hence the honour of the Crown, which it is of the highest importance to the whole Empire to maintain unimpaired, must be compromised by any injustice or violation of good faith, which it has the power to prevent, being committed by the local Authorities. It is therefore the duty of those by whom the Imperial Government is conducted, and to whom, as the responsible servants of the Crown, its honour is entrusted, to take care that this honour does not suffer by the Sovereign's being made a party to proceedings involving a departure from the most scrupulous justice and good faith towards individuals, or towards particular classes of the inhabitants of any of our Colonies.

In the Colonies which are the most advanced in civilization and in the exercise of the powers of self-government, it is not superfluous to insist on this consideration: on the contrary, it is in Colonies having popular forms of government that there is perhaps most danger that, in the excitement of party contests, to which such governments are peculiarly liable, measures not consistent with strict justice may sometimes be attempted, and may require to be checked by the authority of the Crown, entrusted to the Secretary of State. Any interference on the part of that Minister with measures of purely internal administration in the Colonies to which I am now adverting, is to be deprecated, except in very special circumstances, the occurrence of which must be exceedingly rare; but I am convinced that it may sometimes be called for, and that it is therefore expedient to trust, for averting the evils and the dangers which must arise from an improper interference by the Home Government with the local administration, rather to the discretion with which the powers now vested in the Crown are exercised, than to a limitation of these powers by new legal restrictions: In particular, I should regard it as in the highest degree unadvisable to adopt the proposal that has been made to take away, so far as regards certain classes of laws, the general power which the Crown now possesses of disallowing all acts or ordinances passed by the Colonial Legislatures. I shall have to advert to this question hereafter, with reference to New South Wales ; I will therefore abstain from considering it more particularly at present.

I have little doubt that the propriety of regulating the amount of control to be exercised by the Secretary of State over the measures of the local Authorities, by the greater or less infusion of popular power in the constitutions of the several Colonies, will be generally recognized ; it remains to be considered what steps ought to be taken for the establishment of representative institutions where they do not now exist, or for improving them where they exist only in an imperfect form. On this head also I think there can be little difficulty in determining the principles which ought to be acted upon, although there will be a good deal more in their practical application.

Keeping steadily in view that the welfare and civilization of the inhabitants of the Colonies, and the advantage which the Empire at large may derive from their prosperity, are the only objects for which the retention of these dependencies is desirable, and believing also that there can be no doubt as to the superiority of free governments to those of an opposite character, as instruments for promoting the advancement of communities in which they can be made to work with success, I consider it to be the obvious duty and interest of this Country to extend representative institutions to every one of its dependencies where they have not yet been established, and where this can be done with safety ; and also to take every opportunity of giving increased development to such institutions where they already exist but in an imperfect form. But I believe that in some cases representative governments could not safely be created, and also that the same form of representative institutions is by no means applicable to Colonies in different stages of social progress. The principal bar to the establishment of representative governments in Colonies, is their being inhabited by a population of which a large proportion is not of European race, and has not made such progress in civilization as to be capable of exercising with advantage the privileges of self-government.

Of such Colonies Ceylon affords the best example. The great majority of its inhabitants are Asiatics, very low in the scale of civilization, and having the character and habits of mind which have from the earliest times prevented popular governments from taking root, and flourishing among the nations of the East. Amidst a large population of this description there are settled, for the most part as temporary residents engaged in commerce or agriculture, a mere handful of Europeans, and a larger number (but still very few in comparison with the whole population) of inhabitants of a mixed race. In such a Colony the establishment of representative institutions would be in the highest degree inexpedient. If they were established in such a form as to confer power upon the great body of the people, it must be obvious that the experiment would be attended with great danger, or rather with the certainty of failure. If, on the other hand, the system of representation were so contrived as to exclude the bulk of the native population from real power, in order to vest it in the hands of the European minority, an exceedingly narrow oligarchy would be created,—a form of government which experience certainly does not show to be favourable to the welfare of the governed. Were a representative Assembly constituted in Ceylon, which should possess the powers usually entrusted to such a body, and in which the European merchants and planters and their agents had the ascendency, it can hardly be supposed that narrow views of class interests would not exercise greater influence in the legislation of the Colony than a comprehensive consideration of the general good. To anticipate that this would be the effect of placing a large measure of power in the hands of a small minority, implies no unfavourable opinion of the character and intelligence of the European inhabitants of Ceylon, but only a belief that they would act as men placed in such a situation have generally been found to do.

In Mauritius, Trinidad, St. Lucia and Natal, a somewhat similar state of things exists; for although the preponderance of the uncivilized races in these Colonies is far less overwhelming than in Ceylon, still, taking into account the immigrants from India and Africa (whose welfare is entitled to especial consideration), the inhabitants of European origin are but a fraction of the whole population. Hence it appears to me, that the surrender of a large portion of the powers now exercised by the servants of the Crown, and the establishment of representative Legislatures, would not be calculated to ensure the administration of the government upon principles of justice, and of an enlightened regard for the welfare of all classes in these communities. This end may, I believe, be far better attained by maintaining for the present in these Colonies the existing system of government, of which it would be a great mistake to suppose that, because the inhabitants are not entitled to elect any of the members of the Legislatures, it provides no securities against abuse. Other influences are brought to bear upon the government of these Colonies, which answer many of the objects of a Legislature of a representative character.

In the first place, in all of them the Press is perfectly free; the newspapers comment upon all the measures of the Government, not only with entire liberty, but with the most unbounded license; and the force both of local opinion, and also to a considerable degree of opinion in this country, is thus brought to bear upon all the measures of the Administration. Every inhabitant of the Colonies is also entitled freely to address to the Secretary of State any complaints or remarks he may think proper on the measures of the local Authorities, subject only to the rule that such letters shall be transmitted through the hands of the Governor (who is bound to forward them), in order that he may at the same time send such explanations on the subject as appear to him to be called for. This privilege is largely exercised, and is the means of supplying much useful information. It is hence impossible that the Secretary of State can be kept in ignorance of any errors or abuses committed by the local Authorities, while, if he fails to interfere when he ought, he cannot himself escape the censure of Parliament. The greatly increased facilities of intercourse with the Colonies have of late years effected a great practical alteration in the position of Colonial Governors ; and, whatever may have been the case formerly, it undoubtedly cannot be alleged that Parliament is now indifferent to what goes on in the Colonies, or that faults, real or imaginary, which may be committed in the administration of their affairs, can hope to escape the ever-ready criticism of an Opposition eager to find matter for objections to the Government of the day.   Perhaps some persons may think that this disposition has been carried too far for the real interest of the Colonies.

In these Colonies there exist also Legislative Councils consisting partly of persons filling the chief offices of the Government, partly of some of the principal in- habitants, who, though named to their seats in the Legislature by the authority of the Crown, and not by popular election, are yet in the habit of acting with great freedom, and practically express to a considerable extent the opinion of the class to which they belong. It was my object, while I held the seals of the Co- lonial department, without relinquishing the power possessed by the Crown, gradually to bring these legislative bodies more under the influence of the

opinion of the intelligent and educated inhabitants
of these Colonies. With this view, in one or two
cases, the proportion of unofficial to official members
was augmented, and the practice was everywhere
introduced of requiring the whole expenditure to be
provided for by ordinances discussed and passed by the
Legislative Council ; these ordinances being founded
on estimates prepared and submitted to the Legislature by the Governor, and published for general information. In general the fixed establishment of the
Colonial Governments is provided for by permanent
laws, and that part of the expenditure which is of a
more fluctuating character, by Ordinances passed annually, every charge on the Colonial revenue being required to have, in one form or the other, the sanction
of the Legislature. This regulation was adopted, under
my instructions, in all the Colonies to which I am now
referring, in place of the very lax and irregular practice
previously prevailing in some of them, by which the
only authority for a large proportion of their expenditure consisted of instructions given by the Secretary
of State, with the concurrence of the Treasury. The
publicity given to the estimates and accounts of the
Colonial expenditure, and the rule that, except in cases
of great emergency, the drafts of all proposed ordinances should be published before being passed, have
enabled the Colonists to bring under the consideration of the Governors and the Legislative Councils,
and ultimately of the Secretary of State, any objections they have entertained to proposed ordinances or

financial arrangements. Every encouragement has
been given to them to make known their opinions
freely, both to the local and Home Governments; and
the most careful consideration has been given to their
views, especially when these have been stated by
chambers of commerce or municipal bodies, the advice and assistance of which, in the administration of
Colonial affairs, are in my judgement of the highest
value.

These are as effective securities as in the present
state of these Colonies I believe to be attainable,
for ensuring their good government; but I conceive,
that gradually to prepare them for a more popular
system of government ought to be one of the principal objects of the policy adopted towards them,
and it is one of which I never lost sight. It was
more particularly with this view that I endeavoured,
whenever practicable, to create a system of Municipal
organization, entertaining a strong conviction that
the exercise of the powers usually entrusted to municipal bodies is the best training that a population can
have for the right use of a larger measure of political
power.

With regard to Colonies which already possess
representative institutions, I have observed above that
the form of these institutions varies very much in
different cases. In Canada and the neighbouring
provinces the system of government has, within
the last few years, been assimilated as nearly as
possible to that which prevails in this Country, Ex-

ecutive Councils having (as I have already mentioned) been established, composed of persons holding their offices only while they possess the confidence of the Assemblies, and the administration of the government being carried on by their assistance. In the other Colonies the representative bodies do not generally participate so directly, and in some scarcely at all, in the exercise of any power but that of legislation. When I come to treat of the affairs of particular Colonies, I shall have to notice the more important peculiarities in their Constitutions, and the reasons for allowing those peculiarities to continue : for the present I will confine myself to some general remarks, on the inexpediency of adopting the suggestion which has sometimes been made, that the system of government in all the Colonies possessing representative institutions should be assimilated to that which now exists in Canada.

The system now established in Canada is that of Parliamentary Government, that is to say government by means of parties. This form of government is now working well in that and the neighbouring provinces, and is probably on the whole the best plan hitherto adopted of enabling a Colony in an advanced stage of its social progress to exercise the privilege of self-government; it may therefore be regarded as the form which representative institutions, when they acquire their full development, are likely to take in the British Colonies. The experience however of our own Country, in which this system of government has so long flourished, may teach us that its advantages are by no means unmixed, even in communities the best adapted to it, but that there are considerable drawbacks to the benefits we derive from it. We know also that hitherto Parliamentary government has not been carried into successful operation for any considerable time, in any other country in the world but our own, and that it is little more than ten years since it was first attempted in any of our Colonies, while in none of them can it be said to have been brought into full operation until far more recently. Even this short experience of its working in the Colonies, would seem to show that it is suitable only to a community which is not a very small one, to a population in an advanced stage of civilization, which has had the advantage of some training by the working of a free constitution of a simpler kind, and, I should be inclined to add, in which Municipal institutions exist, capable of dividing with the Legislature the very large powers which it would engross, if in the absence of such institutions the representatives of the people had a virtual control over the appointment of the executive officers of the government.

In a small community the successful working of this system of government is rendered difficult, by the necessarily restricted number of members of the Legislature, and of persons qualified by their intelligence and education to fill the principal offices of the government, and at the same time in possession of sufficient means to devote their time to the public service, without adopting such employment as a permanent profession. Where the popular branch of the Legislature necessarily consists of only a small number of members, the increased importance which attaches to individual votes greatly increases the danger of those abuses to which party government is always liable, as will readily be understood by those who have observed the effect produced in this Country by a nearly equal division of parties. Even in the Assembly of Canada, although a numerous body, compared to most Colonial assemblies, it has been remarked that its great inferiority in numbers to the House of Commons has a decided and injurious effect upon its adaptation to the system of government now in force in that Colony. The want of a sufficient number of persons possessing the leisure and competence requisite to enable them to give up their time to the public service without adopting it as a profession, is even a greater difficulty in the way of the adoption in a small society of what has been called in the Colonies "responsible," but what may more properly be termed "party" or "parliamentary," government. Where the persons capable of holding office are very few, party contests have a tendency to run into extreme and dangerous bitterness. It may be questioned whether these considerations have been sufficiently attended to, and whether, in one at least of the North American Colonies, the inhabitants have not required prematurely the establishment of a system of government for which they are not yet sufficiently prepared.

Nor ought it to be overlooked, that the peculiar form of government to which the above remarks apply is by no means necessary for the enjoyment, by a Colony, of the advantages of a free government. If a representative Legislature exists, the people not only possess the power through their representatives of determining all questions relating to legislation, the imposition of taxes, and the expenditure of the public money, but they have likewise the means of expressing their opinion, in a manner which makes it certain that it will not be neglected, on the administration of the executive government. In those earlier days of our Colonial history, to which it is now so much the fashion to look for an example to be followed, these were the only securities for good government; and there can be no doubt that they are now far more effective than in those times, in consequence of the altered state of public opinion in this Country on such subjects, and of the increased facilities which now exist for bringing before Parliament any grievances of which the Colonists may have to complain. Nor is it immaterial to observe, that, even in the United States of America, Congress does not possess any such direct control over the executive government as that which is exercised by the Legislatures of Colonies in which Parliamentary government is established; and the President during the term of his office exercises an authority far larger, and far less subject to any check

against abuse, than that which is vested in the Governor of a British Colony possessing a Representative
Legislature. It is true that the President is elected
by the people he is to govern, whereas the Governor
of a British Colony is appointed by the Crown ; but
as the election of the President renders him in fact
the nominee of a party, and creates many temptations
for the exercise of the great power he possesses for
mere party purposes, it may not unreasonably be questioned whether even greater securities are not required
against its abuse, than are necessary in the case of a
Governor entirely unconnected with all local parties,
and who has the strongest interest in administering
the affairs of the Colony entrusted to his charge with
fairness, and in such a manner as to give general satisfaction to the inhabitants.

These observations on the general principles which
ought to govern our Colonial Administration would
be incomplete, without adding some remarks upon the
important subject of Patronage. It is commonly believed, that one of the principal objects for which the
Colonies are retained is the patronage which they are
supposed to afford. It is impossible to conceive a
greater delusion. It is now many years since the
Colonies have afforded to the Home Government any
patronage which can be of value to it as a means of
influence in domestic politics. Since Parliament has
ceased to provide, except in a very few special cases,
for any part of the expense of the civil government
of the Colonies, the Colonists have naturally expected

that offices paid for by themselves should be filled up by the selection of persons from their own body, when this can be done without inconvenience. Accordingly offices in the Colonies have, for a considerable time, been for the most part practically disposed of by the Governors. It is true that these offices, when their value exceeds £200 a year, are in general nominally at the disposal of the Secretary of State, and, when vacancies occur, can only be filled up by the Governors, subject to the confirmation of the Crown signified by that Minister. But in the great majority of cases the recommendation of the Governors is accepted as a matter of course; the patronage therefore is in effect exercised by them, and offices are filled up by the appointment of Colonists.

This practice prevails more or less completely in different Colonies according to circumstances. In the North American Colonies appointments may be said to have been for a long time given exclusively to residents; and in the other Colonies, having temperate climates and a European population, they have been chiefly so, perhaps with fewer exceptions than would have been for the real advantage of the Colonies themselves. I say with fewer exceptions than would have been for the real advantage of the Colonies themselves, because, until they reach an advanced stage in their progress, I believe that the appointment to some of the principal offices in the Colonies of persons not selected from the narrow circle of their own inhabitants, and imbued with the peculiar feelings and opinions which are apt to prevail in such communities, but chosen from among the well-educated gentlemen of the Mother-country, is calculated greatly to improve the tone of Colonial society, and to prevent it from gradually degenerating from the standard of manners and acquirements to which we are accustomed at home. It is also an advantage in small societies, as tending to mitigate the bitterness of that party spirit which is so often their bane, that some of the offices of most importance should be filled up by persons from a distance, not connected with any of the small knots and cliques into which such societies usually become divided; while the interchange of appointments between different Colonies not only answers this object, but tends also to keep up among them a feeling of connection with each other and with the Empire of which all form a part. These remarks apply more especially to Judicial appointments, which, I believe, it would be wise, as a general rule, to fill up from the Bar of the Mother-country or of other Colonies, until the Colonies have made a considerable advance in wealth and population.

For these reasons it seems to me in the highest degree inexpedient, that a transfer of patronage from the Crown to any Colonial Authorities should be formally made. The existing arrangement enables the Secretary of State occasionally to depart from the restricted field of selection for important offices afforded by the society of the particular Colony, though practically this can be done very rarely; while

the necessity imposed upon the Governor of reporting
the reasons for his recommendations to vacant offices,
and obtaining the confirmation of the Secretary of
State for the provisional appointments he may make,
affords no unimportant check on any abuse of the
patronage thus exercised; especially as those candidates for employment, whose claims have not been
admitted by the Governor, have the right of bringing
their case by letters sent through his hands under the
consideration of the Secretary of State.

In the tropical climates, where the number of residents of European race is comparatively small, and
the Colonial society affords a still narrower field of
selection, appointments are rather more frequently
made from home; but even in these Colonies, the more
important and lucrative situations are usually filled by
the promotion of those who have held inferior appointments; and it is desirable, for the encouragement of
the civil servants of the Government, that this course
should in general be followed; though no positive or
invariable rule can be laid down, and it is sometimes
of great advantage to depart from the usual practice.
The above observations apply to all appointments
under the rank of Lieutenant-Governor, or President,
administering the government of a Colony; and the
effect of the practice I have described, which has
been followed for some years by successive Secretaries
of State, has been to reduce the number of appointments, really at the disposal of this Minister, within
limits so narrow as to render the patronage an object

of no importance as a means of obtaining political support for an Administration.

Governors and Lieutenant-Governors, it is true, are invariably appointed by the Crown, on the advice of the Secretary of State ; but this patronage can only be looked upon as a source of difficulty and anxiety. The welfare of every Colony, and the alternative of success or failure in administering its affairs, are so mainly dependent upon the choice of a Governor, that I can hardly believe that any Secretary of State, even if he were insensible to all higher motives than a regard for his own interest and reputation, would willingly be guided in his selection by any consideration except that of the qualifications of the individual preferred. At the same time, the advantages of these appointments are not such as to lead to their being often accepted by persons who have much distinguished themselves by the ability they have shown ; so that the services of men who have filled other important offices, and who would therefore be preferred for such situations, cannot be commanded. Hence the choice generally lies among persons of less tried fitness.

I certainly shall not in this Letter attempt to canvas the merits of the various appointments to Colonial Governments which were made while it was my duty to advise the Queen on this subject; it would be impossible to do so without entering into considerations quite unfit for public discussion. I will only state generally, and I can with con-

fidence appeal to you for the correctness of the statement, that no pains were spared which it was in my
power to take, in order to secure the services, as
Governors, of the persons who appeared to me most
likely to discharge their important duties with judgement and ability; that the great majority of those appointed were known to me only by reputation and by
their public services; that a very large proportion of
the Governments filled up while I held office, were so
by the promotion of persons already in the Colonial
service, (it being my opinion, that the efficiency of that
service, as a whole, would be increased by thus rewarding those who had distinguished themselves in
it); and that the selection cannot, on the whole, be
regarded as otherwise than successful, looking to the
manner in which the affairs of the Colonies have been
administered by the Governors and Lieutenant-Governors whom I recommended to the Queen. I will
give in the Appendix a list of the persons so appointed, distinguishing those with whom I had no
personal acquaintance previously to their nomination,
and specifying the public services by which they were
known to me*.

I have observed in the earlier part of this Letter,
that if the principles I have endeavoured to establish
are admitted, it will follow that the Colonies ought to
take upon themselves a larger proportion than heretofore of the charges they occasion.

The chief source of expense at present on account

* See Appendix (A) at the end of this Volume.

of the Colonies is their military protection, as the
charges of their civil government are now generally
paid by themselves; and the naval expenditure, which
is frequently charged against the Colonies, cannot in
my opinion be so with any justice, since, if we had
no Colonies, I believe that the demands upon our
naval force would be rather increased than diminished,
from the necessity of protecting our commerce.

Our military expenditure on account of the Colonies
is certainly very heavy, including the charges for the
pay of the troops stationed in them; the cost of barracks and ordnance works, that of transport, and the
large proportion of the dead weight of the army which
is fairly chargeable to the Colonies. This expenditure
ought, I think, to be very largely reduced; and the
Colonies, now that they are relieved from all that is
onerous to them in their connection with the Mother-
country, should be required to contribute much more
than they have hitherto done to their own protection.
This would, in point of fact, be only a return to what
was formerly the practice of this Country. In the
early days of our Colonial history it is well known that
the settlers, in what are now the United States, were
thrown very much upon their own resources in their
contests, not only with the Indians, but with the
French, and that the Mother-country acted rather as
an ally than as a principal in their wars. In the West
Indies the Colonies were also required to contribute largely towards their own military protection;
indeed it is only within the last twenty years that

Jamaica has ceased to provide rations and barracks
for the troops quartered there; and even now there is
a relic of the ancient system, in the charge still borne
by the Island, on account of the forts, though the
keeping up of these forts has, I fear, become little
more than a form.

I believe it was not until the time of the great
revolutionary war with France, that nearly the
whole burden of the defence of the Colonies was
undertaken by this Country; but for the last fifty or
sixty years this has been so generally done, and the
charges on this account borne by the Colonies have
been so few and inconsiderable, that a sudden change
of system could not have been safely effected. The
importance of returning to a sounder system was not
however lost sight of, and we endeavoured to establish,
and by degrees to act upon, the principle that the Colonies can only look to the Mother-country for military
support in any dangers to which they may be exposed
from a powerful foreign enemy; that Her Majesty's
troops are not to be expected to undertake the duties
of police, and of maintaining the internal tranquillity
of the Colonies; and that the Colonies ought to undertake to provide for the expense of barracks for such
of Her Majesty's troops as may be stationed in them
for their protection. I except the case of those important naval and military stations, which are maintained rather with a view to the interests of the Empire
at large, than those of the particular Colony, such for
instance as Malta, Bermuda, etc., where the fortifica-

tions are of far more importance to the Empire than
to the Colony.

As a first step towards carrying these views into
effect, instructions were transmitted to the Australian
Colonies very early in your administration, for a
large reduction of the force quartered there, and for
the transfer of the barracks to the Colonial Authorities, except in Van Diemen's Land, where, on account
of the large number of convicts, a different rule was
of course adopted. The transfer of the charge for
barracks to the Colonial Governments appeared to
be one of the first steps which ought to be adopted
in attempting to reduce our Colonial military expenditure; because the charge for barracks and military
works is a very heavy one, and is also one which it
is impossible effectually to check at the great distance
of many of our Colonies. Copies of the correspondence with the Governor of New South Wales on this
subject, containing a full explanation of the policy
pursued on this subject, will be found in the Appendix*. Although the principle thus acted upon in Australia was one which it was our intention to adopt as
the general guide of our policy, there were strong
reasons for beginning its application in Australia, and
proceeding somewhat cautiously in acting upon it elsewhere. The Australian Colonies are, of all the Queen's
dominions, the safest from attack by any foreign enemy;
their position and the nature of the country render
it impossible that in war such an enemy should do

* See Appendix (B) at the end of this Volume.

more than plunder and burn some of the seaport-towns, and even this would be effectually guarded against by a very small amount of exertion on the part of the Colonists, in erecting batteries and forming volunteer corps of artillery. In peace, there being no warlike natives (I confine these observations to the Colonies in Australia, excluding New Zealand), there is absolutely no danger to apprehend. Hence the amount of force required (except for purposes of police, which I do not conceive to form part of the proper duties of Her Majesty's troops) is very inconsiderable, and the Colonies may without difficulty undertake the charge of keeping in repair the barracks which have already been built. It is also to be remembered that the Australian Colonies have not lost anything by our recent commercial legislation : on the contrary, the effect of that legislation has been only to relieve them from restrictions, without depriving them of any peculiar and gainful privileges.

In other Colonies, though the same principle has already been partially acted upon, and was intended gradually to be so more completely, there were, as I have said, reasons for proceeding cautiously. In the North American Colonies the necessity of maintaining a considerable force arises almost entirely from their proximity to the United States, and from the fact that, if we were unfortunately involved in a quarrel with that Republic, our Colonies would be attacked as a means of injuring us. These Colonies, as I shall hereafter have occasion more particularly to show, had also

suffered more really than any others from the changes
of our commercial policy; and the moment when they
were struggling with the difficulties thus brought
upon them, was not one which could properly be
chosen for calling upon them to submit to an entirely
novel charge on account of their military expenditure. In the West India Colonies the commercial
distress, which has for many years weighed so
heavily upon them, formed a complete obstacle
to their being now called upon for any contribution towards their military defence. But both in
the North American and West Indian Colonies a
large reduction of force has been effected (a part of
this reduction having been only ordered, and not
completed, when we left office), by which a very considerable saving has been made; and, in the former,
the maintenance at the cost of this Country, of
an irregular local force, which formerly cost £16,000
a year, has been discontinued, and steps have been
taken towards the complete adoption of the same
principle as in Australia. I shall have occasion, in
adverting to the transactions of Canada, to return to
this subject, and state more particularly what has
been done there. The other Colonies are chiefly
either garrisons, such as Malta and Gibraltar, or else
already contribute largely to their own military expenditure, as Mauritius and Ceylon.

Other arrangements have also been made, with the
view of gradually diminishing the military expense of
the Colonies; of these one of the most important has

been that for sending out pensioners, instead of detachments from the regular regiments of infantry, as
convict guards, and for settling enrolled pensioners in
Canada, New Zealand, and Australia.

I am persuaded that if the policy which I have thus
slightly sketched is followed up, and if the Colonies,
as they become better able to bear the charge, are
required to take upon themselves a larger share of
their military expenditure, this burden on the Mother-
country may at no distant period be reduced to a
very moderate amount.   Considering that it is little
more than five years since the first steps were taken
towards the adoption of this as a regular system of
policy, and that during that brief period the disturbance of our commercial relations with the Colonies
has imposed upon us the necessity of avoiding any
hasty proceedings in carrying it into effect, the progress already made is as great as could reasonably be
expected.

I fear that this preliminary explanation of the principles on which the administration of Colonial affairs
was conducted while under my immediate direction,
as a member of your Government, must have appeared
tedious to you, to whom these views are so familiar,
and with whom I have so often had to discuss them.
I am, however, writing for the information of persons who have not your knowledge of the subject;
and I trust that the general explanation I have now
given will enable me, by avoiding repetitions, to compress within narrower limits than would otherwise be

possible, without failing to make our policy intelligible to persons not possessing that knowledge, the account I propose to give of the principal events of the last six years in the different Colonies. But here for the present I will stop. In future Letters I intend to advert in succession to the several Colonies or groups of Colonies, and to call your attention to what is of most importance in their transactions, and in the discussions to which they gave occasion during the time of your Administration.

April 27, 1852.

LETTER II.

THE SUGAR COLONIES GENERALLY.

MY DEAR LORD JOHN,

I intend in this Letter to speak only of those Colonies of which sugar forms the staple article of produce. I begin with these, in the sketch which it will be my object to give of the most important circumstances in the history of the various British Colonies since July, 1846, because the earliest measure of your Administration was to propose to Parliament the alteration of the Sugar duties, which was carried into effect by the Act of the 18th of August, 1846, and because the discussions and proceedings arising out of that measure have been amongst the most important of those relating to the Colonies which have since occurred.

It is perhaps not strictly within the design of these Letters to discuss the propriety of a legislative measure which, after much debate, received the sanction of Parliament; since it is obvious that, if the members of the Executive Government are to be considered as

answerable at all for a measure so sanctioned, their
responsibility is very different, both in kind and degree, from that which they incur by the exercise of
their administrative powers. But the passing of this
Act had so material an influence upon all the affairs
of the sugar-growing Colonies, and carrying on their
government became so much a struggle to maintain
the policy of that Act, that some explanation of the
grounds on which it was adopted is necessary for a
right understanding of the transactions of these Colonies in the last six years.

The object of the Act of 1846 was to provide for
the immediate reduction, and the entire abolition at
an early period, of the heavy differential duty which
was levied on foreign sugar as compared to that
produced in the British dominions, and, further, to
put an end to the distinction established by a previous Act, between foreign sugar the produce of countries in which slavery does or does not prevail. The
details of this measure, it may be right to observe,
were subsequently modified, and the period at which
British and foreign sugar were to be placed on a footing of complete equality in the home market was
somewhat postponed, the duties being also generally
lowered by the Act of 1848, which it became necessary to pass in consequence of the commercial disasters of 1847, and the panic they created. The
policy however of the Act of 1846 was adhered to;
and as it is unnecessary for the objects of this Letter
to advert more particularly to the provisions of the

two Acts, and the points in which they differed, I will, without taking further notice of the change in the mode of applying it, proceed to explain the grounds (so far as relates to the Colonies) upon which that policy was adopted and maintained. I have to add, that, in stating the grounds of our policy, I of course can only claim to do so according to my own understanding of them, because it is very probable that the considerations, by which the different members of the Government were led to concur in the measures that were adopted may not always have been the same, though leading to the same practical conclusion, and I have no right to assume that the views which I had myself been led to form many years ago on the state of the Sugar Colonies were on all points in conformity with those of others. I must therefore, at the risk of some appearance of egotism, refer more than I could wish to my own individual opinions.

In addition to those general reasons having reference to our domestic interests, which may be urged in favour of all measures for relieving trade from artificial restrictions (and especially the trade in an article which is now almost a necessary of life), the expediency of ceasing to exclude foreign sugar from our market by heavy differential duties seemed to me to be established by the following considerations. At the period to which I am referring, the British planters had long been in the enjoyment of a monopoly of the home market, which had been but slightly relaxed, by the Act of 1844, in favour of sugar the produce of countries in which slavery does not exist. But not-withstanding this monopoly, ever since the abolition of slavery (and indeed from a much earlier period) there had been constant and loud complaints on the part of the West Indians of the difficulties to which they were exposed and of the distress which they suffered*. Hence there could be no doubt that the "protection" (as it is termed) which had been granted to them had failed at all events to secure their prosperity, if it had not been one of the main causes of their difficulties. It seemed to me probable that this last was the fact, and that the operation of the system of monopoly, to which the West Indians attached so much importance, had really been injurious instead of beneficial to them; because, while it would be easy to show that in all cases what is called "protection" tends to create ex-pectations only to disappoint them, and to inflict loss upon those engaged in branches of industry so fa-voured, by leading them to calculate on prices which

* See particularly the Memorial of the House of Assembly of Jamaica, of the 28th of February, 1844, quoted in Mr. Burge's Letter to Lord Stanley, of the 29th of May, 1844 (House of Commons Sessional Paper of 1844, No. 341); also the further Memorials from the Assembly to the Queen, of the 18th of December, 1846, and the 24th of December, 1847 (House of Commons Sessional Paper of 1847, No. 160, and House of Lords Paper of 1848, No. 250, p. 75); the Report of the Committee of the House of Assembly on which the last Memorial was founded (p. 83), and the Despatch in reply p. 166. See also Lord Harris's Despatch of the 28th of December, 1846 (p. 696 of the same Paper), in which he says, that for the last *ten* years the greater number of estates in the Island have been kept in cultivation at a great loss.

they do not practically realize, this tendency was aggravated in the case of the sugar-planters by other circumstances.

The measure for the Abolition of Slavery, which was passed in 1833, is now generally admitted to have been most unhappily defective, from its containing no provisions calculated to meet what constituted the real difficulty of that great change in the state of society, namely the want of adequate motives to impel the Negroes to labour when the direct coercion to which they were subject as slaves should be withdrawn. Experience has long demonstrated that men, whatever be their race or their colour, will not submit to steady and continuous labour, unless under the influence of some very powerful motive; and that in general they can only be induced to do so either by direct compulsion (that is to say, by being treated as slaves), or by the constraint imposed upon them by their inability to obtain otherwise what their habits lead them to regard as necessary for a comfortable existence. It is notorious that even English labourers, probably the most industrious in the world, relax in their exertions when the power of this motive is diminished; and it has often been remarked, that when, owing to some unexpected demand, or other circumstances, the wages of any numerous class of labourers are suddenly and largely increased, the majority avail themselves of the increase to enjoy a larger portion of leisure than before, and content themselves with working only hard enough to live somewhat, but not greatly, better than they had been previously accustomed to do. Now, during slavery, the Negroes were maintained principally by the produce of their own provision-grounds, which they cultivated in the time allowed them for the purpose by their masters, from whom they received in addition certain allowances, principally of clothing and salt-fish, to the value of a few shillings a-year: that is to say, they worked under the terror of the whip, without receiving any return beyond these few shillings for their labour, since in most of these Colonies land is so abundant that it can be had almost for nothing, and their provision-grounds could not therefore be considered as part of the wages of the Negroes. · By relieving them from the coercion under which they had previously worked, and enabling them to command the full value of their labour, which in three or four weeks would amount to as much as they had received from their masters for a year, it was therefore certain that a change would be made in their position, in comparison to which that experienced by English workmen, in consequence of the most extravagant rise of wages ever known in this Country, under any temporary demand for a particular kind of labour, would be as nothing.

But although this was clearly to be anticipated, the Emancipation Act did not attempt to meet the difficulty that was sure to arise from the want of any adequate motive to induce the Negro to submit to continuous labour. All that it did was to adjourn the

difficulty by continuing slavery in a modified shape*,
under the name of apprenticeship, for a few years
longer; but the people of England, who had paid for
the abolition of slavery, and had been told that it was
effected, when it turned out that this was not the
case, and that slavery was in reality still continued,
though in a mitigated form, would not submit to have
their expectations thus disappointed. It was with extreme difficulty that, in 1838, the House of Commons
was induced to forgo its demand that the apprenticeship should at once be put an end to by the authority
of Parliament, and to rest satisfied with passing an
Act, which so crippled the power of the masters to
enforce compulsory labour, that the right to it was
no longer worth retaining. The consequence was,
that this remnant of slavery was abandoned, and complete emancipation was granted to the Negroes, in the
Crown Colonies by an Order in Council, and in the
others by local Acts. None of these laws contained
any provisions calculated to bring to bear upon the
Negroes other motives to industry when that of coercion was withdrawn. They were also all alike deficient in not attempting to make adequate provision
for the education and religious instruction of the newly
emancipated population, or for the establishment of an
effective police and the inforcement of order.

* See Lord Derby's (then Lord Stanley) speech in the House of
Lords, on the 7th of February, 1848, in which he distinctly states
though this was strenuously denied in 1833) that the apprenticeship
was only a system of modified slavery.—*Hansard*, vol. xcvi. p. 175.

The result was, at first, less difficulty and a smaller diminution of the amount of work done by the Negroes than might have been expected. They accepted moderate wages, not knowing that they could command more; and as, in the early days of freedom, they imitated their masters and incurred expenses altogether unsuited to their condition in life, they were obliged, in order to obtain the means of meeting these expenses, to do more work than might have been anticipated. But they gradually got to know the value of their labour, and wages consequently rose; while at the same time they ceased to think it necessary to show that they were free by indulging so much as at first in fine clothes and luxuries, and their style of living subsided into one less violently different from that to which they had been used as slaves. The unfortunate consequence was, that not only did wages continue to rise, but—contrary to what happens in such a country as this, where an undue rise of wages in any particular employment soon corrects itself, by attracting more labour from other quarters—the higher the wages, the smaller became the amount of exertion by which the Negro could command what he considered necessary for his comfort; and, there being no source whence additional labourers could be procured in sufficient numbers to fill up the void, as the cost of labour increased, its quantity diminished. But the amount of labour which could be commanded being less than was required to carry on cultivation upon its previous scale, while the capital invested in sugar-

plantations, which would be in a great measure sacrificed by allowing them to go out of cultivation, was
very large, it inevitably happened that the competition among the Planters, for the scanty supply of
labour that was available, forced up wages to the
very highest rate which the prospects of the sugar-
market rendered it possible to pay, without incurring
a heavier loss than would have been sustained from
the abandonment of plantations.

In this state of things it is obvious that the tendency of that monopoly of the British market for
which the Planters contended, was really to increase
instead of to diminish their difficulties, because it raised
their expectations as to the price their sugar would
command, and consequently the wages they could venture to pay. So powerfully had these causes operated,
that, in 1846, wages in Guiana * had risen to two
shillings and fourpence for about six hours' labour, the
Negroes scarcely ever condescending to work more
than four days in the week, and often only two or
three†. In other Colonies, where the land is less
fertile, or the supply of labour less deficient, wages
had not been raised to this extravagant height; but
everywhere the tendency of the law by which the price
of Colonial sugar was artificially enhanced in the
British market, had been to raise the wages of the
Negroes, and to diminish the amount of labour which

---

* See House of Commons Sessional Paper, No. 325 of 1847,
p. 93.

† See House of Lords Sessional Paper, No. 250 of 1848, p. 568.

the Planter could even at an increased price command. Nor is this all. The high rate of wages which the Negroes could command, and the absence of any necessity for devoting more than a small portion of their time to labour, instead of proving of real advantage to them, had tended to make them rather retrograde than advance in civilization since the abolition of slavery. They are described in Guiana (where the evil was greatest) as passing their time in shooting and fishing, leading an irregular and wandering life*, much addicted to petty theft, and committing more serious offences when called upon to submit to a very moderate reduction of their extravagant wages, which was imperatively demanded by an alteration in the price of sugar. Education is stated to have made little progress, and it is observed that "the fact of the continued prevalence and undiminished influence of the practice of 'obeah' in this and other Colonies will partially illustrate the slow progress of intellectual improvement amongst them; and there seems to be a general impression that the rising generation are less docile, and more inclined to evil and reckless pursuits, than their elders †."

Such is the melancholy picture, given by a very competent authority, of the social condition of the

---

* See Governor Light's Despatch of the 3rd of May, 1848. (House of Lords Paper, No. 250 of 1848, p. 567.)

† Mr. Walker's Report on the condition of British Guiana, transmitted in Governor Barkly's Despatch of March 21, 1849, in the Appendix to the first Report of the Committee of the House of Commons on Ceylon and British Guiana, p. 308.

Negro population in one of the most important of the former Slave Colonies, more than fourteen years after the passing of the Act of Emancipation, and above ten years after the Negroes had been placed in the enjoyment of entire freedom by the abolition of the system of apprenticeship.   Such a state of things (of which the existence was known in 1846, though the description of it I have quoted was not written till later) seemed clearly to demonstrate that the system which had been pursued towards these Colonies, at the time of emancipation and since, was radically erroneous, and that a totally different one ought to be adopted.   The change which was thus urgently required could not be effected by any single measure ; but, for the reasons I have stated, it was a first and indispensable step toward improvement to alter the duties levied in this Country upon sugar, so as no longer artificially to enhance the price of Colonial produce, and thereby maintain the extravagant wages hitherto received by the Negroes, which had contributed so much to encourage idleness and obstruct the progress of civilization.   A severe temporary pressure upon all concerned in sugar cultivation in our Colonies was no doubt to be anticipated, while this change of policy was in progress ; but, until it had been accomplished, it was certain that society in these Colonies could not be placed in a sound and healthy condition, and the longer it was delayed the more painful would be the crisis which must be passed through.

It was upon these grounds that the abandonment of the policy by which, up to 1846, foreign sugar had been almost excluded from the British market, appeared to me to be no less desirable, with a view to the well-understood interests of the Colonies, than it was clearly expedient for the sake of the fiscal and commercial interests of the Mother-country. The alteration of the sugar duties however was not adopted as a single measure; it formed part only of a general system of policy it was proposed to pursue, and the necessity of taking other means at the same time, in order to promote the success of that policy, was by no means overlooked.

One of the measures adopted with this view was to recommend to Parliament, that the Colonies which were to be deprived of their monopoly of the home market, should be enabled to admit foreign goods to their own markets on the same terms as similar British goods. By an Act of Parliament which was at that time in force, there were levied in the British Colonies, in addition to the duties imposed by Colonial laws, certain differential duties upon articles of foreign origin. These differential duties could not be at once repealed (as they had been imposed) by the authority of Parliament, because in some cases the receipts from them formed no inconsiderable portion of the Colonial revenue, the sudden loss of which would have occasioned serious inconvenience; accordingly, instead of simply repealing the Act of Parliament imposing these duties, a Bill was proposed, and passed into a law, by which the various Colonial Legislatures were empowered to repeal the

duties in question. At a later period the relief of
Colonial commerce from restrictions imposed by the
authority of Parliament was completed by the repeal
of the Navigation Laws. The various restrictions from
which the Colonial sugar-grower was thus relieved were
estimated, in a memorandum officially communicated
to the Board of Trade by the Committee of West India
Planters and Merchants in the year 1830, as equivalent to a charge of no less than five shillings a hundredweight on Colonial sugar; the removal therefore of
this burden could not fail to afford material assistance
to the British Planters, in meeting the competition to
which they were in future to be exposed.

But the chief disadvantage to which they complained
of being subject, in competing with the foreign sugar-
grower, was that created by the continuance of the
Slave-trade, which enabled the latter to obtain a
large supply of cheap labour. From this disadvantage
also the Government endeavoured to relieve them;
and with that view, as well as on the still higher
grounds of humanity, every effort was made to suppress the Slave-trade by the vigorous use of our
naval power,—I rejoice to say, with so much success,
that the last reports received from the coast of Africa,
when we retired from office, represented that detestable
traffic as having been very nearly extinguished; and
I am happy to perceive that Her Majesty's present
Ministers have been able to advise the Queen to inform Parliament, in closing the late Session, that, for
the present, the Slave-trade is entirely suppressed on

that part of the African coast where it was formerly carried on to the greatest extent.

But there were other measures which seemed to be still more urgently required for the restoration of the prosperity of the Sugar Colonies. This prosperity, and the welfare of all classes of the inhabitants of these Colonies, depend upon their being enabled to continue to advantage the cultivation of sugar, not merely because this branch of industry constitutes their chief source of wealth, but because, if it were to cease, there would no longer be any motive for the residence of the European inhabitants in a climate uncongenial to their constitution, while it is certain that they could not be withdrawn without giving an almost fatal check to the civilization of the Negroes.

But in most of these Colonies there was little prospect that the cultivation of sugar could be long continued, unless the amount of labour available to the Planters could be increased, and its cost materially reduced. This was the unanimous opinion of all persons interested in the production of Colonial sugar, nor was there any reason for questioning its correctness. Hence the planters and merchants connected with the West Indies and Mauritius were urgent in their demands for the adoption of measures to increase the supply of labour by immigration. It was our earnest desire to meet these demands as far as possible, though it appeared to us a mistake to depend too exclusively on immigration. Accordingly we did all in our power to encourage the introduction of labourers from India, Africa, and Madeira, (the only quarters from which there appeared any prospect of obtaining them,) insisting upon nothing but the observance of those precautions which a due regard to humanity imperatively required.

It would lengthen this Letter far too much, were I to attempt to state in full the various measures which were taken in order to promote immigration; but as there has been much misconception with regard to the restrictions said to have been put on African immigration, I think it right to observe, that I am aware of no such restriction having been imposed, with the single exception of its having been required that *free* immigrants only should be taken. Some persons (I am happy to say they were very few) earnestly contended that the purchase of slaves in Africa, for the purpose of emancipating them in the British Colonies, should be sanctioned. It was urged that to do this would be to rescue the unhappy creatures so bought from a most miserable condition, and to place them in one highly favourable to them. So far as regards the individuals first purchased, this would undoubtedly have been true; but the further effect of the measure would have been to create a new demand for slaves on the coast of Africa, and, by doing so, to have given a fresh impulse to the internal Slave-trade throughout that continent, and to the wars and cruelties by which that odious traffic is maintained. It was therefore the bounden duty of the Government to take care that no means of procuring immigrants for the West Indies from Africa should be adopted, which involved the purchase of slaves for that purpose, directly or indirectly. No restrictions were imposed for any other object, and none which, I believe, can be shown to have been unnecessary for this.

Unfortunately, no great success attended the endeavours to obtain free immigrants from this quarter. The African is in general attached to his own country; and though the Governors of the British Settlements on the coast were instructed to make known to the population thê much higher wages and the advantages they might obtain, by going to the West Indian Colonies, and though a steamer was sent to what is called the Kroo Coast, whence the Guiana Planters were of opinion that a large number of voluntary immigrants might by that means be obtained, these endeavours proved almost unavailing, and hardly any accession of labourers for the Colonies has been obtained from Africa, except those found on board the slavers captured by our cruizers. Having mentioned the slaves thus liberated, it is proper to add that formerly a large proportion of these poor people used to remain at Sierra Léone; but by our orders means were taken to induce them, when first liberated, to go to the West Indies, and with so much success, that by far the greater part of those found on board ships captured in the last four or five years have consented to do so. Within the same period also improvements have been made in the arrangements of the depôt where liberated Africans are received at St. Helena, and in those for their conveyance to the West Indies, which have put a stop to the excessive mortality that formerly prevailed among these unhappy people, both in that island and in the ships in which they were conveyed. Since the improved arrangements were adopted, the expense of conveying liberated Africans to the West Indies has been reduced, and, instead of being subject to much sickness and a high rate of mortality, their health has generally been excellent, and the deaths singularly few. The expense of conveying these people to the Colonies, which up to 1848 had been a charge on the Colonial revenue, has, by an arrangement made in that year, been since provided for by Parliament. It appears by the annual report of the Emigration Commissioners* for the present year, that no fewer than 13,500 Negroes, liberated from slavers, have been sent, at the cost of the British Treasury, to the West Indian Colonies, where they have proved of great service to the Planters, while the reports of the condition of these immigrants are in the highest degree satisfactory. I have only to add, on the subject of African immigration, that, a few months ago, a proposal for making another attempt to obtain emigrants from the Kroo Coast was sanctioned, and though its result is not yet known, I am not altogether without hopes that it may succeed.

As the supply of labour that could be obtained

* See Appendix to this Report, No. xix., p. 99.

from Africa was so scanty, we did what we could to make up the deficiency from other quarters. For this purpose we continued, and, I trust, considerably improved, the arrangements which had previously been adopted for procuring immigrants from India for those Colonies which thought it expedient to incur this expense. We also endeavoured to open a new source of supply in China. Two or three years ago Dr. Gutzlaff (by whose death the public service has since sustained a great loss) came home from China on leave of absence, and I availed myself of the opportunity of inquiring from him what prospect there was of obtaining emigrants from China, whence I felt persuaded that they might be got, and with advantage, in spite of the failure of such an attempt which had been made a few years ago in Mauritius. He expressed his opinion that a very large number of labourers of a superior description, and accustomed to the cultivation of sugar, might be procured from China, and pointed out the means by which this might be done. This information I communicated to the Governors of Trinidad and Guiana; and I likewise placed Dr. Gutzlaff in personal communication with some of the principal West Indian proprietors in this country. Additional information was afterwards obtained to the same effect from Dr. Bowring (our Consul at Canton), which was also communicated to the Governors; and Mr. White (an exceedingly intelligent gentleman of Guiana, who had been sent from that Colony to Calcutta, for the purpose of inquiring whether the arrangements for procuring emigrants from India, for Guiana and Trinidad, might not be improved,) was directed to proceed to China, and ascertain on the spot what steps should be taken for obtaining labourers from that country. Mr. White furnished a very able report upon the subject, and obtained offers from some highly respectable mercantile houses to undertake the conveyance of Chinese emigrants to the West Indies; and when we left Office, the arrangements were so far matured that, unless they have been subsequently altered, I anticipate that in the course of the present year the first despatch of labourers from this quarter to Guiana and Trinidad will take place.

The mere introduction of immigrants into the Sugar Colonies would however have been of comparatively little use, without the adoption of some means to ensure their performing the labour expected from them in return for the expense so incurred. The facility for obtaining a subsistence by a very small amount of labour, which rendered the emancipated Negroes averse to steady industry, was not without its effect on the immigrants also; and it was absolutely necessary to bring to bear upon them some stronger stimulus to exertion, if the Colonies were to derive from their large expenditure in the introduction of labourers the benefit that was desired. No effective regulations had been adopted for this purpose, when I was called upon to consider the subject. The Planters universally insisted that the only arrangement which could be satisfactory to them would be to legalize contracts for labour for not less than three years, and to induce the immigrants as much as possible to bind themselves by agreements of this duration.

I found, when I received the seals of the Colonial Department, that these long engagements had been disapproved by preceding Secretaries of State. Soon after the Abolition of Slavery, the power of entering into such contracts had been greatly restricted by Orders in Council, applying to Colonies where the Crown possessed legislative authority, and by instructions limiting the discretion of the Governors in assenting to laws which might be passed in those possessing representative Assemblies. Subsequently these restrictions had been withdrawn or modified, and it had been signified to the West Indian Committee in this country, that Her Majesty's Government were prepared to sanction Colonial laws for legalizing and enforcing contracts for labour for three years, subject to certain limitations and provisions against abuse. But though previous Secretaries of State had decided that the sanction of the Crown was no longer to be withheld from laws of this sort, no encouragement had been given to the Planters to rely upon long contracts, as the means of obtaining steady labour from immigrants introduced into the Colonies. In a letter addressed to the Chairman of the West Indian Association by the Under Secretary of State, on the 28th of March, 1846, the following opinion was expressed by my immediate predecessor in office :— " But though willing, in deference to these reasons, to assent to the proposal" (for extending the power of entering into contracts for labour), " Mr. Gladstone directs me to observe that he must be distinctly understood as expressing no opinion that the experiment of entering into contracts for service for three years will eventually fulfil the expectations of those by whom the measure may be adopted. On the contrary, Mr. Gladstone fears that the disappointment of these hopes is far more probable : he believes that the result of attempts to bind free men to continue in any particular service after they have become dissatisfied with it, is very generally fatal either to the interests of their masters, or to their own freedom,—to the interest of the employer, unless severe and formidable coercion be used to overcome the labourer's reluctance to work—to the labourer's freedom, if those methods be taken *."

This opinion appeared to me to be just ; and I therefore believed it to be necessary that, as long contracts for service were unlikely to answer, other means should be adopted, on which more reliance could be placed, for the purpose of ensuring the performance, by labourers introduced at the cost of the Colonies, of the labour expected from them, in return for the expense so incurred. The nature of the measures to which I looked for effecting this object, and my general views on this important subject, will be best explained by an extract

* See House of Commons Sessional Paper, No. 691 of 1846, Part II. p. 4.

from a despatch which I addressed to the Governor of Mauritius on the 29th of September, 1846, and of which copies were sent in a circular to the Governors of the West Indian Colonies. In this despatch, after pointing out in detail the objections to an ordinance for regulating the rights and duties of Masters and Servants, which had been passed in Mauritius, and of which I had been compelled to advise the disallowance on account of the undue harshness of some of its provisions, I proceeded to make the following observations :—

"But while I have on these grounds been under the necessity of advising Her Majesty to refuse her sanction to the ordinance you have transmitted, I am far from being insensible to the force of the reasons which have led the members of the Mauritius Legislature to conclude that some change in the existing system with respect to the introduction and employment of Coolie labourers is urgently required; on the contrary, I entirely concur in that opinion, and my disapprobation of the Ordinance is founded, not on my differing with the Legislative Council as to the necessity of adopting more effectual regulations for securing the continuous labour of immigrants brought to the Colony at the public expense, but upon a conviction that the means proposed for attaining that object are not well adapted to the end which they have in view, whilst at the same time they are open to very serious objections.

" The original error to which all the objectionable

provisions of the Ordinance are to be traced, is that it
proceeds upon the principle of endeavouring by law to
enforce upon the immigrants the due performance of
the obligations to labour which they have contracted
by accepting a free passage to the Colony, instead of
seeking to place them in a situation in which they
might be acted upon by the same motives by which
men are impelled to labour in countries in which industry flourishes.   This I conceive to be a great mistake; all experience tends to prove that no legal regulations, however severe, if they stop short of the extreme compulsion which is the characteristic of slavery,
can succeed in enforcing really efficient labour (even
though it may be in fulfilment of a voluntary obligation) from men who have no interest in being industrious.   On the other hand, where the motives of self-
interest are properly brought to bear upon their conduct, there are few, if any, among the various races
of mankind who may not be stimulated to industry.
Hence I am of opinion that, instead of encouraging
the Indian labourers to enter, before they arrive at the
Mauritius, into contracts to labour for several years
for particular employers, and then endeavouring by
stringent regulations to enforce the performance of
these contracts, under circumstances in which it is the
interest of the immigrants to break them; the true
policy would be to adopt regulations, of which the
effect should be, to make it the decided and obvious
interest of the immigrants to work steadily and in-
dustriously for the same employers for a considerable

time. Nor does it appear to me impossible to devise regulations which would have this effect, while at the same time they would provide, in a manner much less objectionable than heretofore, for a large part at least of the expense of immigration*."

The despatch then proceeded to explain the heads of an ordinance, which were transmitted with it, for the consideration of the Council of Mauritius, and of which the principal provisions were, that immigrants introduced into the Colony at the public expense should be registered, and should be required either to enter into written engagements to work for a year for some planter, or, in the event of their not doing so, to pay in advance a monthly tax of five shillings; the written engagements to be subject to a stamp-duty of forty shillings for an original engagement, and twenty shillings for the renewal of an engagement at the end of the year with the same master. Registered immigrants were not to be allowed to leave the Colony without passports, until they had completed five years' industrial residence—which was defined to be residence during which they had either been under a written engagement to work for some master, or had been paying the monthly tax. At the end of five years' industrial residence, the immigrants were to be entitled to a free passage back to India; but those who chose to return at their own expense at an earlier period, were to pay, before

* House of Commons Sessional Paper, No. 325 of 1847, p. 144.

receiving a passport, one pound for every year wanting
to make up the stipulated term of residence.

By a law of this kind it was anticipated that the immigrants would be placed under an effective obligation
to work, while, at the same time, they would have the
same interest in being industrious as any other free
labourers, and they would be made to repay to the
Colony the expense incurred in bringing them from
India.   As this expense was incurred for the sake of
procuring labour for the planters, and the immigrants
voluntarily accepted a passage to the Colony for that
purpose, it was considered only just that those who
declined to enter into any engagement to work, should
be required to pay in advance the monthly tax I have
mentioned, which would merely amount to a repayment
by instalments of the expense incurred on their account
under a bargain which they had not fulfilled.   The
necessity of finding money to meet this demand would,
it was anticipated, compel them to undertake some
kind of labour to earn it, instead of living in idleness
and vagrancy ; and this was considered even a more
important object than that of securing the Colony
against a pecuniary loss.

The stamp-duty on engagements would also be
virtually paid by the immigrants, since their labour
would come into competition with that of the resident
population, or of immigrants who had completed their
five years' residence ; and the planter would of course
only consent to pay to the immigrants such wages as,
with the stamp-duty, would make their labour not more

expensive than that of men not coming under the provisions of this law. By reducing the stamp-duty on
the renewal of an engagement to half that chargeable
on an original engagement, a great encouragement was
given to the continuance of immigrants in the same
service; since a planter who would only have to pay
twenty shillings stamp-duty on a renewed engagement,
would obviously be able to offer better wages to the
labourer, than another person who could not engage
him without being subject to a charge of forty shillings. Though the continuance of immigrants in the
same service was thus encouraged, their right to seek
a new master, if they thought fit to do so, secured to
them the power of availing themselves of the competition for their labour to obtain its full value, and thus
maintained unimpaired that stimulus to industry which
exists in a healthy state of the relations between
labourers and their employers.

An ordinance founded on these principles was
passed in Mauritius, and has worked exceedingly well,
as I shall have occasion to show in giving an account
of the transactions of that Colony. Somewhat similar
laws were also passed at a later period, (some of them
very lately,) in most of the Sugar Colonies.

Immigration however was not the only, perhaps not
the principal source, from which an increased supply
of labour was considered to be obtainable. It was
still more important, in my opinion, to endeavour
to augment the amount of available labour, by
stimulating the actual population of these Colonies

to greater industry. I have already explained the error which was committed at the time of the Abolition of Slavery in 1833, in not adopting some means of imposing upon the emancipated slaves the necessity of greater exertion. A plan of emancipation, founded upon a consideration of this necessity, had, in the beginning of the year 1833, been submitted on behalf of the Government to the West Indian Committee by Lord Ripon (then Lord Goderich), who at that time held the office of Secretary of State for the Colonies. The assent of the West Indian Committee was refused to this plan, (partly perhaps because Lord Ripon was not authorized to accompany the proposal with the offer of large pecuniary compensation afterwards granted to the holders of slaves) ; and the seals of the Colonial Department having been transferred to Lord Derby (then Mr. Stanley), this scheme was entirely abandoned, and a different one was afterwards carried.

The distinguishing characteristic of the rejected plan* was, that it proposed to stimulate the Negroes to industry by the imposition of a tax on their provi-

---

* This plan, and the correspondence relating to it, will be found in the Appendix to the Fourth Report of the Committee of the House of Commons on Sugar and Coffee Planting, of 1848, p. 158. It had previously been printed in 1833, by the Committee of the West Indian Association, and had been extracted from their Proceedings and added as an Appendix to a corrected report, which I published in that year, of my speech in the House of Commons against the measure proposed by the Government for establishing a system of apprenticeship on the abolition of slavery. I may be permitted here

sion-grounds, while very stringent regulations for enforcing the payment of the tax, and for the prevention of vagrancy, were to have been established. The design of these proposals was to substitute, for the

to quote a few sentences from the remarks by which I introduced the rejected plan in the above Appendix, in order to show that the difficulties which have arisen from the mode of abolishing slavery which was adopted in 1833, are (though less in degree) in kind precisely those which I then anticipated. After expressing my opinion that slavery ought to be abolished, even if it were certain that the production of sugar in our Colonies would in consequence be altogether stopped, I proceeded to make the following remarks :—" If however sugar cultivation can be kept up consistently with the great principle of allowing every man (subject only to the control of the law and of the magistrate) to have the free disposal of his own time and labour, it is, I think, most desirable that it should be so ; and this, not less for the sake of the slaves themselves, than for that of the planters and of the manufacturers and merchants in this country, who are interested in the commerce of our Colonies. The negroes certainly would be infinitely better off than at present if emancipation were to take place without any accompanying measures for imposing upon them the necessity of regular work : in that case it may safely be concluded that they would almost universally become occupiers of land, from which, with very little exertion, they could derive a greater abundance than they now have of the necessaries of life, and of the few comforts to which they are accustomed, so that they might, and in all probability would, pass the greater part of their lives in idleness. This I cannot consider to be what would be most advantageous for them : to be under the necessity of exerting themselves is, I believe, a blessing to men, of whatever country and in whatever situation of life ; while the unavoidable consequence of the general refusal of the negroes to work for wages would be the annihilation of the commerce of the Colonies, and the ruin of all those who directly or indirectly depend upon it,—a result which in the end would be most injurious to the negroes, since it would prevent the residence among them of Europeans or of any other persons raised above the necessity of labouring for their subsistence, and

direct coercion of the whip by which the Negroes
had hitherto been impelled to labour, the indirect
constraint by which the working-classes in countries
where slavery does not exist are driven to exertion,
namely the impossibility of otherwise obtaining such a
maintenance as their habits render necessary to them.

In 1846, when I assumed the direction of the Colonial Department, experience had only too clearly demonstrated the urgent want of some such stimulus to
industry as would have been brought to bear upon the
Negroes by the measures proposed in 1833; but unfortunately the time had passed away in which this want
could be easily supplied.   It was impossible to expect
that, after eight years of almost unrestricted license, the
Negroes would easily be induced to submit to such
heavy demands upon them, and to such stringent regulations, as would have been .accepted with joy and
gratitude on their first emerging from slavery, and as
a substitute for its oppression.   But though the facilities for the reorganization of society (for nothing less
was required) which existed in 1833 could no longer
be commanded, and measures which would then have

thus enabled to diffuse around them the knowledge and the refine-
ments of civilized life. The proposal which has been submitted to
Parliament is, in my opinion, objectionable, not because it would
make it necessary for the negroes to perform a reasonable amount of
labour, but because it would impose this necessity by direct compulsion, instead of by the indirect compulsion (if I may be allowed
the expression) which would arise from placing them in circumstances in which industry would be their only refuge from want."—
Appendix, p. 52 : *Speech on Colonial Slavery, published by Ridg-
way,* 1833.

met with no resistance could only be attempted with
great caution in 1846, it nevertheless appeared to me
that it was still expedient to act, as far as was practicable, on the principles of the rejected plan of 1833,
which I conceive to be generally applicable in seeking
to promote the improvement of a population low in
the scale of civilization, and whose wants are few and
easily supplied.

In all communities of which this is the social condition, (and therefore in several other British Colonies,
besides those where slavery was abolished in 1833,)
I believe that the means of advancing civilization;
at the command of a Government, are of two kinds,
the first being measures having for their immediate
object the maintenance of order and security, and
the prevention of vagrancy by an efficient police,
the construction and improvement of roads, and
the establishment of hospitals, places of worship, and
schools, to provide education for the rising generation, religious instruction for all, and relief for the sick
and destitute; the second, but hardly less important
object, being to stimulate the industry of the people
by having recourse, at least to some extent, to direct
taxation bearing upon them, as the means of raising
the revenue required for the public service, and more
particularly for those important objects which I have
just mentioned—the police, roads, schools, places of
worship, and hospitals.

The necessity of adopting more efficient means for
the maintenance of order and the prevention of

vagrancy in the Sugar Colonies, has long been insisted upon by all connected with them; nor do I believe that the advantage of establishing good roads,
schools, places of worship, and public hospitals, has
been disputed, though I fear that the great importance of institutions for the education of the young,
and for the relief of the sick and destitute, has not
been sufficiently recognized. But the difficulty of providing funds to meet the expense has hitherto stood
in the way of making adequate provision for these
objects; and it has not been understood that not only
might this difficulty have been surmounted, but a
very powerful stimulus at the same time have been
given to the industry of the population, by adopting
the mode of taxation to which I have adverted.

This is a point of such extreme importance, that
I must explain somewhat more fully my views respecting it, which I cannot do better, than by ex-
tracting a portion of a despatch which, on the 24th
of October, 1848, I addressed to Lord Torrington,
on the financial measures that had been adopted in
Ceylon. In that despatch, after pointing out that
from the earliest times the practice had existed in that
Island, and in India, of requiring from the people
direct contributions to the wants of the Government,
principally in the form of gratuitous service, or of a
deduction from the produce of agricultural labour, I
proceeded to make the following remarks* :—

* See Papers relating to the affairs of Ceylon, presented to Parliament by Command, February, 1849, p. 344.

" The methods adopted of imposing this burden on the population may have been objectionable, and it is my own opinion that, both in India and under the native Governments in Ceylon, they were generally either extremely objectionable in themselves or were much abused; but the practice of requiring direct contributions from the mass of the people appears to me to have arisen from a necessity, inherent in the character, circumstances, and habits of the people, which must continue equally to be felt by their present rulers. But, further, it appears to me to be a mistake, to regard the imposition of direct taxation to a moderate amount, upon a population in such circumstances, as really injurious to them. I am persuaded that it may, on the contrary, be conducive to their true welfare. The view of this subject, which I conceive to be erroneous, has probably been adopted from applying to a very different state of society, a judgement founded upon that to which we are accustomed in Europe. In all European countries, the necessity of supplying their daily wants is, to the labouring classes, a sufficient motive to exertion; indeed, the difficulty which they experience in obtaining the means of comfortable subsistence is so great, that it has generally been considered (as it always ought to be) the great object of the Governments of these countries, in their financial arrangements, to avoid aggravating this difficulty by the imposition of taxes calculated to enhance the cost of subsistence. But the case is very different in tropical climates, where the population is very scanty in proportion to the extent of territory; where the soil, as I have already observed, readily yields a subsistence in return for very little labour; and where clothing, fuel, and lodging, such as are there required, are obtained very easily. In such circumstances there can be but little motive to exertion, to men satisfied with an abundant supply of their mere physical wants; and accordingly experience proves that it is the disposition of the races of men by which these countries are generally inhabited, to sink into an easy and listless mode of life, quite incompatible with the attainment of any high degree of civilization.   But if it be admitted, as I think it must, that the real welfare of mankind consists, not alone in the enjoying an abundance of the necessaries of life, but in their being also placed in a situation favourable to their moral improvement and to their advance in civilization, it follows that, in such countries as I have adverted to, it may be for the true interest of the working classes that the contributions demanded from them towards the wants of the State should somewhat increase the amount of exertion required for procuring a subsistence.

"The greater progress which civilization has made in temperate as compared to tropical climates, has always, and I believe justly, been attributed to the power with which necessity, which is proverbially the mother of invention and the mainspring of human exertion, has operated in the former as compared to the latter; hence the obvious policy of giving additional force to this stimulus in those cases in which it is found to be deficient.

"Nor is it to be lost sight of, that while direct taxation is, in such circumstances, calculated to promote the progress of society, indirect taxation has the very opposite effect. To create and to foster a taste for the habits of civilized life in a rude population, it is requisite that they should have before them the example of civilized men, and that the gratification of the wants of civilized life should be rendered as easy to them as possible; but with this view imported articles should be rendered cheap, and those branches of trade and industry which require the direction of civilized and educated men, such as the production of sugar and coffee, should be encouraged. Hence the peculiar importance of avoiding the imposition of any taxes which can interfere with trade, and the expediency of adopting the very opposite policy to that which would be proper in Europe, by endeavouring, in the imposition of taxes, to make them press, so far as prudence will admit, rather upon those who are content with a mere subsistence, than upon the possessors of property and the purchasers of luxuries. I cannot forbear remarking that what is now taking place in the West Indian Colonies, and the difficulties which are there experienced from the deficiency of adequate motives for industry, afford a striking illustration of the justice of the views I have thus explained to you."

It will be observed that this reasoning is not less

applicable to the West Indies than to Ceylon ; indeed
the principle of taxation recommended in the above
extract is far more calculated to be of service in the
former, because in almost all the Colonies in that part
of the world there exists a great deficiency of labour
available for hire (which is not the case in Ceylon,
owing to its vicinity to India), while the practice has
been general of providing for the public expenditure
by taxes which have a direct tendency to increase
that deficiency. Hitherto the principal source of
revenue in the West Indies has been the imposition
of heavy duties on imports, including articles of ordinary food ; and it is obvious that this system of
taxation must tend both to increase artificially the
strength of the motives which lead the Negroes to
prefer working in their own provision-grounds, to
labouring for hire in the cane-fields, as the means
of procuring a subsistence, and also to discourage the
formation of tastes which would afford a new stimulus
to industry.

Unfortunately the opinion of the Planters as a class
has been generally no less unfavourable than that of
the labouring population might have been expected to
be, to a thorough reform of the system of taxation in
the Sugar Colonies upon these principles. Without
the decided support of the former it was impossible
to attempt to carry such a reform into effect ; comparatively little has consequently been accomplished in
this direction (especially in the Colonies having representative Assemblies), although the utmost pains were

taken to press the subject upon the attention of the various legislative bodies through the Governors *, and though the ablest of these officers entirely concurred in the views I have stated, and did all that lay in their power to promote their practical adoption. Hence the financial improvements that have been effected have consisted chiefly of reductions of taxation, not of the substitution of better sources of revenue for objectionable taxes. In some Colonies the reductions of taxation have been large, as will appear when I come to notice what has been done in different Colonies.

In the absence of a thorough financial reform, founded on the principles I have endeavoured to explain, sufficient pecuniary means were not available for carrying into full effect the other class of reforms to which I have adverted, especially as in many cases the existing taxes were so objectionable in their character, that their reduction was imperatively required. But the efforts of the Government were steadily and

* See particularly the following despatches:—To Lord Harris, October 24, 1848, p. 22 (House of Commons Sessional Paper of 1846, No. 160). To Lord Harris, April 15, 1848 (House of Lords Paper No. 250, of 1848, p. 775). To Governor Barkly, June 1, 1849 (House of Commons Paper of 1849, No. 594, p. 188). To the same, September 30, 1849. To Sir Charles Grey, December 22, 1847. To the same, February 15, 1851. The last of these despatches is a recapitulation of the substance of many previous communications to the Governors of the Sugar Colonies, and contains a full explanation of my views on this subject; I shall have occasion again to refer to it, and I have inserted it at length in the Appendix. See Appendix (C) to this volume.

constantly directed towards providing the means, by the strictest economy, of giving increased efficiency to the branches of the Administration in which this was most necessary, and towards ensuring such a use of the powers which belonged to it, as might be best calculated to correct the errors committed since the abolition of slavery. Of these errors the following description is given by Lord Harris, in his able despatch of the 19th of June, 1848; the most important statements in it are not less applicable to most of the other Sugar Colonies than to Trinidad, of which he is immediately speaking. He says, " The affairs of the Colony have now arrived at that state, that it is absolutely necessary that their position should be thoroughly investigated, and then placed on such a footing as that at all events the lavish expenditure and hap-hazard legislation which have been going on for the last ten years should not occur again*." In a subsequent part of the despatch he proceeds to observe :—" One of the many errors which have been committed since the granting of emancipation, is the little attention paid to any legislation having for its end the formation of a society on true, sound, and lasting principles. That such an object could be attained at once, was and is not to be expected; but undoubtedly, had proper measures been adopted, much greater progress might have been made. As the question at present stands, a race has been freed, but a society has not been formed. Liberty has been

* House of Commons Sessional Paper of 1848, No. 749, p. 320.

given to a heterogeneous mass of individuals, who can only comprehend license. A participation in the rights, and privileges, and duties of civilized society has been granted to them; they are only capable of enjoying its vices. To alter such a state of things, vigorous and prompt measures are required, in order that the authority of the law should be felt; greater weight must be given to the Executive; to humanize the people, a general and extensive system of education must be adopted; to assist in civilization, every encouragement should be given to the establishment and to the easy circumstances of a superior class, especially of Europeans, amongst the population. All this requires expense. But what means are ready at hand to effect this? The energy of the lower Authorities has been shaken, by the partiality which has been invariably shown until lately in the transgression of the law, if by a coloured or a black man*."

I have quoted this extract from Lord Harris's despatch, because it contains, in a few words, what I consider to be a singularly accurate exposition of the errors of policy which had been committed in the former Slave Colonies, and because it was the main purpose of the greater part of the voluminous correspondence, which it was my duty to conduct with the Governors of these Colonies, to impress upon them, and, through them, on the leading members of the communities committed to their charge, the necessity of correcting the errors here pointed out. Throughout that correspon-

* Ibid., page 323.

dence the objects in view were, to bring the former slave population under a much stricter discipline than they had hitherto been subject to; to make them understand that the abolition of slavery was not intended to relieve them from the obligation to exertion, but to create motives to industry, to promote education, and to provide for the strict enforcement of the law, at the same time to relieve the Planters by a judicious revision of the system of taxation, and by the reduction of all unnecessary expense, carefully avoiding however all reductions which would either have violated the public faith to individuals, or interfered with the maintenance of the public establishments on that footing of complete efficiency which true economy requires.

Unfortunately the Planters, and others interested in the production of Colonial sugar, were so determined to look for relief from their difficulties only by a return to the former system of monopoly, and were so much encouraged in this temper by those who called themselves their friends, that they were induced to adopt a course which rendered it impracticable for the Government to carry the policy I have endeavoured to describe more than very partially into effect. The course to which I refer, as having been adopted by the West Indian party, led to such serious results, that I must advert to it rather more particularly.

For about a year or a little more after the passing of the Act of 1846, for the alteration of the Sugar-duties, there appeared to be a general disposition, on the part of those who had opposed the measure, tacitly to acquiesce in its continuance; and during the Session of 1847 the subject was almost, if not quite, unnoticed in Parliament. But the commercial disasters, in the latter part of that year, entirely altered the feelings of all connected with the Sugar Colonies, and created a panic among them, which prompted them to endeavour, by every means in their power, to prevail upon Parliament to retrace the steps which it had previously taken. Accordingly the distress of these Colonies became, during the Session of 1848, one of the principal subjects of Parliamentary debate. A Committee of inquiry into the causes of this distress was moved for in the House of Commons by the late Lord George Bentinck, with the avowed object of again excluding foreign sugar from our market; and when the evidence thus obtained came under the consideration of the House, a strong effort was made to prevail upon it to substitute a return to this policy for the measures which were brought forward by the Government.

You must doubtless well remember, that while we freely acknowledged and deplored the severe distress which at that time pressed upon the sugar-growing Colonies, we judged it to be far less attributable to the alteration in the Sugar-duties by the Act of 1846, and to the disturbance of existing relations, which is usually the first result of the abandonment of a vicious commercial system, than to the more general causes, under which all branches of the trade and industry, not only of this Country, but of Europe, were then suffering ; and we were persuaded that a return to the former policy, of excluding foreign sugar from our markets, would aggravate, instead of mitigating, the evils so loudly complained of.

We therefore resolved not to depart from the policy which had been adopted in 1846, but to endeavour to relieve the immediate pressure upon the Colonial interests, partly by a modification of the arrangement with regard to the duties on sugar, which had been made in that year, partly by enabling the Colonies, by the credit of this Country, to obtain loans on favourable terms, for immigration and other objects calculated to promote their improvement. The alteration we proposed, as to the Sugar-duties, involved some postponement of the period at which foreign and British sugar were to be admitted on equal terms, together with a very important reduction of the duties generally, which, by increasing the consumption of sugar, we believed would contribute, more than any other measure that could be adopted, to the real relief of the Planters.

Resolutions, on which to found a Bill for carrying this alteration into effect, were submitted to the House of Commons, and it was at the same time recommended that the Treasury should be enabled to guarantee loans to the amount of £500,000, which the Colonies might raise, in addition to the advances previously sanctioned, of £50,000 to Tobago, on account of the hurricane by which it had been devastated, and of £200,000 to Guiana and Trinidad, to provide for expenses already incurred on account of immigration. These proposals were met by a resolution, moved as an amendment by the present Secretary of State for the Colonial Department, which affirmed the insufficiency of the remedial measures suggested by the Government. This amendment, after a prolonged debate, was rejected by a majority of only 15, the numbers on the division having been 245 in its favour, and 260 against it.

Such a division, and the tone of the discussion by which it was preceded, could not fail greatly to encourage the hopes of those who contended for the restoration of the former monopoly of the British Planter; and it was believed that the accomplishment of this earnestly desired object would be greatly promoted by thwarting as much as possible the measures, and especially the whole Colonial policy, of an Administration pledged to the maintenance of the principles of commercial freedom, and to the application of these principles to the important article of sugar. The difficulties thus thrown in our way prevented our accomplishing much that it would have been desirable to effect; and hence, although I trust I shall be able to show a great improvement in the condition of some of the Sugar Colonies, that improvement has been far less general and decided than I believe it would have been, if those most interested in their welfare had adopted a different course.

Still the effect of the abandonment of the system of monopoly in the article of sugar, with the measures by which it was accompanied, has been the very reverse of that destruction of this branch of industry in the British dominions, which, during the inquiry of 1848, was so confidently predicted, as the inevitable result of refusing to restore protection. I need hardly observe that, nearly six years having now elapsed since Parliament determined that the monopoly formerly enjoyed by the British sugar-grower should be withdrawn, and nearly four since the law still in force was passed, it is clear that there has been time enough for this change of system to produce at least the greater part of its effect, and that if the production of sugar still continues to increase, that increase cannot now be attributed to an extension of cultivation effected under the stimulus of what is called protection. The question as to whether there has been an increase, and whether it is still going on, will be best answered by the following statements, compiled from the latest accessible information.

The first Table to which I have to call your attention is one showing the average annual importation of sugar from the three great divisions of the British possessions, namely the West Indies, Mauritius, and the East Indies, for the five years preceding July 1846, and for the five years succeeding,—that is to say, for the last five years before, and the first five years after, the admission of Slave-grown Sugar to our markets.

Quantities of Sugar and Molasses entered for Home Consumption in each of the Five Years ending July 5, 1846, and July 5, 1851.

WEST INDIES.

	cwts.
Average of Five Years ending July 5, 1846	2,702,730
Average of Five Years ending July 5, 1851	2,821,204
Increase	118,474

EAST INDIES.

	cwts.
Average of Five Years ending July 5, 1846	1,102,067
Average of Five Years ending July 5, 1851	1,343,555
Increase	241,488

MAURITIUS.

	cwts.
Average of Five Years ending July 5, 1846	674,256
Average of Five Years ending July 5, 1851	950,163
Increase	275,907

Total Increase from the British Possessions	635,869

You will perceive from this Table, that there has been a decided increase in the importation of all these descriptions of British sugar in the five years during which it has been exposed to the competition of the foreign grower, as compared to the five years of monopoly.

The next Table is one which has been prepared to exhibit, in periods of three years, the effect of the most important changes that have taken place in the circumstances of our Sugar Colonies, since the abolition of slavery was carried into full effect. For this purpose it compares the amount of sugar imported from the Colonies in the first three years after the cessation of the system of apprenticeship; in the three years immediately preceding the first slight relaxation of the former monopoly, by the Act of 1844; in the three years immediately succeeding, and in which the further relaxation of the monopoly, in the year 1846, can have had but a slight effect; and finally, in the last three years, in which that measure and the subsequent one of 1848 must have had time to exercise a great part at least of the influence they were calculated to have, on the extension or diminution of cultivation.

Sugar imported into the United Kingdom.—Triennial Averages.

Whence imported.	1839 to 1841 inclusive.	1842 to 1844 inclusive.	1845 to 1847 inclusive.	1849 to 1851 inclusive.
	cwts.	cwts.	cwts.	cwts.
West Indies	2,388,362	2,487,297	2,733,714	2,833,698
Mauritius	620,734	568,590	918,313	967,126
East Indies	746,864	1,044,911	1,386,169	1,463,356
Total from British Possessions.	3,755,960	4,100,798	5,038,196	5,264,180

This Return, you will observe, leads to the same conclusion as the preceding one, and shows an increase of production in each successive triennial period.

The last Return, relating to this subject, which it is necessary for me to quote, is one showing the amount of sugar imported from each of the British Possessions, taking them individually, in the two last years[*].

* It will be observed that, in this Return, the quantities of sugar imported are given for the years beginning in January, and therefore

Sugar imported from each of the undermentioned Colonies in the Years 1850 and 1851.

	1850.	1851.
	cwts.	cwts.
Antigua	123,485	200,235
Barbadoes	524,651	583,840
Dominica	51,816	60,239
Grenada	92,803	121,381
Montserrat	1,607	7,675
Nevis	15,508	33,309
St. Christopher's	70,717	122,029
St. Lucia	53,903	69,930
St. Vincent	139,567	163,409
Tobago	44,297	45,130
Tortola	1,406	3,070
Trinidad	366,214	441,772
British Guiana	525,297	595,200
Mauritius	1,003,296	1,000,269
British India	1,359,690	1,574,473
Jamaica	574,796	627,823
	4,949,053	5,649,784

It will be seen, from this Return, that the year ending January 1852 shows an increase, as compared to the preceding year, in the importation of sugar from every one of the British Possessions, without exception.

These Returns taken together prove that, whether we look to an average of several years, or to single years, there is, up to the very latest date, an increase in the

the figures will not correspond with those in the former Return, in which the years are taken from July to July,—the most convenient date when it can be taken, as it is that of the changes in the amount of the duty. These Tables have been prepared from the various Returns laid before Parliament. Tables showing the importation and consumption of Sugar, down to the latest period, are given in the Appendix (D) to this Volume.

production of sugar in the British Possessions, instead of that immediate and total cessation of cultivation which it was asserted must take place, unless the former monopoly were restored; and it is thus demonstrated, that the great fiscal and commercial advantages which are admitted to have been derived from the abrogation of that monopoly, have not been purchased by the lamentable consequences that were predicted.

But while the production of sugar in the British Colonies has thus continued to increase under the influence of competition, its price, as compared to foreign sugar, has continued to fall. It appears, from a Return* lately laid on the table of the House of Commons, that in 1844 (the last year in which the British grower had a complete monopoly) the average prices of British West India and of ordinary yellow Havannah sugar, exclusive of duty, were respectively 34s. 9d. and 21s. 3d. per cwt.; but that, in the half-year ending the 1st of January last, the price of British West India sugar was only 23s. 8d., that of Havannah sugar being 22s.; that is to say, that in the former year, the price of Colonial sugar, to the British consumer, was maintained at a rate 13s. 4d. per cwt. above the price of foreign sugar, by the exclusion of the latter from our market, while under the existing law the difference of price between the two descriptions of sugar has been reduced to 1s. 8d.

It is impossible to account for these two facts—of a

* Sessional Paper of 1852, No. 296.

great reduction in the price of British, as compared to foreign sugar, and of a simultaneous increase in the imports from the Colonies—except by supposing that the abrogation of the former monopoly has produced the effect anticipated by its advocates; and that the reduction in the price of Colonial sugar has been met by greater economy in its production, and more especially by a reduction of wages, or rather by what is still more advantageous to the Planters than a nominal reduction of wages, an increase in the amount of labour obtained for the same money that was formerly paid. It will appear in the sequel that this inference is confirmed by more direct evidence as to the reduction which has been effected in the cost of producing sugar in the Colonies. It will also appear that, instead of any deterioration having in that time taken place in the internal condition of the majority of these Colonies, there are decided symptoms of improvement.

July 13, 1852.

LETTER III.

MAURITIUS.—ST. LUCIA.—TRINIDAD.

MY DEAR LORD JOHN,

The account I have given in my last Letter of the policy pursued towards the Sugar Colonies generally, will enable me, I trust, to review at less length than would otherwise have been necessary, the transactions of those amongst them to which it is needful to refer.

To begin with Mauritius. This Colony, in the year 1846, was in a condition which, judging from the rapid increase in the production of sugar which had been going on for some years, and from the state of the revenue, might have been regarded as exceedingly prosperous; but, on the other hand, both those interested in the cultivation of sugar and the Governor concurred in representing this prosperity as rather apparent than real, and in pointing out the existence of evils and difficulties of a very serious character. In an address to the Governor, dated the 31st of May, 1846, and signed by seven hundred and twenty-five of the principal planters, merchants, and others, the preceding four years are described as "a period of unexampled distress and anxiety for all those concerned in Colonial agriculture*." In their repeated communications, both with the local and home Governments, the Planters and their correspondents in this country insisted principally on the scarceness and dearness of labour, and the consequent necessity of introducing a much larger number of labourers. They complained also that a large proportion of the labourers introduced from India, at a heavy expense to the Colony, did not give it in return the advantage of the labour for which this expense was incurred; many returning to India after comparatively short periods of residence, a still larger number being withdrawn from the cultivation of sugar by other occupations or by habits of vagrancy; while even of those who had contracted engagements with the Planters, many were very irregular in their attendance, the percentage of deserters and absentees being so considerable as greatly to diminish the amount of labour at the disposal of the Planter. The heavy taxation to which the Colony was subject was likewise a matter of complaint †.

The Governor's despatches by no means tended to throw doubt on the justice of these complaints;

* See House of Commons Sessional Paper for 1847, No. 325, p. 292. See also p. 295.

† See House of Commons Sessional Papers, No. 691, Part II. of 1846, and 325 of 1847 *passim*. See also House of Lords Paper of 1848, No. 250.

on the contrary they clearly proved the scarcity of labour, the rise which had taken place in wages, and the failure of the existing regulations to secure a due return in labour, for the heavy expense incurred by the Colony in the introduction of immigrants from India. But on the other hand the Governor, while admitting these evils, pointed out that the growing scarcity and dearness of labour, which had been so constant a subject of complaint, was to be accounted for by the competition of the Planters for labour to enable them to extend their cultivation, and that the production of sugar had rapidly increased by means of borrowed capital furnished by the great agency Houses, and for which very heavy charges were made; and he called attention* to the danger arising from this state of things, and the probability of "extensive embarrassment" being brought upon those engaged in this speculative system, "should a dark day arrive in succession to three consecutive seasons in which the Colony had been wonderfully favoured by Providence." These apprehensions of coming difficulties were but too completely realized by the commercial disasters of 1847, when so many of the great Mauritius Houses in this country fell to the ground; and the fact was disclosed, that the whole system upon which the cultivation of the Colony had been carried on, under the system of protection, .was radically

---

* See Sir W. Gomm's despatch to Mr. Gladstone of August 24, 1846, House of Commons Paper of 1847, p. 217; also his despatches of February 18 and 20, and September 3, of the same year.

unsound, and had been pushed in a spirit of imprudent speculation, far beyond what the real capital and resources available for its support would warrant.

Previously to the occurrence of this commercial crisis, the principal object calling for the attention of the Government was the necessity of placing the system of immigration from India on a better footing; and I have already in my last Letter given an extract from a despatch which I addressed to the Governor of Mauritius, explaining the principles on which I recommended that an ordinance for this purpose should be framed. The suggestions contained in this despatch were adopted with some modifications in an ordinance passed in 1847, and afterwards amended by two ordinances of the following year. By these laws the relations between the immigrants and their employers were placed on a satisfactory footing, and provision was made for meeting a large proportion of the cost of Indian immigration, by a tax which, though nominally paid by the Planters, really fell, as it ought to do, on the immigrants themselves. Regulations for checking the abuses which were complained of, as prevailing at the depôt where the immigrants were received to await being hired, were also established by Mr. Hugon, who was appointed Protector of Immigrants,—an office for which he was peculiarly qualified, by his having passed some years in India in the service of the East India Company, and his being well acquainted with the language of the people.

These measures have been attended with complete

success. In August, 1845, it was complained that many of the immigrants* returned to India long before the expiration of the five years for which they had agreed to come ; and it was estimated that, in addition to those thus lost to agriculture, out of about 35,000 immigrants introduced into the Colony from India in the years 1843–44, not less than 8,700† had been altogether withdrawn from sugar cultivation, by becoming vagrants or having taken to other occupations, while of those who were under engagement to the Planters, eighteen per cent. were to be· deducted as absentees. During the last two years complaints of these evils have greatly diminished, and it appears that in every respect the existing system is working in a highly satisfactory manner‡. I shall have to quote in the sequel a recent despatch from the Governor of the Colony, giving very gratifying evidence to this effect.

On the subject of immigration, I have to add that the heavy expense at which it was conducted had been a frequent subject of complaint on the part of the Planters. It was their wish that all persons should

* See Return of amount lost to the Colony by premature return of immigrants, House of Lords Sessional Paper of 1848, No. 250, p. 922.

† See Report of the Committee of Council of Mauritius, House of Commons Sessional Paper of 1846, No. 361, part ii. pp. 161–3 and 225, and Appendix to the Eighth General Report of the Emigration Commissioners, No. 15.

‡ See Appendix to the Eleventh General Report of the Emigration Commissioners, Nos. 32, 33, and 34, and Appendix to the Twelfth Report, No. 42.

be allowed to introduce as many labourers as they pleased, at their own cost, with a right to their services. But the abuses to which such an unrestricted introduction of labourers by individuals had led at an earlier period, attracted the attention of Parliament, and in 1838 the Government of that day was compelled to put a stop to it; and although there is no obstacle opposed by the law to the free resort to Mauritius of as many labourers as may think fit to come from India or from other quarters, it has been found necessary to require that those who do not come of their own accord, but are brought there, should be so under the immediate charge of the Government. The arrangements for this purpose have been gradually improved, and since 1847 a remarkable reduction has been effected in the cost of introducing immigrants into Mauritius from India. In that year it appears, from a return which the Emigration Commissioners have been so good as to furnish me with, that the cost per head of these immigrants was £6. 13s. 4d., but that for the years 1850 and 1851 it has averaged only £3. 3s. 1d., excluding in both cases the expenses incurred in India. At this reduced cost, the immigration of labourers from India must be nearly, if not quite, self-supporting, since the increased productiveness of the general revenue, which must arise from securing to the Planters an adequate supply of labour, may fairly be set against any excess of the expense incurred in providing passages and return passages for the immigrants, beyond what is paid by them in the form of a stamp-duty on engagements, or of a monthly tax on those not working under engagements. This large reduction in the expense of immigration, it need hardly be observed, constitutes a very important relief to the finances of the Colony. It has been accomplished partly by a relaxation of the rules of the East India Company as to the class of vessels to be used in this service, but far more, as I believe, by the removal of the restrictions imposed by the former Navigation Laws.

I have already made a passing allusion to the commercial difficulties of the year 1847. These disasters, in affecting every branch of our national industry and trade, fell with peculiar severity upon Mauritius, and I have now to give some account of the measures adopted by the Government for the relief of the Colony, in that season of extreme embarrassment and anxiety. In the month of October, 1847, in consequence of the failure of a large proportion of the mercantile houses connected with the Colony, a representation was transmitted to the Colonial Office by the Mauritius Association of London*, pointing out the absolute necessity for some interference on the part of the Government, in order to guard against the calamitous consequences that might ensue from the sudden interruption of the arrangements by which the employment of the large immigrant population, and the importation into the Colony of food for their use, had hitherto been provided for. It was stated that Mauritius annually drew

* House of Lords Sessional Paper of 1848, No. 250, p. 1073.

from India, for the consumption of the immigrants from that country, from 480,000 to 500,000 bags of rice, and that there was reason to apprehend, in consequence of the disasters that had fallen upon Calcutta and Mauritius, that the required supplies might not be regularly forwarded. The Association therefore recommended, as a precautionary measure against the risk of famine, that instructions should be sent to the Bengal Government by the next Overland Mail, to ascertain what shipments of rice had been made to the Colony; and in the event of its appearing that there had been a deficiency in the usual supply, to cause it to be made good by shipments on account of the Colonial Government. The Association further recommended, that, as the usual resources of the Colonists would be cut off by the total disorganization of commercial credit in England and India, an advance of £10 a ton on sugar shipped to this Country should be made by the local Government to the Planters, to enable them to continue the cultivation of their estates, and thus prevent the large number of labourers who had been introduced into the Colony from being thrown out of employment. Lastly, the Association recommended that this advance should be made in notes for one dollar each, payable in twelve months, to afford time for the Colonial agent to send out specie for their discharge.

This letter was dated the 15th of October, 1847; and though we were well aware of the great danger of any interference on the part of the Government with the

ordinary operations of commerce, and that much more
harm than good is usually done by such interference,
for the relief of difficulties of the kind now apprehended, still this case appeared to be so urgent and so
peculiar, as to justify some departure from ordinary
rules. The large number of labourers, who might, as
it was feared, be left altogether destitute, had been
brought to Mauritius on the responsibility and at the
cost of the Colonial Government; while the danger was
increased by the remoteness of the Island from all the
great marts of commerce, and the apparent impossibility of its supplying, without extraneous assistance,
the want of capital which must have been occasioned
by the failure of Houses which had been stated (as it
was believed correctly) to have had in their hands not
less than half the trade of the Colony.

After as much deliberation as the shortness of the
time permitted, it was therefore determined that the
greater part of the measures recommended by the Mauritius Association should be adopted, and despatches
were addressed to the Governor on the 25th of October, acquainting him that instructions had been sent
to the Government of India to forward supplies of
rice to the Colony, if this should prove to be necessary, and authorizing him to make advances to the
merchants and planters of Mauritius, on the security
of sugar to be shipped for this Country, to an amount
not exceeding £150,000. This money was to be advanced at the rate of £9 a ton on the sugar shipped.

* See Paper quoted above, pp. 1070–1078.

The recommendation that the advances should be made in dollar notes payable in twelve months was not adopted, it being considered that this would in fact be equivalent to the establishment of an inconvertible paper currency, against the depreciation of which no effectual security could be provided,—a measure the injurious consequences of which must in the end far outweigh the advantage of any temporary relief it might afford.

But in declining to adopt this proposal, it was considered that some benefit might be derived from the issue of a paper currency, under regulations which should effectually secure its constant convertibility into specie; the object being to give to the Colony the advantage of a medium of exchange which, though more economical than one consisting exclusively of the precious metals, should be equally free from all danger of depreciation. The effect of this, it was anticipated, would be to set free a portion of the capital of the Colony, which was locked up in the specie used in its pecuniary transactions. This was regarded as an object of great importance, at a moment when so large an amount of the capital embarked in the production of sugar was either lost or withdrawn, in consequence of the recent commercial failures. The Governor was accordingly instructed to take the necessary steps for the issue of a paper currency of this description.

These despatches were transmitted to the Governor on the 25th of October, and their substance was communicated to the gentlemen of the Mauritius Association, by whom the subject had been brought under the consideration of the Government. They acknowledged with much gratitude the relief thus afforded*, but at the same time they strongly urged the necessity of adopting further measures for effecting a permanent improvement in the condition of the Island. What they chiefly insisted upon was, that a larger supply of labour should be afforded, and on easier terms; that intercourse with Madagascar should be renewed; that the taxation of the Colony should be greatly diminished, and especially that the export duty on sugar should be repealed; that, with a view to this object, the expenditure should be largely reduced and the system of Government entirely remodelled and simplified; and lastly, that greater advantage should be given to Colonial sugar, in its competition with foreign sugar in the home market. In reply to this communication, they were assured that it was the

* See the letter from the Association dated October 28, 1847, p. 1079 of the Paper quoted above. This letter contains the following passage:—" We now approach your Lordship, to offer our most sincere and very grateful acknowledgments for these timely measures of relief to the Colony in the hour of her extreme need. Whatever may be the result, we must say that your Lordship has responded to our call in the kindest manner, and with a readiness and promptitude of action that has never been exceeded; and we beg, in the name of the Colony, to tender to your Lordship our warmest thanks. These kind acts go far to impress the Association with the idea that the interests of the Colony are still considered of value and dear to the Mother-country, and in the estimation of Her Majesty's Government."

earnest wish of the Government to afford to the Mauritius merchants the utmost practicable relief, by the reduction of taxation, and by facilitating their obtaining a supply of labour upon the easiest terms to the Colony; but that it was impossible to give the peremptory instructions to the Governor which were asked for the immediate removal of particular taxes, and that no expectations could be held out that a return to the policy of excluding foreign sugar from the British market would be recommended to Parliament.

I have already fully explained our views, and the course we adopted, on some of the chief points adverted to in the above correspondence; it remains that I should state that an effort was made, but for the time in vain, to re-establish the former intercourse between Mauritius and Madagascar, and that I should give some account of what was done to meet the wishes of the Mauritius merchants, by improving and simplifying the system of the Colonial Government, and by reducing the public expenditure and taxation. This account must necessarily be a very general one, since to enter into any details would lead me into much greater length than is admissible.

The most important improvements which have been effected in the government of Mauritius have been the commencement of a system of municipal organization, and a reform in the judicial establishments and in the administration of justice. Until very recently there existed no municipal organization

whatever in Mauritius, and much business was thrown
on the various public departments, from which it was
highly desirable to relieve them. By an ordinance
which came into operation on the 1st of January,
1850, a Corporation was constituted for the town of
Port Louis, which was reported by the Governor, in
his despatch of the 16th of May, 1851, to be working in a satisfactory manner*. This measure was
intended to be preparatory to the general establishment of a system of Municipal organization for the
rural districts, as well as for the towns of the Island;
and I trust that this object may not be lost sight of,
as its accomplishment would not only provide for the
management of many affairs of a local character, in a
much more satisfactory manner than at present, but
would also be the best preparation for the future concession to the inhabitants of a larger share of power
in the government of the Island. In the meantime,
while, for the reasons I have mentioned in the
first of these Letters, the state of society in Mauritius does not seem to be adapted to the establishment of popular government, two additional unofficial members have been appointed to the Council
of Government from among the principal inhabitants
of the Colony; the various departments of the Government have also been revised, and considerable
progress has been made in simplifying the arrangements for the transaction of public business, and in
providing for the reduction of the expense of the

* Blue Book Reports presented to Parliament in 1851, p. 272.

several establishments to as great an extent as is consistent with the maintenance of their efficiency, and with justice to the existing holders of office.

With regard to the judicial establishment and the administration of justice, it is only necessary for me to observe, that ordinances have been passed by which very important changes have been carried into effect, with the view of assimilating the forms of procedure to those of this Country, and getting rid of some cumbrous and objectionable parts of the old French system. It is confidently anticipated, that by these changes the administration of justice will be rendered far more prompt and efficient than formerly, with a material reduction of expense both to the Colonial Treasury and to individuals.

A very considerable reduction of taxation has been effected, the taxes abolished or reduced being those which pressed most directly on the industry and trade of the Colony. Of these taxes, the one which has always been the subject of the loudest and most just complaint is that on the export of sugar, which has been reduced from 1s. per cwt., its amount in 1846, first to 9d., then to 6d., and ultimately to 4½d., the Planters being thus relieved from a charge of £37,500 a-year. Other taxes, amounting to no less than £50,734 a-year, have also been reduced, all of them being imposts the removal of which is calculated to afford relief and encouragement to the trade and industry of the Island. This is peculiarly the case with regard to the taxes which formerly rendered the transfer of property in Mauritius exceedingly expensive, and also to some of the Customs-duties and dues upon shipping, which have been abolished. The reduction of the last, coming in aid of the repeal of the restrictions imposed by the former Navigation Law, seems likely to render Port Louis a most important harbour of resort for the ships of all nations, which cannot fail to be attended with much advantage to the Island. The above reduction, amounting in all to nearly £88,000*, has been effected in taxes

* The following is a more detailed statement of the taxes reduced :

Taxes reduced in Mauritius from 1846 to 1852, omitting those suspended only and afterwards re-imposed.

Reduced in 1847 :—

Transcription duty	£2400 per annum	
Market dues	1600	
	—— £4000	

Reduced in 1848 :—

Taxes on horses and carts (deducting £470, the produce of a new tax on horses, from £5740, the gross amount of the tax reduced.) . .	£5270	
Export duty on sugar, reduced from 1s. to 9d.	15,000	
Other export duties	100	
Duties on advertisements, passports, and stamps	1470	
Port charges	1865	
Coals, bricks, etc.	130	
Provisions (Parliamentary duties) .	400	
Tonnage dues and duties on coasters, boats, etc.	9100	
Registration and other fees . .	6000	
	—— £39,335	

Reduced in 1849 :—

Fishing and trading licenses . . .	£6108

which in 1846 produced a total revenue of £328,340, without the imposition of any new taxes except the stamp-duty on engagements and monthly tax on immigrants, and a small increase of the duties on tobacco and spirits or cordials, these last amounting together to about £14,000 a-year. The latter are a tax upon luxuries, which have always been considered one of the fairest subjects for taxation; the former, as I have already explained, cannot properly be considered a tax at all, but ought rather to be regarded as an arrangement for recovering from immigrant labourers, brought into the Colony, a part of the expense incurred by their introduction; and, instead of checking trade and industry, it tends directly to promote them.

Reduced in 1851 :—

Differential import duties .	.	.	£3321
Export duty on sugar, from 9*d.* to 6*d.*			15,000
			——— £18,321

Reductions proposed in 1852 :—

Export duty on sugar, from 6*d.* to 4½*d.*			£7500
Export quay duties .	.	.	5500
Harbour dues .	.	.	1000
Registration dues	.	.	5000
Portal charges .	.	.	1000
			——— £20,000

Making a total of taxes reduced since 1846 of £87,764 per annum, including taxes for the repeal of which ordinances have lately been passed.

The above statement has been made out from a Paper as to the financial arrangements of the Colony for the present year, which was laid by the Governor before the Council, and was republished from a Colonial newspaper in the 'Economist' of the 15th of May, and from an account which was prepared for me some time ago in the Colonial Office, from similar Papers of former years.

The whole therefore of the great relief which has been given to the commercial interests of Mauritius, has been obtained without any drawback by the imposition of new burdens. This relief has also been granted without any detriment to the finances of the Colony. It appears, from accounts laid by the Governor before the Council, and recently received in this Country, that the revenue for 1851, which had been estimated at £292,762, actually amounted to £321,390, and the expenditure to £259,728, leaving a surplus of £61,662, the surplus at the end of the year 1850 having been £42,000.

Such were the chief measures of the Government in the Mauritius during the five years and a half of your Administration. The highest credit is due to Sir G. Anderson and Mr. Higginson for the energy and judgement with which they successively managed the affairs of the Island, and performed the difficult task entrusted to them of working out the policy we had determined to adopt. The results of that policy will be best shown by a despatch from the Governor, which I had the satisfaction of laying on the table of the House of Lords on the eve of our retirement from office. This despatch I think it right to quote at length; and before doing so, I have only to observe that, in order duly to estimate the improvement which has taken place in the condition of the Colony, it should be remembered, that the distress which only four years ago prevailed there, had produced its ordinary effect of political discontent, which was greatly aggravated by the persevering efforts made in this Country to represent the members of your Administration as enemies of the Colonies, on account of our commercial policy. The correspondence laid before Parliament affords ample evidence of the discontented and irritated feelings which prevailed in the Colony during the years 1847 and 1848,—feelings which are in striking contrast with those described as now existing amongst the inhabitants in the following despatch :—

" Copy of a Despatch from the Governor of Mauritius to Her Majesty's Principal Secretary of State for the Colonies, with a Report on the State of the Rural Districts.

"Mauritius, 14th October, 1851.

" MY LORD,

" I beg leave to transmit herewith copies of an address presented to me by the inhabitants of Flacq on my recent visit to that district, and of my reply thereto*.

"I have now completed a tour of the rural districts, during which the favourable impressions that I had been led to form, and to express to your Lordship, of the condition, the progress, and the promise of this valuable, and, at the present period, most interesting dependency of the Crown, have been amply confirmed.

" I found abroad a spirit of self-reliance, a conviction of the adequacy of our growing resources, and a resolution to combat with vigour the difficulties still unsubdued, that to my view present unmistakeable earnests of ultimate success. I saw, in some quarters, luxuriant canes covering lands redeemed within a few years from the forest or the rock, now amply remunerating the labour and capital bestowed upon

* See Appendix (E) to this Volume.

them. I saw in others substantial edifices rising up, new
and powerful steam-engines at work, and improved processes
of manufacture, rewarding the enterprise of their introducers,
and everywhere symptoms of activity, energy, and industry.
I saw the Indian immigrant in the field, working steadily
and with good-will, and when at rest cheerful and contented
in his camp. As it is by him and through him that the
Mauritian Planter must rise or fall, to the character of the
relations subsisting between them the utmost importance
ought, I conceive, to be attached. So far as I could judge—
and I took pains to ascertain correctly—these relations are
highly satisfactory. Complaints on either side grow more
rare, as the language, the character, and the habits of
the Indian become better understood; and from what I
heard and witnessed, I believe that he and his employer
are mutually pleased and satisfied. There appeared no
general scarcity of labour, although in some less favoured
localities it was represented that additional hands were required. Wages continue moderate, and our now open port
generally keeps down the price of rice and other grain to a
reasonable average. The market however is not supplied
with sufficient regularity, but it may be expected that free
competition will soon cure this defect.

" I may perhaps be over-sanguine, but I witnessed so
many significant symptoms of progress and improvement
throughout the island, that I cannot resist the conviction
that the foundation is now being laid of wealth and prosperity, more stable and enduring than ever could have been
attained under the former speculative and artificial system
of labour and of prices, which for a time largely enhanced
profits, and ultimately left the Colony on the verge of
bankruptcy and ruin. I will not dwell upon the painful
sacrifices, the misery and suffering, that followed; very few

escaped unharmed, and many were engulfed in the wreck. I will rather turn to the gladsome prospect that has opened upon us, elevating the hopes of the employers of free labour, and cheering them on to the momentous struggle in which they are engaged, and of which this little Island seems the predestined battle-field. The issue may for a season vacillate, but the ground already won, and the resources available, fully developed and judiciously applied, form no light guarantees of ultimate victory. The discomfiture will prove a mighty engine, an incalculable impetus, to the extinction of slavery, and to the suppression of that accursed traffic.

" I will not pretend to estimate the maximum production of sugar of which this fertile soil is capable ; that it at present falls far short of that limit is unquestionable. By more skilful and economical husbandry, and the larger application of chemistry and improved mechanism to the manipulation of the cane, in both of which directions progress is being made, there is no doubt that the amount of production can be considerably increased ; but for clearing forest lands, and reclaiming large tracts now lying sterile and unproductive, a large accession of capital and labour is required ; and that will assuredly follow the establishment of confidence in the capabilities and resources of the Colony, which the present aspect of both agricultural and commercial affairs is, in my judgement, well calculated to promote.

" Whilst I am enabled to report thus favourably of our material prospects, I believe I am warranted in stating that progress has also been made in ameliorating the moral and social condition of the people, but much more, I apprehend, remains to be accomplished. The great lever, education, has much to contend against, from the heterogeneous ele-

ments by which it is here surrounded. Amongst a community composed of men differing in race, in manners, in
language, and in religion, by none of whom perhaps are the
advantages and value of knowledge sufficiently appreciated,
the march of education must necessarily be slow, and its
harvest of protracted maturity.

" I have recently referred to the Education Committee
the highly important question of devising some provision
for imparting elementary instruction to the Indian section of the population; but its solution is beset with such
formidable difficulties that I at present entertain but faint
hopes of seeing the object accomplished.

" The almost total absence of the emancipated race from
plantation labour is a striking feature in our social economy,
They are now to be sought for in the principal towns and
their neighbourhood, or in retired spots, where they have
located themselves in straggling hamlets, deriving an easy
subsistence from the produce of the ground which they
cultivate, and from the rearing of poultry and other stock,
which they carry to the market of Port Louis, sometimes
from very distant quarters of the island. They also traffic
in firewood and charcoal: and huckstering and peddling
are favourite pursuits. I visited some of these Settlements:
they wear an appearance of comfort and independence:
their inmates are generally orderly and well-conducted;
but they prefer ease to work; and, unstimulated to labour
beyond what their limited necessities demand, they abandon
all field-work for hire, which, unfortunately, they consider
to be a degraded occupation, and which, in their own minds,
they cannot disconnect from the old system of compulsory
labour. This feeling is imbibed by their children, whom
they bring up to follow callings similar to their own, or
some trade or handicraft; so that until the immigrants

become denizens of the soil, to which every possible encouragement is given, planters may be said to be entirely dependent on foreign labour for the cultivation of their estates. There is usually a church or chapel within reach of these Settlements, at which the attendance is, I understand, pretty regular; but I fear that the opportunities for secular instruction are exceedingly limited. Intermarriages between Indians and creoles are very rare, but more frequent now than formerly. The great disparity between the sexes amongst the former is an evil which I have frequently noticed, and which is, I hope, in course of being mitigated. The liberality shown by the local Government, and the readiness with which they sanction the additional expenditure involved in the attempts made to remedy this defect, are, I think, highly creditable to their foresight and philanthropy.

"I rejoice in believing that all classes of the community over whom I have been called to preside are animated by a spirit of loyalty and order; but the sentiments of respectful attachment and genuine regard entertained towards the Sovereign's Representative in the rural districts were as conspicuous as they were highly gratifying to witness. I was cordially welcomed everywhere; and the knowledge, both of men and things, directly acquired by personal intercourse and observation, cannot, I think, fail to be useful and profitable. My visits were gratefully and warmly appreciated by the inhabitants, who looked upon them as the revival of an ancient and popular custom, when relations between governors and governed stood upon a more intimate and less reserved footing. They feel gratified at the occasional presence of the chief of the Colony, from which they also anticipate advantage to their districts, in the opportunity of having their local wants and wishes brought more immediately under his notice. They were freely invited to make these known, and the reasonableness and justice of their demands generally enabled me to take measures for acceding to them without delay and without difficulty. I found no crying grievances to redress, no festering wounds to heal, no grave complaints to inquire into ; peace, harmony, and contentment appeared to prevail. To preserve and improve these blessings will be my unremitting study ; and, possessing the confidence of the people and the continued support of your Lordship, I trust that my efforts will not prove unavailing.

" Some may pronounce the picture that I have attempted to draw too flattering ; but I assure your Lordship that no exaggeration is intended. My only desire has been to describe faithfully what came under my own observation, and to make known to your Lordship the conclusions which I have ventured to deduce, in reference to the condition, both present and prospective, of the districts which I have recently visited.

" I have, etc.,

" J. M. HIGGINSON."

There are two other Sugar-growing Colonies in which the form of government is the same with that which exists in Mauritius, namely St. Lucia and Trinidad. In both a similar course of policy has been pursued to that which I have already described as having been adopted in Mauritius; it is therefore unnecessary that I should advert to more than a few particulars in the correspondence to which their affairs have given rise.

With regard to St. Lucia it will be seen, on reference

to the series of very able Reports upon its condition which were made by the late Lieutenant-Governor, Mr. Darling* (now Lieutenant-Governor of the Cape of Good Hope), that on his appointment at the end of the year 1847 he found the Colony in a state which was very far from satisfactory. The upper classes were divided by feuds and jealousies, which for some years had convulsed society, while the labouring population were not making the progress in civilization which might have been expected since the abolition of slavery. The means of promoting education were exceedingly defective; considerably less than half the population were in the habit of attending any place of worship; and, though serious crimes were rare, petty thefts and other minor offences were lamentably common. Agriculture was in a very rude state, with little improvement apparently going on, and there existed neither municipal institutions of any kind, nor agricultural or other societies, calculated to promote the interchange of ideas and the intellectual improvement of the Colonists. The administration of justice was costly, and in many respects defective.

It is of course impossible that a really satisfactory state of society can be substituted for one so much the reverse except by very slow degrees; and in so short a time as has elapsed since the close of 1847, all

---

* See Blue Book Reports, presented in 1848, 1849, 1850, and 1851; and Lieutenant-Governor Darling's Despatch to Colonel Reid, of the 21st of March, 1848. (House of Lords' Sessional Paper of 1848, No. 250, p. 348.)

that can be expected is that a beginning of improvement should have been made, and that means should have been created for carrying it progressively forward. This has, I think, certainly been accomplished. Party spirit does not run so high as formerly, owing mainly to the judicious and conciliatory conduct of the late Lieutenant-Governor, and in no slight degree also, as I believe, to the course which was taken with reference to the unfortunate differences between a former Lieutenant-Governor and the then Chief Justice. These differences, after greatly agitating the Colony, led to charges being brought against the Judge, which, instead of being decided by any more summary process, were referred for inquiry and adjudication to a Committee of the Privy Council, by whom counsel were heard both in support of the charges and in reply to them. The Committee of the Privy Council ultimately recommended the removal of the Judge who had been accused, expressing at the same time some disapprobation of the course taken by the predecessor of Lieutenant-Governor Darling; and this decision, having been pronounced by a perfectly impartial tribunal, and after an inquiry of a judicial character, was not contested, as it certainly would have been, had it proceeded from any less weighty authority; and it practically put an end to a business of a very troublesome nature*.

I mention this circumstance, because it is an ex-

* These Papers were laid at the time upon the table of the House of Commons.

ample of those personal quarrels between the officers of Colonial Governments, which it is so much the tendency of these small societies to create, and which add so materially to the labour and difficulty of administering the affairs of the Colonies. It illustrates also the advantage of the arrangement to which I shall advert in a future Letter, by which the Secretary of State was enabled to obtain the assistance, on certain occasions, of a Committee of the Privy Council.

The office of Chief Justice, having thus been rendered vacant, was not filled up by the appointment of any resident Judge; but an arrangement was made, with the assent of the Legislature of Barbadoes, for appointing Sir Bouchier Clarke, the very able Chief Justice of that Colony, to the same office in St. Lucia, to which latter Colony he now pays periodical visits, for the purpose of presiding in the Court when cases of importance are brought before it, minor cases being disposed of by the resident Puisne Judge. The expense of the judicial establishment has thus been materially reduced, without depriving St. Lucia of the advantage of having her Courts of Justice presided over by a lawyer of the highest distinction, both for professional knowledge and for the general uprightness and excellence of his character. The economy of this arrangement is the least of its recommendations; its great advantage is that of placing the important office of Chief Justice in the hands of a person not usually resident in the Island, and thus removed from the influence of those local animosities which so constantly arise in such small communities, and oppose a great obstacle to the satisfactory administration of justice, by a judge who is himself a member of the society which is thus divided. The arrangements for the administration of justice have further been improved by the establishment of Trial by Jury in criminal cases, by some important amendments in the laws relating to masters and servants, and by affording increased facilities for the recovery of debts, by less expensive processes than formerly.

Trial by Jury was established upon a system which has been for many years in successful operation in Van Diemen's Land, and which I have omitted no opportunity of recommending for adoption elsewhere. The objections to requiring unanimity in a Jury are palpable and notorious; but, on the other hand, the rule of deciding by a majority is open to the objection, that the majority may overrule adverse opinions hastily and impatiently, and resort to the ready expedient of resolving every question by putting it at once to the vote. The plan which seems best adapted to obviate on the one hand the undue impatience of a majority, and, on the other, the undue pertinacity of a minority, is that of verdicts by majorities lessening as the periods of deliberation lengthen. Thus, if the Jury consist of twelve (which however is a larger number than I would recommend) unanimity is required for the first two hours, unanimity less by one for the second, less by two for the

third, less by three for the fourth, less by four for
the fifth; and if there should then, at the end of ten
hours of deliberation, be a dissentient minority of
more than four out of twelve, a new Jury is to be
impanelled.

Amongst other improvements of a more general
nature which have been effected, the Lieutenant-
Governor points out* that " the basis of an extended
provision for the education of the people, and for
disseminating useful agricultural knowledge, has been
laid." Public works of much utility have been successfully completed; reductions in the civil establishment have been made, without impairing its efficiency;
the objectionable export-duties formerly levied have
been repealed, and the customs-duties generally lowered without reducing the revenue, which is amply
sufficient to meet the expenditure; the beginning of
municipal institutions has been made, by the creation
of a Town Council in Castries; the charge of pauperism
has been greatly reduced, by a careful revision of the
claims for relief; and, lastly, about 1100 Negroes
liberated from captured slavers have been introduced
into the Colony, and most gratifying reports have
been received of their condition and prospects.

Though the measures I have enumerated may not
present any immediate and striking results, they have,
I believe, laid the foundation for a solid improvement
in the condition of this Colony, one of the most highly
gifted by nature in the British dominions. In the

---

* Blue Book Reports for 1849.

meantime it is satisfactory to find that in St. Lucia, where, by the careful investigation of the Lieutenant-Governor, we have more complete means than elsewhere of judging of the actual results of the competition to which the British sugar-grower is now exposed, there is very strong evidence to show that the effects of our altered commercial policy have not been injurious to the Planters. Lieutenant-Governor Darling, with great pains, collected information which throws much light on the practical working of the recent change, and which will be found in his Reports upon the Colony presented to Parliament in the years 1850 and 1851. In the former of these Reports he states that "the fall in wages from an average of 1s. 4d. a day in 1846 to 11d. in 1849 was the direct result of the reduced prices occasioned by the Sugar Duties Act of 1846." He then shows, by a comparison of the rates of wages in St. Lucia with the average prices of Colonial sugar in this Country, as given in the Gazette, "that while in 1846 the rate of wages was to the Gazette price of 1 cwt. of sugar as 1 is to 26, in 1849 the rate of wages stood in proportion to the Gazette price of 1 cwt. of sugar as 1 does to 28 ; or, putting the case thus, if 1s 4d. was the daily wages in 1846, when £1 14s. 5d., or 413 pence, was the Gazette price of 1 cwt. of sugar, then when in 1849 11d. became the rate of wages, £1 3s. 8d., or 284 pence, would be the equivalent price of a cwt. of sugar ; but I find the average price of Muscovado sugar for 1849 to be about £1 5s. 6d. per cwt., being 1s. 10d. a cwt.

in favour of the produce of the year 1849." He proceeds to observe that the cost of labour does not form
the whole cost of producing sugar, but constitutes
from two-thirds to three-quarters of such cost; and
that freight having been reduced from four to three
shillings per cwt. and the prices of some articles of
estates' supplies being also lower, "upon the whole
it may be concluded that the position of the pro-
ducer of sugar, so far as it is affected by the proportion which exists between the cost of production and
the price of produce, is in 1849 at least 2s. 6d. better
than it was in 1846*."

Lieutenant-Governor Darling, in making this statement, frankly acknowledged that the Planters in St.
Lucia then took a very different view of the subject
from himself; but, reverting to the question in his
Report dated the 8th of May 1851, he points out
"that the sales of estates which have taken place since
the commencement of the present year amply prove,
both by the prices realized and the number of contending purchasers, that the opinion I have ventured to
advance, that profitable returns from the cultivation
of the cane may be reasonably expected, are now
acquiesced in by many of the planting body."

* The publication of this statement led to its accuracy being
questioned by one of the principal planters in the Island, a member
of the Legislative Council; but the Lieutenant-Governor met the
doubt thus raised by further details, which fully supported, as it appears to me, the correctness of his original statement, or at least of
that part of it which I have quoted. See this correspondence in the
second part of the Blue Book Reports for 1850.

I have already, in speaking of the Sugar Colonies generally, quoted the opinion expressed by Lord Harris of the condition in which he found the fertile and beautiful island of Trinidad in 1846. The existence of such a state of things as he described, more than eight years after the complete abolition of slavery, affords decisive evidence how little the commercial monopoly which the Planters had enjoyed had contributed to promote their real interest, or, I may add, that of any other class of society. It was also a state of things which rendered the Colony little capable of bearing up against the difficulties of the commercial crisis of 1847. Accordingly these difficulties were felt nowhere with greater severity than in Trinidad; and during the last months of 1847 and the whole of 1848 nothing could exceed the gloom by which its prospects were overhung. In addition to other failures, the stoppage of the West India Bank, which Lord Harris reported in his despatch of the 4th of December, 1847, contributed greatly to increase the embarrassment which was experienced; and the falling off of the revenue, from the interruption of trade, threatened to add the insolvency of the Colonial Treasury to that of a large proportion of those engaged in the commerce and agriculture of the Island.

On the 22nd of May, 1848, the Governor reported the Colonial Treasury to be absolutely empty; and in this and other despatches, while he said that the existing salaries were not higher than they ought to be, and that for the efficient conduct of the public service the civil establishment required to be increased instead of being diminished, he felt it impossible to suggest any mode of meeting the deficiency which the Council anticipated in the revenue of the year, without, amongst other measures, having recourse to a large deduction from the salaries of all the public servants. He proposed* that a deduction, varying from thirty per cent. on the highest salaries, to one per cent. on salaries of £100 a-year, should be made in paying the public servants.

This proposal evinced great disinterestedness on the part of Lord Harris, as the largest percentage of deduction would have applied, under the rule he suggested, only to his own salary : but it did not seem to be a course that ought to be adopted. The instructions that were transmitted to him, therefore, were to the effect, that a deficiency of revenue to meet the indispensable demands of the public service might make a reduction of the salaries of public officers unavoidable, but that, as the salaries of public servants had been determined and accepted on the assumption that the rate of income assigned to them is assured, the salaries of offices which were not vacant could not with justice be reduced in anticipation of an apprehended deficiency, but only for the purpose of meeting one that had actually occurred, and in that case the percentage of deduction must

* House of Commons Sessional Paper of 1849, No. 280, p. 4.

be an equal one from all salaries whatever, or, at all events, from all salaries exceeding £150 a-year.

He was also informed that, to meet the immediate difficulty, which had arisen mainly from the circumstance that the Commissioners who had been authorized to raise a loan for the expenses incurred on immigration had failed in doing so, owing to the great pressure in the money-market, Her Majesty's Government proposed to obtain the sanction of Parliament (which was granted) for making the required advance from the British Treasury, and that the Colony was in future to be relieved (as I have already mentioned) from the expense of the introduction of liberated Africans. Instructions were also given with respect to some reductions of establishment which appeared to be practicable, a large discretion being given to the Governor to adopt such other measures as he might consider to be most expedient for adjusting the balance between the receipts and the expenditure of the Colony.

Lord Harris acted with great firmness and judgement on these instructions. He revised the establishments, and postponed all expenses not of the most pressing nature, but did not make the contemplated deduction from the salaries of the public servants, or postpone the operation of an ordinance which, (availing himself of the power granted to the Colonial Legislature by the Act of Parliament of 1846,) he had passed in 1847, for the purpose of repealing the Parliamentary differential duties, and at the same time considerably reducing the general rate of duties on imports. When the ordinance in question was passed, it was arranged that it should take effect from the commencement of 1849; and notwithstanding the great financial difficulties which were experienced in 1848, this arrangement was not departed from, in the confidence, (which events have proved to be well grounded,) that, notwithstanding the severity of the crisis which the Colony was undergoing, its resources were sufficient to bring it through its difficulties, and that the revival of its trade and industry would be promoted by relieving its commerce from the burdens to which it was subject; so that, notwithstanding the apparent sacrifice of revenue it involved, the proposed alteration of the tariff was a measure to which, for financial not less than for other reasons, it was expedient to adhere.

The anticipated improvement began to show itself, both in the financial and industrial prospects of the Colony, even earlier than might have been expected. On the 1st of February, 1849*, Lord Harris, in giving an account of the condition of the Island for the previous year, had to describe a large falling off in the exports, imports, and revenue of the Colony for 1848. The exports, though not greatly diminished in quantity, were less in value in 1848 than they had been in 1847 by upwards of £211,000; the diminution in the imports exceeded £120,000, and in the revenue £20,000; but at the same time the

* Blue Book Reports, presented to Parliament in 1849.

Governor reported that, notwithstanding these adverse circumstances, and his having been obliged to expend £10,000 on buildings, he had been able to reduce the expenditure within the gross revenue* (viz. £79,425), and that he hoped to have it in his power to carry on the Government still more economically in the year then beginning.   He added that wages had been reduced by one-fourth, and in some places by a third, but that a want of hands was felt more severely than ever.

In this reduction of wages (which, I have already remarked, we always calculated upon as the certain result of the reduction in the price of sugar consequent upon the admission of foreign sugar into the British market), and in the diminution of the other expenses of the Planters by the economy introduced into the Government, and the lowering of the duties upon imports, there were, in the midst of existing difficulties, the certain seeds of speedy improvement. The want of hands which was complained of was met, partly by a small amount of immigration, and especially by the introduction of a certain number of liberated Africans, and partly (as I should infer from various circumstances, though I have no direct evidence of the fact) by increased exertion after a time on the part of the previous population.   Thus the produce of the Island was increased, and at the same time it was raised at less cost than before ; and on the

* It appears that in the *gross* revenue Lord Harris includes the amount received by loan, which must have been about £20,000.

20th of February, 1850*, Lord Harris was enabled to report that for the year 1849 the exports showed in quantity a very good return, having amounted to 49,000,000 lbs.†, being 9,000,000 lbs. above the average of the nine preceding years, and inferior only to the export of one of those years, viz. 1847, in which there had been an extraordinary crop.

The revival of this great branch of Colonial industry naturally led to an improvement in other respects. The revenue for 1849 showed an increase upon that for the previous year of £25,100, and gave an excess above the expenditure of £14,865; the imports also increased by no less a sum than £170,000, nearly coming up to the average of the nine preceding years, —the value of the imports in 1849 having been £481,562, the average of the nine previous years being £500,000. This is a remarkable change for the better, to have taken place in a single year in the state of affairs in the Colony, and affords, as it appears to me, a decisive proof of the soundness of the policy which had been pursued with regard to it —a conclusion which is confirmed by the continuance and progressive increase of improvement up to the present time.

From the two Annual Reports‡ succeeding those which I have already quoted, it appears that the sugar

---

* Blue Book Reports, presented in 1850, Part II. p. 210.

† It may be inferred, though it is not expressly mentioned that this statement includes cocoa and coffee as well as sugar.

‡ Dated February 10, 1851, and May 18, 1852.

crop of 1850 was not a good one, but the exports of sugar and cocoa were larger both in quantity and value in 1851 than in the previous year, the crop of cocoa being considerably the largest ever raised in the Island. The revenue has continued steadily to advance, showing in each year a large surplus over the expenditure; so that the Governor has been enabled first to reduce, and for the present year to abolish altogether, the export duty on the principal articles of produce in the Colony. This tax in the year 1849 produced £13,556, and had ranged in former years from £13,000 to £18,000 a-year; consequently, by its remission, the Planters have been materially relieved. This abolition of an impost very injurious to commerce has been effected, without arresting the progress of various measures calculated to promote the advance of the Colony in civilization and prosperity, but involving no inconsiderable expenditure.

Great improvements have been effected, and are still going on, in the roads; and arrangements have been made for increasing the facilities of intercommunication afforded by the Post-office, and for the better administration of justice, and the maintenance of order by the police. The accomplishment of these most important objects, without an undue addition to the demands upon the general revenue, has been rendered practicable, principally, by a very valuable ordinance, called the Territorial Ordinance, which was passed by Lord Harris, and brought into operation at the close of 1848. By this ordinance the Colony has been divided into wards, and provision has been made for the creation of municipal bodies, whenever the number of inhabitants capable of undertaking the management of their own local concerns, and willing to do so, shall be sufficient for the purpose. In the meantime wardens have been appointed, for the performance of part of the duties which will ultimately devolve upon elective municipal bodies, and rates have been levied and applied under the direction of these officers, for the construction and repair of the roads, and for objects of a similar local character.

The average produce of these rates, for the last two years, has been about £19,000; and the Ordinance has been reported to be working exceedingly well, and to be likely to become more useful as it is brought into more perfect operation. Already it has, I trust, been the means of averting a great danger. In his last annual report Lord Harris mentions that, when it came into operation, " small Settlements were in the act of formation in wild districts of the Island, which are totally incapable of supporting the commonest requirements of civilized society. These would have become the nest of the idle, the dissolute, and the criminal; but I hope an effective check has been administered." The check adverted to by Lord Harris is that created by the imposition of rates on land occupied in the manner he describes, together with the appointment of officers whose duty it is to enforce the laws, and more especially a law which was passed about three years ago, to facilitate the ejection of squatters from land to which they have no legal right. These measures are calculated to prove highly conducive to the improvement of the Colony and the progress of the inhabitants in civilization, especially in combination with the facilities which have lately been afforded for the acquisition by the working-classes of village allotments, in suitable situations, where, under arrangements made by Lord Harris, they can now purchase small freeholds, on terms affording great encouragement to industry.

It will be observed, that the establishment of a system of local rating, and the steps which have been taken to prevent land from being appropriated without being paid for, are in strict accordance with those views which I have endeavoured to explain in my last Letter, as to the best mode of promoting the industry of a population placed in such circumstances as that of Trinidad; but I should be sorry to represent them as more than the first steps towards the adoption of a policy which I believe to be sound, but which, not having been acted upon in proper time, and when it might easily have been so, can now be only brought into operation by degrees, and with very great caution.

That further measures in the same direction are urgently required is, I think, clearly shown by the remarkable account of the results of the census of Trinidad in 1851, contained in Lord Harris's last annual

Report. In that Report, after giving some details with respect to the numbers of different classes of the population, he proceeds to state that, without reckoning children under ten years of age, there are " more than 10,000 persons, out of a population of less than 70,000, having no employment ; and of those, 8000 turn out to be inhabitants of Port of Spain. I think it necessary," he goes on to observe, " to call attention to this fact, because it must be remembered that in a community such as this there are no idlers among the better classes ; so that a seventh of the whole population of the Colony, nearly a fourth of the adult population, and more than half of the total population of the chief town, are composed of persons in the lower ranks of life, and having no visible means of gaining an existence." Lord Harris adds," It appears to me, that such a state of things requires very serious consideration, and urgently demands some remedy,"—an opinion which must command universal concurrence.

I believe the required remedy is to be sought in carrying forward cautiously and gradually, but at the same time decidedly, that course of policy which has been entered upon with so much advantage. I am persuaded that both the advancement in civilization of the lower classes of society, and the prosperity of the Planters, would be promoted by acting, further than has yet been done, on the principle of providing by direct local rates for objects of real importance to the population, but which they are too ignorant, if left to themselves, to care for. It is in the highest degree

desirable to extend and improve the provision made
for the education and religious instruction of the population, and for giving relief and medical aid to the
destitute and to the sick ; and if funds for these important objects were raised, as they easily might be,
by a direct impost from which even the idlest could
not escape, in addition to the direct advantage to be
gained from the expenditure of the money so levied,
an indirect but perhaps not less real advantage would
arise from the effect of such an impost, in increasing
the amount of exertion necessary to obtain a mere
animal existence, since this would also increase the
supply of labour to the Planter.

While the government of Trinidad remains in the
hands of Lord Harris, the utmost reliance may be
placed on his following up the policy he has so well
begun ; and in looking forward to further measures
of improvement, it is a just subject for congratulation that, by what has already been accomplished, the
Colony has been brought safely through the severe
crisis it has had to pass, and that there is no longer
even the slightest pretence for apprehending that
cessation of sugar cultivation in this fertile Island,
which four years ago was confidently predicted as
the inevitable result of the commercial policy adopted
by Parliament. On the contrary, the only question
now is, as to the greater or less degree of rapidity
with which the Colony will advance in that career of
improvement on which it has undoubtedly entered ;
and the probability is that in the next few years

there will be a large increase in its produce. This will be promoted by the measures now in progress, for procuring an additional supply of labour by immigration. Trinidad has obtained a portion of the loan guaranteed by Parliament for the purpose of immigration, and by means of it a considerable number of labourers will be introduced from India, some of whom have already arrived. There is reason to hope that this will be attended with far greater advantage to the Colony than the former immigration from the same quarter, as, by the law now in force, and which is founded on the same principle with the Mauritius Ordinance to which I have adverted above, most of the evils which were experienced in former years have, I trust, been guarded against, and provision has been made for obtaining the repayment from the immigrants, in the manner I have explained, of a large proportion at least of the expense incurred in bringing them from India.

Steps have also been taken within the last two years for procuring immigrants of a far more valuable description. I refer to the free black and coloured inhabitants of the United States. These people are regarded as an encumbrance, and their presence is considered a most serious evil in the States which they now inhabit, while there can be no doubt that many of them would be the best possible settlers who could be introduced into Trinidad. Speaking the English language, with habits of industry and of civilized life, and well adapted by their constitution to the climate, there seems no reason to doubt the success of black and coloured immigrants from the United States. Provided a proper selection is made of the individuals to be brought, their introduction could not fail to be of the highest value to the Colony, not only from the actual accession to its population which would thus be obtained, but from the example which they would afford to its present inhabitants. Such an addition to the existing population of Trinidad would have a tendency to raise the whole community in the scale of civilization, whereas there is precisely the opposite tendency with respect to immigration from almost every other quarter, and this is no slight drawback to the advantage to be obtained from it.

Last year an agent was sent from Trinidad to some of the Southern States of the American Union, for the purpose of inquiring into the practicability of obtaining immigrants of this description; and the information collected by him was, in my opinion, far from discouraging, though I fear this is not the view of the subject which has been adopted by the leading Colonists, without whose active support an experiment, which would be a most interesting one, cannot be tried with any prospect of success*.

* I cannot help here expressing my surprise that the attention of none of our merchants and capitalists has been directed to the Slave States of America as a source from which to obtain a supply of labour, and to the great returns which by means of that labour might be obtained from the fertile lands of Trinidad and Guiana. There is no doubt, I believe, that a large amount of British capital has

I will here close what I rather fear may be found a somewhat tedious account of the progress of Trinidad during the last six years, only apologizing for the length to which this part of my Letter has extended, by observing that I have thought it advisable to enter

been directly or indirectly invested in sugar cultivation in Cuba and Brazil, and it is to be feared that some of that capital may have been employed in the purchase of slaves illegally imported from Africa. The natural advantages of the British Colonies I have mentioned are, as I believe, much superior—most certainly they are not inferior—to those of either Cuba or Brazil, while they have an immense advantage over both in the perfect security they enjoy, and over Cuba at least in the lightness of their taxation. This being the case, the question naturally suggests itself, might not a given sum of money be applied to greater advantage in procuring labour from the Slave States of America to cultivate the rich soils of Trinidad and Guiana, than in purchasing slave-labour in foreign dominions? Why should not the owner of an estate in one of these Colonies liberate by purchase, and settle upon his property, a whole gang of slaves from some of the worn-out tobacco or cotton plantations in Virginia and Maryland, taking from them an engagement to repay out of their wages by instalments an amount sufficient to cover the price of their freedom, the cost of their removal to the Colony, and a fair percentage to meet the risk of loss? Looking to the great sacrifices and dangers willingly submitted to by many of the slaves in the United States to effect their escape to Canada, it seems reasonable to conclude that they would joyfully accept a proposal to obtain their freedom and their removal to another part of the British dominions, of which the climate is far better adapted to their constitution than that of Canada, and to which they might be conveyed without risk or hardship, in company with their friends and relations. The ready concurrence of the slaves in such an arrangement may therefore, I think, be reckoned upon, and in the present state of feeling in the United States on the subject of slavery I believe that many of the slave-owners, more especially in the most northern of the Slave States, would no less gladly avail themselves of such a mode of relieving themselves from a description of property which it is daily becoming into these details, because this Colony affords a more complete illustration than any other, both of the difficulties which have had to be encountered in our Sugar Colonies, and of the policy by which I believe those difficulties may ultimately be surmounted.

July 31, 1852.

more difficult and more painful to them to retain. It might also be well worth inquiry on the part of the non-resident owners of West Indian property, whether they might not derive far more advantage from their estates than they now do (or are ever likely to do under the present system of management) by letting them to experienced American planters, who might be induced to come over and occupy them, at the head of their slaves, emancipated for the purpose, on such terms as I have suggested. Many American planters are known to have gone to Cuba, and I have no doubt they might with far more advantage go to a British Colony, taking their slaves with them, after giving them their freedom on condition of paying by instalments what they would fetch if sold. For the success of measures of this kind, all that seems to be necessary is that the liberated slaves should be treated with the utmost fairness and consideration, and that provision should be made, by laws to be passed by the Colonial Legislatures (if the existing laws are insufficient for the purpose), for the easy recovery of the instalments due from these immigrants. The attention of the local Legislatures was some time since called to the importance of this subject.

LETTER IV.

GUIANA.—JAMAICA.—BARBADOES.

My dear Lord John,

In this Letter I propose to treat of those Sugar Colonies over which the authority of the Crown is more or less restricted by the institutions they possess. The first of these, of which I have to notice the transactions, is British Guiana. It is true that British Guiana is included amongst what are called the Crown Colonies, as it is one of those which were acquired by conquest, and in which the Crown therefore exercises the power of legislation by Order in Council; but it stands in a different position from the other Crown Colonies, inasmuch as it possesses a Constitution, by which the power of the Crown is much more limited than in the Colonies to which I have hitherto referred, especially with regard to the imposition of taxes and the appropriation of the revenue. The Constitution which now exists in British Guiana is a somewhat complicated one; but having been gradually moulded into its present shape, to meet wants and difficulties which have from time to time arisen, I believe it to be far from unsuitable to the existing state of society, and with some modifications, which were in progress when I gave up the seals of the Colonial Department (and which, so far as I can gather from the newspapers, seem still likely to be proceeded with) will probably be as good a form of government as the peculiar circumstances of the Colony will admit of.

It is not necessary for the objects I have in view in this Letter, to give any detailed account of the Guiana Constitution; it will be sufficient to mention, that a body called the Court of Policy, in which the number of official and unofficial members is equal, the Governor having a casting vote, possesses the general power of legislation, but without the right of levying taxes, or making appropriations from the Colonial revenue*. These powers the members of the Court of Policy can only exercise when sitting in what is called "the Combined Court," with certain persons who are known as the "Financial Representatives," and are, as their name implies, elected to the office they hold. Till lately, however, the Financial Representatives were chosen by about·800 persons only, out of a population of 120,000, and were really not the representatives of the people, but of the merchants, planters, and absentee proprietors. In the Court of Policy, the Governor, by the official votes and his own cast-

* This latter limitation is, in strictness, only in force during the continuance of the Civil List.

ing vote, can always command a majority, though this is a power never exercised but with great reluctance. In the Combined Court, on the contrary, the addition of the Financial Representatives leaves him without the power of carrying any measure, unless he can obtain the support of some, at least, of the elective members.

Such being the general nature of the Constitution of Guiana, I propose, in adverting to its transactions, to confine myself almost entirely to giving a short account of the progress and consequences of the unfortunate differences between the Governor and the Combined Court, which for some time interrupted the regular working of the Government. There has been much correspondence, during the last six years, with the Governor of Guiana, on the subjects of immigration and of the means to be employed for promoting the industry of the population; but the measures recommended on these heads, and partially adopted, have been so precisely the same in principle with those suggested to other Colonies, that in speaking of Guiana I may omit any further notice of these important questions, than a mere reference to the despatches which have been written upon them *.

* The following are the most material of these Despatches, which will be found in the Papers laid before Parliament :—Circular of October 23, 1846, to Governors of West Indian Colonies. To Governor Light, January 18, February 28, April 1, May 23, June 30, 1848. To Governor Barkly, June 1, June 16, July 31, September 30, December 15, 1849; February 15 and 16, May 1, June 15, 1850; July 8, 1851.

With regard to the differences which arose between the Government of Guiana and the Combined Court, what has occurred is as follows.

Of the whole expenditure of the Colony, about one-seventh constitutes what is called the Civil List, on which are charged the salaries of the Governor, the Judges, and some of the other public servants. The amount of these various charges is determined by an ordinance, passed by the Combined Court, which is to continue in force until the 31st of December, 1854; and of course, until this law expires, none of these charges can be altered, except by another ordinance, which requires the assent of the Crown. In this respect the Civil List of Guiana resembles the Civil List of this Country, or those parts of the expenditure of the United Kingdom which are charged by Act of Parliament on the Consolidated Fund. The remainder of the Colonial expenditure requires the annual sanction of the Combined Court, like the grants submitted to the House of Commons in Committee of Supply.

No question has ever been raised, as to the full power of the Combined Court to deal as it might think fit with the latter portion of the Colonial expenditure. The differences which have led to so much discussion have been occasioned by a claim put forward by the Combined Court, to insist on a reduction of the charges on the Civil List. The first suggestion of such a reduction was made by the Court of Policy in December, 1847, when the elective members of the Court carried resolutions, in which they prayed for the consent of Her Majesty's Government to a reduction of 25 per cent. on all salaries charged on the Civil List, in consideration of the distressed state of the Colony, arising from the great fall which had taken place in the price of sugar. These resolutions were transmitted to this Country by the Governor, in his despatch of the 1st of January, 1848 *; but before an answer to it could be received, the elective members of the Court proceeded to require the postponement of the consideration of the estimates of the year, in order, as it was stated, that there might be time, before the estimates were passed, to learn what might be the intentions of the Government with regard to the relief of the Colony.

When this course was decided upon, intelligence had reached Guiana, of the efforts which the West Indian party were making in this Country, to prevail upon Parliament to abandon the policy of 1846; and it is perfectly well known, that to promote the success of these efforts at home was the real object of the measure adopted by the leaders of the opposition in the Colony. The Governor, in the postscript of his despatch of the 18th of March, 1848†, says, "It seems to be the general opinion that the measures proposed to be adopted to stop the supplies emanate from the West Indians in England connected with this Colony." In his despatch of the 31st of March

---

* See House of Lords Sessional Paper of 1848, page 451.

† Page 630, House of Lords Paper, No. 250 of 1848.

he transmitted resolutions laid before the Court of
Policy by one of the elective members, in which the
intention of refusing the usual supplies is distinctly
placed on the ground that protection had been denied
to the British Sugar-grower; and Mr. Gordon, one of
the principal planters in the Colony, in his correspondence with the Colonial Reform Association, has since
distinctly asserted that the attempt to cut down the
Civil List "was in the first instance suggested by the
Protectionists, as a part of a general system for embarrassing Government with a view of regaining lost
protection*."

Such was the real object of the proposal to reduce
the salaries on the Civil List; the professed ground
for it was the distressed condition of the Colony.
But, with every desire to adopt any measures calculated really to relieve the distress which undoubtedly
weighed heavily on the Planters, it did not appear to
us that there was the slightest reason for believing that
the reduction which was insisted upon with so much
violence would afford any perceptible relief, or that
there was any necessity for having recourse to it, while
it was open to obvious and strong objections. The
amount of relief which the proposed reduction was
calculated to afford to the Planters could hardly be of
much importance, since the Civil List, as I have stated,
constituted only about one-seventh of the whole expenditure of the Colony; while, of the taxes by which
this expenditure was provided for, only a very small

* House of Commons Sessional Paper of 1851, No. 624, p. 486.

proportion fell on the cultivators of sugar. There was certainly no financial occasion for the measure, since, notwithstanding the difficulties of the proprietors, the Colonial revenue, instead of having fallen off since the Civil List had been settled, had continued to increase; and the measure was open to the greatest objection, not only as a departure from an arrangement deliberately assented to by the Combined Court, but as involving a breach of faith with the public servants, who had accepted the offices of which it was attempted to reduce the emoluments, on the full assurance that their salaries had been secured to them, at least until the expiration of the period for which the Civil List had been granted. Among the persons by whom this would have been felt the most severely, were the Judges and law officers, some of whom, as has since been shown by the present Governor, had sacrificed professional incomes far exceeding their salaries, for the purpose of accepting the offices they held. A diminution of twenty-five per cent. in their salaries would therefore have been an act of extreme injustice*.

For these reasons it was determined not to comply with the demand which was advanced, although it was well understood that, if it were refused, the elective members of the Court of Policy would, in the Combined Court, where they had a clear majority, refuse to pass the annual tax ordinance, by which the greater

* See Governor Barkly's despatch of May 6, 1849, and the answer to it of the 14th of July. (House of Commons Sessional Papers of 1849, No. 594, pp. 161 and 199.)

part of the Colonial revenue is raised, and would thus to a great extent deprive the Government of the means of carrying on the public service. As had been foreseen, after a correspondence, too long to refer to in detail, during which the usual taxes were continued from the 30th of June till the 30th of September, the Combined Court ultimately suffered them to expire from that day, and the Governor was left without any resources (beyond those arising from some comparatively small taxes levied under permanent laws,) to meet the necessary expenses of the Government.

It was probably anticipated, by those who suggested this mode of proceeding on the part of the Combined Court, that the embarrassment in which the Government would thus be placed, would compel us to apply to Parliament for power to continue to levy the usual taxes without the sanction of the Combined Court, or to have recourse to some other expedient involving a departure from the regular and established mode of conducting the Government of the Colony. In the then state of parties in the House of Commons, we should in either case have been exposed to a defeat, which would have greatly promoted the success of those who were struggling to recover for the British Sugar-grower the monopoly of the home market, of which he had been deprived. The course however which, after much consideration, we decided upon adopting, was a very different one from that which seems to have been expected.

The Governor was instructed not to assent to the

desired diminution of the salaries of public servants
actually holding offices charged on the Civil List, so
long as the ordinance providing for them should remain in force; but he was informed that, in the event
of any of these offices falling vacant, Her Majesty's
Government would be ready to listen to any recommendation of the Combined Court for the reduction
of their emoluments, before they were filled up.   The
grounds of this determination were explained, and it
was pointed out, that the adoption by the Combined
Court of the unreasonable course of withholding the
pecuniary means required for carrying on the public
service, would have no effect in inducing Her Majesty's servants to recommend to Parliament, or Parliament to sanction, the change in our commercial
policy which the planters believed would relieve them.
He was informed that he must strictly confine himself
to the exercise of his legal powers, and that those
public services for which he was refused the means of
providing must be discontinued, even if this involved
disbanding the police and shutting up the hospitals,
and an interruption of the regular administration of
justice; and that, if the usual Colonial allowances were
not paid to the officers of Her Majesty's troops serving
in the Colony, the troops would be withdrawn.   The
Governor was further informed, that no more liberated
Africans could be sent to the Colony, so long as no
provision was made for the maintenance of the public
establishments required for taking care of them.

   These instructions were contained in various de-

spatches*, written, some of them before and some
after the final refusal of the Combined Court to vote
the usual taxes. They were dictated by the conviction that it was our duty, as servants of the Crown,
not to allow ourselves to be driven from that commercial policy which we believed to be the right one,
no less for the real interest of the Colonies than for
that of this Country, by a threat on the part of
the Planters to adopt measures, of which the consequences would really fall almost exclusively upon
themselves. For my own part, I greatly regretted the
certain increase of the difficulties of the Colonists,
and the great danger to their lives and property
which might arise from their refusing to the Government the means of meeting the charges of the civil
establishment, including the police ; but I did not think
that those who were determined to proceed to these
extremities ought to be relieved from the consequences
of their own conduct, either by appealing to Parliament to set aside the Constitution of the Colony, or
by yielding to the unreasonable demands which the
measures they had had recourse to were intended
to enforce. On the contrary, I thought it absolutely
necessary that they should be made to feel that we
would not flinch from the course we had deliberately
adopted, and that they must be prepared to meet the

* See particularly the Despatches to the Governor of the 15th of
February, and 11th and 17th of June, 1848, and of the 15th of January, 16th of April, and 14th of July, 1849. These Despatches
will all be found in the correspondence laid before the House of
Commons in 1849.

consequences of their own measures, of which the responsibility would rest solely on themselves. I was persuaded that, by acting with patience and firmness on this policy, those who exercised a predominating influence in the Colony would at length be brought to understand, that they could gain nothing by depriving the local Government of the means of carrying on the public service, and of maintaining establishments, in the existence of which we in this Country have but a comparatively slight and indirect interest, but which are absolutely necessary for the welfare, and even for the safety, of the Colonists.

The result answered my expectation; and after allowing the usual collection of taxes to be suspended for nearly eleven months, the Combined Court, in the month of August, 1849, passed an ordinance (which was afterwards renewed) to revive the tax ordinance of 1847 for three months, until some further arrangement could be made; and on the 1st of December following the Governor was enabled to report the final and satisfactory termination of the controversy relating to the Civil List, and the passing of all the usual financial measures.

The successful conclusion of this harassing affair was much promoted by the circumstance that a Committee, appointed by the House of Commons to inquire into the subject, agreed to a report expressing an opinion in favour of the binding character of the Civil List arrangement in Guiana; but the result was in a far greater degree due to the firmness and judgement with

which the affairs of the Colony were administered by
Mr. Barkly, who had been appointed Governor toward
the close of the year 1848.   It is probable that, but
for the remarkable skill and ability with which, on
his assumption of the Government, that gentleman
applied himself to the settlement of the unfortunate
differences which he found existing between the Executive Government and the Combined Court, the accomplishment of this important object would not
have been obtained without much greater delay.   Far
more serious injury to the Colony must also have resulted from this protracted struggle, but for the success
with which he endeavoured to diminish the demands
upon the Government during the interruption of the
levy of taxes, and to render the very limited pecuniary
resources at that time at his disposal available in carrying on the most essential branches of the public service.

But although the differences which put a stop, while
they lasted, to the regular working of the government, were brought to a close at an earlier period,
and upon the whole with less detriment to the Colony,
than might have been expected, their consequences
have nevertheless been highly injurious to its interests.
In the first place, the loss of revenue to the Colony
by the interruption for above ten months of the ordinary taxes, is calculated by the Governor at upwards
of £150,000*.   Considering that the importation of

* 760,000 dollars. See Governor Barkly's Despatch of December 5, 1849. (House of Commons Sessional Papers of 1850, No. 21,
p. 251.)

goods usually liable to duties was checked for some time before the actual cessation of the power to collect the duties, by the expectation that it would take place, and that while it lasted considerable stocks of these goods were naturally accumulated, which had to be consumed after the tax ordinance was revived, there seems reason to believe that the calculation of the Governor, as to the loss to the revenue, must be rather below than above the truth. By this loss of revenue, a formidable deficiency was created; and although the permanent sources of income were sufficient to avert the actual bankruptcy of the Local Government, a debt had been incurred at the end of the year 1849, of £40,000, which the Governor says would have been quadrupled " if the Combined Court had not at length availed itself of its power to economize on a large scale, instead of persisting in its attempt to strike off a few thousand dollars from a Civil List to which the faith of the Legislature was pledged for a given time*."

Nor did the community derive, from the interruption of the collection of the ordinary duties, that relief which is usually conferred by a remission of taxation. A few individuals, who happened to have goods which could be introduced while the duties were suspended for a comparatively short and uncertain period, obtained the chief advantage from what was thus lost to the public, and no small proportion of it fell to the lot of the foreign holders

* See Despatch above referred to.

of gin and tobacco, the price of which was run up in
the markets of Surinam and St. Thomas by the sud-
denness of the demand. The Governor states in his
despatch, that the debt incurred (which it was fortunate for the Colony was so small) would be paid by
the former taxes, which had been re-established; and
he observes, that this affords a convincing proof of
the elasticity of the Colony's resources, of the continued prosperity of the great bulk of its inhabitants,
and that the leading proprietors were not justified by
the state or prospects of the revenue in stopping the
supplies. He points out, that in doing so they had
acted very unwisely for their own pecuniary interests,
since, by adopting that course, in addition to exciting
ideas of insubordination in the minds of their labourers,
shaking the credit of everybody connected with the
Colony, and aggravating the depreciation of property,
they had also postponed for three years a reduction of
taxation, which it was in their power to have effected
immediately. In 1851 taxes were remitted to an
amount not far short of £40,000, including the repeal
of the Income and Produce Tax, and the reduction of
shipping charges and of the duties on imports. The
material relief which will thus be afforded to the trade
and industry of the Colony, might have been obtained
with equal facility in 1848, if the leading planters, who
exercised a predominating influence in the Combined
Court, would in that year have consented to apply
themselves to a calm consideration of practicable and
judicious financial reforms, instead of embarking in a

reckless struggle with the Executive Government, nominally for an unjust reduction of a few thousand
dollars of annual expenditure, but really for the recovery of their lost monopoly.

But the pecuniary loss which the Colony has incurred by this struggle, into which the Planters were
so ill-advised as to be led by those who called themselves their friends, is by no means the most serious
part of the injury that has resulted from it. A much
greater evil is the delay it has occasioned (I still hope
only a delay,) in the accomplishment of many measures of improvement of the most urgent necessity.
I have, in a former Letter, adverted to the very unsatisfactory condition of the labouring population of
Guiana, and to the startling fact that the emancipated Negroes were reported in 1848 to have rather
gone back than advanced in civilization since the Abolition of Slavery, and I have pointed out the general
character of the measures which I conceive to be
necessary for the correction of so great an evil. How
pressing is the need for such measures, will be seen
on reference to the very able despatches of the Governor* ; but in his despatch of the 2nd of February,
1850, after expressing his "cordial concurrence" in
my views, as to the policy which ought to be adopted,
he goes on to say, "If the fruit of my exertions yet
remains to be developed, in the passing through the
Colonial Legislature a series of measures calculated

* See especially that of the 17th April, 1850, and that of the 24th
September of the same year.

to effect the foregoing objects, I am confident your Lordship will make allowance for the political turmoil to be surmounted before the attention of elective members could be attracted to questions so much less exciting, though so much more useful, than those to which they had unhappily suffered their attention to be diverted."

It is impossible not to recognize the validity of this excuse, for the Governor's having failed to make more rapid progress with the legislation which is required for the improvement of the Colony.   I trust however that this legislation will now be proceeded with ; indeed, since the excitement of the political struggle has subsided, the Court of Policy has been assiduously engaged in the consideration of business of an urgent kind, to which it had previously been impossible to attend, and several useful measures have been carried, calculated to prepare the way for those larger and more important measures which I believe to be necessary.   Amongst those already carried are ordinances for the encouragement of Immigration, founded on the same principle as the Mauritius law, which I have already described ; a valuable ordinance for the establishment of Rural Constables, which is reported to be working very usefully* ; and, in connection with this, a subsequent ordinance for regulating the powers and duties of Justices of the Peace.   To this list may be added the ordinances (which are perhaps the most important of the whole)

* See Blue Book Report for 1850, p. 199.

for effecting the comprehensive legal reforms, of which Mr. Arindell, the late Attorney-General (who now, I am happy to see, has obtained the promotion he so well deserves, and has been appointed Chief Justice), was the author. These Ordinances do the greatest credit to the judgement and ability of Mr. Arindell, and will, I believe, confer on Guiana the advantage of a speedy, cheap, and satisfactory administration of the law.

Some changes have also been effected, or are now in progress, in the Constitution of the Colony. I have already mentioned, that the Financial Representatives (who, with the Members of the Court of Policy, constitute the Combined Court, which has the control of the Colonial finances,) were formerly chosen by a body of electors not exceeding in all eight hundred in number, and so composed as to give a virtual command of the elections to a few of the leading bankers, merchants, and planters. In 1849 an ordinance was passed greatly extending the franchise, and a comparatively large proportion of the population would now be entitled to take part in the election of Financial Representatives, if they took sufficient interest in public affairs to claim their right to be registered as electors. Other changes are still under consideration. During the continuance of the dispute with the Combined Court, an agitation was raised in favour of the entire alteration of the present Constitution, and the substitution of one precisely similar to those which exist in the older West Indian Colonies, which possess

Representative Assemblies, exercising, in conjunction with the Governor and Council, all the powers of legislation. The state of society in Guiana, where there is an extremely small proportion of Europeans, the remainder of the population being made up of various different races, for the most part little advanced in civilization and altogether deficient in the education and intelligence necessary for the safe exercise of political power, rendered such a change in this Colony in my opinion altogether inexpedient. But some modifications of the existing Constitution seemed to be desirable; I therefore, in the course of last year, communicated on the subject with several of the principal proprietors and merchants connected with the Colony, including some gentlemen who usually reside there, but were at that time in this Country. These gentlemen entered with me upon the consideration of the reforms it would be advisable to introduce, in a manner for which I had reason to feel deeply indebted to them; their views were frankly and fully explained to me, and they received in the most friendly and candid spirit the opinions which I thought it right to express on their suggestions. The result was, that they agreed to resolutions recommending certain amendments in the Constitution of the Colony, which met with my entire concurrence; and these resolutions having been officially communicated to me, I transmitted them to the Governor, with a view to their being submitted to the Court of Policy and carried into effect. I gather, from what has appeared in the newspapers, that our retirement from office is not likely to lead to the abandonment of these projected reforms, but that they will still most probably be adopted.

Having thus given an account of our measures with regard to Guiana, I must, before taking leave of that Colony, say a few words as to the effects of the policy on which we acted with regard to it, on its prospects and actual condition. It is of course impossible that so great an improvement should have been effected in the state of society, and in the industrial condition of the Colony, as I believe might have been accomplished, if those interested in its welfare could have been persuaded at an earlier period, that we had the same object in view with themselves, and could have been induced to support, or at all events to abstain from thwarting, our measures; but still the policy which has been pursued has been by no means barren of advantage. Though laws have not yet been passed in Guiana doing all that is required to alter the state of things to which the indisposition to exertion shown by the population may be attributed, the measures which I have mentioned as having been adopted in the Colony have had some effect in this direction; and still more has been produced by the change in this Country in our commercial policy. The wholesome stimulus of competition is beginning to tell on the labouring as well as the other classes in Guiana, in urging them to greater industry (which must be the foundation of all improvement), and in correcting those bad habits which the artificial enhancement of the value of their labour by the monopoly given to British sugar in the home market had so much contributed to create. The Governor, on the 18th of April, 1850, reported that, though "the money rate of wages was unaltered, the real price of labour, measured by quantity and quality, has fallen in a proportion approaching at least the decline in the value of sugar." I must add that there is some remarkable evidence, where it might have been little expected to be found, that labour in Guiana is no longer so extravagantly dear as formerly, and is actually far less expensive than it was during slavery. For the last two or three years a Committee of Officers has been employed in inquiring into our naval and military establishments abroad, for the purpose of reporting to the Treasury on the reductions of expense which may be practicable. In their report upon Guiana the Committee recommend that it should be ascertained whether the contract system of transport might not be adopted in that Colony, on the ground that "the contract rate for a cart, horse, and driver was £1. 5s. 5d. a day in the time of slavery, and is now 8s. 4d*."

I will conclude what I have to say about Guiana, as I have done in the case of Mauritius, by inserting at

* See Reports of the Committee appointed to inquire into the Naval, Ordnance, and Commissariat Establishments and Expenditure in the Colonies, presented to both Houses of Parliament by command of Her Majesty, p. 219.

length two recent despatches from the Governor, giving an account of its actual condition.

" *Government House,* 12 *November,* 1851.

" My Lord,

" I have the honour to transmit the Half-yearly Reports of the Stipendiary Magistrates for the half-year ending the 30th June last, and to explain, that they have been delayed by the desire of most of the magistrates to calculate the centesimal proportions to the population, according to the recent Census, the compilation of which is only just completed.

" From the Consolidated Tables, your Lordship will perceive that the accounts of the moral condition of the peasantry do not exhibit so decided an improvement as that which is going on in the material prosperity of the country; but there appears to be, at any rate, a mitigation of those symptoms which were calculated to cause anxiety, if not alarm ; for the returns show no diminution in the number of labourers at work, and no increase of crime, whilst, notwithstanding the apathy reported to be prevalent amongst parents with respect to the education of their children, six new schools have been opened within the period.

" If indeed the improvement in the condition of the country should be continuous and permanent, there can be no doubt it will soon re-act beneficially on the labouring population, by enabling proprietors to resume those efforts for the promotion of religion and education which in so many cases were interrupted by dire necessity, and by stimulating the Legislature to make more liberal provision for the same purpose.

" The situation of proprietors is unquestionably better

than it has been for some years past; and if they act prudently in not extending their cultivation faster than they can secure the manufacture of its products, either by improved machinery or by the introduction of fresh labourers, there seems no reason for apprehending a reverse; but everything depends upon the cost of production being kept low, a fact which, in their anxiety to increase their crops, they are but too apt to forget, and to raise the great item of the ' wages of labour' by improvident competition.

" General attention, I am happy to state, is now directed to the all-important question of drainage, and I feel confident that in a few years none of the large plantations on the sea-coast will be without its draining engine worked by steam-power, whilst the smaller estates will have to combine for the same object. The only cause of delay at present seems to be the difference of opinion among engineers, as to whether the scoop-wheel or the centrifugal pump is best adapted to the circumstances of this Colony.

" The latter principle, as applied to the very different task of separating sugar from molasses, is not quite so successful in all cases as was at first anticipated; but though requiring improvement, before it can be made applicable to curing sugar boiled by the ordinary process in open pans, it is, as mentioned in the Consolidated Tables (C. 2) rapidly superseding the pneumatic pan as a subsidiary process where the cane-juice has been boiled ' *in vacuo*,' and may, I think, also pave the way for the extended use of Gaddesden and Evans's pan, or other cheaper substitutes for the vacuum, by which the juice is evaporated at so low a temperature as to give the sugar a grain which cannot be injured by the centrifugal machine.

" It is a favourable omen for the future prosperity of

British Guiana, that so much interest should be taken in such improvements, at a moment when confidence is so far restored as to induce capitalists at home to take a less desponding view of its resources as a sugar-growing country, than they have done since it was first brought into competition with Cuba and Brazil.

                              " I have, etc.,
          " (Signed)   HENRY BARKLY."

          " *Government House, 9th January,* 1852.
   " MY LORD,
   " The comparative statements of produce exported from this Colony during the quarter and the year ending 5th instant, which I have now the honour to enclose, prove that I was not more sanguine in the anticipations which I have throughout expressed to your Lordship, of a very considerable increase in the Sugar-crop of 1851, over that of the two preceding years, than I was fairly entitled to be,—the actual excess amounting to 5682 hogsheads, or upwards of fifteen per cent.
   " That that excess is in some degree attributable to a favourable season, and to the consequent richness in saccharine matter of the cane-juice, is proved by the fact of there being an actual diminution both of Rum and Molasses,—the products of the refuse in crystallizable liquor left; but it nevertheless cannot be questioned that the increased production of Sugar is mainly owing to an extension of cultivation, and to the introduction of improvements both in agriculture and in the process of manufacture, and that so far this increase is likely to prove permanent.
   " But for the very low prices current indeed in Great Britain, which will, I much fear, render the 43,034 hogsheads shipped in 1851 of less value than the 37,351

shipped in 1850, I should have anticipated a progressive augmentation of the exports of the Colony, until they were at least equal to those previous to Emancipation; but I fear this event will at any rate be retarded, until confidence in the abilityof our Planters to withstand the increased competition, to which they are every day being subjected, can be restored.

" Looking however to what has been accomplished in this Colony since 1846, in reducing the cost of production, I can see no reason to despair of a very great further reduction being effected ultimately, although, I fervently trust, without the same quota of distress to be undergone in the transition*.

" I have, etc.,

(Signed)   " HENRY BARKLY.

" The Right Honourable Earl Grey, etc."

I have next to call your attention to that which, from the amount of its population, and from the éx-tent and richness in natural resources of its territory, is entitled to be considered the most important of our former Slave Colonies. I refer of course to the magnificent island of Jamaica. This Colony has for two centuries been in possession of a Representative Constitution, and the Assembly not only exercises the ordinary authority of a Legislative body, but performs many of what are usually the functions of the Executive Government, the authority of the

---

* Tables of the quantities of produce exported from the Colony, enclosed in the above despatch, are given in the Appendix (F) to this Volume.

Crown being more restricted than elsewhere by various laws which have at different times been passed and by usages which have grown up. But the actual condition of Jamaica, I regret to say, is far from being such as to show that the possession of the powers of self-government affords that complete security for the welfare of a community, and for the good management of its affairs, which many persons seem to suppose.

You are aware that the accounts which continue to reach this country describe Jamaica as labouring under the severest distress, nor do I believe that there is any reason for imputing much, if any, exaggeration to these statements. The Colonists and owners of property in Jamaica are loud in their complaints, and ascribe all their losses and difficulties to Imperial Legislation. The abolition of the slave-trade and of slavery, and the recent changes in our commercial policy, have been pointed out by the Assembly* in various memorials and petitions to the Queen and to the two Houses of Parlia-

* The following passages occur in the Memorial of the House of Assembly to the Queen, of the 18th of December, 1846. "We, your Majesty's loyal subjects, the Assembly of Jamaica, by permission to approach your Majesty, humbly to remonstrate against the many wrongs which we have sustained by acts of the Imperial Parliament. . . . . The establishment of Slavery was not our act, but that of the parent Government, the lands of Jamaica having been patented by your royal ancestors on the special condition that they should be cultivated by slaves for the promotion of the national wealth; and this policy was continued under sanction of British laws equally sacred as those under which any other class of your Majesty's sub-

ment, as the grievances of which they have had to complain, and the causes of the ruin which they have experienced. I have quoted in a note below some remarkable passages from one of the Memorials addressed to the Queen by the Assembly, of which I regret that the great length prevents my inserting the whole. This Memorial was voted in December, 1846, when the alteration of the sugar-duties, by which sugar the produce of slave labour was admitted to the British market, had only been enacted a very few months, and could have had no effect in producing the distress which is described in this document, in terms not less strong than those which have been

jects held their property. It is unnecessary for us here to enter into the history of the trade by which those slaves were procured; it is enough to say that, after having been most vigorously and profitably carried on for one hundred and fifty years by British ships, British merchants, and British capital, it was abolished by Act of Parliament in the year 1807. *This was the first check to the hitherto extending cultivation and prosperity of Jamaica.* The advocates for the abolition of the African slave-trade then most solemnly disclaimed all intention of seeking to interfere with the existing state of slavery in the Colonies; but scarcely had one object been accomplished, when agitation commenced with respect to the other. The first overt act of the Parliament effected by this new agitation was in the year 1815, by the introduction of a Bill in the House of Commons for registering the slaves, professedly to prevent their illegal introduction into the Colonies, but covertly to pave the way for subsequent emancipation. The next movement was in the year 1823, when Mr. Canning, then a Minister of the Crown, introduced certain resolutions into the House of Commons, conceding to out-door pressure the interests of the Colonists and the principle of slave emancipation." One remarkable sentence in this Memorial I have distinguished by italics. See House of Commons Sessional Paper of 1847, No. 160.

used at a later period. It deserves to be particularly observed, that in this Memorial, which contains an elaborate statement of the grievances of Jamaica, it is complained that the abolition of the Slave-trade by Act of Parliament was the first check to the prosperity of the Colony, and that the various steps by which slavery was first mitigated, and ultimately completely abolished, are insisted upon as the causes of the general ruin of the proprietors of the Island; the fiscal changes which had lately taken place in this Country being only adverted to as likely to become a new source of difficulty.

I believe the view thus taken of the subject by the Assembly to be so far right, that the abolition of the Slave-trade was necessarily fatal to the kind of prosperity (such as it was)* which Jamaica formerly

---

* I say "such as it was," for the former prosperity of Jamaica was always of a very precarious kind, and chequered by periods of severe distress. Even while the British Colonies enjoyed not only the monopoly of our market, but the unrestricted power of using slave-labour and carrying on the slave-trade, the Planters of Jamaica were frequently compelled to make urgent applications to Parliament for relief; and their business was so hazardous, that, in spite of the great gains of some seasons, there were few who realized money by it in a series of years. See the testimony to this effect of Bryan Edwards, in his 'History of the West Indies;' Lord Derby's Speech in the House of Commons, when moving, in 1833, the Resolutions on which the Bill for the Abolition of Slavery was founded; the Reports of Committees of the House of Commons of 1807 and 1832; the Report of a Committee of the House of Assembly of Jamaica in 1804, and the Petition of that House to the Prince Regent in 1811. Some extracts from these documents will be found in the Appendix (G) to this Volume.

enjoyed; and this step once taken, it became, I am convinced, impossible for the Island to enjoy durable prosperity, except by adopting an entirely different system, based, not upon slavery and commercial restrictions, but upon freedom, both personal and commercial. The only wise course therefore for the Colonists to pursue, would have been to apply themselves to the establishment of such a system, and of a new social organization, by the adoption of well-considered and judicious measures for effecting an inevitable change, with as little disturbance and with as little delay as possible. Unfortunately a very different line of conduct has been followed by those who have possessed the chief influence among the Colonists; and the same determined resistance which was made to the abolition of the Slave-trade was, afterwards made to the mitigation and the abolition of slavery, and to the alteration of our commercial policy. These successive changes have been accomplished only after struggles highly injurious to the welfare of the Colony; and thus for the last thirty years the relations between the Local Legislature and the Government at home, under successive Administrations, have, with some brief intervals, continued to be on a very unsatisfactory footing. There has been little of that harmonious co-operation between these Authorities, without which it is impossible that the affairs of the Island can be properly and efficiently conducted.

During your Administration, no effort that we

could make, without abandoning the commercial policy we thought it our duty to maintain, was omitted, for the purpose of establishing a good understanding with the Colonists and especially with the Assembly ; but our endeavours to effect this object were unsuccessful. Unhappily the Colonists were led to believe that nothing would be of any avail for the relief of their difficulties, except a restoration of some portion at least of their former commercial privileges; and that this object was one that might be obtained by the assistance of a powerful party at home, and of which the accomplishment might be promoted by embarrassing and thwarting as much as possible an Administration pledged to a policy directly opposed to their views.

It would be unjust to blame the Colonists for having been induced to adopt this opinion, and the line of conduct to which it led, considering how much they were encouraged in doing so by persons of great influence in this Country, and how natural it is for those who are suffering from distress to listen to advice and suggestions such as were addressed to the West Indians by their professed friends. But though it would be unfair to censure the Assembly of Jamaica and the leading Colonists with any great severity, for the course they pursued, there can I think be no doubt that it has proved a most unfortunate one for their own interest. This is the only conclusion that can be drawn from the fact, that while Jamaica enjoys advantages which I consider to be much superior, and which certainly are not at all events inferior, to those of any other Sugar Colony, it alone continues to exhibit no signs of any improvement in its condition; while in other important Colonies, equally dependent for their prosperity on the cultivation of sugar, there has been, as I have shown, a manifest abatement of the difficulties with which they have had to contend, and a dawning of brighter prospects for the future.

Jamaica has greatly the advantage of Trinidad and of Guiana in the amount of her population, and still more in the comparatively advanced stage of civilization which that population has reached; while of her natural fertility and resources, I am not aware that any but a very high opinion has ever been expressed; yet Guiana and Trinidad, without those extensive powers of self-government, which it is the fashion to represent as alone necessary for the welfare of a Colony, and which Jamaica possesses, have completely surmounted their financial difficulties; their revenue already exceeds their expenditure, notwithstanding large reductions of taxation, and their production of sugar is rapidly increasing. In Jamaica, on the contrary, the state of the Colonial finances is getting from bad to worse; and we are assured that, without some change, of which there is as yet no appearance, the cultivation of sugar cannot be much longer continued. There must have been serious errors in the management of the affairs of Jamaica, to account for so unfortunate a difference.

Nor is it difficult to perceive what these errors have

been. Although the need of well-considered legislation, to meet the wants of an entirely new state of society, was not less urgent in Jamaica than in the other former Slave Colonies, and though Jamaica has far greater facilities than most of these Colonies for carrying into effect such measures as are required, the Statute Book of the Island for the last six years presents nearly a blank, as regards laws calculated to improve the condition of the population, and to raise them in the scale of civilization. And unfortunately the errors to be imputed to the Legislature are not merely negative; the management of the finances, on which so much depends, has been most defective. Taxes have been reduced without any proportionate reduction of expenditure, which has been allowed habitually to exceed the income; and an increasing load of debt has thus been incurred, partly in the very objectionable form of issues of an inconvertible paper currency, under the name of "Island Cheques," partly in other ways. While this has been going on, no attempt has been made to relieve the finances and the industry of the Colony, either by the practice of a judicious and systematic economy, or by substituting less objectionable taxes for the very impolitic and onerous ones, both general and parochial, which now exist. Yet, by well directed efforts of this kind, it is certain that much might have been done for the relief of the Colony and for the encouragement of productive industry.

The mismanagement of the Colonial finances must in part at least be attributed to the mode in which their administration is conducted. The Assembly not only retains strictly in its own hands its constitutional privilege of deciding upon the amount of grants to be made for the service of the Colony, and the taxes by which they are to be met, but it resents, as contrary to its privileges, any interference on the part of the Governor, even by way of advice, with its exercise of its authority over the public purse. It is not required in Jamaica, as it is in this Country, in Canada, and in the Australian Colonies, that every grant of money should be recommended by the Crown's Representative before it is voted; but every member of the Legislature proposes any vote which he considers to be advisable, nor is there any person responsible for preparing an estimate of the probable receipts and expenses of the Colony, and taking care that the latter shall be covered by the former. It is obvious that such a mode of conducting financial business is calculated to lead to great irregularity, and it has been found to do so in all the Colonies in which it prevails. In the absence of any effective individual responsibility, it is too commonly the practice for each member of the Assembly to push forward every grant for objects interesting to himself or his constituents, without much regard to the amount or comparative urgency of other claims on the public purse ; so that the appropriation of the revenue comes to be determined rather by a kind of scramble amongst the members of the Legislature, than by a careful consideration of what the public interest requires.

Jamaica is not singular in allowing this mode of appropriating the public money to continue, notwithstanding the manifest objections to it; but it is the only Colony in which I am aware of the existence of a further departure from the principles of the Constitution on this subject, which has greatly aggravated the evils of the practice I have described. In this Country it has long been considered to be a constitutional principle of great importance, that all grants of public money made by Parliament are to be regarded as grants to the Crown; and though the House of Commons has established its right to define very strictly, in making grants, the objects to which they are to be applied, and will not consent to even the most minute alterations by the House of Lords in the Bills sent up for that purpose, it has never disputed that the collection of the revenue, the custody of the public money, and its application to the objects for which it is voted, should be entrusted to the servants of the Crown. No such rule has been observed in Jamaica.

By various local Acts, most of them of somewhat remote date, the collection and application of the revenue have been almost entirely taken out of the hands of the Governor, and certain persons known by the name of the Commissioners of Public Accounts exercise, under scarcely any control, the powers which ought properly to belong to the Governor, and to the public servants who act under his authority. So far has this been carried, that these Commissioners actually possess, and have repeatedly used, the power of issuing, without the concurrence of the Governor, large sums in the inconvertible paper called Island Cheques, to which I have already adverted; and the Governor has also, more than once, had occasion to remark on the irregular and imperfect manner in which the revenue is collected, without having any means of interfering to enforce a more efficient performance of this very important duty. All the members of the Assembly are *ex officio* commissioners of public accounts; in reality therefore the Assembly, under another name, exercises all the anomalous powers which belong to these Commissioners, and which include a complete control over the audit of the accounts of the expenditure which they vote as legislators. As the Commissioners are authorized by law to continue to meet and act, notwithstanding a prorogation of the Assembly, and retain their power even after it is dissolved, until a new one has been elected, another check, which in this Country is imposed on the power of the House of Commons, by the authority of the Crown, to arrest its proceedings by a prorogation or dissolution, is virtually got rid of in Jamaica. The irresponsible and irregular power exercised by the Assembly, and by its members as Commissioners of Public Accounts in matters of finance, would alone have been quite enough to prevent the financial affairs of the Colony from being administered with that judgement and steadiness which the difficulties of the times urgently required; but there were other circumstances also which had still more effect in diverting the attention of the Assembly from all useful measures, whether financial or of any other description.

The commercial calamities of the latter months of the year 1847, together with the proceedings in Parliament on the subject of West Indian distress in the beginning of 1848, produced great excitement in Jamaica, as well as in other parts of the West Indies, and inspired the leading Planters with a determination to make every effort in their power to overthrow the Home Administration, to the measures of which they were persuaded that the distress which weighed so heavily upon them was attributable. Public meetings were held at various places in the Island, at which very violent language was used, and very strong resolutions were adopted, condemning the measures of Parliament affecting the Colonies; and in the Spring and Summer of 1848 many petitions were presented to the Governor, praying that he would summon the Legislature at an earlier period than usual, "to take into consideration" (such are the words of one of these petitions) "the state of the country, and to deliberate and determine what measures ought to be adopted to avert or ward off the baneful effects of Imperial Legislation*."

Although, in the state of feeling which was thus manifested, it was not likely that the Assembly, when called together, would act with the judgement and moderation which could alone have rendered its proceedings really useful, the Governor did not think

* See House of Commons Sessional Paper of 1848, No. 685.

it expedient to decline complying with the applications
made to him, and he accordingly summoned the Assembly to meet for the despatch of business on the
3rd of August. The Session proved as unproductive
of good as might have been anticipated; but even
before it began, the violent proceedings, to which I
have referred, had an effect which might have been
very serious.   In the end of June and the beginning
of July considerable alarm was created by rumours of
an approaching rebellion of the Negroes; and, upon
inquiry, it turned out that this alarm was not entirely
unfounded. Though there is a strong spirit of loyalty
to the Crown amongst the Negroes, who are easily
managed, if judiciously and justly treated, they are at
the same time ignorant, very credulous and excitable,
and capable when excited of most reckless and dangerous conduct.   Upon a population of this kind—
entertaining also towards the White inhabitants of the
island the feelings naturally engendered by the recol-
lections of slavery, and a knowledge that the abolition of that odious system had been forced upon their
masters, whose reluctant submission to the change had
never been concealed—the proceedings of the Planters
were calculated to have a very agitating effect; and
there seems no reason to doubt that such an effect
had been produced to a very considerable extent, and
that some, though probably only a few, of the Negroes
were contemplating measures of violence against the
Whites.

Dr. Williams, the Archdeacon of Cornwall, in a

letter to the Bishop, which is enclosed in Sir Charles Grey's despatch of the 22nd of July, 1848*, after mentioning " a prevalent report that there was to be a rising of the peasantry," states that " the groundwork of the whole matter is the belief of the peasantry that the United States of America are likely to take possession of this Island, and to reduce them to slavery. This belief, it is supposed, has originated from the mention which has been made in some of the American papers of the distressed state of this Island, and the good which would result from its annexation, with Cuba, to the United States; and I fear the Planters have not themselves been prudent in what they have said on the subject of relief from Great Britain, as well as other persons, some very influential." The indications of this state of feeling created for a short time much apprehension among some of the White inhabitants; and some of the very party whose intemperate proceedings had occasioned whatever danger existed, were anxious for the adoption of measures which would no doubt have increased it, by adding to the excitement of the Black population. The Governor however firmly refused to take any steps which might have had this effect, and in his despatch of the 22nd of July he states, " I am now pretty well satisfied that there has been no other danger than that of the alarm being propagated to such an extent as might have induced precipitate and erroneous measures, such as calling out the militia and the enrolment of volunteers,

* See Parliamentary Paper quoted above.

and the distribution of arms to partisans. If this had been done, collisions must almost inevitably have taken place, and there is no saying to what extremities the mischief might have been carried." He proceeds to state, that "he had resolutely abstained from giving the sanction of the Government to any other measures" than certain precautionary ones which he described. These consisted in making arrangements to have a sufficient force promptly available, if any disturbance should occur in the districts where it was apprehended, and in the issue of a proclamation, to quiet the minds of the Negroes, by assuring them that there was no danger that any attempt would be made again to reduce them to slavery. These measures were successful, and all cause for alarm soon passed away; but it is due to Sir Charles Grey to state, that this result is mainly to be ascribed to his firmness and prudence, and that, had he listened to the suggestions of some whose apprehensions obscured their judgement, such was the state of men's minds, that Blacks and Whites might easily have been led, by unfounded fears of each other, to very deplorable acts of mutual violence.

I have said that the Session of the Legislature, which the Governor had been pressed to hold at an unusual season, was unproductive of any good. After having sat for more than a month, the Assembly adjourned from the 20th of September to the 24th of October, not a single Act of any kind having passed the Legislature; but though the addresses and resolutions of the Assembly showed much irritation, nothing occurred which necessarily precluded the expectation that the ordinary business of the Colony might be proceeded with in due time. The Governor stated, that though the financial prospect was far from satisfactory, and Her Majesty's Government ought to be prepared to say in what manner the local government of the Island was to be carried on in case of the usual annual supplies for 1849 being refused, he did not despair of the difficulty being averted. He believed the Island to be as capable as ever of yielding a revenue, though in a different manner from former times; and he thought the Assembly might be prevailed upon to take the requisite measures for raising it, if there were not parties at home who urged the Members to withhold the Supplies, as a means of influencing and embarrassing the administration of Colonial affairs by Her Majesty's Government*.

On the 4th of November the Governor reported, that the Assembly having met again, the tone and character of their communications with him were better than in the August Session, which he thought had been of great use in dissipating the irritation, which had been increasing and accumulating for several months before; and that he then had good hopes of the ordinary Supplies being voted, and the ordinary business transacted before the end of the year; though he did not feel quite confident that a

* Sir C. Grey's Despatch of August 19,1848. (House of Lords Sessional Paper of 1849, No. 111, p. 14.)

different course might not be adopted under the directions of a party in England, who certainly had recommended the stoppage of the Supplies*. Unfortunately this doubt proved too well founded: the same tactics were adopted in Jamaica as in Guiana; and the Assembly, after coming to a resolution†, on the 13th of December, that they would "not pass any Bill raising a revenue beyond the 15th of February next, until a measure of retrenchment, consonant with the impoverished condition of the Island, be passed into a law," adjourned to the 23rd of January. The intention of this resolution obviously was to convey a menace, that if the Governor and Council should fail to pass a Bill of Retrenchment, of which the nature had not then been determined, the Assembly would stop the Supplies. By adjourning for so long a period after passing this resolution, the Assembly allowed, as the Governor observed, "just three weeks after their re-assembling as the period within which its plans of economical reform are to be brought forward and considered, and the momentous question is to be determined whether four-fifths of the revenue of the Island are not all at once to cease‡."

When the Assembly again met, it soon appeared that their plans of reduction were founded upon the same principle of injustice, and were no doubt adopted

* See Sir C. Grey's Despatch of November 4, 1848, p. 71 of the same Papers.
† See the above Paper, p. 143.
‡ Sir C. Grey's Despatch of January 4, 1849, p. 145.

upon the same advice, and with the same object, of embarrassing the Government at home, as the measures
to which I have adverted as having been proposed in
Guiana. A Retrenchment Bill, as it was called, was
passed by the Assembly, and sent to the Council on
the 2nd of February, the effect of which was to subject
the salaries of the holders of certain offices to reductions, varying from 10 to 33⅓ per cent. By this measure, a saving in all of about £14,000 a-year would
have been effected, one-half of which would have fallen
upon twelve individuals. The Judges and Vice-Chancellor would have suffered a loss of one-third of their
salaries, and the Chairmen of Quarter Sessions of one-
fourth,—all these salaries having been granted by
permanent Acts, passed within a comparatively recent
period by the Colonial Legislature. The salaries of
the Assistant Judges had been thus settled only six
years before ; and it was shown that, of the gentlemen
who had accepted the office, one at least was at the
time making a larger income at the Bar, which he
was induced to forgo, in the confidence that his salary
would be permanently secured to him*. In the same
manner the Chairmen of Quarter Sessions, who had
been selected with great care from the English Bar, in
consequence of an Act passed only eight or nine years
previously, were to have their salaries reduced from
£1200 to £900 a-year.

* See the debate in the Council, on the Retrenchment Bill, enclosed in Sir C. Grey's despatch of February 19, 1849. (Papers presented by Command, May 10, 1849, p. 37.)

The injustice of these proposals is too obvious to require to be urged; and there was the less excuse for the Assembly's insisting upon them, inasmuch as, if the restoration of the finances had been their real object, measures might easily have been found, free from all objection and calculated to produce far more substantial benefit, than the contemplated Act of confiscation, directed against a comparatively small number of individuals. The Governor had pointed out, that the person who had lately held the office of Receiver-General had died, leaving a large deficiency in the Colonial Treasury, and that an early examination of his accounts was desirable *. The Governor also showed that there had been no falling off in the revenue which might not be accounted for either by a reduction of duties or by the " imperfect, lax, and neglectful collection of the taxes." The whole system of taxation, both general and parochial, was also very faulty, and much of the expenditure wasteful, and susceptible of large reduction without injury to the public service. But though there was so much room and such urgent need for measures of real financial reform, none were attempted by the Assembly, the members of which, either in that character or as Commissioners of Accounts, have practically in their hands the whole power of dealing with financial affairs. The Governor has so little substantial authority, even of an administrative kind, with regard to them, that he could take no measures for recovering from the securities of the late

* House of Lords Sessional Paper of 1849, No. 111, p. 10.

Receiver-General the amount of the deficiency left in the Treasury by that officer, which was neglected by the Assembly. Nor had he the means of correcting such a gross abuse as that of allowing the taxes to be very irregularly collected, the largest arrears, as he states, being supposed to be due from those who were best able to pay them*. The only power which the Governor possesses, with regard to the pecuniary affairs of the Colony, is that of expressing his opinion and offering advice and suggestions in his speeches and messages to the Assembly; and that body is so jealous, and is so apt to resent any interference even of this kind, as a breach of their privileges, that it is necessary to act with great caution in attempting it.

While the Assembly altogether neglected those measures of real improvement which were within their power, they pressed forward with reckless violence the unjust and ineffectual plan of retrenchment which I have described; and when the Bill for carrying it into effect was unanimously rejected by the Council, they endeavoured to accomplish their object by indirect means. In Jamaica there is not, as in this Country, a public revenue derived from taxes imposed by permanent laws, sufficient to meet the expenses charged by such laws on the Colony. With us it is well known that the greater part of the taxes are levied under the authority of Acts of Parliament which are not limited in duration; formerly the sugar

* See Sir C. Grey's Despatch of March 31, 1849. (Papers presented by Command, May 10, 1849, p. 70.)

duties, and latterly the Income-tax, have been an exception to this rule ; but there are permanent taxes more than sufficient to meet those fixed expenses which are charged by law on the Consolidated Fund. In Jamaica, on the contrary, by far the larger part of the revenue is derived from taxes, the levying of which is authorized by Acts of which the duration does not in general exceed a year.

Taking advantage of this circumstance, the Assembly endeavoured to overrule the other branches of the Legislature ; and, though the Council and Governor had not concurred in altering or repealing the laws regularly passed by the whole Legislature for granting certain salaries, it attempted to defeat the operation of these laws by declining to provide any funds from which the payments sanctioned by them could be made. With this view the Assembly, in passing Bills for the renewal of two of the principal sources of the Colonial income—the duties on imports and on rum—inserted clauses specially appropriating the proceeds of those taxes to particular objects, amongst which the payment of the salaries they insisted on reducing was not included. Notwithstanding the manifest objections to the course thus taken by the Assembly, the Import Duties Bill was passed by the Council and assented to by the Governor ; that for imposing duties on rum was rejected.

I will not follow through its several stages the long struggle that ensued, in the course of which different Retrenchment Bills were proposed and failed, and the

Assembly was once dissolved and several times pro-
rogued. A detailed account of these miserable proceedings would be at once wearisome and useless ;
it will be sufficient to give a very brief summary of
their result. As the point in dispute was the same,
so our policy was also the same, as that which I
have already described as having been adopted with
regard to Guiana. We came to the conclusion that it
was our duty to maintain the honour of the Crown, by
advising Her Majesty to withhold her sanction from
any measure involving a violation of justice towards
individuals, or a breach of the public faith ; and if, in
consequence, the Assembly should refuse to provide
the means of carrying on the public service, to leave
to that body the responsibility for the results to which
this might lead. We also thought it right, not to purchase a temporary respite from the difficulties which
would arise from such a refusal on the part of the
Assembly, by allowing the Governor to give his assent
on behalf of the Crown to any Bills which might be
tendered to him, and which should be at variance
with the recognized principles of the Constitution or
the standing instructions to Colonial Governors. At
the same time we were not only ready, but anxious,
to concur in any just and reasonable measures of
reform, whether financial or constitutional, which the
Assembly might think fit to propose. To constitutional reforms we also declared our readiness to
advise Her Majesty to accede, if proper measures of
the kind should be passed : but on its being pointed out

that this would involve the relinquishment of some of the irregular powers which had been assumed by the Assembly, that body tacitly abandoned the request it had preferred to have the system of Government assimilated to that which prevails in Canada.

Instructions in accordance with these views (which were fully explained to him) were addressed to Sir Charles Grey, in various despatches, and particularly in those of the 11th of October, 1848, and the 16th of April, 1849, which will be found amongst the papers laid before Parliament. The last of the two despatches I have mentioned contains so complete a statement of the grounds upon which we acted, that I have thought it right to give it at length in the Appendix*.

The policy which was thus pursued proved, as in Guiana, ultimately successful. The Assembly was dissolved in 1849, and, though at first this measure appeared to have had little effect in changing the conduct of that branch of the Legislature, there was a considerable change in its composition; there was a change also in public opinion, as was shown by a petition numerously signed, which was presented to the Council in support of that body's proceedings; and it seemed to have become understood both by the Planters resident in Colony, and by the Jamaica proprietors in this Country, that the course taken by the Assembly had been ill-judged for their own interest. The consequence was that after different modifications of the objectionable Retrenchment Bill had been attempted,

* See Appendix (H) at the end of this Volume.

it was at length abandoned, and matters returned pretty much into their usual course.

This result is, I think, in no small degree to be attributed to the calm and temperate manner in which the Governor conducted himself in all his communications with the Assembly, to the able manner in which the objections to the measures they rejected were exposed by the Members of the Council in their debates*, and perhaps most of all to the fact that none of the West Indian party, or of the advocates of commercial monopoly in this Country, ventured, in either House of Parliament, to bring the proceedings which had taken place in Jamaica under discussion, in such a manner as to elicit an expression of the opinion of Parliament on the matters in dispute between the Government and the Assembly. When the controversy came to a crisis, all the papers on the subject, including the instructions which had just been addressed to Sir C. Grey, were laid before both Houses of Parliament on the 10th of May, 1849, with the express object of challenging a discussion, if the course we had thought it our duty to take were objected to. The challenge was not accepted,—a circumstance which could not fail to have its effect in Jamaica.

Unfortunately however, although we succeeded in resisting the objectionable measures which were pressed upon us, and also in maintaining our commercial policy,

* A report of the debate (or rather of the speeches, for the members of the Council were unanimous) on the rejection of the Retrenchment Bill, will be found in the Papers laid before Parliament.

which the proposal of those measures was intended to be an engine for overturning, the struggle into which the Assembly was led by those who called themselves their friends in this country, effectually paralysed, as I have already mentioned, every attempt to effect any of those numerous improvements in the laws, and in the financial and administrative arrangements of the Colony, which were needed, in order to raise it from that deep depression to which it has been reduced. An irreparable injury has thus been done to Jamaica, and an opportunity has been lost, which it may not, I fear, be easy to regain; nor can I look forward without very gloomy anticipations, as to what may be the result of having allowed so many more years to slip away, without taking effectual measures to improve the condition, both moral and physical, of the Negro population, and thus to prepare them for that position, and for that increasing power and influence in the Colonial society, to which they must necessarily advance.

Under the law as it stands the Negroes must soon acquire a predominant power in the Assembly. Looking then at what the Constitution of Jamaica is, and to the state of things which is likely to arise, when the Assembly, possessing as it does such large powers by law, shall represent those who possess also an overwhelming superiority of physical force, and who will not, I fear, be guided by much knowledge or judgement, or have a very kindly feeling to the absentee proprietors, I am at a loss to understand how the latter can have been so blind to their obvious interest, as not to avail themselves of the power and influence they still possess in the local Legislature for the purpose of co-operating with the Crown to introduce the many reforms which are wanted, and the neglect of which during these precious years may be productive of so much danger. While I held the office of Secretary of State, I had frequent occasions to deplore that the majority of those connected with Jamaica, with whom it was my duty to communicate, could not be induced to believe either in the serious character of this danger, or in the sincerity of our wish to promote the true interest of themselves and of the Colony. The delusive hope they were encouraged to entertain, of recovering some portion at least of that commercial monopoly on which their desires were so earnestly fixed, obscured their judgement, and great is the responsibility of those by whom they were thus misled.

During the last year and a half or two years of your Administration, there was a great change in the temper of the persons to whom I advert; and those connected with Jamaica, in this Country at least, showed latterly much more disposition than formerly to co-operate with us, and to look to practical measures, rather than to vain attempts to recover their lost monopoly, for an improvement in the condition of the Colony. At the end of 1850* intelligence was received in this country of the outbreak of cholera in Jamaica, and many of the principal proprietors and

* On the 20th of November: see House of Commons Sessional Paper of 1851, No. 104.

merchants connected with the Island lost no time in entering into communication with us as to the measures which should be adopted for its relief. I am happy to say that they carried on these communications in the best possible spirit and temper, and the measures which were taken were adopted with their concurrence and support. In the first instance three medical officers, recommended by the General Board of Health, were sent out to the West Indies, to assist the local Authorities by their advice in framing measures to check or avert the pestilence, and the Governor was authorized to draw upon the Treasury for £3000 to afford assistance to the most distressed of the families reduced to destitution by the death of those on whom they depended for support.

But it was felt by those with whom we had communicated, as well as by ourselves, that the most serious result of the pestilence, and that with which it was most difficult to deal, was the diminution it had caused in the already scanty supply of labour available in Jamaica, and it became matter of the most anxious consideration to us what steps could be taken to meet this evil. On mature deliberation we were of opinion that little could be done towards this end except by the Local Legislature, but that much was in its power, and that we ought to give to it all the assistance we could, in devising the measures best calculated to meet the exigency. A despatch, to be laid by the Governor before the Legislature, was accordingly prepared with as little delay and as much care as possible, explaining very fully the various measures which it seemed to me would be most likely to effect an improvement in the condition of the Colony. In the preparation of this despatch I availed myself largely of the suggestions and information given to me by the gentlemen with whom I had been in communication, and they were put in possession of it before it was sent to the Governor. If I am not mistaken, they concurred generally, if not entirely, in the advice thus given to the Legislature, and gave it their support by letters which they addressed to their friends in the Colony. I have already adverted to this despatch in what I have said of the Sugar Colonies generally, and it will be found at length in the Appendix*.

Though the recommendations thus addressed to the Assembly were approved by a large proportion at least of the principal gentlemen in this country connected with Jamaica, I regret to say that hitherto no steps towards acting upon them have been taken in the Colony; and it appears, from resolutions adopted by the Assembly in February last, and by a pamphlet called 'A Statement of Facts relative to the Island of Jamaica,' which was published in the month of June by three delegates from the Assembly who had been sent over, that the resident Colonists are still looking, not to what they can do for themselves, but to some assistance they hope to obtain from Parliament, for relief from their difficulties.

* See Appendix (C) to this Volume.

This is greatly to be lamented, since the more carefully the circumstances of Jamaica are considered, the more reason there will be found for believing, that while Parliament can do little to improve its prospects, there are measures which it is in the power of the Local Legislature to adopt, and by which it might fairly be hoped, that its difficulties would be conquered and prosperity be ultimately restored to an Island which, in spite of its present distress, I regard as possessing in great abundance all that is necessary for becoming at no distant period a rich and flourishing Colony. But in order that this result may be attained, it is absolutely necessary that dependence for extraneous assistance, should be exchanged for strenuous exertion on the part of the Colonists and of the Colonial proprietors at home. There is no hope of improvement while those whose interests are at stake continue to manifest only apathy and neglect of what is in their own power, while they are calling for aid from others. Nothing shows more strongly the want of energy on the part of the Colonists, than the absence of any decided efforts to ward off from the Island, in future, the disease by which it has lately suffered so severely. The medical officer who was sent there, found that all the known causes of disease exist in Jamaica in great abundance, and that much might easily be done for their removal. But, though this has been shown very clearly, I do not learn that anything has yet been done toward carrying into effect the precautionary measures recommended by Dr. Milroy. It is however only fair to add that, considering how slow the towns of this Country have generally been to avail themselves of the power given to them by Parliament to adopt measures of sanatory improvement, it is not perhaps surprising that the inhabitants of Jamaica should have been equally dilatory in attending to the subject, notwithstanding the awful warning they have had in the recent visitation of cholera.

I have entered at so much length into the transactions of some of the Sugar Colonies, that I must abstain from adverting to the others, except so far as to refer to the remarkable increase of the production of sugar in Barbadoes since 1846, which affords perhaps a more signal refutation, than even the facts I have mentioned with regard to Mauritius, of the predictions made in that and the following years as to the results which must, it was said, follow from the admission of slave-grown sugar into our markets. In spite of these predictions, I find that the crops of sugar exported from Barbadoes in the three years up to 1846, and in the three last years, have been as follows* :—

1844	23,146 hhds.	1849	33,077 hhds.
1845	24,777 „	1850	35,302 „
1846	21,996 „	1851	38,730 „
Average	23,306 „	Average	35,703 ,,

This is an increase of production which may well excite surprise, and which clearly demonstrates that the production of sugar by free labour can be carried

* See Blue-Book Report for 1852.

on with success, in spite of the competition with slave-labour to which it has been exposed.

Perhaps it may be said that Barbadoes enjoys advantages in the great density of its population, which the other Sugar Colonies do not possess, and that therefore what has been done in that Island, forms no criterion of what is possible in others. To a certain extent this is true; but on the other hand I must express my opinion, that the greater success of the Barbadoes Planters is not by any means exclusively due to the advantage they possess from the Colony being so populous; I cannot but believe that it is in part at least attributable to the fact, that they never resorted to those unwise means for the purpose of extorting from the Government à restoration of the former monopoly of the British sugar-grower to which the planters of Jamaica had recourse, and never either allowed the public business to be interrupted, or ceased cordially to co-operate with the able officers who have held the post of Governor in adopting such measures as have been found necessary for promoting the welfare of the community.

I must further observe, that the absence of any difficulty in carrying on the cultivation of sugar in Barbadoes, in consequence of the density of the population, affords another striking proof of the soundness of the views I have so fully stated in the earlier part of this Letter, as to the nature of the legislation which is required in the other Sugar-growing Colonies. If the free Negro is found to be so capable of exerting himself when placed in such circumstances as he is in Barbadoes, and if experience in that Island clearly proves that, when both planters and labourers are compelled by the restricted area of the territory they occupy to concentrate their efforts within a space proportioned to their capital and numbers, they can successfully compete with slave-grown sugar, does it not follow that in the other Colonies, where the population bears a very different proportion to the extent of land, it should be the aim of legislation as far as possible to correct the tendencies thus created, and to prevent the bounty of nature from being abused, and becoming, instead of an advantage, only an encouragement to idleness and an obstacle to civilization?

August 14, 1852.

P. S. Since this Letter was written, I have, within these few days, been much gratified by finding that my opinion as to the ability of the British Colonies to compete successfully in the growth of sugar with countries in which the labour of slaves is still employed, has been confirmed by no less an authority than the present Chancellor of the Exchequer, the biographer of Lord G. Bentinck. In Mr. Disraeli's speech on the Budget, on the 3rd of this month, I find the following most remarkable passage:—" It may be said that these are merely figures " (he had just been comparing the entries for home consumption of Foreign and British sugar for the first ten months of 1851 and of 1852), " but I beg to observe that in this instance

figures constitute the case. This is a question of
figures, and the result of the figures I have quoted
is, that there being, in 1851, 4,126,000 cwt. of British sugar against 1,487,000 cwt. of foreign, in 1852
there were 5,378,000 cwt. of British against only
814,000 cwt. of foreign. In other words, British production has increased by 1,250,000 cwt. and foreign
production has decreased by about 600,000 cwt.   I
may be called a traitor—I may be called a renegade
—but I want to know whether there is any gentleman in this House, wherever he may sit, who would
recommend a differential duty to prop up a prostrate
industry which is actually commanding the metropo-
litan market*."

The argument is conclusive; but how much loss
would have been saved to the unfortunate West
Indians, how much better would the state of Colonial industry have been at this moment, even than
that which the Chancellor of the Exchequer describes,
if the party with which he is connected had for
the four years preceding February, 1852, taken a
juster view of the prospects of the Colonial Planter !
Had they done so, the Colonists of Guiana and of
Jamaica, instead of being encouraged to enter upon
that unfortunate struggle with the Government for the
recovery of protection, which I have described, would
no doubt have co-operated with us in effecting the
many much-needed improvements which we were
anxious to assist them in accomplishing; and many an

* See the report of Mr. Disraeli's speech in ' The Times.'

unhappy Planter, who has been compelled to sell his property for one-half or one-fourth of its real value, because the confidence of English capitalists in the possibility of his continuing his business with advantage was destroyed, would have obtained assistance that would have enabled him to surmount his difficulties. Well may the West Indians say, " Save us from our friends ! "

December 7, 1852.

LETTER V.

BRITISH NORTH AMERICA.—CANADA.

My dear Lord John,

I will now turn to those large and flourishing provinces which constitute the British territory in North America. In the history of these provinces the last six years will form a memorable epoch, since within that period their system of government, which was previously in a state of great doubt and uncertainty, may be said to have been established on what there is good reason to hope may be a permanent footing, and the difficult and embarrassing questions which had arisen, as to the rules to be observed in conducting their affairs, have received a solution in which all parties have practically acquiesced. This has not been accomplished without discussions and controversies which, during their progress, were the source of much anxiety; but we may congratulate ourselves upon having succeeded, before the breaking up of your Administration, in bringing all these various discussions

and controversies to a satisfactory termination, and
upon having left these, the most important of the Colonial dependencies of the British Empire, in a state,
not only far better than that which we found existing
on our assumption of office, but such as to afford the
most encouraging prospects for their future welfare
and rapid progress, both in moral and material prosperity. A very slight sketch of the various transactions and events through which this result has been
attained is all that I can attempt.

Without going back to occurrences of an earlier
date, I would begin by observing, that a new era in
the history of British North America may be said to
have opened with the passing of the Act of 1840, for
the union of the former Provinces of Upper and Lower
Canada, and with the consequent re-establishment in
the latter of constitutional government, of which the
unhappy insurrections of 1837 and 1838 had necessarily occasioned the temporary suspension. A simple
return to the former system of constitutional government was impossible after these events. They had
been the bitter fruit of defects and abuses in that
system, which had been fully exposed in Lord Durham's well-known Report; and its publication had
naturally created a desire for the reform of the evils
it pointed out, not only in Canada, but in the Lower
Provinces, to which many of Lord Durham's remarks
were equally applicable.

When our lamented friend Lord Sydenham (then
Mr. Poulett Thomson) went to Canada as Governor-

General, in the Autumn of 1839, there was much excitement on the question of establishing what was called " Responsible Government ;" while the notions generally entertained as to what was meant by these words, and as to the manner in which such a Government was to be carried on, were exceedingly vague and ill-defined.   You held at that time the office of Secretary of State for the Colonies, and made the first attempt to give something like shape and consistency to these vague ideas, and to carry into effect the reform desired by the Colonists so far as this could be done with safety.   In two despatches addressed to Mr. Poulett Thomson, on the 14th and 16th of October, 1839, you pointed out the necessary distinctions between the Government of this Country and that of a Colony ; but at the same time you observed that, while you saw insuperable objections to the adoption of the principle of the responsibility of the Local Government to the Assemblies in the manner in which it had been stated in the Colonies, you saw none to the practical views of Colonial Government recommended by Lord Durham, as you yourself understood them ; and you announced that for the future the principal offices of the Colonial Governments in North America would not be considered as being held by a tenure equivalent to one during good behaviour, but that the holders would be liable to be called upon to retire whenever, from motives of public policy or for other reasons, this should be found expedient.   You explained that this rule was to be applicable without limitation to persons appointed to the offices in question subsequently to the date of your despatch, and to the existing holders of office so far as was clearly necessary for the public good; but at the same time with due regard to the fair expectations of individuals, to whom pecuniary compensation should be awarded when it might appear unjust to dispense with their services without such an indemnity*.

These instructions were written in apparent contemplation of the adoption of some such mode as that now established of carrying on the government of the North American Colonies; but up to July, 1846, the problem of bringing into satisfactory operation this system of administration had certainly not been solved. In Canada, during the early part of Lord Sydenham's administration, the insurrection was too recent, and its effect in creating animosity and disaffection among one division of the population had been too great, to allow of the re-establishment of constitutional government in the Lower Province, where the power of legislation had been entrusted by Parliament to a Special Council. Even when the union was accomplished, the state of the country was still such as to prevent the French Canadians from acquiring their just weight in the House of Assembly elected for the first Parliament of the United Provinces; and the circumstances of the time, together with his own talents

* See, for the two despatches containing these instructions, the House of Commons Sessional Paper, No. 621 of 1848, pp. 3–6.

for business, combined to give Lord Sydenham great influence over the Legislature, and to render it necessary for him to take upon himself a larger personal share of the administration of affairs than would have fallen to him according to the strict theory of the Constitution.

In the then state of things, and of men's minds, it would have been impossible otherwise to carry on the Government; and the power which was thus in fact assumed by Lord Sydenham, was wisely used in passing various measures calculated to promote the material welfare and improvement of the country. He endeavoured also to prepare the way, by a firm and just administration, which should allow the passions and animosities excited by previous events to subside, for the safe introduction of a more constitutional system of government. In this respect the policy of Lord Sydenham was highly successful, and it contributed greatly to facilitate the adoption of the liberal and enlightened measures taken by his successor, Sir C. Bagot, during whose brief government a much nearer approach was made to the establishment of a really constitutional system; but the death of Sir C. Bagot took place so soon, that the establishment of such a system could be only imperfectly effected by him, nor is it easy to judge whether, if he had lived, he would have been able to avoid those difficulties in which his successor, Lord Metcalfe, became involved.

A difference of opinion arose between Lord Metcalfe and his Council upon a question relating to the distribution of patronage, into which it is neither necessary nor expedient that I should enter; it is sufficient to state, that this difference led to the retirement of the members of the Executive Council, who were supported by a majority of the Assembly. Eventually, though not without considerable delay, Lord Metcalfe was enabled to form another Council, for which, by means of a dissolution of the previous Parliament, he obtained the support of a new Assembly. But this was only accomplished by Lord Metcalfe's personal popularity and influence, which were employed to procure the return of members favourable to his policy: the effect of this was to place him in direct hostility with one of the great parties into which the Colony was divided. Though the difficulty of carrying on the Government was thus obviated for the moment, as the party into whose hands he had thrown himself possessed a small majority in the Assembly, this advantage was dearly purchased by the circumstance that the Parliamentary opposition was no longer directed merely against the advisers of the Governor, but against the Governor himself and the British Government, of which he was the organ.

Hence, as it is the nature of all popular Assemblies to undergo from time to time changes, by which the minority of one year becomes the majority of another, and as there could be no doubt that sooner or later the party with which Lord Metcalfe had quarrelled would recover its ascendency, there was a certain prospect of great future embarrassment from the state of things which had arisen. Nor was this all; the Governor, by his rupture with one party, was placed to a far greater degree than was desirable in the power of the other, by which he was supported, and lost the means of exercising his proper authority in checking any departure from moderation on the part of those by whose assistance he was compelled to carry on the Government. The danger of his position was fully understood by Lord Metcalfe, and it is apparent that he foresaw difficulties in the future administration of the Colony, which he had not succeeded in discovering any means of surmounting.

When Lord Metcalfe was at length compelled to relinquish his post, by the frightful disease in spite of which he had continued to the last to discharge his public duties with heroic patience and resolution, Lord Cathcart succeeded him, first as Administrator of the Government in virtue of the military command which he held, and afterwards as Governor-General, to which office he was appointed on the advice of Mr. Gladstone, shortly before the formation of your Administration. Lord Cathcart had, as it appeared, been appointed Governor-General in consequence of the threatening state of our relations with the United States, which rendered it desirable, at the time the appointment was made, that the chief civil and military authority in Canada should be vested in the same hands. But when we assumed the direction of affairs, the Oregon dispute had just been happily settled, and the danger of an interruption of peace with the United States had passed away. On the other hand, as regarded the internal affairs of Canada, the position to which Lord Cathcart succeeded, on assuming the Government, was calculated, as I have explained, to create much anxiety for the future, and seemed to require that the management of these affairs should be entrusted to a person possessing an intimate knowledge of the principles and practice of the Constitution of this Country, some experience of popular assemblies, and considerable familiarity with the political questions of the day. These qualifications could not reasonably be expected from a military officer who, like Lord Cathcart, had hitherto been almost entirely occupied by the duties of his profession, and had not been accustomed to take any active part in English politics.

Accordingly it was my opinion, in which you and our colleagues agreed, that another Governor-General should be appointed, and after much consideration it was determined that Lord Elgin should be selected for this important post. He was at that time personally altogether unknown to me; but he had conducted the government of Jamaica, whence he had just returned, with great ability and success, and had also during the very short time he had sat in the House of Commons, given proof of no ordinary talents. The speech by which he had principally distinguished himself in the House of Commons was certainly not one to give him any claims upon us as a party, since it was made in seconding the amendment on the Address which led to the downfall of Lord Melbourne's Administration, in August, 1841 ; but as our object was not to make selection with a view to party interests, but to entrust the management of the largest and most important of the British Colonies, in a season of great difficulty, to the ablest hands we could find, Lord Elgin was recommended to the Queen for this appointment, in preference to any of our own party or personal friends. I cannot forbear remarking, that, as the Government of Canada is literally the only civil office in that Colony in the gift of the Home Government, and is the greatest prize in the Colonial service, the manner in which it was on this occasion disposed of affords a proof of the injustice of the common allegations, that the Colonies are retained only for the sake of the patronage they afford.

As Lord Elgin, though appointed at an earlier period, did not leave this country to assume the Government of Canada until the month of January, 1847, I had the opportunity of communicating with him very fully previously to his departure, with respect to the line of conduct to be pursued by him, and the means to be adopted for the purpose of bringing into full and successful operation the system of constitutional government which it seemed to be the desire of the inhabitants of British North America to have established among them. He was thus, before he assumed the duties of his office, placed completely in possession of our views on the various questions which the introduction of this system of Government naturally raises. The best explanation I can give of these views, and of the principles which have guided our whole policy toward the North American Colonies, will be afforded by an extract from a despatch which I had occasion to address to Sir John Harvey, the Lieutenant-Governor of Nova Scotia, on the 3rd of November, 1846, in answer to an application from him for instructions as to the course he should adopt in circumstances of considerable difficulty in that Province.

It had appeared, from Sir John Harvey's report on the state of affairs in Nova Scotia on his assumption of the Government, that the Executive Council was incomplete, that there was reason to doubt its being able to continue to conduct the affairs of the Province with advantage, and that he had been urged by the Members of the Opposition, with whom he had been in communication, to dissolve the existing Assembly, in the belief that by so doing a new Assembly would be elected, in which they would have a majority showing public opinion to be in their favour. With reference to this state of things, I transmitted to Sir John Harvey the following instructions, which, it will be observed, involve principles of general application to all Colonies having a similar form of government*. " I am of opinion that under all the circumstances of the case, the best course for you to adopt is to call upon the Members of your present Executive Council to propose to you the names of the gentlemen whom they would recommend to supply

* See House of Commons Sessional Paper, No. 621 of 1848, p. 8.

the vacancies which I understand to exist in the present Board. If they should be successful in submitting to you an arrangement to which no valid objection arises, you will of course continue to carry on the Government through them, so long as it may be possible to do so satisfactorily, and as they possess the necessary support from the Legislature. Should the present Council fail in proposing to you an arrangement which it would be proper for you to accept, it would then be your natural course, in conformity with the practice in analogous cases in this Country, to apply to the opposite party; and should you be able, through their assistance, to form a satisfactory Council, there will be no impropriety in dissolving the Assembly upon their advice; such a measure, under those circumstances, being the only mode of escaping from the difficulty which would otherwise exist, of carrying on the government of the Province upon the principles of the Constitution. The object with which I recommend to you this course, is that of making it apparent that any transfer which may take place of political power from the hands of one party in the Province to those of another, is the result, not of an act of yours, but of the wishes of the people themselves, as shown by the difficulty experienced by the retiring party in carrying on the government of the Province according to the forms of the Constitution. To this I attach great importance; I have therefore to instruct you to abstain from changing your Executive Council until it shall become perfectly clear that they are unable, with such fair support from yourself as they have a right to expect, to carry on the government of the Province satisfactorily, and command the confidence of the Legislature.

" Of whatever party your Council may be composed, it will be your duty to act strictly upon the principle you have yourself laid down, in the memorandum delivered to the gentlemen with whom you have communicated,—that, namely, ' of not identifying yourself with any one party,' but, instead of this, ' making yourself both a mediator and a moderator between the influential of all parties.' In giving therefore all fair and proper support to your Council for the time being, you will carefully avoid any acts which can possibly be supposed to imply the slightest personal objection to their opponents, and also refuse to assent to any measures which may be proposed to you by your Council which may appear to you to involve an improper exercise of the authority of the Crown for party rather than for public objects. In exercising however this power of refusing to sanction measures which may be submitted to you by your Council, you must recollect that this power of opposing a check upon extreme measures proposed by the party for the time in the Government, depends entirely for its efficacy upon its being used sparingly and with the greatest possible discretion. A refusal to accept advice tendered to you by your Council is a legitimate ground for its Members to tender to you their resig-

nation,—a course they would doubtless adopt, should
they feel that the subject on which a difference had
arisen between you and themselves was one upon
which public opinion would be in their favour.
Should it prove to be so, concession to their views
must sooner or later become inevitable, since it cannot be too distinctly acknowledged that it is neither
possible nor desirable to carry on the government of
any of the British Provinces in North America in
opposition to the opinion of the inhabitants.

" Clearly understanding, therefore,. that refusing to
accede to the advice of your Council for the time
being, upon a point on which they consider it their
duty to insist, must lead to the question at issue
being brought ultimately under the decision of public
opinion, you will carefully avoid allowing any matter
not of very grave concern, or upon which you cannot
reasonably calculate upon being in the end supported
by that opinion, to be made the subject of such a
difference.   And if, unfortunately, such a difference
should arise, you will take equal care that its cause
and the grounds of your own decision are made
clearly to appear in written documents capable of
being publicly quoted.

" The adoption of this principle of action by no
means involves the necessity of a blind obedience to
the wishes and opinions of the Members of your
Council; on the contrary, I have no doubt that, if
they see clearly that your conduct is guided, not by
personal favour to any particular men or party, but

by a sincere desire to promote the public good, your objections to any measures proposed will have great weight with the Council, or, should they prove unreasonable, with the Assembly, or, in last resort, with the Public.

" Such are the general principles upon which the Constitution granted to the North American Colonies render it necessary that their Government should be conducted. It is however, I am well aware, far easier to lay down these general principles than to determine in any particular case what is that line of conduct which an adherence to them should prescribe. In this, your own judgement and a careful consideration of the circumstances in which you are placed must be your guide; and I have only, in conclusion, to assure you that Her Majesty will always be anxious to put the most favourable construction upon your conduct, in the discharge of the arduous duties imposed upon you by the high situation you hold in Her service."

The despatch, from which the above is an extract, was communicated to Lord Elgin previously to his proceeding to Canada; and, in conformity with the principles there laid down, it was his object, in assuming the Government of the Province, to withdraw from the position of depending for support on one party into which Lord Metcalfe had, by unfortunate circumstances, been brought. He was to act generally upon the advice of his Executive Council, and to receive as Members of that body those persons who might be pointed out to him as entitled to be so by their possessing the confidence of the Assembly. But he was carefully to avoid identifying himself with the party from the ranks of which the actual Council was drawn, and to make it generally understood that, if public opinion required it, he was equally ready to accept their opponents as his advisers, uninfluenced by any personal preferences or objections.

In adopting this rule of conduct, it was of peculiar importance to make it manifest that all past contentions and the unhappy events of 1837 and 1838 were buried in complete oblivion; and that all the inhabitants of Canada, who would for the future act as loyal subjects of the British Crown, would be regarded with equal favour by the Governor, without reference to their national origin or to the party to which they might belong. Upon this policy Lord Elgin has steadily acted, and, after passing through a crisis of great difficulty, it has been crowned with complete success. On his assumption of the Government he found the Provincial Administration in the hands of the party which had supported Lord Metcalfe; and for the first Session, as the Members of this Administration were enabled, though with much difficulty, to maintain their majority in the Assembly, they remained in office, receiving from Lord Elgin all the constitutional support they could ask for, and every facility for the attempts they thought it right to make to strengthen their position by a junction with some of the leaders of other parties. These attempts were not successful, and at the close of the year 1847 the then Canadian Administration, finding that they could neither form a new and stronger combination of parties, nor reckon any longer upon even the bare majority they had previously had in the Assembly, applied to Lord Elgin for power to dissolve the Parliament : no objection having been made on his part, the dissolution took place, and was followed by a general election, which gave a complete triumph to the party previously in opposition.

When this result was ascertained, Lord Elgin gave to the Members of his Council the option of immediately retiring, or of calling the Parliament together at once. They chose the latter course. The Parliament met, a vote was carried against the Administration, which retired, and a new one was formed from the ranks of their opponents, the Members of both parties concurring in expressing their sense of the perfect fairness and impartiality with which Lord Elgin had conducted himself throughout these transactions. With his new Council he acted in the same spirit as with their predecessors : without in the slightest degree committing himself as their partisan, he freely gave them his confidence, and the assistance of his judgement and experience in preparing measures for the benefit of the Province ; and without attempting by direct authority to prescribe to them the course which they should follow, he practically exercised a great and most useful influence on the conduct of affairs.

The consequence of this was, that the French

Canadians, and the Liberal party in the Western Division of the Province, seeing that their leaders and friends were admitted to their just share of power and influence, that no distrust of them was evinced by the Governor, and that the government really was to be carried on strictly in the spirit of the Constitution, without any preference being shown to men of any one party or national origin, became on their side reconciled to the Imperial authority which was thus exercised, and proved themselves worthy of the confidence which had been placed in them, by the loyalty and attachment they manifested to the Crown. So soon and so decidedly were the healing effects of this policy experienced, that, when the news of the French Revolution of February, 1848, reached the Province, it occasioned no disturbance or alarm. In the state of public feeling and opinion which Lord Elgin found prevailing on his arrival in Canada, little more than a year before, there can be no doubt that the intelligence of this startling event would have produced most formidable excitement, if not actual disturbance. Instead of this, there was the most perfect tranquillity and security*. All efforts

* The state of the Province about this time is thus described in the presentment of the Grand Jury of Montreal, enclosed in Lord Elgin's despatch of May 3, 1848 :—"Le Grand Jury ne peut s'empêcher de manifester le bonheur qu'il éprouve de voir le pays jouissant d'une paix et d'une tranquillité profonde, tandis que les peuples de la vieille Europe se trouvent engagés dans les troubles et le feu des révolutions. Cette paix dont jouit notre pays, qu'il sait apprécier et qu'il saura maintenir, est due à la forme de notre Gou-

to create opposition to the Government amongst the French Canadians utterly failed; they heartily and steadily supported the Government, and took every opportunity to manifest, by addresses and resolutions, the strongest spirit of loyalty to the British Crown. The Liberal party in Upper Canada manifested a similar spirit, and during the Irish movement in the Summer of 1848, the attempts of the American-Irish sympathizers to obtain support in Canada met with nothing but discouragement.

If a different spirit had prevailed, and if the European events of 1848, falling like a spark on a population disaffected to the Government, had provoked any corresponding movement in Canada, it is probable that disturbances there, even if slight in the first instance, would have been followed by very disastrous consequences; since it can hardly be doubted, from what has happened in other cases, that the Government of the United States, however sincerely it might have had the wish, would have wanted the power, to restrain the lawless adventurers whom any outbreak in Canada would have attracted from all quarters of the Union to take

vernement, et surtout à la sagesse, à l'habileté, et à la fermeté des hommes appelés par le Représentant de notre Souverain à le faire fonctionner. Avec de tels hommes à la tête des affaires, soucieux comme ils le sont des intérêts de tous, sans distinction, le pays ne peut que prospérer, et jouir de cette paix si nécessaire au déploiement de son industrie et de son commerce. Le Grand Jury est donc persuadé que cette paix, si nécessaire au bonheur du pays, ne sera jamais troublée; le Gouvernement pouvant compter sur la sympathie et l'appui cordial et sincère de tous ses habitants.—Chambre du Grand Jury, Montreal, Avril 29, 1848."

part in it.   In the insurrection of 1837 and 1838 the
only serious danger arose from the " sympathizers" (as
they were called) from the United States ; and since that
time the Mexican war had added largely both to the
number and to the dangerous character of the class of
men in these States whom the love of excitement and
the hope of plunder are sure to gather together in any
part of North America where there may be a prospect
of that irregular warfare in which they delight.   An
insurrection in Canada would therefore most likely
have involved us also in a war with the United States;
and it is my conviction that the Country could hardly
have escaped from these calamities, but for the policy
upon which, under our direction and with our support, Lord Elgin so ably acted in the government of
Canada.

But although this policy was thus successful in recon-
ciling the alienated French Canadians to the Imperial
Government, and in gaining the affections of the great
body of the people, it was not to be expected that it
should not lead to some dissatisfaction on the part
of those who had been accustomed to consider themselves as entitled to the exclusive possession of the
favour of the Government.   However necessary it was
for the peace and welfare of the Colony that former
events should be buried in oblivion, and that all who
would for the future conduct themselves as faithful
subjects of the Queen, should be regarded as possessing equal claims on the favour of the Crown, it was
impossible that this rule could be acted upon without

creating irritation and discontent in those who saw in
it an improper forgetfulness of their own services to
the Crown during the insurrection, and in supporting
Lord Metcalfe as the Queen's Representative.

By the change of Administration which had taken
place, the party long accustomed to ascendency, and
to consider themselves as the party of the English
Government, had seen the power and influence, which
they had grown to regard as rightfully belonging to
themselves, and which, by the support of the Home
Government, they had been enabled, with a brief
interval, to exercise for a long period, transferred to
a party composed principally of persons whom, on
account of their democratic opinions or of their national origin, they had been in the habit of regarding and representing as disloyal and as the natural
enemies of the British Crown.

It was natural that such a transfer of political power
should create feelings of great displeasure and indignation in the minds of those from whom it was taken,
and there was another circumstance which contributed to exasperate these feelings. The party which
was thus deprived of power happened to include in
its ranks a large proportion of those who were most
deeply interested in the trade of the Province, and
1848 and 1849 were years of great mercantile distress in Canada, which was attributed, not altogether
unjustly, to the recent change in the commercial
policy of this Country. Thus the same persons who
felt most the transfer of political power from one

party to the other, were those on whom the heavy pecuniary losses of a period of extreme commercial difficulty fell also with the greatest severity; hence it is not surprising that, as in the Mother-country political parties were at that time divided principally on the question of free trade or protection, the irritation of the party in the Colony which had been deprived of political power should have been greatly increased by the fact, that the commercial policy to which they attributed their losses was maintained by the Administration at home, under which they had been refused that active support against their political rivals which had been given to them by Lord Metcalfe.

This was the more strongly felt, because Canada had a real grievance to complain of: it had suffered severely from the want of steadiness and consistency in our commercial policy. By the Canada Corn Act of 1843, in consideration of a duty of 3s. a quarter having been imposed by the Provincial Legislature on the importation of foreign wheat, not only the wheat of Canada, but also its flour, which might be manufactured from American wheat, were admitted for consumption into this Country at a nominal duty. The effect of this enactment was obviously to give a large premium for the grinding of American wheat in Canada for the British market. The consequence was, that much of the available capital of the Province was laid out in making arrangements for carrying on the lucrative trade which was supposed to be thus opened to its merchants and millers. But almost before these arrangements were fully completed, and the newly-built mills fairly at work, the Act of 1846 swept away the advantage conferred upon Canada in respect to the corn-trade with this Country, and thus brought upon the Province a frightful amount of loss to individuals, and a great derangement of the Colonial finances.

These evils were naturally attributed by the sufferers to the legislation of 1846, though in my opinion they might more justly have been so to the short-sighted and unwise Act of 1843, of which many members of the House of Commons (of whom I myself was one) predicted the consequences at the time it was passed, and therefore opposed it, on the ground that even then it was obvious that a general repeal of the existing Corn-law could not long be withheld, so that the adoption of the partial measure recommended by the then Government must eventually bring great losses upon Canada, by creating expectations which would certainly be disappointed. But whether the mistake was in passing the Act of 1843 or that of 1846, it is clear that one or the other must have been grievously wrong; and there can be no doubt that the Province had been greatly injured by that inconstancy of purpose which had induced the Imperial Legislature, within the short period of three years, to pass two Acts entirely opposed to each other in principle. It was only natural that the sufferers by this rapid change of policy should condemn, not the original and imprudent grant of the privilege which had been conceded to the Colony, but its abrupt and unexpected withdrawal.

From all these causes the party opposed to the Canadian Administration were disposed, when the Provincial Parliament met in the year 1849, to carry their opposition beyond the usual bounds of political hostility, and to direct it not only against the Governor's advisers, but against the Governor himself, and the Administration then existing in this country. With such a disposition, it was not likely that grounds for attack would be wanting; and they were soon found, in a Bill which was submitted by the Government to the Assembly, for making compensation to persons in Lower Canada who had suffered losses in the rebellion. I am anxious to avoid, as far as possible, the risk of reviving the excitement on this subject, which at the time rose to a great height and led to very deplorable consequences; I will therefore give as brief an account as I can of transactions, some explanation of which is indispensable in a review of Colonial affairs during the last six years.

The Rebellion Losses Bill, as it was called, was brought forward in the Provincial Parliament in the Session of 1849, by Lord Elgin's then advisers, for the purpose of completing what had already been done by their predecessors towards giving effect to the wish expressed by the Assembly in an Address to Lord Metcalfe, which had been voted so long since as the year 1845. The prayer of the Assembly in that Address was, " that His Excellency would be pleased to cause proper measures to be adopted, in order to ensure to the inhabitants of that portion of this Province, formerly Lower Canada, indemnity for just losses by them sustained during the rebellion of 1837 and 1838." It is to be observed that compensation for losses of this description had already been given in Upper Canada, and that, before this Address was voted, under Ordinances passed in 1838 and 1839 by the Special Council (to which at that time the power of legislation in Lower Canada was entrusted), the losses sustained by the loyal inhabitants of the latter Province while supporting the Government had been ascertained and reported upon*. It was clearly therefore the intention of the Government, which had concurred in the above Address, and of the Assembly, by which it had been voted unanimously, to extend the indemnity beyond the limit assigned to it by the Ordinances of the Special Council, and to give it not only to those who, when supporting the Government, had suffered losses from the rebels, but also to those whose property had been destroyed or injured by the troops or volunteers, where such destruction of property could be shown to have been wanton and unnecessary, which was held to be the meaning of the somewhat awkward expression "just losses," which occurs in the Address of the Assembly already quoted.

* See Lord Elgin's Despatch of the 5th of May, 1849, in the "Further Papers relative to the Affairs of Canada," presented to both Houses of Parliament, on the 25th of May, 1849.

In consequence of this Address, Commissioners were appointed by Lord Metcalfe, to inquire into the claims of persons in Lower Canada whose property had been destroyed during the rebellion ; and the Commissioners, in reporting upon these claims, were directed to distinguish the cases of those who had joined in the rebellion, or had been aiding or abetting therein. Upon inquiring in what manner this classification was to be made, they were answered by Mr. Secretary Daly, under the authority of the Governor in Council, in the following terms :—" In making out the classification called for by your instructions of the 12th of December last, it is not His Excellency's intention that you should be guided by any other description of evidence than that furnished by the sentences of the courts of law."

In entire accordance with the proceedings adopted during the earlier stages of these transactions, the Bill passed through the Provincial Parliament under the auspices of Lord Elgin's advisers, excluded absolutely from participation in the indemnity fund only those persons whose guilt in the rebellion had been established by legal conviction or by their own confession ; leaving it to the Commissioners, who were to be appointed to carry out the Act, to determine, in cases which came before them, how far the destruction of property complained of had been wanton or unnecessary. This was a duty obviously of the greatest delicacy, for the faithful and loyal discharge of which the best security was afforded by the re-appointment as Commissioners of the same gentlemen who had been named to that office by Lord Metcalfe. The Rebellion Losses Bill therefore had its origin in an Address of the Assembly, which was passed with the concurrence of Lord Metcalfe's Conservative Administration; its provisions were adopted from the Report of Commissioners appointed by that Administration in pursuance of the Address; and after it became law, its execution was confided by Lord Elgin's advisers to the same individuals.

But all these circumstances were not sufficient to prevent a violent outcry from being raised against the measure, as one of which the object was to reward and encourage rebels. In the House of Assembly, notwithstanding a very determined resistance, the Bill passed by large majorities, by no means composed exclusively of French Canadians; since Lord Elgin has shown, that in the final division of forty-seven to eighteen on the passing of the Bill, seventeen Members from Upper Canada voted in its favour, and fourteen against it; and of ten Members for Lower Canada of British descent, six supported, and only four opposed it*. In the Legislative Council the measure encountered much opposition, but it was the opposition out of doors which was of the most importance. In different parts of the Province petitions were got up against the Bill, the great majority of which, though it was still in progress when they were prepared, were addressed, not to either branch of the Legislature, but to the Governor, and generally

* See the Despatch quoted above.

concluded with a prayer that he would either dissolve the Parliament, or reserve the Bill, when it reached him, for the signification of Her Majesty's pleasure.

Lord Elgin, feeling on the one hand that an appeal to the people would be futile, and on the other that he would not be morally justified in throwing on Her Majesty's Government at home the responsibility of accepting or rejecting the Bill, most properly determined to adopt neither of these courses; and when the Bill was presented to him, he gave the Royal Assent to it in the usual form. Unhappily his doing so was made the occasion of serious riots, in which he was himself attacked and insulted, and the public buildings in which the Provincial Parliament held its sittings were burnt, with the valuable libraries they contained. For a considerable time after these deplorable occurrences, the most violent attacks were directed by the newspapers of the Opposition personally against Lord Elgin; and so strongly were the feelings of a part of the population of Montreal excited against him, that he could not go into the town without the risk of insult and of a disturbance of the public peace, but was compelled almost to confine himself to Monklands, the country residence of the Governor.

By taking this line of conduct Lord Elgin incurred much obloquy at the time; but he acted on the conviction that, although it would have been easy, with the military force which he could command, to put down any riotous proceedings which might have taken place, and he might with perfect security to himself have braved the popular feeling by going into Montreal; still, for the permanent welfare of the Colony it was of the utmost importance to avoid, if possible, any occasion for the employment of force against the mob; since, if blood had been shed in the necessary suppression of acts of violence, this could not have failed to exasperate the animosities already excited, and still further to inflame one class of the population against another. He was also in no small degree influenced by the reflection, that among those who were carried away by the excitement of the moment, some at least were worthy men, actuated by feelings of wounded pride, which were entitled to all possible consideration; he preferred therefore to submit in silence to all the imputations that were directed against him, and waited patiently until the excitement which had been created should subside. At the same time however he expressed his opinion, in reporting these transactions to the Government at home, that the clamour and disturbances raised out of doors ought not to be allowed to prevail against the deliberate decision of the Provincial Legislature, and that submission to such dictation would render the government of the Province by constitutional means impossible*.

In this opinion we concurred, and we agreed with-

* See Lord Elgin's Despatch of the 30th of April, 1849, in the Papers presented to both Houses of Parliament in May, 1849.

out hesitation to advise Her Majesty to signify to Lord Elgin Her undiminished confidence in his ability and judgement, and Her entire approbation of his conduct, which was done by my Despatch* of the 18th of May. Lord Elgin had remarked that, if he should be " unable to recover that position of dignified neutrality between contending parties which it had been his unremitting study to maintain," it might be for the interests of Her Majesty's service that he should be removed from his high office, to make way for a Governor less personally obnoxious to any section of Her Majesty's subjects within the Province. In the despatch I have referred to, he was informed, in reply to his suggestion, that his relinquishment of his post would be regarded as a most serious loss to Her Majesty's service, and that no doubt was entertained that he would succeed in recovering his position of " dignified neutrality."

To this end his efforts were directed; but their success was greatly hindered for some time by the manner in which the intelligence of the events which had taken place in Canada was received in this Country. These events were made the subject of discussion in both Houses of Parliament. In the House of Commons, after some incidental notice of the subject on previous occasions, it was more formally brought under consideration by Mr. Gladstone, on the 14th of June, when, on the motion for bringing up the Report of the

* See further Papers presented to Parliament on the 25th of May, 1849.

Committee of Supply, he made a long speech of severe censure on the Colonial Government, which however was not followed up by submitting any distinct proposal to the House. But although he proposed nothing, after your reply to his speech, Mr. Herries, taking nearly the same line of argument as Mr. Gladstone, but following it out to its natural conclusion, moved an Address to the Crown, praying that Her Majesty's assent to the Canadian Act might be withheld, until satisfactory assurances had been obtained, that no persons implicated in the rebellion would be allowed under its provisions to receive compensation for their losses. After two nights' debate, in the course of which Sir Robert Peel spoke strongly in defence of Lord Elgin's conduct, and against the motion of Mr. Herries, it was rejected by a large majority.

A few days later, resolutions condemning the proceedings of the Canadian Government were moved in the House of Lords by Lord Brougham; and, being supported by the whole strength of the Opposition, were only rejected, by the aid of proxies, by a majority of three,—of the Peers present, a majority having voted for them.

When the intelligence of these discussions, and especially of the close division in the House of Lords, reached the Colony, it had naturally the effect of keeping up the excitement which had previously been created. In the month of August the arrest of some of the persons accused of having been engaged in the riots in April, led to a fresh and serious riot in Montreal, when a violent attack was made by the mob on the house of Mr. Lafontaine, in resisting which one man was shot, who afterwards died of his wounds; this, owing to the extreme forbearance of Lord Elgin and his advisers, was the only life lost throughout these unhappy disturbances.

But the violence of the passions which had been excited was displayed, not merely by the riotous conduct of an ignorant mob, but by proceedings of a more really dangerous and objectionable character on the part of persons of superior education and station in life. In the course of the Autumn of 1849 there was got up in the Province a movement, somewhat formidable in the first instance, in favour of what was called the annexation of Canada to the United States. An address to the people of Canada, bearing a large number of signatures, and advocating this measure (the necessity of which was rested in part on the withdrawal of the commercial privileges formerly granted to the Colony by the Mother-country), was printed and extensively circulated through the Province. Though it was the object of the Government, both in Canada and in this Country, to act with the utmost forbearance, in the conviction that the excitement would subside, and that those whose passions had for the moment betrayed them into very objectionable. proceedings, were not really insensible to their duty as British subjects; it was still considered necessary clearly to show that this forbearance did not proceed from any disposition to yield to the intemperate opposition which had been offered to the constituted Authorities.

One of the most important measures adopted with this view was the removal of the seat of Government from Montreal. Soon after the riots in April, an address to the Governor had been carried in the Assembly, praying that in consequence of these outrages, and of the destruction of the building in which the sittings of the Legislature had formerly been held, he would in future summon the Provincial Parliament to meet alternately at Toronto and Quebec.

When the intelligence reached this Country of the renewal of disturbances in Montreal in August, a despatch was addressed to Lord Elgin, pointing out that the existence of such a spirit of insubordination in that city rendered it a very unfit place for the seat of the Provincial Government and for the meeting of the Legislature *; and, on the 18th of November, the Governor reported, in reply, that after full and anxious deliberation he had resolved, on the advice of his Council, to act on the recommendation of the Assembly that the Legislature should sit alternately at Toronto and Quebec, and with that view to summon the Provincial Parliament for the next session at Toronto †. The removal of the seat of Government from Montreal,

* See Papers relating to the removal of the seat of Government and to the annexation movement in Canada, presented to both Houses of Parliament, April 15, 1850.

† See the above Papers, p. 6.

which was decided upon in this deliberate and un-impassioned manner, was calculated to give a useful lesson to the inhabitants, not only of that city but of the whole Province, as to the natural consequences of acts of violence and insubordination to those who were guilty of them.

About the same time that this measure was decided upon, the Governor caused a circular letter to be addressed to all the persons holding commissions at the pleasure of the Crown, whose names had ap-peared amongst the signatures to the address to the people of Canada recommending the annexation of the Province to the United States, with the view of ascertaining whether their names had been attached to that document with their own consent. Some of these letters were answered in the negative, some in the affirmative, and others by denying the right of the Government to put the question, and declining to reply to it. Lord Elgin* resolved, with the advice of the Executive Council, to remove from such offices as are held during the pleasure of the Crown, the gentlemen who admitted the genuineness of their sig-natures, and those who refused to disavow them.

In this course we thought it right to support him, and a despatch was addressed to him, signifying the Queen's approval of his having dismissed from Her service those who had signed the address, and Her Majesty's commands to resist to the utmost any at-tempt that might be made to bring about a separa-

* See the above Papers, p. 10.

tion of Canada from the British dominions, to mark in the strongest manner Her Majesty's displeasure with all those who might directly or indirectly encourage such a design, and to adopt legal proceedings against those whose conduct might, in the opinion of the law officers, afford grounds for doing so*. This policy was attended with complete success. From the first the Governor had received the decided and energetic support of the great majority of the inhabitants of the Province; addresses to the Queen and to the Governor were transmitted in great numbers from all parts of the Province, condemning the riotous proceedings at Montreal, and expressing a strong determination to maintain the connection between the Colony and the Mother-country; and by degrees both the excitement which had been created and the annexation movement died away, the authors of that movement having apparently, on cooler reflection, become ashamed of it.

Before we retired from office, the state of public feeling throughout the Province had become in the highest degree satisfactory. There are of course those party divisions which must be expected to exist in all free governments; but there has been a remarkable abatement of the former bitterness of party spirit, and still more so of the animosities arising from difference of national origin, while there is every indication that all parties are becoming daily more sensible of the advantages they derive from the form

* See the above Papers, p. 23.

of their Government and from their connection with
the British Empire. The arrangement by which the
seat of Government and the sittings of the Legislature were fixed alternately at Toronto and Quebec has
contributed not a little towards removing the feelings
of alienation from each other of the inhabitants of
French and of British descent. The French Canadians
have thus been brought into closer communication
than formerly with the inhabitants of the western
division of the Province, and an increase of mutual
esteem and respect, with the removal of many prejudices by which they were formerly divided, have
been the result of the two classes becoming better
acquainted with each other.

The improved state of feeling generally is however,
no doubt, in a great measure to be attributed to the
recovery of the commercial and industrial interests of
the Province from the depression under which they
laboured for a time. I shall almost immediately have
to call your attention to the evidence which exists of
the present prosperity of Canada; but before doing
so, it is fit that I should mention some of the other
matters relating to this Colony, which during the last
five years have occupied the attention of its Government and Legislature.

Within that period questions of much importance
have required and received consideration; and notwithstanding the degree to which, during a part of the time,
public attention was occupied and distracted by party
dissensions, useful legislation and measures of improve-

ment have by no means been neglected. The Provincial Parliament at an early period availed itself of the power granted to it by the Act of 1846, to repeal the differential duties formerly imposed on imports from foreign countries by Imperial Legislation ; and Canada has now a tariff of duties levied for revenue only, and in such a manner as to interfere as little as possible with the natural direction of capital and industry. It has also passed laws extending and improving the system of Municipal organization, which is now very complete in the western division of the Province, and is beginning to be brought into operation in the eastern division also. The District Councils have been assisted in adopting effective measures for improving their means of communication, both by ordinary roads and by railroads : of the former many have already been made, and steps have been taken which there is every reason to believe will ensure the speedy construction of various important lines of railway. In the western division of the Province an admirable system of general Education has been brought, by recent improvements, into complete and effective operation; and measures are in progress for extending and improving in like manner the means of education in Eastern Canada.

In the years 1847 and 1848, at the instance of the Local Government, we recommended to the Imperial Parliament the repeal of certain parts of the Act of Union, which were considered by the inhabitants of Canada to involve an improper restriction of

the powers of the Provincial Legislature to deal with
their own local affairs. Accordingly, by the Act of
the 10th and 11th of Victoria, chap. 71, the provisions in the Act of Union relating to the Civil List of
Canada were repealed, and Her Majesty was enabled
to give her assent to a Provincial Act to supply
their place; so that the whole expenditure of the
Colony now takes place under the authority, not of
Imperial, but of Provincial Legislation. In the following year (by the Act of the 11th and 12th of Victoria, chap. 56) other clauses of the Act of Union,
which require that the English language only should
be used in instruments relating to the Legislative
Council and Assembly, were also repealed. These measures were not of very great practical importance
in themselves, but considerable consequence was attached to them by the inhabitants of Canada, as a
proof of the confidence of the Imperial Government
and Parliament, and as removing the last traces of
that distrust which the insurrection had necessarily
left behind it, and which was evinced in the clauses
of the Union Act now repealed.

Laws have also been passed for the protection, both
of the Province and of the immigrants themselves,
from the evils which arose from the manner in which
Emigration was formerly carried on. This subject is
one of the highest importance, both to the Colony
and to the Mother-country, and has occupied a very
large share of public attention. In the year 1847,
the arrival in the Colonies of large numbers of Irish

immigrants had been attended with great calamities. These unhappy people, flying from famine, flocked to every port that was open to them in North America. The passage to the British possessions being at that time considerably cheaper than that to the United States, the poorest and most destitute of the starving multitude made the former their destination. Neither the Imperial Passengers Act, then in force, nor the Colonial laws, were calculated to meet such an emergency. The regulations imposed by the former, as to the number of persons to be embarked in a given space, as to the accommodation to be afforded, and the precautions to be taken on board emigrant-ships, though they had sufficed under ordinary circumstances, proved altogether inadequate when such vast numbers of emigrants were striving to escape from starvation, many of them carrying with them the seeds of disease from the sufferings they had already undergone. The consequence was that a frightful fever broke out in the emigrant-ships, and at the quarantine stations where the emigrants were landed in the Colonies, and especially in the St. Lawrence; and the mortality, which in former years had been only at the rate of about five in every thousand emigrants, was increased elevenfold, and there were no less than fifty-five deaths in the same number of passengers.

The Colonial Government and the members of the medical and clerical professions made the most strenuous and laudable efforts for the relief of the crowds of miserable beings thrown upon their care by the arrival of the emigrant-ships. Every arrangement, which the limited means that were available rendered practicable, was made for the reception of the emigrants, and for supplying their wants and relieving their sufferings. The Colonial Government incurred a heavy expenditure in the measures adopted for this purpose, while several of the medical men and clergy of different persuasions fell victims to their humane exertions, and died of the fever which they caught in attending to the emigrants, whose sufferings, in spite of all that could be done for them, were of the most heart-rending description.

It was obviously necessary to take precautions against the recurrence of such calamities ; accordingly, a temporary Act for the regulation of emigrant-ships to North America was passed by Parliament early in the Session of 1848, to afford time for the full consideration of a permanent law, which has since been passed. An application was also made to Parliament, to relieve the North American Colonies from the heavy expense incurred by them in the relief of emigrants, and a sum of no less than £140,000 was voted for that purpose. In Canada (and a similar course was adopted in the other North American Colonies) a local Act was passed, founded on suggestions contained in a despatch which I addressed to Lord Elgin.   The principal objects of this Act were to provide for the expenditure to be incurred by the Colony on account of emigration, by an increase of the emigration-tax already levied ; and at the same time to make it the interest of owners and masters of ships to take all the precautions in their power against disease, by augmenting the tax in cases where there·should be such sickness on board ships as to render it necessary to prolong their detention in quarantine. There were also other stringent regulations, to meet the most serious of the evils which had arisen. These measures were attended with complete success. There has been no recurrence of the calamities of 1847; and the severity of the restrictions judiciously imposed by the Legislature in the first instance has been relaxed, as experience has shown that this might safely be done, while at the same time effective arrangements have been made for the protection of ignorant emigrants from the heartless and cruel frauds to which, in New York, they are too often exposed.

I cannot leave this subject of Emigration without reminding you that, in the midst of the alarm and distress of the Irish famine of 1847, we were most urgently pressed to take measures for increasing the tide of emigration, by applying to Parliament for a grant of money to promote it; and that it was with considerable difficulty that we were able to resist the very general wish that was expressed, that something of this kind should be attempted. We were however so strongly convinced, that it would be utterly impossible for the Government to interfere directly in transferring the distressed population of Ireland to the other side of the Atlantic, without doing far more harm than good, and without giving rise to great abuses, that we steadily refused to engage in such an undertaking. We were persuaded that the effect of any interference by the Government in the manner desired, would have been to paralyse the exertions of individuals, by which alone so vast a movement of the population, as was required and was in progress, could be safely accomplished.

Had the Government undertaken the removal of the distressed inhabitants of Ireland, it would have brought upon itself a responsibility of the most formidable kind, both as to the selection of those who should be allowed to emigrate at the public expense, and the arrangements to be made for providing for them on their arrival. If the most destitute and helpless had been taken as would have been requisite for the relief of Ireland, the evil inflicted on the places to which they were sent would have been so great, that the United States would doubtless immediately have availed themselves of their right as an independent Nation to take measures for their own protection, and would have passed laws effectually to prevent a destitute multitude from being cast on their shores. The Colonies would have claimed, on such irresistible grounds of justice, a right to adopt similar measures, that they could not have been refused permission to do so, without producing an alienation of their affections, fatal to the authority of the British Crown.

As it was, there were great complaints as to the description of emigrants that went to the North

American Colonies; and it was only by showing that the Government had neither the power nor the right to interfere as to the selection of emigrants, that these complaints were met*. If the emigrants had been sent out by the Government, it would also have been universally felt that the Government could not possibly repudiate the responsibility of providing for them on their arrival in the Colonies; and the experience of what occurred in Ireland during the famine but too clearly shows how readily the multitude of destitute emigrants, who in the year 1847 reached the shores of America, would have thrown themselves upon the public, had this been possible. Nothing but the pressure of absolute necessity would have compelled them to make the exertions and submit to the hardships through which they were in fact provided for.

Nor should it be overlooked, that if destitute labourers arrive in such a country as Canada in greater numbers than can be absorbed by the existing demand for labour, they must be exposed to quite as much distress, and there will be as much difficulty in maintaining them, for a time at least, as if they remained at home. In a new country, where additional land is continually being reclaimed from the wilderness, it is impossible to assign a limit to the number of labourers who may be received with advantage, if they are really industrious and arrive in due succession,

* See Report of the Colonial Land and Emigration Commissioners enclosed in the Despatch of December 1, 1847, already quoted.

because the labourers of one year become the employers of labour of a few years later; but those who arrive without capital to enable them to settle, and who cannot find employment, are exposed to still more hopeless destitution than at home,—a destitution moreover which it is even more difficult to relieve. It has been clearly proved by experience that, without incurring an expense far beyond what could be justified by the object in view, it is impracticable for the State to undertake to provide in a Colony, any more than at home, employment for large numbers of labourers, and that it is still more impossible to furnish to such labourers capital to enable them to become settlers.

Hence we judged it to be our duty to confine the measures we adopted on the subject of emigration to those which had for their object to enable individual proprietors or Poor Law Unions, under certain restrictions, to send out emigrants, to guard against the abuses which experience had shown to be likely to arise, and to facilitate, on the other side of the Atlantic, the distribution of those who arrived seeking work, to the places where they could most easily find it. We were anxious also to have adopted measures to encourage emigration indirectly, by providing for the more regular settlement of the unoccupied lands of the Colonies, and thus increasing the demand for labour; but the opinion of all the local Authorities was so adverse to the plans of this kind which were suggested, that none of them were carried into effect.

The result has shown the soundness of the views upon which we acted. Without any interference on the part of the Government, and without any expense to the public, the tide of emigration has now set in so strongly from Ireland to America, that many persons are beginning to fear that the drain of the population, instead of being insufficient, will be too great. I see no reason for apprehending this; but with the present facilities for communication, I believe that the drain will continue, until the great disparity between the value of labour in Ireland and on the other side of the Atlantic shall be put an end to, and till the wages paid in Ireland shall be such as to afford a comfortable subsistence to the labourer. There is every reason for desiring that, till this has been accomplished, emigration should go on at its present rate, or even more rapidly ; and, on the other hand, it can hardly be doubted that, as this alteration in the relative value of labour takes place, emigration will reach its natural limit, and gradually decline.

It is a remarkable circumstance, in the present emigration from Ireland, that it is effected not only without charge to the public revenue, but with comparatively little demand upon the private means of individuals in the United Kingdom. The Emigration Commissioners have ascertained that the remittances made by former emigrants to their friends and relations in this Country amounted last year to nearly a million of money*, taking into account only

* £990,000 : see the Commissioners' Report for 1852, p. 12.

those remittances made by channels which admit of their being traced, and without reckoning the sums sent by private hands, or other means, of which it is known that the aggregate amount must be very large, though individually the sums so sent are usually small. The money thus transmitted from the United States and the British Colonies is chiefly for the purpose of assisting those to whom it is sent to emigrate; and it is now a common practice for several friends or relations in Ireland to club their means, so as to enable one or more of their number to emigrate; and the individuals so sent save out of their wages what is necessary to carry out the rest in succession. The able-bodied son or husband frequently emigrates in the first instance, and then remits to his wife or parents the means of joining him in America; and it has been clearly ascertained that, of late years, the great majority of Irish emigrants who have landed at New York, or in Canada, have been proceeding to join their friends or relations who had gone before them. It is highly to the credit of the Irish national character that there should exist so generally amongst the lowest classes of the population such strong feelings of family affection, and such fidelity and firmness of purpose, as are implied by the great extent to which this mode of conducting emigration has been carried.

The result of leaving emigration to proceed spontaneously, has thus been to effect a transfer of population from one side of the Atlantic to the other, to an extent far beyond what could have been thought of, if it had been to be accomplished by the direct agency of the State; and at the same time avoiding the enormous expense, and the abuses,. which no care could have prevented, had such an operation, even upon a comparatively small scale, been carried on at the public expense, by any machinery that could have been devised. But it has been objected that, although these advantages of the policy which has been pursued cannot be denied, they are to a great extent counterbalanced by the fact that, under this system, the greater part of the emigrants from the United Kingdom, instead of increasing the population and wealth of British Colonies, have gone to promote the progress of the United States. If the United States were to be regarded as a hostile Power, the force of this objection could not be denied; but their interests are now so intimately bound up with our own, that the emigrants from our shores, in augmenting the wealth and population of the United States, are in effect contributing to promote British trade and British prosperity. Canada also, it must be remembered, has, in proportion to her previous population and to her means of employment, received full as many, if not more, of the emigrants from the United Kingdom than the neighbouring Republic.

I shall have occasion to make some further observations upon emigration when I come to speak of the Australian Colonies; but for the present I must revert to the affairs of Canada, with reference to which there still remain two or three matters which it is proper for me to mention. Of these I will first notice the endeavours that have been made, to place the commercial intercourse between Canada and the United States on a more satisfactory footing. The Parliament of Canada having availed itself of the authority granted to it by the Act of 1846, to repeal the differential duties formerly levied on imports from foreign countries, the merchants and manufacturers of the United States have now had for some time as free access as those of this Country to the markets of Canada, while the agricultural produce of the United States has also, as it is well known, been allowed to compete upon equal terms with that of the Colony in the British market.

In these circumstances the inhabitants of Canada have naturally felt it as a great grievance, that their own agricultural produce should not be admissible for consumption into the United States, except on the payment of what is practically a prohibitory duty. It has therefore for the last four or five years been an object, sought with great earnestness by the inhabitants of Canada and the other British Provinces, that an arrangement should be concluded with the United States, for allowing a reciprocally free trade between those States and the British dominions in North America in agricultural produce and a few other articles. In order to effect this object, negotiations have been carried on with the United States Government; but although no pains have been spared by the British

Minister at Washington, with the assistance of gentlemen deputed for that purpose by the Provincial Governments, in endeavouring to induce the Government of
the United States to make a concession which is manifestly one which in all fairness this Country is entitled
to ask, hitherto these efforts have been fruitless. It is
not surprising that this refusal of the United States, to
meet the just expectations of the people of Canada,
should have created among the latter a strong disposition to enforce retaliatory restrictions on the trade
carried on between themselves and their neighbours ;
and I consider it by no means one of the smallest
services which it was in our power to render to the
Colony, while we were entrusted with the direction of
affairs, that we succeeded in preventing the adoption
of any measures of this kind, not by a direct and
formal refusal to sanction them, but by unofficially
discouraging their being brought forward.

Though the restrictions upon Canadian commerce still
maintained by the United States, are marked by a spirit
of selfish unfairness far from creditable to the Republic,
or rather to those by whose influence in its councils
they are kept in force, nothing I think can be more
clear than that they are infinitely more injurious to the
United States themselves than to Canada, and that,
on the other hand, the consequence of any retaliatory measures to which Canada might be provoked to
have recourse, would fall chiefly on herself. It is of
the exclusion of their agricultural produce, and particularly of their wheat, from consumption in the United

States, that the Canadians principally complain; and as wheat is at times dearer in the adjoining States of the Union than in the Province, the Canadian farmer is no doubt a loser by the restriction, to the extent of this difference of price, whatever it may be. But as the United States are upon the whole exporters of agricultural produce, and must probably for many years to come continue to be so, it is certain that the price of corn in their own markets must in general be regulated by that which they can obtain for the surplus they export, in the foreign market, in which they meet the Canadian produce on equal terms. Hence it is impossible that the price of corn in the Union can be kept for any length of time much higher than it is in Canada, and the loss to the Canadian farmer, from being deprived of this additional market, must be comparatively trifling.

The injury to the United States themselves, from the restriction, is by no means so trifling. Since the completion of the St. Lawrence Canals, and the repeal of our Navigation Laws, Canada is becoming a formidable rival to the United States, in the great trade carried on in the export of flour to the various markets of the world which draw their supplies from the fertile lands of Western America. Of the two lines of communication between the great lakes and the sea, the one by the St. Lawrence to Quebec, the other by the Erie Canal to New York, the former possesses the great advantages of not requiring any trans-shipment of goods and produce between the most remote of the

Western Lake ports and the sea, and also of admitting of the use of much larger vessels than can be employed in the Erie Canal. The consequence is that a great saving of time, and probably a saving of money also, can be effected by the use of this line in bringing produce from the West to the port of shipment, and likewise in sending the various goods required for consumption in the interior from the seaport to the place of their destination. New York has a countervailing advantage over Quebec and Montreal, in the lower rate of freight to the European and other principal markets of the world; but since the repeal of the Navigation Laws, and the opening of the Canadian ports to the flags of all nations, this advantage has been greatly reduced, and there is reason to believe that the trade between the far West and the principal ports of the world will be most cheaply carried on through the St. Lawrence. This being the case, it is clear that a competition is just beginning, which promises to be a very severe one, on the part of the Canadian ports with New York, for the enormous trade which is already carried on, and is daily increasing, in the exchange of the surplus agricultural produce of the industrious settlers on the lands washed by the great American lakes, for the various supplies which they require.

In this exciting competition it is obvious that the Canadian miller and merchant must be directly assisted by the maintenance, on the part of the United States, of restrictions on the import of Canadian wheat; since, if these restrictions have any effect at all, they must tend to keep the price of wheat in the United States at a higher level than in the adjoining provinces; and, in so close a race, a slight difference may be material in determining which of the rivals for the trade shall be able to supply the foreign consumer on the easiest terms. If it were possible that the law of the United States could succeed in its object, and maintain a rate of prices in the Republic materially higher than in Canada, the effect of this would probably be, that in no long time a large part of the trade in flour from New York to Europe, to Cuba, and to Brazil, would be transferred to Canada, and that the manufactured goods, the sugar and other supplies required in return by the settlers in the West, would be conveyed to them by the same route. So clear does it seem to me that this is the tendency of the existing restriction on the importation of the agricultural produce of Canada into the United States, that, in the interest of the former I should wish these restrictions to be maintained for a few years, until her trade with the West can be thoroughly established, were it not that I have unlimited faith in the general rule, that in every case the removal of restrictions upon the freedom of trade is certain to be attended with advantage to all whom those restrictions affect.

Looking at the subject in this light, I believe that the true policy for this Country and for Canada to pursue, would be to abstain from any further negotiation or communication whatever with the United

States, respecting the duties imposed by them on Canadian produce, leaving them to deal with the question as they may think best for their own interest, and not allowing their decision to have any influence in regulating the Canadian tariff: this should be determined solely by a consideration of what rates of import duty on different articles may be best calculated to raise the revenue required for the public service, with the least pressure upon the community, and the least diversion of capital and industry from their natural channels. Perhaps it is hardly to be expected that the people of Canada should acquiesce in a policy so different from that which nations have hitherto almost universally agreed in following; but at all events it is earnestly to be hoped, that the Provincial Parliament will be wise enough to abstain from any legislation of a retaliatory character. To exclude the United States from the markets of Canada, because they are so injudicious as not to admit Canadian produce to their own market, would, on the part of Canada, be simply to punish herself for the faults of her neighbour, and to deprive herself of the advantages of the trade she now enjoys, because she is not allowed to carry on a still larger one. The Canadian consumer only purchases goods imported from the United States, because they cost him less than similar goods obtained from any other quarter; and there would surely be no sense in taking from him this advantage, because the Government of the United States will not on their side allow their own people to purchase from Canada what could be most cheaply obtained there.

I have entered into this question further than I should otherwise have done, because it involves a general principle to which I attach the highest importance, and also because it affords an example, which proves that without depriving the Colonies of the full enjoyment of political liberty, and of the right of managing their own affairs, the Government of this Country does possess the means of exercising a powerful influence over their councils, and that the connection of the various parts of the British Empire need not be rendered so merely nominal as some persons suppose, by the abstinence of the Mother-country from exerting an imperious control over her Dependencies. There can be no doubt that a Government, acting upon opposite views of commercial policy from those which, with the support of Parliament, your Administration maintained, would have led Canada into the adoption of measures of retaliation against the United States, for their restrictions on her commerce; and, as I have said, I believe that we have rendered no slight service to the Colony and to the Empire by giving a different direction to her policy*.

Another question which has lately occupied public attention in Canada, is that relating to the Clergy Reserves. It is well known that by the Canada Act

* Since this was written I have observed, with regret, in the Colonial newspapers, that different views are now likely to be acted upon by the Provincial Government.

of 1791, one-seventh of the un-granted lands of the
Colony were set apart for the support of a Protestant
Clergy, reserving however to the local Legislatures
of the two Provinces the power, with the consent
of the Imperial Parliament, of varying or repealing
this enactment. For many years this provision had
excited much discontent in both Upper and Lower
Canada, but especially in the former. In the hope
of allaying this feeling, it was enacted by Parliament
in 1840, when the Provinces were united, that these
lands should be sold, and the proceeds applied in
certain proportions to the endowment of the Clergy
of different denominations ; those of the National
Churches of England and Scotland receiving a share
far exceeding that which would have been assigned to
them had the division been regulated by the number
of members of the several Churches.

I regretted this arrangement at the time it was made,
fearing that, from the opinions prevailing in Canada, it
would not long be acquiesced in as a permanent settlement of the question. You may perhaps remember
that, not being myself in office, I communicated to
you the opinion I entertained, but abstained from
any public opposition to the measure, because it was
obvious that such opposition to an arrangement on
which you, as leader of the Government, were agreed
with the leaders on the other side, must have been
ineffectual, and could only tend to diminish any little
chance there might be that the arrangement would be
accepted permanently in the Colony.

My anticipation that it would not be so received has proved correct; it has been found impossible to prevent the subject being again agitated in the Province; and in the year 1850 an Address to the Queen was voted by the House of Assembly, praying that Her Majesty would recommend to Parliament a measure for the repeal of the Imperial Act of the 3rd and 4th of Vict. c. 78, and for enabling the Canadian Legislature to dispose of the proceeds of the Clergy Reserves, subject to the condition of securing to the existing holders for their lives the stipends to which they were then entitled. This Address was answered by a despatch to Lord Elgin, which he was instructed to lay before both Houses of the Provincial Parliament, and in which he was informed that it had appeared to Her Majesty's Government, on mature deliberation, that the desire expressed by the Assembly ought to be acceded to, and that a recommendation would be made to Parliament accordingly. He was told that, "in coming to this conclusion, Her Majesty's Government have been mainly influenced by the consideration, that, great as in their judgement would be the advantages which would result from leaving undisturbed the existing arrangement, by which a certain portion of the public lands of Canada are made available for the purpose of creating a fund for the religious instruction of the inhabitants of the Province, still the question whether that arrangement is to be maintained is one so exclusively affecting the people of Canada, that its decision ought not to be withdrawn from the

Provincial Legislature, to which it properly belongs to regulate all matters concerning the domestic interests of the Province."

It would have been impossible, in conformity with the principles which I have endeavoured in the first of these Letters to explain, as those on which our whole Colonial Policy was founded, to come to any other decision. It shows in my opinion the advantage of acting on those principles, and of confining the exercise of the authority of the Imperial Government to cases really calling for it, that the local Legislature, in this instance, was induced to abstain from attempting to carry measures to which the Crown could not have been advised to assent, principally by the confidence entertained, that no attempt would be made to over-rule the wishes of the People of Canada in a matter of purely domestic interest, provided that their Representatives showed due respect for the honour of the Crown, and the authority of the Imperial Parliament. There were not wanting in the Assembly Members who urged that the vested interests of those actually in the receipt of incomes from the fund with which it was proposed to deal, should be disregarded and that, without waiting for the repeal of the Imperial Act, the local Legislature should proceed at once to alter the arrangement, resting on its authority. Fortunately the Assembly listened to the more moderate counsels of those who urged, that to give the Royal Assent to an Act depriving existing incumbents of their incomes, would be regarded by the advisers of the Crown as inconsistent with its honour, and would therefore be refused ; and that to pass, without express authority for doing so, a Provincial Act for the purpose of altering the provisions of an Act of the Imperial Parliament, would be to assume for the local Legislature a power with which the Constitution does not invest it.

From the tone of the debates which took place, it may be inferred, that this judicious advice would have been little likely to prevail in the Assembly, but for the reliance placed on the adherence of the Imperial Government to the principles which had of late been observed in the exercise of its authority in the Province. I must not omit to mention also that, in the discussions on this question, which had much excited the popular passions, the French Canadians, though the interests of the Protestant churches were at stake, were generally on the side of respecting vested interests and the authority of the Imperial Parliament,— an additional proof of the good effects produced by treating them with confidence and kindness. I have only further to add upon this subject, that it had been our intention to have brought under the consideration of Parliament, in the Session of 1851, a Bill for carrying into effect what we had promised ; but we were prevented from doing so by the circumstance, that the attention of the House of Commons was so long occupied by matters which could not be postponed, that there was no opportunity of submitting to it the intended Bill, until it was too late in the

Session to proceed with the measure with any prospect of success : it was therefore postponed till the
present year, and was to have been brought forward
in a few days, when the division took place which
led to the breaking up of your Administration.

In practically recognizing, by the course we adopted
on the various matters to which I have adverted, the
claim of the Canadians to exercise the powers of self-
government, we did not lose sight of the views I
have stated in the preliminary part of this Letter as
to the corresponding duties, which the exercise of
the powers of self-government imposes upon the Colonial dependencies of the Empire, and to the propriety of their relieving the Imperial Treasury from a
part of the charges it has been subject to on their account. The manner in which we proposed to act upon
these views will be best explained by an extract from
a Despatch which was addressed to Lord Elgin in
the Spring of last year, in reply to one in which
he had sent home an elaborate Minute, by his Executive Council, on the finances of the Colony. This
Minute was founded on certain reports, presented to
the Assembly in its previous Session by a Committee appointed to inquire into the public income
and expenditure of the Province. Amongst other proposals for saving expense, a reduction of the salary
attached to the office of Governor-General had been
brought under consideration ; and with reference to
this suggestion we thought it advisable to explain
fully to Lord Elgin, for the information of his Council

and of the Canadian Parliament, the changes which the altered state of their relations in other respects seemed to render expedient in the pecuniary arrangements between the Province and the Mother-country. The instructions sent to Lord Elgin upon this subject were so important that I must quote them at length. They were as follows.

" That portion of the Minute of your Executive Council which relates to the amount of the salary at present attached to the office of Governor-General, and your own remarks upon this important point, have attracted the more particular attention of Her Majesty's Government. The present salary of that office does not appear to me to be unduly high ; on the contrary, believing it to be an object of the greatest importance to Canada that the post of Governor-General should be filled by men of political experience and of the highest ability that can be found, I regret that the salary is not at present such as in general to afford any temptation to those who have taken a lead in public affairs in this Country, to abandon their prospects at home for the purpose of accepting this office. But I concur with your Lordship and with your Council in considering the amount of the salary as of far less importance, than that this amount, whatever it may be, should be fixed, and should cease to be the subject of perpetual discussion in the Province ; since such discussion, it is justly remarked by your Council in their Minute, is calculated to impair the dignity of the Queen's Representative. It might have been hoped, that the manner in which the present salary of the Governor-General was granted for Her Majesty's life by the Provincial Legislature, by an Act of Parliament freely and deliberately passed for that purpose, would have had the effect of permanently settling a question the agitation of which is attended with so much evil.

" Experience has however proved this hope to be unfounded ; nor can I see the slightest reason for believing that, if the existing arrangement were to be departed from, and any possible reduction in the salary of the office assented to by Her Majesty, the question would then be set at rest, or that a still further reduction would not be proposed as soon as it might suit the views of any political party to renew the discussion.

" There is but one mode, that I am aware of, by which any further agitation of this question in the Province may be effectually prevented, and that is, by making the salary of the Governor-General a charge, not upon the Canadian, but upon the British Treasury. This is an alteration which for many reasons I have long regarded as advisable ; and it appears to Her Majesty's Government, that a fitting occasion for proposing it is now presented, in consequence of the desire manifested by the Canadian Parliament for a revision of the Civil List. But it is impossible that such an alteration can be recommended to Parliament, except as part of a general measure for placing the fiscal relations of the Mother-country and the Colony on a footing adapted to the greatly altered circumstances of the present time, as compared to those under which the existing arrangement of those relations has grown up.

" Canada (in common with the other British provinces in North America) now possesses in the most ample and complete manner in which it is possible that she should enjoy it, the advantage of self-government in all that relates to her internal affairs. It appears to Her Majesty's Government that this advantage ought to carry with it corresponding responsibilities, and that the time is now come when the people of Canada must be called upon to take upon themselves a larger share than they have hitherto done, of expenses which are incurred on this account, and for their advantage. Of these expenses, by far the heaviest charge which falls upon this Country is that incurred for the military protection of the Province. Regarding Canada as a most important and valuable part of the Empire, and believing the maintenance of the connection between the Mother-country and the Colony to be of the highest advantage to both, it is far from being the view of Her Majesty's Government, that the general military power of the Empire is not to be used in the protection of this part of Her Majesty's dominions. But looking to the rapid progress which Canada is now making in wealth and population, and to the prosperity which she at this moment enjoys, it is the conviction of Her Majesty's Government that it is only due to the people of this Country, that they should now be relieved from a large proportion of the charge which has hitherto been imposed upon them, for the protection of a Colony, now well able to do much towards protecting itself.

" In adopting this principle, I need hardly observe to you, that Her Majesty's Government would merely be reverting to the former Colonial policy of this Country. You are well aware, that up to the period of the war of the American Revolution, the then British Colonies which now form the United States, as well as the West Indian Colonies, were required to take upon themselves the principal share of the burden of their own protection, and even to contribute to the military operations undertaken to extend the Colonial possessions of the British Crown. The North American Colonies defended themselves almost entirely from the fierce Indian tribes, by which these infant communities were frequently imperilled, and furnished no inconsiderable proportion of the force, by which the contest of British power with that of France was maintained on the continent of America ; and the West Indian Colonies did not, in proportion to their means, make less exertions.

" Her Majesty's Government would have thought it right at an earlier period to revert to this former policy of the Empire, and to extend to Canada measures of the same description with those which have already been adopted as respects the Australian Colonies, had it not been that till lately there were circumstances connected with the commercial and general condition of Canada, which seemed to render the time unfavourable for effecting so important a change. The difficulties under which commerce and industry laboured, were of a very aggravated description, and produced their usual consequences of political excitement and discontent ; nor ought it to be concealed, that much of the prevailing distress was attributable to the changes which had taken place in British legislation. The combined effect of the stimulus given by the Act of 1843 to the investment of capital in preparations for supplying this Country with flour from Canada, and of the subsequent general repeal of all restrictions on the importation of corn and flour into the United Kingdom, had undoubtedly been to cause very heavy losses in Canada, and till these had been recovered, it would have been inexpedient to add to the burdens of the Province.

" But the season of commercial depression in Canada has now passed away ; the repeal of the Navigation Laws, and the opening of the St. Lawrence Canals, which the Province has been enabled to construct, by a loan raised on highly favourable terms, on the credit of the British Treasury, has given a great impulse to its trade ; and the remarkable increase of the Customs' revenue, which you have lately reported to me, affords a clear and striking proof of the return of prosperity. Under these circumstances, it appears to Her Majesty's Government that no more favourable opportunity could be found for placing the fiscal relations of the Mother-country and the Colony on a permanent and equitable footing. They are the more induced to adopt this view of the subject, because they are prepared to recommend to Parliament, that assistance of the same kind with that which has proved so eminently useful to Canada in the construction of the St. Lawrence Canals, should be extended to her in respect of another public work, calculated to be hardly less beneficial to her than these Canals. In another despatch I will explain to your Lordship the views of Her Majesty's Government with regard to the means by which it is hoped that the construction of the Quebec and Halifax Railway may be accomplished. I only advert to this subject at present for the purpose of observing, that while the credit of this Country is exerted to enable Canada to extend her public works and to develop her resources, I feel confident that the Parliament of Canada will readily co-operate with Her Majesty's Government, in adopting measures for diminishing the charge on the British Treasury for the defence of the Province.

" Having thus explained to your Lordship, the principles of the policy which Her Majesty's Government propose to adopt, I will now proceed to state more particularly the measures by which it is contemplated that this policy should be carried into effect. In the first place, it is intended that in future, with the exception of a certain number of enrolled pensioners, for whose location in the Province arrangements are in progress, the troops maintained in Canada should be confined to the garrisons of two or three fortified posts of importance, probably only Quebec and Kingston. The terms of amity upon which this Country now is with the United States, and the fortunate termination of all the questions in dispute between the two nations, removes, as I trust, all risk of any attack upon Canada from the only power from which there could be any danger; and it appears to Her Majesty's Government, that if the Provincial Militia is maintained upon a proper footing, so long as peace continues, enough would be done to provide for the security of the Province, by maintaining garrisons of regular troops in the two important posts I have mentioned. In the unfortunate, and I trust improbable, contingency of a war with the United States, it is obvious that both the Colony and the Mother-country would be called upon to submit to great sacrifices, and to make great exertions for their defence; but I have no doubt that these would be cheerfully made by both, if the exigency should unhappily arise.

" Upon the reduction of the British force in Canada to the garrisons of these fortified positions, it would become necessary that the warlike stores which are kept in the Colony should be reduced, and that the barracks and other buildings which are no longer required should be disposed of; but if the Parliament of Canada should be willing to undertake to keep up these barracks and buildings, in case of their being hereafter required, there would be no objection on the part of Her Majesty's Government to make them over to the provincial Authorities ; and if the maintenance of a British force at any of the posts now occupied should be desired, for the preservation of internal security, such a force would be readily supplied by Her Majesty's Government, if the actual cost thus incurred were provided for by the Province.

" Another charge which Her Majesty's Government would also expect that the Province should take upon itself, as part of the above arrangement, is that of maintaining the canals, now in charge of the Ordnance Department. You are aware, that these canals were executed at the sole expense of this Country, and at a very heavy cost, chiefly with a view to the military defence of the Province. Her Majesty's Government conceive, that the charge of maintaining them ought now to be undertaken by the Province, and I trust that no difficulty will arise on that head. With regard to the Indian Department, as by the arrangement lately made, the extinction of the charge (except so far as regards some payments for their lives to individuals) is provided for within five years, no further steps are required to be taken.

" In conclusion, I have now only to assure you that —while Her Majesty's Government consider that justice to the people of this Country requires that Canada, which is now so well able to support whatever establishments are necessary for her own defence and for her own advantage, should cease to occasion so heavy a charge as formerly to the British Treasury, and that it is a fitting opportunity for introducing the change when, in consequence of proceedings which have taken place in the Province, it becomes expedient to call upon Parliament to provide for the salary of the Governor General—it must not for a moment be supposed, that these measures are contemplated under any idea that the connection between the Mother-country and the Colony could be dissolved without great injury to both, or that there is any probability that it will be so. On the contrary, these measures are regarded as safe, because Her Majesty's Government are persuaded that the great body of the people of Canada are so fully satisfied of the great benefits they enjoy from the system of constitutional government, now happily established in the Province under the authority of the British Crown, that it may properly be left to themselves to take their share of the burden of maintaining and defending an order of things from which they reap so much advantage. Under this impression, and in the earnest hope and confident belief that Canada may long continue to form an important member of the British Empire, Her Majesty's Government have adopted the conclusions which I have now explained to you*."

Our retirement from office took place before these instructions could be fully acted upon. The call upon Canada, to take upon herself a larger share than here-

* See Despatch to Lord Elgin of the 14th of March, 1851, in the Papers relating to the Civil List and Military Expenditure in Canada, presented to both Houses of Parliament by Command, on the 8th of April, 1851.

tofore of the charges incurred on her account, was intended to be coupled with an application to Parliament, not only to provide for the salary of the Governor-General, but also to give the assistance of the credit of the British Treasury towards the execution of the projected line of railway for connecting the British Provinces in North America. The final result of the communications between the several Provinces on this last subject was not received, until we had ceased to be the advisers of the Crown. While this remained uncertain, we were not in a position to bring the question under the consideration of Parliament; I will therefore say nothing further with respect to it, except that I learned with deep regret that the scheme for the execution of the projected railway, to which the three Provinces had with much difficulty been brought to agree, had not received the approbation of our successors.

Without however waiting for the time when the whole of the proposed arrangement could be submitted to Parliament, we had already for some time been taking measures for largely reducing the expenditure of this country in Canada. With this view a local corps of cavalry which had been employed was discontinued, and a further reduction of the regular force stationed in the Province, beyond that which we had previously made, was ordered in the beginning of this year, and has, I believe, since our retirement from office been carried into effect, steps having been at the same time taken to enroll and settle upon land, in such a manner that their services may quickly be obtained when wanted, a considerable number of pensioners from the army. Plans previously under consideration for building barracks for the troops in Canada, and which, if I remember right, were to have cost not far short of a million of money, were abandoned*. Instead of building new barracks at the expense of the Mother-country, the Provincial Government was called upon to provide accommodation for the troops which it appeared to that Government desirable to retain in other places than the fortified posts, and in this manner quarters were provided for a regiment at Montreal. The Provincial Government was also called upon to defray the expense of moving detachments of troops, when they were required in aid of the civil power. An arrangement was also made for immediately reducing, and altogether stopping at the end of five years, the expense of what is called the Indian Department in Canada, which had hitherto cost this Country between £13,000 and £14,000 a-year. I have not the means of ascertaining what is the total saving to the British Treasury thus effected, but it must amount to a very considerable sum.

With regard to Canada, it only remains that I should sum up in a few words the results of the course of policy which I have described. In the pre-

---

* In the second Report (1849) of the Select Committee on Army and Ordinance Expenditure, and in the Evidence given, much information will be found as to the expense which must have been incurred in providing barracks for troops in Canada, had the former system of military defence been adhered to.

ceding pages I have shown that, within the last few
years, there has been a most gratifying improvement
in the state of political affairs and of public feeling
in the Province ; that the affections of a large part of
the population which had been alienated, have been
regained; and that all classes now evince an ardent
attachment to the British Crown, and to the institutions under which they live; that the hateful animosities and rancour, created by civil war and differences
of national origin, have almost disappeared ; and that
the party divisions which still remain, are not greater
than those which are to be found under other free
Governments ; that a system of constitutional government, copied from our own, has been firmly established
and is universally acquiesced in, while its principles
are now generally understood and appreciated; and
that the best evidence of the successful working of
this system of government has been afforded by the
passing of a variety of useful laws, all tending to promote the welfare of the people and the progress of
society. Nor has the improvement been less marked,
or less rapid, in what relates to the material interests of
the Province. The temporary difficulties occasioned by
a sudden change in the commercial policy of the Empire having passed away, the removal of restrictions
and regulations, by which the industry of the Province
was hampered or diverted into artificial channels, has
produced its natural effects, and the trade and agriculture of Canada have risen from their depression, to a
prosperity both greater than that which they formerly

enjoyed, and more secure, since it does not depend
upon any monopoly or partial advantages granted to
them in the British market, but is the result of exertion and enterprise called forth by the wholesome
stimulus of competition.

The most striking evidence of the degree to which
Canada is now prospering is afforded by the state
of her finances and public credit. When we were appointed to office, in July 1846, we found Canada in a
situation of some financial difficulty, the large expenditure occasioned by her great public works (though,
I believe, wisely incurred) had for the moment pressed
heavily on her resources, and a member of the Provincial Administration (Mr. Cayley), who had come
to England for the purpose of endeavouring to raise
money to meet some pressing demands on the Colonial Treasury, experienced the greatest difficulty in disposing of the 6 per cent. Debentures of the Province,
though the state of the English money-market was
still by no means unfavourable ; and, if I remember
right, no large amount of these Debentures could be
sold even at a price somewhat below par.   In the
present year Mr. Hincks, who now fills the office formerly held by Mr. Cayley, has been in this country,
and it was his duty, as it had been that of his
predecessor, to raise money for the Provincial Government ; but so greatly has its credit improved, that no
difficulty whatever has been experienced in procuring
all that was required, and the 6 per cent. Debentures,

which could not formerly be disposed of at par, have commanded a price of 115 to 116 *.

The revenue, the income derived from the tolls on the canals, and the trade of the Province as shown by the amount of exports and imports, have all increased with extraordinary rapidity†, and the indications of

* It appears, from the following Price-list of American Securities, which I have extracted from a recent newspaper, that the credit of Canada now stands fully as high as that of her republican neighbours; her inferiority in this respect having, a very few years ago, been one of the main arguments used by those who contended that her connection with this Country was an obstacle to her prosperity.

	Redeemable.	Prices.
United States 5 per cent. Bonds . .	1865	95 to 98
United States 6 per cent. Bonds . . .	1862	$103\frac{1}{2}$,, $104\frac{1}{2}$
United States 6 per cent. Bonds . . .	1868	$108\frac{1}{2}$,, 109
Ditto 6 per cent. Stock	1867–68	$106\frac{1}{2}$,, $107\frac{1}{2}$
New York State 5 per Cents. . .	1858–60	97 ,, 98
Pennsylvania 5 per Cent. Stock . . . ——		87 ,, 88
Ohio 6 per Cents.	1870–75	104 ,, $105\frac{1}{2}$
Massachusetts 5 per Cent. St. Bonds .	1868	109 ,, $109\frac{1}{2}$
Maryland 5 per Cent. State Bonds . . ——		$96\frac{1}{2}$,, 97
Virginia 6 per Cent. Bonds	1886	$99\frac{1}{2}$,, 100
Kentucky 6 per Cents.	1868	99 ,, 100
Tennessee 6 per Cents.	1890	98 ,, 99
Canada 6 per cent. Bonds	1874	115 ,, 116

† I subjoin some statements showing the extent of the increase which has taken place :—

Year.	Gross Revenue Customs.	Total Nett Revenue of Province.	Gross Revenue Welland Canal.			Gross Revenue St. Lawrence Canals.			Value Imports Customs.	Value Exports Customs.
	£.	£.	£.	s.	d	£.	s.	d	£.	£.
1846	422,215	512,993	27,410	1	6	8,894	10	1	2,510.869	
1847	414,633	506,826	30,549	17	8	15,375	14	6	2,350,978	
1848	333,029	379,645	29,064	7	3	14,539	14	3	3,191,328	2,521,599
1849	444,547	513,431	34,741	18	8	17,855	4	8	3,002,599	2,498,773
1850	615,694	704,234	37,925	17	7	20,393	0	10	4,245,517	2,990,428
1851	737,439	824,184	50,460	6	8	22,812	12	1	5,358,697	3,241,180

prosperity and of rapid progress everywhere to be seen,
are such as to strike the most careless observer.   The
advance of the Colony has been most rapid during
the last three years ; but I think it right to add, that
its progress from very small beginnings, during the
whole time it has formed part of the British Empire,
has been most unjustly depreciated ; and although it
has been a sort of fashion to draw an unfavourable
comparison between Canada and the flourishing Republic of which she is the neighbour, careful inquiry
has recently shown that, so far from Canada having
anything to fear from such a comparison, it is one
which, if fairly made, is greatly to her advantage.   She
has advanced and is advancing even more rapidly than
her republican neighbour in population, in wealth, and
in commerce.   I do not wish to encumber this Letter
with unnecessary statistics ; I therefore abstain from
going into the details which would support what I
have asserted ; and instead of doing so, will refer you
to the exceedingly able lectures delivered in March
last, at Toronto, by the Reverend Adam Lillie, and
published in the ' Journal of Education ' of Upper
Canada.   In these lectures it is demonstrated, by a
minute comparison of the statistics of Canada and of
the most flourishing States of the Union, that the rate
of advance has been decidedly more rapid in the
former than in the latter.

I would add, that the opinion of an impartial
and intelligent observer, who has lately published a
highly interesting volume, giving an account of the

impression made upon his mind by what he observed during a short tour in the United States and Canada, is still more decidedly in favour of the latter. I allude to Mr. Tremenheere, who, in his ' Notes on public subjects in the United States and in Canada,' has shown that the Canadians are far from having any reason to envy their neighbours, with respect either to their progress in wealth and material prosperity, or, to what is of still higher interest, the degree to which they enjoy the blessings of freedom and good government, and their comparative exemption from those abuses from which no human institutions can be entirely free. I believe you are acquainted with this very interesting volume; if not, I cannot better conclude these remarks on the affairs of Canada than by recommending it to your notice. In my next Letter I shall have to speak of the other British Provinces in North America.

September 10th, 1852.

LETTER VI.

My dear Lord John,

Having in my last Letter entered so fully into the affairs of Canada, I may notice more briefly those of the other British Provinces in North America, since much of what I have said respecting Canada applies equally to them. In two of these Provinces— Nova Scotia and New Brunswick—the same system of government which has been established in Canada, has been brought into successful operation ; and I am willing to hope that the same may be said of Prince Edward's Island, though I fear in the latter the experiment has been tried somewhat prematurely, and that the population of this Colony is hardly sufficient for the effective working of the machinery of a form of government better adapted to a community in a more advanced stage of its social progress.

In carrying into effect the changes which have been made in the mode of administering the affairs of these Provinces, though there have been various protracted discussions and much correspondence, but one question has been raised, involving a general principle of importance, which has not already been adverted to in considering the transactions of Canada. The question to which I refer, is that as to the extent to which the actual holders of situations in the public service should be regarded as having vested interests; that is, whether they have a fair right to expect not to be deprived of their employment without compensation, unless for misconduct.

This is a matter upon which a very different feeling prevails on the whole continent of North America, from that which exists in this Country. In the United States it is well known to be the practice to treat the holders of office, from the highest to the lowest, as having no vested interest whatever in their employments, and as being always liable to dismissal at a moment's notice, at the pleasure of the party in power. The proverbial ingratitude of Republics to those who serve them has been manifested in these States in the strongest manner, and little or no consideration has been shown for the interests of even the most distinguished of their citizens who have devoted themselves to the public service.

In this Country, on the other hand, although with very few exceptions all offices in the public service are held legally and technically at the pleasure of the Crown, yet the rule, that only the holders of what are called political offices are to be removed without

compensation for any other cause than misconduct
or inefficiency, has been so completely established by
public opinion, that there is scarcely an instance of
its being departed from. The adoption of a similar
rule in Nova Scotia was recommended in a despatch
to Sir John Harvey, of which the following is an extract. After describing the practice in this Country,
I proceeded to observe :—" Though it is not without
some inconveniences, I regard this system as possessing, upon the whole, very great advantages. We owe
to it, that the public servants of this Country, as a
body, are remarkable for their experience and knowledge of public affairs, and honourably distinguished by
the zeal and integrity with which they discharge their
duties without reference to party feeling ; we owe to
it, also, that as the transfer of political power from one
party in the State to another is followed by no change
in the holders of any but a few of the highest offices,
political animosities are not in general carried to the
same height, and do not so deeply agitate the whole
frame of society, as in those countries where a different practice prevails. The system, with regard to
the tenure of office, which has been found to work
so well here, seems to be worthy of imitation in the
British American Colonies ; and the small population
and limited revenue of Nova Scotia, as well as the
general occupation and social state of the community,
are in my opinion additional reasons for abstaining,
so far as regards that Province, from going further
than can be avoided without giving up the principle

of executive responsibility, in making the tenure of offices in the public service dependent upon the result of party contests *."

Since the date of the despatch from which the above extract is taken, the rule which it recommends as to the tenure by which offices in the public service should be held, has been recognized by all parties in these Colonies, as that which is to be observed. I may be permitted to remark, that until the reasons for adopting this practice, and the limits within which it should be followed, had been thus distinctly explained, there was a strong disposition amongst many of the Colonists to prefer a different system, and to follow rather the example of their neighbours in the United States than that of the Mother-country ; but for the last three or four years no such disposition has been shown ; the offices which are to be considered political have been in general determined and limited to a very small number, and the propriety of not removing the holders of other offices, except for misconduct, has been received as an admitted principle of the Government. It is not, in my opinion, easy to over-estimate the advantages of the establishment in the Colonies of this rule, which I believe, in this Country, to be one of our chief securities against corruption in the administration of public affairs, and against that over-violence of party spirit which is the great danger of all free governments. What I have

* See Despatch to Sir John Harvey of the 31st of March, 1847, page 30, House of Commons Sessional Paper, No. 621 of 1848.

learnt of the working of the opposite system in the
United States, from the reports of the most judicious
observers, strongly confirms me in this opinion, and
increases my satisfaction that it has not been adopted
in British America.

A more difficult part of the same general question
has been, whether these Provinces should also conform to the practice of the Mother country, according
to which it is held that, when the public interest
requires an office, which is not one of those known
as political offices, to be abolished, or its nature
to be so altered as to call for the removal of the
holder, the person thus deprived of it shall receive
compensation for his loss.   This rule has been very
strictly followed in this Country, and I believe with
great advantage ; but the prevailing opinion on the
other side of the Atlantic is by no means favourable
to it, nor was it without some reluctance that the
Assemblies in the different British North American
Provinces were induced to recognize it, and to make
compensation to those persons whom the introduction of the new system of government has rendered
it necessary to deprive of their offices.   This object
has however been accomplished, and some provision
(in general an adequate provision, though in one
or two instances it might have been wished that it
had been on rather a more liberal scale), has been
made for all those who have lost offices which they
had previously a right to regard as permanent, but
which under the present system of government are

included amongst those considered as political. The settlement of these questions, and the policy which has been pursued in the administration of these Provinces, have been followed by a marked improvement in their condition, and in retiring from office we had the satisfaction of leaving them in a state of high prosperity, and with a loyal and contented population.

Having thus described the progress and results of the discussions which have taken place as to the mode of conducting the government of the Provinces of British America generally, I will abstain from adverting to various matters relating to their separate concerns, which, though far from being devoid of interest, would lead me into greater detail than would be convenient, if I were to attempt to enter into them. But there is one subject which, though immediately affecting only an individual Colony, involves principles of wider application, and of so much importance that I cannot leave it unnoticed.

In New Brunswick a question, which has given occasion to much discussion, has been raised, as to whether the authority of the Crown can be exercised with propriety in order to prevent the grant of bounties by the local Legislature, for the purpose of encouraging certain branches of industry. It was our opinion that the grant of such bounties ought not to be permitted, and an Act of the Legislature of New Brunswick granting a bounty for the cultivation of hemp having been sent over for confirmation, the Lieutenant-Governor was informed that, as the Act was of limited duration, and inconvenience might result from its disallowance to those who had undertaken the cultivation of hemp in the expectation of the bounty, Her Majesty would not be advised to disallow it; but he was instructed to refuse his assent to any Act having a similar object which might in future be passed. The House of Assembly, in April 1849, voted an Address to the Queen, in which they represented that this was a matter "purely local," on which "the Legislature of New Brunswick might safely be left to the free exercise of its discretion," and prayed that the instructions given to the Lieutenant-Governor might be reconsidered. We did not, after full deliberation, agree in this view of the subject, nor regard the question as merely local.

It has always been held to be one of the principal functions of the Imperial Legislature and Government to determine what is to be the commercial policy of the Empire at large, and to prescribe to the various Colonial Legislatures such rules as are necessary for carrying that policy into effect. Thus, while the policy of what is called protection was adhered to, very severe and onerous restrictions were imposed on the commerce of the Colonies by the Navigation Laws, and by various Acts of Parliament under which differential duties were levied upon the produce of foreign countries, as compared to the same articles, the produce of the British dominions. To enforce these regulations the administration of the Customs department in the Colonies was kept almost entirely in the hands of the Treasury, as I have already had occasion to notice.

But even while this restrictive policy was adopted, the Colonial Legislatures were not permitted to increase the amount of differential duties levied on goods, the produce of any particular countries. In the year 1843 a circular was addressed by Lord Derby, then Secretary of State for the Colonies, to the Governors of the British North American and West Indian Colonies, instructing them not to give their assent to any Acts which might be tendered to them, " by which duties might be imposed on goods in reference to their place of production, or to the place from which they might be exported." These instructions were given on the ground, that the various local Legislatures of the Colonies could not pass laws for this purpose, without the risk of creating confusion and inconvenience by the want of consistency that could hardly fail to arise in the legislation of so many independent authorities on such a subject.

When Parliament, after a protracted discussion of many years, finally determined upon abandoning the former policy of endeavouring to promote the commerce of the Empire by an artificial system of restrictions, and upon adopting in its place the policy of Free Trade, it did not abdicate the duty and the power of regulating the commercial policy, not only of the United Kingdom, but of the British Empire. The common interest of all parts of that extended Empire requires that its commercial policy should be the same throughout its numerous dependencies ; nor is this less important than before, because our policy is now directed to the removal—instead of, as formerly, to the maintenance—of artificial restriction supon trade. The benefits of a liberal commercial policy will be greatly increased by its general adoption by the principal nations of the world, which we may hope to see eventually brought about ; but it would materially interfere with the attainment of this happy result, if it should be observed by foreign countries that the former and narrower policy of endeavouring by bounties or restrictions to divert capital and industry to other than their natural channels, was adopted with the assent of the Imperial Government in any part of the Queen's dominions.

On these grounds we came to the decision, that the Lieutenant-Governor should be instructed to inform the Assembly that we were not prepared to advise Her Majesty to comply with the prayer of their Address by recalling the instructions he had received, and to point out that we had thought it the more necessary to come to this determination, because we were persuaded that measures of the kind which had been proposed would be not only injurious to the Empire at large, but peculiarly so to New Brunswick herself. The argument of the Assembly, that because capital was scarce in the Province, and its resources comparatively little developed, the granting of bounties was necessary, instead of supporting the conclusion drawn from it, afforded on the contrary a strong reason against their policy. The more scarce capital may be in any country, the more obvious is the propriety of turning it to the best account; while the effect, and indeed the object of bounties is to cause capital to be withdrawn from those branches of industry to which, if left to itself, it would be applied as the most remunerative, in order to be employed in pursuits which, without such assistance, would not yield sufficient returns to induce individuals to follow them. The funds also from which alone bounties can be paid must be derived from taxes, which of course must in some shape or other fall upon the general industry of the community.

Considerable dissatisfaction was manifested in New Brunswick at this decision, and in September, 1850, the Lieutenant-Governor reported that the prohibition of differential duties and bounties by the Imperial Government was regarded as a capricious interference with the right of the Colonists to regulate their own taxation, and dispose of their own money for the purposes of internal improvement. In the despatch containing this report, the Lieutenant-Governor transmitted a Minute of his Executive Council intimating a strong wish that the Legislature of the Province should be allowed to impose differential duties on importations from the United States, to the extent of those imposed by that country on importations from New Brunswick, in the belief that nothing would tend more speedily to bring about a liberal interchange of commodities than such a retaliatory act as was contemplated.

It thus clearly appeared that the question as to whether bounties should be allowed was (as we had from the first regarded it) one of very great importance. It would have been necessary, in order to meet the wishes of the inhabitants of New Brunswick, to withdraw not only the instructions to the Lieutenant-Governor of that Province, with respect to the grant of bounties, but also the more general instructions contained in Lord Derby's circular of 1843, on the subject of differential duties. The question, in short, was nothing less than whether the Imperial Government (using the word government in its widest sense) should abandon the authority it had always exercised of regulating the commercial policy of the whole Empire, and should permit every separate Colony to legislate without restriction on commercial subjects. We came to the conclusion that this change ought not to be acquiesced in; that, for the reasons I have stated, the power of determining the general commercial policy of the Empire ought to be retained by Parliament, and that it was the duty of the responsible servants of the Crown to advise such an exercise of the Royal authority as should be necessary to prevent the policy which Parliament had deliberately adopted, from being counteracted by the measures of the local Legislatures.

We were also satisfied that we had been right in considering the grant of bounties by the Colonial Legislatures, as one of those measures from which the sanction of the Crown ought to be withheld on this ground, since the attempt thus artificially to foster particular branches of industry, at the expense of others, is altogether inconsistent with the principles of that commercial policy which has been sanctioned by Parliament. It also appeared to us, that bounties were further objectionable, because they might be granted by one Colony in such a manner as to derange and injure the trade of another; indeed in neighbouring Colonies they could hardly be granted without having this effect to a greater or less extent. A despatch was addressed to Sir Edmund Head on the 1st of November, 1850*, explaining these views, and expressing our regret that the instructions he had received should have created dissatisfaction, but declining to withdraw or modify them.

The Assembly adhered to its views, and on the 28th of April, 1851, voted some strong resolutions in assertion of its right to pass measures of the kind objected to. These resolutions were voted at so late a period of the Provincial Session of 1851, that no decision upon the subject was required from us until that of the present year should be about to commence. There were also various circumstances, which made it expedient that the consideration of the question should be deferred as long as possible, and it consequently remained undecided when the change of Administration took place, nor do I know what the determination of your Cabinet would have been. My

* The Despatches on this subject have not, I believe, been laid before Parliament, but they were communicated to the Local Legislature.

own individual opinion is, that there was no reason for abandoning the view of the subject we had taken in the first instance, and that the right course for us to have followed, would have been to adhere to the instructions originally given to the Lieutenant-Governor of New Brunswick, issuing similar instructions for their future guidance to the Governors of the other Colonies.

This question was connected with another and very important one with respect to the adoption of more stringent measures to prevent foreign vessels, and especially those of the United States, from fishing within the limits of the fisheries to which British subjects have an exclusive right. There had long been a general, though far from a unanimous wish, on the part of the Colonists, that more effectual means than have hitherto been employed should be made use of, to enforce the exclusive rights of fishing which belong to British subjects; but no necessity for giving any fresh instructions on the subject had arisen previously to our retirement from office. When that event took place, the question had been brought under our consideration by the proceedings of the local Legislatures; but I know not to what conclusion we should have come upon it. My own belief is that, while the right of this Country to exclude any but British subjects from fishing within a certain distance of the coasts of the British territory is beyond dispute, the enforcement of that right would not be calculated to promote the well-understood interests either of the Mother-country or of the Colonists.

The rights of private property in the mouths of rivers, and in other situations where the fisheries must, by their very nature, be appropriated by a limited number of individuals, ought of course to be protected, and respect for the general regulations, which are made for the preservation of the fisheries and the maintenance of order, ought also to be strictly enforced. But I am persuaded that, to prevent the fishermen of the United States from pursuing their occupation within the limits reserved by treaty to British subjects, where there is ample room for all, because the British fishermen fear the competition of their active rivals, is an error founded upon the old and narrow views of monopoly and commercial jealousy. The inhabitants of the Colonies, in their close proximity to the fishing-grounds, and from their being thus enabled to carry on the fishery from their own homes, possess advantages of which they cannot be deprived, and which will always secure to them as large a share of the fishery of their own coasts as their population and disposable capital will allow them to take. But there are other and more attractive occupations open to the Colonists, and the number of hands they can spare for the fisheries is very small in proportion to the apparently inexhaustible supply of fish on their shores. The two Houses of the Legislature of Prince Edward's Island, in a joint petition to the Queen, in the year 1847, attribute the neglect of the fisheries "principally to the people employing themselves in the more congenial pursuits of agricul-

ture," and justly observe, that as a recent Census had
shown little more than a seventh of the total area of
the Island to be in cultivation, it was improbable that
there would be any material alteration in this respect
during the present generation. In the same petition
they point out that, in these circumstances, it is an
advantage to the Colony that the fisheries they cannot
carry on themselves should be carried on by the
fishermen of the United States, who create a demand
for the produce of the farmers, and give a general
stimulus to the trade and industry of the Island.

In the other Colonies, and particularly in Nova Scotia,
the nature of the country and the habits of the population do not lead to such a preference of agriculture
to the prosecution of the fisheries; on the contrary,
they contain a numerous body of hardy, enterprising,
and successful fishermen. But it has never been alleged,
so far as I am aware, that the resort of fishermen
from the United States to the shores of the Colonies
interferes with the Colonial fishermen by depriving
them of ample space for fishing. The only interference on the part of the former, of which the latter
complain, is their competition with them in disposing
of their fish; and I see no more advantage in protecting fishermen from competition than in protecting
farmers, planters, or manufacturers from the same
wholesome stimulus.

I am aware that the desire on the part of the Colonists to exclude the fishermen of the United States
from a participation in their fisheries, arises in no

small degree from the circumstance that the Government of the United States gives a bounty to its own fishermen, and at the same time imposes a heavy duty on the importation of fish taken and cured by those of other nations. The maintenance of these regulations is considered to render it impossible for the British fishermen to meet their rivals on equal terms, and thus to make it necessary for their protection strictly to enforce the exclusive rights of fishing given to them by treaty.

There can be no doubt that the present laws of the United States on this subject are injurious to all parties, and therefore it would be very desirable to make an arrangement with that Government, by which our fishermen should be placed on equal footing in their markets with their own, in consideration of our consenting not to enforce our exclusive right to the coast-fisheries of the Colonies; but if no such arrangement can be made, I do not see that it at all follows that we should be taking a wise course for our own interest, in rigidly enforcing our rights of exclusion. On the contrary, I believe that, by permitting the United States fishermen to share with our own the fisheries of our coasts, without further restriction than is necessary for the maintenance of order, we should soon practically render the regulations of the United States so onerous to themselves that they could not be persevered in. In their competition with each other, the fishermen of the United States would not confine themselves to fishing, but would purchase from the British fishermen fish to make up their cargoes as soon as possible; the vessels also would often, though nominally belonging to the United States, be really manned and owned, in part at least, by British subjects, and the general trade of the Colonies would be increased (as the Legislature of Prince Edward's Island has pointed out) by the demand of the United States fishermen for supplies. In these different ways a large proportion of the bounty paid to encourage the fisheries by the United States Government would find its way into the pockets of the Colonists; and fish, the produce of British capital and labour, would be largely introduced into those States as their own, and on the same advantageous terms. No doubt the fishery would be principally carried on under the United States' flag; but the wealth of which it would be the source, and the maritime population it would nurse up, would be found to a great extent to be really British.

This is by no means mere speculation. In the Bay of Fundy, that which I have described as likely to happen is already taking place on a small scale; and in a memorial addressed to the Lieutenant-Governor of Nova Scotia by the corporation and the representatives of the city and county of Halifax, bearing so late a date as the 2nd of September last, it is urged as an objection to the admission of American fishermen to the British fishing-grounds, that such an irregular trade would take place between the fishermen of the two nations, "to the great injury," as it is said, "of

Colonial traders, and loss to the public revenue."
These apprehended evils there is, I believe, no real
reason to fear; while it is important to observe that this
memorial against the policy of admitting the fishermen of the United States to the British fishing-grounds
contains what amounts to a distinct admission, that
the bad consequences of that policy would extend
only to the Colonial traders and curers, while to the
Colonial fishermen it would open a new market for
the produce of their labour.

This is precisely in accordance with our experience of what has occurred in a similar case on
our own coasts at home. Some twenty years ago
repeated applications were made to me, as Member
for the county of Northumberland, by the fishermen
of that county to press upon the Government the necessity of taking more effectual measures to prevent
the alleged encroachments of the French fishing-boats,
which annually come over for the herring-fishery on
the east coast of England and Scotland. I remember
that, upon inquiring into the subject, I found that,
although the curers of fish might have some reason
to apprehend injury to their trade from the visits of
these foreign boats, to our fishermen they afforded,
on the contrary, the great advantage of an additional
demand and competition for all the herrings they
could catch. At first it was impossible to convince
the Northumberland fishermen that this would be
the case, but there soon ceased to be any doubt on
the subject. Though I believe, by the laws of France,

the bounty given by that country for the cure of herrings can only be claimed for those which are sworn
to have been caught by French subjects, the French
boats on our coasts, finding they can procure their
cargoes more speedily and more cheaply by purchase
than by fishing for themselves, ceased in general even
to take the trouble of shooting their nets*, and for
several years past have been acknowledged by our
fishermen to be their best customers.

So notorious has this become, that in the present year the French Government has sent an armed
steamer to watch the proceedings of their own fishing-
boats, and to enforce their obtaining their herrings
boná fide with their own nets, instead of buying
them from the British fishermen. With this striking
example before our eyes of the value of custom-
house oaths, of the manner in which regulations for
artificially forcing a trade are evaded, and of the
absurd extent to which the interference of the Government with the occupations of individuals must be
carried, in order to have even a chance of preventing
such evasions, it seems to me clear that the best way
of defeating the unwise measures of the United States,
with regard to the fisheries, would be simply to ab-

* I have heard, though I cannot vouch for the fact, that the
master of one of these French boats was seen, after he had obtained
his cargo by purchase, busily employed in wetting his nets and beat-
ing a few holes in them with stones; and being asked what he was
doing, he answered, that he was making the nets look as if they
had been used, that his application for the bounty might be passed
by the Custom-house of his own Port.

stain from attempting to control the natural course of trade and industry, and to offer on the contrary every facility to the United States fishermen, for resorting to the coasts of British America, and for carrying on unrestricted intercourse with the Colonists.

But though this would, as I believe, be the wisest policy with a view to the real interests of the British Provinces, it is one which the opinions generally prevailing among their inhabitants would have rendered it difficult for the Government to adopt during the last five years. I therefore consider it to have been a great advantage to the Public that, during that time, we were not compelled to decide upon either effectually asserting or abandoning the British claims to these fisheries. This is one of the many questions in the solution of which the aid of time was calculated to be useful, and with respect to which it was a gain to postpone as long as possible the adoption of any decisive measures.

The question of the Fisheries affects Newfoundland even more than the continental Provinces of British America; but, in other respects, this Colony has but little resemblance to them. Though its occupation as a fishing-station dates from a very early period of our Colonial history, until within a comparatively recent period the policy of our Government was not to promote, but as much as possible to discourage, the regular colonization of Newfoundland. Settlements grew up there in spite of what was done to prevent them; and in these, for a long time, the powers of

Government were exercised by the officers in command of ships-of-war on the station. It is only about twenty years since any form of representative government was established in the Island; and at first the experiment was so little successful, that Parliament was compelled to interfere, and partially to withdraw the privileges which had been conceded to the Colonists. By an Act passed during your Administration, in the year 1847, the Constitution originally given to the Colony was, with some amendments, restored to it, and placed on a permanent footing. Newfoundland was not therefore considered by us as yet ripe for the system of government now established in the other North American Colonies. We thought it highly desirable that, in its present social condition, the experiment of applying to it arrangements which have only very lately been brought into successful operation even in Canada, should at all events be deferred; and that in the meantime it should be governed in the same manner that all our Colonies having representative institutions used to be, until about ten years ago. There was however a disposition in the Colony to press for the adoption of the same system which is in force in the other North American Colonies, and the question still remained under discussion when we retired from office.

There are a few more particulars which deserve to be mentioned with respect to Newfoundland, before I pass to the Colonies in a different part of the world.

Your Administration commenced in a year of great

calamity to this Island. In 1846 the town of St. John's was almost destroyed by fire, and a great number of the fishing-craft by a hurricane in the Autumn; while both the fishery and the potato-crop fell far short of their usual produce, the failure of the latter arising from the same disease which, in the same year, was so destructive in Ireland. By this combination of misfortunes Newfoundland suffered so severely (the loss by the fire alone having been reported, by Commissioners appointed to ascertain its amount, to fall little short of £890,000*), that it may well be matter of surprise that she should already have recovered from them to the degree that she has. A sum of £30,000 was voted by Parliament for the relief of the distress occasioned by the fire, and a very considerable amount of money was obtained for the same purpose by a collection made in the churches of this Country under a Queen's Letter, and by subscriptions both here and in the other North American Colonies. From these various sources sums amounting altogether to £102,500 were received.

The distribution of this money was attended with the difficulties which are always experienced in guarding against abuses in applying large sums as charity for the relief of distress, however real and urgent that distress may be. To the poorer sufferers by the fire, direct pecuniary grants were made in proportion to their losses, to the amount of about £64,000;

---

* See Sir J. Harvey's Despatch of the 6th of August 1846. House of Commons Sessional Paper of 1851, No. 679, p. 27.

but half the amount of the church collections, under the Queen's Letter (£14,500), was reserved for rebuilding the Protestant Church, which had been destroyed by the fire, and the balance of the whole amount available was applied to meet the most urgent wants of the Colony, which must otherwise have been provided for by taxation, which would have fallen principally on the higher class of the sufferers by the fire, to whom no direct assistance had been given. A good deal of agitation was got up in the town of St. John's, against the decision not to distribute the whole sum which had been raised in consequence of the fire, in direct grants to the sufferers; the retention of half the money raised by the Queen's Letter for building a new Protestant Church being especially objected to. It was however shown by the Governor, that the sums distributed by the Relief Committee to the sufferers by the fire had by no means conduced so much as they ought to the real benefit of the community, which would be much more promoted by a different application of the available balance; while, with regard to the rebuilding of the Protestant Church, it seemed impossible, with justice, to refuse to devote to this object a considerable proportion of the sums collected in the churches of this Country under the Queen's Letter, since it was clear that the money had been given under the full expectation, on the part of the donors, that this would form one of the principal purposes for which it would be used.

The refusal to apply the balance of the money collected for the relief of the Colony in making additional grants of money to those of the sufferers who were anxious to obtain this kind of compensation (which, much to their credit, the merchants and superior classes of the inhabitants had declined) was founded on different but very important considerations. When Sir Gaspard Le Marchant, who had been appointed Governor, reached Newfoundland, in the early part of 1847, he found that the money already distributed by the Relief Committee had produced a demoralizing effect, and, what was still more serious, this was closely connected with a most mischievous system of pauperism which had grown up in the Colony.

Though the ordinary earnings of a working-man in Newfoundland, during the spring and summer, are so high that, in the absence of sickness or some unlooked-for calamity, he ought to be able to maintain himself and his family for the whole year in far greater comfort than falls to the lot of the labouring population in most countries of the world, yet the habits of the people were so improvident, that in every recurring winter they were exposed to extreme distress, which it had become the practice to relieve by small money-payments to the most destitute, from a grant made by the Legislature for that purpose. Almost as soon as he reached the Colony, Sir Gaspard Le Marchant saw the absolute necessity of putting an end to this system, not only because the expense it occasioned pressed heavily on the finances of the Colony, which were in a state of great embarrassment, but still more because it was producing the usual effects of pauperism by encouraging habits of improvidence and demoralizing the population.

It also appeared that the distribution of money in small sums, to the poorer class of occupiers who had suffered by the fire, had tended to aggravate this evil, and to increase the disposition of those to whom this aid had been afforded, to depend rather upon the assistance to be given to them by others, than on their own exertions, for an improvement in their condition.　　Hence it was considered that the balance still available of the sums voted by Parliament, or raised by subscription for the relief of the Colony, ought not to be distributed in the same manner, but might be turned to far better account by being differently applied.　　A portion of this money was accordingly made use of to provide for the repair of the Government House, and for some other urgent expenses, including the relief of the destitute, which could not otherwise have been met without either increasing the debt or adding to the weight of the taxation of the Colony ; and the remainder was reserved for " any unforeseen exigencies which might arise either from a shortness of the fisheries, or a repetition in the failure of the crop, more especially in the outports, as in the present crippled state of the finances of the Colony the Government would have no resources to fall back on*." This course was attended with much

* See Sir Gaspard Le Marchant's Despatch of the 10th of May 1847, pp. 75 and 76 of the Paper quoted above.

advantage. By obviating the necessity of increased taxation, the money sent to the Colony was made to contribute to the benefit of all classes of the inhabitants, in the manner which was at once the most safe and the most just, since any other application of it would have done little for the merchants, who had been the greatest sufferers by the fire, and had not, like the labouring classes, been compensated for their losses by the rise of wages occasioned by the great demand for labour created by the works rendered necessary by the fire. By leaving the relief of the destitute to be provided for from funds entirely under the control of the Executive Government, the correction of the mode of administering that relief which had previously been in use, was also rendered less difficult than it otherwise would have been.

Availing himself of the power thus placed in his hands, Sir Gaspard Le Marchant adopted the principle of giving relief to able-bodied labourers, only by employing them in the formation and construction of roads, taking care to exact from those who asked for such assistance a full return in labour, for which he generally paid, not in money, but in provisions, and always lower wages than those usually current in the Island. In this manner the demoralizing effects of the former system of giving gratuitous assistance to the destitute were avoided, while at the same time works of great importance to the progress of the Colony were executed. Roads had been much wanted, and by those thus made the town of St. John's was brought within comparatively easy reach of other parts of the Colony, giving to these districts the advantage of a better market for their produce, and to the capital the benefit of a more abundant supply of some of the chief articles of consumption. The precaution adopted at the suggestion of Sir Gaspard Le Marchant, in the early part of 1847, of reserving a portion of the available funds for unforeseen exigencies, turned out to have been highly necessary; for, in the Autumn of that year, the potato-crop was more extensively injured by blight than it had been in the previous season, and the effect of this calamity was much aggravated by a like failure of the crop having occurred in Nova Scotia and Prince Edward's Island, from the latter of which Colonies Newfoundland had been accustomed to draw a considerable part of the supplies of food it required. The distress in the Colony during the following winter was consequently very great, and its finances were in a condition which would have rendered it exceedingly difficult, from its own resources, to afford to the population the relief that was urgently required; but the money which had been reserved, being applied with rigid economy and strict precautions against abuse, was sufficient to meet the deficiency of its own means, and enabled the Governor to carry Newfoundland successfully through this trying and anxious season.

But the efforts of Sir Gaspard Le Marchant to improve the condition of the Colony were by no means limited to the measures which it was in his power to carry into effect by his authority as Governor; he endeavoured to inspire both the Legislature and individuals with energy and enterprise; and, mainly owing to his judicious advice and encouragement, successful attempts have been made to increase the resources of the Island. Formerly, the climate of Newfoundland being supposed to be too severe for the growth of corn, none worth mentioning was grown there, and very few cattle were reared. Wheat, barley, and oats have now all been cultivated to some extent, and have been found to answer well, yielding abundant crops of very good quality; and the recent shows of stock have afforded gratifying evidence of the increased attention paid to the rearing and fattening of cattle. This result has been brought about chiefly by the efforts of Sir Gaspard Le Marchant; he urged upon the inhabitants of Newfoundland the importance of attempting the cultivation of corn; and with the assistance of the Legislature and of the Agricultural Society of the Colony, he caused seed-corn and agricultural implements to be imported and distributed, especially in the minor Settlements commonly known by the name of the Outports, where the use of even the most ordinary implements was almost unknown. He himself imported from England cattle of improved breeds, and offered prizes for stock, which excited a useful emulation among the inhabitants in rearing and feeding cattle. He also procured the establishment of two mills in the town of St. John's, none having previously existed in the Island.

By these and similar measures Agriculture, as dis-tinguished from the mere rude cultivation of pota-toes, was established as a branch of industry in the Colony, which was thus rendered less exclusively dependent than formerly upon the fisheries and the cultivation of the potato,—resources which, however valuable, are too precarious to be relied upon alone. From the accounts laid before Parliament, which extend up to the beginning of the present year*, it appears that the distress under which the Colony was labouring had passed away, and that it was then advancing towards a prosperity which bade fair to be both greater and more stable than that which it formerly enjoyed. But I am sorry to learn from the newspapers that the inhabitants, encouraged by two or three good seasons, have this year again trusted too much to their potatoes, which have suffered not less than in former years, and it is to be feared that they will in consequence be much distressed.

October 2, 1852.

* See Sir Gaspard Le Marchant's Despatch of April 12, 1852, in the Annual series of Reports on the Colonies presented to Parliament in the last Session.

LETTER VII.

AUSTRALIAN COLONIES.—SALE OF LAND.— EMIGRATION.

My dear Lord John,

I now turn to a different and distant quarter of the globe, in which, as in North America, the Possessions of the British Crown are fast rising into a great nation. I refer to Australia, in which the last six years have likewise been marked by rapid progress and by important events. The subjects relating to the Colonies in this part of the world, which chiefly occupied our attention during your Administration, were those of the constitution of their governments, the regulation under which land is disposed of, emigration, and transportation.

Upon our accession to office, both the system of disposing of Crown lands in these Colonies, and the state of things with regard to the transportation of offenders, required our immediate consideration. With regard to the Crown lands, there had been for some time much discussion as to the propriety of maintaining the minimum price and the regulations

as to the sale of land which had been established
by the Act of Parliament of 1842, and also on the
claims of the persons who, under the name of squatters, occupy very large tracts of land for pastoral purposes, and who had loudly demanded to be allowed
to hold this land under such conditions as would
enable them to make improvements upon it.   The
policy we adopted was that of adhering to the principles of the Act of 1842, but at the same time acceding, partially at least, to the wish of the pastoral
occupiers of land for an improvement in their tenure.
We proposed, and carried through Parliament, during
the short remainder of the Session of 1846, after our
appointment to Office, a Bill, by which the Crown
was authorized to make regulations for granting leases
of land for periods not exceeding fourteen years.

Under the authority of this Act, Orders in Council
were afterwards framed, by which the leasing of land for
pastoral occupation was provided for, on terms which
depended on the situation and character of the land.
The whole of the Crown lands in the Colony of New
South Wales were divided into three classes, distinguished from each other by being situated in what
were termed the settled, unsettled, and intermediate
districts.   In the first, land was only allowed to be held
from year to year, as it was considered that it might
be wanted within a comparatively short period for
purchase.   In the unsettled districts, where any such
demand was for a long time unlikely to arise, the land
was to be held for fourteen years, and the lessee entitled,

if it should afterwards be sold, to be repaid the value of improvements he might have made. In the intermediate districts, the terms granted to occupiers were of the character which the name given to these districts implies. Regulations, different in form but the same in principle, were also established under the authority of the Act of Parliament in South and Western Australia*.

Subject to the change made by allowing land to be thus let, we thought it our duty steadily to resist the strenuous efforts which were used to induce us to propose the repeal of the Land Sales Act, of 1842, and to abandon the policy on which it is founded. In this course we were supported by Parliament, nor can I entertain any doubt that it was the one best calculated to promote the advantage both of the Colonies and of the Mother-country. The subject is one of so much importance, and on which there has been so much misrepresentation, that I must say a few words as to the nature and origin of the system of disposing of the Crown lands which is now in force in the Australian Colonies, and which we maintained against a strong opposition.

The system is a very simple one; it requires that the Crown lands (except those wanted for public purposes) shall only be alienated by sale, and shall be sold

* See Sessional Papers, House of Lords, No. 114, and House of Commons, No. 252, of 1847, and Papers relative to the Occupation of Crown Lands in New South Wales. Presented to both Houses by Command, in 1848.

without favour or partiality to the best bidder or the first applicant. All land is required to be put up for sale in the first instance at public auctions, which are held periodically, and where it is offered at an upset price of not less than £1 an acre. What is not disposed of at these sales, is afterwards open for purchase at the upset price to the first applicant; and the Governors are instructed to endeavour to keep the surveys so far ahead of the demand for land, that considerably more than is likely to be purchased may be offered at the periodical auctions, and may remain afterwards open for purchase by the first applicant at the upset price; so that persons desirous of buying land may always be able to do so at once, without waiting for these auctions. I may observe, in passing, that a careful attention to this point is of great importance, in order to obviate one of the few real inconveniences which in the first instance arose from the adoption of this system. By having as large an extent of land as possible surveyed before it is wanted, and held in readiness to meet the demands of purchasers, after having its value tested by being offered for sale by public auction, (an essential security against even the suspicion of jobbing,) the object is gained of defeating those schemes for extorting money from Settlers, by threatening to run up the price of the land they want at the public sales, which were at one time complained of. Of the proceeds of the land sales, one half at least is required to be spent on immigration; the other half is applicable to such objects of public utility as may be thought advisable by the Governor and the Secretary of State, with the sanction of the Treasury.

Such are the rules (omitting details immaterial for my present purpose,) now in force, under the authority of the Act of Parliament of 1842, in those of the Australian Colonies to which it applies. The policy to which these regulations are intended to give effect was first adopted by Lord Ripon, who, being then Secretary of State for the Colonies, promulgated at the beginning of 1831 rules, which substituted the system of disposing of the Crown lands in New South Wales and Van Diemen's Land by public sale, for the former mode of doing so by grant. This change was made partly for the sake of raising funds for emigration to these Colonies, but far more with the view of ensuring the distribution of land to those by whom it is really wanted, and preventing those abuses which experience had proved to be inseparable from the system, of disposing of land by grant, in a territory which is in the course of being settled. In spite of stringent regulations, and of honest and strenuous efforts, as I believe, on the part of the public servants in the Colonies to enforce these regulations, it was found practically impossible in New South Wales and Van Diemen's Land, under the former system, to prevent land from being acquired by persons to whom either the means or the inclination to turn it to account were wanting. Nor could the conditions under which land was granted, and which required that it should be improved, be enforced. It is hardly necessary to point out, that this was an evil urgently requiring correction, since there is no such fatal obstacle to the progress of a Colony, as having a large proportion of its lands engrossed by persons who make little use of the estates they have acquired.

By adopting the system of disposing of land only by sale to the best bidder, or, where there have been no bidders by auction, to the first who offers the minimum price, this evil is in a great measure got rid of, since few will pay down money for land which they do not really intend to use. At the same time the money received for land may be so laid out, that the *boná fide* settler may receive, in the increased value for occupation of the land he buys, full compensation for the price he has been required to pay for it. It is, in my opinion, an essential part of the policy which ought to be pursued with regard to the alienation of land, that the proceeds of the land sales should be always so applied as to give this advantage to the purchaser.

In the Australian Colonies, the application of the receipts from land, in the introduction of immigrants of the labouring class, has been in conformity with this principle ; there can be no doubt, that the value of the land which has been sold has been greatly increased by the supply of labour thus furnished to the purchasers. Land obtained by free grant, but without that supply, would have been acquired by Settlers on terms far less really advantageous than what they have purchased with money which has been applied to immigration. The substitution of public sale for grants, as the mode of disposing of the Crown lands, had the further object (which it has completely attained) of relieving the local Government from imputations of favouritism, which were highly injurious to its character and authority. The grants necessarily differed greatly in value, and every man who thought his own less good than his neighbour's, naturally imputed the favour supposed to have been shown to another to improper partiality. There were also continual attempts to evade the regulations, which the local Government incurred much hostility by resisting. Few comparatively as the settlers then were, the amount of correspondence, and the frequency and bitterness of the complaints against the acts of the Colonial Authorities, in the administration of the Crown lands previously to the change of system in 1831, were so great as almost to exceed belief.

Great as had been the evil of the former practice, of disposing of land by grant, yet its abrogation was met by loud remonstrances on the part of those connected with Australia, whether resident there or in this Country; and they almost unanimously joined in representing to Lord Ripon that the measure would be ruinous to these Colonies. Notwithstanding these remonstrances, the change of system which had been determined upon was adhered to, and from this may fairly be dated the great and almost marvellous advance which the Australian Colonies have made in population, in wealth, and in prosperity. The system which was adopted has effectually answered its purpose of ensuring a just and fair distribution of the Crown lands, to those most capable of turning them to account; and at the same time it has afforded the means of meeting, in some degree, the greatest want of the Colonies, by providing a fund to meet the sending out a large number of free labourers.

Prior to this period, there was scarcely any emigration whatever of persons belonging to the working classes to Australia; and the supply of labour in New South Wales and Van Diemen's Land (the only British Colonies which then existed in that part of the world, except the infant settlement of Western Australia,) may be said to have been exclusively furnished by convicts. I had the honour of serving as a member of the first Commission, appointed to promote emigration, in the year 1831, with the Duke of Richmond, Sir Francis Baring, Sir Henry Ellis, and Mr. Hay; and we found that at that time there were no vessels trading with Australia in which passages could be obtained at a price suitable to emigrants of the working classes. The cheapest passage that could then be procured cost, if my memory does not deceive me, from £35 to £40. It was by means of this first Board of Emigration Commissioners, and the application of the small sum of £10,000 derived from the first land sales (or rather by the expenditure of that sum in anticipation of what these sales would produce,) that a commencement was made, in the despatch of vessels to New South Wales fitted for giving passages at a moderate cost to emigrants of the rank of labourers*. From this apparently feeble beginning, emigration to Australia has grown up to the great importance it had attained even before the recent gold discoveries; so that at the end of 1850 the population of New South Wales, which twenty years before did not probably much exceed 50,000†, had increased to 265,000, or more than fivefold. The number of free immigrants who had arrived from the 1st of January 1832, to the 1st of January 1851, were upwards of 123,000 ; and the expenditure of the Colony, in the introduction of immigrants, has in the same time fallen little short of a million and a half‡, the whole of which large sum had been derived from the land revenue, or obtained as advances on its credit.

These results are not a little remarkable, and are entirely due to that system of disposing of the Crown lands by sale, which was commenced, as I have said, in 1831. In that year the upset or minimum price was only five shillings an acre, which was subsequently advanced to twelve shillings, and ultimately to a pound. At first the regulations rested only on the authority of the Crown ; but in 1836 the subject

---

* See the Papers relating to Emigration and the disposal of Crown lands in the Colonies, presented to Parliament in 1831 and 1832.

† See Porter's 'Progress of the Nation,' p. 758.

‡ See Reports on Colonial Blue Books for 1850 and 1851.

was inquired into by a Select Committee of the House of Commons, which recommended that the principle of disposing of all Colonial lands by sale and for ready money should be affirmed by an Act of Parliament.

The subject was again investigated by the Select Committee on the affairs of South Australia, in 1841, which also came to a conclusion in favour of the system which had been adopted, and even intimated an opinion that the price of land might be raised with advantage beyond the rate of £1 an acre, at which it was then fixed in South Australia. It was believed by this Committee that the purchase of land in the Australian Colonies had been retarded by the apprehension of purchasers that the value of the lands they bought might be depreciated by the reduction of the minimum price which might at any time be made by the Crown, on the advice of a Secretary of State taking a different view of the subject from that which had of late been acted upon. To remove this feeling of uncertainty, it was recommended by the Committee that an Act of Parliament should be passed, prohibiting the disposal of the Crown lands otherwise than by sale (except for public purposes), and providing that, while the Crown should have the power of increasing from time to time the upset price of land as circumstances might seem to require, no reduction of a price once established should take place without the authority of Parliament. An opinion was also expressed by the Committee, that the upset price of land, which was then twelve shillings an acre, might be raised with advantage*.

Having been myself one of the Committee from which this recommendation proceeded, I can vouch for the great care with which the subject was investigated by its members, amongst whom were Lord Derby, Mr. Gladstone, Sir William Molesworth, Sir George Grey, Mr. Vernon Smith, and Sir Henry Wood, who had all been accustomed to take great interest in Colonial questions. The latter was the Chairman of the former Committee on the disposal of Colonial Lands (1836). By the Committee thus constituted, the recommendation I have mentioned was agreed to, with little or no difference of opinion; and, in accordance with it, the Land Sales Act was afterwards passed by Parliament without any opposition, on the recommendation of Lord Derby, who had then become Secretary of State for the Colonies in succession to yourself.

I have thought it right to mention these circumstances, because it is one of the standing topics of declaimers against the Colonial Office, to dwell on the maintenance of the present price of land in the Australian Colonies, as a glaring instance of what is called the tyrannical and overbearing conduct of that Office; the fact being, as will be perceived from what I have stated, that it is not by the authority of the Colonial

* See Report of the Select Committee of the House of Commons on South Australia, of 1841.

Office (that is, of the Secretary of State), but by the
authority of Parliament, that the existing regulations
are maintained, and that the Act by which they are
enforced is one which was passed after no ordinary
amount of deliberation and inquiry, with the general
concurrence of the public men of all parties who have
paid most attention to Colonial affairs.

The working of the Act, far from showing that
there was anything erroneous in the views of those
by whom it was recommended and passed, seems to
me to have proved the soundness of the principles on
which it was founded; but at the same time, as might
have been expected, some improvements in its details
were suggested by experience. Of these the most important was that which has, I trust, been accomplished
by the Act I have mentioned, as having been passed
at our instance in 1846, and the Orders in Council
founded upon it, by which the leasing of land is permitted under certain regulations. By these regulations, a difficulty which stood much in the way of the
successful prosecution of pastoral pursuits, hitherto
the most important branch of Australian industry,
has been removed, without prematurely alienating the
Crown lands. Though the soil and climate of these
Colonies are peculiarly favourable to cattle and the
production of wool, yet the amount of stock which
can be maintained by the land in its natural state is
so small, in proportion to the extent occupied, that it
would be hardly possible to name a price for the land
sufficiently low to enable the stockholder to purchase

the large tracts of land requisite to support his flocks and herds. Hence the practice had arisen of allowing the sheep and cattle farmers to occupy, under license from the Government, the lands still remaining in the possession of the Crown; but from this practice another inconvenience arose.

Under the law, as it stood previously to 1846, it was held that, except by sale, no right to land for any longer term than a year could be conferred on the occupier by the Governor, acting on behalf of the Crown; nor could the occupier be enabled to obtain any compensation for improvements made by him on the land, in the event of its being ultimately sold to another person. Hence the holders of " Runs," (as tracts of land occupied for pastoral purposes are termed,) could not prudently expend money in enclosing and cultivating any portions of their Runs, so as to diminish the heavy expense of bringing supplies from the settled districts; in erecting adequate buildings for carrying on their business, and the proper accommodation of their servants; or in constructing dams or wells to increase the supply of water, the want of which diminishes very much the power of some of the best land to carry stock.

By the system now introduced this difficulty has been obviated; in the unsettled districts the Squatter can obtain a lease of his Run for fourteen years, and is secured compensation for the improvements he may make whenever it may be sold; and in the settled districts a similar result is obtained, by giving a right to occupy the Crown lands, until they are wanted for sale, to the owners of the adjoining lands. In this manner, all the encouragement they could fairly require has been given to the sheep and cattle farmers, who have declared themselves quite satisfied and grateful for what has been done for them*; while at the same time the Crown lands have not been improvidently alienated, before they have acquired the value they must ultimately derive from being wanted for an increasing population. It was indeed denied that this would be the operation of the regulations I have described, by those who contended that, instead of adopting them, the minimum price of land ought to be reduced. They asserted that, by the regulations, the Squatters were virtually put in possession of the land, which could never be resumed, if wanted. Experience has however demonstrated, that there was no ground for such an apprehension; and it has been

---

* See a letter to me from several gentlemen occupying Crown lands beyond the settled districts, enclosed in Sir C. Fitzroy's Despatch of the 29th of June, 1849, in the papers relating to the Australian Colonies Government Bill, presented by Command, on the 1st of March 1850, p. 104. In this letter the writers say :—" We cannot, in the first place, refrain from sincerely thanking your Lordship for the part you have taken in having satisfactorily settled this long discussed question, and having conferred so great a benefit on ourselves and the Colony in general. We are satisfied your Lordship would derive very great pleasure, could you see the advantages which have already accrued from fixity of tenure in the superior buildings which have since been erected, and in the general improvement in society beyond the limits of location ; and this, notwithstanding the unprecedented depression of the times, which you must be well aware of, but which is wholly beyond the control of any Government."

found, as was anticipated, that by giving to the Squatters all they could fairly ask, and at the same time clearly defining their claims, the best security has been obtained against their establishing, by degrees, a right of property in the land they occupied. Already, in Victoria, above £20,000 has been laid out by one individual, in purchasing the fee-simple of land which had been occupied as a Run by another person.

Two very important objects have been gained by thus avoiding the premature disposal of these lands; in the first place, the sacrifice of the future receipts from the land sales has been averted, and the public will thus hereafter have the benefit of a very large fund, applicable to immigration or to other objects of general utility, which would otherwise have been lost; in the second place, the still greater advantage has been obtained, of preventing the available lands of the Colony from being engrossed by speculators, and thus securing to future settlers the power of obtaining land within a reasonable distance of the seats of trade and population, at a moderate price. This is, in my opinion, by far the most important object to be gained by maintaining a comparatively high price for land. There can be no doubt that, by reducing the price as much as would be necessary to meet the views of the chief opponents of the existing system, a powerful impulse would be given to the spirit of land-jobbing,—the curse of countries of which the settlement is in progress. Speculators would soon buy up (if it were sold at a very low price) the land eligible for the occupation of Settlers ; and thus persons here-after proceeding to the Colony to settle, would be compelled to pay for land the highest price which the greediness of the land-jobber could extort, instead of paying a moderate price for land purchased direct from the Crown, with the advantage of having the money so paid expended in the introduction of labour, in the construction of roads, or in other works of utility, and thus virtually returned to them in the increased value given to their property*.

Both the Mother-country and the Colonies are deeply interested in preventing the improper and premature alienation of Colonial lands ; since it is the interest of both, that every possible facility should be given to those who may be disposed to leave this country for the purpose of seeking a new home in our Colonial dominions. And it is on this account, that it seems to me both just and wise that the Imperial Government and Legislature should not, at too early a period, transfer to the local Authorities the power of determining under what regulations the Crown lands

* The evil of land-jobbing is much felt in the United States, but it is greatly checked, and the great inconvenience of having large tracts of land engrossed by persons who do not improve them, and yet refuse to sell them unless at exorbitant prices, is prevented by the system of local rates, which prevails universally in these States. The township rates and direct taxes imposed by the State, fall so heavily on land, which is held without being improved in a district which is becoming settled, that it is forced into the market as it is wanted. Unfortunately the inhabitants of the Australian Colonies have resolutely resisted the introduction of any system of local rating or of direct taxation.

in the Colonies should be disposed of. These lands constitute a vast estate, which has been acquired, and to which all the value it possesses has been given, by the very large expense which has been incurred by the Mother-country in establishing, maintaining, and protecting its Colonies. This estate the Crown holds as trustee for the benefit of all its subjects, not merely of the few thousands who may at this moment inhabit a particular Colony, but of the whole British people, whether resident at home or in the Colonies; and it is the duty of the servants of the Crown, and of Parliament, to take care that the magnificent property thus held in trust for the good of the whole Empire, shall be wisely and carefully administered with a view to that object, and not improvidently wasted, or sacrificed to the rapacity of a few individuals. But if the power of altering the regulations under which the Crown lands are disposed of, were given too soon to every Colonial Legislature, nothing is more probable than that the small society of a young Colony might think it for their interest to share among them, to the exclusion of the other inhabitants of the Empire, the lands which properly belong to all; and it is still more probable that, in such a Colony, a few rapacious speculators might have sufficient influence to carry changes, which would conduce to their personal gain, under the plausible but delusive pretence of promoting the interest of their fellow-colonists.

No doubt there is a stage in the progress of a Colony, when the power of regulating the disposal of the

Crown lands may be safely entrusted to a representative Legislature, and when inconvenience may result from withholding it. Peculiar circumstances may also, in some cases, make it proper that this should be done sooner than would in general be desirable; but I am persuaded that hitherto Parliament has acted wisely, in not giving this power to the Legislatures of the Australian Colonies.

I will not pursue this branch of the subject further, although I have given only a very slight sketch of the arguments in favour of maintaining the present price of land in these Colonies. Those who wish to enter more deeply into the question, will find it fully discussed in the Papers relating to the occupation of Crown lands in the Colonies, which have been laid before Parliament*.

It is another matter of complaint connected with the Land Sales Act, that the proceeds of these sales are not placed at the disposal of the local Legislature. I conceive that the principle for which I have contended, of regarding the Crown lands as an estate in which the whole Empire is interested, justifies the Im-

* See particularly Sir C. Fitzroy's Despatch of January 18, 1848, enclosing the Report of a Committee of the Legislative Council of New South Wales; and the Despatch in reply, of August 11, 1848, enclosing the observations of the Emigration Commissioners on the above Report. Papers presented by Command in 1848, pp. 55 and 123. A further Report from a Committee of the Legislative Council in reply to the Emigration Commissioners, and their rejoinder, will be found enclosed in Sir C. Fitzroy's Despatch of November 5, 1849, and mine, of August 14, 1850, in the Papers presented to Parliament in June and August 1850.

perial Authorities in prescribing the objects to which
the money derived from the sale of these lands should
be applied; and this principle, if I am not mistaken,
is recognized in the United States, where, I believe,
that the revenue accruing from the sale of the public
lands is appropriated by Congress, and not by the
State Legislatures. But, as I have already said, I
believe it to be good policy to apply the proceeds of
Colonial land in such a manner that the price may virtually be returned, by the advantages conferred upon
them, to those purchasers who really occupy the land
they have bought. Parliament has provided for this,
so far as regards half the produce of land sales in the
Colonies, to which the Land Sales Act applies, by
requiring that so much of the receipts should be expended on the conveyance of immigrants to the Colonies whence the funds are derived.

The remaining portion of this revenue, it is true,
is placed at the disposal of the Executive Government,—an arrangement which I concur in thinking
open to objection. Though in practice a fairer and
better employment of this money, than could otherwise have been ensured, has probably been obtained
by leaving it at the disposal of the Crown, the exercise
of an unlimited discretion in the appropriation of such
large funds by the Executive Government is hardly
consistent with the strict principle of a representative
Constitution; and it is therefore highly desirable that
a better mode should be adopted, of determining to
what objects that portion of the land revenue which

Parliament has not set apart for emigration should
be applied. Accordingly we proposed that, whenever
District Councils should be established, they should be
allowed to dispose of what remains of the proceeds of
the land sold within their own boundaries, after the
appropriation of the proportion required by the Act
of Parliament to immigration, and after defraying the
cost of surveys and the expense of measures for the
benefit of the Aborigines, whose claim on this fund is
the first of all. We hoped in this manner to encourage the formation of Municipal bodies, and the practical establishment of that system of local organization
which it had been the purpose of Parliament in 1842
to create, but which it failed to accomplish, as the
clauses on this subject in the New South Wales Constitutional Act had never been brought into operation,
in spite of all the efforts, of even so able and energetic
a Governor as Sir George Gipps, to enforce them. We
conceived that, while the execution of public works of
improvement, in the districts where the land is sold,
would in principle be the most proper application of
the funds so raised, the chief obstacle to the creation
of Municipal bodies would also be removed, by thus
placing at their disposal funds for the accomplishment
of these local objects, without the levy of rates, to
which there has always been a strong objection among
the Australian Colonists*.

* See, in the Papers presented to Parliament, the Report of the
Committee of Privy Council on the Constitutions of the Australian
Colonies, and the Despatches to Sir William Denison of the 27th of

In the meantime, I am persuaded that, far from being an improvement on the existing arrangement, to place the funds derived from the sale of land at the disposal of the local Legislatures, would work great injustice to those from whose pockets these funds are derived. The land sold is principally in the more remote and partially settled districts of the Colonies; and the inhabitants of these districts and newly arrived settlers are the chief purchasers, and the persons for whose benefit the money ought to be laid out. But they are precisely those who have least weight in the local Legislatures, in which it is notorious that, from various circumstances, the inhabitants of the Colonial capitals exercise far more than their due share of influence. The effect therefore of making over these funds to the local Legislatures would be to place the money at the disposal, not of those from whose contributions it is derived, but of others who, it might be feared, would apply it to objects in which they are themselves interested, rather than for the benefit of the contributors.

Circumstances have lately occurred in South Australia, affording a significant indication of the spirit which might influence the application of these funds, if they were entrusted to the local Legislatures. It is well known that, although the river Murray is for a great part of its course well fitted for internal naviga-

July, and to Sir Charles Fitzroy, of the 30th of August, 1850. I shall have again to refer to these Papers in my next Letter, and they will be found in the Appendix (I) to this Volume.

tion, and passes through a country capable for many hundred miles of supporting a large trade, its utility is at present destroyed by the want of any communication with the sea. The Lieutenant-Governor of South Australia some time ago proposed that, to remedy this defect and render the river available for internal communication, a sum of money should be applied from the land revenue in the improvement of a harbour on the coast, called Port Elliot, and the establishment of a communication by a railway between the harbour so made and a point on the river, before it spreads out into the shallow lake in which it terminates, and where it is navigable by steamers. It was clear that, regarded merely as an investment of money, this was calculated to be a very advantageous one, since the amount proposed to be expended was far short of what would certainly be received, from the enhanced value of the lands belonging to the Crown on the line of the railway and the river; it was a scheme also eminently calculated to promote the general prosperity of the Colony. Yet to a measure of this kind a strenuous opposition was raised in the Legislative Council,—an opposition unquestionably dictated by a narrow spirit of jealousy, on the part of the inhabitants of Adelaide, to what might prove a rival port to their own.

This was before the Legislative Council of South Australia possessed a representative character; but I believe that, since its Constitution has been altered, the same spirit is likely to prevail in it not less strongly than before, while it undoubtedly possesses greater power to give weight to its wishes. As the expense of the projected improvement was to be defrayed from a source over which the Legislature has no control, its opposition could not arrest it, and measures for carrying it into execution were in progress when we retired from office. What happened on this matter seems to me to afford a useful warning, as to the expediency of entrusting the appropriation of the funds in question to a different authority from the local Legislature.

In what I have said on the subject of the regulations for the disposal of land in the Australian Colonies, I have mentioned the large amount of money which has been derived from the land revenue of New South Wales, and applied to the introduction of immigrants. On the general subject of emigration to Australia I have to observe, that this service was carried on during your Administration upon a very large scale and with great success. When we came into office, we found that emigration to New South Wales had been suspended since 1844, because, owing to the falling off in the land sales which had succeeded the extravagant speculative purchases of a few years before, the funds applicable to this service had been for a time exhausted. In South Australia, on the contrary, the land revenue had already recovered from its depressed condition of two or three years before; and by means of the funds thus available, a steady stream of emigration had been again directed to that Colony. On the 1st of January, 1847, the Governor of New South Wales reported that the debentures issued on the credit of the land revenue, to pay for the previous emigration, would be entirely discharged in the course of the year; and he recommended that another sum of £100,000 should be raised for emigration, which was assented to; and the renewal of emigration to that Colony, including Victoria, (which, as the Port Philip district, still formed part of New South Wales,) was sanctioned on the 30th of August of the same year.

From that time emigration to the Australian Colonies has been steadily carried on, as rapidly as the funds would permit; and in five years, to the end of 1851, the Emigration Commissioners sent there, in ships chartered by them, nearly 60,000 emigrants*.

It is unnecessary for me to give any detailed account of the manner in which this large emigration has been carried on; I believe it is not disputed that the service has been admirably performed by the Emigration Commissioners, and the results afford the best evidence of its having been so, and of the ability and unremitting care with which those gentlemen have performed their duty. Of upwards of two hun-

---

* The numbers sent to each Colony have been as follows :—

New South Wales	19,841
Victoria	17,561
South Australia	20,786
Van Diemen's Land . . .	871
Western Australia	357
Total . .	59,416

See Twelfth General Report of the Emigration Commissioners, p. 18.

dred and thirty ships, in which these emigrants were sent to the Colonies, only one was wrecked, and that almost within sight of the port of its destination, and happily without any loss of life ; the rate of mortality on board the vessels has been singularly low, and the complaints of misconduct on the part of the officers in charge of them have also been very rare, especially when it is considered how difficult it must be to find a sufficient number of persons both willing to serve for the very moderate remuneration that can be allowed, and also duly qualified to discharge the exceedingly arduous duties of the surgeons, to whom the charge, not only of the health of the passengers, but of the maintenance of order on board emigrant ships, is entrusted. The selection of the emigrants is also shown, by the reports received of them after their arrival, to have been good[*]; though of course it is impossible that, in sending out such large numbers, the Commissioners should be able to escape being sometimes imposed upon, and induced to give passages to persons who would be rejected if their want of the requisite qualifications were known. This applies particularly to the single women ; of this class it is so difficult to obtain emigrants of a proper description, and also to guard against deception as to their character, that, were not an increase of the female population in the Colonies so urgently required, it would probably have been better to send no single women.

* See Appendix No. 28 to the Twelfth Report of the Emigration Commissioners.

Referring to the Annual Reports of the Emigration Commissioners, for a detailed account of the measures adopted with respect to Australian emigration, I think it will be right that I should offer a few general observations on the principles by which our course on this subject was guided. You are aware that there have been few more popular subjects for attacks on the Government, while we were entrusted with the duty of conducting it, than that afforded by describing in the most vivid colours the urgency of the want of labour in the Colonies on the one hand, and its supposed redundancy in this Country on the other. Our incompetency, if not wilful and perverse determination to reject measures we knew to be right, have been constantly represented as the sole reason why the alleged surplus of labour and population at home was not remedied, and the prosperity of the Australian Colonies at the same time assured, by transferring to them some of the industrious but starving multitudes, by whom our streets and our workhouses were represented to be crowded. I have no doubt that those who have held the sort of language to which I refer, and which is so often to be found in the columns of newspapers, and in speeches at public meetings, sincerely believed what they were in the habit of saying; and it is certain that the opinion is very generally held, both in this Country and in the Colonies, that, although it may possibly not be the fault of those by whom the Government has been administered, that the transfer of a very large number of our labouring population to Australia has not been effected, yet that it is highly desirable such a transfer should be accomplished, and that, if it were practicable, it ought to be undertaken by the Government*.

But, generally as this opinion has been entertained, I believe it to be entirely erroneous. Instead of seeing any indication of an excess of population in this Country, I observe on every side strong symptoms of the reverse. I know that in every county of England (I might almost say in the United Kingdom), labour and capital, to a far larger amount than are available, might be laid out in the improvement of the land, so as to yield an ample return. In those parts of the country with which I am myself acquainted, I am certain that the draining alone, which is urgently required, would occupy for many years more hands than can be spared from other work; and as the land becomes better drained, it will pay for higher cultivation, requiring the permanent employment of more labourers. In every other branch of national industry there is also an evident and rapid increase in the means of profitably employing labour. No doubt the demand for labour is at this moment much greater than it was only a short time back, and it must be admitted that four or five years ago there was much more appearance than at present of the market for labour being glutted; and

---

* I am speaking of what was the state of opinion on this subject a short time ago; already there appears to be a great change, and perhaps the tendency is now rather towards an unfounded apprehension of injury to the Country by an undue abstraction of population.

even now there are probably particular places where it may be difficult to find profitable employment for all the labourers who are seeking for it. But even during the times when industry was most depressed, and our population was suffering the greatest distress, it was I think clear that the real difficulty arose, not from any deficiency in the field for employment, or any want of capital to make use of the resources which the country affords, but from circumstances (such as the deficiency in the crops of both potatoes and corn in 1846, and the re-action after the over-speculation in railways), which had deranged our social economy, and above all from injudicious laws, which prevented industry from flowing into its natural channels, and the effect of which could not be expected to cease immediately on their repeal.

The present state of the Country affords the most conclusive evidence that this view of the subject was just ; since, with the same field for employment as before, labour is notoriously so far from being re-dundant, that a want of hands is becoming a very general complaint among employers ; and it may be safely asserted, that at this moment there is no effi-cient and healthy labourer in this country who may not calculate on earning a comfortable subsistence by his industry, if he conducts himself well, and exerts himself as he ought to find employment. If there are particular parishes in which there is still an ap-parent want of work for the population, it is only because there are still obstructions from the law of settlement to the natural distribution of labour. Far from its being true (as the inhabitants of the Australian Colonies have been continually told), that there are in our workhouses large numbers of industrious labourers who have been reduced to the condition of paupers only by the impossibility of finding employment, and who, if enabled to emigrate, would at once become useful members of society, I do not hesitate to express my conviction that, except those who have been reduced to distress by age or sickness, there is hardly one to be found among the inhabitants of our workhouses who has not been brought there either by want of industry or by some fault or misconduct, which, having prevented him from succeeding as an independent labourer at home, would in all probability equally prevent him from succeeding as an emigrant in any of our Colonies*. Hence I am per-

---

* There can be no greater mistake, than to suppose that the qualities necessary to secure success in life at home are not equally necessary in Australia, or that those Colonies are a sort of paradise for the working man, where he is never exposed to difficulties either by his own faults, or by those fluctuations of trade, which sometimes for a time leave particular classes of workmen without employment. On the contrary, in the Australian Colonies (I am speaking of the time before the discovery of gold, for it is difficult to judge of the present state of things), the labouring man was exposed to difficulties from both these causes ; and the position of most skilled labourers I believe to have been much more precarious, and, in spite of their higher nominal wages, not really so good as it now is at home, since even with their high wages they cannot there command many advantages they here enjoy. The commonest labourers can no doubt obtain much higher wages and be altogether much better off in Australia than at home, if they can make up their minds to the

suaded, it is not for the interest of the Colonies that
they should look to the workhouses of this Country as
a source whence an increased supply of labour may
be obtained. It appears to me still more clear, that
it would have been highly inexpedient, even when
our labour-market seemed most glutted, that relief
should have been afforded by the State to those who
alleged themselves to be in distress owing to the want
of employment, by giving them free passages to
Australia. It may safely be asserted that in ninety-
nine cases out of a hundred, even in the worst times,
it would be found, on strict investigation, that some
fault or imprudence on the part of the labourer complaining that he could not find work, was the cause
of his difficulty, and that the really steady and industrious man has seldom been out of work. To establish
the practice of giving relief to those who cannot find
work at home, by sending them to Colonies where
wages are higher than they are here, would therefore
be to reverse the position of the good and bad labourers
under the wholesome operation of the natural laws of
society, and actually to give an advantage over the
best labourers to the indifferent ones, on account of
their inferiority, by considering their inability to compete with the others in the labour-market at home, a
reason for giving them the means of carrying their
labour to a higher market in the Colonies. I can

solitude of the bush: even to this class there are, in the various
privations to which they must submit, many drawbacks from the
advantages they obtain.

conceive no policy more fatal than this would be, and no course better calculated to discourage the formation of industrious and provident habits in our labouring population.

Nor is this the only consideration on which grants of public money to promote emigration to Australia (except in some very special cases, and to a very small amount) would have been objectionable, even when the home market for labour was apparently the most overstocked. It is obvious that such grants, drawn as they must be from taxes paid by the people of this Country, would only be justifiable if it could be clearly shown, that the advantage to those on whom the charge must fall would be fully equivalent to the cost incurred. And the greater the pressure upon the Country at the time when such grants are asked for, the greater is the necessity of strictly adhering to this rule. But the only advantage (at all events the only direct and immediate advantage) which the Country could gain by sending some of its inhabitants to Australia, would be that of relieving the labour-market from some of the hands supposed to be superfluous. Now a very slight calculation would suffice to show that the cost of the long voyage to Australia would be so great, in proportion to the number of labourers who could be sent there, that the relief to the labour-market at home would bear no proportion to the expense incurred in such a scheme of emigration.

More than this, I have endeavoured to show that there is not (and never has been) any real redundancy of labour in this Country; consequently it would be most mistaken policy to seek relief from any temporary difficulties we may experience, by artificially promoting emigration at the public expense, instead of by removing any obstacles to the natural extension of the field of employment at home. It must be borne in mind that active and industrious labourers, by being sent to Australia, cease to become contributors to the wealth and revenue of the Mother-country. They will no doubt continue to be contributors to the wealth and greatness of the British Empire, and will help to increase the trade of this Country by adding to the productive power of the Colony to which they go, and to its demand for British manufactures. But if they remain at home, and find here an adequate field for their industry, they will still contribute to increase the wealth and trade of the Empire, with this further and material advantage, so far as the Mother-country is concerned, that they will also continue to be contributors to its revenue, and help to bear those heavy charges which former wars and the necessity of keeping up large establishments, entail upon the parent State, but of which no portion falls upon its Colonial dependencies. It is clear, that the more the population and wealth of the British Islands increase, the lighter will become to their inhabitants the burden of our national debt, and of the taxes to which it compels us to submit. Hence (except when there is some special object to be gained by it) to spend any part of the national income in stimulating emigration, is unjust to those who remain at home, since it is applying money levied from them to an object not calculated to relieve them, but rather to check that natural increase of the wealth and population of the Country, to which alone we can look for real relief from our burdens.

For these reasons it appears to me that Parliament would not have been justified in granting, and that we should have done wrong had we asked it to grant, money to carry on any large measure of emigration to Australia. But in the absence of Parliamentary grants, it is obvious that the Government has no means of sending out emigrants to these Colonies beyond those furnished by the funds which can be raised in the Colonies themselves. Our duties, therefore, with reference to Australian emigration, were reduced to encouraging and assisting spontaneous emigration as far as we could, and applying the money available for that purpose from Colonial sources in sending out emigrants. In the last, we considered ourselves called upon to act as trustees for the Colonies, in which character we had to take care that the funds they supplied, should be laid out for them to the best advantage.

It was this simple principle of regarding the Government as a trustee, bound scrupulously to consult the interest of the Colonies in the expenditure of the money they contributed, which regulated all the measures adopted on the subject of emigration while they were under our direction. My instructions to the Commissioners who are immediately charged with this

branch of the public service, were, that they should on
no account deviate from this principle ; and it is only
due to them to say that they entered most fully into
it, and showed in my opinion great judgement and
ability in applying it. General rules were drawn up,
based upon the advice and information afforded by
the Colonial Authorities, defining as strictly and as
clearly as possible the classes of emigrants who were
to be considered eligible for free passages, or rather
to passages towards the cost of which only a small
contribution is expected from the emigrant. In these
rules, and in the amount of contribution required from
the emigrants, variations were made from time to
time according to varying circumstances at home and
in the Colonies.   The reports received from the Colonies determined to what description of labourers
a preference should be given, and to what extent.
The complaints so frequently made in Parliament, of
the exclusion from the benefit of a passage in the
Commissioners' ships, of persons who would have
made excellent emigrants, because they did not come
strictly within the rigid rules laid down, may be answered by observing that a public Department can
only act on fixed rules ; that the rules of the Commissioners as to the emigrants to be taken are carefully
framed on the advice of the Colonial Authorities respecting the description of emigrants most wanted at
the time ; and though it may be true that some of the
persons excluded by these rules would make excellent
emigrants, still they have no right to complain that,

in the expenditure of Colonial money, a preference is given to those who in the opinion of the Colonists will be most useful to them.

When there is any difficulty in obtaining the required number of emigrants of the most eligible class, the rules are relaxed, so as to extend the field of selection; and in the same manner the amount of contribution required from emigrants is made to vary according to the demand for passages. Thus in the year 1848, when the check to railway enterprise and the generally depressed state of industry, by bringing a heavy pressure on the working classes, had greatly increased the number of applications for passages, the amount of deposit required from emigrants was increased, which of course tended both to limit the number of applications, and to make the funds at the disposal of the Commissioners go further. A year or two afterwards, when the revival of trade and industry at home diminished the disposition of the working classes to emigrate, it became necessary again to reduce the amount of deposit, in order to obtain the number of emigrants that was wanted; the Commissioners being instructed to endeavour always so to fix the amount of deposit, as to maintain, as nearly as possible, an equality between the number of passages which the funds at their disposal would allow them to grant, and that of applications made to them by eligible emigrants.

I may further mention upon this subject that, in 1848, being persuaded that the difficulties of the

Country were merely temporary, and that the revival
of its prosperity would cause a great abatement in
the disposition to emigrate, I thought it advisable to
sanction the anticipation, to an extent which under
other circumstances I should have thought objectionable, of the funds applicable to emigration; and
the Commissioners were thus enabled to take advantage of an opportunity not apparently likely to recur,
of obtaining a large number of the most eligible emigrants on very favourable terms.   The result proved
the advantage of this course, for the revival of the
demand for labour at home led, as I had foreseen, to
a great diminution in the candidates for emigration;
and so marked was the effect produced in this respect
by the renewed prosperity of the Country, that up to
the time of our leaving Office, notwithstanding that
the discovery of gold in New South Wales had been
known for some months, there was still much difficulty in filling the Commissioners' ships.   Since that
time, it appears from the newspapers that the almost
marvellous accounts of the success of the gold-seekers
in Victoria has produced an eager desire for emigration, of which the Commissioners will no doubt have
availed themselves, by again raising the deposit required from emigrants, if they found it in their power
to do so.

I have said that, as a rule, the Commissioners take
only those emigrants who are of what is considered the
most eligible class; but under certain circumstances,
the payment of an additional proportion of the cost

of their passage from some other source, (thus econo-
mizing the Colonial funds,) has been thought to render
it advisable for the interest of the Colonists to accept emigrants not belonging strictly to the required
classes. Thus after the French Revolution of February,
1848, a considerable body of English workmen and
their families, who had been employed in the manufac-
tories in the neighbourhood of Calais, were driven out
of France. If they had been compelled to go to their
native places in this Country, in the then state of
trade, they would have been exposed to much distress ; while at the same time they were represented as
being a remarkably intelligent and industrious body
of people, likely to prove a great acquisition to any
of our Colonies to which they might be sent. But
from having been employed in manufactures, they
were less likely to be immediately useful than agricultural labourers, and were not qualified according
to the Commissioners' rules to be accepted as emigrants. In these circumstances a departure from the
ordinary practice was sanctioned, and in consideration
of a part of the expense incurred being paid from
another source, passages to New South Wales in ships
taken up on account of the Colony were granted to
these people by the Commissioners. This arrangement was made, in concert with Lord Shaftesbury,
who took much interest in the matter, and assisted
in raising the subscription by which the means of
making the payment required by the Commissioners
were provided. I am happy to say that these emi-

grants justified what was done for them, by their
good conduct and industry in the Colony.

It was further regarded by us as the duty of the
Government, to adopt all the means in our power
to promote spontaneous emigration to these Colonies.
For while it appears to me, that, for the reason I
have stated, it would not be just to the tax-payers
at home to apply money derived from their contributions, in the conveyance of large numbers of emigrants
to Australia, yet there are advantages to be anticipated from the extension of colonization in that part
of the globe, which make it desirable to give every
encouragement to emigration thither, which can be
afforded, without any heavy demands on the public
purse. With that view measures were adopted, which
are, I think, likely hereafter to lead to more important results than have yet followed from them. In my
last Letter I mentioned the remarkable fact, that the
greater part, if not the whole cost of the vast emigration now going on to North America is provided for
by remittances made by previous emigrants to the
friends and relations they have left behind, to enable
them to join them in their new home. No such remittances were usually made from Australia, apparently because there existed no simple and easy mode
by which Settlers there could send money to their
friends at home, or provide for their being brought
to the Colony. As it is certainly easier for a labouring man to save money from his wages in the Australian Colonies, than either in Canada or in the United

States, there seemed reason to anticipate that those who have gone to the former, would not be less ready to assist their friends to follow them, if the means of doing so were easily within their reach, than those who have gone to the latter are found to be. Accordingly an arrangement was made, by which persons in the Australian Colonies, wishing to apply money in assisting their friends to emigrate, are enabled to do so by paying, through the agency of the Post-office, into the Military Chest, the amount they intend to devote to this object, to which the sums so received are then applied by the Emigration Commissioners in this Country, to whom credit is given by the Treasury for the sums so paid into the Military Chest in the Colony. In this manner a perfectly simple and easy mode of remitting money for emigration is afforded to those who have already reached the Colonies ; and they can thus assist their friends at home in paying for the outfit of the voyage, and the deposit required by the Commissioners from candidates for emigration.

With a similar object, it has also been provided that purchasers of Crown lands in these Colonies, may require that a certain proportion of the price paid by them for land, shall be applied in giving passages to such persons at home as they may nominate, provided that those selected are duly qualified, under the Commissioners' rules, to be received as emigrants in their ships. To this was added a regulation, by which depositors in the savings-banks are entitled to a slight increase in the rate of interest on their deposits, upon their agreeing to receive repayment ultimately in land. The amount of their deposits would thus become immediately applicable to emigration, while this regulation was calculated to assist the most industrious and frugal labourers in acquiring land; and they were also allowed to nominate emigrants for free passages on similar conditions with the purchasers of land. The privilege granted to the latter has already been largely made use of, so much so as to create some apprehension that it may be abused; but with the precautions that have been adopted, I see no reason for uneasiness on this head. I think it indeed very likely that, if the desire to emigrate to Australia should continue to be as great as it has lately become, owing to the accounts received from the gold-fields, land-purchasers may stipulate for some payment from those whom they may enable to reach the Colony, by nominating them for passages in the Commissioners' ships. But far from seeing any objection to such an arrangement, as a private one between the parties concerned, I think it would be a very natural and proper agreement for them to make; and, so far as the public is concerned, it would clearly be only an advantage to the Colony, since it would promote the more rapid sale of the Crown lands, and a proportionally increased rate of emigration. Such agreements, in fact, would virtually to a certain extent accomplish what has always been considered a very desirable object, that namely of enabling persons in this Country who wish to emigrate, to obtain the means of doing so, on the credit of their future earnings.

Having adverted to this as an object which has been considered desirable, I am reminded that it has often been represented as a fault in the existing system of conducting emigration, that no attempt is made to recover from emigrants sent out by the Commissioners, a portion at least of the expense so incurred. It is obvious that, if this were done, a large addition would be made to the funds applicable to emigration, and it is contended that, if part of the cost of passages provided for emigrants were considered as a loan, they would have no difficulty in repaying it by instalments from the high wages they can earn in the Colonies. It is urged that such loans have often been made by private individuals, and have almost invariably been honestly repaid; and a Society, which has attracted a good deal of public attention, has been formed by that energetic and benevolent lady Mrs. Chisholm, for conducting emigration upon this principle. I have no doubt of its being quite true that such loans made by private individuals have been generally paid; it is, I think, what might have been expected; nor does it seem impossible that this Society may be equally successful in recovering the advances it may make, provided the emigrants it sends out are well selected, and that the services of trustworthy and efficient agents in the Colony can be secured.

But the case would be very different if the advances

were made from public money, and if the Colonial Government, instead of private individuals, or the agent of a private Society, were the creditor to whom repayment was to be made. It is unfortunately only too certain that debts to the Public are regarded in a very different light from private debts, and that a disposition to evade the payment of the former is shown by many, who would be ashamed not to pay what they owe to private creditors. But unless the advances were paid willingly, the difficulty and expense would be so great, as to render it impossible to recover money by petty instalments, from a multitude of persons scattered over so wide a territory as that of the Australian Colonies.

In fact, such was found to be the case when the experiment was tried some twenty years ago. On the recommendation of the first Emigration Commission, (which I have mentioned as having been appointed in 1831,) an attempt was made to supply the urgent want at that time existing in New South Wales of artisans of some of the more ordinary trades, by sending out a certain number of men of this description with their families, under an engagement to repay a part of the expense so incurred. The wages then paid in New South Wales for such labour were so high, that these men could have had no difficulty in making these stipulated payments had they desired it; yet the Governor, Sir Richard Bourke, reported that it was impossible to enforce the claims of the Government, and by his advice they were abandoned.

The great changes which have since taken place in the Colony, only tend to render the attempt to recover debts of this sort more hopeless at the present day than it was then. I mention this circumstance because it is a prevalent notion, that the Government has been culpably remiss in not taking measures to recover from emigrants sent out at the expense of the Colonies some part of the cost of their passage; and I believe that few persons are aware that the experiment was tried so long ago, and that it failed in the hands of so able a Governor as Sir Richard Bourke.

In my next Letters I will call your attention to the subject of Transportation, to the changes which have been made in the constitution of the Australian Colonies, and to their general condition.

October 1st, 1852.

APPENDIX.

A.

List of Officers appointed to the Government of Colonies while I held the Office of Secretary of State, showing the nature of their Previous Services. Those marked thus (*) were personally unknown to me at the time of their Appointment.

COLONY.	GOVERNOR OR LIEUTENANT-GOVERNOR APPOINTED.	PREVIOUS SERVICES OF OFFICES APPOINTED.
Canada, etc.	Governor-General, the Earl of Elgin*	Governor of Jamaica.
New Brunswick	Lieutenant-Governor, Sir Edmund Head, Bart.*	Poor-Law Commissioner.
Prince Edward's Island	Lieutenant-Governor, Sir Donald Campbell*	
Ditto, on Sir D. Campbell's death	Lieutenant-Governor, Sir Alexander Bannerman	Member of Parliament; Commissioner of Greenwich Hospital.
Newfoundland	Governor, Sir Gaspard Le Marchant*	Military service, and Command of a Regiment.
Bermuda	Governor, Captain Elliot	Protector of Slaves in Guiana, previously to the abolition of Slavery; Diplomatic service in China.
Jamaica	Governor, Sir C. E. Grey	Judge in India; Commissioner in Canada; Governor of Barbadoes.
Turk's and Caicos Islands	F. H. Forth, Esq., President of Council of Government*	District Magistrate in Convict Service, Van Diemen's Land.
Honduras	Superintendent, P. E. Wodehouse, Esq.	Civil Service, Ceylon.
Bahamas	Governor, J. Gregory, Esq.*	Van Diemen's Land.
Barbadoes and Windward Islands	Governor, Lieutenant-Colonel Reid	Military Service, as Officer of Engineers; Governor of Bermuda.

COLONY.	GOVERNOR OR LIEUTENANT-GOVERNOR APPOINTED.	PREVIOUS SERVICES OF OFFICER APPOINTED.
Barbadoes and Windward Islands, on the resignation of Colonel Reid	Sir William Colebrooke, C.B.	Military Service, as Officer of Engineers; Commissioner of Eastern Inquiry; Lieutenant-Governor of New Brunswick.
St. Vincent	Lieutenant-Governor, R. G. Macdonnell	Governor of the Gambia.
Tobago	Lieutenant-Governor, D. R. Ross*	Formerly Member of Parliament.
Ditto, on the death of Mr. Ross	Lieutenant-Governor, D. Daly, Esq.*	Secretary to the Government, Canada.
St. Lucia	Lieutenant-Governor, C. H. Darling, Esq.*	Stipendiary Magistrate; Agent-general for Emigration, Jamaica.
Ditto, on Mr. Darling's promotion to the Cape	Lieutenant-Governor, M. Power*	Member of Parliament.
Antigua and Leeward Islands	Governor, R. J. Mackintosh, Esq.	Lieutenant-Governor of St. Christopher.
St. Christopher	Lieutenant-Governor, R. J. Mackintosh*	Private Secretary to the Earl of Carlisle, when First Commissioner of Woods and Forests.
Ditto, on the promotion of Mr. Mackintosh	Lieutenant-Governor, E. Drummond Hay*	Administrator of the Government of the Virgin Islands.
Virgin Islands	Administrator of the Government Sir J. Macgregor	Military Service.
Ditto, on the death of Sir J. Macgregor	Administrator of the Government, Lieutenant-Colonel J. C. Chads	
Dominica	Lieutenant-Governor, Major Blackall	Military Service; Member of Parliament.
Montserrat	Administrator of the Government, Captain J. R. Booth	Naval Service.
British Guiana	Governor, H. Barkly, Esq.	Member of Parliament.
Gibraltar	Governor, Sir R. W. Gardiner, K.C.B.*	Military Service.
Malta	Governor, the Right Hon. R. More O'Ferrall	Member of Parliament; Secretary to the Treasury; and Secretary to the Admiralty.

COLONY.	GOVERNOR OR LIEUTENANT-GOVERNOR APPOINTED.	PREVIOUS SERVICES OF OFFICER APPOINTED.
Malta, on the resignation of Mr. O'Ferrall	Governor, Sir W. Reid, K.C.B.	Governor of Bermuda; Governor of Barbadoes.
Ionian Islands [not a Colony, but the government carried on by the Lord High Commissioner, under the directions of the Secretary of State]	Lord High Commissioner, Sir H. Ward	Member of Parliament; Secretary to the Admiralty.
Cape of Good Hope	Governor Sir H. Pottinger, Bart.	Services in India and China.
Ditto, as successor to Sir H. Pottinger	Governor, Sir H. Smith, Bart., G.C.B.	Military Service at the Cape, etc.
Ditto, as successor to Sir H. Smith	Governor, the Hon. G. Cathcart*	Military Service.
Ditto, Eastern districts	Lieutenant-Governor, Sir Henry Young	Colonial Secretary, British Guiana.
Ditto, Civil, Lieutenant-Governor under General Cathcart.	Lieutenant-Governor, Darling	Lieutenant-Governor of St. Lucia.
Natal	Lieutenant-Governor, B. C. Pine, Esq.*	Queen's Advocate, and Administrator of the Government of Sierra Leone.
St. Helena	Governor, Sir Emerson Tennant	Military Service.
Ditto, on the resignation of Sir E. Tennant	Governor, Colonel Browne*	
Gold Coast	Governor, Major Hill	Military Service on the Coast of Africa, etc.
The Gambia	Governor, R. G. Macdonnell, Esq.*	Chief Justice of the Gambia.
South Australia	Lieutenant-Governor, Sir H. Young	Lieutenant-Governor of the Eastern division of the Cape of Good Hope, etc.
Western Australia	Captain Fitzgerald, R.N.	Governor of the Gambia, Naval Service.

COLONY.	GOVERNOR OR LIEUTENANT-GOVERNOR APPOINTED.	PREVIOUS SERVICES OF OFFICER APPOINTED.
New Zealand:—		
New Munster	Lieutenant-Governor, E. J. Eyre, Esq.	Magistrate in South Australia.
New Ulster	Major-General Pitt [appointed by the Governor in Chief]	
Ditto, on the death of Major-General Pitt	Lieutenant-Colonel R. H. Wynyard.	
Mauritius	Governor, Sir George Anderson*	Civil Service of the East India Company.
Ditto, [on transfer of Sir G. Anderson to Ceylon]	Governor, J. M. Higginson, Esq.	Governor of Leeward Islands; Secretary to Lord Metcalfe in Canada; Civil Service of East India Company.
Ceylon	Viscount Torrington.	
Ceylon [as successor to Lord Torrington]	Governor, Sir G. Anderson, K.C.B.	Governor of Mauritius, etc.
Hongkong	Governor, Sir S. G. Bonham, K.C.B.*	Governor of Singapore.
Labuan	Governor, Sir James Brooke, K.C.B.	Borneo, etc.
Falkland Islands	Governor, G. Rennie	Member of Parliament.
Vancouver's Island	Richard Blanshard, Esq.*	
Ditto	James Douglas, Esq.*	

B.

Copy of a Despatch from Earl Grey to Governor Sir C. A. Fitzroy.

"*Downing-street, November* 24, 1846.

" Sir,

" I have the honour to inform you that in consequence of the information recently received from New Zealand, Her Majesty's Servants have determined that an increase of the military force now in that Colony should be effected with the least possible delay. With that view, I have to instruct you to make immediate arrangements, in concert with the officer commanding the troops in New South Wales, for sending the whole of the disposable force now serving there to Wellington, with the utmost practicable despatch. It will, I calculate, be in your power, without danger, to send at least 900 men for this service, still retaining a small force at Sydney, which, under the present circumstances of New South Wales, is all that I consider indispensable. New South Wales may be regarded as being perfectly safe, for the present at least, from any attack from a foreign enemy; there are no native tribes capable of engaging in serious hostilities with the Colonists; and the Convict establishment is now reduced so low, while so great an increase has taken place in the numbers of the free population, that there is no longer the necessity which some years ago existed for maintaining a considerable military force to guard against the risk of an attempt to rise on the part of the convicts. Under these circumstances there is no part of Her Majesty's dominions in which there is less occasion for a large body of troops. Accordingly I find that, with the exception of those at Sydney, the troops now serving in New South Wales are broken up into small detachments, and obviously performing duties more analogous to those of a police corps than of a part of Her Majesty's regular army.   But these are duties which the heavy demands upon the services of the British army do not admit that it should be called upon any longer to undertake.   Her Majesty's confidential Servants will consider it their duty to take care that the naval and military forces shall afford efficient protection from the attacks of any foreign enemy to so important a part of her dominions as New South Wales; but for the maintenance of internal order and tranquillity it is only reasonable that the Colonists should themselves be called upon to provide, by the formation of an adequate force of Police, or, if necessary, of militia.   You will bring this subject under the immediate consideration of the Legislative Council; and under no circumstances will you consider yourself authorized to delay sending to New Zealand the force I have already named.

" I do not propose that for the present there should be any alteration in the amount of force in Van Diemen's Land, including Norfolk Island, or in Southern or Western Australia; nor is the arrangement for sending the 96th Regiment to India to be disturbed.

" I have, etc.

" (Signed)   GREY."

Copy of a Despatch from Earl Grey to Governor
Sir C. A. Fitzroy.

" Downing-street, October 19, 1847.

" SIR,

" I have to acknowledge the receipt of your Despatch, No. 100, of the 30th April last, with its enclosures, reporting the steps proposed to be taken by the Lieutenant-general commanding Her Majesty's troops in the Australian settlements, in obedience to my instructions to yourself of the 24th November last, for increasing the force in New Zealand, and by the reduction of that in New South Wales, and also pointing out the difficulty which exists in organizing an efficient police corps for the last-named colony.

" Although the force which you propose to retain in New South Wales is somewhat larger in amount than I have directed you to keep there, it is not my intention to withhold my approval from this arrangement, as one of a temporary nature. Viewed in this light, I see no sufficient reason for objecting to the arrangement, because the force which it provided for New Zealand will be raised nearly to the amount that was intended, while the restoration of tranquillity in that Colony has greatly diminished the want of troops which seemed to exist there, when I addressed to you my despatch above referred to. At the time the arrangements which you now report were adopted, there was a further reason for departing in some degree from those which had been directed, in consequence of the demands which still continued on the services of the troops in New South Wales to keep the convicts in subjection. This demand will however now cease, as orders have been given for breaking up the Convict establishment in that colony. Hence, and taking also into consideration the fact that this Colony is peculiarly exempt from the danger of being attacked by a foreign enemy, I am of opinion that the amount to which I last year directed that the garrison of New South Wales should be reduced will ultimately be amply sufficient; and I cannot accordingly hold out to you the expectation that so considerable a force as that to which you refer will long continue to be kept there, merely for the purpose of supporting the police in the maintenance of order, this being a service for which the Colony must provide. You will do well, therefore, to bring under the consideration of the Legislative Council of your Government the propriety of taking early measures to increase the Police, so as to be prepared for the further reduction in the number of regular troops maintained in the Colony, which will probably be effected at a very early period. In taking any measures for this purpose, you will suggest to the Legislative Council that it deserves to be considered whether the difficulty which is described to exist in obtaining the services of an adequate number of effective policemen might not be met by causing men to be engaged for this purpose in England. I have no doubt that men well fitted for the duty might easily be engaged here, under a stipulation to serve for seven or ten years for reasonable wages; and in order to secure their performance of the agreement, some bonus should be held out to them on the completion of their term of service, while, on the other hand, in the event of their either leaving the service voluntarily or being dismissed for misconduct before the expiration of the stipulated period, they should be made subject to a penalty equal to the probable cost of their conveyance to the Colony, for the recovery of which stringent and summary powers should be given to the Governor by the Act authorizing the measure.

" I have, etc.

" (Signed)   GREY."

Copy of a Despatch from Earl Grey to Governor Sir C. A. Fitzroy.

"*Downing-street, March* 4, 1848.

" Sir,

" I have to acknowledge the receipt of your Despatch, No. 166, of the 20th August last, with the copy therein enclosed of a report from the Commanding Royal Engineer in New South Wales, relating to the defences of Port Jackson.

" I cannot coincide in the opinion which you inform me exists in New South Wales, that the circumstance that Halifax and Quebec have been fortified at the cost of this country, affords a precedent for an application being made to Parliament for a vote for the protection of Sydney. The situation of those places, by which they are so much more exposed to attack than any of the Australian cities, affords a sufficient reason for the expense incurred for their defence. You will inform the Legislative Council that, while the right of the Australian Colonies to look for their fair share of that protection which it is object of Her Majesty's naval and military forces to extend to all parts of the British Empire is fully recognized by Her Majesty's Servants, they are of opinion that these Colonies have now made so much progress in wealth and population, that their inhabitants may reasonably be expected to bear also a part of the heavy charges which, with a view to that protection, are imposed upon their fellow-subjects residing in the United Kingdom ; and that the smallest contribution towards these charges which ought now to be required from the Colonists is that of providing any additional means of local defence which may be required. I can therefore hold out no expectation whatever to the Legislative Council of New South

Wales, that Her Majesty's Government will be able to render any assistance towards the erection of the works which have been suggested at Sydney, unless they think proper to vote the requisite funds for their construction, and, on that condition, Her Majesty's Government will be happy to direct the Board of Ordnance to appoint officers to plan and execute the works.

With regard to the want of an artillery force in New South Wales, adverted to by the commanding Royal Engineer, I have to observe that, as a force of this description would only be required in the very improbable event of an attempted invasion, this danger might be met at a very moderate expense by forming in Sydney a volunteer artillery corps. If some of the principal gentlemen would exert themselves in forming such a corps, I should approve of your granting them commissions. It has been found in this country that without interfering materially with their ordinary avocations, the workmen employed in our dockyards can, by devoting to this object a few hours in the week, be trained so as to form a very effective force, both of artillery and of infantry. Similar corps might be formed at Sydney and Melbourne, composed of the labouring population of these towns, and officered by the inhabitants of higher station. The only expense for which the Legislative Council would be called upon to provide would be that of uniforms for the men, and pay during the hours of training. I send you herewith, in order to assist you in the consideration of the question whether a measure of the nature above averted to might not be adopted with advantage, a copy of the regulations respecting the dockyard battalions.

" I cannot conclude this despatch without expressing my confidence that the inhabitants of New South Wales have too much of the spirit which has always distinguished the British nation, to be slow in coming forward to answer this invitation to organize themselves for their own defence.

" I have, etc.

" (Signed) GREY."

Extract of a Despatch from Earl Grey to Sir C. A. Fitzroy, dated Downing-street, June 1, 1848.

" I have to acknowledge the receipt of your Despatch, No. 247, of the 18th December, with the copies therein enclosed, of a Report, with its annexures, of a Select Committee of the Legislative Council of New South Wales, relative to the question as to the expediency of making some addition to the police force, in consequence of the reduction in the numbers of the troops stationed in that Colony.

" My Despatch, No. 11, Military, of the 4th March last, will have apprised you of the views which Her Majesty's Government entertain on the subject of the military defence of the Colony under your Government. I cannot however assent to the remarks which have been made by the Committee, that Her Majesty's Government have afforded protection to New Zealand by depriving New South Wales of the amount of protection to which it is fairly entitled. The force which was withdrawn from New South Wales was sent to New Zealand only to meet a pressing emergency, and Her Majesty's Government do not contemplate the permanent maintenance of a large regular force in the latter, any more than in the former Colony."

Copy of a Despatch from Earl Grey to Governor
Sir C. A. Fitzroy.

"*Downing-street, November* 21, 1846.

" Sir,

" In my Despatch of the 24th of November 1846, No. 2, Military, I instructed you to make immediate arrangements, in concert with the officer commanding the troops in New South Wales, for sending the whole of the disposable force now serving there to Wellington, with the utmost practicable despatch. I calculated that it would be in your power, without danger, to send at least 900 men for this service, still retaining a small force at Sydney, which, under the circumstances of New South Wales at that time, was all that I considered indispensable. I was of opinion that New South Wales might be regarded as being perfectly safe from any attack from a foreign enemy, there being no native tribes capable of engaging in serious hostilities with the Colonists, and the Convict establishment having been reduced so low, while so great an increase has taken place in the numbers of the free population, that there was no longer the necessity which some years ago existed for maintaining a considerable military force to guard against the risk of an attempt to rise on the part of the convicts; and that, under these circumstances, there was no part of Her Majesty's dominions in which there was less occasion for a large body of troops. I found that, with the exception of those at Sydney, the troops serving in New South Wales were broken up into small detachments, and were obviously performing duties more analogous to those of a police corps than of a part of Her Majesty's regular army. I considered that these were duties which the heavy demands upon the services of the British army did not admit that it should be called upon any longer to undertake. I informed you that Her Majesty's confidential servants would consider it their duty to take care that her naval and military forces should afford efficient protection from the attack of any foreign enemy to so important a part of her dominions as New South Wales, but that, for the maintenance of internal order and tranquillity, it was only reasonable that the Colonists should themselves be called upon to provide, by the formation of an adequate force of police, or, if necessary, of militia. I instructed you to bring this subject under the immediate consideration of the Legislative Council, and under no circumstance to consider yourself authorized to delay sending to New Zealand the force I had named.

" In my Despatch of the 4th March 1848, No. 11, Military, I instructed you to inform the Legislative Council of New South Wales, that while the right of the Australian Colonies to look for their fair share of that protection which it is the object of Her Majesty's naval and military forces to extend to all parts of the British Empire was fully recognized by Her Majesty's Servants, they were of opinion that these Colonies have made so much progress in wealth and population, that their inhabitants might reasonably be expected to bear also a part of the heavy charges which, with a view to that protection, are imposed upon their fellow-subjects residing in the United Kingdom, and that the smallest contribution towards these charges, which ought now to be required from the Colonists, was that of providing any additional means of local defence which might be required ; and I suggested to you the propriety of inviting the principal gentlemen of the Colony to exert themselves in forming a volunteer artillery force.

" In my despatch of the 1st of June following, No. 16, Military, after noticing the Report of the Committee of the Legislative Council of New South Wales, on the question how far it might be expedient to make some addition to the police, in consequence of the withdrawal of a portion of the troops, I explained that the force so withdrawn was sent to New Zealand to meet a pressing emergency; and I stated that Her Majesty's Government did not contemplate the permanent maintenance of a large regular force in that Colony, any more than in New South Wales.

"These communications will have fully prepared you for the reduction which Her Majesty's Government find it absolutely necessary to make of the military expenditure of the Australian Colonies, and I have accordingly to acquaint you that Her Majesty's Government propose to transfer to the Colony of New South Wales the barracks and all military buildings and lands not immediately required for the preservation of stores, and that the charge of providing, maintaining, and repairing quarters for Her Majesty's troops in New South Wales must in future be undertaken by that Colony, and that the force to be retained there, will be reduced to a guard in the capital of the Colony, and in the town of Melbourne, which will be the capital of the proposed province of Victoria. If a greater amount of force is required, the Local Legislature must either make provision for raising a more considerable body of police than is now maintained, or some other description of local force, or else provide for the pay and allowances of an additional number of Her Majesty's regular army, in which case there would be no objection to allow additional regiments to serve there.

"In adopting the policy which I am thus called upon to prescribe to you for your future guidance, Her Majesty's Government are swayed by the consideration that New South Wales already possesses representative institutions, that these will, it cannot be doubted, very speedily be extended to the other Australian Colonies, and that all the restrictions heretofore imposed on Colonial trade by Imperial Legislation have now been removed.

" It is my duty to apprise you that, if the Colonial Legislature should not think proper to make adequate provision for the maintenance of the necessary barracks in a manner in which the health and comfort of the troops will be as well secured as at present, it will be incumbent on Her Majesty's Government to remove them altogether.

" I have only further to acquaint you that, in giving to the Colony the barracks and other buildings which are to be transferred to it under the present instructions, it must be distinctly understood that Her Majesty's Government reserve to themselves the right of resuming possession, if at any future time it should in their judgement become necessary to do so; some nominal rent must therefore be reserved as a recognition of the title of the Crown to the property.

" You will take an early opportunity of reporting to me the arrangements which you shall make in pursuance of the present instruction.

" I have, etc.
" (Signed)   GREY."

---

*Copy of a Despatch from Earl Grey to Governor
Sir C. A. Fitzroy.*

" *Downing-street, June* 21, 1850.

" SIR,

" I have the honour to acknowledge the receipt of your Despatch, Military, No. 227, of the 7th November last, with the minute therein enclosed, of the deliberations of

the Executive Council of New South Wales, on the de-
fenceless state of Port Jackson.

" Having attentively considered that minute, I am compelled to state that, so far from finding any reason for altering my previous view of the subject, I conceive that the
facts which are set out in it are calculated to confirm that
view.   I have no doubt that prudence does prescribe the
erection of works sufficient to protect the city of Sydney
from a predatory attack ; but the great value of the property
it contains, and the wealth and prosperity evinced by the
very large sums of money stated to be in the·banks, afford
proof no less of the ability of the Colony to meet the expense of providing such protection, than of the necessity of
doing so.

" On this subject I have to remind you, that many of
the great commercial cities of this Country are even now
not less open than Sydney to predatory attacks, while some
even of our arsenals and important military stations are
as yet but very imperfectly protected; and it is altogether
unreasonable to suppose that Parliament could be asked to
vote money from the revenue of the United Kingdom for
the defence of Sydney, while there is still a want of similar
works at home, more especially as it must be borne in
mind how much more lightly the inhabitants of New
South Wales are taxed than those of Her Majesty's subjects
who remain in this Country.

" Her Majesty's Servants are prepared to take measures
for affording to the inhabitants of the Colonies their fair
share of protection as a portion of the British Empire.
Any attack made upon New South Wales, or any injury
to any inhabitant of the Colony, would be resented in the
same manner as an attack upon any other part of Her
Majesty's dominions, or an injury to any other of Her

Majesty's subjects. But while we admit this as a rule to be observed, we consider that Her Majesty's subjects inhabiting the Colonies must take their fair share with their fellow-subjects at home in bearing the common burden of providing for the safety of the Empire as a whole, and that the smallest contribution which they can be expected to make towards this object is that of undertaking the local expenses which are required.

" It appears to have escaped the notice of yourself and the Executive Council, that in the earlier days of British colonization the Colonists were left to depend in a far greater degree than at present on their exertions. The inhabitants of what are now the United States of America were left, up to the time of the separation, with exceedingly little assistance from the Mother-country, to defend themselves from the numerous and warlike tribes of Indians by whom they were surrounded; nay, even during the war with France, a large part of the burden of maintaining the arduous contest with that powerful monarchy with its Indian allies, fell upon the British Amercian Provinces, and not upon the Mother-country. At the present time the Legislature of Jamaica has the entire charge of the fortifications of the island.

" New South Wales has now advanced so far in wealth and population, that, without further aid from the Mother-country than you will have learned from my recent despatches it is intended to afford, the Colony is well able to do what is necessary in order to provide for its own defence.

" At the same time Her Majesty's Government will be glad to afford such assistance as can be given with justice to the rest of Her Majesty's subjects, in carrying into effect such measures as the Colonial Legislature may consider expedient with a view to its defence. It is not possible to comply with the request that the troops lately sent to New Zealand should be brought back, because measures have already been taken for the reduction of the force in that Colony; but if it should be considered desirable to execute any fortifications by military labour, Her Majesty's Government would willingly take steps for stationing an additional regiment in New South Wales, and also a detachment of sappers and miners, provided the Legislative Council would vote the amount required for their pay, including both their ordinary pay and the working pay to which they would be entitled. No charge would be made upon the Colony for the conveyance of the troops there, nor on account of the claims to pensions which the soldiers would acquire during their stay in the Colony; and further, whenever it became necessary to relieve a regiment so stationed in New South Wales, encouragement would be given to the soldiers belonging to it to take their discharge, thus effecting, without cost to the Colony, a useful addition, not only to its population, but to its means of defence, as men so discharged could, under the existing regulations, be called upon to serve against an enemy in case of need. Her Majesty's Government would also willingly take measures for increasing the number of enrolled pensioners in the Colony, if the Local Legislature would provide for the cost of conveying them there, and settling them in the situations where they might be most useful.

" You will take an early opportunity of communicating these observations to the Executive Council; and you will concert with that body the course which it may be expedient to pursue with the view of bringing the subject under the consideration of the Legislative Council.

" I have, etc.

" (Signed)   GREY."

C.

Copy of a Despatch from Earl Grey to Governor Sir C. Grey.

" Downing-street, February 15, 1851.

" SIR,

" I have had the honour of receiving your Despatch, No. 94, of the 13th of December last, transmitting a memorial addressed to the Queen by the House of Assembly of Jamaica, expressing great alarm as to the difficulty of obtaining a supply of labour for the cultivation of the land, which was anticipated from the frightful mortality, principally among the labouring classes, which has been lately occasioned in the island by cholera, and praying that Her Majesty will order all captured Africans to be sent to Jamaica, and will adopt such other measures for the speedy and adequate supply of free emigrants from Africa, as Her Majesty's Ministers may deem most advisable. I have also received your subsequent Despatch of 16th December, No. 96, transmitting a similar memorial from the Legislative Council of Jamaica. I have not failed to lay both these memorials before Her Majesty, and Her Majesty has been pleased to receive them very graciously.

" In former despatches I have already expressed to you the great concern with which Her Majesty's Servants received intelligence of the very severe calamity by which Jamaica has been visited, and I directed you to adopt such measures as appeared to be immediately practicable for mitigating the sufferings it must have occasioned. But I concur with the two branches of the Colonial Legislature, in believing that the aggravation of the scarcity of labour previously existing in Jamaica, by the loss of so large a number of labourers by the disease which has ravaged the island, is likely to prove one of the most serious consequences of the calamity, unless prompt measures are taken to avert the evil. I have always been of opinion that the labouring, no less than the proprietary classes in Jamaica, are deeply interested in the success of the great branches of industry which are carried on there, because, unless the production of its staple articles of export can be continued with advantage, the most civilized of the inhabitants of the island would have no inducement to reside in it, while their departure could not fail greatly to retard, if not to arrest, the progress of improvement in that part of the population which has so recently emerged from slavery and barbarism. Hence it is my most anxious wish to co-operate with the Colonial Legislature (to which the power and duty of adopting measures to meet the emergency mainly belong) in the endeavour to obviate the new difficulties with which the planters of Jamaica are now threatened, and by which the prospect of improvement in their condition, which I had hoped was beginning to appear, has been again obscured.

" I have thought it right, upon a subject so deeply affecting the welfare of Jamaica, to communicate with some of the gentlemen resident in this country who are most largely interested in the Colony, and I have derived much assistance from the information and suggestions I have received from them, in considering the measures it would be advisable to adopt. The most important of their suggestions are embodied in a memorandum addressed to the Speaker of the House of Assembly, which will be transmitted to Jamaica by the present mail, and of which, and of the letter in which it was communicated to me, I enclose copies for your information. The suggestions of the gentlemen who have signed this memorandum are well deserving of the consideration of the Assembly: and in the hope of giving some further assistance to the Legislature in dealing with a subject of so much difficulty and urgency, I will proceed to state my views on these proposals, and on those of the Legislature, as well as on some others which have occurred to myself, or have been suggested to me from other quarters. In doing so, I may repeat observations already addressed to yourself, or to the governors of other Colonies in the West Indies, in despatches of which you are in possession; but, at the risk of such repetition, I think it will be convenient that I should state in a connected form the conclusions as to the means which should be resorted to for supplying the existing deficiency of labour in Jamaica, to which I have been led, by a close and anxious study of the working of the various plans, which during the last few years have been tried for a similar object in different Colonies.

"Though I am far from believing (for reasons which I shall have occasion to state in a subsequent part of this despatch) that immigration is the only practicable mode of increasing the available supply of labour in Jamaica, it is undoubtedly the first and most obvious resource which suggests itself. I do not doubt the expediency of adopting all practicable means for the introduction of a large number of immigrants of a suitable description into the Colony. With this view, it is the prayer of the Assembly in their memorial to Her Majesty, that all Negroes liberated from slavery by Her Majesty's cruizers should be sent to Jamaica, and that such measures as may be considered most advisable should be adopted for obtaining free emigrants from the coast of Africa. With regard to the Negroes found on board slave-ships captured by Her Majesty's cruizers, I have to observe that already all those who, without improper constraint, can be induced to go to the West India Colonies are sent to these Colonies free of expense to them by Her Majesty's Government; the number therefore to be sent to Jamaica could only be increased by depriving some of the other Colonies of the share of this advantage which they now enjoy; and considering that in these Colonies the want of labour is not less urgent than in Jamaica, though they have hitherto been spared from the disease which has visited that Island, this is a course which Her Majesty's Government could not with propriety adopt. With respect to the introduction of free emigrants from Africa, I concur with the Assembly in thinking that it would be highly beneficial if it could be accomplished; but you are aware that every endeavour which has hitherto been made to procure free emigrants from Africa has failed; and a report which has very recently reached me of the last attempt, which was made only a few months ago, to obtain emigrants from the Kroo Coast, is not encouraging as to the prospect which exists of greater success attending any further experiments of the same kind.

" In the memorandum transmitted to me by Mr. Macgregor it is suggested that an endeavour should be made to induce the free black inhabitants of some of the United States to settle in Jamaica. I have already, in my circular despatch of the 16th of October last, called your attention to the subject; and since that despatch was written I have obtained further information, which tends to confirm the opinion that there is a reasonable prospect that, if proper arrangements were adopted for the purpose, a large number of immigrants might be obtained from among the coloured and black inhabitants of the United States and of Canada. I need hardly observe that there is no immigration which would be attended with so many advantages as that of the class of persons now adverted to. These people are in general trained labourers, accustomed to the usages of civilized society, and speaking the language of the Colony in which it is proposed that they should settle; it is obvious therefore how much more useful they would be than a much larger number of the rude inhabitants of Africa, or even than the natives of India or of China. The distance also from which these immigrants would have to be brought is inconsiderable, so that their introduction would not be attended with heavy expense, and there is reason to believe that their removal is earnestly desired by the communities of which they now form a part, and in which their presence in the actual state of society is a source of discomfort both to themselves and to others.

" The question then arises, What are the steps which it would be advisable to adopt in order to set on foot an extensive immigration of persons of this description from the continent of America ? and after much consideration, I am led to believe that the best course which can be adopted is that of endeavouring to enlist private enterprise in the undertaking. I am of opinion that the exertions of individuals would be more likely to be successful than any public agency which could be made use of in obtaining immigrants well suited to the wants of the Colony, provided proper facilities were afforded to those who stand in need of labour to procure labourers for themselves wherever they can be found.

" But to encourage the efforts of individuals to obtain labour for themselves, it would be necessary to make some arrangement for securing to those who incur the trouble and expense of introducing labourers the advantage they have a right to expect from doing so. It is probably with this view that the gentlemen who have signed the memorandum transmitted to me by Mr. Macgregor have suggested, that contracts for three years should be legalized in Jamaica, as they have been in some other Colonies. You have already been informed that if the Legislature of Jamaica should think fit to pass a law for this purpose, I should not consider it necessary to advise Her Majesty to withhold her sanction from it ; but in repeating that I am prepared to abstain from objecting to such legislation, I must also repeat the expression of my strong opinion as to the extreme impolicy of encouraging contracts of this description. It is obvious that the only advantage which can result to the employers from having their labourers bound to them by contracts for three years, is that of obtaining the labour of those who are so bound on better terms than they could expect to get the same amount of labour from persons under no engagement. This advantage may be expected to arise more from the regularity with which labour can be commanded, than from the rate of wages to be paid to the persons so engaged ; still the return for the expense incurred in the introduction of labourers is looked for in some form or other, from the right to their service for a certain time. No doubt at first sight the scheme appears sufficiently plausible; but the experiment has been repeatedly tried, and contracts of this kind have invariably disappointed those who have entered into them. More than twenty years ago, when the want of labour in New South Wales was exceedingly urgent, some gentlemen having property in that Colony engaged labourers in this Country, and sent them out under contracts to work for them for a term which had been agreed upon. One of the persons by whom this experiment was tried, and who had been most sanguine as to its success, described to me its utter failure; nor were the causes of that failure difficult to understand. It is a truth too obvious to escape the most ordinary observation, that men in general can only be impelled to strenuous and persevering industry by some very powerful motive, while no such motive is brought to bear upon men engaged by long contracts to work at a fixed rate of wages, not higher at all events, if it is not lower, than that which, unfettered by such long engagements, they can command. If men so employed should labour carelessly and inefficiently, the employer has no adequate means of enforcing increased exertion, since to discharge them and cancel the contract, which, in a wholesome state of the relations between the employer and labourer, is a sufficient punishment, would be a reward and not a punishment to the labourer, who would thus be set free from an engagement which prevents him from making the most of his labour. No doubt the master whose labourer does not perform his contracted task, may carry him before the magistrate for punishment; but punishment so inflicted will not enforce industry that will be remunerative to the employer, and the labourer who is not subject to the stern compulsion of slavery, cannot be impelled to real exertion except by making it his interest to exert himself. In this Country, which for successful industry may justly claim to stand at the head of all the nations of the world, it is well known that the employers of labour find it expedient to bring self-interest to bear as directly as possible on the labourers, and that piece-work, whenever it is practicable, is greatly preferred to day labour; though, in the state of the demand and supply of labour which exists here, the power of discharging an idle labourer gives great authority to the master in enforcing exertion on the part of labourers engaged by the day. I must add, that the state of feeling created by the existence of slavery in the United States would, I believe, render the most eligible emigrants who might be obtained there, peculiarly averse to entering into contracts for labour for three years.

" I have entered thus fully into the objections which, in my judgement, render it inexpedient to attempt to bind by long engagements immigrants who may be induced to resort to the British Colonies, because I entertain a strong conviction that such an attempt would be certain to lead to the failure of any plan of immigration of which it formed a part, while at the same time the legitimate object which is aimed at by such engagements is capable of being attained by other means which are not liable to the same objection.　Nothing can be more reasonable than that those who incur the trouble and expense of introducing labourers into Colonies where labour is in great demand, and consequently bears a high value, should be repaid out of the earnings of the labourers so introduced; and I should strongly recommend to the Legislature of Jamaica that every facility which can possibly be given by law should be afforded for making and enforcing contracts founded on this principle.　For this purpose, I am of opinion that a law should be passed, rendering valid in the Colony engagements entered into by immigrants before their embarkation, to repay by instalments such a sum of money as may be agreed upon between them and the persons by whom they are conveyed to the Colony.　It would probably be convenient that such engagements should be in the form of simple notes of hand, promising to pay the sum agreed upon by certain weekly instalments, and that they should be witnessed by the master of the vessel in which the immigrants are embarked, and probably also by some public authority at the port of embarkation.　If that port is a foreign one, the British consul would probably be the best person to perform this duty. It would also, I think, be advisable to provide that when, on the arrival in Jamaica of a ship conveying immigrants embarked upon these terms, none of them should be permitted to land until they had been identified before the immigration agent, or some officer acting under him, as the persons who had signed or affixed their marks to the engagements previously witnessed by the master of the vessel, and a certificate to this effect should then be added to the engagement. Without some such provision as this, it would probably be difficult, after the departure of the vessel, to prove the signature of the immigrant, so as to enforce his promise to repay the cost of his passage. It would further be necessary to provide that every immigrant introduced under such a contract should be bound to give notice to the person with whom he had entered into it, or to the immigration agent, through the police, where he intended to reside, and that till his debt was discharged he should be liable to the penalties attached to fraud if he should, without previous notice to the same parties, go more than five or ten miles from the place where he had signified his intention to reside.

" Great care would be necessary in framing an enactment of this kind, so that on the one hand it might be effectual for its purpose, and on the other it might not press with undue severity on the immigrants, so as to discourage the immigration of the coloured people from the United States and from Canada. This class would not fail speedily to learn from the first immigrants what treatment they had experienced in the Colony; and nothing would be so impolitic as to allow this treatment to give just ground for complaint, since this would infallibly put a stop to an immigration, which is calculated to be so

highly beneficial to the Colony, and which, if properly
encouraged, is, I believe, capable of being established on
a very large scale. I have only to add, on this point, that
the objection I have urged to long contracts for labour
would not apply to contracts entered into with immigrants
thus bound to repay the cost of their introduction into the
Colony, to give them employment at the full wages of
the Colony, but with a power reserved to the immigrant
of cancelling the engagement at his pleasure, on giving a
month's notice of his desire to do so. An assurance of
employment on such terms might be necessary to induce
the labourer to emigrate; and if the wages agreed upon
were such as to make his being discharged a punishment
instead of an advantage, a power might be reserved to the
master, in the case of misconduct or idleness on the part
of the emigrant, to cancel, before a magistrate, this part
of the agreement, leaving in full force the engagement to
repay the debt contracted by the immigrant.

" I am of opinion, that the passing of a simple law of
this kind, by enabling proprietors to make arrangements
for themselves, and to engage labourers wherever they
might be found, whether on the continent of America, in
some of the southern countries of Europe, or in China,
would afford the best means of supplying the present deficiency of labour. But I should see no objection to combining a law of this kind with the adoption of the recommendation of the gentlemen whose memorandum I have
sent you, by taking measures also for the introduction of
labourers at the public expense. If this is done, it appears
to me that it would be advisable to pass a law placing such
immigrants under regulations similar to those which have
been for some time in force with much success in Mauritius, and which have lately been adopted also in Trinidad

and Guiana. Or, what would perhaps be still simpler, the amount advanced from the Colonial Treasury to cover the cost of introducing these immigrants might be made a debt, recoverable from them in the same manner as similar debts would be recoverable by individuals under the law I have suggested. In this case the immigration agent, on behalf of the public, should make the advance, and should have the same power as a private creditor, of recovering the amount by instalments from the immigrant.

" But I have already observed, that I do not consider immigration as by any means the only source from which an increase in the supply of available labour may be obtained in Jamaica. Every account which has reached me of the actual state of society in the Island, tends to confirm my impression that the laws and arrangements now in force are not calculated to call forth the energies of the existing population, and that, if proper inducements to exertion were held out to them, they might, without being at all overtasked, be made to perform much more useful labour than at present. I am unwilling to touch upon topics calculated to revive the memory of controversies now happily forgotten ; but at the same time, in order more clearly to explain my views as to the policy which ought now to be adopted, I hope I may without offence observe, that experience has confirmed the opinion which I expressed at the time, that it was a great and unfortunate error, when slavery was abolished, not to place the emancipated population under regulations calculated to impose upon them the necessity of greater exertion, and at the same time to provide for various objects necessary for their real welfare, but the importance of which it was not likely that they would be able to understand.

" It was not sufficiently understood at the time, that as

during slavery the greater part of the food consumed by the Negroes was derived from their provision-grounds, and the value of the supplies they received from their masters was trifling, compared to that of the labour they performed, the effect of suddenly releasing them from the obligation of performing gratuitous labour, was to leave them without any adequate motive to work for wages for more than a small portion of their time. By devoting a comparatively small part of the week to hired labour, and working as before in their provision-grounds, they were able to live much better than they had ever been accustomed to do, and this being the case, their conduct would have been unlike that of men in any other country of the world, if they had continued to exert themselves as formerly. In this Country, when an unexpected demand for some particular article occasions a sudden and great increase in the wages of any one description of workmen, it is generally found that, in the first instance, the men do not work as long and as hard as before, but take out a part of the greater value of their labour in the enjoyment of more leisure; in like manner, the Negroes of Jamaica naturally availed themselves of being suddenly made masters of the whole returns of their labour, to indulge largely in the luxury of idleness. They did so, indeed, to a less extent than might have been anticipated, as they adopted for a time habits of profuse expense, which could only be met by labour; but still the immediate and very great falling off in the produce of the Island, notwithstanding the economy of labour which was introduced when it became dearer, proves to how great an extent the amount of work done by them was diminished.

" But it certainly was not calculated to promote the real welfare of the emancipated population, that they should be allowed thus largely to indulge in idleness. To men, whatever may be their colour, their country, or their rank, idleness is ever a source of corruption, and I fear it is not to be doubted that the Negroes have been no exception to the rule, and that their advancement in civilization and morality, in the seventeen years which have nearly elapsed since slavery was abolished, have been by no means equal to that which might have been expected, had they been placed in circumstances which would have imposed upon them the necessity of greater industry; nor can it be doubted that they might have been called upon to submit to a greater amount of labour for objects of the utmost importance to themselves. Though their mere animal instincts led them to work sufficiently to obtain the means of gratifying their rude desires, and for the supply of their immediate physical wants, there are other wants of human nature no less real, which they were incapable of understanding, and for which therefore they made no provision. Education, religious instruction, and the procuring of medical advice for themselves and for their children, were unfortunately neglected. It is true they did subscribe what upon the whole amounted to considerable sums, for the support of chapels and schools; but the information which has been obtained on the state of education in the Island, proves beyond all doubt that, notwithstanding the assistance rendered by this country, the provision which has been made for education and for religious instruction, has fallen far short of the wants of the population. The deficiencies with regard to medical aid have not been less striking : during slavery medical aid had been furnished at the charge of the master, and the emancipated slaves did not understand the necessity of paying for such assistance for themselves and for their children; and to this, and to their bad management of their children during sickness, and the consequently large proportion of deaths during infancy, it is, I believe, to be attributed that the population of Jamaica has not, since the abolition of slavery, increased with the rapidity which might have been expected, in a country where all the necessaries of life are in such extreme abundance.

" Hence it appears to me greatly to be regretted, that on the abolition of slavery the emancipated population were not required to make some small weekly payment for the the support of schools, of churches and chapels, and of public dispensaries and hospitals.   Such institutions would have greatly contributed to their civilization and moral improvement; and the necessity of earning in each week the means of making the required payment, would have been a wholesome stimulus to industry, and would have supplied that motive for labour which was unhappily wanting.   It is not, however, for the mere purpose of expressing regret for the past, that I have referred to the error which was in my judgement committed at the period of emancipation; my object is rather to point out, that if these views are just, it may not yet be too late to adopt, partially at least, the policy which ought then to have been acted upon.   It is true that the difficulty of doing so is greatly increased.   At that time the weekly payment which I have suggested might have been required from the emancipated slaves, would have been a substitute for the galling yoke of slavery, and it would therefore have been gladly and cheerfully submitted to, while at the present moment it would be felt as a new burden unjustly imposed on a particular class, and could not therefore be safely required in its simplest form.   But it deserves to be considered by the Assembly, whether the present moment is not favourable to the adoption of measures founded upon the principle which I have endeavoured to explain.

" The recent calamity has naturally called public attention to the great deficiency which exists in the means of supplying medical assistance to the population of Jamaica; it seems therefore to be a good opportunity of reviving the consideration of a measure (suggested, but not adopted, on a former occasion) for establishing parochial hospitals and dispensaries. I am persuaded that such institutions would be found highly useful; and the expense of maintaining them, as they would be established mainly for the benefit of the labouring classes, might, with great propriety, be defrayed by a rate upon houses; the amount levied upon each house being made to depend upon the number of its habitual inmates. In public hospitals and dispensaries thus maintained, every rate-payer should be entitled to obtain gratuitous treatment in sickness for himself and his family, thus rendering the arrangement, in effect, equivalent to the establishment by law of medical clubs, such as those which exist in many English parishes, with the single but important difference, that in Jamaica it would be legally obligatory on every inhabitant of the parish to contribute to the institution. For this difference there would be ample ground in the fact that experience has too fatally proved, that the provision made voluntarily for the treatment of the sick in Jamaica is lamentably deficient. The benefit to be derived from such institutions as I have mentioned would be much increased, if the proposed hospitals were combined with the parochial workhouses, which would be put upon a proper footing for affording relief in cases of destitution, on the system now adopted in well-regulated workhouses in this Country. In Jamaica, where the demand for labour is so great, and a subsistence so easily obtained, it is scarcely possible that any but the sick or the infirm can suffer from want, if they are willing to exert themselves for their own support, and real distress will generally be found to proceed from sickness. Still it will be impossible to enforce, with due strictness, laws against vagrancy, unless the means exist of offering relief in well-regulated workhouses to those who profess, however untruly, that they are driven to vagrancy by distress. Hence the obvious advantages of combining in one establishment the hospital and the workhouse, in which relief is given both to real and pretended distress.

"The want of schools has been no less clearly established than the deficiency of the existing arrangements for the medical treatment of the sick. This absence of any proper provision for the education of the rising generation is an evil of a very serious kind; and when it is considered that, by the existing constitution of Jamaica, the acquisition of political power is no less open to the negro than to the white man, and that in a few years the former race, from their great numerical superiority, can hardly fail to become possessed of a predominating influence, it cannot be doubted that to the future welfare of the community it is of the greatest importance that those who must possess this power should be prepared by education for its exercise. Effective schools ought therefore, in my judgement, to be established throughout the Island; and the expense of doing so is one which might, with the strictest justice, be provided for by such a rate upon houses as I have already described. I should not recommend that any attempt should be made to require the population to send their children to the schools to be thus established; it would be sufficient that all the inhabitants of the several parishes should be called upon to pay their share for the maintenance of effective schools, with the privilege of sending their children to them without any additional payment, if they thought proper to do so. I need hardly observe that the system of maintaining schools by rates has existed in Massachusetts and some other states of the American Union since their first settlement, and has been attended with the best results. I am aware that, in establishing such a system in Jamaica, much difficulty would arise from religious differences; but this difficulty has been successfully contended with in Canada, where, without neglecting religious instruction, the children of parents of various persuasions are educated together; and when the need of some improved system of education is so urgent as it has been proved to be in Jamaica, I should hope that the members of all the different religious communities which exist in the Island would concur in not allowing their differences to stand in the way of that improvement. I cannot leave this part of the subject without adding, that I conceive education to be of great importance to the industrial prosperity of Jamaica, since agricultural improvement can hardly be carried on with spirit and effect except by means of instructed and intelligent labourers.

" In proposing that the expense of providing medical assistance and education for the population of Jamaica should be met by a rate imposed upon houses, according to the number of their inmates, I have had in view both the justice, considering the purposes for which the money is required, of this mode of levying it, and also the advantage to be derived from it by its being calculated to stimulate the labouring classes to industry. I have not, however, forgot the observations in your Despatches of the 20th and 21st of October 1848, on the discontent and irritation which you state to have been produced by the system of parochial assessments, pressing heavily, and in galling manner, on the occupiers of small tenements and holdings of land. I am well aware of the great danger which might result from rousing feelings of this kind in an ignorant and excitable population; they ought not therefore to be subjected to a new burden of the kind I have suggested, without taking care that it is both light in amount, and collected in the manner least onerous to those by whom it is paid, and also that the utmost pains should be taken in explaining that this payment is made for objects in which they are deeply interested. Hence the penalties for default of payment should be as moderate as possible, not exceeding two days of forced labour for every shilling left unpaid; and the magistrates and special Justices should be instructed carefully to explain to the people the advantages they would receive in return for the payment demanded from them before the period fixed for its collection. It would likewise be most desirable that while this new demand is made upon the population, they should at the same time be relieved, if possible, from some of the most objectionable of the present taxes. I would more especially recommend a revision of the duties upon ordinary articles of food, such as flour, butter, and cheese. The duties upon these and upon other articles of a similar kind, I should consider it highly expedient to abolish or to reduce, if the state of the revenue should render it practicable to do so. It is I think impossible to doubt that duties of this kind must have a tendency very injurious to the great staple branches of Colonial industry. While the sugar and coffee planters are suffering so much from a deficiency of labour, it is obvious that in levying the revenue required for the public service the utmost pains should be taken to avoid every tax which has a tendency to divert labour from these occupations. But taxes upon imported provisions have this tendency in the highest degree; by raising the price of such provisions they must necessarily increase the consumption of provi-

sions grown in the Colony, and therefore the demand for
the produce raised by the Negro in his own ground, thus
artificially increasing the profit to be derived from this description of labour, and at the same time making an equally
artificial reduction in the amount of food which can be
purchased by the wages earned in the cane-field. Thus
these duties are directly calculated to discourage the labourer from working for hire, and to lead him to prefer
working in his own provision-ground. It is hardly neces-·
sary to observe, that in the actual state of society in Jamaica, it would be desirable that whatever revenue is
required should be raised by taxes having precisely the
opposite effect.

" For these reasons I consider it to be of great importance that the duties in question should be reduced, if they
cannot be entirely abolished. I am not ignorant that the
present state of the Colonial finances opposes considerable
difficulty in the way of the reduction of any taxes. But
from the information contained in your Despatches of the
9th and 22nd of December 1849, I am led to believe that
by a more exact collection of existing taxes, and particularly the land-tax, and by reverting to the former practice
of the Colony, and leaving certain local charges to be defrayed by parochial instead of by general taxes, the deficiency which would be occasioned by repealing the duties
to which I have pointed out the objections, would be more
than covered. I must add, that on other grounds I conceive it to be of the utmost importance that both these
modes of replenishing the Colonial treasury should be resorted to. Nothing is so prejudicial to the public interest
as to allow taxes which are not repealed to be negligently
and imperfectly collected, since this affords a direct encouragement to fraud, and a premium to dishonesty. The

land-tax also is, of all the public taxes in Jamaica, that to which there is the least objection, as its tendency must be rather favourable than the reverse to industry, in a Colony in which the great difficulty with which the Planters have to contend, is that arising from the too easy terms on which the use of land can be obtained by the labouring population.

" I am no less persuaded of the impolicy of diminishing the parochial burdens at the expense of the general revenue: parochial taxation properly imposed is calculated, for the reasons I have already stated, to act as a stimulus to industry; whereas import duties, unless kept within the most moderate limits, must tend to discourage the formation of a taste among the people for the comforts and luxuries of civilized life, and such a taste could not be developed without creating new and powerful motives for exertion. I have reason to believe, indeed, that the existing mode of levying parochial taxes requires to be revised; it seems objectionable that they should be charged upon stock and upon wheels, a mode of assessment which might fall most heavily upon the most active and enterprising cultivators. Whether rates should be levied, as in this country, according to the value of the property assessed, or rather, as you have formerly suggested, according to the extent of land occupied by the ratepayers, is a question on which I have not the means of forming a judgement.   The principle of apportioning the charge according to the value of the property on which it is imposed would seem to be the fairest; but on the other hand, I can easily understand that to make a valuation which shall not only be really correct, but which shall satisfy those concerned that it is so, may in Jamaica be a matter of insuperable difficulty; even in this country it is not very easily accomplished.   Perhaps a middle course might be the best, and land might be assessed at different rates, according to the nature of the cultivation, one rate per acre being imposed on all pasture land, another on land growing canes, and another on provision grounds, taking as the basis of the calculation the average value of the return derived from the land by those several modes of occupation.

"I am persuaded that the various measures I have suggested would tend, by their combined effect, to stimulate the industry of the working classes in Jamaica, and would greatly contribute to increase the advantage which may be derived from an addition to the number of labourers by immigration. But it is obvious that this is a policy of which the success must entirely depend upon a firm and equal administration of the law, and upon the efficient maintenance of order and obedience to authority throughout the Colony. It is not to be expected that the Negro population would willingly submit to the new burdens imposed upon them, if they should perceive that the land tax and other charges falling upon the higher classes of society were negligently collected and imperfectly paid, and if they were not satisfied that the produce of the rates were properly applied to their professed objects. Nor would it be possible to enforce a rate upon houses, if any part of the population were allowed to wander about without any recognized place of abode, thus escaping the charge which would fall upon the settled and industrious inhabitants of the various parishes. I would therefore most strongly recommend to the Legislature to adopt such regulations, as may ensure the punctual and exact collection of the rates and taxes, both general and parochial, and may subject the collectors to an effective responsibility for the due performance of their duty. The constitution of vestries and other bodies to which the

expenditure of parochial and other local rates is entrusted
should be considered, and if necessary improved in such a
manner as to give the lower class of ratepayers some share
in the management of their own affairs, and the proceedings
of these local bodies should be subjected to the supervision
of some superior authority, and their accounts to an independent audit.   Lastly, if the existing law against vagrancy
is insufficient to check that offence, its faults should be corrected, and it should be considered whether the reductions
which have been made in the police have not been carried
too far, bearing in mind that there can be no such short-
sighted and injudicious economy as that, which would refuse
the necessary outlay for maintaining the police in a state
of complete efficiency, for the preservation of order and the
enforcement of the law, without which industry can never
flourish.

" In conclusion, I have to desire that you will lay before
the Assembly a copy of this despatch, with my assurance
that in making the various suggestions which I have now
offered for their consideration, it is far from my wish to
dictate to them what measures to adopt, on which it is
their duty and their right to determine according to their
own judgement.   My only object has been to afford them
any assistance in my power in considering what are the
legislative measures best calculated to promote the welfare
of all classes of the inhabitants of Jamaica, and to enable
them to turn to account the great natural advantages of
this magnificent island.   The present appears to be an im-..
portant crisis in the history of the colony, and its future
prosperity will mainly depend upon the judgement with
which the measures now to be taken are adapted to its real
wants.   It is incumbent therefore upon the Legislature to
which the destinies of Jamaica are mainly entrusted, well

and maturely to consider the course which should now be adopted; and I have thought it my duty to lay before them somewhat fully my own views as to the policy which ought to be pursued, because these views are founded on an experience now extending over a very considerable number of years, and on a careful study of the state of society both in Jamaica and in other colonies from a period antecedent to the abolition of slavery, with a close observation of the various changes which that measure and others consequent upon it have produced. I entertain a firm conviction that whatever errors I may have fallen into as to the practical measures I have suggested, the principles on which these suggestions rest are sound, and I therefore confidently recommend them to the consideration of the Assembly, with the earnest desire that that body, with the assistance of the other branches of the Legislature, may succeed in adopting such measures as may enable Jamaica to rise from her present difficulties to that prosperity to which I believe she is capable of attaining.

" I have, etc.

" (Signed)   GREY."

D.

SUGAR.

QUANTITIES IMPORTED.

Years ending July 5	Produce of British Possessions			Total Produce of British Possessions.	Foreign Produce.	Aggregate Importations.
	West Indies.	Mauritius.	East Indies.			
	cwt.	cwt.	cwt.	cwt.	cwt.	cwt.
1842......	2,289,005	722,458	1,031,359	4,042,822	581,156	4,623,978
1843......	2,677,816	552,070	1,184,466	4,414,352	757,769	5,172,121
1844......	2,663,779	478,618	835,914	3,978,311	884,609	4,862,920
1845......	3,040,492	699,631	1,263,137	5,003,260	978,162	5,981,422
1846......	2,842,555	801,913	1,531,418	5,175,886	1,307,635	6,483,521
1847......	2,530,333	1,131,108	1,349,639	5,011,080	1,952,555	6,963,635
1848......	3,151,031	881,915	1,432,563	5,465,509	2,087,387	7,552,896
1849......	3,086,357	935,935	1,330,294	5,352,586	2,136,505	7,489,091
1850......	3,222,869	1,028,440	1,549,733	5,801,042	2,033,990	7,835,032
1851......	2,661,513	1,003,033	1,358,228	5,022,774	2,658,179	7,680,953
1852......	3,638,388	1,071,929	1,605,440	6,315,757	1,807,032	8,122,789

Aggregate of Sugar and Melasses—(Melasses being converted into Sugar at the rate of 3 lb. of Melasses to 1 lb. of Sugar).

SUGAR.

QUANTITIES ENTERED FOR HOME CONSUMPTION.

Aggregate of Sugar and Melasses— (Melasses being converted into Sugar at the rate of 3 lb. of Melasses to 1 lb. of Sugar).

Years ending July 5.	Produce of British Possessions.			Total Produce of British Possessions.	Foreign Produce.	Aggregate of the Entries for Home Consumption.
	West Indies.	Mauritius.	East Indies.			
	cwt.	cwt.	cwt.	cwt.	cwt.	cwt.
1842......	2,476,782	826,629	1,022,374	4,325,785	2,189	4,327,974
1843......	2,548,692	521,873	1,019,028	4,089,593	498	4,090,091
1844......	2,721,509	487,559	935,976	4,145,044	93	4,145,137
1845......	2,890,122	722,404	1,236,534	4,849,060	34,584	4,883,644
1846......	2,876,548	812,817	1,296,427	4,985,792	60,064	5,045,856
1847......	2,369,485	906,110	1,447,637	4,723,232	1,256,421	5,979,653
1848......	2,936,181	905,230	1,161,907	5,003,318	865,752	5,869,070
1849......	2,997,141	881,187	1,355,401	5,233,729	1,021,065	6,254,794
1850......	3,105,115	1,094,469	1,370,877	5,570,461	752,027	6,322,488
1851......	2,698,098	963,822	1,381,952	5,043,872	1,522,405	6,566,277
1852......	3,565,714	1,036,705	1,512,791	6,115,210	1,540,308	7,655,518

Account of Duty Received in the United Kingdom on Sugar and Melasses.

Years ending July 5.	Aggregate Receipts of Duty on Sugar and Melasses.		
	Of British Possessions.	Foreign.	Total.
	£.	£.	£.
1842.........	5,476,987	8,026	5,485,013
1843.........	5,176,631	1,665	5,178,296
1844.........	5,253,687	319	5,254,006
1845.........	4,955,221	40,777	4,995,998
1846.........	3,514,354	70,335	3,584,689
1847.........	3,326,947	1,336,615	4,663,562
1848.........	3,522,288	877,378	4,399,666
1849.........	3,430,527	993,407	4,423,934
1850.........	3,371,976	699,969	4,071,945
1851.........	2,793,894	1,343,624	4,137,518
1852.........	3,077,561	1,276,042	4,353,603

Parliamentary Paper 296, 1852. Ibid. 97, 1852.

E.

" *To his Excellency James Macaulay Higginson, Esquire,*
C. B., Governor of the Island of Mauritius and its
Dependencies, etc.

" We, the undersigned inhabitants of Flacq, beg leave respectfully to approach your Excellency, to offer a heartfelt welcome upon the occasion of this your first visit to our District.

" It is many years since the inhabitants of the country

Districts of the Island, have enjoyed the satisfaction of receiving among them the representative of their Sovereign ; we therefore feel the more grateful to your Excellency for having now revived the practice of Sir Robert Farquhar and Sir Lowry Cole, your former much respected predecessors, and afforded us the opportunity of expressing our feeling of loyalty and attachment to our most gracious Queen, and of freely communicating to you personally our wants and wishes, unembarrassed by the shackles of official formality, which are too apt to give rise to misunderstanding and distrust.

" We hail this as the dawn of a new era of confidence and of frankness in the intercourse between the Mauritians and their Governor ; and if the Colonists find reason to be grateful for the benefits that never fail to attend a wise Administration, your Excellency will, on the other hand, enjoy the satisfaction and the glory inseparable from the successful exercise of your exalted functions. To attain this result one of the most important Preliminaries is, to be well acquainted with the field of action and with the population to be dealt with ; and we flatter ourselves that when your Excellency comes to know us well, you will, as we have reason to think was the case with your late honourable Predecessor, acknowledge that no body of people can be more easy of government than the Colonists of Mauritius.

" Sensitively alive perhaps to the appearance of slight, and prompt to resent injustice and calumny, they are easily won by the smallest approach to kindness, and are ever ready to bless the hand extended for their relief, and the heart that sympathizes with their sorrows, or interests itself in their welfare. Slow to claim even their just rights, you will have observed that when forced to make known their wants, their endeavour has always been to afford information to, but never in any way to obstruct the measures of those in authority.

" Animated with such feelings, the inhabitants of Flacq seize the occasion of your presence among us to bring to your Excellency's notice some observations calculated to assist your inquiries, and to make you acquainted with the more immediate wants of the District.

" The question of Municipal Institutions has so recently engaged your Excellency's attention, that it is unnecessary for us now to do more than recall it to your recollection. We may say the same with respect to establishments for charitable and educational purposes, with which we feel sure you will find the District sufficiently enlightened to be entrusted ; the cordiality and union which you will find reigning among all classes of its inhabitants afford a powerful pledge for the punctual exercise of such rights.

" The mere statement of the fact that our District contains twenty thousand inhabitants, and extends over a surface of upwards of a hundred square miles, is enough to satisfy your Excellency of the utter insufficiency of the police guard allotted to it, amounting to only thirteen or fourteen men, notwithstanding all the zeal and activity of the single officer placed in charge of it.

" It will be sufficient also to mention the public roads, of which, extensive as is the district, only the main one receives the regular attention of the civil engineer ; the others are left to the care of the adjacent proprietors, and absorb considerable sums of money, as well for the repairs to make them passable, as for making good the damage and destruction of carriages, carts, and draught animals, caused by the dilapidated state of the public ways.   For want of practicable means of communication many fertile tracts of land lie unproductive, as under present circumstances they are utterly inaccessible.

" The Ordinance respecting the establishment of a District Magistracy has probably already received the approbation of Her Majesty, and may be expected ere long to be put in execution. Our confidence in your Excellency's wisdom and discernment relieves us from any apprehensions on the subject of the selection of persons fully qualified for such responsible and important offices ; but we beg respectfully to suggest the desirableness of the choice of some central spot for the new Magistrate's Court, where also might be fixed the offices of the other public servants of the District.

"There also it is essential to establish a prison, with somewhat more effectual arrangements for the security and health of the prisoners than are to be found in the building at present temporarily used for that purpose.

" In approaching the subject of Indian immigration— perhaps the most important and vital of all to the inhabitants of this Colony—we hasten to express our grateful sense of the efforts your Excellency has unceasingly made for the promotion of this great object. Your endeavours, successful we would fain hope, to place this question in its true light before the Home and the Indian Governments,—your readiness to sanction the introduction of an increased number of labourers, when called for by the wants of the Colony,—your promptitude in taking measures to alleviate the mischief caused by the culpable betrayal of his duties (to use no stronger expression) by our agent at Calcutta, and by the surreptitious competition in the Madras territory of a foreign Colony,—and the wise instructions you have issued to the stipendiary magistrates with a view to ensure the most effective labour with the least possible employment of coercion, demand our warmest acknowledgments.

"Your Excellency has expressed your opinion, that when an immigrant has violated his contract of service by inexcusable desertions, instead of resorting to the unprofitable penalty of imprisonment, it is preferable to compel him, after the expiration of his contract, to replace the labour he has illegally withheld from his master. We entirely concur with your Excellency on this point; but we beg leave to suggest that it would be furthermore necessary, so as to allow no misconstruction to go abroad, as to the true intent of your instructions, to inform the stipendiary magistrates that the penalty of imprisonment is not to be absolutely refrained from, although it be deemed not to produce as wholesome an effect in the above case as the obligation of completing the full extent of labour due. Recourse to measures of compulsion certainly is a painful necessity; but since it is a necessity recognized inseparable from the administration of labour, imprisonment as a penalty should not be entirely suppressed, and would be rightly resorted to in such an instance, as when the delinquent refuses to return to his master to replace the time of his desertions. This course, however, of requiring the immigrant to complete the full time of his contract, and perform the labour he owes to its full extent, as your Excellency has wisely advised, we consider to be the most desirable and salutary, whenever the employer has not indemnified himself according to the law.

"And we venture also to suggest that it be part of the instructions to stipendiary magistrates to encourage as much possible engagements for three years. No measure is better calculated than this, for creating among the immigrants settled and orderly habits, and to lead ultimately to the establishment of a resident peasantry. There is little variety in the different districts and estates, either in the labour or in the wages and other allowances offered to the immigrants, and it cannot be doubted that it would be greatly to the advantage of these people to be spared the loss of time, and the interruption of their habits and occupations, attendant on annual changes of their employers and residences. If the Indians are to be regarded as so far in a state of pupilage as to be interdicted from forming contracts without the sanction of a magistrate acting as their guardian and protector, that officer, it seems to us, should be empowered to advise, and as much as in him lies to encourage, a system so decidedly advantageous to them. Your Excellency's recommendation to this effect will, we are persuaded be attended with very beneficial results.

"We beg your Excellency not to consider these remarks as reflecting even in the most distant manner on the conduct of the public functionaries of our District, the uprightness of whose intentions it is far from our meaning to impeach; but we consider it to be our duty, even towards them, to draw your Excellency's attention to measures that require to be explained and understood ere they can effect all the beneficial results they are intended for.

"These observations, we trust, will be favourably received by your Excellency, although it needed not our voice to awaken you to the extreme importance of the question of Immigration. A country whose wealth, nay, whose very existence, depends upon agriculture, would indeed be lost, if left without a labouring population. We are now, and for the last five years have been, engaged in a struggle with slave-owning and slave-trading Colonies, and, with the blessing of Providence, may yet be victorious in the strife ; but for this we must have labourers, and that at a moderate expense. At present, with an insufficiency for the land actually under cultivation, and surrounded with extensive tracts of country calling only for the fertilizing hand of man, how can we hope to obtain such sufficiency of labour ? It is for your Excellency to restore us that calm and security without which our best efforts must be unsuccessful.

" Your Excellency, as did your worthy predecessor, has rendered justice to the humanity with which our labourers are treated, and we hope that the more you see of us the more you will be confirmed in this opinion, and convinced of our earnest desire still further to ameliorate the lot of those so indispensably necessary to our own welfare. Continue then to represent the truth ; and when the clouds of error and prejudice are dispelled, as they must be by such testimony as your Excellency's, the governments both of the metropolis and of India will no longer hesitate to throw open to their subjects free access to those moral and physical advantages so liberally offered to India by this Colony.

" We now conclude ; and if we do not apologize for the length of our Address, it is because we are well assured of your Excellency's willingness and desire to learn all that interests us. It only remains for us to repeat our hearty welcome, and to assure you that we are, with great respect, your Excellency's most obedient and humble servants.

" (Here follow the signatures.)"

His Excellency's Reply.

" I request, Gentlemen, that you will accept my warmest thanks for this cordial and generous welcome which you have given me to Flacq.

" My visit has been deferred longer than I had intended; it completes my tour of the rural districts, from which I have derived much personal gratification, and the most favourable impressions of the loyalty and good-feeling that animate all classes of the community.

" My object has been to see and to judge for myself; to ascertain the real wants and wishes of the inhabitants, in order that the measures of the Government may harmonize with the voice of the people. The expression of your opinions, and the information which you have afforded me on the several important topics of local interest noticed in your Address, will conduce to this end; and you may rest assured that your suggestions shall have my anxious and attentive consideration.

" It is very gratifying to me to learn, that the measures which have been adopted to secure a more adequate and regular supply of labour have met with your approval. In the absence of a native population to cultivate our soil, our attention should be directed, not only to obtaining a sufficiency of labour for our immediate wants, but also to the more valuable and permanent benefits to be gained by inducing the natives of India, who now come here, and carry their earnings back after a few years, to settle in the Colony; and from my own experience of both countries, I can affirm that by adopting this as their future home, they will, with their own common industry, improve their social and physical condition unmeasurably beyond what they can ever hope to attain in their own.

" I bear willing testimony to the kind and just treatment received by the immigrants at the hands of their
employers, of which I have reason to believe they are
themselves fully sensible.

" They are a tractable and well-disposed people; and
the satisfaction with their conduct which I have heard
generally expressed by the Planters, implies that they are
mutually well-pleased with each other. I know no country in the world in which the position of the agricultural labourer is superior to that of the Indian immigrant
here, and very few indeed in which the same degree of
comfort and independence is enjoyed by him.

" The erroneous impressions of the character of our immigration system, that previously existed both in India
and in Europe, have, I trust, been removed, and the un-
exceptionable footing on which it now stands, promises
greater permanence and security for those advantages
which are unquestionably conferred on the inhabitants of
both countries, by the labour and capital that are inter-
changed.

" The crisis of the severe struggle in which you have
been engaged has, I confidently believe, been overcome,
and that you will now reap the fruits of that energy,
industry, and enterprise which enabled you to maintain
it; and having accepted the new conditions imposed upon
agriculture both here and in the Mother-country, you are
wisely seeking, in more skilful husbandry and improved
processes of manufacture, compensation for that protection
which has, I believe, irrevocably passed away.

" Favoured by a soil of surpassing fertility, and a most
genial climate, as well as by her geographical position,
Mauritius, with hands equal to her resources for produc-
tively employing them, and with judgement and economy

in the disposition of their labour, must move onward, and need not fear competition with other producers, whether slave or free.

"I esteem it no ordinary privilege to be permitted to watch over your interests at a period so full of promise; and I highly value the assurance of your approbation and appreciation of my efforts to promote your welfare which this Address conveys to me.

"(Signed)   J. M. HIGGINSON."

F.

An Account of the Quantity of Produce exported from the Colony in the Year 1851 as compared with that of the Year 1850.

	Sugar.	Rum.	Molasses.	Coffee.
1851.	*hhds.*	*punch.*	*casks.*	*lbs.*
Exported from this port, the production of Demerary and Essequibo .	34,875	14,922	6,186¾	2,868
Exported from this port, the production of Berbice	3,196	674	2,719	180
Total	38,071	15,596	8,905¾	3,048
Exported from the port of New Amsterdam, Berbice, the production of Berbice . . .	4,963	252	625	150
Total Exports for Year .	43,034	15,848	9,530¾	3,198
1850.				
Exported from this port, the production of Demerary and Essequibo .	30,330	11,803	7,932	20,286
Exported from this port, the production of Berbice	2,890½	999	2,724	4,500
Total	33,220	15,802	10,656	24,786
Exported from the port of New Amsterdam, Berbice, the production of Berbice . . .	4,131	139	1,151	30
Total Exports for Year .	37,351½	15,941	11,807	25,086
Increase . . .	5,682½	...		
Decrease . . .		93	2,276¼	21,888

Custom-house, Demerary,
   9th January, 1852.

         (Signed)   C. BAGOT, Comptroller.

PORT OF GEORGETOWN, DEMERARY.

An Account of the Quantity of Produce exported from this Colony, in the Quarter ended 5th January, 1852, as compared with the corresponding Quarter of 1850.

	Sugar.	Rum.	Molasses	Coffee.
1851.	*hhds.*	*punch.*	*casks.*	*lbs.*
Exported from this port, the production of Demerary and Essequibo .	16,275	6,146	3,189½	450
Exported from this port, the production of Berbice	1,833	405	1,397	...
Total	18,108	6,551	4,586½	450
Exported from the port of New Amsterdam, Berbice, produce of Berbice	1,890	160	206	150
Total Exports for quarter	19,998	6,711	4,792½	600
1850.				
Exported from this port, the production of Demerary and Essequibo .	13,251	5,612	3,965	4,086
Exported from this port, the production of Berbice	1,259	474	1,165	...
Total	14,510	6,086	5,130	4,086
Exported from the port of New Amsterdam, Berbice, produce of Berbice	1,913	54	607	...
Total Exports for quarter	16,423	6,140	5,737	4,086
Increase . . .	3,575	571	...	...
Decrease . . .			944½	3,486

Custom-house, Demerary,
   9th January, 1852.

(Signed)   C. BAGOT, Comptroller.

G.

Extracts from the Representation and Petition from the House of Assembly of Jamaica to the Prince Regent, dated December 10, 1811.

"The ruin of the original possessors has been gradually completed. Estate after estate has passed into the hands of mortgagees and creditors absent from the Island, until there are large districts, whole parishes, in which there is not a single proprietor of a sugar plantation resident.

" In the discharge of a most painful duty your Petitioners have laid before your Royal Highness the calamitous situation of themselves and their constituents. It is not to be concealed, and cannot be denied, that a crisis has at length arrived when nothing but the immediate and powerful interposition of the Supreme Authority of the Empire can prevent the utter destruction of a part, not altogether unworthy of attention from its former value.

" Exactions, debasement, and privations have been long and patiently endured by the proprietors of the soil; a large proportion of them now see approaching the lowest state of human misery, absolute want to their families, the horrors of a gaol to themselves."

Extract from the ' History of the West Indies,' by Bryan Edwards. (Vol. II., book 4, ch. 1, p. 15, 4to edit. 1794.)

" This anticipation of imaginary wealth is so prevalent as to become justly ridiculous; yet I am inclined to think it is a propensity that exists independent of the climate and atmosphere, and that it arises principally from the peculiar situation of the West Indian proprietors as landholders. Not having, like the proprietors of landed estates in Great Britain, frequent opportunities of letting their plantations to substantial tenants, they are, for the most part, compelled to become practical farmers on their own lands, of which the returns are in the highest degree fluctuating and uncertain. Under these circumstances a West Indian property is a species of lottery. As such it gives birth to a spirit of adventure and enterprise, and awakens extravagant hopes and expectations; too frequently terminating in perplexity and disappointment."

Extracts from a Report of a Committee of the House of Commons on the West Indies in 1807.

"From their testimony it appears that since the year 1799 there has taken place a progressive deterioration in the situation of the Planters, resulting from a progressive diminution of the price of sugar, although, at the same time, the duty and all the expenses attending the cultivation have been increasing, till at length the depression of the market has become such that the prices obtained for the last year's crop will not pay the expense of cultivation, except upon estates on a very great scale, making sugar of a very superior quality, or enjoying other extraordinary advantages. Calculations have been laid before your Committee, from the accounts of estates both in Jamaica and the other islands, by which it appears that the British Supplies and Island Expenses amount to 20*s.* 10*d.* in the former, and to 19*s.* 6*d.* in the latter, on the cwt. of sugar, after accounting and giving credit for the amount received for the sale of rum. As these calculations are formed upon an average of years, and upon estates of the ordinary scale, and in no respects unusually circumstanced, it appears to your Committee, that these sums per cwt. of sugar may be taken as the average expense of cultivation, independent of interest upon the capital; and your Committee are confirmed in this opinion by finding a similar calculation in the Report made by the Sugar Distillery Committee in the last Parliament. To this must be added the expense of from 15s. 6d. to 16s. per cwt. necessarily incurred for freight, insurance, and other mercantile charges, between the shipping the goods in the Colonies, and their being offered to market in this kingdom, forming together an amount of from 35s. to 36s., which appears, upon this evidence, to be the absolute cost to the planter per hundredweight of sugar, before any return of capital can attach. Upon a reference to the average prices, published in the 'Gazette' for the last eight months, which vary from 36s. to 31s., giving a mean price of 33s. 6d., it appears evident that the planters must have cultivated their estates at a loss.

" The interest which has been stated to your Committee as what should be the fair profit upon a capital of such a nature as that of a sugar estate, consisting not merely of land and negroes, but of buildings of great extent and cost, necessary for the carrying on of such a manufacture, and subject to various and peculiar risks and vicissitudes, is not less than ten per cent.

" During the period of prosperity, previous to 1800, it is stated, that in general the profits did not exceed that sum; and that from that period they have gradually diminished to two and a half and one and a half per cent., till, at the present moment, there is no return of interest whatever.

*   *   *   *   *   *

" Your Committee having briefly stated the distressed situation of the West Indian Planter,—the causes which have gradually produced his distress, which are beyond his reach to remedy, and which must continue to operate with increased effect,—and having stated such measures of relief as have been suggested to them, and such as, from the best sources of information, appear most adequate to the end in view,—have only to add, that if those remedies are liable to objections and difficulties, there is, on the other hand, the strongest concurrent testimony and proof, that unless some speedy and efficient measures of relief are adopted, the ruin of a great number of the Planters, and of persons in this country holding annuities, and otherwise dependent upon those properties for their income, must inevitably very soon take place, which must be followed by the loss of a vast capital advanced on securities in those countries, and by the most fatal injury to the commercial, maritime, and financial interests of Great Britain."

Extracts from the Report of the Committee of the House of Commons, " On the Commercial State of the West Indies," 1832.

" The case submitted to them in these Papers is one of severe distress, affecting the proprietors of the soil.

" Your Committee have received abundant evidence of the distress which is said to have existed, in a considerable degree, for ten or twelve years past, and to have been greatly aggravated within the last three or four.

" In concluding their considerations of the causes of the depressed state of the West India Colonists, your Committee have not forgotten that their depression has existed in former times, and at periods anterior to the abolition of the Slave-trade. To one of these periods their attention has been specially called by the reference of the report of the Committee of 1807, whence it appears that during the late war, and while still supplied with slaves from Africa, the Planters complained of inadequate returns, and of un-equal competition in foreign markets. These results were then ascribed to the circumstances of the war which has long ceased, and which were necessarily independent of the causes now alleged. Your Committee are well aware that this similarity of complaint and discrepancy of assigned reasons has occasioned some distrust of the accuracy of those which are now put forward."

Extract from a Report of a Committee of the Assembly of Jamaica, dated November, 1804.

"That every British merchant holding securities on real estate is filing Bills in Chancery to foreclose, although, when he has obtained a decree, he hesitates to enforce it, because he must himself become proprietor of the planta-tions of which, from fatal experience, he knows the con-sequences. No one will advance money to relieve those whose debts approach half the value of their property, nor even lend moderate sums without a judgement in ejectment and release of errors, that, at a moment's notice, he may take out a writ of possession, and enter on the plantation of his unfortunate debtor. Sheriff's officers and collectors of internal taxes are everywhere offering for sale the pro-perty of individuals who have seen better days, and now must view their effects purchased for half their real value, and less than half their original cost. Far from having the reversion expected, the creditor is often not satisfied. All kind of credit is at end. If litigation in the Courts of Common Law is diminished, it is not from increased ability to perform contracts, but from confidence having ceased, and no man parting with property, but for an immediate payment of the consideration. A faithful detail would have the appearance of frightful caricature."

The above extract was quoted by Lord Derby, in his speech in the House of Commons, on moving the resolutions for the Abolition of Slavery, on the 14th of May, 1833.—See the ' Mirror of Parliament' for that year, vol. ii. p. 1773.

H.

Copy of a Despatch from Earl Grey to Governor the Right Hon. Sir C. E. Grey.

" *Downing-street, October* 11, 1848.

" SIR,

" I received your despatch, No. 75, of the 19th August, with copies of the Votes of the House of Assembly of Jamaica from the 4th to the 16th August, to which it refers.

" It is satisfactory to me to find that you take the same view as myself as respects the capability of Jamaica to yield a revenue adequate to its wants. I have never doubted that an island so rich in natural resources, and possessing a considerable population, which I have no reason to believe to be indisposed to industry, must be able to raise such an amount of revenue as would be required to meet the expenses of its Civil Government, provided proper means were adopted for this purpose, and for that of encouraging industry and of stimulating the inhabitants to exertion. It rests however entirely with the Assembly to consider what are the proper measures to be adopted with this view; and considering how vitally the interests of their constituents are concerned in their deliberations on this subject, I cannot doubt that they will earnestly apply themselves to the task of devising such measures as may appear to them best suited to the present condition of the Colony.

" With reference however to your observations that ' Her Majesty's Government ought to be prepared towards the end of this year to say in what manner the local Goverment of the Island is to be carried on, in the event of the usual annual supplies for 1849 being refused,' I think it right at once and distinctly to inform you, that this is a responsibility which Her Majesty's Government cannot accept.   The Constitution of Jamaica has placed in the hands of the representatives of its inhabitants, the exclusive power and duty of raising in the Colony such an annual income as is necessary for the support of the various public establishments they have judged proper to be maintained for the benefit of the Island; and if those representatives will no longer provide the means of keeping up such establishments, the Colony must unavoidably be deprived of the benefit derived from them.   Parliament undoubtedly could not with propriety be asked to supply the deficiency, nor would it in my judgement be consistent with its duty, to grant from the taxes levied from the inhabitants of the United Kingdom, any money for such a purpose.   The different public establishments have been created by the Colonial Legislature on a scale which I believe to be by no means beyond what is required to provide for the due adminstration of justice, for the enforcement of the law, the maintenance of order, the security of person and property, and the due performance of various other services required for the welfare of the community. Recent events have shown, in a striking manner, the necessity of these establishments, and of the police more especially ; and I should therefore deeply regret any injudicious measures which should prevent their being maintained; but as they are kept up exclusively for the benefit of the inhabitants of Jamaica, it is for the Assembly by which those inhabitants are represented, to weigh the loss which might be sustained by failing to provide an adequate revenue for their support, against the difficulties which may exist in imposing the taxes required for this purpose. The Governor's own duty, and that of Her Majesty's Government, is confined to doing what lies in them towards preventing an increase of the existing difficulties, by refusing to assent to any ill-considered and imprudent measures of legislation. I therefore entirely approve of the intention which you have expressed in your despatch, of refusing your assent to any Acts which may be tendered to you for affording assistance to the Planters' Bank, in the mode which you mention as having been suggested. The measures alluded to would plainly be most objectionable, and I am at loss myself to discover any mode in which such assistance could be given which would not be open to great objection, though I shall of course reserve my judgement upon this point until I know what measures may finally be considered advisable by the Legislature.

" I have, etc.,
" (Signed)   GREY."

———

Copy of a Despatch from Earl Grey to Governor the Right Hon. Sir C. E. Grey.

" *Downing-street, April* 16, 1849.

" SIR,

"I have received and laid before the Queen your Despatches, Nos. 21, 24, and 25, the first dated the 19th February, with a Postscript of the 21st February, enclosing the votes of the Assembly from the 2nd to the 17th of February, with other documents; the others enclosing Memorials to the Queen from the Council and from the Chief Justice, the Vice-Chancellor, and the Judges of the Supreme Court, which have reference to the course taken by the Assembly in refusing to pass bills for the renewal or imposition of taxes sufficient to provide for the ordinary expenditure of the Island, authorized under permanent or unexpired acts; the charges thus left unprovided for, including the salaries of the Governor, the Judges, and the other public officers, and the stipends of the clergy.   This refusal was founded, it appears, on the rejection by the Council of a bill by which the Assembly had proposed to reduce the salaries of all officers paid from the public funds (with the exception of their own speaker, clerk, and sergeant-at-arms, and certain other specified officers) in the proportions of 10 per cent. on salaries between £100 and £300, 15 per cent. on those between £300 and £500, 20 per cent. on those between £500 and £1000, 25 per cent. on those between £1000 and £2000, and 33½ per cent. on those above £2000.

" I am to acquaint you that Her Majesty was pleased to receive the Memorials of the Council and of the Judges very graciously.

" By a later mail I have also received, and I have laid before the Queen, your Despatches, Nos. 33 and 34, of the 10th of March, transmitting further accounts of the proceedings of the Assembly and of the prorogation of the Legislature of Jamaica.   Her Majesty's Government have given their best consideration to the subject of these several despatches and their enclosures, and I am to convey to you Her Majesty's approval of the communications which you had occasion to make to the Assembly in the course of the proceedings set forth in their votes.   Her Majesty entirely approves the substance of those communications, and also the tone and temper by which they were characterized.

"I am further to acquaint you that the course pursued by the Council in the rejection of the Retrenchment Bill, appears to Her Majesty's Government to have been taken in the constitutional exercise of their proper functions, and in the exercise also of a sound judgement. The bill was insufficient (under the reduction of the import duties recently enacted and an imperfect system of collecting the taxes) for the purpose of equalizing the expenditure with the revenue of the Colony, and it was justly objected to, because it imposed an unfair and unequal tax exclusively on the incomes of public servants, though these incomes were, in many cases, secured to those by whom they are enjoyed, by Acts passed for periods which have not yet expired.

" With regard to the result of these proceedings in leaving various urgent demands on the Colonial Treasury unprovided for, you are aware that Her Majesty's Government have no authority to interfere. They can refuse to join in acts of injustice, and it is their duty to do so ; but beyond this the Constitution of Jamaica invests them with no power, and therefore imposes upon them no responsibility. By that Constitution, and by the laws now in force in the Colony, the entire control over the public expenditure, and the exclusive right of levying taxes upon the inhabitants for the purpose of meeting that expenditure, are vested in the Colonial Legislature. Hence, for whatever evils may result from the refusal of the Assembly to renew the taxes usually levied under annual Acts, that body will have to bear the undivided responsibility. It will devolve upon you to administer any revenue which may remain available for the public service, according to any laws which may continue in force, and may impose that duty upon you, and to do the

best you can towards the support of order and justice under
the circumstances; keeping strictly within the bounds of
your lawful authority.   It will also be your duty to adopt
the most efficient means in your power for the strict collection of any taxes still in force, and of any arrears which
may be due to the Island Treasury, requiring all persons
engaged in the collection of the revenue (so far as your
legal authority extends) to give you for that purpose their
best assistance.   For the rest, of course it will not be possible for you or for Her Majesty's servants to regard with
indifference the great public mischief and individual distress which must result from the proceedings of the Assembly; on the contrary, we cannot but feel deep concern
at the injury inflicted upon the credit and upon the permanent interests of the Island, and sincere sympathy with the
present sufferers; but the Constitution of the Island, as by
law established, not calling upon us, or indeed permitting
us, to take any part in these matters, we are at least relieved from the anxiety which would attend a more extended authority and more active duties.

" It appears, however, from your later Despatches that
there exists on the part of a considerable number of the
inhabitants of Jamaica, a strong desire for some change in
the system on which the Government of that Colony is at
present conducted, with the view of securing a better administration of its affairs, and putting an end to those unfortunate differences which now threaten such serious injury
both to public and private interests.   It is satisfactory to
me to find that this desire has been awakened; for while it
is impossible to consider the actual condition of the Colony,
and the general conduct of its public affairs for the last few
years as bearing upon that condition, without coming to
the conclusion that a reform in the system of administration

is urgently required, it is at the same time evident that it is only by the inhabitants themselves, that such a reform can be accomplished. The institutions and the laws of Jamaica have invested its inhabitants with such ample powers in all that relates to its internal Government, that any improvement in that Government must be mainly their own work, though I need hardly assure you of the earnest desire of Her Majesty's Government to afford them their best assistance and co-operation in any attempts they may make to effect it.

" The only specific suggestions which I can find to have been made for changes in the existing arrangements are, first, those relating to the Legislative Council; and secondly, that the system of Government now established in Canada should be introduced into Jamaica. As to the first I must remark, that while I am not aware of any good reason for objecting to such an enlargement of the Legislative Council as has been described as desirable by yourself, it does not appear to me that such a measure would have any tendency to remove the difficulties which have arisen in the Administration of the Colony; since these are not in any degree attributable to the conduct of the Council, that Board having done no more than its duty in rejecting the Retrenchment Bill which was tendered to it for its acceptance; at the same time apparently showing every disposition to concur in any general plan of economical reform involving a just measure of retrenchment, which might have been tendered to it. The same consideration applies with far greater force as an objection to the demand of the Assembly for a change not only in the number but in the constitution of the Legislative Council, as it has existed for nearly two hundred years. It is altogether impossible for Her Majesty's Government to entertain a demand of this kind, brought forward upon such grounds.

" The proposal to assimilate the system of administration
in Jamaica to that which is now established in Canada is
of a very different character, and it is one which, if not in
all respects free from objection, has yet so much to recommend it that if it were the general desire of the people
of Jamaica that such a change should be introduced, Her
Majesty's Government would not be disposed to withhold
their consent to its being so.   I am not certain, however,
that those who have originated this proposal are aware
that its adoption would involve the surrender by the Assembly of much of that power which in the process of time it
has acquired, but which, by the theory of the Constitution, ought rather to belong to the Executive Government
than to the Legislature.   In Jamaica the Members of the
Assembly, under the name of Commissioners of Accounts,
have practically taken upon themselves those duties with
respect to the administration of the public expenditure,
which in Canada are entrusted to responsible Members of
the Executive Government.   In Canada, no vote of public
money can be made by the Assembly except on the recommendation of the Governor ; in Jamaica, the Assembly is
altogether free from any such control.   In Canada, again,
provision has been made by the creation of a permanent
Revenue for the payment of a considerable Civil List; in
Jamaica the Assembly has made the greater part of the
Revenue dependent upon taxes only imposed for a year at
a time, and of late for even a shorter period.

" I am far from being of opinion, that, judging of the
two systems of administration by their practical results,
that of Jamaica is to be preferred; on the contrary, in
expressing my belief, in an earlier part of this Despatch,
of the necessity for a reform in the administration of Jamaica, it was the management of its finances which I had

principally in view, and which, I am compelled to observe, appears to me to have been exceedingly defective, mainly in consequence of the retention by the Assembly, in its own hands, of powers little suited to any popular body. A careful review of the information which you have now transmitted to me, and of that previously to be found in the records of this office, leaves no doubt in my mind, that the financial difficulties with which Jamaica has now to struggle have been greatly aggravated, if not occasioned, by the want of a steady and persevering adherence to a system of judicious and well considered economy. I find that a debt has been incurred, which though not perhaps very large in amount compared with the natural resources of the Island, yet bears a high rate of interest, the charge for which is a heavy item in the annual expenditure. I find also that recourse has been had to the expedient of meeting a part of that expenditure by the issue of what are called Island Cheques, which constitute in fact an inconvertible paper currency, now considerably depreciated, and which acts most unfavourably on the general trade of the Colony, and must necessarily subject the Colonial Treasury to a heavy loss in the collection of the revenue. I find likewise that while debt, in its most burdensome form, has thus been accumulated, little has been done to prevent the expenditure exceeding the revenue. Within a few years Acts have been passed by the Colonial Legislature, by which very large additions have been made to the public establishments, and this increase, which was probably called for by the exigencies of the public service, has not been met by the adoption of efficient means to ensure the punctual collection of the taxes, to enforce a strict audit of the public accounts, and to maintain a proper check upon the incurring of new expenses without due inquiry, and a real and proved neces-

sity.   What you have stated to me, as to the large arrears
of taxes still uncollected, the circumstances under which
the deficiency in the accounts of the late Receiver-General
took place, (which remains, I believe, still unsatisfied,) and
the nature of many of the charges annually voted by the
Assembly, without the recommendation of any responsible
authority, afford conclusive evidence, how little true economy has been studied in the financial administration of
the Colony.   It is also, I think, hardly less clear that this
faulty administration of the colonial finances is mainly to
be attributed to the absence, under the system which has
been adopted, of any effective responsibility bearing upon
individuals for the errors which have been committed.

  " Hence, if in order to secure a better administration of
their affairs, and especially of their finances, the people of
Jamaica should think proper by their representatives either
in this, or in a newly elected Assembly, to ask Her Majesty's sanction for the adoption of a similar mode of conducting the Government of the Colony to that which now
exists in Canada, I am not aware that any obstacle, which
might not easily be overcome, would stand in the way of a
compliance with their wishes.   The only legislative measures which would be necessary for this purpose, would be
such as the Colonial Legislature would have full authority
to pass, and would consist mainly of acts to repeal the
various laws heretofore passed, for vesting in the Assembly,
or in its members in the character of Commissioners of
Account, some of the anomalous powers they now possess,
and to create and provide salaries for the offices to be held
by responsible public servants, by whose assistance the Governor would have to conduct the affairs of the Island.

  " Considering the great natural advantages possessed by
Jamaica, and the amount of its population, I cannot doubt

that if by this, or by any other means, a steady perseverance in a well-considered and consistent system of financial policy could be secured, great relief might be afforded to the industry of the Colony in the difficulties with which it has now to struggle. But for this purpose it is especially necessary that all the measures of the Legislature should be governed by a calm and deliberate consideration of the real wants and interests of the Island, and that these measures should not be liable to frequent changes adopted upon slight grounds. I need hardly remind you that some of the salaries which it has lately been proposed to reduce by no less than one-third of their amount, were only a few years ago secured, by Acts passed apparently after full deliberation, to the holders of offices which were at that time created, and that some of these offices were accepted by gentlemen at a considerable sacrifice of the incomes they then enjoyed from other sources, solely from a consideration of the security they believed they should possess for the official salaries thus granted to them. Whether the Legislature at that time acted wisely in creating these offices, and in assigning to their holders the remuneration which was determined upon, it is not necessary for me to inquire: for be this as it may, it is obvious that in addition to the injustice of the sweeping reduction of these salaries which has been proposed, that measure is utterly inconsistent with that true economy which consists in obtaining for the public the best possible service at a moderate cost. If it shall once be known that the Legislature of Jamaica cannot be depended upon for maintaining the salaries which it has secured, by Acts deliberately passed, to the holders of certain offices, it is certain that these offices will no longer be accepted by men of superior qualifications, at the same moderate salaries which would suffice if their permanence were not exposed to hazard.

" In the same manner there can be little doubt that the charge of the debt might be diminished, and the inconvenience arising from the circulation of inconvertible Island Cheques might be got rid of on moderate terms, if the credit of the Colony were improved, by providing, as in this Country, a permanent revenue equal to the fixed charges upon it, instead of leaving the public creditor almost entirely dependent upon annual taxes, the renewal of which may be interrupted by any such differences between the branches of the Legislature as those which have now occurred.

" I have thus indicated (studiously avoiding all details) the general character of the measures by which it is in the power of the Legislature of Jamaica to promote the welfare of its inhabitants and alleviate the pressure of the difficulties with which they have now to contend. The cordial concurrence of yourself, of the Council, and of Her Majesty's Government in measures of this description is not doubtful; and if the people of Jamaica desire their adoption, they can have no difficulty in causing their wishes to be attended to by their Representatives. It rests, therefore, with the people themselves to determine what course is to be followed, since it will be their own interests which will mainly suffer from any error which may be committed by their Representatives, as I trust they will distinctly understand when you shall again call together the Legislature. I have no doubt, from your past conduct, that you will judge rightly when the proper time is come for doing so, and also as to whether or not it may be right, previously, to dissolve the present for the purpose of causing a new Assembly to be elected. But with reference to the next meeting of the Legislature, whenever it may take place, I think it indispensable to direct that the clause of the Royal Instructions, forbidding you to give your assent to any laws enacted for a less term than one year, unless to meet some special and unforeseen emergency, shall be in future strictly adhered to. This is a clause of very old date in the Royal Instructions to the Governors of Jamaica and of other Colonies, founded on strong grounds of permanent policy; and although I am not surprised that you should have thought a deviation from it expedient, under the difficult circumstances in which you were placed, and though I am far from disapproving of your having done so, I am satisfied that for the future a steady adherence to it will be the course best calculated to promote the public interests. The result of the concession you have made upon this point is the clearest proof that it ought not to be repeated, and you will cause it to be distinctly understood by the Legislature that Her Majesty has left you no discretion upon this head, but has commanded you strictly to adhere to the letter of the Instructions which have for so long a time been given to all the Governors of Jamaica, as to the duration of any Acts which they are at liberty to accept.

" And although I am equally aware of the cogency of the motives which induced you to assent to the Import Duties Bill, notwithstanding the Clauses of Appropriation attached to it, I have to instruct you not in future to admit of any innovation on the regular and constitutional practice of keeping Revenue and Appropriation Bills separate from each other ; assuming that to have been, as I understand to be the case, a practice as fully established in Jamaica as it has been in this country, and in the other Colonies whose Constitutions have been modelled on our own. It is a practice which cannot be departed from without danger.

"I have received Her Majesty's commands to cause

copies of the Despatches before me to be presented in both
Houses of Parliament.

"I have, etc.,

"*Governor Sir C. E. Grey,*   (Signed)   Grey."
"*etc.   etc.   etc.*"

I.

At the Court at Buckingham Palace, the 1st day of May,
1849.   Present, The Queen's Most Excellent Majesty in
Council.

Whereas there was this day read at the Board a Report
of the Right Honourable The Lords of the Committee of
Council, appointed for the consideration of all matters
relating to Trade and Foreign Plantations, dated the 4th
day of April last, in the words following, viz :—

"Your Majesty having been pleased by your Order in
Council of the 31st January last, to refer unto this Committee copies of a correspondence between Earl Grey, one
of Your Majesty's principal Secretaries of State, and Sir
Charles Fitzroy and the other Governors of Your Majesty's
Australian Settlements, on the subject of the introduction
to Parliament, in the ensuing session, of a Bill for the
better government of those Colonies, to consider the same,
and report to Your Majesty our opinion as to the steps
which it would be advisable for Your Majesty to take on
the subject of the said correspondence.

"In obedience to Your Majesty's commands we have
taken into consideration the subject so referred to us, and
humbly submit to Your Majesty the following Report of
the conclusions which we have adopted.

"In order to render intelligible the grounds on which our opinions on this subject proceed, we must briefly advert to the distinctions between the practice which has been observed during the present century, and the practice which was observed in earlier times, respecting the establishment of systems of civil government in the colonial dependencies of the British Crown.

"In those ancient possessions of Your Majesty's royal predecessors, which at present form so large a part of the United States of America, and in all the other British Colonies (whether acquired by the occupation of vacant territories or by cessions from foreign powers), there prevailed until the commencement of the nineteenth century the almost invariable usage of establishing a local legislature consisting of three estates—that is, of a Governor appointed by the Sovereign, of a Council nominated by the Sovereign, and of an Assembly elected by the people. Although in some cases other schemes of colonial polity had been at first established, yet those schemes had all, with one exception, progressively been brought, before the end of the eighteenth century, into conformity with this general type or model. The Colonies of Ceylon, Trinidad, and Guiana, do not form exceptions, for although conquered, they had not been ceded before the beginning of the present century. Nor is Newfoundland an exception, because it was in those times regarded and governed as a mere fishing station, and not as a colony. Neither can Malta and Gibraltar be referred to as exceptions, because they were regarded not as colonies, but as mere military fortresses, and were governed by military laws. The only real exception was in the case of Sierra Leone, which at the era in question was governed by an incorporated company.

"Further, these colonial constitutions were all (except

in the Canadas) created by letters patent under the Great
Seal either of England or of Great Britain, and those letters patent were issued in the exercise of an unquestionable
and undisputed prerogative of the Crown. But in Lower
and Upper Canada, the three estates of Governor, Council,
and Assembly, were established, not by the Crown, but by
the express authority of Parliament. This deviation from
the general usage was unavoidable, because it was judged
right to impart to the Roman Catholic population of the
Canadas privileges which in the year 1791 the Crown could
not have lawfully conferred on them. There is also reason
to believe that the settlement of the Canadian Constitution,
not by a grant from the Crown merely, but in virtue of a
positive statute, was regarded by the American loyalists as
an important guarantee for the secure enjoyment of their
political franchises.

" But during the nineteenth century the British Crown
has acquired, by conquest and cession from foreign states,
three transatlantic Colonies, one Colony in Southern Africa,
and four Colonies to the eastward of the Cape of Good
Hope. During the same period the British Crown has acquired, by the occupation of vacant territories, two Colonies on the western coast of Africa, three in New Holland,
one in Van Diemen's Land, one in New Zealand, and one
in the Falkland Islands. In no one of these sixteen Colonies has the old colonial polity of a Governor, Council, and
Assembly been introduced. In no one of them (except
New South Wales) has any electoral franchise been granted
to the colonists, or any share in the local legislation to their
representatives.

" In all these conquered Colonies, the ancient system of
internal government remains such as it was at the times
of the respective conquests, excepting that by letters patent

under the Great Seal, a Governor and a Council appointed
by the Crown have in each of them been authorized to
make local laws. In Guiana, indeed, no such letters patent
have been issued, because the ancient Dutch legislature
still retains in that Colony its ancient forms and powers.

" In all the Colonies acquired during the nineteenth century by the occupation of vacant territories, the same system of internal legislation by a Governor and a Council
appointed by the Crown has been introduced by the authority of Parliament.

" In Colonies so acquired, the Royal prerogative was
competent only to the establishment of systems of civil
government, of which a Legislature, composed in part at
least of the representatives of the people, formed a component part. To dispense even for awhile with such a Legislature, Parliamentary aid was requisite. But in sanctioning that departure from the general type or model of
the earlier colonial Constitutions, it has been the practice
of Parliament to recognize the ancient principle, and to
record the purpose of resuming the former constitutional
practice so soon as the causes should have ceased to operate, which in each particular case had forbidden the immediate observance of it. Nor has the pledge thus repeatedly given been forgotten. It has been redeemed in
New South Wales, except so far as relates to the combination which has taken place there of the Council and Assembly into one Legislative House or Chamber. It has
been redeemed with regard to New Zealand, although peculiar circumstances have required a temporary postponement of the operation in that Colony of the Act passed by
Parliament for establishing in it a Representative Legislature.

" We are of opinion that the time has not yet arrived

for conferring this franchise on the Colonists of Western Australia, because they are unable to fulfil the condition on which alone, as it appears to us, such a grant ought to be made; the condition, that is, of sustaining the expense of their own civil government by means of the local revenue, which would be placed under the direction and control of their representatives. Whenever the Settlers in Western Australia shall be willing and able to perform this condition, they ought, we apprehend, to be admitted to the full enjoyment of the corresponding franchises, but not till then.

"The Colonies of South Australia and Van Diemen's Land, being on the other hand at once willing and able to provide by local resources for the public expenditure of each, or at least for so much of that expenditure as is incurred with a view to colonial and local objects, the time has in our judgement arrived when Parliament may properly be recommended to institute in each of those Colonies a legislature in which the representatives of the people at large should enjoy and exercise their constitutional authority.

"In submitting to Your Majesty this advice, we are only repeating an opinion so familiar and so generally adopted by all persons conversant with the government of the British Colonies, that it would seem superfluous to support it by argument or explanation. The introduction of this constitutional principle into every dependency of the British Crown is a general rule sanctioned by a common and clear assent. The exception to that rule arises only when it can be shown that the observance of it would induce evils still more considerable than those which it would obviate and correct. We are aware of no reason for apprehending that such a preponderance of evil would follow on the introduction of such a change in South Australia and Van Diemen's Land. The contrary anticipation appears to be entertained by all those who possess the best means and the greatest powers of foreseeing the probable results of such a measure. We therefore recommend that, during the present session of Parliament, a Bill should be introduced for securing to the representatives of the people of South Australia and Van Diemen's Land, respectively, their due share in the legislature' of each of those Colonies.

" We apprehend however that it would be found highly inconvenient to consider this question as it regards those two settlements, without at the same time adverting to the effects with which such a change in them must be followed in the whole range of the Australian Colonies.

" New Holland is at present divided between the three governments of New South Wales, South Australia, and Western Australia. The most cursory inspection of the maps and charts of those regions will sufficiently show, that as they shall become more populous and more extensively settled, it will be necessary to divide them into a greater number of distinct Colonies. But confining our immediate attention to the case of New South Wales, we observe that the cities of Sydney and of Melbourne, lying at a great distance from each other, form the respective capitals of districts of great extent, separated from each other by diversities of climate and by some corresponding differences in their natural resources, and in the agricultural and commercial pursuits followed in each of them. The inhabitants of the southern districts have long and earnestly solicited that Melbourne should be made the seat and centre of a Colonial Government separated from that of Sydney ; and so decided has this wish become of late, that on the recent general election of members of the

Legislature of New South Wales collectively, the inhabitants of the southern district have virtually and in effect refused to make any such choice. The reluctance which was at first so naturally entertained at Sydney to the proposed innovation, appears to have gradually but effectually yielded to the progress of knowledge and reasoning on the subject. The Governor and the Executive Council, the existing Legislature, and, as we believe, the great body of the Colonists, now favour the contemplated division of their extensive territory into a northern and a southern Colony.

"Nor is it surprising that such should have been the ultimate conclusion of such a debate. The inhabitants of countries recently and imperfectly settled are exposed to few greater social evils than that of the remoteness of the seat of government from large bodies of the settlers. The effect is virtually to disfranchise a large proportion, if not a majority, of the Colonists, by excluding them from any share in the management of public affairs, and in the inspection and control of the conduct of their rulers. In such circumstances the inconveniences of the centralization of all the powers of Government are experienced in their utmost force. The population of the districts most distant from the metropolis are compelled to entrust the representation of their persons and the care of their local interests to settled residents at that metropolis, who possess but a very slight knowledge of their constituents, and a faint sympathy with their peculiar pursuits and wants.

"We propose therefore that Parliament should be recommended to authorize the division of the existing Colony of New South Wales into a northern and a southern province. Sydney would be the capital of the northern division, which would retain the present name of New South Wales. Melbourne would be the capital of the southern division, on which we would humbly advise that Your Majesty should be graciously pleased to confer the name of Victoria. In former, times Your Majesty's royal ancestors or predecessors permitted a similar use of their names to designate provinces on the North American continent. Venturing to presume that it will be Your Majesty's pleasure to follow those precedents on the present occasion, we shall take the liberty in the sequel of this Report to use the name of Victoria to describe the same province ; and the name of New South Wales to describe the northern province of the great territory to which, collectively, the latter of those appellations at present belongs.

"The line of demarcation between New South Wales and Victoria would coincide with the existing boundary between the two districts into which, for certain purposes, the Colony is already divided. It would commence at Cape How, pursue a straight line to the nearest source of the River Murray, and follow the course of that river as far as the boundary which now divides New South Wales from South Australia.

" In each of the two proposed provinces of New South Wales and Victoria, we apprehend that provision ought now to be made by Parliament for creating a Legislature, in which the representatives of the people should exercise their constitutional authority and influence. We do not advise that resort should be had for these purposes to the ancient and unaided prerogatives of Your Majesty's Crown, because it is not competent to Your Majesty, in the exercise of that prerogative, to supersede the Constitutions which Parliament has already established in the Australian Colonies. Parliamentary intervention is therefore indispensable.

" If we were approaching the present question under

circumstances which left to us the unfettered exercise of
our own judgement as to the nature of the Legislature to
be established in New South Wales, Victoria, South Australia, and Van Diemen's Land, we should advise that Parliament should be moved to recur to the ancient constitutional usage by establishing in each a Governor, a Council,
and an Assembly. For we think it desirable that the political institutions of the British Colonies should thus be
brought into the nearest possible analogy to the Constitution of the United Kingdom. We also think it wise to
adhere as closely as possible to our ancient maxims of government on this subject, and to the precedents in which
those maxims have been embodied. The experience of
centuries has ascertained the value and the practical efficiency of that system of Colonial polity to which those
maxims and precedents afford their sanction. In the absence of some very clear and urgent reason for breaking
up the ancient uniformity of design in the government of
the Colonial dependencies of the Crown, it would seem
unwise to depart from that uniformity. And further, the
whole body of constitutional law which determines the
rights and the duties of the different branches of the ancient Colonial governments having, with the lapse of time,
been gradually ascertained and firmly established, we must
regret any innovation which tends to deprive the Australian Colonies of the great advantage of possessing such a
code so defined and so maturely considered.

" But great as is the weight that we attach to these considerations, the circumstances under which we actually ap -
proach the question are such as to constrain us, howeve r
reluctantly, to adopt the opinion that the proposed Act of
Parliament should provide for the establishment in ea ch
of the four Australian Colonies of a single House of Legis -

lature only ; one-third of the members of which should be nominated by Your Majesty, and the remaining two-thirds elected by the Colonists.

" For such is in point of fact the system which now prevails throughout the territories which will compose the two provinces of New South Wales and Victoria. It was the pleasure of Parliament, in the year 1842, to establish that system. Custom appears to have attached the Colonists to it. Public opinion in New South Wales would appear to be decidedly opposed to an alteration, in this respect, of the existing Constitution of the Colony by the authority of Parliament.

" Of this fact the most conclusive proof is to be found in the petitions recently presented to Your Majesty and to Parliament, from a large body of the Colonists, praying that no change may be made, without the consent of the inhabitants at large, in the constitution and form which the local Legislature has already received from Parliament. In the absence of any counter-petitions we think it reasonable to conclude that such is the deliberate judgement of the great body of the settlers in New South Wales and Victoria, and we are of opinion that it would be unwise and unjustifiable to force such a change upon them. All that in our judgement can be reasonably done, is to leave to the legislatures, now to be established, the power of amending their own Constitutions, by resolving either of these single Houses of Legislature into two Houses. The weight which is justly due to the arguments in favour of that measure will, we trust, not be without its proper influence on both the electoral and the elected bodies.

" But even if the state of public opinion in New South Wales were less distinctly ascertained, the adoption of the course which in itself we regard as the most wise, would be forbidden by the pledge into which Your Majesty's Executive Government have already entered on the subject. Proceeding, as we apprehend, in the same view which we have ourselves taken of the wishes and judgement of the inhabitants at large, and anticipating, as we believe, our own view of the impropriety of any direct encounter with that opinion on the present subject, Your Majesty's Secretary of State having the department of the Colonies, in a Despatch of the 21st July last, informed the Governor of New South Wales, and through him the existing Legisla- ture and the Colonists at large, that this was not such a ' reform as it was at all incumbent on the Legislature at home to press on an unwilling or even on an indifferent people.' The language of this Despatch (in the wisdom of which we entirely concur) will of course be regarded by Your Majesty as implying an engagement, to which it is necessary strictly to adhere.

" The considerations to which we have thus adverted in favour of thus establishing a single House of Legislature in each of the two proposed provinces of New South Wales and Victoria, may perhaps appear applicable to those provinces only. For neither in Australia nor in Van Diemen's Land has Parliament introduced any such Constitution ; nor has Your Majesty's Executive Government entered into any pledge on the subject to either of those Colonies ; nor have any petitions been received ascertaining what is the state of public opinion in either of them on the question whether the Legislative Houses should be combined into one Chamber or separated into two. But we cannot from these considerations conclude that a real freedom remains to Your Majesty and to Parliament of selecting that which may appear on abstract grounds and on general principles to be the wiser course. We apprehend that the inconvenience of settling the forms of government simultaneously in Colonies so closely adjacent and so intimately connected with each other, with any diversity in regard to a principle so fundamental as this, is a much more formidable inconvenience than any which could follow, from maintaining a strict uniformity in that respect.   As therefore, for the reasons which we have already assigned, it appears necessary to constitute a single House of Legislature only, both in New South Wales and Victoria, we are of opinion that the same system must prevail in regard to South Australia and Van Diemen's Land.

"We recommend therefore that the proposed Act of Parliament should provide for convoking in each of the four Colonies a Legislature comprising two estates only, that is, a Governor and a single House, composed of nominees of the Crown and of the representatives of the people jointly.   We also think that in South Australia and Van Diemen's Land, as in New South Wales and Victoria, the Legislatures now to be established ought to have the power of amending their own Constitutions, by resolving either of these single Houses of Legislature into two Houses.   Whatever the result may be in either of the four Colonies, Your Majesty will thus at least have the satisfaction of knowing that free scope had been given for the influence of public opinion in them all; and that this constitutional question has been finally adjusted in each, in accordance with that opinion.

" For the same reason we think it desirable that the Legislatures now to be created should be entrusted with the power of making any other amendments in their own Constitution which time and experience may show to be requisite.   We are aware of no sufficient cause for withholding this power, and we believe that the want of it in the other

British Colonies has often been productive of serious inconvenience.

" On the other hand we do not think it right that a subordinate Legislature should have the power of enlarging or altering any of the constitutional franchises conferred on it by Parliament, without either the express or the implied assent of the Queen, Lords, and Commons of the United Kingdom. We should object to such an unrestrained permission, not for technical or legal reasons merely, but on broad and substantial grounds. Changes in the Constitution of any Colony may be productive of consequences extending far beyond the limits of the place itself. They may affect the interests of other British settlements adjacent or remote. They may be injurious to the less powerful classes of the local society. They may be prejudicial to Your Majesty's subjects in this country, or they may invade the rights of Your Majesty's Crown. We think therefore that no Act of any Australian Legislature which shall in any manner enlarge, retrench, or alter the Constitution of that Legislature of its rights and privileges, or which shall be in any respect at variance with the Act of Parliament or other instruments under which the Legislature is constituted, ought to be of any validity until it had been expressly confirmed and finally enacted by Your Majesty in Council. And we are further of opinion that it should not be lawful to make any Order in Council so confirming any such Act, until it had been laid before each House of Parliament for at least thirty days.

" Such being the general views we entertain as to the creation of the proposed Australian Legislatures, it seems necessary to advert, however briefly, to the subordinate and auxiliary enactments requisite for giving effect to that design. We shall however indicate the principal topics of this class to which it will be necessary to advert, without entering into any minute examination of the particular course which it would be desirable to follow in regard to each of them.

" The Statute-book abounds in recent precedents of such enactments. They will especially be found in the Acts establishing the existing Legislature of New South Wales, and in the recent Act for establishing a Legislature in New Zealand. The main objects of them are the division of each Colony into convenient electoral districts; the determining who shall be qualified to vote and to be elected; the settling whatever relates to the registration of votes, the conduct of elections, and the making returns; the ascertaining all the rules to be observed respecting the nomination of such of the members as are not to be elected; the defining the powers of the Governor as to the acceptance or rejection of bills; the defining the powers of Your Majesty with regard to the confirmation or disallowance of any such bills; and the securing to the Executive Government of each Colony the initiation of all money votes. It would be easy to enlarge this catalogue of subordinate topics demanding attention in framing the proposed Act of Parliament, but, for the reason already mentioned, we apprehend that it would be a needless addition to the length of this Report.

" We should think it prudent, if we thought it practicable, to confine the proposed Act to those provisions which are necessary for constituting Legislatures in the four Colonies in question, and for enabling those Legislatures to perform the duties to which they will be called. For we contemplate with great reluctance any departure from the general principle which leaves to the local Legislature of every Colony the creation of other local institutions, and the enactment of any laws which are to have their operation within the local limits of the Colony. But there are circumstances which seem to render unavoidable some deviation from that principle in the case of the Australian Colonies.

" Thus throughout New South Wales there are at present existing (at least in point of law) municipal corporations called District Councils. In point of fact, and for every practical purpose, these bodies may be regarded as extinct. Nevertheless, their legal rights, founded on an Act of Parliament, might at any time be called into action. It becomes therefore inevitable that Parliament should, in some form or other, dispose of the claims of these bodies to corporate powers and privileges.

" The most obvious course is that of a simple repeal of so much of the existing statute as relates to the District Councils, leaving the local Legislatures to deal with the subject afterwards at their discretion. The objection to this method of proceeding is, that it would not really be the mere removal from the British Statute-book of a series of ineffectual enactments. It would be regarded, and not unreasonably regarded, in these Colonies, as a significant intimation of the judgement of Parliament, that local municipal corporations might safely be dispensed with in their system of government. We think that it would be highly inexpedient to afford any countenance to such an opinion.

" We are of opinion that the existence in Australia of municipal bodies in a state of efficiency is scarcely less necessary to the public welfare, than the existence there of representative Legislatures. A large part of the benefit to be derived from such Legislatures, seems to us to depend on the simultaneous establishment and co-existence of incorporated municipalities. It is the only practicable security against the danger of undue centralization. It is the only security for the vigilant and habitual attention by the local Legislature to the interests of the more remote localities. It is by such bodies alone that in those secluded societies public spirit is kept alive, and skill in the conduct of public affairs acquired and exercised. It is in such corporations that the Colonists are trained to act as legislators in a larger sphere. By them, and by them alone, can any effectual resistance be made to the partial and undue dedication of the public resources, to the advantage of districts peculiarly fortunate in the zeal and authority of their representatives in the Legislature.

" For these reasons we cannot think it right that the legal existence of the existing District Councils should be abolished by Parliament.

" We think it would be a better course that the Act of Parliament passed in 1842 should be amended, by enacting that the District Councils which it contemplated should not be brought into operation, unless upon the petition of the inhabitants of the several districts; and that the Governor should be invested with the power of issuing charters for creating these corporations, in the districts from which he should receive petitions for their establishment, such petitions fairly representing the prevailing and deliberate wishes of the inhabitants of any such district. We apprehend that this arrangement, by which the grant of corporate powers would be left to the Governor, as the representative of Your Majesty, would be in strict accordance with the practice of this country from the earliest period. The ancient charters of incorporation were granted, on the petition of the towns, to which they were accorded by the Sovereigns. The early charters invested the corporations with the right of holding markets and of levying tolls, and landed property was also frequently conferred upon them, and they were thus placed in a possession of such resources as were necessary for the proper performance of the duties assigned to them.

"When, in the progress of society, a different state of things had arisen, and it was no longer possible to provide any new corporations which might be created, with the pecuniary means of discharging the functions belonging to them, without the imposition of rates, as it was held that the authority of the Crown did not extend to empowering corporations created by it to levy rates, the practice of granting charters fell into disuse, and many of our largest towns experienced much inconvenience from being without any adequate local organization. To meet this difficulty, Parliament, in reforming the ancient corporations, invested the Crown, in the year 1835, with the power of granting charters, by which the corporations so created should be authorized to levy rates for local purposes.

"Charters of incorporation have in this country, it is true, been confined to the towns; but, without charters, the rural districts have possessed from the earliest times an organization enabling them to manage their own local affairs with but little interference on the part either of the Crown or of the Legislature, except for the purpose of from time to time extending or regulating the exercise of the powers of their local authorities.

"The parish vestries, from very ancient times, have exercised the power of levying rates for the repair of churches, to which was afterwards added the relief of the poor. The magistrates, also, who may be regarded as the virtual representatives of the counties, have been empowered by Acts of Parliament, passed at various times, to levy county rates for the purpose of building bridges, gaols, lunatic

asylums, and court-houses; also for the custody of prisoners, for maintaining a police, and for various other purposes of local interest. It has always been held that this
system of local government has been one of the main elements of our national greatness and of the stability of the
British Constitution.

" In Australia it seems impossible, from its peculiar circumstances, to create so complex a system of local organization as that which prevails in this Country ; in their present
state of progress, inconvenience only could result from
attempting to create in these Colonies, parishes, poor-law
unions, and corporate towns, with their distinct powers ;
the same localities being, for different purposes, under the
jurisdiction of two or three different local authorities. But
we are of opinion that it would be both practicable and
desirable that so extensive a territory should be divided
into districts, each possessing some body of a representative character, constituted in some simple manner, to which
should be entrusted all the powers of local administration
which are required. Such a body ought to possess the
power of levying rates, but we would recommend that the
exercise of this power should not be made imperative, and
that the provision of the existing Act of Parliament, which
renders it necessary that half the expense of the police in
each district should be thus levied, should be repealed.
The Colonial Legislature ought, we think, to have full
power to pass laws, making any regulations it may think
fit as to the mode of assessing and levying rates ; also for
making any alterations which may be found necessary in
the constitution and in the duties assigned to these municipal bodies. We recommend that the provisions we have
now described should be made applicable to Van Diemen's
Land and South Australia, as well to the provinces into

which New South Wales will be divided, and should likewise be extended to Western Australia, whenever that settlement may be capable of receiving a representative legislature.

" It may however be questioned, and with great apparent reason, whether there exists, or is likely to arise in any of these Colonies, a disposition to bring into action the dormant powers of the existing municipalities, or to solicit the grant of any new powers of that nature. It is at least certain, that there has hitherto been a strong disinclination in the rural districts of New South Wales to assume the privileges and to undertake the responsibilities of such incorporations, and that reluctance may of course be found insuperable hereafter. If so, we should regard it as a conclusive objection to the project of reviving the old or of creating new municipalities. Neither Your Majesty nor Parliament would desire to force unwelcome duties on the Australian Colonists under the name of franchises. If such duties are not undertaken with alacrity, and performed with zeal, and controlled by public vigilance, and rewarded by public applause, they would be undertaken to no good purpose, and would be better declined.

" But the acknowledged want of alacrity and zeal in this service in the municipal corporations already established, has been publicly and generally ascribed to a cause which we are disposed to regard as remediable. In order to the effective execution of the powers of these bodies, it would be necessary to raise large local rates, and to devote a large part of the produce of them to an expenditure unfruitful of any considerable or immediate advantage to the ratepayers. If, for example, a road or a drain should be formed through a district imperfectly settled, by the produce of rates levied on the present settlers, that outlay would confer on the ungranted lands, in proportion to their extent, a benefit equal to that which the settled lands would derive from it. Eventually, indeed, those ungranted lands would be sold at prices enhanced by this application of the local rates, and the general territorial revenue of the colony would to the same extent be enhanced; but the ratepayers of the district would receive no peculiar benefit excepting that of the more rapid increase of settlement in their immediate vicinity. Persons living in a new country, to whom the command of capital is of such urgent importance, can never be expected to find in such remote, uncertain, and inappreciable benefits as these, a motive strong enough to induce them to impose on themselves rates to which the wild lands could contribute nothing.

"To remove this very reasonable objection, we would observe that one-half of the territorial revenue of the Australian Colonies is at present appropriated by Act of Parliament to the cost of introducing emigrants. The remaining half, subject to a deduction of certain enumerated charges, has been placed by Parliament at the disposal of the Lords Commissioners of the Treasury for the public service of the respective Colonies. We recommend that of the territorial revenue realized in each district, the proportion thus left under their Lordships' control, should be placed by them at the disposal of the District Councils for objects of local concern, reserving only such a percentage as might be necessary for any purposes of general interest which ought to be charged upon this fund. We should further propose that the sums so placed at the disposal of the District Councils should be applicable exclusively to public works within their respective districts. We also think that no such work, if effected at the expense or by the aid of the land-fund, should be undertaken without a previous report on its probable advantages, and a previous estimate of its cost by official persons duly qualified to prepare such reports and estimates. Further, we would advise that no such work should be actually undertaken without the previous sanction of the Governor in Council, founded on the proposed estimates and reports. Finally, we think that the proper officers of each District Council should render, annually, accounts of the grant of the last preceding year, which accounts should be published for general information. No additional grant ought to be made to any such body so long as any such account was in arrear.

" It appears to us that by dedicating to these purposes that part of the land-fund which Parliament has left at the disposal of the Crown, many important ends would be answered. The Executive Government in this Country would be relieved of a responsibility which is as needless as it is invidious. A powerful motive would be called into action for the acceptance and employment of the proposed corporate franchises. The great principle of devoting the land-fund to the utmost possible extent to the improvement of the land would be observed. The manual labourers introduced into the Colony by the one-half of that fund would not more directly contribute to the improvement of the territory than the remaining portion would contribute to that end by the creation of roads, drains, and other similar works. The price of all ungranted lands in the district would be enhanced by such works, and of that increased price the Colony would receive the benefit in an augmented emigration fund, while the particular district would also receive a particular benefit from it in an augmented dividend of the part of the fund which we propose to dedicate to these services. It would operate as an inducement to purchase waste lands to *bonâ fide* settlers, as every such purchaser would, through the Council of his district, virtually receive back again a large part of his payment for the land, in improvements of the locality in which it was situate. Thus every district in which sales of Crown lands could be effected would be in a state of progressive improvement. As, by means of successive sales, the waste lands of the Crown in any district became small in comparison with the improved lands of actual settlers, this source of local revenue would indeed diminish; but the value of the rateable property would be continually increasing. The resource afforded by this use of the funds at the disposal of the Lords of the Treasury would thus come in aid of the local resources of a district when such aid was most essential to its welfare, and would cease to avail the district as it became more and more independent of all resources but its own. Thus District Councils would be rescued from the necessity of contracting debts in the infancy of the settlement of their district, when the lenders of the money would demand a very high rate of interest, and such loans would be necessary only in districts wealthy enough to be able to make them on moderate terms.

" As however the proposed application of this fund must be contingent on the acceptance or non-acceptance by the districts of the proposed Charters, we apprehend that until that contingency shall be determined by the event, it will be premature to ratify by the authority of Parliament the contemplated dedication of the fund to these purposes. Nor is there any present necessity for the intervention of Parliament, as under the existing law Your Majesty possesses the power of directing this appropriation of the funds in question.

" Among the appropriations of the public revenues of New South Wales by Parliament, is that of a sum of

£30,000 per annum for the support of public worship, it
being however referred to Your Majesty to apportion that
fund between the different Christian Churches amongst
which the Colonists are divided. Your Majesty has already
determined that this sum shall be distributed between the
Churches of England, of Scotland, and of Rome, and the
Wesleyan Society. To each of those bodies has been assigned an income bearing to the entire income the proportion which, according to the census of the year 1841,
the number of the members of each of those bodies bore to
the collective number of the members of all of them. The
census of 1846 has however shown such a change in these
numerical proportions, or such an inaccuracy in the census
of 1841, as renders the division of the fund somewhat more
favourable to the Church of England than, according to the
strict principle of that division, it ought to be.

" We are of opinion that the proposed Legislatures
ought not to possess the unrestricted power of altering the
existing arrangements. The vested rights which individual
clergymen hold under the New South Wales Constitutional
Act, ought, we apprehend, to be maintained inviolate.
And in the absence of very weighty reasons, clearly and
fully established, it would, we think, be inexpedient to deprive any one of the four Churches in question of any part
of the temporal support to which it is at present entitled
under that statute. The existing arrangement however,
which appears to have contemplated a periodical revision
of the number of the members of each Church, and a consequent readjustment from time to time of their respective
dividends, is in this respect open to much objection, and
the effect of adopting that principle would inevitably be to
bring discredit on the efforts made by those Churches for
the diffusion of ʰhe opinions peculiar to and characteristic

of each of them. Such efforts would be ascribed, however unjustly, to other motives than the disinterested desire for the propagation of truth, or of supposed truth, and a spirit of competition and rivalry would be excited, which every devout member of each of these Churches would earnestly deprecate.

" We should therefore propose to secure to each of the four Churches, not for a definite, but for an indefinite period, that share of the common fund which has been assigned to it under the existing arrangement. If at any future time the local Legislature of either province should see fit to endow any other Church than those four, or to augment the endowment of any one of the four, any such new or augmented endowment ought, we apprehend, to be made by an additional charge on the revenue of the province, and not by a deduction from the revenue of any one of the four endowed Churches. Whatever fluctuations may occur in the comparative numbers of the members of those Churches, the steady and rapid increase of the population of the Australian Colonies renders it eminently improbable that the absolute wants of any one of those Churches will ever be less than they are at present, or that the existing endowment of any one of them will ever be found to be excessive.

" In giving this permanent character to the existing apportionment, it seems however necessary to guard against one error which has already been brought to light. That apportionment was founded on the census of 1841. But there is reason to conclude that the subsequent census of 1846 was not only taken with much greater care, but was drawn up with much greater accuracy, and affords a much safer basis on which to erect a scheme of indefinite duration. We subjoin a schedule showing the results of the census of 1846, as far as respects the numerical proportion between the adherents of the different Churches. From that schedule it will appear that the present apportionment of the fund for the support of public worship is less favourable to the other endowed Churches, as compared to the Church of England, than according to the census of 1846 it ought to be. In pursuance of the principle already stated, we propose that Parliament should be recommended to redress that inequality, not by a deduction from the share of the latter, but by an additional charge on the public revenue. Such a charge would not be of great amount, and would not raise the whole appropriation for public worship to the same proportion to the existing resources of New South Wales, as that which subsisted between the former appropriation for that service, and the resources of the Colony at the time when it was made.

" In distributing between New South Wales and Victoria the total amount of the proposed annual charge for public worship, we apprehend that in pursuance of the principle of respecting, as far as possible, all vested interests and existing arrangements, the census of 1846 should be taken as the guide to be followed. We therefore propose that the proportion of the grant for each of the four Churches to be charged on the revenue of each province respectively, should be determined by the comparative numbers of the members of these Churches in the two districts at the time the census was made. We add, in an Appendix to this Report, a schedule, showing the amount which, following this rule, would be charged on the revenues of both provinces in favour of the several Churches.

" With regard to Van Diemen's Land and South Australia, in neither of which Colonies has any Parliamentary provision been made for the support of public worship, we conceive that it will be sufficient that Parliament should

now provide that the proposed Act shall not in any manner interfere with the operation of the laws existing on
that subject in either of those Colonies; but that those
laws shall continue in force as fully as if no such Act had
been passsed.

"Passing to the subject of a Civil List, we have to
observe that the very large proportion of the revenue of
New South Wales, at present withdrawn from the control
of the Legislature by the permanent appropriation of Parliament, has been a continual subject of complaint and
remonstrance in the Colony since the passing of the Constitutional Act of 1842; and we cannot conceal our opinion
that these complaints are not without some foundation.
It appears to us hardly consistent with the full adoption
of the principles of Representative Government, that as
to a large part of the public expenditure of the Colony,
the Legislature should be deprived of all authority; nor
does there appear to us to be any real occasion for imposing a restriction upon the powers of that body which manifests so much jealousy as to the manner in which those
powers may be exercised.   The expenditure thus provided
for is all incurred for services in which the Colonists alone
are interested.   The Colonists themselves are mainly concerned in the proper and efficient performance of those services; and it appears to us that they ought to possess,
through their representatives, the power of making such
changes from time to time in the public establishments as
circumstances may require.   But while we are of opinion
that there is no sufficient reason for refusing to the Legislatures of the Colonies a control over the whole of their
expenditure, we also think that great inconvenience and
very serious evils might be expected to arise from leaving
the whole of the public establishments to be provided for

by annual vote. In this country Your Majesty's Civil List is settled upon Your Majesty for life, and, in addition to this, Parliament has thought fit to provide, by a permanant charge on the Consolidated Fund, for a very considerable part of the establishments kept up for the public service, including the whole of those of a judicial character, leaving to be defrayed by annual votes those charges only which have been regarded as requiring the more frequent revision of the Legislature. The reasons which have induced the British Parliament in this manner to withdraw various heads of expenditure from annual discussion, and to make provision for them in a manner which can only be altered by an Act of the whole Legislature, apply, as we apprehend, with much increased force in favour of adopting a similar policy in the Colonies. It is not be denied that in these smaller societies party spirit is apt to run still higher than amongst ourselves, and that questions respecting the remuneration of public servants are occasionally discussed, rather with reference to personal feelings than to a calm consideration of the real interest of the community. We believe also, that true economy is promoted by giving to those who are employed in the public service some reasonable assurance for the permanence of their official incomes. It is thus only that efficient service can be secured in return for a moderate remuneration. With these views the arrangement which we should recommend is, that Parliament should, in the first instance, charge upon the revenues of the several Colonies an amount sufficient to defray the expense of those services which it would be inexpedient to leave to be provided for by annual votes of the respective Legislatures, leaving however to those Legislatures full power to alter this appropriation by laws to be passed in the usual form. It would remain for

Your Majesty to determine what instructions should be given to the governors of these Colonies, as to their assenting on behalf of the Crown to any laws which might be tendered to them by the Legislatures, for repealing or altering any of the charges created by Parliament on the revenues of the respective Colonies. We conceive that it might be advisable by such instructions to restrain the Governors from assenting to Acts making any alterations in the salaries of their own offices, or of those of the Judges and some others of the public servants, unless these Acts contained clauses suspending their operation until they should be confirmed by Your Majesty's immediate authority. It appears to us that this course ought to be adopted, because we consider that the salaries of the principal officers of the Colonial Governments ought not to be changed without Your Majesty's direct concurrence; and because the present holders of some of the offices of lower rank have received their appointments under circumstances which give them a strong claim to the protection which would be thus afforded to them. Men who have abandoned other prospects for the purpose of accepting Colonial employment, which they had reason to expect would be permanent, and who have since faithfully discharged their duties, must be regarded as having claims which rest upon the grounds of public faith, and on contracts which on their side have hitherto been strictly fulfilled, to retain their present salaries, so long as they shall conduct themselves properly, or to receive adequate compensation for their loss. We doubt not that such claims would be respected by the local Legislatures, whatever reductions they might see fit to make in other cases: but we think that Your Majesty ought to secure them even from the risk of a hasty and ill-considered decision to their prejudice, occasioned by some temporary excitement; subject to these qualifications, we are of opinion that complete control over the Colonial expenditure ought to be given to the respective Legislatures.

" There yet remains a question of considerable difficulty. By far the larger part of the revenue of the Australian Colonies is derived from duties on customs. But if, when Victoria shall have been separated from New South Wales, each province shall be authorized to impose duties according to its own wants, it is scarcely possible but that in process of time differences should arise between the rates of duty imposed upon the same articles in the one and in the other of them. There is already such a difference in the tariffs of South Australia and New South Wales; and although, until of late, this has been productive of little inconvenience, yet with the increase of settlers on either side of the imaginary line dividing them, it will become more and more serious. The division of New South Wales into two Colonies would further aggravate this inconvenience, if the change should lead to the introduction of three entirely distinct tariffs, and to the consequent necessity for imposing restrictions and securities on the import and export of goods between them. So great indeed would be the evil, and such the obstruction of the inter-colonial trade, and so great the check to the development of the resources of each of these Colonies, that it seems to us necessary that there should be one tariff common to them all, so that goods might be carried from the one into the other with the same absolute freedom as between any two adjacent counties in England.

" We are further of opinion that the same tariff should be established in Van Diemen's Land also, because the intercourse between that Island and the neighbouring Colonies in New Holland has risen to a great importance and extent, and has an obvious tendency to increase. Yet fiscal regulations on either side of the intervening strait must of necessity check, and might perhaps to a great extent destroy, that beneficial trade.

" If the duties were uniform, it is obvious that there need be no restrictions whatever imposed upon the import or export of goods between the respective Colonies, and no motive for importing into one goods liable to duty, which were destined for consumption in another ; and it may safely be calculated that each would receive the proportion of revenue to which it would be justly entitled, or, at all events, that there would be no departure from this to an extent of any practical importance.

" Hence it seems to us that a uniformity in the rate of duties should be secured.

" For this purpose we recommend that a uniform tariff should be established by the authority of Parliament, but that it should not take effect until twelve months had elapsed from the promulgation in the several Colonies of the proposed Act of Parliament. That interval would afford time for making any financial arrangements which the contemplated change might require in any of them ; and by adopting the existing Tariff of New South Wales (with some modifications to adapt it to existing circumstances) as the General Tariff for Australia, we apprehend that there would be no risk of imposing upon the inhabitants of these Colonies a table of duties unsuited to their actual wants. We should not however be prepared to offer this recommendation, unless we proposed at the same time to provide for making any alteration in this general tariff, which time and experience may dictate, and this we think can only be done by creating some authority competent to act for all those Colonies jointly.

" For this purpose we propose that one of the Governors of the Australian Colonies should always hold from Your Majesty a commission constituting him the Governor-General of Australia. We think that he should be authorized to convene a body to be called the General Assembly of Australia, at any time and at any place within Your Majesty's Australian dominions which he might see fit to appoint for the purpose. But we are of opinion that the first convocation of that body should be postponed until the Governor-General should have received from two or more of the Australian Legislatures addresses requesting him to exercise that power.

" We recommend that the General Assembly should consist of the Governor-General and of a single House, to be called the House of Delegates. The House of Delegates should be composed of not less than twenty, nor of more than thirty members. They should be elected by the Legislatures of the different Australian Colonies. We subjoin a schedule explanatory of the composition of this body, that is, of the total number of delegates, and of the proportions in which each Colony should contribute to that number.

" We think that Your Majesty should be authorized to establish provisionally, and in the first instance, all the rules necessary for the election of the delegates, and for the conduct of the business of the General Assembly, but that it should be competent to that body to supersede any such rules, and to substitute others, which substituted rules should not, however, take effect until they had received Your Majesty's sanction.

" We propose that the General Assembly should also have the power of making laws for the alteration of the number of delegates, or for the improvement in any other respect of its own Constitution. But we think that no such law should come into operation until it had actually been confirmed by Your Majesty.

" We propose to limit the range of the legislative authority of the General Assembly to the ten topics which we proceed to enumerate. These are :—

" 1. The imposition of Duties on Imports and Exports.

" 2. The Conveyance of Letters.

" 3. The formation of Roads, Canals, or Railways, traversing any two or more of such colonies.

" 4. The erection and maintenance of Beacons and Lighthouses.

" 5. The Imposition of Dues or other Charges on Shipping in every Port or Harbour.

" 6. The establishment of a General Supreme Court, to be a court of original jurisdiction, or a court of appeal for any of the inferior courts of the separate provinces.

" 7. The determining of the extent of the jurisdiction and the forms and manner of proceeding of such Supreme Court.

" 8. The regulation of Weights and Measures.

" 9. The enactment of laws affecting all the Colonies represented in the General Assembly on any subject not specifically mentioned in the preceding list, but on which the General Assembly should be desired to legislate by addresses for that purpose presented to them from the Legislatures of all those Colonies.

" 10. The appropriation to any of the preceding objects of such sums as may be necessary, by an equal percentage from the revenue received in all the Australian Colonies, in virtue of any enactments of the General Assembly of Australia.

" By these means we apprehend that many important

objects would be accomplished which would otherwise be unattainable; and by the qualifications which we have proposed, effectual security would, we think, be taken against the otherwise danger of establishing a central Legislature in opposition to the wishes of the separate Legislatures, or in such a manner as to induce collisions of authority between them. The proceedings also of the Legislative Council of New South Wales, with reference to the proposed changes in the Constitution, lead us to infer that the necessity of creating some such general authority for the Australian Colonies begins to be seriously felt."

SCHEDULE 1.

	Distribution of £30,000 according to Census of 1841 (existing arrangement).			Distribution of £30,000 according to Census of 1846.	Sums which, according to the Census of 1846, will correspond with the sum now enjoyed by the Church of England, according to the Census of 1841.
	1			2	3
	£	s.	d.	£	£
Church of England	17,581	2	4	15,715	17,581
,, Rome .	8,510	14	6	9,333	10,441
,, Scotland	3,136	9	11	3,634	4,066
Wesleyans . . .	771	13	3	1,316	1,472
Total	29,998	0	0	29,998	33,560

In the present undivided Colony of New South Wales

Distribution of the Sums in Column 3 *between New South Wales (present Sydney District) and Victoria (present Port Philip District), according to the Census of* 1846.

	New South Wales.	Victoria.	Total.
	£	£	£
Church of England . . .	14,812	2,769	17,581
,,　　Rome	8,757	1,684	10,441
,,　　Scotland . . .	2,979	1,087	4,066
Wesleyans	1,176	296	1,472
Total	27,724	5,836	33,560

Census of 1841 *and* 1846, *upon which the above calculations are founded.*

	1841.		1846.	
Church of England :—				
Sydney District . . .	67,537		79,810	
Port Philip District .	6,190	73,727	14,921	94,731
Church of Rome :—				
Sydney District . . .	33,249		47,187	
Port Philip District .	2,441	35,690	9,075	56,262
Church o Scotland :—				
Sydney District . . .	11,009		16,053	
Port Philip District .	2,144	13,153	5,856	21,909
Wesleyan3 :—				
Sydney District . . .	2,586		6,338	
Port Philip District .	650	3,236	1,597	7,935

SCHEDULE 2.

Composition of the House of Delegates.

Each Colony to send two members, and each to send one additional member for every 15,000 of the population, according to the latest census before the convening of the House.

On the present population the numbers would be as follows:—

	Population by last Census.	Number of Members.
New South Wales	155,000	12
Victoria.	33,000	4
Van Diemen's Land (deducting convicts)	46,000	5
South Australia	31,000	4
		25

" Her Majesty having taken the said Report, together with the Schedules thereunto annexed, into consideration, was pleased, by and with the advice of Her Privy Council, to approve thereof.

" (Signed) W. L. BATHURST."

Copy of a Despatch from Earl Grey to Governor Sir C. A. Fitzroy.

" *Downing-street, August* 30, 1850.

" SIR,

" The Act for the better Government of Her Majesty's Australian Colonies having at length received the Royal assent, it is with much satisfaction that I have now the honour of transmitting it to you. It was my earnest desire to have been enabled to do so at an earlier period; but the delay which has occurred in finally enacting this measure has been attended with this advantage, that it has given room for the thorough and repeated discussion of its provisions, both in Parliament and by the various organs of public opinion in the Colonies. These protracted discussions, and the detailed Report of the Committee of Her Majesty's Privy Council, of which you are already in possession, and of which the recommendations have been closely followed in this Act, must have rendered both its principle and its details so well known to yourself and the public, that it is necessary for me, on the present occasion, to do little more than advert to some of the changes which the measure underwent during its progress through Parliament.

" These changes, with one or two exceptions only, which I will presently notice, involve no departure from the fundamental principle of the measure, which is that of maintaining the existing Constitution of New South Wales, with as little alteration as possible, in the separate Colonies into which it is now about to be divided, and extending that Constitution to the other Colonies to which representative Constitutions are, under this Act, to be granted.

" The reasons which induced Her Majesty's Government to take this course in the first instance, and to adhere to it notwithstanding the objections which were urged against it in Parliament, have been fully stated in the report already alluded to, and in the debates which took place during the progress of this measure. We were of opinion that changes in an existing Colonial Constitution ought not to be made, without very strong reason, by the Legislature of the Mother-country. The supreme power with which the British Constitution invests that Legislature ought, in our judgement, to be thus exercised only when called for by a case of clear and urgent necessity, or of

great abuse, or by an authentic expression of the wishes of
the community to be affected by the change. The proper
authorities to introduce those gradual improvements which
are really likely to be safe and profitable are those which
may be brought into action by the natural development
of the Colonial community itself. You are aware that,
except in a very few cases which have occurred within the
last century, the various forms of government established
in the British Colonies have not been determined by Parliament, but have been settled by the Crown, in concert
with the inhabitants of the Colonies, and that any alterations and amendments of the Constitution originally adopted
have been effected from time to time as they have been required by the same authority.

"On full examination of the subject before them, Her
Majesty's Government could find no evidence of any necessity, or of any abuse, which would, in their opinion,
have justified a departure, with regard to New South
Wales, from this principle of our early Colonial policy, by
having recourse to the authority of Parliament in order to
effect in the Constitution of that Colony a change which
has not been demanded by its inhabitants. We were by
no means insensible to the force of the arguments commonly adduced against legislation by a single Chamber.
But, on the other hand, we were acquainted with the peculiar difficulties which, in the Australian Colonies, at present impede the attendance of members from distant districts, and render it unadvisable to adopt for their legislature a Constitution which would have increased the number
of persons required for the satisfactory transaction of business. We could not discover in the record of the proceedings of the existing Legislature any reasons for supposing that it had substantially failed in its duty to its

constituents, or had worked in a manner disadvantageous to their interests and the progress of the community. The evidence in our possession seemed to lead to very different conclusions; and above all, we had no reason whatever to believe that the community were dissatisfied with the present Constitution of the Colony, nor any means of judging in what manner, if that Constitution were to be altered, it could be so with advantage and in accordance with the wishes of the inhabitants. Though we were aware that in New South Wales, as elsewhere, there undoubtedly existed differences of opinion as to the best means of constituting a Legislature, yet we did not find, in the numerous petitions which the subject of this Act has elicited, any expressions whatever of discontent with that now established, or any prayer except for its substantial maintenance.

" But while thus maintaining the existing Constitution of New South Wales, Her Majesty's Government were, as I have stated, anxious to give to the Legislature the fullest power, consistent with safety, of amending that Constitution, and of modifying from time to time, without the intervention of Parliament, the political arrangements which may be suitable to existing circumstances, but which are likely to require adaptation to the changes which must take place in so rapidly advancing a society. The necessary powers for this purpose are given by Section 32 of the Act. You will observe that they extend, among other things, to the formation of two Chambers, of which one or both may be elective. The only restriction, in short, on the general power of alteration appears to be this, that, if the present single Chamber is retained, the proportion of elective and non-elective members cannot be varied, nor can the manner of appointment of the non-elective members be interfered with. The power of the existing Legislature, of effecting minor alterations in the arrangements for the election of members of the first Legislative Councils of New South Wales and Victoria, is defined by Section 11. The control of Her Majesty's Government and of Parliament over the more extensive changes which may be hereafter made in the Constitution is provided for by the 32nd Section, which enacts that these changes shall only be effected by reserved bills.

" On the important subject of the use which may be made of these powers, it would be premature now to address you in detail. In my own opinion (strengthened undoubtedly by the general consent of the various petitions and addresses which have reached me in their expression of confidence in the existing Legislature), it would be most advisable to abide for a time by the Constitution as it now stands. I think that there will probably be more danger from the over-eagerness of some to make use of the power of change now placed in their hands, than from the reluctance of others to venture on untried experiments. I think, moreover, that the progress of most of the Australian Colonies is so rapid, and the changes both in the general frame of society and its component parts so continual, that any attempt to establish a more elaborate form of Legislature, if too hastily entered upon, is likely to be found defective in some unforeseen particular ; so that another Legislature might probably find it necessary to commence the work of change anew, and that there would thus be danger of the institutions of the country becoming the subject of a succession of experiments, injurious to the public interest by the excitement they would be calculated to keep up, and by their tendency to divert public attention from measures of a more practical kind.

" These are the views which my observation of public

affairs, and especially of the course of events in Europe of late years, would lead me to impress on you; they are those of one deeply anxious for the continuance of that advance in material and moral prosperity, of which the Australian Colonies have on the whole exhibited so striking an example, but like all general views, they must be received subject to the exigencies of times and events.

"I have only to add, in reference to this part of the subject, that, under the definition of 'reserved bills,' given in Section 33, you will observe that you retain the power of refusing your consent to all bills, and are in no case under the necessity of reserving them for the signification of the Queen's pleasure, if you think them clearly inadmissible, and that they ought therefore to be at once rejected.

"The most important deviations from the general principle of leaving the existing Constitution unaltered are to be found in Section 4, which was introduced in the progress of the bill through the House of Lords. It was strongly urged on Parliament that the existing franchise was originally fixed on too high a scale, and that, from changes in the money value and distribution of property, it had become even more restricted than was contemplated. There existed, moreover, no legal means for the admission to the franchise of persons holding pasture licenses, or of persons residing beyond the boundaries of location. It is true that by this bill, as originally framed, the new Legislatures, after the division of the Colony, would have possessed the power of lowering the franchise, and of admitting these voters; but it was felt that leaving these changes to be effected by the exercise of this power must cause some delay in the redress of what was clearly shown by petitions and other representations to be felt as a practical grievance. If, moreover, the same franchise was to be fixed for the several Colonies at the outset (and any other course would have been manifestly inconvenient), it was thought objectionable to establish one recognized as too high.

" You are therefore empowered, under Section 3, with the assistance of the existing Legislative Council of the whole Colony, to form new electoral divisions for both New South Wales and Victoria, admitting such districts as you think proper, without regard to the ' boundaries of location.' And the first election in each Colony will take place under the new franchise provided by Section 4.

" I will next direct your attention to the clauses of the Act which relate to the power of the Legislature as to the imposition of taxes and the appropriation of public money.

" The expenses of collecting the Revenue will be defrayed, as hitherto, out of the gross Revenue, and the charges incurred on this account will, for the present, continue to be audited as they now are in the manner which has been directed by the Commissioners of the Treasury, under Act 7 and 8 Vict., c. 72. But in my Circular Despatch of the 8th instant, I have informed you that the management of the establishment of customs is henceforth to be placed under the Local Government, and the Lords of the Treasury concur with me in the desire that the Local Legislature should have the fullest information respecting the details of the charges on the gross Revenue for the cost of collection. I enclose, for your information and guidance, the copy of a letter from the Treasury on this subject.

" The effect of Sections 13, 17, and 18, is to give the Legislature a considerably increased control over that part of the Colonial expenditure now charged on what is called the Civil List. The Legislatures will have the power to alter, by Acts passed for that purpose, all or any of the sums specified in the schedules. In the case of these alterations affecting the salary of the Governor, or the appropriation for public worship, it is required by the present Act of Parliament that the Colonial Acts should be reserved for the signification of Her Majesty's pleasure.

" In the former Act there was a power given to the Governor, by the 38th Section, of varying the sum appropriated to the purposes of Schedule B, and the savings accruing from such alteration were exempted from the control of the Legislative Council. This latter proviso has been omitted in the present Act, as there appeared to be no sufficient reason why the ordinary power of the Legislative body should not extend to these particular savings.

" This extension of the authority of the Legislature has been rendered expedient in the view of Her Majesty's Government, by the evidence of the hitherto successful progress of Constitutional Government. The manner in which the people of New South Wales have hitherto exercised the powers they possessed through their Representatives seemed fully to justify the grant of the enlarged power which will now be entrusted to them in relation to their financial affairs ; but it has been deemed right by Parliament, in order the more completely to maintain the independence of the Judges of the Supreme Court, to provide that no diminution of judicial salaries by Colonial enactments shall affect Judges appointed previously to the passing of such enactment.

" All other salaries, except those of the Governor and Judges, are placed by Parliament under the ordinary control of the Legislature. With regard to the mode of exercising this control, you will however observe that reductions of fixed establishments, or of any expenditure provided for by permanent laws, can only be effected by Acts of the Legislature, which of course require the assent of the

Crown, signified by yourself, and confirmed by Her Majesty; but I wish you distinctly to understand that there is no desire on the part of Her Majesty's Government to prevent prospective reductions of charges which, in the opinion of the Colonists, will safely admit of being diminished.   The interests of existing office-holders must be protected, because they accepted those offices with expectations which cannot justly be disappointed.   But, subject to these interests, there is no objection to the Legislature fixing whatever scale of emoluments they may think fit for public servants to be hereafter appointed.   I should, for my own part, consider it highly injudicious to reduce the salary of an office so as to render it no longer an object of ambition to men of ability and of respectable station.   But this is a matter in which the interests of the Colonists only are involved, as they will be the sufferers from any failure to provide adequate remuneration for those by whom the public · service is carried on; the determination, therefore, of what is sufficient must be left to the Legislatures, with whom will rest the responsibility for the judicious exercise of the power.

"I consider it, however, absolutely essential that, whatever may be the rate of payment, the salaries of all the principal officers of the Government should, for the reasons stated in the Report of the Committee of the Privy Council, be permanently granted; that is, not voted from year to year, but provided for in the same manner as charges on the Consolidated Fund in this country by Acts, and therefore only susceptible of alteration by Acts of the Legislature passed in the ordinary manner, with the consent of the Crown.   You will therefore understand that you are not at liberty to give the assent of the Crown to any Act which may be passed reducing the salaries of those who are now in the public service, or rendering dependent on annual votes any of the charges now provided for by permanent appropriations. Any Acts of this sort you will reserve for the signification of Her Majesty's pleasure, unless you consider them so manifestly objectionable as to call for their rejection. Subject to this restriction you are authorized to exercise your own judgement in giving or withholding your assent from Acts for the reduction of the fixed charges on the Colonial Revenue.

" With regard to the Land Revenue, I am aware that much jealousy has existed of its being appropriated, as it hitherto has been, by the Authority of the Crown, and it is therefore necessary that I should explain that though the Act of Parliament which I now transmit to you makes no alteration in the existing law upon the subject, Her Majesty's Government have no desire to exercise any control over the appropriation of this Revenue beyond that which is necessary in order to ensure its being expended on the objects to which it is legitimately applicable, and in a manner consistent with justice towards those from whom it is raised. But this Revenue is of a very different character from that which is raised by taxation; and my views with regard to it will be best explained by the enclosed copy of a Despatch which I have lately had occasion to address to the Lieutenant-Governor of Van Diemen's Land. The principles there stated are, with very slight modification, applicable to New South Wales. The most important differences between the two Colonies are—first, that in New South Wales the expenditure of half the income derived from the sale of land on emigration, as required by the Land Sales Act, is, in the absence of any other source from which a sufficient supply of labour could be obtained, an appropriation of this fund which tends directly to increase the value of the land from the sale of which it is derived; and, secondly, that in Van Diemen's Land there is no longer occasion for any expenditure on account of the aboriginal natives, while in New South Wales the cost of the best arrangements which can be made for their protection and civilization ought to be regarded as a charge prior to all others on the Revenue derived from the appropriation of the lands of which they were the original inhabitants. After providing for this charge and those incurred on account of surveys and the cost of collection, such proportion of the Revenue derived from the sale or leasing of the Crown lands as is not required for emigration, ought, as far as possible, to be applied in Local Improvements in the district in which it arises; and I propose communicating with the Lords Commissioners of the Treasury on the steps which should be adopted in order to carry these views into effect.

" The provisions of the Act respecting District Councils, which are closely connected with the subject to which I have just adverted, appear to require no further explanation, as they are in exact conformity with the detailed recommendations of the Report of the Committee of Privy Council.

" The effect of Sections 27 and 31 is to give the several Legislatures that full power, which is understood to have been hitherto curtailed by the restrictions of various Acts of Parliament, to impose such customs-duties as they may think fit, provided only that they are not of a differential kind, and do not contravene certain other regulations of minor importance.

" The provisions of Section 29 were introduced on account of doubts which appeared to exist, whether a Supreme Court could be established in the new Colony of Victoria without contravening the enactments of former statutes, and whether full liberty to make alterations in the existing Supreme Courts would, without these provisions, have been vested in the Legislatures of the altered Colony of New South Wales and of Van Diemen's Land. The effect of the clause is, that complete freedom of action in this respect is left to the several Legislatures, and that the Legislature of Victoria may either continue for the present the judicial arrangement now in force, or proceed forthwith to establish a new one.

" The boundary between New South Wales and Victoria is the same with that now existing between the Sydney and Port Philip districts. The mode by which any alteration is to be effected is pointed out in Section 30. In the case of one Legislature only petitioning, the Privy Council cannot take such a petition into consideration until six months after notice of the petition has reached the Legislature which has not petitioned : a provision which appears to afford ample opportunity for any counter petition.

" The provisions of Sections 34 and 35 were introduced on consideration of the peculiar circumstances of that large and important portion of the Colony which lies to the northward, particularly in the direction of Moreton Bay. The centre of the peopled part of that district is as far from Sydney as Melbourne itself; and it is impossible not to foresee that the same inconveniences which have led to the separation of Victoria from New South Wales, may at no distant time be felt in the north. It has been thought, therefore, expedient that the Crown should possess the power of forming a new Colony or Colonies so as to include Moreton Bay, and of communicating representative institutions to the inhabitants of any district so divided from New South Wales. But this power is only to be exercised on petition from the householders of the territory affected by the arrangement. Her Majesty's Government can have no interest in promoting the formation of any such new Colony, and the clauses adverted to merely secure the means of carrying into execution the distinct wish of the inhabitants themselves.

" The clauses giving power for the establishment under certain circumstances of a General Assembly for two or more of the Colonies were omitted from the bill in its progress through the House of Lords. This omission was not assented to by Her Majesty's Government in consequence of any change of opinion as to the importance of the suggestions on this point which are contained in the Report of the Committee of the Privy Council. But it was found on examination that the clauses in question were liable to practical objections, to obviate which it would have been necessary to introduce amendments entering into details of Legislation which there were no means of satisfactorily arranging without further communication with the Colonies.

"Her Majesty's Government have been the less reluctant to abandon for the present this portion of the measure which they proposed, inasmuch as even in New South Wales it appeared, as far as they could collect the opinion which prevails on the subject, not to be regarded as of immediate importance, while in the other Colonies objections had been expressed to the creation of any such authority.

" I am not, however, the less persuaded that the want of some such central authority to regulate matters of common importance to the Australian Colonies will be felt, and probably at a very early period ; but when this want is so felt, it will of itself suggest the means by which it may be met. The several Legislatures will, it is true, be unable at once to give the necessary authority to a General Assembly, because the Legislative power of each is confined of necessity within its territorial limits; but if two or more of these Legislatures should find that there are objects of common interest for which it is expedient to create such an authority, they will have it in their power, if they can settle the terms of an arrangement for the purpose, to pass Acts for giving effect to it, with clauses suspending their operation until Parliament shall have supplied the authority that is wanting. By such Acts the extent and objects of the powers which they are prepared to delegate to such a body might be defined and limited with precision, and there can be little doubt that Parliament, when applied to in order to give effect to an arrangement so agreed upon, would readily consent to do so.

" In framing the Schedules to this Act, some difficulty was necessarily experienced from the imperfection of the materials at the command of Her Majesty's Government for ascertaining distinctly the division of the existing appropriations between the services of New South Wales and Port Philip. We had no wish to increase the sum reserved by way of Civil List, but we felt that it was above all desirable that no existing interest should be sacrificed, or placed in a less secure position than at present. This circumstance, and the inevitable increase in the establishment of Victoria on being raised to a separate Government, have produced an augmentation of nearly £12,000 on the whole amount of the charge for the fixed establishment. But if you find on examination that the amount required for any particular services, and charged on the Civil List, has been unnecessarily added to in the process of framing these Schedules, so that there is a surplus at your command consistently with justice to existing interests, the Act provides the means of making a reduction accordingly.

"I have now gone through all the observations which appear to be requisite in order to fully explain to you the details of the measure which has just received the sanction of Parliament, and which it will be your duty to take the necessary steps for bringing into operation at as early a period as may be practicable. I have only in conclusion to assure you that in framing this measure and recommending it to Parliament, Her Majesty's Government have had no other object in view but that of establishing in the Australian Colonies a system of government founded on the same principles of well-regulated freedom, under which the inhabitants of this country have enjoyed so large a measure of security and of prosperity, and under which the British Empire has risen to so high a pitch of greatness and of power. It is my earnest and confident hope that by this Act of Parliament, the foundation is laid upon which institutions may gradually be raised, worthy of the great nation of British origin which seems destined rapidly to rise up in the Southern hemisphere, and to spread our race and our language, and carry the power of the British Crown over the whole of the vast territory of Australia.

"I have, etc.,

"*Sir C. A. Fitzroy,*   (Signed)   GREY."
    "*etc., etc.*"

Enclosure.

Earl Grey to Sir William Denison.

" *Downing-street, July* 27, 1850.

"SIR,

"In my Despatch on the general subject of the finances of Van Diemen's Land, I have thought it right to reserve for separate consideration the general principles by which the application of the Land Fund is to be governed. The question is one of so much importance that I am anxious that my views upon it should be thoroughly understood. I will accordingly proceed now to explain them. The money derived from sales of land I regard not as constituting a part of the Revenue of the Colony, in the proper sense of the word, since these receipts do not periodically recur, but arise from the permanent alienation of part of the public property, and ought therefore to be dealt with as capital to be invested in the accomplishment of objects of permanent public benefit. The proper object also of disposing of land by sale instead of by free grant, according to my view of the subject, is that of regulating the distribution of the Crown Lands among those who will turn them to the best account, not that of realizing a large sum of money for general purposes. Experience has demonstrated that when a Colony is in progress of settlement, if land is disposed of either by free grants or by sales at a low price, no precautions can prevent its being engrossed by persons who acquire possession of it, not with a view to its occupation and improvement, but on the speculation of deriving a profit from its increase in value as the Colony advances in wealth and population. In the meantime, land thus left unimproved, is a great obstacle to the general progress of the Colony, and the settlement of emigrants is checked and discouraged by the high price they are compelled to pay for land to the speculators by whom it has been bought up. This evil is guarded against by selling land at a price too high to allow of its being acquired with any expectation of profit by persons who mean to let it lie idle. But as the object of imposing such a price is to ensure the gradual distribution of land to settlers as it is wanted, it has always been my opinion that the sums received for it should be applied in such a manner as to add to the value of the land to purchasers who mean really to occupy and improve it. The popular objections to the comparatively high price which has for some years been required for the Crown Lands in the Australian Colonies would in my judgement be well founded, and it would be highly impolitic to withdraw from settlers so much of their available capital, if this money were not in fact restored to them by its being applied in such a manner as to increase the value of the land they acquire. With this view, in the other Australian Colonies, half the sums so received are by law devoted to the introduction of emigrants, by which a supply of labour is obtained, and a value is given to the land which it would not otherwise possess. In Van Diemen's Land it is not necessarr, as there is an abundant supply of labour from another source, to apply any of the receipts from the sale of land directly to this purpose; but upon the same principle they ought to be applied to public works, such as roads, bridges, and buildings, which will conduce to the profitable occupation of the lands alienated. The Committee of Privy Council on the proposed Constitutions of the Australian Colonies has advised, that whenever local bodies are constituted representing the inhabitants of the different districts, the application of half the Land Fund to objects of this kind should take place under their superintendence. I am strongly impressed with the importance of adopting this recommendation, and I should anxiously desire to see the establishment of such municipal bodies at the earliest possible period; and whenever they are established, it would be highly expedient that the expenditure of a portion of the Land Fund, in the manner I have described, should take place under their direction, subject to the approval of the Lieutenant-Governor. In the meantime this application of the money should take place under the directions of the Government, since, if it were placed at the disposal of the Legislature, it is almost certain that due regard would not be shown to the interests of the inhabitants of the remoter districts, whence it is principally derived, who are too few to have much influence in that body. In Van Diemen's Land, in consequence of the absence of any considerable demands for emigration, a larger proportion of the Fund ought probably to be applied locally than in the other Colonies; still a certain proportion of it ought, I think, to be retained for purposes of a similar character, but of more general advantage,—such as improvements of the great lines of communication, and of the principal harbours,— by which the general trade of the Colony may be benefited. These instructions must, however, be regarded as subject to those contained in another Despatch which I have this day addressed to you, and in which I have informed you that instalments of £5000 annually, in payment of the Colonial Debt to this country, must constitute a first charge on the Land Revenue.

"I have, etc.,

"*Sir W. Denison,*   (Signed)   GREY."
  "*etc., etc.*"

END OF VOLUME I.

COLONIAL POLICY.

VOL. II.

THE

COLONIAL POLICY

OF

LORD JOHN RUSSELL'S ADMINISTRATION.

BY EARL GREY.

IN TWO VOLUMES.

VOL. II.

LONDON:

RICHARD BENTLEY, NEW BURLINGTON STREET,

Publisher in Ordinary to Her Majesty.

1853.

CONTENTS.

VOLUME II

APPENDIX.

THE COLONIAL POLICY

OF

LORD JOHN RUSSELL'S ADMINISTRATION.

———◆———

LETTER VIII.

AUSTRALIAN COLONIES.——TRANSPORTATION.

My dear Lord John,

I propose to devote this Letter exclusively to the very difficult and important subject of Transportation. This question has long occupied the attention of Parliament and of successive Governments; and various modes of punishing criminals have from time to time been tried, in the hope of discovering some method of doing so, at once effectual for the protection of society, by creating a salutary dread of the consequences of violating the law, humane towards criminals, and just towards the inhabitants of our Penal Colonies. When we succeeded to office, none of the attempts to introduce a system of punishment answering this description had proved successful, and none less so than the very last that had been made. The consequences in Van Diemen's Land

of this latest experiment had been so unfortunate as
to render it a matter of extreme urgency for us, immediately on our appointment, to consider and decide
what course should be adopted in order to correct
with the least possible delay the frightful evils which
had been brought to light.   We found that the intelligence received from this Colony had led the preceding Secretary of State (Mr. Gladstone) to the conclusion that, if the stream of transportation thither
could not be entirely arrested for the next eighteen
months or two years, at all events not less than two-
thirds of the male convicts who would have been sent
there in that time must be diverted to some other
quarter; and it was stated, that he could not estimate
the number for whom it would be necessary to make
provision elsewhere, at less than from five to six thousand*.   The preceding Government had adopted the
views expressed by Mr. Gladstone in the official letter
to which I have referred; and there seemed to us no
room for doubting the correctness of their judgement
as to the absolute necessity of relieving Van Diemen's
Land, for a time at least, from the influx of convicts,
who had for the last five or six years been sent there
in such overwhelming numbers.

Nothing could be more lamentable than the state
of things in that Colony, according to the best
information which had been received.   The convicts
in gangs were in a state of extreme demoralization;

* See Papers on Convict Discipline presented to Parliament by
Command, February 16, 1847, pp. 10, 11.

their discipline was relaxed and ineffective, and the amount of useful labour performed by them exceedingly small. The number of male convicts in the Colony on the 31st of December, 1845, was about 25,000, of whom nearly 12,000 were on the hands of the Government; and of these no less than 3268 were passholders waiting for hire* but unable to obtain employment, while the Comptroller-General of Convicts reported that in the course of the ensuing twelve months 3852 more would emerge from the probation gangs, and become eligible for employment as passholders, without his seeing any fair probability of the demand for labour being much increased. The Comptroller-General pointed out that the condition of these passholders waiting for hire was little better than that of convicts who were still worked in the probation gangs, which could not fail to have a bad effect on the discipline of the gangs. He also stated that much evil arose from having large bodies of passholders collected together in the hiring depôts†.

While the state of the Convict establishment was thus unsatisfactory, the general condition of the Colony was not less so. The finances were in a state of extreme embarrassment, the expenditure of the Government having so much exceeded the revenue, that the Lieutenant-Governor had been compelled to

* See the same Papers, p. 23.

† For an account of the state in which the Convict establishment in Van Diemen's Land was found by Mr. Latrobe and Sir William Denison, see their Despatches of May 31 and July 10, 1847, in the Papers presented May 5, 1848, pp. 33, 79.

obtain considerable loans both from the Bank and from the Military Chest, without any authority for doing so. Trade and every branch of industry were likewise greatly depressed, and large numbers of the free inhabitants were leaving the Colony. This disposition to abandon Van Diemen's Land was not confined to the working classes, who were naturally attracted by the higher wages of the neighbouring Colonies in the glutted state of their own labour-market, but extended to not a few of the higher classes also.

Such, when we assumed the direction of affairs in July, 1846, was the condition of the Colony, as shown by the accounts, both official and private, which came before us. Nor was it difficult to trace the causes to which this state of things was to be attributed. Up to the year 1840 the whole number of convicts transported from this Country to Australia had been divided between New South Wales and Van Diemen's Land. In that year an Order was made by the Queen in Council, on your advice (you being then Secretary of State for the Colonies), discontinuing New South Wales from being one of the places to which convicts might be sent. I must candidly tell you that it has always appeared to me that this was an error, and that the whole territory of New South Wales should not have been closed against the reception of convicts,—not, at all events, until more complete arrangements for otherwise disposing of them, than had then been made, had been matured and brought into operation.

Probably however the bad consequences of the measure would have been far less serious, had it been carried into execution according to your original plan, of
which it was a material part that the whole number of
criminals sent to Australia should be greatly reduced,
a much larger proportion than heretofore being kept
for punishment at home. But in the last year of
Lord Melbourne's Administration a vote was carried
against the Government in the House of Commons,
for an Address to the Queen praying that this change
of policy might not be continued, and that a large
number of the convicts who had been detained in
this Country might be sent abroad. In consequence of this vote, it became necessary to send
many more convicts to Van Diemen's Land than
you had contemplated when the Order in Council
of 1840 was made; the result was, that, whereas in
the twelve years from 1829 to 1840, both inclusive,
the whole number of male convicts who arrived in
Van Diemen's Land had been 19,878, giving an
annual average of 1658; the number who arrived
in the succeeding five years was 17,637, the annual
average being 3527, or more than double that of
the preceding period*.

Nor was this all. Formerly the great majority of
convicts sent to the Australian Colonies were assigned
as servants to the settlers; and though this system was
liable to some very serious objections, which I think
justified its condemnation by the Committee of the

* See Papers presented by Command in July, 1849, p. 84.

House of Commons on transportation in 1838, it was at all events attended with this great advantage, that it prevented the congregation together of large numbers of these men in the charge of the Government. But in consequence of the opinion which had been given by the Committee to which I have referred, and of a similar opinion which had been pressed upon the Government by Sir John Franklin, the Lieutenant-Governor of Van Diemen's Land, the practice of assignment was finally discontinued in July, 1841. Hence, while the number of convicts annually sent to Van Diemen's Land was more than doubled, as compared to former years, the number for whose safe custody and management the Government was called upon to provide, was increased in a very much larger proportion.

It is obvious that with the best possible arrangements it would have been extremely difficult to provide adequate buildings (without which the maintenance of proper discipline among a large body of convicts is impossible), and a sufficient staff of able and efficient officers, to meet the wants of a service so suddenly and so greatly extended; and unfortunately it is clear that Lord Derby (then Lord Stanley), who succeeded to you in the office of Secretary of State, had greatly under-estimated the amount of the increase of the buildings and establishment which was called for, in order to provide for the proper management of the very large number of criminals, which his measures placed in the immediate charge of the local Government. In the year 1842 he issued full instructions as to the system (known as

the probation system) on which the convicts sent to
the Colony were in future to be managed; and in
doing so he made a very proper and much-needed
addition to the provision formerly made for the religious instruction of these unhappy men, but unfortunately he omitted to give directions for the immediate
erection of suitable prisons for their reception; nor
did he send out a sufficient number of really able and
efficient officers to carry his regulations into effect. It
is only just to Sir Eardley Wilmot, in whose hands
the system of punishment established in 1842 so sig-
nally failed, to observe, that he was not furnished with
the means which he considered necessary for the effective working of the plan; and that he has stated, that
" too much economy " was, in his opinion, the mistake
of the Commissariat, which had not " either in extent
or with sufficient despatch furnished the buildings
required."

He attributes this mistake to the injunctions
which he quotes from Lord Derby's despatch of the
22nd of March, 1844, that " the primary object to
be kept in sight in the employment of convicts is the
raising by them of the produce necessary for their
subsistence, and the consequent diminution of the expense now entailed upon the Mother-country;" and
that " the benefit to accrue from their labour to Van
Diemen's Land, important as I acknowledge it to be,
is still but a secondary and subordinate consideration*." The importance of rendering the necessarily

* See Papers of February, 1847, p. 117.

large expense of the convict establishment as little burdensome to this Country as possible, cannot of course be doubted ; but it is, in my opinion, equally beyond all doubt, that in Van Diemen's Land still higher considerations were sacrificed to an economy which proved in the end to be a fallacious one. I am persuaded that, if it were possible to make the calculation, it would be found, that ultimately an increase of expense has been occasioned by the error of sending out such large numbers of criminals, to be retained in the charge of the Government, without making adequate preparations for their reception. Nothing was really saved at last by not erecting at first, proper buildings where they might have been placed, if not in separate cells during the night, at all events in apartments so arranged and lighted and guarded, as to prevent the most revolting offences against morals and decency. Nor were the consequences much less serious, of omitting to send out from this Country a sufficient number of really efficient officers, capable of enforcing strict discipline among the convicts, and also of directing their labour, so as to render it as useful as it certainly might have been.

The endeavour to reduce the expense to the Mother-country of the convict service, likewise led to the adoption of a regulation, which also contributed to prevent the labour of this large body of men from being turned to much account. In a despatch dated the 23rd of August, 1842, the Governor was

instructed that the convicts were not to be employed
either for the Colonial Government or for private individuals, without their services being fully paid for
to the British Treasury. The Lieutenant-Governor
strongly objected to this rule; and during the latter
part of 1843 and the beginning of 1844 he continued
to urge its being abandoned, in consideration of the
universal distress in the Colony, and the impossibility
that either the local Government or private individuals
should employ convicts, even at the moderate sum
charged for them per day by the Commissariat. In
a despatch of May, 1844, he said that the difficulty
of getting into service continued, and that the passholders, " being thus thrown on the world with nothing
but their labour to support them, and no labour being
in demand, either starve or steal." He concluded as
follows :—" Unless some means are adopted to employ
the ticket-of-leave men and conditional-pardon men,
who, as they receive their indulgences, are thrown on
their own resources, I am fearful we shall not only
have a pauper population, but a thieving population,
thrown upon us."

These remonstrances were not successful, nor did
the Government of that day think it consistent with
their duty to accede to Sir E. Wilmot's suggestion,
that the payment of the superintendants and overseers
required to direct the labour of convicts employed on
Colonial works, should be accepted as an equivalent
for its value. The unfortunate consequence was, that
as the Colonial finances were not in a situation to bear

the cost of public works executed by convicts, on the terms required by the Home Government, the labour of these men was not made available, for the many works of this sort, which might have been undertaken, and which would have increased the demand for labour, by affording additional facilities to the settlers for the prosecution of various branches of industry. The labour thus withheld from the Colony, was employed in the endeavour to raise the agricultural produce required for the supply of the convicts, and in other ways, by which it was expected that the charge they occasioned to the British Treasury would be reduced. But either from the inability of the officers to enforce discipline and proper exertion on the part of the convicts, or from want of skill in the application of their labour, the returns obtained from it were of little value in comparison with its cost.

In Norfolk Island, which is a dependency of Van Diemen's Land, things were in 1846 even worse than in the latter; the demoralization of the convicts and the relaxation of discipline, both amongst them and the officers employed, having reached a pass which was truly frightful, and which led, on the 1st of July, 1846, to a formidable outbreak of the convicts, in which some of the overseers were murdered. This mutiny was put down by the interference of the troops, and twelve of the ringleaders were afterwards hanged.

I have already stated that our predecessors in office had considered it absolutely necessary, in the circumstances I have described, that transportation to Van

Diemen's Land should be greatly diminished, if not entirely arrested, for two years, and that we concurred in this decision. Mr. Gladstone had further considered it necessary that Sir Eardley Wilmot should be at once relieved from the Government of Van Diemen's Land, and he had accordingly directed Mr. Latrobe, the Superintendant of Port Philip, to proceed thither and take charge of the Island, as administrator of the Government, until a new Lieutenant-Governor should arrive.

For this post Mr. Gladstone had selected Sir William Denison, who had been appointed Lieutenant-Governor, but had not yet left England or received his final instructions at the time of our accession to office. Dr. Hampton had also been appointed to the office of Comptroller-General of Convicts in Van Diemen's Land, in succession to Mr. Forster, whose death had not long before been reported. A very judicious choice appeared to have been made in both cases. Sir William Denison, in addition to his general ability and high character, had the advantage of great professional skill and experience as an engineer officer, in which capacity he had for some years superintended the construction of very important works and buildings for the Admiralty, several of them being executed partly by convict labour. He was thus peculiarly qualified for the office of Lieutenant-Governor of Van Diemen's Land, where one of the first objects to be attended to at that time, was to render the labour of several thousands of convicts

more useful than it had hitherto been, and more
especially to employ it, in supplying the deficiency
of proper buildings for the convict service, which I
have described. Dr. Hampton also had had experience under the Commissioners of Pentonville, and in
the superintendence of convict ships, which was calculated to be of much service to him in the office to
which he was appointed.

This being the state of things with which we had
to deal, instructions were in the first place prepared
for Sir William Denison, after much personal communication with him. The general object of these
instructions was, to direct him to take such measures as appeared best calculated to remedy, with as
little delay as possible, the evils I have described. For
this purpose, he was to provide proper buildings for
the reception of the convicts necessarily retained in
the hands of the Government, he was to endeavour to
improve the discipline of these men, and to stimulate
them to industry by the introduction of a system of
task-work, and at the same time to aim at turning
their labour to better account by directing it more
judiciously. To assist him in accomplishing this
object, he was authorized to take with him to the
Colony, ten or twelve non-commissioned officers of
Sappers and Miners and of the Royal Artillery, whose
services as overseers, in carrying on the works he
might undertake, it was anticipated would be of great
value. He was also, by means which were pointed out
to him, to find work for the convicts, as they emerged

from the probation-gangs, to the extent which the deficiency of private employment might require. The particular modes of proceeding, to be adopted for the attainment of the objects contemplated in these instructions, (which were embodied in a Despatch dated the 30th of September, 1846, addressed to Sir William Denison on the eve of his departure for the Colony*), were subsequently altered in many important respects, in consequence of changes in the circumstances of the Colony and of suggestions derived from experience, and it is not necessary therefore to go into their details.

A more important and a much more difficult task remained to be performed. We had to consider and decide upon the arrangements to be made, for carrying into effect for the future, the sentences of transportation which are passed upon offenders according to the existing law, unless we should judge it necessary to recommend to Parliament an alteration of the law, and the substitution of some other secondary punishment. After much anxious deliberation, we came to the conclusion, that the mode of dealing with criminals sentenced to transportation ought to be materially changed, but that the law as it stood, gave ample powers to the Crown for effecting the required alterations. This being the case, although the new mode of inflicting the punishment of transportation, which we proposed to adopt, would eventually require the formal sanction of Parliament, we judged that the introduction of a Bill for that purpose, had better be

* See Papers presented to Parliament, 1847.

postponed until the proposed changes had been tried, in order that any defects in our plan might be ascertained by experience, and corrected, before legislating on the subject. This seemed to be the most prudent course, because we could hardly hope to succeed at once, in devising a system of secondary punishment, effectual for its purpose and free from objections, thereby solving a problem, which has for many years engaged the attention of the legislators and statesmen of most civilized countries, and has hitherto proved too difficult for them all. A full explanation of the manner in which we proposed that criminals sentenced to transportation should in future be punished, and of the considerations on which the plan was founded, was embodied in an official letter from Sir George Grey, as Secretary of State for the Home Department, to myself.

Without entering into details, I must remind you of some of the leading principles of the measures we proposed. We considered that transportation, as hitherto conducted, was not a simple punishment, but included the two very distinct punishments of exile, and of subjecting the offender in some shape or other to penal labour, either in the service of a master to whom he was assigned, according to the practice which prevailed prior to 1841, or else under the immediate charge of officers of the Government at home or in the Colonies. We believed that both these elements of punishment were useful, and ought to be retained.

Exile, by relieving the Country from a dangerous class, and at the same time affording to the offender the best chance of again becoming a useful member of society, was regarded as highly advantageous; but by itself it was plainly not a sufficient punishment for serious offences, since it is notorious that thousands of persons annually submit to it of their own accord, merely from the desire of improving their condition. Even voluntary emigration however is still a painful effort to the great majority of those, who from this motive make up their minds to have recourse to it; and that compulsory banishment from their native country, is still more acutely felt by a large proportion of those sentenced to it, is sufficiently proved, by the urgency of the petitions which are often addressed to the Government, not to remove convicts from this Country or to exchange conditional for free pardons, so as to enable them to return. Hence, viewing exile as in itself a substantial punishment, and one which upon other grounds it was desirable to retain, but as being quite insufficient in itself, it appeared to us that the sentence of transportation should continue to involve the same two penal elements as heretofore.

But we thought that experience had shown ample reasons, for altering both the mode and place of inflicting that part of the punishment, which consists in subjecting the offender to forced labour. The Committee of the House of Commons on transportation had, in the year 1838, for very good reasons, advised the discontinuance of the system of assignment. Since that time, the attempt to enforce penal labour on offenders kept under the charge of officers of the Government in the Colonies, had failed still more completely.   There was room indeed to hope, that guided by the experience gained from that failure, there would be no difficulty in taking precautions that should prevent the recurrence of the evils which had arisen in Van Diemen's Land, at least in so aggravated a form, but still there were inherent difficulties in carrying into execution a system of penal labour in a remote Colony.   In such a situation the Government could neither exercise a sufficiently close superintendence over the working of the system, nor yet command with the same facility as at home, the services of trustworthy and energetic subordinate officers, on whom the discipline and success of a penal establishment mainly depends.   There could be little doubt that, if the large number of convicts in the penal gangs in Van Diemen's Land had been in penal establishments at home, the abuses which grew up would have been far sooner discovered and corrected, and that the difficulties which arose in getting an efficient staff of officers, would not have been experienced. Hence we considered that so much of the punishment of transportation as consists of penal labour, should be inflicted at home, or in comparatively neighbouring Colonies.

It was true, that for a long time many of the offenders sentenced to transportation had been punished at home, by confinement in the hulks with work in the dock-yards, and that the result had been the reverse of satisfactory. But, on the other hand, the experiment of the separate system at Pentonville had been eminently successful, and there was reason to hope that, by improvements which might be introduced, convicts, after going through a period of separate imprisonment, might be employed on public works, within reach of the constant inspection of the Government, without the evils which generally attend the congregation together of large bodies of men in such circumstances.

With these views, it was stated in Sir George Grey's letter to which I have referred, that the punishment of transportation was intended in future, to consist of " a limited period of separate imprisonment, succeeded by employment on public works, either abroad, as at Gibraltar or at Bermuda, or in this Country; and ultimately followed, in ordinary cases, by exile or banishment for the remaining term of the original sentence*." In a subsequent part of the letter, the advantages offered by the Australian Colonies for the ultimate reception of convicts, after they had undergone the more strictly penal part of their sentence, were insisted upon; and in conclusion it was stated that " the plan itself must for the present be considered as experimental, and power will be reserved to the Government to modify it according to the results of experience. But, if permanently adopted, it

* See page 197 of the Papers already quoted.

will be necessary to embody it in a Bill to be submitted to Parliament*." In my official reply, after
expressing my entire concurrence in the views explained in Sir George Grey's letter, I added that de-

* As we have been charged with a breach of faith towards the
people of Van Diemen's Land for the resumption of transportation
to that Colony, after a different intention had been expressed, it is
right that I should explain precisely how the case stands on this
matter. The claim of the Colonists to have received a promise that
transportation to Van Diemen's Land should never be renewed,
is founded on the fact that, in my despatch to Sir William Denison
of the 5th of February, 1847, there are to be found the words, " I
have to inform you that it is not the intention [of Her Majesty's
Government] that transportation to Van Diemen's Land should be
resumed at the expiration of the two years for which it has already
been decided that it should be discontinued." This expression may
have been an unguarded one ; but it is impossible to read the despatch in which it occurs, without perceiving that it was meant to
apply only to transportation on the former system, and that it was
still intended that convicts should ultimately be removed to the Australian Colonies, though not for the purpose of undergoing forced
labour in the penal gangs. In the sentence immediately preceding
that containing the words on which the claim to a promise is founded,
it is said, " The best and only hope of restoring convicts to society,
as virtuous, industrious, and useful members of it, consists in their
being removed as exiles, and as freemen, after having undergone a
penal imprisonment and servitude in the United Kingdom." This
passage, and the whole context of the despatch, clearly imply that
the ultimate removal of convicts to the Colonies was an essential
part of the plan which had been decided upon ; and if any doubt
could still have existed on this point, it must have been removed by
the correspondence with Sir George Grey containing the expressions
quoted in the text. This correspondence was printed and laid before
Parliament, and transmitted to the Lieutenant-Governor, for the
purpose of more clearly explaining to him the intentions and views
of the Government. The plan thus explained was never departed
from, except on one point. Originally it was intended that convicts,

spatches recently received afforded " new and conclusive proof that, while the Australian Colonies are far
from possessing any advantages for carrying into effect
the strictly penal part of the sentence inflicted upon
convicts, they do possess the highest advantages for
the reception of criminals, whom it is desirable, both
for their own sake and for that of society, to remove,
after their punishment has been completed, from the
danger of being again brought into a criminal course
of life in this Country, by the difficulties and dangers
to which here they are unavoidably subject, but from
which in the Colonies they are in a great measure
exempt."

after undergoing a preliminary punishment at home, should be sent
out as "Exiles," with conditional pardons. Subsequently it was
found advisable that they should rather be sent as holders of tickets-
of-leave. This was the only change which took place, and it is precisely one of those modifications of the original plan the probable
necessity of which had been anticipated in the passage of Sir George
Grey's letter quoted in the text. It is true that the Lieutenant-
Governor, from misapprehending his instructions, as to the extent
to which the former policy was to be abandoned, was induced to declare to the Legislative Council, in terms much more positive than
these instructions were intended to warrant, the determination of the
Government not to send any more convicts to Van Diemen's Land.
This however was an error which could not commit the Government, even if the words used by Sir William Denison had been
much stronger than they really were. In point of fact, what he said
amounted to no more than an explanation of what he conceived to
be the intentions of the Government at the time. Indeed, it was
manifestly beyond the power of any Minister to make such a promise as has been claimed ; and we had expressly recognized the
necessity for having our measures eventually sanctioned by Parliament.

Sir George Grey's letter was dated the 20th of January, 1847, and my despatch, informing Sir William Denison of the intentions of the Government, the 5th of February following; and almost immediately afterwards (on the 16th of the same month), papers on the subject of convict discipline were presented to both Houses of Parliament. The letter and despatch in question were included in these papers, and our plans and views were thus fully explained to Parliament and the Public. The subject was speedily brought under discussion in both Houses, and in the House of Lords a select Committee was appointed to inquire into it, on the motion of Lord Brougham. Much valuable information was collected by this Committee, especially from the Judges, and from many of the persons most experienced in the administration of the criminal law and in the charge of convicts, whose evidence was in general strongly adverse to the abolition of transportation as a punishment, and the same opinion was expressed by the Committee in their report. In the course of some incidental discussions, it was clearly shown that the House agreed with their Committee; and, as far as it could be gathered, this was also the prevailing opinion in the House of Commons.

In the course of the year 1847, important information was received from the Colonies, which also tended to show the propriety of some change in the plan which we had experimentally adopted. During the two or three preceding years, a good many selected convicts, after going through a period of separate confinement in Pentonville prison, had been sent to Port Philip with conditional pardons and with the name of exiles. Although upon the whole this measure had answered well, and the exiles had, for the most part, conducted themselves to the satisfaction of the settlers and of the local Authorities, this had not always been the case, and the conduct of some had afforded grounds for thinking, that a modification of the terms on which they were sent out, would be attended with advantage. As exiles, no control could be exercised over them; and so long as they neither returned to this Country, nor were legally convicted of any new offence, they had a right to the same freedom of action as any other of the Queen's subjects. Ticket-of-leave holders, on the contrary, could be required to reside in any part of the Colony that might be pointed out to them, and to conform to various regulations; while, for any misconduct, they were liable to have their tickets-of-leave withdrawn. It was shown by experience, that the change from the state of strict restraint of a prisoner in a penal establishment, to the unlimited freedom o the holder of a conditional pardon, was too sudden; and that the temptations to which exiles were exposed in the towns, where they were generally too much inclined to remain, were often found to be more than they could withstand.

With the additional information which was before us, and bearing in mind the expression of opinion in Parliament during the previous Session, we again took the whole subject into consideration in the latter months of the year 1847 and the beginning of 1848, and came to the conclusion that, although in the main it would be right to adhere to the principles of the plan we had originally adopted, yet it ought to be subject to this very important modification, that convicts should in future be sent out, not as the holders of conditional pardons, but of tickets-of-leave. This change in our measures was determined upon ; and it involved the necessity of this further change, that convicts could only be sent to Colonies which had been declared by Order in Council, under the authority of the Transportation Acts, places for the reception of transported offenders, and where a penal establishment was maintained. It was necessary, in order to give effect to the intended modification of the system of punishment at first adopted, to restrict the sending of convicts to such Colonies, because in no others would there be either the legal power, or the means, of exercising over them that control which makes the distinction between the holder of a ticket-of-leave and an exile. The system thus altered has continued to be since acted upon, but with progressive improvements in the details of the regulations which have been adopted, as these have been suggested by experience. Without troubling you with an account of the successive steps, by which the system of punishment was brought into the form it had attained when we retired from office, it will be proper that I should give a brief summary of the regulations which we left in force.

Under these regulations all convicts*, except those whose bodily or mental health renders them unfit for it, are in the first instance subjected to a period of separate imprisonment, varying from six to eighteen months, according to their sentences, to the circumstances of their several cases, and to the manner in which they bear their confinement; eighteen months being apparently the longest period for which this severe punishment can be safely inflicted.

After they leave the separate prisons, they are ordinarily removed to one of the penal establishments at home, or at Gibraltar, or Bermuda, where they are detained and subjected to hard labour for a time, which varies according to their sentence, and to the greater or less degree of good conduct and industry they manifest. A system of task-work, with a daily record of the work they do and of the manner in which they behave, has been established, by which convicts are enabled to abridge considerably the period of their detention, by industry and good conduct, and to pass to the next stage, that of ticket-of-leave holders in the Colonies. They are found to look forward with intense anxiety to obtaining this boon ; and the hope of doing so, is thus a powerful instrument for the

* I ought to mention that I refer only to male adult convicts ; this is the class which comprises the great majority, and it would lead me into details unsuitable to this Letter, from their length, if I were to advert to other classes.

maintenance of discipline, among those still under coercion, whether at home or abroad. A few, who prove altogether unmanageable at home, are sent to Norfolk Island, instead of with tickets-of-leave to another Colony, and some are also sent to Van Diemen's Land or Western Australia without tickets-of-leave; but these two classes form only a small proportion of the whole. Sending any convicts to the Colonies without tickets-of-leave, was a departure from our original plan; but it was found necessary to send a few in this manner, in order to keep up the establishments required in the Colonies for the reception and punishment of men whose tickets-of-leave might be withdrawn for misconduct; and it also appeared that a valuable addition might thus be made, to the means of maintaining discipline among the large bodies of convicts at home.

In the Colonies, those to whom tickets-of-leave are granted, are not allowed to leave the custody of the Government, until they have made an agreement with some settler, to serve him for not less than a year; the employers being responsible for paying to the Government a certain sum annually from their wages. The ticket-of-leave holders are not considered eligible for conditional pardons, until they have paid a certain sum in this manner, and have behaved well for a time, varying according to the length of their sentence. Thus a man transported for seven years, must behave well, as ticket-of-leave holder, for not less than a year and a half, in which a deduction from his wages, at

the rate of £5 a year, or £7. 10s. in all, must be paid
to the Government. A man transported for twenty
years, or for life, is not eligible for a conditional
pardon, until he has behaved well for five years, and
has paid £25 to the Government. By this regulation,
together with those, by which a prisoner can abridge
the period passed by him in the preliminary stages
of his punishment, by industry and good conduct, he
may obtain a conditional pardon when he has completed about half the term of his sentence, a sentence
for life being reckoned for this purpose equivalent
to one for twenty years. The holders of tickets-of-
leave are required to reside in certain districts, and,
as a general rule, at a distance from the towns and
more settled portions of the Colonies.

The above is a summary of the regulations to which
the holders of tickets-of-leave were to be subject,
according to the latest instructions which had been
sent to the Governors of the Penal Colonies when we
left Office; but at that time, though these instructions
had been acted upon in Western Australia, this had
not been completely accomplished in Van Diemen's
Land; and I do not know what may have since been
done. You are aware, that the object of these regulations is to assimilate the condition of the ticket-of-
leave holders to that of the assigned servants of former
days, except in those particulars in which the system
of assignment was open to objection. It is impossible to doubt, from the evidence of facts, and from
the all but unanimous opinion of the Colonists, that,

with all its faults, the old system of assignment worked admirably in many cases, and that it was the means, both of greatly advancing the wealth and prosperity of the Colonies in which it prevailed, and also of rescuing from their criminal career, and rendering once more useful members of society, a larger proportion of the offenders so treated, than, I believe, any other system of punishment hitherto tried.

A close investigation of the circumstances in which a convict was placed as an assigned servant, and of the manner in which they generally affected him, will show that the advantages of the system consisted mainly in its effecting two objects.   It dispersed the convicts over a wide territory, at a distance from the temptations of their former life, and without the means of indulging their old and bad habits, with little or no command of money, but with an abundant supply of all they really want ;—and it brought to bear upon them strong incentives to good conduct, both in the hope of entire freedom, to which this was sure to lead, and in the salutary dread of the prompt and severe punishment, to which conduct of an opposite description would expose them.   On the other hand, the disadvantages of the system were, that it placed assigned servants far too much in the power of their masters, in whose characters there was necessarily much variety.   The assigned servants were in fact slaves, and there is only too painful proof that in many instances the evils inseparable from slavery were experienced.

Now it will be observed, that the regulations I have mentioned, as having been prescribed with regard to the holders of tickets-of-leave, are contrived for the purpose of retaining as much as possible of what was good, and rejecting what was evil, in the old system of assignment. They provide for the dispersion of the convicts, for their being kept at a distance from the towns, and in the districts to which free labourers will least willingly go. They also provide against these men having the command of much money, while they yet give them an interest in being industrious, by making the deduction from their wages a fixed amount, so that the more they earn the larger will be the surplus to be paid to them ; and they have the same inducement to good conduct as the assigned servants, as they know that by such conduct they may certainly expect to obtain conditional pardons, while if they behave ill, not only will they lose this advantage, but even their tickets-of-leave can be withdrawn.

At the same time the effect of the regulations is not to reduce them to the condition of slaves : they have the privilege of free labourers in agreeing for themselves with their employers, and making the best bargain they can as to the wages they are to receive. The Crown, which has by law a property in the services of persons sentenced to transportation, instead of assigning this property to the master, makes it over to the man himself, subject to the condition of his submitting to a certain annual deduction from his wages, for the payment of which his employer is responsible.

This difference is very material, and is an effectual
security against an abuse, which was not unknown
under the old system of assignment.   The very fact
of his behaving well, was sometimes made to delay
the period of a convict's obtaining his freedom, as
an unscrupulous master, to avoid losing a good servant, has been known to make a report of his conduct which postponed the period of his being enlarged.   To complete this account of the regulations
we adopted, I have only to add, that it was provided
that the wives and families of married convicts should
be sent out to join them, whenever either the men
themselves or their families could pay half the cost of
their passage, and that the deduction made from the
wages of convicts while holding tickets-of-leave, should
be allowed to reckon towards the proportion of this
expense, which they were required to contribute.   The
Governors were instructed to apply the remainder of
the money received from these men for the benefit of
the Colonies, either in promoting free immigration or
in public works.

Such, in its complete form, was the system which
we established for carrying into effect the punishment
of transportation, which has so long been known
to our law, and this system has received somewhat
more than the tacit approval of Parliament.   Not
only has the fullest information, as to every step of
importance which we took, been regularly laid before
Parliament, without any attempt having been made
to obtain from either House a disapproval of our

measures ; but the Convict Prisons Bill of 1851, which we submitted to Parliament, for the purpose of giving greater facilities for the execution of that part of our plan which related to the punishment of prisoners at home, was passed without opposition. But though nothing like serious opposition to our policy was attempted in Parliament, we had, in acting upon it, to encounter difficulties of the most formidable kind.

I have already mentioned that, at the time of our accession to office, it was necessary, according to the calculation of my predecessor, to make provision elsewhere for not less than from 5000 to 6000 convicts, who, in the next two years, if no change had been made in the arrangements of the five previous years, would have gone to Van Diemen's Land, but whom it was now impossible to send there. But the previous Administration had not had time to take any steps for meeting this exigency, so far as regards prisoners who must for a time be retained in that condition, beyond instituting a preliminary inquiry as to the Colonies to which they might be sent, and giving directions for sending as large a number as possible to Bermuda and Gibraltar. The first question therefore which pressed upon us was, how we were to provide for the large body of convicts who, in a comparatively short time, must be " diverted," to use Mr. Gladstone's expression, from Van Diemen's Land.

There were two distinct objects to be provided for, with regard to these men, in applying the system

of punishment which we contemplated. It was necessary to make arrangements, in the first place, for
their safe custody under proper discipline, while they
should be in a state of punishment properly so called;
and, in the next, for their reception abroad, when they
should emerge from this preliminary state of punishment. Both these objects presented many difficulties;
but the most urgent and embarrassing question was,
how to dispose of the offenders sentenced to transportation, who would be thrown upon our hands by
succeeding Assizes. The exigency had arisen suddenly, and there existed very insufficient means of
meeting it; there were no proper buildings, no adequate convict establishments or machinery for carrying
on the service on the scale that was required; everything had to be created, and was wanted at once. It
was obviously impossible that at first the arrangements should be otherwise than exceedingly imperfect, and it was only by degrees that they could be
improved, and that adequate means could be provided
for the custody and discipline of convicts, while kept
under coercion.

Our difficulties and embarrassment were also
much increased, in the first years of the new policy,
by the sudden augmentation of the number of convicts sentenced to transportation in Ireland, in consequence of the famine. The average annual number
of persons sentenced to transportation, in that part
of the United Kingdom, in the three years before the
famine, was 681; in the years 1847, 1848, and 1849

this average rose to no less than 2658. It would be foreign to the objects of this Letter to enter into any detail as to the arrangements for the punishment of convicts at home, which were made under the direction of Sir George Grey. But the effect of sending these men to the Colonies under the existing system, greatly depends upon the manner in which the preliminary stages of their punishment are passed through by them in this Country. I may therefore be permitted so far to deviate from my immediate subject as to mention that, during your Administration, the Secretary of State for the Home Department succeeded n providing the means of subjecting all prisoners sentenced to transportation in England and Scotland, to a certain period of separate imprisonment, and that the great penal establishments at Portland and Dartmoor were created and brought into operation, in which, at the date of the last Report, there were no fewer than 1845 convicts* in the highest state of discipline. A prison has also been built at Portsmouth, as a substitute for the Hulks formerly used, for the convicts employed in that Arsenal; and we looked forward to the time when we should be able to get rid entirely of Hulks, which must always be bad, and at the same time expensive, prisons.

In Ireland the Mountjoy Prison has been built, and

---

* In Portland Prison, December 31, 1851 829
In Dartmoor Prison 1,016

1,845

(See Reports of Directors of Convict Prisons for 1851.)

is managed, on the model of that at Pentonville; and a large establishment has been formed on Spike Island, for the custody and employment of convicts when they are removed from separate confinement. The difficulties with regard to Irish prisoners, owing to the sudden increase in the number sentenced to transportation, have been partly met by passing an Act of Parliament, authorizing the Crown to send convicts from that country to Gibraltar and Bermuda. An Act was also passed, abolishing the punishment of transportation, in cases of a first conviction for simple larceny, which considerably reduced the number of such sentences.

Such are the measures which have been adopted in this country. The establishments at Gibraltar and Bermuda have always been regarded as on the same footing as the Hulks at home, since convicts are not allowed, after their release, to remain at either of these places. Every effort was made, in the early years of your Administration, to increase the accommodation, and to receive as large a number of convicts as possible at both.

At Bermuda, the erection of prisons on shore is in progress, to supersede the Hulks which have hitherto been in use, and which are even more objectionable in that climate than elsewhere. A great part of the work in building the new prisons, at Bermuda, Portland, and Dartmoor, has been done by the prisoners themselves. By the various measures which I have thus slightly sketched, we succeeded in keeping down the number of convicts sent to Van Diemen's Land, sufficiently to avoid embarrassing the efforts of Sir William Denison to effect the reform so urgently needed in the penal establishment in that Colony. This, as I have said, was accomplished with great difficulty in the first years of your Administration; but I am happy to think that, when we gave up the direction of affairs, we left the convict establishment in such a condition as to afford ample means for inflicting the first stages of their punishment on offenders, and at the same time to render the accomplishment of the further improvements which are still needed, comparatively easy.

But our greatest difficulty was to find means by which to provide in a satisfactory manner for the ultimate disposal of prisoners, when they should no longer be under the direct charge of the officers of the Government. This difficulty did not press upon us quite immediately, because the system of punishment I have described, as that which we decided upon adopting, involved their detention for a considerable time in penal establishments elsewhere, before they were sent on to the Colonies, in which the hope of ultimate freedom was to be held out to them. But it was necessary at once to look forward, and to take the requisite steps to enable us at the end of a year or two to meet the expectations which the offenders sentenced for the shortest terms would be encouraged to entertain, and the strict fulfilment of which was the key-stone of the whole system. How to effect this, by finding places to which convicts might, at

the proper time, be sent with tickets-of-leave or conditional pardons, with a fair prospect of maintaining
themselves by honest labour, was a most embarrassing
question, but one with which it was necessary to deal.

I have shown that the House of Commons, in the
year 1841, by a formal vote carried against the Administration of the day, had declared its objection to
the retention in this country of any large proportion
of the offenders sentenced to transportation ; and that
in 1847 the House of Lords, though it came to no
formal vote, had clearly indicated a similar opinion,
by its appointment of a Select Committee, and by the
tone of the discussions which took place on the system of punishment we had proposed.   Such being
the opinion manifested by both Houses of Parliament,
while transportation beyond the seas was the principal secondary punishment known to the law, and our
own judgement was in favour of the ultimate removal
of criminals from this Country, it was clearly incumbent upon us to make every exertion in our power
to discover some means by which this object could
be accomplished.

But since the revocation in 1840 of the Order in
Council, by which New South Wales had been declared a place for the reception of criminals sentenced to transportation, there remained no Colony to
which they could be sent, with a view to their remaining there, except Van Diemen's Land, of which
the labour-market had, as I have shown, been so
completely glutted that it was quite unsuited for the

purpose. The inquiries instituted by Mr. Gladstone, and afterwards by myself, as to the possibility of sending criminals to other Colonies, were attended with little success, in finding new and permanent openings for disposing of them; none such has yet been found, except in Western Australia, in which Colony it was not until 1850 that we were able to make the necessary arrangements for their reception. Hence we were inevitably compelled to rely mainly on the effect of the measures which we determined to adopt, in order to restore Van Diemen's Land to a more healthy state, and to create a demand for the labour of the convicts we might send there.

The steps which we took with this view, and which I shall presently describe, proved more successful than might have been anticipated. What perhaps contributed more to this result than anything else was, that for a time we were enabled to avail ourselves to some extent of New South Wales, as a place to which convicts might be sent, on emerging from the earlier stages of their punishment. I have already mentioned that, for two or three years previously, some had been sent to Port Philip as exiles, and in the Spring of 1847 we received from Sir Charles Fitzroy a remarkable report from a Committee of the Legislative Council of New South Wales, on this subject. A despatch of Mr. Gladstone's, which directed the Governor to ascertain and report whether a limited number of convicts might not be sent there with advantage, was laid before the Legislative Council by the Governor ; and having been referred to a Committee, a very able report was made upon it, so immediately before the close of the Session, that the Legislative Council had no opportunity of considering it ; but it was nevertheless transmitted to this country by Sir Charles Fitzroy, in his despatch of the 6th of November, 1846 *. The Committee in this report began by observing, that if transportation from this Country to any part of Australia could be entirely put an end to, this would be what, in their opinion, would be " most conducive to the interests and most agreeable to the inclinations " of the Colonists ; but they stated that it was plainly not the intention of the Home Government thus to put an end altogether to transportation to Australia. On the contrary, convicts were still to be sent to Van Diemen's Land, and to the then proposed new penal settlement of North Australia. That the question therefore for the inhabitants of New South Wales to consider practically was, not whether convicts should be altogether excluded from their Colony, but whether they should be received directly and on equitable conditions, or whether they should come indirectly through other Colonies, and without the adoption of the measures which might be taken to compensate for their presence, if transportation were openly renewed. Looking at the question in this light, the Committee reported decidedly in favour of allowing transportation to New South Wales to be

* See Papers presented to Parliament, April 15, 1847, p. 3.

renewed upon certain conditions, of which the following are the most material.

" That the transportation of male convicts be accompanied, as a simultaneous measure, with the importation of an equal number of females, to consist of female convicts as far as they will go, and the balance to be made up of female emigrants.

" That, as a further simultaneous measure, such transportation be accompanied with an equal importation of free immigrants, as nearly as possible in equal proportion as to sexes.

" That the wives and families of all convicts receiving permanent or temporary indulgences, should be brought out and count as part of this free immigration.

" That not fewer than 5000 male convicts be annually deported to this Colony."

Then followed certain conditions as to the expenses to be provided for by the Mother-country, and other matters to which I need not now refer; after which the Committee proceeded to state that the descriptions of convicts who should be received were,—

" 1st, Young delinquents who have committed first offences after little or no probation.

" 2nd, Convicts who have committed grave offences after a probation considered adequate to the crime; the probation meant being probation under the separate system.

" 3rd, Convicts at the commencement of their sentences, who have committed various crimes.

" 4th, If any convicts be received from Van Diemen's Land, convicts with tickets-of-leave."

The Committee proposed that the third class of convicts mentioned above should be assigned as servants to
the Settlers, according to the former system, but with
some additional regulations to guard against abuse.
Of that system the Committee expressed the highest
approbation, and a still stronger condemnation of all
plans for working convicts in gangs in the Colony,
under any regulations that could be devised.

On these conditions the Committee recommended
that transportation to New South Wales should be
renewed, and described in such glowing terms the
advantages which would result from this, both to the
Colony and the Mother-country, as to make it obvious
that the compulsion to receive convicts in some way
or other, to which they professed to yield, was not one
to which they submitted with any great reluctance.
They stated :—" Your Committee indeed feel satisfied
that, under the conditions thus to be imposed on future transportation, all the hulks, prisons, and peni-
tentiaries of England might be at once emptied of
their inmates, and those inmates readily employed in
the boundless fields of profitable occupation, at present
shut up from Colonial enterprise, and destined to remain so, until a sufficient supply of labour from some
source or other shall arrive among us to open them
out."   They proceed afterwards to state :—" Nor are
your Committee at all apprehensive that any moral
evil of serious account would flow in upon the Colony

from the large importation of criminals, which would
be consequent on so great a revolution in the administration of the penal discipline of England. The
free population have now obtained so great a head
and mastery over the convict population, that if this
preponderance be only maintained in any future
scheme of transportation, the absorbing and dispersing powers of the community will be so vast and
will so rapidly augment, that there will be no chance
that transportation here, whatever its amount, will be
able to swamp the free population of this Colony as it
swamped it formerly, and as it has latterly swamped
the free population of Van Diemen's Land."

In their peroration the Committee warm into en-
thusiasm on the advantages to be anticipated from
adopting their suggestions. They say :—" Such, your
Committee conceive, would be the immense gains and
mighty influences for good, which would result at home
from the change here recommended in the administration of the penal discipline of our common Country ;
whilst, on the other hand, the seeds of a great community would be sown on this continent, which would
shoot up with a vigour and rapidity unexampled in the
history of our race,—a community which, from its very
outset, would re-act powerfully on the whole frame of
her internal industry, enlarging the field of her employment at home, extending the circle of her commerce abroad, until, in the rapid progress and ultimate
immensity of this beneficial interchange, a mighty Colony would arise, linked to her by the strong ties of

common origin and mutual interest ; a faithful subject and never-failing customer, that would be attached to her in peace, would not desert her in war—that would multiply her resources, increase her numbers, consolidate her strength, and be the mainstay, not only of her supremacy and dominion in these seas, but probably of her continued supremacy and dominion in the world."

This Report was signed by Mr. Wentworth, as Chairman of the Committee, of which the other members were Mr. Lowe, Dr. Bland, Captain O'Connell, Mr. Robinson, Mr. Foster, Mr. Dangar, Mr. H. H. M'Arthur, Mr. Windeyer, and the Colonial Secretary. I give the names, because those acquainted with the affairs of New South Wales will see from the list how much importance was due to the Report of a Committee so composed*.

In a despatch written a little later (on the 20th of December, 1846), Sir C. Fitzroy transmitted a report from the Acting Superintendent of Port Philip, stating that a ship with exiles having arrived at Melbourne, the whole of the men had been engaged in three days at high wages, and enclosing a return of two thousand "Expirees," as they a retermed, who had been introduced from Van Diemen's Land at the expense of certain land and stock proprietors of Port Philip. The Acting Superintendent added that, "Could more ample funds have been raised, the importation of Ex-

* See Convict Papers presented to both Houses of Parliament, April 15, 1847, pp. 6–14.

pirees from Van Diemen's Land would have been much greater*;" and it appears from the local newspapers, that associations had been formed by the leading Colonists for the purpose of bringing over these men, for which object assistance was afforded by the Royal Bank of Australia, and that one of the first to avail himself of this assistance was Mr. Charles Cowper, the present Chairman of the Anti-Convict League.

It was obvious from this information, and from applications for the renewal of transportation to New South Wales, which reached us from more than one quarter, that there existed a strong desire among many of the Colonists for a supply of labour of this description; but the Governor had also transmitted many memorials, expressing in strong terms the opposite wish, and had stated that he was " entirely unprepared as yet to say on which side the opinions of the generality of the more respectable and influential portion of the community will preponderate." In these circumstances we thought it our duty to make no change in the arrangements as they then stood ; that is, to allow occasionally small numbers of exiles to be sent to the Colony, but not to take measures for sending a larger number of convicts with tickets-of-leave until we should know the determination of the Legislative Council on the report submitted to them by their Committee. Our view was, that a Colony, not originally founded as a convict Colony, or in which the Order in Council making it

* See Convict Papers, presented May 5, 1848, p. 10.

so had been formally repealed, could not properly be
made a place for the reception of offenders unless with
the assent of the inhabitants ; and that in a Colony
having a Legislature of a representative character,
that body was entitled to be regarded as alone competent to express with authority the wishes of its constituents.

Accordingly we determined, as I have said, to wait
for the decision of the Legislative Council; and in
the meantime a despatch was written to Sir Charles
Fitzroy, on the 3rd of September, 1847, explaining
the views of the Government on the Report of the
Committee which he had transmitted to us, stating
that we could not entirely accede to the proposals it
contained, but that we would consent to the renewal
of transportation to the Colony, under an arrangement, the heads of which were fully given, and which
was in its essential principles, though not in its
details, the same with that suggested by the Committee.   He was informed that we proposed to send
out convicts to New South Wales with tickets-of-
leave, after having undergone previous punishment
at home ; and also to take measures for sending out,
at the cost of the British Treasury, a number of
free emigrants equal to that of the offenders who
might go to the Colony. The most important conditions proposed by the Committee, to which we
did not assent, were those which would have involved
the partial re-establishment of the system of assignment, and the imposition upon the Mother-country

of two-thirds of the charges incurred by the Colony for police, gaols, and the administration of criminal justice*.

In the meantime, while we were considering the Report of the Committee of the Legislative Council, and coming to this decision, that Council had also been considering the same Report at Sydney, and had come to a resolution rejecting the recommendation of its Committee, and deprecating the resumption of transportation. This resolution was transmitted to this Country by the Governor, in his despatch of the 25th of September, 1847†, which was answered by my informing him that no further steps would be taken on the subject, until we should know the decision of the Legislative Council on the proposals contained in my despatch of the 3rd of September, 1847. As soon as that despatch reached the Colony, Sir Charles Fitzroy laid it before the Legislative Council, which, on the 7th of April, 1848, came to resolutions, on the motion of Mr. Wentworth, in favour of acceding to the proposals it contained. In transmitting these resolutions, the Governor recommended " the immediate commencement of the system ;" expressing his conviction, that it would be " received as a boon by a large majority of the people of this Colony, where the want of a sufficient supply of labour is becoming daily more apparent, and is operating most injuriously

* See Despatch to Sir C. Fitzroy of September 3, 1847, in the Papers presented May 5, 1848.

† See the above Papers, p. 31.

on the prospects of many of the largest and most respectable landholders in it*."

This despatch reached England on the 7th of August, 1848. Unfortunately, the near approach of the end of the Session rendered it impossible for us then to propose to Parliament a vote for sending out free emigrants to the Colony, in consideration of its consenting to receive convicts; and the financial situation of the country at that time was such, that we could not rely on being able to propose such a vote even in the following Session. In these circumstances the course that was adopted was that of explaining to Sir C. Fitzroy our inability, for the above reasons, to adhere in this respect to the arrangement we had proposed in the previous year, and informing him that, on finding that we could not fulfil the expectations we had held out, of a boon to be granted to the Colony in consideration of its receiving convicts, we should have abstained from sending any, until there had been time to communicate with him again, had we not feared that serious injury to the Colony must arise from our taking that course. We inferred from his despatch, and from the information which had reached us from other quarters, that the want of labour was so urgent, that the largest supply which could be furnished by funds raised in the Colony for free immigration, would be altogether inadequate. We therefore judged that the Colonists would prefer having some ticket-of-leave holders, calculated to prove very useful as labourers, sent to them

* See Convict Papers presented in February 1849, p. 38.

at once, even though unaccompanied by the promised free labourers, to suffering the great inconvenience of having any accession of labour, beyond what they could obtain by their own resources, delayed for the many months which must be lost, before an answer could be received to another despatch addressed to him. Accordingly a moderate number of convicts of the above description would, he was informed, be sent out ; and for the purpose of investing him with the necessary legal power to maintain the control over them, to which we concurred with the Committee of the Legislative Council in thinking that they ought to be subject, the Order in Council of 1840, by which New South Wales had ceased to be a place for the reception of convicts, was revoked.

Sir Charles Fitzroy was further told that, if the Legislative Council should object to receive convicts without the free immigration at the expense of this Country which had been stipulated for, the transmission of any more convicts to the Colony would at once be stopped, and application would be made to Parliament for the means of fulfilling our original promise, by sending out as many free immigrants at the cost of this Country as the Colony might be entitled to by the number of convicts sent off before the decision of the Legislature could be known*. No doubt was entertained, when these instructions were written, that, even if for pecuniary reasons it should be thought inex-

---

* See Despatch to Sir C. Fitzroy of September 8, 1848, p. 50 of the above Papers.

pedient to adopt permanently the principle of sending
out free emigrants to the Colonies receiving convicts,
Parliament would enable us to send to New South
Wales the number required to make good this engagement.

The Governor having published this despatch for
general information, a great opposition to allowing
convicts to be sent on any terms to the Colony immediately arose; attacks were made upon us in speeches
at public meetings and by the newspapers, for what
was termed a gross breach of faith; and on the 1st of
June, 1849, the Legislative Council voted an Address
to the Queen, in which, without any reference to their
vote of the previous year, in favour of the resumption
of transportation, they not only expressed their objection
to it on the terms proposed in my Despatch of the 8th
of September, 1848, but strongly protested " against
the adoption of any measure by which the Colony would
be degraded into a penal settlement ;" at the same
time entreating Her Majesty " to revoke the Order in
Council by which New South Wales has been again
made a place to which British offenders may be
transported*."

It is hardly necessary to observe, that the reproach
directed against us for an alleged breach of faith, in
sending out convicts unaccompanied by free immigrants, was perfectly idle. By undertaking that, if
the promise was claimed, it should be strictly fulfilled
(as was afterwards done), all grounds for such a com-

* See Convict Papers, presented January 31, 1850, p. 19.

plaint were completely obviated. Nor in point of fact do I believe, that the omission to send out the free immigrants stipulated for, had really much to do with the storm of popular indignation which was raised against the renewal of transportation.

The Legislative Council, it will be observed, does not ground its refusal of the proposal of September, 1848, on its differing from that to which it had previously given its assent, but protests " against any measure by which the Colony should be degraded into a penal settlement." There had, in truth, for many years been a strong party against the reception of convicts in New South Wales,—a party composed of very different elements, and including, with many who sincerely entertained the repugnance they professed on moral grounds to the introduction of such persons into the Colony, a great number of the labouring classes, especially in the towns of Sydney and Melbourne, who were influenced by jealousy of the competition of convicts, and a fear that their coming might lead to a reduction of the extravagant wages they had been in the habit of obtaining ; and others again who, for personal or electioneering objects, thought it their interest to excite the popular passions, and found in this question the easiest means of doing so. The anti-transportation party, thus composed, had in the interval since the subject was last considered in the Legislative Council, gained the ascendency, assisted in no small degree by the diminished urgency of the demand for labour, in consequence of the large free

immigration which had for some time been carried on
under the direction of the Commissioners.   Having
gained the ascendency, the opponents of transportation carried with them many whose sincere opinions,
looking to their previous language and conduct, can
hardly be believed to have been in unison with the
prevailing sentiment of the hour.   Nor is this surprising, as the moral courage to oppose the tide of
popular feeling when it appears to be wrong, is a rare
virtue everywhere, and especially in small Colonial
societies, new to the exercise of the powers of representative government.

I am confirmed in my belief that this is a correct
explanation of the agitation, by the fact that the outcry against the reception of convicts from the best-
managed penal establishments at home, was most violent in the Port Philip district, where only two years
and a half before public associations had been formed,
and subscriptions to a large amount collected, for the
purpose of importing two thousand " Expirees " from
Van Diemen's Land,—men whose punishment had
been gone through in the probation-gangs of that
island, at the time they were notoriously in the lowest
state of demoralization.

But, although I do not believe that our having
thought it necessary somewhat to modify the proposal we had made in 1847, and to which the
Legislature had given its assent, had in truth
much to do with its change of opinion, yet our departure from what had been agreed to, afforded a

plausible ground for that change; and it is not improbable that, if this ground had been wanting, and
if what had been proposed had been strictly fulfilled, the Legislature would not have been induced
to retract the assent it had given to the reception
of convicts. I am therefore bound in candour to
admit that, on looking back to what took place at
the time, with the advantage of our subsequent experience, it now appears to me that, in not adhering
to the arrangement precisely as it had been agreed
upon, and announcing when we sent out the first
convicts with tickets-of-leave to New South Wales
that we would take the earliest opportunity of applying to Parliament for the means of sending out
a corresponding number of free emigrants, we were
guilty of one of those errors of judgement from which
I suppose that no Administration will claim to have
been altogether exempt, in the very difficult task of
conducting the affairs of this Country.

It is the more to be regretted that a different course
was not taken, as, in point of fact, we were enabled
in the following Session to propose to Parliament a
vote for sending free emigrants to the Colonies which
received convicts; the grant was made without difficulty, and has been renewed in subsequent years.
The result was unfortunate, since the Legislative
Council eagerly availed itself of the opportunity of
withdrawing its consent to the resumption upon any
terms of transportation to New South Wales, which,
—greatly as I am persuaded to its own loss, as well

as to the disadvantage of this Country,—was thus closed to the reception of convicts. It was obvious that the Colonists who were in favour of receiving them, notwithstanding their being a minority, included no small proportion of the most intelligent and enterprising members of society; but we thought it our duty to adhere to the principle I have stated, of looking to the constitutional representatives of the Colonies, as alone authorized to declare the wishes of the community, to which we had announced our determination to conform on this subject.

Despatches were accordingly written to Sir Charles Fitzroy*, pointing out how little foundation there was for the complaints against the course we had taken, and informing him that, the wishes of the Legislature having been now clearly expressed, no more convicts would be sent to the Colony. Eventually the Order in Council, making New South Wales a place to which convicts might be transported, was again revoked. It seems to me that this was the only course we could properly take; but that the Legislature of New South Wales, in requiring us to take it, has deprived the Colony of a class of labourers peculiarly suited to its circumstances and its wants. The estimation in which their services are held by employers may be judged of by the fact, that the ' Hashemy ' convict-ship having arrived at Sydney, in June, 1849, when there were four emigrant-ships

* See Despatches to Sir Charles Fitzroy of the 10th and 16th of November, 1849, pp. 46, 51.

lying in the harbour, with about one thousand souls on board, all the convicts (with the exception of four, whose tickets-of-leave it was considered necessary to withhold, and fifty-nine who were sent to Moreton Bay, where labour was urgently required) were within six days, and even before the emigrants, hired by respectable landholders and sheep-farmers* at high wages. The superintendent of convicts added, that he had at the time applications in his office for the services of a larger number of this class of labourers than could be supplied by the arrival of several convict-ships ; and in concluding his report, he expressed his great satisfaction " at the high state of moral feeling exhibited in the conduct and bearing of the convicts by the ' Hashemy,' one which made itself apparent to all who went on board that vessel to engage servants." I should mention, that it was the convicts by this ship whom the Governor was called upon, by resolutions passed at a public meeting, to send back to England.

In thus entirely stopping the admission of convicts into New South Wales, the Legislature disregarded the opinions and wishes expressed by the inhabitants of the northern part of the Colony, who have evinced a strong and, as I think, a most reasonable wish for the services of convicts. In the splendid pastoral country communicating with Moreton Bay the want of labour is daily felt more severely by the flock-owners. There is no prospect that this want can be adequately supplied by free immigration,—for this among other rea-

* See Convict Papers, presented January 31, 1850, p. 27.

sons, that free immigrants, even before the discovery
of gold, generally preferred other employment to that
of undertaking the care of sheep in the remote regions
where they are pastured, and leading the solitary life
which this imposes upon them.   But for the holders
of tickets-of-leave, this is precisely the most suitable
employment, and one which completely answers the
object with which they are required to pass some
time in that condition, before they obtain more
unrestricted freedom ; and as they are under the
obligation of residing in the districts pointed out to
them, their services may be depended upon, where
those of free immigrants could not be so.   Hence
this district combines every possible advantage for
the reception of offenders in this stage of their punishment : it would be for the benefit of the men
themselves that they should be sent there, because
they would find ample employment of the best kind ;
it would be greatly for the pecuniary interest of the
Settlers, and of the community to which they belong,
of which the prosperity mainly depends on the increased production of wool ; and lastly, it would be
much to the advantage of the Mother-country, now
that large supplies of Australian wool have become so
necessary to our manufacturers.

The inhabitants of the Northern district of the
Colony seem to be convinced, that its being again
opened for the reception of convicts is for these reasons desirable.   Strong representations to that effect
were made by many of the principal landholders two or

three years ago ; and public meetings have been held at various times, at which resolutions to the same purport have been carried : in a late newspaper from Moreton Bay I have seen an account of a meeting recently held, at which the absolute necessity of the measure is insisted upon, and very gratifying testimony is borne to the utility and good conduct of the convicts who were sent there during the short interval that this was practicable *.

In this district, as elsewhere, there is a division of opinion on the subject ; but there seems no reason to doubt that a large majority of the inhabitants are decidedly in favour of again receiving convicts. It is to be hoped that this wish will not be resisted by the Legislature ; but if so, the inhabitants of Moreton Bay have a remedy within their reach, by renewing their application to the Crown for the separation of that district from the rest of the Colony of New South

* One of the speakers, Mr. A. Hodgson, made the following statement, in moving one of the resolutions : "In regard to the introduction of exiles into this district up to the present time little need here be said. They had, with few exceptions, been found to be most useful and valuable servants, particularly the 400 per the ship Bangalore. They were all earning an honest livelihood, at a remunerative rate of wages, and would shortly regain the freedom to which their good conduct so justly entitled them. The recent muster of ticket-of-leave holders was most satisfactory, and proved the assertion of the Anti-Transportationists, that a large number had left this district, to be a fallacy (hear, hear). The exciting news from the gold mines had not had the effect of causing them to absent themselves from their district, and thus risk their liberty for some imaginary gain."

Wales, for which Parliament has provided in the recent Constitutional Act.

This further division of the Colony of New South Wales, was applied for by memorials to the Queen, signed by a large proportion of the inhabitants of the Northern district, many of whom openly declared that their principal object was to obtain the services of con-victs. Quite apart from that object, the measure will, probably at no distant period, become necessary on other grounds; and this district is likely to require to be formed into a distinct Colony, for the same reasons that Port Philip has already been so. When we were called upon to consider the memorials to which I have referred, the time however seemed hardly come for this separation. In answering the Governor's des-patches transmitting the petitions, an opinion to that effect was expressed, and Her Majesty was advised, without absolutely rejecting their prayer, to refer them back to the Colony for further consideration.

So matters rested when we left Office, and I neither know what may have been since done by our succes-sors, nor what further would have been decided upon by your Cabinet, had it still remained in existence, when the answers to the despatches which had been written were received. But I may be permitted to express my own opinion, that if it had then appeared, that the admission of convicts to the district of Moreton Bay, was as decidedly called for by the wishes of the inhabitants as there was reason to believe, while owing to the opposition of Sydney it could only be accomplished by a division of the Colony, it would have been right to adopt that measure. At the same time, I think it was to be desired that this division should be deferred, and that the Legislature of New South Wales should be induced to consent to the opening of the squatting districts for the reception of convicts. Could the Legislative Council have been induced to do so, it would have been easy, without dividing New South Wales for other purposes, to have framed an Order in Council, providing for the introduction of convicts into the Colony, but only into a part of it strictly defined, and limited so as to exclude the towns and more settled districts.

It is, I know, considered that the discovery of gold is an obstacle to such a measure, and that it is absurd to punish a man by sending him to a country where gold is to be obtained. Those who make this objection seem to forget, that a man sentenced to transportation cannot hope to be relieved from constraint, so as to be able to join in the exciting search for gold, until he has completed at least half the term of his sentence. It is surely an absurdity to suppose that any man will, from the desire of ultimately making his way to the Diggings, deliberately expose himself to several months of the stern discipline of Pentonville, followed by a year or two, and perhaps much more, of severe labour at Portland, in order to be sent to Australia, where on his arrival he will be required to work hard, far from the gold regions, without receiving all his earnings for a further period, which may extend to five years or even more.

Those who wish to reach the mines, may do so far more easily than by the road of transportation, nor do I believe that the dread of the punishment will be in the slightest degree diminished by its being known that, after a period of severe endurance, at the end of a time in no case less than three years and a half, and which in general will be far more, convicts who have passed through this ordeal, will find themselves within somewhat easier reach of the gold-fields than they were, before they committed the crimes for which they have suffered. Criminals, of all men, are those who least look forward to advantages so distant, and to be purchased by so much previous privation and suffering; the immediate gratification of their passions is the ruling motive of their lives. But while the discovery of gold affords no valid objection to the removal of criminals to Australia, it has greatly increased the want which is felt there, of the only class of labourers whose services can be calculated on, in order to carry on other and not less important occupations than the search for gold, which draws away by its seductions so many of those who are free to join in the pursuit.

To return, however, from this digression. New South Wales, after the correspondence of which I have given a summary, was, at the end of 1849, entirely closed against convicts from this Country; and the attempt to find new openings for them in other Colonies had likewise failed everywhere, except in

Western Australia, where, after much correspondence and consideration, we succeeded in making arrangements for their reception. That Colony, owing to the original and fatal error of making profuse grants of land to the first Settlers, had dragged on a miserable and doubtful existence, and, at the end of twenty years after its foundation, had a population of little more than 4,600; while South Australia and Port Philip, founded several years later, had grown into thriving communities, attracting annually from the Mother-country, by the aid of their land fund, about twice as many emigrants as there were inhabitants of all kinds in the elder Settlement. At length the prospects of Western Australia had become so hopeless, that there was every prospect of the Colony's being abandoned; when the inhabitants determined, as their only resource, to apply to the Government to have it made a place to which convicts should be transported. This proposal was acceded to, and the necessary arrangements were made for giving effect to it.

The great object we had in view was to provide another place, in which criminals may, after being punished for their offences, be restored to freedom, with a reasonable prospect of maintaining themselves in comfort by honest industry. But it is obvious that at first, so small a community, as one consisting of only between four and five thousand inhabitants, could not afford a demand for the labour of more than a very limited number of such men. It was also abso-

lutely necessary, before convicts could with advantage
be sent there as the holders of tickets-of-leave, that a
penal establishment should be formed, to which those
deprived of that indulgence for misconduct could be
sent. Such an establishment also (for practical reasons into which I need not enter,) cannot without inconvenience be formed on a very small scale : hence
our plan was to erect the necessary buildings for the
accommodation of five hundred prisoners, with the
officers and military guard required for their custody
and management. A much smaller number were to
be sent in the first instance, and chiefly by their
labour, the accommodation wanted for the whole was
to be gradually provided. The first prisoners sent
out, were to be men selected for their good conduct, to whom the grant of tickets-of-leave, at an
earlier period than they would otherwise have been
entitled to them, was to be held out as an incentive
to continued good conduct and exertion. This was a
precaution exceedingly necessary, inasmuch as the first
who arrived, would find buildings so little suited for
the safe custody of prisoners, that much reliance would
unavoidably have to be placed upon their indisposition
to attempt escape or resistance, from their looking
forward to obtaining tickets-of-leave soon after their
arrival. The first convicts who arrived, were to be
employed in providing, as soon as possible, for the
proper reception of those who were to follow ; afterwards the labour of those still under coercion was
intended to be used in the improvement of the Port.

With regard to their subsequent disposal, it was calculated that the demand of the convict establishment for the various supplies which would be required, would give so great a stimulus to the agriculture and trade of the Colony, that a considerable proportion of those who obtained tickets-of-leave would readily find employment from the Settlers; while for a time it was determined that, to those who could not, employment should be given by the Government. They were to be employed in various works of improvement, such as the construction of roads, calculated to increase the future field for industry, and the erection of cottages for themselves, which they were to be allowed to occupy on the payment of a moderate rent, with the privilege of purchasing them when they could accumulate sufficient means. This could be done at a very moderate expense, since, beyond the supplies they required, their wages would not be in general paid to them in money, but would go in abatement of that debt to the Government with which I have, in an earlier part of this Letter, explained that all convicts were to be charged, as holders of tickets-of-leave. Means were also to be taken for dispersing them through different parts of the Colony, as they were released from coercion.

A military Guard of Pensioners was to be sent out with each convict-ship; measures being taken to settle these men and their families in the Colony, to the free population of which they would form a very useful addition. Each Guard, it was afterwards arranged,

was to continue doing military duty after its arrival
in the Colony, until relieved by the next that came;
thus giving to the men the advantage of having pay
in addition to their pensions, until they had had
time to become acquainted with the Settlement, and
the means of employment which it afforded. Subsequently the military force was increased by sending
out a company of one hundred Sappers and Miners;
and as they were selected from men of the trades most
wanted in the Colony, the deficiency of skilled labour,
which had been one of the great difficulties experienced in carrying on the buildings and other works,
was supplied by the same measure, which placed at
the disposal of the Governor a military force amply
sufficient for any exigency likely to occur. The command of the Sappers was combined with the general
management of the whole convict establishment, in
the hands of Captain Henderson, an able officer of
Engineers, who, before he proceeded to the Colony,
went to Portland, to make himself thoroughly master
of the system of discipline and of employing the prisoners, which has been pursued there with so much
success. Lastly, a grant was obtained from Parliament
for sending out a certain number of free emigrants, to
guard against the inconvenience of having the population of the Colony composed in too large a proportion of those who had been convicts.

The religious instruction of the convicts sent to the
Colony was a subject of some difficulty. While they
remained under coercion, they were of course under

the care of the Chaplain; but on their obtaining tickets-of-leave, their dispersion over a wide territory, though in other respects attended with great advantage, was a serious obstacle to their receiving the attention of clergymen, of which it was very important that they should not be deprived. It was ultimately arranged that some additional clergymen should be sent out, whose salaries should be charged partly on the Colonial revenue, partly on the vote for the convict establishment, and who were to be stationed in the districts where their services would be most useful to the holders of tickets-of-leave, but with the care of the free population also.

I have thus given merely the outline of the measures which were adopted : there were of course many details to be provided for, the arrangement of which was a work of much time and labour, in which the able assistance of Mr. Elliot and Colonel Jebb was of the utmost value. These matters were so well attended to, that far fewer difficulties arose in carrying the plan into operation than could have been expected. The principle of the whole scheme, and the object to which every part of it was directed, was not merely to find a mode of disposing of a certain number of convicts immediately, but also to provide a constantly increasing field for their employment hereafter. We believed that, by affording to the small number of Settlers already in the Colony both a supply of labour and an enlarged market for their produce, and undertaking to execute, by convict-labour, the works most wanted for the profitable occupation of the territory, the great natural advantages of the Colony would be developed, settlers with capital would be attracted, and capital would be accumulated by the present settlers and the most industrious of the convicts when released from punishment, as happened formerly in New South Wales. We expected that a trade with India and the other Australian Settlements would spring up, and that, in the course of a few years, Western Australia would grow into a wealthy and flourishing community, adding to the power and greatness of the British Empire, and affording a wide field for the profitable employment and settlement of large numbers of those who have undergone punishment for their offences.

Hitherto this process has been going on with almost unhoped-for rapidity and success. The first instructions to the Governor, as to the measures to be adopted, were transmitted to him on the 22nd of October, 1849; the first vessel for the conveyance of convicts to the Colony was chartered in the January following, was despatched in the beginning of March, and reached the Colony with seventy-five convicts, and fifty-four pensioners and their wives and families, on the 2nd of June, 1850. Before the close of 1850, 384 convicts had been sent there, all men who were for a time to be detained as prisoners; and in 1851, before the end of July, 598 with tickets-of-leave were sent. By that time, I had learned, that by the active and judicious exertions of Captain Fitzgerald and Captain Henderson (the Governor of the Colony and the Comptroller-General of Convicts), ample accommodation had been provided for 500 prisoners, and that they were usefully employed. Those who have obtained tickets-of-leave have readily found employment, and it appears from the Governor's annual Report, dated the 12th of April, 1852, which has been laid before Parliament, that they are now gradually becoming good farm-servants working at moderate wages; that the Colony is prospering in every respect; various public works which were urgently wanted have been completed; the sale of land, and the taking on lease of that which is available for pastoral purposes, are increasing; a regular trade with Madras and Calcutta has been opened; and, what is most important, the Governor states "that the amount of crime as yet committed in this Colony among all classes, is so slight that I do not feel it necessary to make any unfavourable remark whatever *."

* The following extract from a private letter, which I have received permission to publish from the gentleman to whom it was addressed, gives an interesting account of the success which has thus far attended the experiment of sending convicts to Western Australia.

[Received February 21, 1852.]
                    " Perth, Western Australia,
                         " November 1, 1851.

"The Pyrenees had then just arrived, with three hundred ticket-of-leave men, who have since been distributed, and nearly all are now in private employ, besides others that have become entitled to 'tickets' from the establishment at Freemantle; and it is a matter of

Such is the progress which has been made in Western Australia, in opening a new field for the reception of convicts, when they are released from the first stages of their punishment. It is now the only Colony, except Van Diemen's Land, which is open to them; and though it is, I think, to be regretted that they cannot be dispersed through a greater number of our Colonial possessions, I see no reason to apprehend that these two Colonies may not, with proper management, suffice for the purpose.

But with reference to this point, it will be proper, before I proceed to give an account of transactions in Van Diemen's Land, that I should notice an objection which has been made to our reversal of the decision of

much congratulation that their conduct has been hitherto most exemplary, affording to the working part of the free community in this Colony a most wholesome example, not only in respect to good conduct, but they appear to have imbued them with a degree of activity they did not possess before the introduction of convict labour. The Settlers are not the most sober people. Possibly this may arise from their former want of occupation, and indigency: when the Colony was in a languishing state, and little or no employment offered, the people contracted habits of drunkenness to drown care. At present everything begins to assume a cheering aspect: I see it; though only four months here, I see the change. Everybody is affected by the introduction of convict labour, and the expenditure it brings with it. At first a feeling of distrust and opposition was evinced: this is fast wearing away, and giving place to confidence. The ticket-of-leave men are engaged in private families indiscriminately with the free servants, and are otherwise employed in common with free men. Their general conduct is very superior to that of others in the same sphere of life. This may possibly arise from one or other of two causes,—in some from a determination to alter their course, and in others from a fear of returning to prison.

our predecessors to form a new Penal Colony under the name of North Australia, on the eastern coast of New Holland and north of the 26th degree of south latitude. The plan which had been determined upon, and in which we did not think it advisable to persevere, was to send a certain number of convicts, " emancipated by pardon, by length of service, or as exiles," to form a settlement on a part of the mainland of New Holland which was still unoccupied. It was, in the first instance, to be occupied by exiles from England, who were to be settled on small lots of land ; and when, by the assistance of these men, sufficient preparations had been made, convicts from Van Diemen's Land,

" The Settlers, even those who were most opposed to the introduction of convicts, admit that they are more orderly and obedient, and work better, than most of the free men. This was told me by one of the most wealthy farmers here, who has spent several thousands of pounds, and is now, after twenty-two years, reaping some benefit from his labour and capital. His family and himself have experienced great vicissitudes. He had serious intentions, two or three years ago, of abandoning his property, and quitting the Colony.

" I was afforded ample means of judging of the state and working of the system carried out by Captain Henderson and the Superintendant, Mr. Dixon. It appeared to me that much of the good and orderly conduct of the men may be attributed to their treatment in depôt. They are well cared for, have good food, and are well worked ; I never saw men work better, or look in better condition. The discipline is excellent : cleanliness, order, and regularity are most conspicuous in every branch ; and all this is arrived at under the mildest form of moral restraint. I am informed by Mr. Dixon that the behaviour of the men-in and out of barracks is very creditable. The reports from the rural depôts are as satisfactory ; they will do much good eventually."

whose sentences had expired, or who had obtained conditional pardons, were to be sent there.

To this scheme it appeared to us, that there were
the following decisive objections. In the first place,
if convicts were sent to a still unoccupied territory,
where there were no Settlers to employ them, no
buildings prepared for their reception, no roads of
any kind, no fit site for a town yet fixed upon,—in
short, where everything was in a state of nature,—it
was obvious that the expense to be incurred must
be very large (as every fresh attempt to form new
Settlements has clearly demonstrated), and that the
whole of the convicts who might remain in the
Settlement would for a long time be entirely dependent upon the Government for their support. The
necessity of providing for them would not be averted
by giving them allotments of land. From these
allotments they could not possibly procure a subsistence, until much time and labour had been expended in reclaiming and cultivating the land; in
the meantime they must be provided for by the Government, and could only cease to be so, when by industry and good management they should have been
enabled to obtain a living from the soil. It has
always been found a difficult and a costly undertaking,
to establish men who have no capital of their own as
settlers on wild land, even when this has been tried
with carefully selected labourers from rural districts.
The experiment was little likely therefore to succeed

with emancipated convicts, whose habits are almost always improvident, and of whom much the greater number know nothing of agriculture.

If it was necessary to provide for these men by settling them on land, it was clear that this might be accomplished with infinitely greater facility in Van Diemen's Land. There is plenty of good land still belonging to the Crown in that island, well adapted for the purpose, and far more accessible than North Australia. In Van Diemen's Land there were likewise available for the undertaking all the resources offered by an existing Colony and by a large Government establishment. Roads to the new Settlements might have been formed by convict labour, in Van Diemen's Land, at a comparatively trifling expense; and no new establishment of Police, Judges, or Commissariat, no additional troops, with the barracks and buildings necessary for all these departments of the public service, would have been required. The enormous amount of the charges which must have been provided for under these heads, if any considerable number of these people had been settled in North Australia, may be judged of by the heavy expense unavoidably incurred in the formation of the penal establishment in Western Australia; although in that Colony there were very considerable resources of all kinds available, and many of the most costly preliminary preparations for taking possession of an unoccupied territory, had already been accomplished.

But further, the great object in the transportation

of offenders is, to avoid forming a society mainly composed of those who have been criminals.   It is well
known how great were the evils produced, in the
earlier days of New South Wales, by the preponderance of the "Emancipist" element in the Colonial
society.   North Australia would have been a society
consisting exclusively of men who had suffered punishment for their offences, unless a few free Settlers
were attracted by the Government expenditure.

Against these objections there was to be set but
one real advantage, that I am aware of.   North Australia was to have been peopled by "Emancipists,"
that is, by convicts over whom the Government no
longer possessed the legal power of exercising any
control, unless they should commit some new offences ;
these men clearly therefore would not have remained
in the new Settlement, but would have crossed the
mere conventional line dividing it from New South
Wales, to seek employment in that Colony, where
no doubt there would have been ample demand for
their labour.   But if this was the object of the proposed new Penal Settlement, I cannot think that it
was a legitimate mode of attaining it.   Had it been
determined, in spite of any objection on the part
of the Legislative Council of New South Wales, to
make arrangements for giving free passages to the
"Expirees" from Van Diemen's Land to Moreton
Bay, and to have opened at Brisbane a depôt for the
reception of such of these men as might wish to go
there while waiting for hire, the demand for labour in

the northern part of the old Colony, would have been made available for those of the emancipated convicts in Van Diemen's Land who could not there find employment, in a manner far less open to objection than the establishment of a new Colony in a portion of territory cut off for that purpose from New South Wales. It would not have been difficult to find arguments of no slight weight in favour of overruling the objections felt, by only a portion of the Colonists of New South Wales, to allowing those who have been convicts to come there; but if this course was considered unadvisable, and an intention of respecting these objections was professed, I do not think that it could be right to send the same class of persons, whose direct removal to New South Wales was abandoned, to a new Settlement immediately adjoining it, where there was nothing to detain them even for a single day, and whence there was no room to doubt they would immediately resort to it.

I have now to give an account of what has taken place in Van Diemen's Land with reference to transportation,—the Colony to which of all others the measures adopted on this subject have been of the most vital interest. I have already described the condition in which we found the Island on our accession to Office; and I have stated the substance of the instructions with which Sir William Denison was furnished, as to the measures he was to adopt in order to correct so frightful a state of things. These instructions were very ably acted upon. A complete reform in the buildings, in the staff of officers, and in the system of discipline and of employing the convicts, was rapidly accomplished. By reducing as much as possible the number sent to the Colony, and afterwards giving the majority of those who went there tickets-of-leave, instead of sending them to the probation-gangs, the Lieutenant-Governor was enabled to reduce the number of convict-stations, and to provide, without incurring any very large expense, for putting those which were retained on a proper footing both with respect to buildings and officers. At the same time by introducing a system of task-work and a strict but just discipline, active industry and good order were made to take the place of idleness and the grossest irregularity among the prisoners.

These measures of improvement were extended to Norfolk Island, where, as I have shown, they were even more necessary than in Van Diemen's Land. My first impression was, that this island ought to be abandoned as a penal settlement altogether; but this could not be immediately accomplished, from the total want of any means of disposing of a large proportion of the criminals who were there; and afterwards a strong opinion against giving it up was expressed by Sir William Denison and Dr. Hampton, on the ground of the great assistance derived from the existence of such a further place of punishment, in maintaining discipline in Van Diemen's Land. This opinion carried with it so much weight, that we decided (though not without reluctance) that the penal establishment in Norfolk Island must, for the present at least, be continued. I am not unaware of the advantages this Island possesses, in some respects, for penal purposes ; but, on the other hand, from its remoteness and the delay and difficulty of communicating with it, there must always be danger of abuses arising there (as they have done before) which may too long escape discovery and correction. If the establishment should be permanently retained, much care and vigilance will be necessary to guard against this danger.

Important as it was to re-establish discipline among the convicts in charge of the Government in Van Diemen's Land, it was perhaps even more so to restore that Colony to a condition in which it might afford them employment and an eligible abode, when they should be relieved from direct coercion, and become entitled to tickets-of-leave or conditional pardons. With this view the Lieutenant-Governor had been instructed to take measures for settling on land, those for whom employment could not be otherwise found. But as we were well aware of the great difficulty of doing this, it was only to be attempted as a last resource, and the great object was, if possible, to create a demand for their labour. This, it appeared, could only be done by developing the natural resources of the Colony, and by undertaking various public works and improvements which were calculated, by affording new facilities for agriculture and trade, to give a stimulus to private enterprise and industry.

By the instructions which had been given by our
predecessors for requiring payment from the Colony
for the labour of convicts so employed, an unfortunate obstacle had been opposed, as I have mentioned, to undertaking works of this description ;
the more so as, from the same desire to reduce the
charge to the British Treasury on account of the penal
establishment, when the application of £24,000 towards the expenses of the Colonial Police, from the
Parliamentary vote for convict services, was sanctioned, it was required that, in consideration of this
grant, the land-revenue should be paid into the
Military Chest, instead of into the Colonial Treasury.
We considered it right to remove these obstacles to
the more useful application of the labour of the
prisoners ; we therefore adopted the rejected suggestion of Sir Eardley Wilmot, that, for convicts
employed on works of the description alluded to, the
charge against the Colony should be limited to the
cost of tools and of the extra superintendence required in directing their labour.

With regard to the territorial revenue, we instructed the Lieutenant-Governor that, after repaying by instalments the advances obtained by Sir
Eardley Wilmot, the remainder was to be applied
in improvements calculated to increase the value of
the land sold, on the principles which I have fully
explained in my last Letter.   It was our expectation
that, by so expending the territorial revenue, we
should encourage the sale of land and the settlement

of the districts still unoccupied, and should promote the accumulation of capital, thus increasing the demand for labour. By these instructions the Lieutenant-Governor has been enabled, since he reached the Colony, to accomplish many works calculated greatly to promote the object we had in view. He has commenced, and I hope made considerable progress in, a more regular and correct survey of the Colony than had yet been attempted; thus removing an obstacle to the easy and safe acquisition of land by Settlers, and getting rid of a fertile source of difficulty and litigation, by ascertaining correctly the boundaries of land sold or granted to different individuals. He has undertaken the construction of wharfs and basins, which, when completed, will greatly increase the facilities for carrying on the trade of the two principal ports of the Island, and already do this to a considerable extent. By various roads and bridges he has opened additional land both for agriculture and for pastoral occupation. There is, more especially, a fine pastoral district to the westward of Hobart Town, which had hitherto been entirely inaccessible, and which works of considerable magnitude, now approaching to completion, will render easily available.

These various measures have been attended with a success far beyond what could have been hoped, when the Colony was in the state of extreme depression to which it had been reduced in 1846. Even before the discovery of gold in the neighbouring Colonies had stimulated the demand for labour, the worst

of the difficulties the Lieutenant-Governor had to encounter were completely surmounted. The number of
convicts eligible for hire on the hands of the Government had been greatly reduced, few remaining but
those whose inefficiency as labourers prevented any
demand for their services. The new arrivals (except
some of the Irish, in whose case also want of skill
as labourers was the obstacle to their being employed)
were in general speedily engaged; and the success
with which various branches of industry were prosecuted, and the great extension of trade, afforded
every reason to hope that the demand for labour
would continue to increase.

Since the discovery of gold in New South Wales
and Victoria, I need hardly say that the command
of convict labour has been of the greatest benefit
to Van Diemen's Land. If the Settlers had depended
chiefly on the supply of labourers free to go to the
Diggings, which were within easy reach, it is difficult
to see how it would have been possible to prevent
the entire interruption of many of the most important
branches of the industry of the Colony. As it is,
with the supply of labour they derive from transportation, and the unlimited market for their produce,
which the sudden influx of population into the adjoining Colonies has occasioned, the prospects of
the Settlers in Van Diemen's Land are in the highest
degree promising, and the only ground they have
for apprehension is that the supply of convict labour
will probably fall far below their wants.

So far as their material interests are concerned, I am not aware that any difference of opinion can exist, as to the very great advantage which Van Diemen's Land, in its present circumstances, must derive from receiving convicts. But it is alleged that these material advantages are far more than counterbalanced by the great moral evils arising from transportation ; that the Colonists feel the latter so acutely, that they would willingly forgo any pecuniary benefit they may derive from the continuance of the existing system ; and that it is unjust and tyrannical in the British Government and Parliament to compel them to submit to what is so injurious and hateful to them.

Confidently as assertions to this effect have been made, I am persuaded there is little foundation for them. Looking back at the history of Australia for the last sixty years, I see nothing to justify the conclusion that, upon a fair balance being struck between the good and the bad moral results of transportation, even as it has actually been conducted, the bad would be found to preponderate. No doubt great evil resulted from the creation of a society in which the convict element (if I may use the expression) predominated so much as it formerly did in New South Wales. No doubt great moral corruption and great physical suffering were produced, by the manner in which convicts were formerly conveyed to the Colony, and by the system (or rather absence of all system) of management to which they were subject, both during the passage and on their arrival. Before public attention had been seriously directed to the subject, frightful abuses certainly occurred in the transportation of offenders; even when the practice of assignment was established, there were still abuses; and, as I have shown, the probation system, which was substituted for it in 1842, was still more open to objection. But with all these errors in the mode of conducting transportation, when we look at what the Australian Colonies are at this moment, and consider that these communities have been created by it (for it is notorious that the penal settlements afforded the means of founding the others), I think it would be difficult to deny that, if the scheme of sending convicts to Port Jackson has worked much evil, it has worked still greater good.

There is another light in which the subject may be considered. In the year 1850 I caused a calculation to be made, from the various sources of information to be found in the Colonial Office, to ascertain, as nearly as possible, what might be the total number of persons then living in the Australian Colonies, who had originally been prisoners, but who were actually in the enjoyment either of entire freedom, or of that degree of freedom which is conferred by tickets-of-leave and conditional pardons. The result of the investigation was to show that the number of such persons in those Colonies could not be less than 48,000; and out of this large number, those who were not in some way or other maintaining themselves honestly, either by their labour or by the property they had acquired, were so few, that they formed a mere fraction of the whole. Had they remained in this country, the case would have been very different; and I fear that, instead of its being the majority that would have been doing well, and the few who were still living by habitual violation of the law, the latter would have been the rule, and the former the exception.

It has been repeatedly proved that, when a man has once been led into living by dishonesty and plunder, nothing is more difficult for him, after having been punished for his offences, than to find the means of honestly maintaining himself in this country. However anxious he may be to do this, and to abstain from breaking the law, his previous course of life closes against him almost every honest career, while it is hard for him to shake off his old associates, who drag him back again into his evil practices. There are many well-authenticated and remarkable accounts of the sincere but fruitless efforts made by men who have been habitual criminals, to take to a different and honest course of life. Hence, if we look to the Empire as a whole, it seems to me that in a moral point of view far more good than evil has resulted from a system by which the 48,000 persons, now for the most part maintaining themselves honestly in Australia, have been sent there, instead of being allowed to remain in this country a burden on society and to themselves, like the *forçats libérés* in France.

It is said however that this is not the light in which the subject should be considered, and that, even grant-

ing the moral advantages of transportation to preponderate over its evils, looking at the Empire as a whole,
still it is not just to the Colonies to continue the
system when the evils fall exclusively on them, while
the advantages are all on our side.   Even if it were
true that all the advantages (in a moral point of view)
derived from the system of transportation fell to the
share of this Country, the above argument would not
perhaps be conclusive; but it must fail altogether, if
it should appear (as I have no doubt it will on careful
investigation) that, without looking beyond the Colonies, it is not the fact, that the moral evils arising
from transportation have been nearly so great as they
have been represented, while its compensating advantages have been overlooked.   With regard to its compensating advantages, I would call your attention to
an important remark in a Report made in the year
1847, by a Committee of the Legislative Council of
New South Wales on immigration.   It is stated in
this Report* that "the advanced rate of remuneration
for labour is not the only evil attending its deficient
supply; nearly all the witnesses concur in the statement, that the absence of competition amongst the labourers is productive of restless and unthrifty habits;
they are becoming less efficient and less attentive to
their duties, because a servant of any description now
knows, if he be discharged from his place even without
a character, he can obtain other employment immedi-

* See Papers on Emigration to the Australian Colonies, presented
by Command, in August, 1848, p. 7.

ately." There is much other information to the same effect, and I believe it cannot be doubted that, in Colonies where there has been a great scarcity of labour, the competition of convicts has had a decidedly good effect on the conduct of the free emigrant labourers.

I would further observe, that the arguments commonly used upon this subject by speakers at public meetings in the Colonies, would seem to imply that they suppose all free immigrants to be moral and excellent persons, and all convicts irredeemably vicious. There can be no greater error than such a supposition : it by no means follows that, because a man has never been convicted of any offence against the law, he must necessarily be a person of virtuous habits and irreproachable conduct ; and, in point of fact, it is notorious that among those who emigrate from this Country, as among those who in the United States act as the pioneers of civilization in the far West, there is a much greater variety of characters than among an equal number of persons in our, Home population. It is impossible that it should be otherwise, since the energy and enterprise which best fit a man for the hardships of a settler's life, are by no means most commonly found in those who are also distinguished by steadiness of character and of conduct.

On the other hand, among the convicts there are very many who have not been habitual criminals, but who have been led into the commission of some offence for which they have incurred the sentence of the law, by bad example or by some sudden temp-

tation; and such men, after having undergone their
punishment, are perhaps less likely again to misconduct themselves than those who have never experienced
the consequences of doing so.   Even of those who
had been habitual criminals in this Country, and whose
living had long been obtained by plunder, it has been
ascertained beyond all doubt that a great majority,
when removed from their former temptations and dispersed over the territory of New South Wales as assigned servants, very generally became once more useful
members of society.   If this occurred under a system
confessedly most imperfect, it is surely only reasonable
to expect that it will be still more generally the case
now, when it is considered how greatly the prisons of
these days are superior to the hulks from which convicts were formerly sent to New South Wales, and
how great is the contrast between the order and discipline of a modern convict-ship, and the confusion
and license of one of former times.   Indeed the existing regulations have been long enough in force to
enable us to judge of their results, and I have noticed the very satisfactory testimony which has been
borne to the singularly good conduct of the prisoners
sent out under them to the Colonies.   I do not mean
to express my belief that, in any large proportion of
cases, convicts are changed in heart and disposition.
Many of them I trust are so by the blessing of God
on the exertions of the chaplains, and the time for
reflection afforded during the period of separate imprisonment.   But I fear that in all societies the really

good and religious, those who do what is right, and from a right motive, are a minority; it would therefore be unreasonable to expect more from the generality of those who have incurred the sentence of the law by their offences, than that they should have learnt, by the punishment they have gone through, to conform outwardly to the laws they had been in the habit of breaking, and should conduct themselves peaceably and properly towards those among whom they live.

Now that the emancipated convicts do so conduct themselves in Van Diemen's Land, and that in this Colony there exists a perfectly orderly state of society, with complete security for person and property, there is abundant testimony; and I might cite the evidence to that effect of many trustworthy witnesses, including naval and military officers, who have recently visited the island, and have expressed the highest satisfaction with all they have seen. But without referring to any other witness, it will be sufficient to call your attention to the following extracts from a private letter I received some months ago from a gentleman in Van Diemen's Land, which contain an amusing and graphic description of the fears of a new comer, founded on the accounts of the state of the Colony that have been so diligently published, contrasted with the real security which exists. I have not scrupled to publish these extracts, without any express permission, as I cannot doubt, from other parts of his letter, that no objection to my doing so would be felt by the writer, —a gentleman, I would add, upon whom the utmost reliance may be placed. After stating that he left England and went to Van Diemen's Land "with the worst forebodings and prejudices," and after describing all the attempts which were made on his arrival to enlist him in the Anti-Convict League, he proceeds as follows :—

" In the dearth of accommodation within the rounds of the police, I was glad, after living three weeks in the ship, to take a lone house three miles from Launceston, on a road not patrolled, with a navigable river in its front, and dense bush behind it. My neighbours, at the distance of a long half mile, are a farmer who was a convict, a smith, a shoemaker, and a joiner, all of whom had been in the same predicament; and thus, with my seven dogs, and my pistols distributed amongst my English and German servants, I awaited my fate. My German governess, whose father is a captain in the Frankfort service, loaded a double-barrelled gun; and my German butler contrived to have a complete armament in his bed-room : he put strings to a miserable dinner-bell, and on the least alarm we went our nightly rounds. We have a nasty ugly hill between us and the town, where the horses must walk, and where there is cover for highwaymen, so it was long a question whether I, the master of the house, ought to be out after dark, and whether we could safely accept dinner and dance invitations in the town.

" Tomorrow I shall have been six months in my lone house. I went into my pantry yesterday, and my butler's pistols were not loaded. My German governess sent her double-barrel to be cleaned, and has not asked for it again. The plate is no longer brought regularly into my bed-room. I leave my forty-guinea 'Mortimer' double-rifle in my study at the other end of the house. I have a convict coachman, a convict gardener, and some farm labourers, who were sent out here. My coachman and gardener live on the premises; we seem to have altogether ceased to feel alarm. We are out at all hours of day or night, without precaution and without apprehension. I have begun this letter in this somewhat trivial manner, because I think that one personal case is better than a quantity of generalization. But I may go on to say, that we have spent days and nights in other settlers' houses, far more lonely and unprotected than our own,—houses built at different times, like our old English manor-houses, full of corners and crevices, steps up and steps down, with fastenings to doors and windows of most untrustworthy description. I have walked through the dense bush, and driven miles and miles over roads where escape by means of speed had been impossible. Cheap living, a healthy climate, abundance of pleasant employment, a firm Government, an active police, and, I may add, comfort even in the prisons,—these, and especially the three first, guarantee safety to our lives and property. . . . .

. . . . . "I have lived in three country towns in England, and three years in London. I was one winter in Paris. I have spent, altogether, five years in Germany. I am competent to say conscientiously, that I have never been in better regulated, more quiet towns, than Hobart Town and Launceston. The country districts are the same. The road-side inns stand open, there are all sorts of shops in the villages, and people of all vocations go about their work as cheerfully and pleasantly as they do anywhere in England."

I think that this letter, supported as it is by so much concurrent evidence, especially in Sir William Denison's despatches, completely negatives the supposition that the Colony of Van Diemen's Land is suffering, in the manner asserted, from the continuance of transportation. It is however contended, that even if the Colonists are mistaken as to the extent of the injury inflicted upon them, still it is not right to compel them against their will to submit to the continuance of a system to which they so much object. I confess I doubt very much whether the opinion of the Colonists is so much against transportation as is supposed. In the Colonies even, more than at home, real public opinion—the opinion which is entitled to consideration and respect—is not always to be gathered from clamour and from the newspaper press; and there are not wanting strong symptoms of the artificial character of the agitation got up by the Anti-Transportation League, and of its being supported by no earnest and sincere opinion on the part of many of those who have, from various motives,

thought fit to join it. The most decisive indication of this is to be found in the fact, that every ship
laden with convicts which has lately arrived, has led
to applications for their services two or three times
more in number than the men who have been
brought; and that although one of the rules of the
League is that none of its members are to employ
convicts, yet practically many of them are found not
the least eager of the numerous candidates for this
description of labour.

Even, however, if there were a much greater concurrence of genuine opinion in Van Diemen's Land
against the continuance of transportation to that
Colony than I believe there really is, I should not be
prepared to admit that, under all the circumstances
of the case, this Country is called upon to defer to
that opinion, by taking a course of which it is at
least doubtful whether it would not be really injurious to those who ask for it, while it clearly would
be very much so to the Empire considered as a
whole. It is to be remembered that Van Diemen's
Land was founded for the express purpose of receiving convicts; that it has been fitted to answer that
object by an enormous expenditure on the part of the
Mother-country, by which not only all the buildings
required for the penal establishment, but the greater
part of the roads and public works throughout the
Island, have been provided. The free inhabitants
consist either of those who have of their own accord
settled there for the sake of the advantages to be
derived from this large expenditure and from con-

vict labour, or of the children of those who have
done so ; and for these persons now to prefer a claim
to have the sending of convicts to the Island discontinued, just when it has been brought into the condition in which it is best suited for receiving them,
seems to me to be a pretension which is altogether
unreasonable.   The demand of the inhabitants of the
other Australian Colonies, that convicts should no
longer be sent to Van Diemen's Land, because when
they become free they cannot be prevented from going
to the neighbouring settlements, is not more tenable.

Australia was originally occupied by this Country
exclusively for penal purposes.   When it was decided
that New South Wales, in deference to the wishes
of its inhabitants, should cease to be a penal Colony,
a concession was freely made to them which could
not have been demanded as a right, and which gives
them no claim whatever to ask that the whole of that
extensive region of the earth should, for their convenience, be closed against British offenders.   What is
now the Colony of Victoria, was first settled as a part
of New South Wales while still a convict Colony ;
and the means of forming the settlement, and the resources by which it was carried forward to such early
prosperity, were drawn from Van Diemen's Land, and
derived mainly from the labour of convicts.

South Australia was also voluntarily placed by its
founders in the neighbourhood of existing penal Colonies, for the sake of the assistance to be obtained
from the various resources they afforded.   With what
justice then can those who have for their own conve-

nience settled in that part of the world, which the Government and Parliament of this country had previously selected for the reception of convicts, now claim that, when they have obtained from the system all the advantages they desire, it should, to meet their wishes, be discontinued, though this would be attended with great and manifest injury to the interests of the Empire?

For these reasons I must maintain that this Country is perfectly justified in continuing the practice of Transportation to Australia; the Colonies being only entitled to ask, that in the arrangements for conducting it, their interests and welfare should be consulted as far as possible, and that, with regard to the expense incurred in these arrangements, they should be generously dealt with.   The statement I have made will show that these conditions were not neglected during your Administration, and the whole policy of this Country towards the Australian Colonies, while it was conducted by us, will, I am persuaded, be pronounced by those who will take the trouble to investigate the facts in a candid spirit, to have been just and considerate as well in what relates to the transportation of offenders, as in all other matters*.

October 30th, 1852.

* See Mrs. Meredith's interesting work on Van Diemen's Land, published since this Letter was written, for strong evidence in support of the statements I have made as to the effect of transportation to that Colony.

LETTER IX.

MY DEAR LORD JOHN,

There still remain to be considered, with reference to the Australian Colonies, the proceedings which have taken place as to the changes in the form of their government, and their general condition at the end of your Administration. The measure we brought forward for settling their constitutions, was very fully discussed in both Houses of Parliament in the Session of 1850 ; and I should be compelled far to exceed the limits within which I am anxious to confine these Letters, if I were to attempt to give even an outline of the Bill we proposed to Parliament, of the considerations by which we were guided in framing it, and of the arguments which were urged against many of its provisions. I will therefore content myself with making a few somewhat desultory remarks on the origin of the Bill, and on some of the most important points which arose in the debates upon it.

We found, when we came into office, that there had been much correspondence on the propriety of dividing what was then the district of Port Philip from the Colony of New South Wales, of which it still formed a part; and it was apparent that there had come to be a tolerably general concurrence of opinion as to the necessity of this measure, which had in the first instance been vehemently opposed in the older part of the Colony. It was also our opinion, that the time was come when a representative form of government, which already existed in New South Wales, ought to be established also in Van Diemen's Land and South Australia, and that provision should be made for extending the same boon to Western Australia as soon as its inhabitants should be prepared to take upon themselves the expenses of their civil government, instead of having them provided for by an annual Parliamentary vote. Neither of these objects could be accomplished without the aid of Parliament, and there were many obvious reasons for including in a single Act the provisions required for both.

In the year 1847 a despatch was therefore addressed to Sir Charles Fitzroy, informing him of our intention to submit to Parliament a Bill upon this subject; and that in this Bill we should endeavour to amend the existing constitution of New South Wales, as established by the Act of 1842, in two material respects.

We proposed, in the first place, to revert to the ancient form of Colonial Constitutions, and to divide the Legislature, in which the representatives of the people and the nominees of the Crown had hitherto sat together, into two Houses.   In the second place, adverting to the obstacles which had hitherto prevented the important clauses of the Act of 1842, for the establishment of Municipal bodies, from being brought into effective operation, the Governor was told that, " it will be necessary to consider what changes ought to be made in the existing law for the creation of municipalities in order to secure to those bodies their just weight and consideration, and especially whether, with that view, they may not be made to bear to the House of Assembly the relations of constituents and representatives*."

The publication in the Colony of the Despatch conveying to the Governor the above information as to our intentions, was followed by strong manifestations of opinion against the contemplated measure ; and petitions, very numerously signed, against any change in the constitution which had not been previously assented to by the Colonists, were transmitted home by Sir Charles Fitzroy.   It appeared to us that this was a reasonable demand, and that, when representative institutions have once been conferred upon any Colony, the form of those institutions ought not, without some very grave reason, to be altered by Parliament contrary to the wishes of those to whom they

* See House of Commons Sessional Paper of 1848, No. 715, p. 5.

have been granted. A Despatch was accordingly addressed to Sir Charles Fitzroy, in which he was informed that, in recommending to Parliament the division of the Colony, no change in its constitution, beyond what might be necessary to give effect to that measure, would be proposed.

Before submitting to Parliament any Bill upon this subject, we were of opinion that it would be expedient it should be carefully inquired into by a Committee of the Privy Council. At the time when there was no separate Secretary of State for the Colonies, the most important matters relating to them were habitually referred by the Crown to the Committee of Council for Trade and Foreign Plantations; but although this Committee retained its ancient name, and though, with reference to the confirmation or disallowance of Colonial laws, the decision of the Crown was always made in the form of Orders in Council founded on the reports of this Committee, for many years the real functions of this department had been confined to matters of trade, and it had been in the habit of rendering very little assistance to the Secretary of State in the administration of Colonial affairs. We considered that, upon certain Colonial subjects, the ancient practice of calling upon the Committee for Trade and Foreign Plantations to act as a deliberative body might be usefully revived; that this would be the means of rendering valuable aid to the Secretary of State and the Cabinet in deciding upon questions of importance, and also

would afford an opportunity for placing the reasons
for the decisions adopted by the Crown, on the advice
of its Servants, on record, in a more formal shape
than that of a mere despatch.

With this view the Queen was advised to add to
the ordinary members of the Board of Trade, Lord
Campbell, then Chancellor of the Duchy of Lan-
caster, Sir James Stephen, and Sir Edward Ryan;
and to refer to the Board thus augmented, amongst
other questions, that as to the best mode of effecting
the contemplated changes in Australia. In the beginning of 1849 this Committee, after much careful
consideration of the subject, made a Report, in which
they stated their views as to the course which ought to
be adopted; and this Report, having been approved,
was submitted to the Queen in Council for confirmation, after which it was laid before Parliament, and
transmitted to the Colonies*. A Bill, framed in strict
accordance with the recommendation of the Committee, was prepared and brought into the House of
Commons the same Session; but, from the pressure
of other business, it was impossible to proceed with
it, and it was postponed till the next year.

In 1850 the subject of the Australian constitutions was recommended to the attention of Parliament
in the Queen's Speech, and it occupied a large portion
of the time of the House of Commons during the
Session. Several provisions of the Bill encountered
in that House much opposition, and it gave rise to

* See Appendix (I) of the First Volume.

exceedingly protracted debates, but was eventually passed without any material alteration. In the House of Lords it was also very fully discussed, and passed with two somewhat important amendments, to which we thought it right to agree. The one was an alteration of the franchise of electors, calculated to give a fairer share in the representation to the occupiers of pastoral land; the other was the omission of the clauses by which it was intended to empower the several Colonial Legislatures to constitute a sort of Congress, in which matters affecting the interest of more than a single Colony might be dealt with. The first of these amendments effected a change which we had always considered to be expedient in itself, and our only reason for not having originally introduced it into the Bill, was a doubt whether it would not be more in accordance with the principle of the measure, to leave this change in the franchise to be made by the Colonial Legislature. The second amendment involved the postponement of an arrangement, of the ultimate necessity for which no doubt can, I think, be entertained; but it was successfully shown that the clauses, as they stood in the Bill, would not have been sufficient for their object, and that it was hardly possible to correct them in this respect, without previous communication and concert with the local Legislatures. With these alterations the Bill was finally passed.

To this slight account of the origin of the measure, and of the proceedings upon it while it was before Parliament, I will add a few remarks on its substance,

and on some of the points which led to most discussion during its progress.   The principle of the
Bill was that of making the least possible change
in the actual constitution of New South Wales, when
dividing that Colony into two, and of establishing the
same form of government in the new colony of Victoria, and in Van Diemen's Land and South Australia; with a provision that it should also be extended
to Western Australia whenever the latter should be
prepared to take upon itself the charges of its civil
government.

But in maintaining unaltered the form of government actually existing in New South Wales, and extending it to the neighbouring Colonies, we induced
Parliament to invest the local Legislatures with large
powers of making (subject to certain conditions) whatever changes in their institutions or in their laws
might from time to time be found necessary.   Hitherto
the power of amending Colonial constitutions, which
have been granted by Act of Parliament, had always
been reserved by Parliament to itself.   By the New
South Wales Act of 1842, no power was given to the
Legislative Council of altering any clauses in that Act,
however inconvenient they might prove, or of making
even the most minute variation, in the amount of
the large sums, which the schedules of that Act had
made applicable to certain heads of service.   This
had led to no little embarrassment, particularly in
respect to the Municipalities which the Act of 1842
proposed to create, but which it had been found

impossible to bring into effective operation. In our opinion it was improper that the power of the Colonists to adapt their institutions, to the changes in the circumstances which are taking place so rapidly, should be thus restricted.

In our older Colonies, the constitutions of which were originally granted by charters from the Crown, there is no such restriction on the power of the local Legislatures to effect, with the concurrence of the Crown, the reforms which may be found necessary. We saw no reason why a different rule should be applied to Australia, and we therefore introduced into the Bill clauses investing the Legislative Councils with the most ample power of amending the constitutions thus granted, and of altering the appropriation of the sums which, by the schedules of the Act, are made applicable to certain purposes. It is only required that changes of this kind should be effected by laws passed for the purpose, to which of course the assent of the Crown is necessary. Whether it can properly be advised to give that assent, is a question on which the responsible Servants of the Crown must in all cases exercise their discretion. With respect to bills for effecting constitutional changes, Parliament has reserved to itself the power of exercising some control, by requiring that they shall be laid before both Houses before they receive the Royal confirmation. This extension of the power of the local Legislatures was much objected to in the House of Lords; but I observed with satisfaction, in the last Session, that upon further consideration, Her Majesty's present advisers thought it right to introduce the same provision into the New Zealand Bill of this year, and it passed the House of Lords without opposition.

The part of the Bill which met with most opposition was that, by which the Legislatures of these Colonies were to be formed on the model of that of New South Wales, which, by the Act of 1842, was a single Chamber, of which two-thirds of the members were elected by the inhabitants, and the remainder nominated by the Governor on behalf of the Crown. It was vehemently contended that both the opinion of the greatest political writers and experience, were clearly in favour of the division of the Legislature into two Chambers, and various motions were made with the view of altering the Bill accordingly.

Even if the validity of the arguments in favour of dividing the Legislature into two Chambers had been admitted to their full extent, it would have been impossible to accomplish this by the Bill then before Parliament, without entirely altering the principle upon which it was founded. It was the object of the measure to meet the wishes strongly urged by the Colonists in numerous petitions*, by making no material alteration in the constitution of New South Wales, upon which they had not had a previous opportunity of express-

---

* Several of these petitions will be found in the " Correspondence on the subject of Australian Colonies Government Bill, presented to both Houses of Parliament by command of Her Majesty, on the 1st of March, 1850."

ing their opinion. It was true that the question of
dividing the Legislature into two Chambers had been
discussed in the Colony, enough to show that if there
was no decided opinion in favour of such a change,
there was at all events no general objection to it.
Still it was quite clear that the alteration would be
very unpalatable, unless the upper Chamber were
made in some way or other elective; while no mode
of introducing the principle of election into the composition of this branch of the Legislature had yet
been suggested, of which it could be said that any
considerable number of the Colonists were likely to
approve.

This was undoubtedly the main reason which led us
to bring forward the Bill in the shape we did, and to
resist its alteration*. But I must add, that the close
attention it was my duty to give to the working of
various Colonial constitutions, while I held the office
of Secretary of State, led me to alter a good deal the
opinion I at first held, in common with most other persons, that a Legislature divided into two branches is
in itself greatly to be preferred in all cases to one composed of a single Chamber. I now consider it to be
very doubtful, at least, whether the single Legislature
ought not under many circumstances to be preferred.
If an Upper Chamber could be constituted in such

---

* See the Debates; also the Report of the Committee of the
Privy Council, already referred to, and the Despatch to Sir C. Fitzroy of July 31, 1848 ; p. 39 of the papers presented to Parliament
on the 1st of March, 1850.

a manner, as to have substantial weight and authority, and to be thus capable of exercising a salutary check upon the representative Assembly, while, at the same time, effectual provision were made against the machine of government being brought to a stand by differences between these two bodies, the advantage of such a constitution of the Legislature could not well be contested. But to accomplish this, is a problem not yet solved by any Colonial constitution of which I am aware.

The attempts hitherto made to create in the Colonies a substitute for the House of Lords, have been attended with very moderate success. Legislative Councils composed of Members appointed by the Crown have, in general, had little real influence over public opinion, while they have been attended with the great disadvantage of rendering the Assembly less efficient, by withdrawing from the scene where their services might be most valuable, some of the persons best qualified, by the enjoyment of a certain degree of leisure, by their character and their ability, to be useful members of the popular branch of the Legislature. The number of such men in the small circle of Colonial society is necessarily limited; hence it seems inexpedient that any of them should be taken away from the Assembly, which must always exercise the largest share of power and influence. And as it is found, that the character of every legislative body is greatly altered for the worse, by its being composed of too small a number of members, the effect of dividing the Legis-

lature into two Chambers, in a community not numerous enough to furnish more than a few persons
qualified for such duties, is to substitute two comparatively ineffective bodies for one of a superior
character.

On the other hand, the experience of the few years
that the Constitution of New South Wales has been
established, has shown that very considerable advantage arises from the presence in the Legislature, of a
certain proportion of members, who do not owe their
seats to popular election. The members appointed by
the Crown, being only one-third of the whole body,
can never prevent the passing of measures which are
strongly supported by public opinion, as they might
(and as experience elsewhere shows they often would)
if they sat by themselves, as a separate branch of the
Legislature. But though they cannot defeat such
measures, they can ensure their being fully discussed,
and not passed, without a previous consideration of any
objections, to what may be the mistaken demands of
an excited and ill-informed popular feeling.

It is of the utmost importance, that in all legislative
assemblies both sides of all disputed questions should
be heard, and that those who hold what is not the
popular opinion of the day, should be represented.
But from the nature of Colonial societies, there is a
great danger that this may not always be the case,
if all the Members of the Assembly must be returned
by popular election ; since there are occasions when
able and upright men may fail to be elected, from

the very qualities which render it most desirable that
they should be so, in consequence of their being too
judicious to be misled by some delusion of the moment,
and too honest and independent to profess to share in
it, contrary to their real opinion.   To prove that the
Members of the Legislature nominated by the Crown
are not those who stand lowest in public estimation,
it may be sufficient to mention, that the first Legislative Council of South Australia, under the recent Act,
by a unanimous vote, chose for its Speaker a member
of this class.

While there are these advantages in the form of constitution originally given to New South Wales, and
now extended to the neighbouring Colonies, it also
makes provision, by another arrangement, for that revision of laws before they are finally passed, which it
is considered one of the chief objects of the division
of the Legislature into two branches to ensure.   By
the Act of 1842, the Governor is invested with the
power, when any Bills are tendered for his assent on
behalf of the Crown, of returning them for the consideration of the Legislative Council, with any amendments he may think it right to suggest; instead of
being compelled, as in other Colonies, to give or withhold his assent, from measures in the precise form in
which they are presented to him.   There is a further
security against hasty legislation, in the power which
belongs to the Crown of disallowing Colonial laws,
even after they have been passed by Governors.   It
not unfrequently happens, that the Servants of the

Crown advise Her Majesty to delay her confirmation of Colonial laws, until the local Legislatures have had an opportunity of reconsidering and amending them; nor would it be difficult, in the records of the Colonial Office, to find repeated instances of great improvements in the legislation of the Colonies having been due to the exercise of this power*.

Another part of the measure which has led to much discussion, but perhaps more in the Colonies than in

---

* Since this Letter was written, I have seen reports of discussions in the Assembly of Canada on proposals for reforming the Legislative Council of that Province, tending strongly to confirm the opinion I have expressed above. It appears, from the debates in the Provincial Parliament, and from the articles on the subject in the Canadian newspapers, that the present constitution of the Legislative Council is almost universally disapproved, but that there is much conflict of opinions as to the manner in which it should be altered. I have not had an opportunity of following the discussion very closely, but, from what I have read of it, I should infer that all who have taken part in it have been far more successful in pointing out objections to the schemes they have opposed, than in defending their own, and that there is not one of these plans which would be likely to answer. I observe, that this has led to the question being raised, whether it is necessary to have any second Chamber at all. I believe that there is good reason for this doubt, and that, in the present state of Canada, the best mode of dealing with the subject would be to abolish the Legislative Council altogether, and to enlarge the Assembly, giving to the Governor the power of nominating a small proportion of the members (by which seats would be secured for the members of his Executive Council), and also the right of returning Bills with amendments, as in Australia. The Provincial Parliament is not invested, by the Union Act of 1840, with the power of altering its provisions or introducing constitutional reforms ; but it is not probable that Parliament will withhold, from the largest and most advanced in its social condition of all our Colonies, a power which they most of them now possess.

this Country, is that relating to the appropriation of certain amounts of money from the revenue of the several Colonies for the maintenance of their religious establishments. I believe the great majority of persons in this Country, will concur in thinking it highly desirable that these establishments should not only be maintained, but increased. For my own part, I entertain the strongest opinion of the necessity of making some provision from the public revenue of the Colonies, for the religious instruction of their inhabitants, and that this vital object cannot safely be left altogether to the spontaneous efforts of individuals, by adopting what is called the voluntary system. But all important, as I consider it to be, that the Colonists should provide, from their public revenue a part at least of the expense of maintaining adequate religious establishments for the population, it is no less clearly demonstrated by experience, that to impose this obligation upon an unwilling people by the authority of Parliament, in addition to other objections, is open to this conclusive one, that, instead of being advantageous, it is really injurious to the cause of religion, by indisposing men to receive the instruction which they are compelled to pay for unwillingly, and, as they think, in violation of the principles of a representative Constitution. The Bill, as we proposed it, went, I think, as far as was for this reason expedient, in maintaining grants for religious purposes in these Colonies. It provided that the existing grants should continue, until altered by some new law passed by the local Legislature, and required that Acts for making such alterations should not be at once assented to by the Governor, but should be reserved for the special signification of Her Majesty's pleasure. The object of this provision, was to take away all just ground of complaint from the Colonists, on the score of their being deprived of the constitutional power of controlling the expenditure of the whole revenue levied from them by taxes, but at the same time to oppose some check to hasty legislation on this subject, and to confer upon the Crown the power of guarding the vested interests of individuals from being unjustly dealt with.

The enactment we proposed on this point received the sanction of Parliament, and is now the law; and I would fain hope that the Colonies will not exercise unwisely the power with which they have been invested, though I grieve to observe, that in South Australia there seems to exist at present a strong disposition to adopt, in its most absolute form, what is called the voluntary system, and to put an end to all grants whatever for religious purposes. Perhaps however, strong as the disposition is, the inhabitants may upon further reflection be led to take a different view of the subject. Independently of all higher grounds of objection to the course they contemplate, it is one which, looked at merely as a pecuniary question, can hardly fail to be injurious to them, as nothing assuredly would so much tend to induce the best class of settlers to avoid South Australia, and to give a preference to other Colonies, as finding that in the

former they would not enjoy, for themselves and their
children those facilities for public worship, to which
the people of this Country attach so high and so just
a value.   In the meantime it is satisfactory to know,
that the effect of abstaining from any attempt to force
the Colonists to pay for the maintenance of a religious
Establishment, has not been unfavourable to the real
influence and prosperity of our own Church; its usefulness has been not a little extended by the appointment of three additional Bishops in Australia, for
whom endowments were provided by the exertions and
generosity of members of the Church, during your Administration.   The zealous and able clergymen who
have accepted these arduous offices have already done
much, (and still greater success will, I trust, attend
their labours as they continue,) in increasing the
number of clergymen and promoting the building of
churches and schools.

A strong desire was expressed by some members
of both Houses of Parliament, that clauses should be
added to the Australian Constitutional Act, for the
purpose of assisting and encouraging the voluntary exertions of the Church of England in these Colonies, by
relieving its members from difficulties under which
they are supposed to labour.   The authors of these
proposals did not succeed in showing, that any legislation was required for the benefit of the Church of
England in this part of the Empire, which could be
undertaken by Parliament, without trenching on the
proper province of the local Legislatures, and the

clauses which had been suggested were not adopted. It is, I think, well for the interests of the Church of England in the Colonies, that such was the result of the discussion, and that the Act passed, without containing clauses which could have been attended with no advantage that would not have been dearly purchased, by wounding the sensitive jealousy felt by the Colonists, of any interference by the Imperial Legislature in their local concerns.

The importance of this subject has led me rather further than I had intended, in adverting to one provision of the Bill we submitted to Parliament for the better government of the Australian Colonies. I have only to add, with respect to this measure, that during its progress through Parliament it was strongly urged that it ought to be amended, so as to deprive the Crown of its ancient power of disallowing Colonial laws, at least so far as relates to a certain class of acts. I have already noticed this question in my first Letter, and some additional arguments against the proposed important change in our Colonial system will be found in a despatch I am about to quote. We thought it, for the reasons there stated, our duty to resist the proposed alteration of the Bill, and no amendment of the kind was made; but the manner in which it was urged during the debates, and the general tone of these discussions, had an unfortunate effect on the success of the measure, when passed, in New South Wales.

When the Report of the Board of Trade, on which

the Bill was founded, reached the Colonies, it was received with an expression of entire satisfaction; the approbation of all its essential recommendations was indeed so general that it might almost be said to have been unanimous; and I have now before me a collection of extracts, made from the Colonial newspapers at the time, from which it appears that these newspapers, various as are the general political views of their writers, concurred in approving highly of the measure which was proposed, except as to a few of its minor details, on which there was some difference of opinion. When the Bill founded on the Report, which was introduced but not proceeded with in the Session of 1849, was received in the Colonies, it met with the same favour, and much disappointment was occasioned by the subsequent intelligence that it had been necessary to postpone it.

But in New South Wales (for in the other Colonies it was different*), the debates in Parliament altered the feeling of many of the inhabitants, whose fault it is to be somewhat easily led away by unsound but plausible arguments when their vanity is appealed to. They were induced to suppose, that the privileges

---

* In Victoria the general feeling seems to have been the very opposite to that which prevailed in Sydney.   See the Address of the inhabitants of Geelong, in which they express their gratitude, not only for the Act of Parliament which had been passed, but also for the instructions, which had been sent to the Governor, as to the mode of carrying it into operation.   Further Papers, relative to the alterations in the Constitution of the Australian Colonies, presented to Parliament, July 1, 1852, p. 3.

granted to them by Parliament were less than those enjoyed by other Colonies, and to believe in the reality and importance of the faults which theoretical observers in this country had detected in the Constitution under which they had lived for several years, although in that time they had apparently been unconscious of the existence of many of the alleged defects in the form of their government, which had not been manifested by their practical effects. Accordingly, though only two years before they had almost unanimously petitioned Parliament not to make any change in their Constitution without their previous assent, when the Act of 1850 reached the Colony, preceded by the reports of the debates in Parliament, it immediately became the object of indiscriminate censure. The Legislative Council—echoing, as I believe, not the real opinion of the majority or most intelligent part of the population, but rather that of the most noisy and easily excited—voted what they called a " Declaration and Remonstrance against the New Constitution Act, 13 & 14 Vict., chap. 59." This document, and the despatch in reply to it, will be found at length in the Appendix* ; they ought to be carefully read, and compared with the Report of the Board of Trade, on which the Australian Constitutional Act was founded, by all who would form a correct judgement on the merits of that measure. Those who will take this trouble can hardly fail to be convinced that the Legislative Council, in their Declaration and Remon-

* See Appendix (A) to this Volume.

strance, have fallen into errors, both of reasoning and
of fact, so obvious that it is difficult to account for
them otherwise, than by supposing this State Paper to
have been drawn up and voted rather under the influence of excited feelings than with the care and deliberation which would have befitted its importance.   If the
people of New South Wales wish really to benefit by
the powers of self-government which their Constitution confers upon them, they must make their Representatives feel the necessity of evincing greater calm-
ness of judgement, and regard for the dictates of sober
reason, in the exercise of the high functions intrusted
to them.

The inhabitants of New South Wales may be assured that the success of free institutions in any
country depends far less upon the particular form of
those institutions, than upon the character of the
people upon whom they are conferred, and the use
they make of the power placed in their hands.   Nor
are there any qualities more necessary to a people
who possess such a Constitution, than the judgement
and good sense which will prevent them from following blindly those who seek to obtain popularity by
declaiming on alleged grievances, and which will
lead them strictly to examine, and to reject, when ill-
founded, the claims of such pretenders to their favour.

I have but a few words to add on the subject of
the Australian Colonies, among which I have thought
it more convenient not to include New Zealand, to
which I shall call your attention separately.   You

will perceive that I have made little reference to the discovery of gold in New South Wales and Victoria. This discovery was only known in this Country a few months before we retired from Office, and in that time we were not called upon to take any measures upon the subject, beyond approving what had been done by the local Authorities, and pointing out to the Governor of New South Wales, that the revenue derived from gold ought to be employed in adding to the strength and efficiency of the police, and making the other arrangements required by the very novel state of things that had arisen. The changes produced by the extraordinary abundance in which gold has been found, bid fair to be so great as almost to defy conjecture as to their ultimate result; hence I have thought it advisable to speak only of what had been done prior to this discovery, and of the state of things which existed on the eve of its taking place, which affords the best means of judging of the results of our policy. That state of things, I am happy to say, was in the highest degree satisfactory. In my Letter upon Transportation, I have had occasion to show the very remarkable improvement that has taken place in the condition and prospects of the two Colonies to which convicts are still sent; and, in my account of our measures with respect to Emigration, I have stated to how large an extent we had been able to add to the population of New South Wales, Victoria, and South Australia, by means of the territorial .revenue. In all other respects these Colonies were equally prosperous, and the annual reports up to the end of 1850 (the last year in which their condition had not been affected by the discovery of gold) show an extraordinary progress to have been made by them.

I find that the receipts from the sale of Crown lands in New South Wales (including Victoria), which, after the extravagant sales of a few years before, had been reduced in 1844 to £7402, and had only recovered to £27,060 in 1846, had risen in 1850 to no less than £156,698, while the revenue derived from licenses and leases to occupy Crown lands was at the rate of about £51,000 a-year; and the general revenue, which in the year 1846 had been £270,550, was in 1850 £371,394. The most important branch of industry in the Colony, the production of wool, had also increased very rapidly. The number of sheep in the Colony in 1846 was 7,906,811, and in 1850 it amounted to 13,059,324. The wool exported in 1846 was 16,479,520 lbs., worth £1,019,985; in 1850 the export of wool had risen to 32,361,829 lbs., worth £1,614,241. The progress of South Australia has been even more rapid. The Customs revenue of that Colony, which in 1846 was £37,643, had increased in 1850 to £102,523. The extent of land in cultivation had increased from 33,292 acres in 1846, to 174,184 in 1850. The number of sheep assessed in 1846 was 681,374; the number depastured on the Crown lands, (within and without the part of the Colony divided into hundreds,) amounted in 1850 to 1,152,039. The export of wool in 1846 was 1,473,186 lbs., in 1850 it was 3,289,232 lbs. The total value of the exports of all descriptions was in 1846 £190,669, and in 1850 it had risen to £571,348*.

I might have quoted other Returns, but those I have selected are sufficient to show with what extraordinary rapidity these Colonies were advancing in wealth and importance even before the discovery of gold had occurred. Their prosperous condition, and the progress they have made, justified the measure which I have mentioned in my first Letter, that we had taken, in calling upon them to contribute more than heretofore to the expense of their military defence; and it also affords us, I think, conclusive evidence that the art of colonization has not been, as it has been said, lost in modern times.

November 1, 1852.

* See the Annual Blue Book Reports presented to Parliament.

LETTER X.

NEW ZEALAND.

MY DEAR LORD JOHN,

I have hitherto had to speak of Colonies which, during the whole period of your Administration, have been in the enjoyment of uninterrupted peace. I have now to call your attention to those which have been disturbed by war or insurrection. The British Colonies which during the last six years have suffered from events of this kind are New Zealand, Ceylon, and the Cape of Good Hope. I do not add the Ionian Islands, because, though Cephalonia has also been the scene of insurrection, these islands are not a British Colony, but a distinct State, under British protection; and though their government is presided over by a British Commissioner, who acts under the directions of the Secretary of State for the Colonial Department, their system of administration is in many respects different from that of a Colony. Hence, as I find the task I have undertaken, in proposing to give an account of the transactions of the

Colonies properly so called, is more than enough for me, I will take advantage of the circumstance of the Ionian Islands not forming part of the British dominions, to abstain from entering into their affairs. I do this the more gladly, because the most important subject connected with their administration which we were called upon to deal with, had not been disposed of when we retired from Office, but was still pending.

With respect to New Zealand, you cannot fail to recollect that the accounts received from that Colony were so unsatisfactory and alarming during the years 1844 and 1845, that, after having been the subject of a Parliamentary inquiry and of much discussion, Lord Derby, who was then Secretary of State for the Colonies, thought it necessary, in June 1845, to recall the former Governor, and to direct Captain (now Sir George) Grey, then Governor of South Australia, to proceed with the least possible delay to New Zealand, and take upon himself the administration of its affairs. When the new Governor reached the Colony, in November 1845, he found the British troops and settlers engaged in hostilities, (of which they had had greatly the worst,) with the Natives in the northern part of the islands. Sir George Grey's first object on his arrival in New Zealand, was to avail himself of the naval and military force at his disposal, to put down the dangerous rebellion in the district of the Bay of Islands, and his account of the complete success which attended the measures he took for this purpose, had reached the Colonial Office three or four months before we were appointed to Office. The war was not renewed in that district, though it long continued to give cause for much anxiety ; but in the southern province a few months later there were serious disturbances, which broke out at intervals, and did not finally cease until August, 1847.

It is unnecessary that I should give any detailed account of these disturbances ; it is sufficient to state that, during the whole of 1846 and the greater part of 1847, though the Governor was making steady progress towards establishing permanent tranquillity, and succeeded in maintaining friendly relations with the great majority of the natives, some of the principal Chiefs continued to show a spirit of disaffection and insubordination, which on two or three different occasions broke out into open and very serious hostilities.   By the energy and judgement of the Governor, admirably supported as he was both by the troops and by the naval force on the station, any general insurrection was averted, and all the military operations it was necessary to undertake were brought to an early and successful close.   Among the most remarkable events of this period were the seizure of the famous Chief, Te Rauparaha, in July, 1846, and the rebellion at Wanganui, in April, 1847.   Te Rauparaha, who was one of the most noted warriors in New Zealand, and had been a chief actor in the massacre of Captain Wakefield and his companions in 1843, was detected by the Governor in concerting with his old ally, Rangihaeata, hostile proceedings against the British Settlers in the neighbourhood of Wellington, while professing friendship to them. When this was clearly ascertained, the treacherous Chief was seized without resistance, by a prompt and well-executed surprise, and he was detained a prisoner on board one of the ships-of-war until all danger from him was at an end, when, on the intercession of two of the friendly Chiefs, he was released. There is every reason to believe, that this measure prevented a very formidable outbreak from taking place.

At Wanganui, in April, 1847, the murder of the wife and children of a Settler led to another insurrection. The murderers were promptly taken, and delivered into the hands of the British Authorities, by our native allies; when some of the most powerful Chiefs in the district, who were nearly related to the culprits, assembled a war-party of no less than 600 men for their rescue. The British force at Wanganui consisted of only 170 men, notwithstanding which, Captain Laye, the officer in command, did not hesitate to try the murderers by court-martial, and, on their conviction, to have four of them hanged with as little delay as possible. The Governor reported, that this firmness and decision on the part of Captain Laye probably saved the country from a serious rebellion*. The execution of the culprits was followed, as was to be expected, by an attack on the Settlement, which however Captain

* See Papers presented to Parliament, December 1847, p. 71.

Laye, with the small force at his command, gallantly repulsed, and with the assistance of the Settlers he defended the place successfully until the Governor arrived with reinforcements. There were afterwards two or three severe skirmishes, and it was not until the 3rd of September, 1847, that the Governor was able to report that the disturbances at this place were at an end, and not likely to be renewed*. Since that time tranquillity has been maintained throughout the Colony, and it has continued to advance steadily and rapidly in prosperity. The policy by which this result has been obtained, and the difficulties the Governor has had to contend with, are so well described by himself, that I may be permitted to quote nearly the whole of the very interesting Despatch in which he has done so. In this Despatch, dated July 9, 1849†, he states that the two Colonies, into which New Zealand was then divided,

" are composed at present of what may be termed nine principal European settlements, besides smaller dependencies of these. The largest of the settlements contains about seven thousand (7000) European inhabitants; and their total European population may be stated at about twenty thousand (20,000) souls. These settlements are scattered over a distance of about eight hundred (800) miles of latitude; they are separated from each other by wide intervals; and communication, even for persons on horseback, exists only between three of them. Their inhabitants are chiefly

* See Papers presented to Parliament, February 1848, p. 12.
† See Papers presented January 1850, p. 190.

British subjects, but there are amongst them many Americans, French, and Germans. The majority of them have never been trained to the use of arms. The settlers, both in the main Colonies and the subordinate dependencies, have occupied the country in so scattered and irregular a manner, that it would be found impossible to afford them efficient protection. They are generally without arms, and would probably be deprived of them by the aboriginal population if they possessed them at any remote stations.

"The wide intervals between these European Colonies are occupied by a native race, estimated to consist of one hundred and twenty thousand (120,000) souls, a very large proportion of whom are males, capable of bearing arms. These natives are generally armed with rifles or double-barrelled guns; they are skilled in the use of their weapons, and take great care of them; they are addicted to war; have repeatedly, in encounters with our troops, been reported by our own officers to be equal to any European troops; and are such good tacticians that we have never yet succeeded in bringing them to a decisive encounter, they having always availed themselves of the advantage afforded by their wilds and fastnesses. Their armed bodies move without any baggage, and are attended by the women, who carry potatoes on their backs for the warriors, or subsist them by digging fern-root, so that they are wholly independent of supplies, and can move and subsist their forces in countries where our troops cannot live.

"I should correct here a popular fallacy, which, if ever acted upon, might prove ruinous to these settlements. It has been customary to compare them to the early American Colonies, and the natives of this country to the North American Indians. There appears to be no analogy between the irregular manner in which these islands were partially

peopled by whalers and persons from all portions of the
globe, and the Pilgrim Fathers who founded the early settlements in America. And I have been assured by many
excellent and experienced officers, well acquainted with
America and this country, that there is, in a military point
of view, no analogy at all between the natives of the two
countries; the Maories, both in weapons and knowledge of
the art of war, a skill in planning and perseverance in
carrying out the operations of a lengthened campaign, being
infinitely superior to the American Indians. In fact, there
can be no doubt that they are, for warfare in this country,
even better equipped than our own troops.

"These natives, from the positions which they occupy
between all the settlements, can choose their own point of
attack, and might even so mislead the most wary Government, as to their intended operations as to render it extremely difficult to tell at what point they intended to
strike a blow. They can move their forces with rapidity
and secresy from one point of the country to another;
whilst, from the total absence of roads, the impassable
nature of the country, and the utter want of supplies, it is
impossible to move a European force more than a few
miles into the interior from any settlement.

"The natives moreover present no point at which they
can be attacked, or against which operations can be carried
on. Finding now that we can readily destroy their pas or
fortifications, they no longer construct them, but live in
scattered villages, round which they have their cultivations;
and these they can abandon without difficulty or serious
loss, being readily received and fed by any friendly tribe to
whom they may repair. They thus present no vulnerable
point. Amongst them are large numbers of lawless spirits,
who are too ready, for the sake of excitement and the hope

of plunder, to follow any predatory chief. To assist in anything which might be regarded as a national war, there
can be little doubt that almost every village would pour
forth its chiefs and its population.

"With these characteristics of courage and warlike
vagrancy, the Maories present however other remarkable
traits of character. Nearly the whole nation has now been
converted to Christianity. They are fond of agriculture,
take great pleasure in cattle and horses; like the sea, and
form good sailors; are attached to Europeans, admire their
customs and manners; are extremely ambitious of rising
in civilization, and of becoming skilled in European arts;
they are apt at learning, in many respects extremely con-
scientious and observant of their word, are ambitious of
honours, and are probably the most covetous race in the
world. They are also agreeable in manners, and attach-
ments of a lasting character readily and frequently spring
up between them and Europeans.

"A consideration of these circumstances will, I think,
lead to the conclusion that any attempt to form, in those
portions of these islands which are densely peopled by the
natives, an ordinary European settlement, the inhabitants
of which produced all they required, and were wholly independent of the native race, must end in failure. The natives
in the vicinity of such a settlement, finding themselves excluded from all community of prosperity with its inhabitants, would soon form lawless bands of borderers, who, if
they did not speedily sweep away the settlement, would
yet by their constant incursions so harass and impoverish
its inhabitants, that they would certainly soon withdraw to
the neighbouring Australian settlements, where they could
lead a life of peace and freedom from such incursions.
Upon the other hand, however, it would appear that a race

such as has been described could be easily incorporated into any British settlement with mutual advantage to both races; the natives supplying agricultural produce, poultry, pigs, and a constant supply of labour (although yet rude and unskilled), whilst, upon the other hand, the Europeans would supply the various manufactured goods required by the natives, and provide for the manifold wants created by their increasing civilization. Such a class of settlements might easily grow into prosperous communities, into which the natives, with characters softened by Christianity, civilization, and a taste for previously unknown luxuries, would readily be absorbed.

" The questions to be solved have therefore been, how to induce the native race cordially to assist in the attempt to create so desirable a state of things, and how to provide the funds requisite for governing so many isolated settlements, spread over so vast a tract of difficult country, the intervals between which are occupied by so warlike a race, over whom it was necessary to exercise some control? It is worthy of remark here, that the united population of New Zealand is as large as that of New South Wales has until very recently been, and that it is a population, from its mixed and peculiar elements, infinitely more difficult to govern than that of New South Wales, whilst the cost of the machine of government is greatly increased from the number of the settlements and their distance from each other. In point of fact, the several settlements are distinct colonies, and, both in the difference of feelings and interests of the Europeans and of the respective native tribes, inhabiting each, differ much more widely from each other than many British Colonies do. It appears, therefore, that it would be imprudent and unjust to attempt to draw any parallel in these respects between New Zealand and any other British Colonial Possession.

"In carrying out any plan, having for its object the amalgamation of the two races, the following difficulties have, until recently, presented themselves:—

"1stly. Hostile encounters had taken place between the settlers and the natives in the south of New Zealand, and between Her Majesty's forces and the natives in the northern portion of the country, in all of which the number of killed and wounded on our side had been comparatively so large, and the loss of the enemy so small, that they had been led to form an exaggerated notion of their own prowess and strength; and a desire of emulating the example of those chiefs who were imagined by their countrymen to have gained great successes, had excited a spirit of exultation and dissatisfaction throughout the greater portion of the islands; so that whilst a rebellion was actually raging in one portion of the islands, it was too probable that the natives would speedily break out into similar excesses in other portions of them.

"2ndly. Disputes existed between the settlers and the natives in various places regarding their respective rights to certain lands. These disputes, relating to the personal interests of the parties concerned, created between them feeling of hostility and bitterness which was gradually raising race against race, and which threatened ultimately to become a feeling which could only be put a stop to by the extermination of one party or the other.

"3rdly. As a necessary result of the difficulties existing under the two previous heads, the revenue had almost disappeared, and by the issue of paper money a large debt had been contracted; there was thus an absence of the funds requisite for the re-establishment of order and good government, whilst the settlers had also, to a great extent, lost all confidence in their future prospects, and were in a disheartened and desponding condition.

" 4thly. A very great difficulty had been created by the Crown's right of pre-emption having been waived in favour of certain individuals over large tracts of land, and by the inordinate demands of other persons to extensive tracts of country having been entertained by the Government, the result of which was, that a party of land-claimants had been called into existence, who made demands so extravagant and illegal that no Government could accede to them; nor did it appear practicable to make a settlement of these claims, even upon the most liberal basis, without incurring for the Government such a degree of hostility from a large number of persons as would probably exceedingly embarrass and impede any subsequent Administrations.

" In determining the line of policy the Government should pursue, in reference to the first class of the difficulties above named, that is, in reference to the war which existed in New Zealand, and the rebellion which appeared likely to to break out, the following considerations seemed naturally to present themselves :—

" It appeared to be clearly the duty of the Government, in a firm and decided manner, to crush the existing rebellion, and to put down without delay any disturbances which might afterwards break out; but yet it also seemed clear that its ruling line of policy should be, not to embark in any operations in which an absolute certainty did not exist of speedy and complete success, and rather to delay engaging in hostilities which might appear necessary, than hurriedly to embark in any contest the result of which could not be foreseen.

" Indeed, delay in engaging in hostilities was, wherever practicable, obviously the first duty of the Government of this territory. No knowledge of the country, of such a nature as to enable an officer to move with certainty a body of troops even to a few miles from any of our settlements, was possessed by the Government.

"The number of persons who possessed a competent knowledge of the native language was so few that it was impossible to secure the services of the requisite number of interpreters. The two races had so recently been brought into close contact, that their ignorance of their respective appearance, of their language, customs, and manners, filled them with mutual distrust, whilst their disputes, in relation to land, embittered their feelings of hostility. It appeared very probable that, as the two races became more accustomed to each other, as their knowledge of each other's language and customs increased, and as their private differences were adjusted, so would all necessity for war and conflict between them wear away; whilst, should these anticipations of a delay in military operations rendering a war unnecessary, prove correct, it would clearly have been an uncalled for measure of severity to hurry on a contest with the natives. And in the case of each individual who fell in such a conflict, it might have been said that, from his ignorance, a man had been destroyed, whom a few months' enlightenment would have rendered a good subject, a valuable consumer of British manufactured goods, and a contributor to the revenue. The loss to Great Britain by engaging in an unnecessary war would also have been great; every hundred soldiers that had fallen must have cost at least £10,000. Moreover Great Britain, in despatching two regiments to this country, had made great exertions, which it could not continue or repeat without considerable inconvenience to the public service. Yet even a very few false movements might have entailed so considerable a loss upon the small force in this country, as to have rendered large and continued reinforcements necessary. It is per-

haps not too much to say, that during a considerable period
of time, any signal failure in an operation which had been
entered upon, would have led to a simultaneous and almost
general rising, the effects and cost of which may be easily
conceived.

" It was also certain that, even if the anticipations which
had been formed, of the benefits which might spring to
both races from delaying military operations, had not been
realized, and it had proved ultimately necessary to embark in a war, yet that each month's delay, by increasing
our knowledge of the country and of the native language,
and by enabling us to complete our roads and to consolidate our establishments, would be of the greatest advantage to Great Britain, by enabling it to enter on the contest
with greater means and more certainty of success.

" Mercy, justice, and prudence, all appeared therefore to
point to delay as the general rule on which the Government should act. This line of policy has therefore been
in all instances unswervingly pursued, and the result has
quite equalled the anticipation which might reasonably
have been formed; for whilst the rebellion which existed
and the disturbances which naturally sprang from that
rebellion have been in all instances crushed, the total loss,
of all ranks, sustained on our side through so long a period
of time has amounted to only 28 killed and 53 wounded;
and in as far as human judgement can form an estimate
of such matters, no probability exists of any extensive
rebellion ever hereafter breaking out in the country; and
even should such disturbances again unhappily break out,
our knowledge of the country is now so much more accurate, our alliances with the natives have become so much
more numerous, our military roads have already been so
far completed, the number of persons acquainted with the

native language and customs so increased, and the natives' supplies of arms and ammunition have been so much diminished, that we should enter on such a contest with infinitely greater advantages than we formerly possessed.

" The efforts which have been made by the Government of this country for the removal of the second class of difficulties alluded to were of two kinds :—

" 1st. The resumption of the Crown's right of pre-emption, which had unfortunately been abandoned, and

" 2nd. The adjustment of many of the almost innumerable land questions which existed. The task of resuming the Crown's right of pre-emption appeared to be one of great difficulty and danger, but the natural good sense of the natives, and their continually increasing confidence in the Government, have rendered its accomplishment much less difficult than was anticipated. The various steps which have been taken, for the adjustment of the disputes in reference to land, have been so fully detailed in the Despatches from the various authorities, and the large mass of documents which have been transmitted to the Home Government, that it may be unnecessary to say more than that, with very few and trifling exceptions, every land question in the southern province has been already disposed of, whilst in the northern province nearly all questions connected with lands have been also arranged, with the exception of those which, resting upon grants issued by the Crown, can only be dealt with by our Courts in the ordinary manner.

" The measures taken to remedy the difficulties detailed under the third head, namely the want of a revenue, the existence of a depreciated paper currency, and the failure which had taken place in the confidence and expectations of the settlers, have also all been fully detailed in the

Despatches which relate to those subjects. The objects contemplated by the Government, in reference to these subjects, may be generally stated to have been, the imposition of duties, which, by a system of indirect taxation, might raise from the native as well as from the European population a revenue which would increase with every successive step of their advancement, and yearly yield the means for their more efficient control and government, whilst, in aid of and in connection with these plans, the depreciated paper currency was partly withdrawn, and the remaining portion of it was converted into a funded debt.

" In order to remedy, inasfar as possible, the evils enumerated under the fourth head, namely the difficulties which had been created by the Crown's right of pre-emption having been waived in favour of certain individuals over large tracts of lands, and the claims of others having been entertained to enormous tracts of country, every effort has been made to adjust these claims upon the most liberal terms, and to carry out these arrangements in the most conciliatory manner; this being, however, one of those cases in which individuals have been led to form extravagant expectations which it was impossible for any Government to realize, no efforts could probably have prevented much disappointment and bitterness of feeling ensuing, and it is probable that nothing but time can completely eradicate this evil, although, from the settlement of so large a number of these claims, and from the arrival of so many disinterested persons in the Colony, the proportionate number of individuals, whose expectations have been disappointed, is gradually decreasing, and their influence as a party will soon cease to be felt.

" But little would, however, have been accomplished if

the Government had confined itself simply to an attempt to remove the various evils under which these islands were labouring. It was necessary that active measures should at the same time be taken, without delay, for the amalgamation of the two races ; that the confidence of the natives should be won ; that they should be inspired with a taste for the comfort and conveniences of civilized life ; that they should be led to abandon their old habits ; that the chiefs should be induced to renounce their right of declaring peace and war ; and that the whole of the native race should be led to abandon their barbarous modes of deciding disputes and administering justice, and should be induced for the future to resort to our Courts for the adjustment of their differences and the punishment of their offenders.

" Thoroughly to accomplish a change of this nature would require a long series of years and a succession of generations.

" The utmost therefore that any Government could hope to do was, to establish institutions which might imperceptibly but certainly lead to so complete a change of manners in a barbarous nation as was contemplated ; and to secure these institutions by such laws and by such a constitution, as appeared to afford a reasonable guarantee for their perpetuity ; the first step to be taken to ensure these ends appeared to be, to convince the natives that our laws were better than their own, as affording more perfect security for life and property, and a much more ready means of adjusting differences which might arise either between natives and Europeans or amongst natives themselves.

" To attain these ends, the Resident Magistrate's Ordinance was passed, and Mixed Courts were constituted for the settlement of disputes betwixt natives. At the same time a considerable number of their young chiefs and most promising young men were enrolled in an armed police force, and thus habituated to act as actual administrators in the lowest offices of the law, and were made acquainted with the practical administration of the law in our inferior Courts. This latter measure, at the time it was introduced, excited unbounded ridicule, yet probably no measure has been so totally successful in its results. The native armed police force has furnished gallant men, who have led our skirmishing parties, and who have fallen like good soldiers in the discharge of their duty; and it has furnished intelligent, sober, and steady constables, whose services, under various circumstances, have been found of great utility. The actual result of the two measures combined is sufficiently attested by the number and importance of the cases in which natives were concerned which have been recently decided by our tribunals, to which until lately the natives never resorted.

" To bring the natives under the influence of the Government, and to gain their confidence and attachment, various measures have been resorted to by the Government. Hospitals have been established in the principal districts, to which both races have been equally admitted, and in which they have been tended with equal care; savings-banks have been instituted for the benefit of both races; a considerable number of natives have been employed in the minor offices of the Government establishments; pensions have been conferred on those chiefs who, during the first rebellion, were most distinguished by their gallantry, fidelity, and devotion to the British cause. Large numbers of natives have been employed on public works and in the construction of roads, thereby securing to the Colony the advantage of excellent lines of communication, whilst, from the discipline maintained amongst those employed upon public works, those works formed in fact industrial schools, in which the natives were trained to European habits of order and obedience, were accustomed to use European tools instead of their own rude implements, and were thus gradually trained to become useful labourers for the colonists. The natives have also been encouraged to pursue improved modes of husbandry, to construct mills, to acquire vessels, to attend to the breeding of cattle and horses, and a newspaper is fortnightly published by the Government, for the purpose of giving them useful information and plain practical directions on all those points to which the Government is anxious they should direct their attention.

" These various measures may be however said to aim only at the present improvement and advancement of the native race, and to make no adequate provision for their continual advancement in the arts of civilized life, and for the education of the native children upon such a system that they might have a prospect of standing on terms of equality with the European race, and of understanding and speaking their language.

" Fortunately the task of the Government in this respect has been an easy one. There existed in this country three Missions, established by different Christian Denominations, amongst whom there is perhaps an emulation as to which should achieve the greatest amount of good ; and it may reasonably be doubted whether at any period of the world there has existed in one country, amongst so large a number of men who had devoted themselves to the holy calling of a missionary, so many persons who were eminently qualified by piety, ability, and zeal to discharge the functions of the office upon which they had entered : the result has been that these gentlemen, scattered throughout the country, have exercised an influence without which all the measures adopted by the Government would have produced but little effect. Won by their teaching, the natives have almost as an entire race embraced Christianity, and have abandoned the most revolting of their heathen customs. Instructed by their missionaries, probably a greater proportion of the population than in any country in Europe are able to read and write; and encouraged by the precept and example of the same gentlemen, they have, in all parts of the islands, made considerable progress in the rougher branches of civilized life. The Government therefore, in establishing schools, thought it most desirable not to attempt to set up a system of its own, which might have required years for its development (during which a generation might have melted away, and an opportunity have been lost which could never be recalled), but rather to join its exertions to those of the missionaries, and to endeavour, whilst it established its own educational institutions, to render the system of the missionaries more complete and effective than hitherto. It therefore provided considerable funds which should be set apart for educational purposes, but determined that these funds should be applied under the direction of the heads of the different Denominations who had missions established in New Zealand; it being provided that the several institutions, which received any portion of these funds, should be conducted upon the industrial system; that the English language should be taught there, and that a sound religious education should be imparted to the pupils. Provision was also made for the appointment by the Government of inspectors, who will examine into the state of the schools, and will ascertain that the various requirements which are imposed by the laws relating to these institutions are strictly complied with.

" All these measures appeared calculated to secure a permanent and constantly increasing, instead of a scanty and superficial, civilization for the native population; and in order still further to increase the chances of success, two laws were passed, the first of which prohibited the natives from procuring arms or ammunition, and the second of which debarred them from the use of spirituous liquors. These regulations appeared stringent and likely to create discontent, but it was thought probable that, united with so many other measures of a character which were agreeable to the natives, and clearly calculated to promote their welfare, their strong natural good sense would lead them to see that these more distasteful restrictions had originated in the same care for their welfare, as had suggested the other portions of the system; and the result has justified the anticipations which were formed, as they have without complaint acquiesced in these regulations, and generally and cheerfully acknowledge their beneficial tendency.

" In the course of the past eighteen months the natives have, on several occasions, shown in the most striking manner their increasing confidence in our institutions, and their knowledge of the rights they have gained by their incorporation into the British Empire, by carefully considering the effect that proposed measures are likely to have upon their future welfare, and by evincing their gratitude or dissatisfaction by forwarding congratulatory addresses for benefits received, or by transmitting memorials against proposed measures to the Queen, on whose justice and desire to promote their welfare they evidently relied with the most implicit confidence.

" The most cursory consideration of the large number of objects which the Government proposed to itself, in carrying out the system of policy which has just been detailed, must have shown that it relied upon receiving, at east for some years, considerable moneyed assistance from some extraneous source, until the improvement which might naturally be looked for, in the internal traffic and external commerce of the Colony, had so far improved the revenue that it would suffice to defray the necessary expenditure of the Government.

" Such assistance was, in point of fact, most generously supplied by the Imperial Parliament, and it hence became an important object for the local Government so to conduct the financial operations of the Colony, that it might, at the earliest possible period, dispense with the assistance which was afforded to it, and thus cease to be a burden upon the parent State, which had so liberally aided it during its early struggles. This end may be said to be so far attained, that in the ensuing year the resources of the country will suffice to defray the whole of its expenditure with the exception of £15,000, if the proposed financial operations are approved of which were detailed in the Despatch named in the margin*, whilst, as in each succeeding year, an increase of revenue may be looked for, and no corresponding increase in the expenditure will be requisite, the amount of assistance received from Great Britain can be still further rapidly diminished in each year subsequent to 1850.

" In order that every guarantee might be afforded that the state of prosperity to which these Colonies were attaining might have a character of permanency, it was still necessary that institutions should be devised, which would ultimately constitute a form of government which was likely to be adapted to the circumstances of this country, and to be

* Papers presented to Parliament, No. 52, April 20, 1849, page 134.

satisfactory to its mixed and peculiar population. It also appeared to be a matter of great importance, that continual advances should be made towards such institutions, so that their introduction might be gradual, and that they might, as it were, imperceptibly grow with the growth of the Colony.

" Such a form of institutions had already in their main outline been sketched by your Lordship, and these in their main features presented a constitution than which nothing better could be devised here, although alterations in the details appeared necessary to adapt them to this country and to the feelings of its inhabitants. These alterations were made, and the form of constitution which appeared best adapted to New Zealand was fully reported on in the Despatches named in the margin*, whilst several steps preparatory to their introduction have already been taken in this country; and in point of fact, with the exception that the assemblies, instead of being elective, are nominated by the Crown, the proposed system may be said already to be in full operation in New Zealand. The great error which the local Government is in this respect thought by one party in the Colony to have committed, is too great a delay in introducing the elective principle. It may perhaps upon the other hand be urged that, looking to the peculiar condition and population of this country, it is better to err on the side of prudence, and not to incur the risk of the fearful evils which would ensue from another rebellion, for the sake of acquiring one or two years earlier that which must certainly within so short a period be obtained."

* Papers presented to Parliament,—No. 106, Nov. 29, 1848, page 9 ; No. 4, Feb. 2, 1849, page 21 ; No. 23, March 15, 1849, page 56 ; No. 27, March 22, 1849, page 59.

Enclosure.

Return of Killed and Wounded in New Zealand from March 4 to
July 2, 1845.

Date.	Name of Place.	Killed.	No.	Wounded.	No.
1846.					
March 4	Kororarika .. {	Soldiers	4	Soldiers..	1
		Seamen	6	Seamen..	8
May 8.	Okaihan .... {	Soldiers	13	Soldiers & } 39	
		Seamen	—	Seamen }	
		Soldiers	32	Soldiers..	60
July 1.	Ohaiowai ... {	Seamen	2	Seamen..	2
		Pioneers....	—	Pioneers .	4
	Total to July 2, 1845.....		57	.....	114

Return of Killed and Wounded from January 11, 1846, to
July 20, 1847.

Date.	Name of Place.	Killed.	No.	Wounded.	No.
1846.		Soldiers ..	3	Soldiers..	11
Jan. 11	Ruapekpeka ... {	Seamen ..	9	Seamen ..	17
		Pioneers..	1	Pioneers .	2
May 11	Boulcott's Farm, } Valley of the } Hutt.	Soldiers ..	7	Soldiers..	3
June 16	Valley of the } Hutt....... }	Soldiers ..	1	Soldiers..	4
Sept. 10	Howkewi ..... {	Soldiers ..	2	Soldiers..	6
		Seamen ..	1	Seamen..	—
1847.					
May 10	Wanganui	Soldiers..	1	Soldiers..	—
July 19 and 20.	Ditto	Soldiers..	3	Soldiers..	10
	Total to July 20, 1847 ...		28	.....	53

Grand Total, from March 4, 1845, to July 20, 1847 :—
85 killed, 167 wounded."

A Report upon the condition of the Island, bearing
a date more than two years subsequent to that* which

* October 10, 1851.

I have quoted, has since been laid before Parliament, and it shows that the prosperity of the Colony has continued to increase during that period, and to become more firmly established. The revenue from Customs, which is the principal source of the Colonial income, had in the northern province been abandoned altogether in the hope of conciliating the Natives, in the latter part of 1845. The present Governor re-imposed duties on imports almost immediately after his arrival, and in 1846 they yielded a revenue of £21,888, which in 1850 had increased to no less than £48,945. It is a remarkable fact, showing the soundness of the present prosperity of the Colony, that this revenue has continued to increase, notwithstanding the large diminution in the naval, military, and civil expenditure of this Country in New Zealand. In the year 1850 the value of the exports had also risen to £115,441, having been no more than £44,215 only two years before; from the diminution of British expenditure the imports, as was to be expected, showed a comparatively small increase. The European population (exclusive of the troops and their families) was 22,408 in 1850, having been 16,996 in 1848*. The Natives have shown increasing confidence in the Government and in British law; they are rapidly acquiring the habits of civilized life, and becoming possessed of property, including water-mills and coasting vessels, and are carrying on a large trade with the Settlers,

---

* See Papers presented to Parliament, May 3, 1852.

to their mutual advantage*. In short, the contrast between the state of things at the end of 1850, and that
which the present Governor found existing on his arrival at the end of the year 1845, is so marked and
so gratifying, that it is difficult to believe that so great
a change should have been accomplished in the short
space of five years. No general report of the state of
the Colony, up to a later period than the end of 1850,
has been laid before Parliament; but from the accounts
in the newspapers it appears that, up to the date of
the latest advices, nothing had occurred to check the
progress of the Colony.

It is to the Governor, Sir George Grey†, that New
Zealand is mainly indebted for this happy alteration
in its condition and prospects. Nothing but the
singular ability and judgement displayed by him during the whole of his administration, and especially in
its commencement, could have averted a war between
the European and Native inhabitants of those Islands.
It would have been one of the same character with
that which has been raging so long at the Cape of

* See Papers presented in August 1851, and especially Mr. Kemp's
Statistical Returns, in the Appendix.

† As I have expressed so strongly the admiration I feel for Sir
George Grey's services in New Zealand, I ought perhaps to say,
that my opinion has not been influenced by any private feelings of
partiality. Notwithstanding the name he bears, there is no rela-
tionship between Sir George Grey and myself, nor have I the advantage of any personal acquaintance with him. I never had the
pleasure of seeing him, and know him only by his conduct and my
correspondence with him in the public service.

Good Hope, but still more arduous, since the New Zealanders would have been yet more formidable enemies than the Kafirs, and the scene of the contest so much more remote. The war which had already begun when Sir George Grey reached New Zealand, and in which at that time all the advantage had been with our adversaries, would have been converted into a mortal struggle between the European and Maori races by the slightest error of judgement on his part, and by his failing to unite with the most cautious prudence, equal firmness and decision. Such a struggle, once commenced, could hardly have been closed except by our abandonment of the Islands in disgrace, or the extermination of their aboriginal inhabitants.

The best proof of the wisdom of Sir George Grey's policy towards the Natives is afforded by the almost unbounded influence he has established over their minds, notwithstanding the severity he has been compelled to exercise upon some occasions. He has never attempted to conciliate their favour at the expense of justice to the Settlers, or by showing indulgence to lawless proceedings; on the contrary, he has maintained his authority over them with an exceedingly high hand, and has strictly enforced various regulations calculated to be very unpalatable to them, especially his prohibition of any trade with them in arms and gunpowder. Yet he has succeeded in impressing them with a conviction that he is their best and truest friend, and commanded thus their willing obedience to all his measures. There are, in the voluminous papers which have been laid before Parliament, many remarkable proofs of the degree to which he has secured their affection and confidence. I will mention but two. When the Government House at Auckland had been destroyed by fire, a body of Natives came forward with an entirely spontaneous offer of their unpaid labour to rebuild it; and afterwards, when a report that he was to be recalled had been circulated by some of the White opponents of his Government, petitions to the Queen that he might be allowed to remain were signed by the Natives; and it is a curious circumstance that the first signature to one of these petitions was that of the Chief Te Rauparaha, whom he had kept so long in confinement. Some of the letters written by Chiefs to the Queen, expressing their earnest desire that he might not be removed, and the gratitude and affection they felt for him, are very interesting*.

* See Papers presented to Parliament in July, 1849, p. 27; Papers of January, 1850, p. 66; of August, 1850, pp. 106, 109; of August, 1851, pp. 44, 49, 134–141, 142. I add two of the letters referred to.

Copies of two letters from bodies of New Zealanders to the Governor Sir George Grey, after the burning of the Government House on the 22rd of June, 1848.

Auckland, June the 24th, 1848.

Friend the Governor,

Salutations to you. Great is our love and sympathy to yourself and Mrs. Grey because your dwelling has been destroyed by fire. Had we been awake at the commencement of the fire we should have come to your aid, but we reached the place when the

Giving then to the Governor the chief credit for having brought New Zealand in safety through the perilous crisis of the last seven years, the merit which we are entitled to claim, is what belongs to us for having supported him in the policy he has pursued, and co-operated with him to the utmost of our power. His previous administration of South Australia, under difficulties of another kind, but hardly less formidable than those he had to encounter in

fire was in full vigour. Our object was to save your property. There are forty of us working at the Barracks, and this is the love of us people at the Barracks for you, because you are the directing, upholding, controlling, etc., parent of all the people. Do you hearken! With yourself is the thought relative to our building a new house of stone for you, as we have been instructed in this good work, and we know how to perform it, as we have learnt the art of building. If you consent to this, will you write to us, and we will talk with the Chiefs about it.

From your loving children. Written by Te Taranu for the Workmen of the Barracks. Concluded to our Father the Governor.

(True translation, C. V. DAVIES.)

Second Letter.

Wakoia, June 24, 1848.

FRIEND THE GOVERNOR,

Salutations to you. Great is our love to you. We have heard of your distress (or loss) by fire. Friend, this is the love of the people of the quarry to you. Friend, we are here pleased with you. We are willing or anxious that the stones of the Quarry should be taken by you, so that a stone house may be built for you. It will not take many weeks to build it; perhaps one, perhaps two. This is our thought relative to the stones for you; but there must be no payment given us. This is a token of affection from the people of the Quarry to our Governor.

(True translation, C. V. DAVIES.)

New Zealand, and the justness of all his views with regard to the latter as explained in his despatches, entitled him to our unreserved confidence. This being the case, I am persuaded that we adopted the only course likely to lead to a happy result, in resolving to embarrass him by few positive and no minute instructions, but to leave it almost entirely to his own judgement to determine upon the measures to be taken by him, and to be guided mainly by his advice in what we were ourselves called upon to do.

This was the principle upon which we acted; and accordingly, when, a few weeks after we came into Office, we received despatches in which he expressed his opinion that, for four or five years, a larger force than he had previously applied for was required, we lost no time in taking measures to meet his demand, though there was much inconvenience in providing the 2500 men he had asked for, in addition to a naval force, for this distant Colony. 900 men, in addition to the 1100 already in New Zealand, were immediately ordered to join him from New South Wales; and 500 discharged soldiers from the army were raised and formed into a corps, called the New Zealand Fencibles, to make up the amount required*. As this last was rather a novel measure, and has proved eminently successful, it is proper that I should give some account both of the reasons by which we were

---

* See Despatch to Sir G. Grey, of November 24, 1846, in the Papers presented to Parliament by Command, January 1847, p. 81.

governed in adopting it, and of the manner in which
it was carried into execution.

What Sir George Grey required, was rather to be
enabled to command at a short notice an overwhelming force, to put down any resistance which might
be attempted to the authority of the Government,
than the constant service of a large body of troops.
Hence it appeared desirable that a part of the force
sent to the Colony should consist of men well trained
as soldiers, but who, instead of being kept constantly
under arms and in the receipt of military pay, should
be established in the Colony as settlers, in such a
manner that their military services when wanted
might be commanded on the shortest notice, and yet
that they might be enabled to maintain themselves
principally by their own labour. By such an arrangement it was anticipated that the Colony would gain
the double advantage, of protection in the event of
war, and in peace of a supply of labour and a permanent increase of its White population.

Such were the objects with which it was proposed
that the New Zealand Fencibles should be raised.
The Pensioners of the army, who, under the authority
of Lord Hardinge's Act, had been organized for service in this Country under the direction of Colonel
Tulloch, together with soldiers who had been discharged before they had acquired a right to pension,
would, it was ascertained, afford ample means of
raising a corps of the required strength, without admitting into it any but men of good character and

still vigorous constitution. In insisting upon the
last condition, it was not of course expected that the
men composing this force, however carefully selected,
should be from their time of life as capable of enduring the toils of active warfare as the soldiers of
a regular regiment. But as there would always be
many posts which must be garrisoned for the protection of the capital and of the depôts, (where all the
supplies of the troops in the field require to be left in
safety,) it was considered that a certain proportion of
the force in the Colony might be of this description,
without at all diminishing the number of regular
troops which, on an emergency, could be employed
in active operations. Nor was it overlooked that,
though the experiment had been more than once tried,
discharged soldiers had not hitherto proved good
settlers ; but there was nothing in these former failures
to justify unfavourable anticipations as to the result
of the present attempt. They were easily to be accounted for by the fact, that men accustomed during
the greater part of their lives to be constantly under
the care of their officers, and to be left very little
dependent on their own forethought and prudence,
had been sent to the Colonies under no superintendence whatever, and left to shift for themselves
in circumstances altogether novel to them, and under
difficulties with which they were little fitted to contend.

We trusted that, by avoiding this error, a different
result might be obtained ; and it was determined that
the men embodied for service in New Zealand, al-

though they were not to be constantly receiving pay, and employed in military duty, should be under the continual care and superintendence of officers in permanent pay. Six Companies of about 500 men were to be raised, and established in two or three villages, to be prepared for their reception, probably in the neighbourhood of Auckland. The men were to be accompanied by their wives and families, and each was to have a cottage prepared for him, with one acre of land, one quarter of which was to be cleared. A larger quantity was to be reserved, which they were to have the right of purchasing at a moderate price if able to do so; but it was not intended that they should look to the cultivation of this land as their principal means of support, at least in the first instance. Their land was expected to be used as a garden, to assist them in maintaining their families, and employment as labourers was meant to be their chief dependence.

Such employment there was no difficulty in assuring them that they should have, since, in addition to the private demand for labour, there would be that of the Colonial Government in the construction of roads, which were urgently wanted both for civil and military purposes. Much importance was attached to keeping the men together in villages, not only to render their services promptly available when wanted, and with a view to defence, but also to make it easier to provide religious instruction and education, for the men and for their children. A school-house, which was also to serve as a chapel, was to be erected in each village. At the end of seven years' service their cottages and land were to become the property of the men ; in the meantime they were to have the use of them rent free, in consideration of their attending regularly for military exercise twelve days in each year, and mustering under arms on Sundays for Church parade. They were to receive pay, if called out for service, like the Pensioners in this Country.

These views, and the conditions on which the men were to be raised, were fully explained to the Governor*, and they were sent to the Colony as soon as the necessary arrangements could be completed. The measure has entirely answered our expectations. The establishment of these men in the neighbourhood of Auckland has been successfully accomplished ; they are doing so well, that a considerable number of them have already been able to buy a part of the land reserved for them, and others have purchased their discharge from the corps, by defraying the expense of bringing other Pensioners from England to take their place. Their presence has given quite the same feeling of security as that of an equal number of regular troops, while it has been clearly shown by the Governor that a very great saving to this Country has been effected by the substitution of a force of this description for an ordinary regiment of the same strength†.

* See page 19 of the Papers quoted above.

† See the Governor's Despatch of February 8, 1851. Papers of August, 1851, p. 144.

Though the original cost of settling these men on their land, and building their cottages, was much heavier than was found to be necessary when two more Companies were sent out at a later period, with the advantage of the experience that had been gained by the first attempt; this charge has already been much more than covered, by the saving in the pay to which regular troops would have been entitled. The advantage which the Colony has obtained from this increase of its population may be best judged of by the fact, that the Crown land in the hundreds in which these military settlements are situated, is now estimated to be worth upwards of £67,000, though at the time the settlements were commenced its value was not above £5000 or £6000, judging in both cases of the value from the prices which have been obtained for land sold at the time. No doubt a part of the increased value of this land is owing to the generally improved condition of the Colony, but it has been principally occasioned by the formation of these settlements. At a later period the Governor permitted eighty-one families of Natives to occupy some land adjoining the military villages rent-free, on condition of the men serving, armed at their own expense, under the command of the Officer of the Fencibles, whenever the latter may be called out for drill or military service. This arrangement, the Governor states, is intended, in the event of renewed disturbances, " to secure for each division of Pensioners the co-operation and assistance of a body of Natives accustomed to be drilled with them and attached to them from inhabiting the same locality and serving under the same officers, whose activity and knowledge of the country will in some degree compensate for the age and unfitness of the pensioners for rapid movements. In fact, the two combined ought to compose a force of a very useful description."*

I must further observe as to this measure, that I regarded it as one of very great importance, not merely on account of its immediate results, but as an experiment on the practicability of combining the two objects, of providing for the military defence of the Colonies at a cheap rate, and increasing their British population and their supply of labour, by forming settlements of men under certain obligations of military service, but not retained constantly in pay or in the performance of military duty. If the experiment succeeded in New Zealand, I looked forward to the same principle being applied elsewhere, as it already has been to a certain extent in Canada, Van Diemen's Land, and Western Australia, but not yet by any means on the scale on which it is capable of being acted upon. It is not necessary that the men sent out as military settlers should be Pensioners; they might be soldiers of comparatively short service, still in the vigour of their age, and equal to any military duty they might be called upon to perform; nay, men

* See Sir George Grey's Despatch of the 22nd of June, 1849, p. 169 of New Zealand Papers, presented to both Houses of Parliament, in January 1850.

might be raised for the purpose, and after being thoroughly disciplined in this Country, might be settled in the Colonies on the same terms as the New Zealand Fencibles.

In the Australian Colonies, where an increase of the means of military protection is desired by the inhabitants, a portion of their large emigration funds might be spent in carrying out and establishing on land Settlers of this description, instead of ordinary emigrants, with the further advantage of being thus enabled to place bodies of labourers where they are most wanted, which, in the event of the construction of railways being undertaken, might be of no small use. In all our Colonies possessing temperate climates this plan might, with modifications according to their several circumstances, be acted upon; and even in some of the tropical Colonies there are situations in the mountains perfectly adapted to European constitutions, and where the establishment of a British population would both morally and politically be of inestimable advantage. Not to mention other Colonies, in Ceylon, Mauritius, and Jamaica there are undoubtedly to be found situations in the high grounds, where there is no reason to doubt that British military settlers, with their families, might expect to enjoy as good health, and to be as capable of labour, as at home.

But I am sensible that this subject, in which I have long taken great interest, has led me too far from that which is my immediate concern. To return to New Zealand, I have shown that we gave to the Governor all the support he asked in the way of increased military force. We did so in the full confidence that he would not apply for more than was really required, and because we concurred with him in believing that, if a sufficient force were sent in the first instance, in four or five years' time, by the measures he contemplated, it would become safe to reduce it; but that it was to be feared, "if a sufficient force were not at once stationed in the country," to use his own words, "sanguinary and expensive yet petty wars may take place, which will entail on Great Britain a large and useless expenditure of blood and money, and retard the advancement of this country almost indefinitely; whilst, on the other hand, should a sufficient force be at once sent here, I feel satisfied that no further disturbance of any consequence will take place, and that in a few years the country will be able to defray the expense of its establishments*." On this sagacious advice we acted, and the result was precisely what the Governor had anticipated; the large force placed at his disposal answered its purpose; so early as 1849 it became safe to commence its reduction, and before we left Office the military expenditure of this Country in New Zealand had been reduced within very moderate limits.

With regard to the civil expenditure of the Colony, the advice of the Governor was founded on the

* See the Governor's Despatch of May 14, 1846. (Parliamentary Papers of January, 1847, p. 16.)

same principle, and we followed it with the same good effect. He pointed out that he was called upon to govern, not only the European population, estimated at that time at 12,000 souls, but the much larger native population, which was supposed to be 120,000 ; and that New Zealand was not therefore in the ordinary position of a young country, the establishments of which could grow in extent in the same proportion as its population, revenue, and commerce. A large population rapidly becoming civilized, and capable of immediately affording a considerable commerce and revenue, already existed there; but no establishments had been formed for the protection of life, property, or commerce, or for the control and government of this large population, who, if their energies were not directed into proper channels, and if they were not kept under proper control, would certainly attempt to set up the government of various ambitious Chiefs, and would keep the country in a constant state of disturbance and war. He urged that it was "therefore absolutely necessary that a considerable annual expenditure in excess of revenue should be sanctioned for a few years by the British Parliament, to provide for the formation of the public buildings, roads, and establishments which are absolutely requisite for the assertion and preservation of British supremacy, for the control of the turbulent, the protection of life, property, and commerce, and the security of the revenue which the country can at once yield*." He expressed

* See the Governor's Despatch of May 12, 1846, in the Papers presented January, 1847, p. 15.

his strong confidence that, if the grants he considered requisite for these purposes were given, the revenue of the Colony would rapidly increase, and the demands upon the Imperial treasury would proportionally diminish, and in a very few years would cease altogether.

We concurred in these views, and therefore, though the demand we were compelled to make upon the liberality of Parliament was a very heavy one, we did not shrink from making it ; nor did Parliament decline to accede to it.   By means of the large grants which were voted upon these grounds for the service of New Zealand, the Governor was enabled to prosecute with vigour the various measures of improvement he had described as necessary ; and among these there were none which both on civil and military grounds he considered so important as the construction of roads. With reference to these it is a remarkable circumstance which I hope there can be no objection to my mentioning, that at the very time when Sir George Grey was writing from New Zealand to represent the absolute necessity of roads with a view to military security, the great man whose recent loss the Nation has had to deplore was in this country expressing precisely the same opinion.   The Duke of Wellington, who had of course been consulted on the military arrangements which were to be adopted in New Zealand, had strongly advised that one of the very first objects to be aimed at should be the construction of roads, so as to afford easy means of communication, and for the march of troops and artillery between the most important points.   These works were accordingly carried forward as rapidly as possible; and as early as October, 1847, the Governor was able to report, "that the great lines of communication which were absolutely requisite to connect the town and port of Wellington with the good country lying beyond the ranges of mountains covered with forests, which surround Wellington, are rapidly progressing, and will probably be quite completed in about eight months from the present date; after which time that town may be regarded as in a state of comparative security, and I think it will then advance rapidly in wealth and prosperity."

In addition to the utility of roads when completed, both for military and civil objects, a very important incidental advantage was obtained from their construction by the employment thus afforded to a large number of the Natives.   They eagerly accepted this employment, on account of the wages they earned; and the occupation and the pay they received were very useful, in withdrawing them from the temptation to join those of their countrymen who were inclined to turbulence and plunder; the work at the same time was very valuable, from the industrial training it afforded, as the Governor has remarked in the Despatch which I have quoted.   The instruction of the Natives, and the influence over them acquired by the officers who directed their labours, was by no means one of the least valuable results of these undertakings; and Captain Russell, under whose charge they were carried on, deserves very great credit for the remarkable success with which he availed himself of the labour of the Natives, and for the pains he took in training and instructing them. His reports upon the progress of the work entrusted to his care, which will be found in the Parliamentary Papers, are very interesting; and it speaks highly in favour both of his intelligence and ability, and of the industrious disposition of the Natives, that he has been able to show that the roads he constructed with their help have been made at a very low cost, compared with that of roads in other countries. Major Marlow was equally successful in teaching a considerable number of Natives to work as masons and quarry-men; and he built by their assistance the enclosure-wall of the barracks at Auckland, as well as it would have been done by European labour*, and much more cheaply. It was the Natives employed under him who made the offer I have mentioned, of their gratuitous labour in rebuilding the Government House.

The expenditure for this and the other objects pointed out by the Governor as being important, has completely answered the purposes for which it was incurred. He had, as I have shown, recommended this outlay, in the confident expectation (which we shared with him) that Parliament, by providing liberally for the wants of the Colony for a few years, would be adopting the course of truest economy, because it would thus be enabled the more speedily to diminish the

* See Papers of December, 1847, p. 51.

naval and military force employed there, and also soon to reduce, and before long to discontinue altogether, the annual grants for the charges of the Civil Government of New Zealand. We trusted that this would be rendered practicable by the secure establishment of peace, the rapid increase of the Colonial revenue, and the diminution of expenditure, as the public works most urgently wanted should be completed.

This anticipation has been amply verified by the result. The amount voted by Parliament in 1847 for the service of New Zealand was £57,000; in the three next years, including a vote for arrears in 1850, it averaged about £27,000 a year; in 1851, the vote was reduced to £20,000; in the present year to £10,000, and in the estimates of this year it is stated that the Governor is of opinion that if Parliament should next year make a final grant of £5000, New Zealand will afterwards be able to maintain its own civil establishment without any further assistance. The fact that it has been found possible to provide at so early a period for relieving the Mother-country from any charge on account of the Civil Government of the Colony, is the best justification of the large votes we proposed in the first years of your Administration.

We also deferred to the opinion of the Governor upon another subject of extreme importance: I refer to the question as to the proper time for establishing representative institutions in the Colony. On our appointment to Office, at so late a period of the Session of Parliament as the beginning of July, we had but very little time to consider what measures of legislation were so immediately required as to render it expedient that they should be brought forward at once, instead of being deferred to another year. It was probably owing to our being compelled to come to a decision without an opportunity of full deliberation, that we were induced to adopt, what proved to have been a hasty and erroneous conclusion as to the propriety of giving a Representative Constitution at once to New Zealand.

There were not wanting what appeared to be very powerful reasons in favour of this course. The form of Government which existed in New Zealand had undoubtedly altogether failed in securing, for the last five or six years, a wise and vigorous administration of its affairs ; on the contrary, there had been during that time a series of mistakes committed by the local Authorities, producing the worst effect on the interests of the Settlers, amongst whom a strong feeling of discontent with the whole system of government had thus been created, and an eager desire to take the management of their own concerns into their own hands. We were of opinion that there was so much substantial ground for these feelings, that we were extremely unwilling to defer till another Session obtaining from Parliament authority to make the desired change in the system of Government in New Zealand. We believed also, that the obvious difficulty of giving to a representative Legislature the power of legislating for the Natives, in the election of which they could have no influence, might be obviated, by empowering the Crown to define districts within which the laws and customs of the Natives, so far as they are not repugnant to the general principles of humanity, should be maintained in force.

Influenced by these considerations, we proposed to Parliament a Bill, which was passed into a law, by which the Crown was empowered to establish representative institutions in the Colony. The leading principle of the measure was, that there were to be two Provinces having distinct Legislatures, with authority to make laws on most subjects, but restrained from doing so on some, which were to be reserved for the consideration of a general Legislature acting for both Provinces. Within those portions of the territory not occupied by Europeans, provision was made for the government of the aboriginal inhabitants of New Zealand by their own laws and customs. The Act which was passed, prescribed only what was to be the general nature of the new Constitution, and conferred upon the Crown exceedingly extensive powers for filling up the outline thus traced, and making all the regulations of detail that were required for bringing the proposed system of government into operation. In the exercise of these powers, a Charter under the Great Seal and instructions to the Governor under the Sign Manual were prepared. By these he was authorized to summon the representative Legislatures which were to take the place of the existing Legislative Council, and all the arrangements necessary for that purpose were provided for. These instruments were transmitted to the Governor in an explanatory despatch, which bore date the 23rd of December, 1846 *.

When the above despatch reached the Colony, the Governor immediately wrote to represent in strong terms the danger which, in the then state of New Zealand, would have arisen from the discontent that would infallibly be excited among the Natives, by the proposed change in the form of government. He pointed out, that they were large contributors to the revenue, the disposal of which was to be entrusted to a Legislature in which they would be altogether unrepresented,—that they were quite intelligent enough clearly to perceive this, and the injustice to them of such an arrangement. Adverting to the disturbances which had just taken place, to the unsettled state of their minds, and the disposition to turbulence that still existed, he deprecated in the strongest terms the immediate introduction (at least into the Northern Province) of the proposed form of Government, which he said might probably, in a few years, be safely and with advantage established †.

The Governor's despatches to this effect reached this Country in November, 1847, and we did not hesitate to act upon his advice. He was at once informed that we would propose to Parliament a Bill, to sus-

* See Papers presented to Parliament in January, 1847, p. 64.

† See his Despatches of the 3rd and 13th of May, 1847, in the Papers presented in December, 1847, pp. 42, 47.

pend for five years the operation of so much of the Act of 1846 as related to the establishment of Representative Legislatures in New Zealand, and to enable Her Majesty for the same time to reconstitute the former Legislative Council. As it appeared however from his despatches to be desirable, that the proposed division of the Colony into two Provinces with distinct Legislatures should take place, while it seemed doubtful whether, in the Southern Province, that Legislature might not be in part of a representative character, we intended that the Bill to ·be submitted to Parliament should contain provisions by which the revived Legislative Council for the whole Colony should be empowered to establish Provincial Legislatures, of which it should be at liberty to determine the constitution*.

A Bill to this effect was accordingly brought in and passed. The authority thus entrusted to the Governor has been used with great discretion and advantage; he established subordinate provincial Legislatures, and by passing various important and useful laws, in furtherance of that general system of policy which I have described, he removed all obstacles to the establishment of representative government in New Zealand, even before the five years for which it had been suspended had expired; and if the pressure of other business in the House of Commons had not rendered it impossible, we should have brought in a Bill for this purpose in the Session of 1851. In the

* See Despatch to the Governor, of November 30, 1847, p. 47.

Session of this year it was one of the subjects recommended to the attention of Parliament in the Queen's Speech; and, after the change of Administration, a Bill was brought forward and passed by our successors, by which the intended grant of representative institutions to New Zealand has been accomplished, —not precisely in the manner I could have wished, but in one to which I see no material objection.   The leading principle of the Act of 1846—the division of authority between subordinate Provincial Legislatures, and a general Legislature for the whole Colony—has been adhered to.

I must not quit the subject of New Zealand, without saying a few words on the relations between the New Zealand Company and the Government.   Whatever may have been the merits or demerits of the original scheme of that Company, it was universally acknowledged that its chances of success had been greatly diminished by the ill-judged measures of the local Authorities, who had thrown difficulties in the way of the enterprise from its very beginning to which it ought not to have been exposed.   Hence it had been acknowledged by Lord Derby, that the Company had a fair right to expect from the Government assistance, which might in some degree make up for the disadvantages to which it had thus been exposed.   Before he went out of Office, he had commenced an arrangement, which was confirmed and completed by his successor, Mr. Gladstone, bywhich a considerable sum of money was to be advanced to them with this view.

The Company however did not admit the sufficiency of this compensation; and, after much communication with them, it was agreed that a proposal should be submitted to Parliament, the principle of which was that a further advance of money, and very large powers of administering the Crown lands in the southern division of the Colony, should be entrusted to them; under an agreement that, if in three years they should fail in placing themselves in a situation to carry on with advantage their colonizing operations, they should be at liberty to resign their functions and all their claims to land into the hands of the Government. Should they decide on doing so, they were to receive in return for the surrender of their Charter and of all their other property and rights, a release from their obligation to repay the sums advanced to them, and a claim to have their original capital, which had been sunk in the colonization of New. Zealand, repaid to them from the proceeds of the sales of land in the Colony.

A Bill to give effect to this arrangement was submitted to Parliament, and passed. I do not think it advisable, on this occasion, to enter into further particulars on this subject, partly because the transactions between the Government and the Company were so exceedingly complicated, (in consequence of proceedings which had taken place prior to our appointment to Office,) that an intelligible statement of what has taken place could not be made without protracting this Letter to a most tedious length, while the few persons who would be likely to take an interest in the subject will find all I could say upon it in a speech which I made in the House of Lords in June last, on the second reading of the New Zealand Bill, and which is of course recorded in the Debates*. But my chief reason for abstaining from giving any more detailed account of the transactions in question is, that I understand it to have been arranged that they are to be investigated by a Committee of the House of Commons as soon as possible, and that, in the anticipation of such an inquiry, it would be hardly proper for me in this form to state my own view of the case. Here therefore I will close my Letter on the subject of New Zealand.

November 20, 1852.

* I add in the Appendix an extract from the Report in Hansard's Debates of the speech in question. See Appendix (B) to this Volume.

LETTER XI.

CEYLON.

My dear Lord John,

I have next to speak of the affairs of Ceylon; and although, in the last three years, they have occupied a very large space both in the leading articles of the newspapers and in the reports of the debates in Parliament, and though the papers relating to this Colony, which have accumulated on the table of the House of Commons, form an enormous mass, I yet hope to restrict what I must say on the subject within a moderate compass.

The principal difficulties we had to contend with in Ceylon were those which arose, directly or indirectly, from the embarrassed condition in which we found its finances; and I must therefore look back to a time a little earlier than our coming into Office, to explain the origin of this disorder in its pecuniary affairs. The evil is to be traced to the too great reliance which was placed on the apparent prosperity occasioned by the sudden extension given to what might almost be called a new branch of industry in the Colony. The cultivation of coffee first began to be of importance in Ceylon soon after the equalization, in 1835,of the rates of duty levied in this Country on East and West India coffee, and it received an additional impulse from the subsequent reduction of the duty in 1842*. Large profits must probably have been made by those who first engaged in the business, as a great amount of capital speedily flowed into it. The total number of acres planted with coffee in the Island prior to 1845 was only 26,429, and in the two years 1845–1846 this extent of coffee plantation was nearly doubled; the new plantations made in those years having amounted to 22,319 acres.

Before a new coffee plantation can be made, very heavy expenses have to be incurred in the preparatory operations, of clearing the land and erecting the necessary buildings; the fact therefore that so great an extent of land was planted in these two years, proves that there must have been a previous large investment of capital in this business. While that investment was in progress, it gave to the Colony an appearance of great prosperity; for whatever might be the ultimate profit or loss to those who brought the capital into the Island, their expenditure, while it lasted, could not fail to give a great stimulus to trade and to the revenue. The greatest effect was

* See Porter's 'Progress of the Nation,' p. 752. The quantity of coffee imported into this Country from Ceylon was in 1835, 1,870,143 lbs.; in 1846, 17,735,406 lbs.; in 1849, 35,640,958 lbs.

produced on the revenue derived from the sale of land. The system of disposing of the Crown lands by sale had only been introduced in 1837. In the first three years the receipts from this source increased about £7000 a year ; in 1840 the amount received was £19,994 (being rather more than double that in the preceding year); and in the years 1843, 1844, and 1845, the money received for land rather exceeded £94,000 *.

During this time of excitement the revenue derived from Customs was also suddenly and unnaturally increased: it rose from £78,000 in 1843, to £88,000 in 1844, and to £110,000 in 1845†. The inevitable revulsion soon followed, and when Lord Torrington, who had been appointed Governor, reached Ceylon in the month of May, 1847, he found that the balance of £200,000 in the Colonial Treasury, which the latest accounts received in England prior to his departure, had encouraged him to expect would be available for effecting improvements in the system of taxation, was already virtually disposed of. The revenue had fallen as suddenly as it had increased, the receipts from land had fallen from an average of above £30,000 a year, for the three previous years, to £13,054 in 1846, and in the current year were producing at the rate of less than half this reduced amount‡. The

* See Appendix to Third Report of the Committee of the House of Commons on Ceylon, p. 252.

† Ibid. p. 246.

‡ The amount received in 1847 was £6471.

other branches of the revenue were affected in like manner, but to a less extent, and the result was that in 1846 there had been an excess of expenditure over receipts of above £74,000, and it was probable that the deficiency would be still greater in 1847 ; while it was found on investigation, that a part of what had been returned as the available balance in the Colonial Treasury consisted of notes of the Government paper currency, the issue of which would, in fact, be equivalent to raising money by loan, as the payment of these notes might be claimed at any time*.

In these circumstances very decided measures were obviously necessary, in order to preserve the Colonial Government from impending bankruptcy. Unfortunately it was extremely difficult to do anything effectual for that purpose. In the past years of prosperity, the expenditure of the Colony had been increased more than in proportion to the increase of the revenue, though it certainly might have been foreseen that the latter had been much too sudden to last. The income of the Colony had risen, in 1845, to £454,146, being £89,000 above the average of the five preceding years, and £10,000 above the income of 1844, which was itself considerably in excess of that of any previous year. Of this large receipt no less a sum than £37,946 was derived from the sale of land, a source of income necessarily precarious and fluctuating, since very large sales of land for two or

* See Lord Torrington's Speech in the House of Lords on the 1st of April, 1851.

three years, are invariably followed by a proportionate falling off in the demand. Though the increase in the revenue was of a nature to hold out so little prospect of permanence, it had been considered by the previous Government to justify a still larger increase in the expenditure, which in the same year, 1845, had been carried up to £448,232, being within less than £6000 of the amount paid into the Colonial Treasury in that year of unusual receipts, and being £105,000 above the average of the five preceding years [*].

The circumstances of the Colony were no doubt such as to make some addition to the expenditure unavoidable. The purchasers of land had a right to expect from the Government, that the large amount paid by them for the land they had bought, should be applied in making roads, by which supplies might be sent to their estates, and the produce carried back to the port of shipment. The expense however incurred in making new roads was far larger than the receipts for land, and the money had also been laid out in such a manner as to render it impossible at once to diminish the expense when the altered state of the Colonial Treasury required it. Many roads had been begun and not completed, which, if left in that state, would soon have been destroyed by the tropical rains to which they would be exposed; and

---

[*] See Lord Torrington's Despatch of November 15, 1849, and its enclosure. (Appendix to Third Report of the Ceylon Committee, pp. 244–252.)

in that climate roads even when finished require such constant attention, that the expense of constructing them, far from being all that is to be considered, ought to be regarded as leading to a permanent charge for their maintenance.

But the increase of expenditure had by no means been confined to that which had been occasioned by the measures taken for supplying the want of roads which was so urgently felt. Lord Torrington found, on his assumption of the Government, that the annual fixed charge of the Civil Establishment had been augmented by not less than £40,000* since the year 1841, a large part of this increase being the consequence of a complete re-modelling of the civil service of the Colony, which had been made by the authority of Lord Derby in the year 1845. This had occasioned a very considerable addition, not only to the immediate charge of the Civil Establishment, but also in the prospective one for pensions. From the nature of the civil service of Ceylon, it was difficult to make immediate reductions to a large amount in the cost of the establishment, without giving just ground of complaint to those who had adopted this service as a profession, under regulations which give them a right to look to it, as a secure provision, so long as they should discharge their duties properly.

It will be seen that the facts I have mentioned

* See Blue Book Reports presented to Parliament in 1848, p. 293.

would of themselves have been sufficient to render
the financial condition of the Colony one of great
embarrassment; but there were other circumstances
which aggravated the difficulties to be contended
with. At the very moment when, even if he could
retain the whole of the existing sources of revenue,
it was hard to see how Lord Torrington could bring
the expenditure within the income, and put a stop to
the excess of the former, which, by the end of the
current year, must absorb the whole surplus accumulated in the Treasury in better times; it also became
evident that, in addition to the falling off in the land
sales, another of the chief sources of revenue was
no longer to be depended upon. Hitherto the export
duties had contributed a large sum annually to the
Treasury, the most important articles upon which
these duties were levied being cinnamon and coffee.
The former of these articles in particular (of which
Ceylon was long supposed to possess a natural
monopoly) had, from the time when the Island belonged to the Dutch, always yielded a large though
fluctuating revenue, either as a Government monopoly, or by the imposition of an export duty. But
the time was now come when it was clear that
this could not be maintained. The competition of
cassia from China and India, and of cinnamon, which
the Dutch had succeeded in growing in Java, had so
reduced the price and the demand for the cinnamon
of Ceylon, that it was obvious the latter could no
longer be produced without loss, if it continued to

be burdened with the heavy export duty then levied in the Colony. The proceeds of the duty had fallen to £20,000 in 1846, and, from the information collected, there appeared no room to doubt, that the only effect of continuing the tax would be, not to preserve the revenue, but to put an end to the cultivation of cinnamon in the Island; whereas, by at once abolishing, or greatly reducing the export duty, there was every probability that a valuable branch of industry would be saved.

The necessity for affording some relief to the coffee-growers was little, if at all, less urgent. When Lord Torrington reached the Colony, the re-action from the excitement of 1845 had already begun, and the prospects of the coffee-grower, which had some time before been supposed to be so brilliant, were assuming a very gloomy appearance. A few months later things became much worse, and the growers of coffee in Ceylon were scarcely less severely affected than the sugar-planters in other Colonies, by the commercial disasters of the latter part of 1847; though the distress of the former could not be attributed to their having been deprived of protection, inasmuch as there had been no change in the rates of duty levied in this Country on coffee since the year 1844. Hence it was clear, that the distress must have been occasioned by those general causes which at that time disturbed the trade of the world, and by the want of caution with which coffee-planting had been undertaken upon so large a scale, and conducted in so expensive a manner. But although the difficulties of the Planters had arisen chiefly from their own want of prudence in embarking in the speculation, it was not the less important that whatever was practicable should be done for their relief; and there was no measure so well calculated to answer this object, as the repeal of the export duty on coffee, or more called for by a variety of considerations.

Such was the state of things with which Lord Torrington found himself called upon to deal, immediately upon his arrival in the Colony. The course which he took was at once to issue a circular to the different departments of the local Government, enjoining the reduction of the expenditure within the very narrowest limits that might be practicable*; and he set himself earnestly to the task of retrenching every item of charge which could be dispensed with or deferred, without injury to the public service. He also applied himself, with the assistance of his Executive Council, to a careful investigation of the general condition of the Island, with the view of being enabled to propose to the Legislative Council, when it should assemble toward the close of the year, such measures of legislation as should seem best adapted to meet the difficulties of the times.

After much deliberation, the conclusion arrived at was, that a bold policy would be the best and safest; that, notwithstanding the apprehended deficiency in the revenue, it was necessary, for the relief of trade

---

* See Lord Torrington's Speech quoted above.

and the encouragement of commercial enterprise, to submit to a further considerable loss of income by the repeal or reduction of some of the most injurious taxes. It was determined that the export-duties should be abolished, except that upon cinnamon, which was to be reduced by two-thirds, a duty of fourpence instead of a shilling a pound on the export of this article being (reluctantly) retained for the present. It was further resolved that the differential duties upon imports should also be abolished, by reducing the duties on foreign to the same rate as those on British goods. The total loss of income from these reductions was calculated to exceed £40,000. To meet the deficiency which would be thus occasioned, or rather increased, the Governor and his advisers looked partly to the exercise of the most rigid economy, and the postponement of every expense which could possibly be deferred, until the Colony should rally from its actual state of depression; partly to the imposition of some new taxes of a less objectionable character than those which were to be repealed; but, above all, to a measure they contemplated, by which the general revenue should be relieved from a part of the expense of making and keeping up roads throughout the Island, by converting this into a local charge under local superintendence*.

This policy was strictly in accordance with our views,

* See Lord Torrington's Speech in the House of Lords, and the Despatch of November, 1849, already quoted, and also his various Despatches from the 8th of June, 1847, to the 6th of May, 1848, in the Papers laid before Parliament in February, 1849.

which had been fully explained to Lord Torrington
previously to his departure from this Country; and
when the Legislative Council met, at the end of 1847,
he brought before it a series of Ordinances, which were
in due time passed, for giving effect to the proposed
measures. The new taxes imposed were, a stamp-duty
(which was not strictly a new tax, but an alteration
and increase of an old one), a shop-tax, some slight
increase of the customs-duties on wines, opium, and
some other articles, together with some minor taxes,
including license-duties on guns and dogs. The imposition of some of these taxes, particularly the last,
was afterwards made the subject of severe censure on
the Governor, which it would not, I think, be difficult
to show to have been altogether unfounded. I do
not however consider it worth while going into the
subject. That Lord Torrington's financial policy as
a whole was in the highest degree successful, is a
matter of fact on which there can be no dispute; and
this being the case, it is but of little consequence
whether or not errors were committed with regard
to the minor taxes which were afterwards repealed or
modified, namely the taxes on shops, guns, and dogs,
the last of which was rather intended to abate a nuisance than to raise a revenue.

Leaving these petty points, which nothing but personal or party animosity could ever have magnified
into matters worthy of serious notice, I have to observe that by far the most important of the series of
measures to which I have adverted, was that which

was known by the name of the Road Ordinance. The construction and maintenance of roads was one of the heaviest charges upon the Colonial Treasury; yet, so far from its being advisable to curtail the work of this kind which was done, it was of the highest importance to the progress and prosperity of Ceylon that the roads should be improved and many new ones made. The imperfection of the existing means of transit, and the consequently heavy expense of bringing down their produce and of sending supplies to the higher country, which is the best adapted for the growth of coffee, was one of the greatest difficulties with which the Planters had to contend. At once therefore to relieve the Colonial Treasury from a heavy burden, and to provide for an extension and improvement of the means of communication, the Road Ordinance enacted that every male inhabitant of the Island between eighteen and fifty-five years of age should be required, either to perform six days' labour on the roads, or to commute that service for a payment in money, the amount of which varied according to the value of labour in different places, but was nowhere more than three shillings.

A local organization was likewise established, for regulating the application of the money or labour thus contributed by the population to the roads. In each of the six Provinces into which the Colony is divided, there was to be a Provincial Road Committee, of which the Government agent was to be chairman, the Commissioner of Roads or one of his assistants a member, and at least two of the other members were to be persons not holding office under the Crown. The main lines of communication, under the name of " Principal Roads," were to be under the general direction of the Provincial Committee, which were annually to allot two-thirds of the labour or money contributed by the inhabitants, to the works they considered most necessary. The arrangements proposed for this purpose by the Commissioners were to be subject to the approval of the Governor. The minor roads and paths were to be under the direction of District Committees appointed by the Provincial Committee, and to this class of roads one-third of the labour and money contributed by the population were to be applied. In order to ensure a due return of advantage to those who were thus required to give money or labour, it was provided that on principal roads the work done should be within twenty miles of the residence of the contributors, and on minor roads within seven. The District Committee were to be assisted in the performance of their duties, and more especially in making out the lists of the persons on whom the obligation to contribute money or labour was to be imposed, by " Division Officers," who were to be elected by the householders in the " Divisions" into which the several districts were to be subdivided.

Such were the leading enactments of this very important Ordinance; a full explanation of its provisions, and of the objects contemplated by its framers, will

be found in Lord Torrington's Despatch of the 6th
of May, 1848*.   It will be seen, on reference to that
Despatch, that although in the first instance the Division Officers were to be the only persons elected to
their offices, employed in the execution of the law, the
measure was intended as the beginning of a system
of Municipal organization, by which the population
might gradually be brought to take a greater share in
the management of their own affairs.   The appointment of the Division Officers by election, was a step
of no slight consequence towards acting upon the
views explained by Sir William Colebrooke in the
report made by him in 1832, as one of the Commissioners of Eastern Inquiry, and in his memorandum
of 1834, which are referred to in Lord Torrington's
Despatch.   Sir William recommended that an attempt
should be made again to bring into use the ancient
village councils, or " Gansabes," of Ceylon, " institutions once popular among the inhabitants of the interior, and requiring little regulation to render them an
efficient means of providing for the police, the registration of lands, and other objects of local interest."
It is well known that the organization of village
communities which has existed in India, and generally among the Eastern nations from the earliest ages,
has been regarded by the most competent judges as
productive of very great advantages.   Sir Stamford
Raffles, during the short occupation of Java by the
British, contemplated restoring to these original native

* Papers of February, 1849, p. 113.

institutions some portion of the effective character they had lost; and by his regulations of 1814 (which were abolished by the Dutch) he gave to the inhabitants of every village the right of electing their own Headman, subject to the confirmation of the Resident, whose duties in Java were analogous to those of the Government Agent in Ceylon. It would certainly have been impossible to select a Governor of an Eastern people, affording a better model for imitation than Sir Stamford Raffles, and in providing for the election of Division Officers by the people, Lord Torrington followed closely the steps of that distinguished man, in allowing the " Headmen" to be chosen by the villagers of Java. The Road Ordinance therefore I consider to have been a very valuable one, and to have supplied a means of communication between the Natives of Ceylon and the officers of the Government, which had hitherto been wanting.

Another important feature of the measure was, that it proposed to raise the means for the construction and improvement of roads by direct taxation, since to require statute labour commutable for a money payment, is in fact to impose a direct tax. I have already, in speaking of the West India Islands, quoted part of a Despatch which I addressed to Lord Torrington, explaining my reasons for believing that, in such a state of society as that which exists in Ceylon, direct taxation is the most advantageous system of raising the money required for carrying on the public service. A capitation tax is not perhaps in itself the

best mode of imposing a direct tax, but it was probably
the only one which could have been made promptly
available, owing to the various obstacles which existed
in Ceylon to the levying of any other tax. An assessment on land, which would in many respects have
been preferable, could not be attempted without a
survey, the completion of which would have taken
much time; and it is also a great difficulty in the way
of a land-tax, that land is frequently held in Ceylon
by joint tenants and in very minute portions. I
may add, that from the first the Road Ordinance has
worked well, and that, in the last Report upon the
state of the Colony, which bears the date of April,
1852, it is stated by the present Governor to have
been " a very beneficial law for the practical and general good of the people."

This measure however was not to come into operation until the beginning of 1849, nor could much, if
anything, be expected from the new taxes at an earlier
period. It was therefore mainly to the reduction of
expenditure that the local Government was compelled
to look in the meantime, for averting the very serious
consequences to be apprehended, from allowing the
outgoings from the Colonial Treasury to continue to
exceed the receipts, to the extent they were doing
when Lord Torrington arrived in Ceylon. But, for
the reasons I have mentioned, the Governor and his
Council believed it to be impracticable to bring the
expenses of the Colony within its income, at least for
a considerable time; and they therefore concurred

in making an urgent application to us for relief from the annual payment of £24,000, required from the Island on account of the military charges, and also for an advance from the Imperial Treasury*.

These proposals, though very urgently pressed upon us, we considered it quite impossible to agree to. Our opinion, for the reasons I have mentioned in a former Letter, being that the contributions from the Colonies generally towards the cost of their own military protection ought to be increased instead of diminished, we could not acquiesce in forgoing the annual payment into the Military Chest which had for many years been required from Ceylon, and from which successive Governors had earnestly but in vain endeavoured to get it relieved. An advance from the Imperial Treasury would have been still more inadmissible. The only answer therefore that could be returned to the Governor, was one informing him that what he asked could not be granted, approving his various financial measures, enjoining a yet more severe economy, and authorizing him, if in spite of all his endeavours he should be unable otherwise to find the means of meeting the demands upon the Colonial Treasury, to raise a loan, in order to give time for the various measures of retrenchment which had been adopted to be brought into full operation. A despatch, stating fully the views of Her Majesty's Government on the financial condition of Ceylon, was addressed to the Governor on the 17th of July, 1848, which he

* See Papers of February, 1849, pp. 92, 99.

was directed to lay before his Executive Council, and he was desired with their assistance to prepare a plan for the revision of the civil establishment, so as to bring the expenses of the Colony within its means. This plan, after being submitted to the examination of the Legislative Council, was to be sent home for approval*.

The Governor, without waiting for these instructions, had from his first arrival in the Colony applied himself very vigorously to the work of retrenchment; but unhappily this was a work not less ungracious than it was necessary. The indispensable reductions of the public expenditure could not be accomplished, without affecting the interests of many individuals, and this was felt directly or indirectly by a large proportion of the persons employed in the public service. Those engaged in the trade of the Colony, and in its principal branch of industry, were also suffering severely from the commercial difficulties of the times. Thus both these classes, of which the European society of Ceylon is chiefly composed, were in 1848 in circumstances which almost invariably create a disposition in men to find fault with the Government under which they are living. In this state of things it is not perhaps surprising, that when, in the summer of that year, the central provinces were disturbed by an insurrection which, after creating much alarm for a short time, was put down by prompt and vigorous measures, a cry was raised by a small number of

* See the above Papers, p. 333.

persons in the Colony (and afterwards taken up with greater violence by a party at home) that the insurrection had been occasioned by the oppressive character of the taxes imposed by Lord Torrington. It was loudly asserted that, after having thus driven the people to rebel, he had displayed wanton and cruel severity in suppressing the rebellion and punishing those engaged in it.

The assertion that the taxes produced the rebellion is so far true, that there is little reason to doubt that the imposition of new taxes, of which little was yet known, afforded an opportunity to the discontented classes of the natives to misrepresent the intentions of the Government. Absurd tales as to the nature of the new taxes were circulated, to excite the ignorant population, and induce them to revolt. But it most certainly is not true that the oppressive character of the burden imposed upon the population drove them to rebellion. So little was there in these taxes calculated to create discontent if they had been understood, that the one which might have been supposed to be most obnoxious—the Road Ordinance—has appeared, since it came into operation, to be a popular measure, the people willingly contributing the small amount of labour or money required from them, for the sake of the advantage they derive from obtaining improved means of communication.

But while the population only knew that some new taxes had been imposed, but were still almost entirely ignorant of their nature, it was not difficult for the

chiefs and priests, who for other reasons had long
been discontented, to spread abroad false reports as
to the oppressive character of the burdens to which
the people were about to be subjected, in order to
drive them into revolt. Nor is it difficult to account
for the discontent of the chiefs and priests, which had
already shown itself more than once in treasonable
plots*. They felt that their influence over their countrymen was gradually fading away, from their being
brought into contact with European civilization, and
from the restrictions imposed by our laws, on the
exercise of the unchecked power they had once possessed over the lower classes of their countrymen.
The extension of coffee-planting, by bringing many
Europeans into districts in the interior where, till
lately, they had seldom if ever been seen, had greatly
accelerated the change in the state of society which
was obviously in progress; and it was only natural
that, to those who saw in this change the certain loss
of their own former station and consequence, it should
be in the highest degree distasteful, and that they
should be anxious to overthrow British authority, by
which they were aware that it was brought about.

I believe that from the same causes a similar spirit
of disaffection has been found, in the earlier years of
British supremacy, to prevail very generally among the
higher classes of native society in the various countries
of British India which have been successively brought

* There had been actual or attempted insurrections in the following years:—1817–18, 1823, 1824, 1834, 1843.

under our dominion ; and that something very similar may be observed wherever a semi-civilized or a barbarous people is brought under British rule. That rule is generally a blessing to the population at large ; but it is not less generally obnoxious to those who, as priests, or chiefs, or nobles, have been at the head of the native society, because, in addition to their feeling painfully their inferiority to the ruling race, they also find that they can no longer maintain their station among their own countrymen, when British authority interferes with the exercise of their former tyrannical power, and when British example and the diffusion of education gradually emancipate the minds of the mass of the population from the superstitions by which they were enthralled.

Perhaps more might have been done in Ceylon and elsewhere to render the spread of civilization, and the establishment of a system of government by which the lower classes of the people are protected from oppression, consistent with the maintenance of the relative position in the native society of those who have hitherto been at its head. This would have been highly desirable, because it would avert much danger and greatly promote the progress of improvement, if the natural leaders of such a native society could be made friends instead of secret enemies to British authority, by finding their interests attended to and their feelings consulted. But how this is to be accomplished is a problem of extreme difficulty, which has, I fear, nowhere been very satisfactorily solved.

In addition to those usual causes which, in Ceylon, as in other countries in similar circumstances, tend to alienate certain classes of the population from their rulers, there was in that Island a further source of disaffection. The priests have very considerable influence over the population, and they were much discontented with the effect of the steps which had been taken for several years, for the purpose of disconnecting the Government from any share in the management of the temples devoted to the Buddhist worship, or of the lands with which they are endowed. Nothing can be more proper than that the Government of a Christian nation should refuse to undertake the appointment of the priests of an idolatrous religion, or the management of their temple lands. But hitherto successive Governors of Ceylon have failed in discovering any mode of practically applying the rule to this effect laid down for their guidance, without giving the Buddhist priests some right to complain of the non-performance of the engagement, entered into by treaty when the country came under our dominion, that the people should be allowed the free exercise of their religion, and that the endowment of the temples should be maintained.

Under the native Kings, the maintenance of the national religion was so identified with the Government, and the religious establishment was so closely connected with the supreme authority of the State, that when power passed into the hands of a Government which, regarding the national worship as idolatrous and superstitious, thought itself bound to refuse any active assistance in carrying it on, the priests were altogether at a loss how to act for themselves, and unable, without the aid, which was refused to them, to make any satisfactory arrangement for filling up vacancies in their own body, or for protecting the temple lands from encroachment. The difficulty of providing for the appointment of priests to the temples, when the Government refused to take this duty upon itself, has been more particularly embarrassing, in consequence of the peculiar tenets of the Buddhist religion and of the state of society. Sir Colin Campbell could not discover any satisfactory mode of acting upon the instructions on this point which he had received from Lord Derby; and Lord Torrington, to whom the same instructions were repeated, was equally embarrassed. It is doubtless one of the most difficult questions that can arise in the government of any country, and I much doubt whether it admits of any perfectly satisfactory solution. Certain it is that the attempt which was made (and after all with very partial success) to disconnect the Government of Ceylon from an idolatrous religion, contributed not a little to increase the discontent of the priests.

Such are the causes which, from the best information that has been obtained, seem to have made the chiefs and priests of Ceylon for many years discontented; nor can it be doubted that the rebellion of 1848 is to be traced to this discontent, and not to any grievances to which the great body of the natives were subject. The latter only followed those whom they had been accustomed to follow, and whose influence, aided by misrepresentations as to the intended taxes, was still sufficient to lead the population into rebellion. On the part of the real authors of the revolt, it was an attempt to use, while it still lasted, the power they felt to be gradually slipping out of their hands, for the overthrow of British authority. But though the people at large had no real interest in the success of this attempt,—since, instead of being oppressed by their present rulers, they have been released by them from the grinding tyranny to which they had been subject under their native princes,—they were at the same time so ignorant, so easily led by the disaffected chiefs and priests, and so numerous, whilst the force at the disposal of the local Government was in comparison so exceedingly small, and the nature of the country and its extent were so unfavourable to military operations, that the danger when the rebellion broke out was most serious; and, if it had not been crushed at once, it would in all probability have led to a protracted and doubtful contest.

After various rumours of disturbance and symptoms of agitation and disaffection, a pretended descendant of the former Kings of Kandy was crowned by the priests in the Temple of Dambool, on the 26th of July, 1848. Large numbers of men assembled in arms in different places, one party of whom attacked the town of Matelle, drove away the magistrate, sacking and plundering various public buildings. The town of Kurnegalle was also attacked, and was for a short time in the power of the insurgents.

In these circumstances Lord Torrington acted with vigour and decision. He proclaimed martial law in the disturbed districts; he lost no time in sending a steamer to Madras to obtain reinforcements, which were promptly furnished by the Government of that Presidency; and he made, in concert with Major-General Smelt, who commanded the troops, arrangements for placing as large a proportion as possible, of the small force at his disposal, under the orders of Colonel Drought, the Commandant of the Central Province. Colonel Drought and the officers under him acted with no less vigour, and in a very few days all open resistance to the authority of the Government was at an end, though it was some time before the pretended King could be taken. Eighteen of the most guilty of the rebels were sentenced to death by courts-martial and executed, and minor punishments were inflicted upon a considerable number of others.

These decided measures, and the prompt example that was made of some of the ringleaders, produced the desired effect; tranquillity was completely restored, and has not since been disturbed. Many lives and much misery were saved by this speedy re-establishment of order. Though, compared with averting a great destruction of human life, it was very secondary, yet it was not of small importance, that a very heavy pecuniary loss to the Colony was prevented, by the early return of a feeling of security, after the great alarm which had existed at first.   A crop of coffee, of great value, was nearly ready for gathering when the insurrection occurred : if the alarm had continued only a little longer, the labourers would have been deterred from coming as usual from India to secure it, and the loss to many of the Planters must have been almost ruinous.   The infliction of so severe a check on this important branch of industry, just as it was showing the first signs of recovery from the difficulties it had gone through, was happily avoided, and the Coolies came from India with their usual confidence.   As soon as we received information of these events, we thought it our duty to advise the Queen to signify her approval of Lord Torrington's conduct in suppressing the rebellion.

But the danger was hardly over, before Lord Torrington became the object of violent attack both in the Colony and at home.   In the Colony, however, his assailants were rather noisy and bitter than numerous ; the great majority of the European community were too sensible how much they owed to him, and how serious the peril had been, to take any part in these attacks ; and, on the contrary, a very large proportion of the most respectable planters and merchants signed addresses, expressing in strong terms their gratitude for the protection they had received, and their sense of the services which Lord Torrington had rendered to the Colony.   A similar address was also unanimously voted by the Legislative Council.

In this Country the events which had occurred in Ceylon were used as a political engine against the Government. The leaders of the Opposition did not indeed generally take an active part in the attacks made upon Lord Torrington, but they had not the generosity to discourage these attacks, which were made, with a degree of rancour of which there are happily few examples, by persons of less note, and by the daily and periodical press connected with the parties opposed to the Government.

It was represented, that the insurrection had been occasioned by measures which were described as oppressive and unnecessary; it being studiously concealed that, whether the new taxes were good or bad, except the insignificant gun-tax, they had not begun to be levied when the rebellion broke out, and that the necessity of raising some new taxes or other, to meet the difficulties occasioned by the imprudence of preceding Administrations, was undeniable. It was still more loudly asserted that the insurrection, produced by misgovernment, had given occasion for acts of wanton and disgraceful cruelty, for which no terms of reprobation were too strong to be heaped upon Lord Torrington and the Government at home, by whom his conduct had been approved and supported.

I cannot forbear expressing my surprise (and I must add, for the sake of the persons to whom I allude, my regret) that some of those who countenanced these charges, were induced to do so. I am at a loss to understand how such accusations could ever gain credit with men capable of forming an impartial judgement, considering how unsupported they were by anything like trustworthy evidence, and how utterly improbable they were in themselves. I should have thought that no one could fail to perceive, that it was the obvious interest of Lord Torrington to suppress the insurrection as speedily and with as little severity as possible, and that he must have wished to do so, if for no higher motive, at all events for the credit of his Government. On the other hand, he could have no conceivable motive for the cruelty imputed to him, but that of a love of blood for its own sake, and a wanton pleasure in the infliction of suffering, which are fortunately rare even in the worst men; while, even if it could be supposed that Lord Torrington was actuated by such feelings, he could not have gratified them, except by the assistance of officers of the British army.

All the rebels who suffered death were convicted by Courts-martial, composed of officers of the regiments employed in Ceylon; the sentences pronounced by these Courts were duly approved by the officers in command at the places where the trials were held; and Lord Torrington's responsibility is confined to that of having declined to exercise his power as Governor, to remit the punishment of death, which the Courts-martial had thought it right should be inflicted on a comparatively small number of the ringleaders in the rebellion. In some of the cases, I believe that Lord Torrington would not have had

the power to interfere, even had he wished it, because, if I am not mistaken, some of the capital sentences were carried into execution before there was
time to report to him upon the subject, it having
been justly considered that the effect of the punishment greatly depended upon its being prompt, and
that by making it so the public safety would be sufficiently secured, by inflicting it on a smaller number
of persons than might otherwise be necessary. When
it is remembered, that the British army has always
been distinguished no less for its humanity than for
its courage, and that an officer guilty of wanton
cruelty would, from the general feeling which per-
vades the Service, meet from his brother-officers the
same contempt and scorn which he would incur by
showing cowardice in face of the enemy, these accusations against Lord Torrington seem to be sufficiently refuted, by observing, that if true, his guilt
must have been shared, not by one or two, but by
several British officers of acknowledged merit and
unstained honour.

His acquittal however does not rest upon this. These
charges were brought before the House of Commons,
and referred to the investigation of a Select Committee, of which I will only say that its proceedings
were of a very unusual character, and that it certainly
spared no pains to obtain evidence criminatory of
Lord Torrington. The inquiry was protracted during
two Sessions, and was concluded by the Committee's
agreeing to a very short Report, expressing no definite

opinion on the subject referred to them, but certainly
giving no countenance to the charges they had inquired
into. In 1851 the evidence was laid before the House;
and at length, on the 31st of May, the whole subject was brought to the test of a discussion, by resolutions condemning the conduct of Lord Torrington
and of the Government, being moved by the gentleman who had been chairman of the Select Committee.
The resolutions were supported, as a party question,
by the Opposition, the leaders of which did not think
it unworthy of them to make use of such charges
against an individual, for the purpose of injuring the
Government; but there were many of those who
were in the habit of voting with the Opposition, whose
sense of honour and justice revolted against this mode
of carrying on party warfare; and the resolutions
were consequently rejected by a majority of no less
than eighty, the debate having been even more trium-
phantly in our favour than the division.

After such a decision by the House of Commons,
I consider it to be quite unnecessary to enter into
any particulars as to these alleged cruelties. Instead of doing so, I think myself bound to express
my firm conviction that, in cases of rebellion, the
infliction of prompt and severe punishment on a
small number of the most guilty, is the truest mercy.
Armed resistance to the constituted Authorities of
the State, on account of the wide-spreading calamities
to which it leads, and of the amount of suffering it
occasions, ought to be regarded as one of the most

heinous crimes of which men can be guilty. It is therefore a false and sickly humanity which would shrink from inflicting prompt and condign punishment on the leaders in the commission of such a crime, in order both to protect the thousands of innocent persons who must suffer from leaving it unchecked, and also to avert the necessity of inflicting more numerous punishments in the end, by preventing the contagion of rebellion from spreading among the deluded followers of those who begin it. Among a barbarous or semi-civilized people this is more especially necessary; and I am persuaded that any hesitation or want of vigour and firmness, in the circumstances in which Lord Torrington was placed, would probably have cost the lives of as many hundreds, possibly of as many thousands, as there were individuals capitally punished under his authority*.

I must add, that the Governors of distant Colonies, in times of rebellion, are placed in situations of so much difficulty and responsibility, that every generous mind will be disposed to put the best construction on their conduct, and to believe, till

---

* Major Forbes, in his 'Eleven Years in Ceylon,' states, that in the insurrection of 1818 the loss on our side (chiefly from climate and fatigue, as very few fell in action) was estimated at 1000, and on the side of the natives at 10,000. On that occasion there were above 6000 troops employed in the Kandian Provinces, and near 10,000 in Ceylon. The rebellion began in September, 1817, and was not subdued till the 2nd of November, 1818. In 1848 the force in these Provinces little exceeded 1500 men.

the contrary is clearly proved, that they have acted to the best of their judgement.   Even if this consideration, and a sense of what is due to men on whom such arduous duties are imposed, is insufficient to restrain the disposition to carry on party warfare by such means, a regard for the safety of our Colonial Empire ought to prevent the repetition in future of such attacks as those which have been directed against Lord Torrington and Sir Henry Ward, for having performed a painful duty in putting down rebellion.   Is it possible that the expectation of being exposed to this sort of obloquy should fail to exercise some influence over the mind of a Colonial Governor, called upon suddenly to act in the trying emergency of a rebellion threatened or begun ?   Must it not of necessity add to his difficulty in forming a correct judgement as to the course he ought to take ? and would it be unnatural, that he should be induced to shrink from the prompt exercise of a necessary severity, by knowing that the very success of that severity in averting the danger is likely to be wrested into the means of injuring him ?   In my next Letter I shall have occasion to remark, that it is by no means certain that the interests of the Country may not already have felt elsewhere, some of the injurious effects which the attacks directed against Lord Torrington were calculated to produce.

In Ceylon these attacks, and the appointment of a Committee of the House of Commons to inquire into them, were productive both of injury to the Colony and of embarrassment to the local Government. Even if the proceedings of the Committee had been conducted with the utmost judgement and discretion, an inquisitorial investigation, intended to support such serious charges against the Governor of a distant Colony, could not fail to impair his authority, and to interfere with his devoting his time and thoughts to the various measures of improvement, which were required and were contemplated, both in the legislation of Ceylon and in its system of administration. This inevitable inconvenience was far from being diminished, by the manner in which the inquiry was carried on by the Committee, and it was greatly aggravated by the publication, in the Colonial newspapers, of selections from parts of the evidence most hostile to Lord Torrington, notwithstanding the refusal of the House of Commons to allow the evidence to be published in its incomplete state at the end of the Session of 1849.

It would be superfluous to comment on the gross impropriety of furnishing the Colonial newspapers with the means of making this publication, or on the difficulties which, from the nature of Colonial society, it was calculated to throw in the way of the Governor. Nor can it be matter of surprise, though it is deeply to be regretted, that the inquiry, carried on as it was, should have created great irritation in the mind of Lord Torrington. This irritation was increased by circumstances connected with differences, of long standing, between two of the principal civil servants of the Colony, in which the Governor became involved, and which were brought before the Committee. The subject is so painful a one, that I will not refer to it further than to say, that the disclosure of certain private and confidential letters, which were laid before the Committee, produced a state of things which seemed to render it impossible that Lord Torrington should continue to act with Sir Emerson Tennent and Mr. Wodehouse, (the two gentlemen to whom I have alluded,) with advantage to the public service in the situations which they respectively held in Ceylon; it was therefore considered expedient that they should all cease to be employed in that Island, and arrangements were made accordingly.

Lord Torrington left Ceylon in the beginning of November, 1850; but, previously to his departure, he received addresses from the leading merchants and planters, expressing in most gratifying terms their sense of the services he had rendered to the Colony, their approval of his policy, and their regret at his relinquishment of the Government of the Island*. This was a tribute to the ability and success of his administration, highly honourable to those from whom it proceeded, and which had been well earned by Lord Torrington. I have shown that he found Ceylon, on his arrival, in circumstances of the greatest difficulty; its finances were in a condition which was leading rapidly to bankruptcy, while its trade and industry

* See pp. 29—33 of Papers presented by Command, February 4, 1851.

were suffering from extreme depression. I have given a slight sketch of the measures which he promptly adopted to arrest these evils, and I have the satisfaction of being able to state that, though he held the Government somewhat less than three years and a half, when he gave it up, these measures had already produced a complete and most favourable change in the aspect of affairs.

The acting Governor, who administered the affairs of the Island until the arrival of Sir George Anderson, was able, on meeting the Legislative Council shortly after Lord Torrington's departure, to congratulate that body on what he termed " the remarkable, and of late years quite unprecedented, state of financial prosperity and promise" which the Papers he laid before the Council showed the Colony to have attained. There had been a surplus of revenue above expenditure of £10,000 in the half-year; a debt of £50,000 to the Oriental Bank, which it had been necessary to contract in the embarrassment of 1848, had been paid off, principal and interest, with the exception of about £11,000; the charges connected with the rebellion had all been provided for out of the local revenue; the expenditure of 1849 had been brought down no less than £78,000 below that of 1846, and in the first nine months of 1850 a further reduction of £16,000 was effected, exclusive of the Road department[*]. Nor

* See Lord Torrington's Speech in the House of Lords, and the Papers of February, 1851, p. 36.

was this reduction of expenditure accomplished at the cost of the efficiency with which the public service was carried on ; on the contrary, every department of the Civil Administration was conducted with greater vigour and regularity than before.

The trade and industry of the Colony also felt the beneficial effects of the measures judiciously adopted by Lord Torrington (apparently not without considerable risk) for their relief. The prospects of the coffee-planters and cinnamon-growers had again become brighter when he left the Island, and have since continued to improve. The difficulties, in short, of 1847 and 1848 had been completely surmounted, and the Colony was fast rising to a prosperity which, having nothing artificial or unsound in its character, appeared likely to be more durable than that of 1845. I rejoice to say, that hitherto the expectations justified by the aspect of affairs on the retirement of Lord Torrington have not been disappointed, and Sir George Anderson, who succeeded him as Governor and has ably followed up the policy he began, has in his annual Report, dated April, 1852, expressed a favourable opinion of the condition of the Colony.

December 2nd, 1852.

LETTER XII.

CAPE OF GOOD HOPE.——NATAL.

MY DEAR LORD JOHN,

Of the Cape of Good Hope, which is to form the subject of this Letter, you will easily perceive that I must necessarily speak with much reserve. I shall be content to give an exceedingly imperfect account of its transactions, and to omit the mention of many circumstances and considerations which would tend to explain and justify some of our measures which have been the most severely criticized, in order that I may avoid reviving animosities which are, I hope, subsiding, or wounding feelings which I desire to respect.

At the time when your Administration was formed, accounts had not very long been received of the breaking out of a Kafir War; and almost as soon as I was installed in the Colonial Office, I was called upon to receive a deputation of Cape merchants and proprietors, who gave me a heart-rending account of the devastation of a wide extent, of what had been the most flourishing districts in the Colony. They described to me the destruction of property to a vast amount, by which great numbers of persons had been reduced from comfort, and in some cases from wealth, to ruin, and the loss of no small number of valuable lives by the murder of unprotected Settlers; and they made most urgent representations of the necessity of taking immediate and effectual measures for the defence of the Colony. There was but too much ground for these representations; it appeared, from the despatches of the Governor, and from information received from various other quarters, that the attack upon the Colonists by their savage neighbours had been entirely unprovoked, and had been the cause of a fearful amount of misery. Our first measure therefore was to send additional troops to the Cape, with the least possible delay. We also thought it right to advise the Queen to appoint Sir Henry Pottinger to be Governor of the Cape, in place of Sir Peregrine Maitland. Without meaning to find any fault with the measures of the latter in the office he held, we were of opinion that the state of the Colony was one of so much danger and difficulty as to require the services of a Governor of the greatest ability and energy that could be found; and the fact that no less than fifty-four years had elapsed since Sir Peregrine Maitland had entered the Army, proves that he must have attained an age at which scarcely any man is equal to the exertions required from an officer who has to conduct the active operations of such a war as we were engaged in*.

For these reasons Sir Henry Pottinger was appointed Governor of the Cape, to which was added the office of Her Majesty's High Commissioner for settling the affairs of the territories adjacent to the Colony.

---

* I think it right to take this opportunity of expressing my opinion of the very great danger to which the Country is exposed by the existing rules of our Army, by which in time of peace no officer can expect to attain the rank of major-general under the age of fifty, and the great majority must be considerably older before they do so. Thus the youngest major-general in our service is above the age at which it was the opinion of Napoleon that men generally ceased to be fit for active service in war (which, if I am not mistaken, he put at forty-five). I know that the highest military authorities are very averse to any departure from the existing rule, by which the rank of major-general is granted only to full colonels who rise to it (from that rank) by strict seniority, and I am also aware that these authorities are scarcely less averse to entrusting an important command to an officer before he becomes a major-general. But notwithstanding the professional objection which exists to any change of system, I am persuaded that it is imperatively demanded by the interest of the Country; that at present the field of selection for officers for important commands is unduly limited; and that many of these commands have of late years been held by officers who no longer possess the vigour and energy of body as well as of mind which are necessary in war. The great Lord Chatham did not allow professional etiquette to stand in the way of his entrusting the honour of the British arms to young and enterprising officers. Wolfe was a lieutenant-colonel of only seven years' standing, when, in preference to many of his seniors in that rank, he was made colonel by brevet, in October, 1757, and three months afterwards was appointed brigadier-general; and he only held a local commission as major-general in America, when he led the force which effected the conquest of Canada, and fell at the moment of victory, at the age of thirty-five, on the 13th of September, 1759.

As he was not in the military service of the Crown, but in that of the East India Company, the rules of the Army did not admit of his being invested with the military command of the troops employed there, which was conferred upon Sir George Berkeley.

Sir Henry Pottinger performed the duty entrusted to him most ably. While the military operations were prosecuted under the command of the General, the Governor kept the communications with the hostile Kafirs under his own immediate direction, and applied himself to the task of increasing and rendering as efficient as possible the irregular force, levied in the Colony to assist the regular troops; and at the same time he endeavoured to check the abuses which are so apt to arise, and which it is so difficult to prevent, when a force of the former description is suddenly called for in time of danger. Such abuses had prevailed largely at the Cape, but Sir Henry Pottinger dealt with them in a vigorous and determined manner. He also perceived, and was bent upon correcting, the vices of the system on which the Hottentot settlements on the Kat River and other places had been formed, —a system the deplorable results of which have been experienced in the present war.

The war, which was supposed to have been finished when Sir Henry Pottinger reached the Colony, did not prove really to have been so; there was merely one of those delusive intervals of comparative quiet, which are so common in wars with barbarous tribes: the contest soon broke out again, and was not entirely concluded until the month of December, 1847. In the meantime Sir Henry Pottinger (who had only accepted the Government of the Cape, on the express understanding that his doing so was not to interfere with his prospects in India) had been appointed Governor of Madras, and Sir Harry Smith was selected to succeed him at the Cape. When the latter reached the Colony, the war had been virtually terminated by the unconditional surrender of the Chief Sandilli, and it was soon completely finished by that of Pato. It was one of the first acts of the new Governor to release the former, thus extending to him a clemency of which he has since shown himself very little deserving.

The war being thus concluded, it devolved upon Sir Harry Smith to act upon the instructions which had been originally given to Sir Henry Pottinger, and were renewed to himself, as to the policy which should be adopted, in order to prevent, if possible, a recurrence of the calamity which had just been experienced. The substance of these instructions was, that experience having demonstrated the futility of treaties with the Kafirs, no more were to be made; but that, as the only mode of providing for the future security of the Colony, the tribes inhabiting the district between the Keiskamma and the Kei, who had made so unprovoked a war upon the Colonists, must be deprived of their political independence, and the territory taken possession of on behalf of the Crown. It was not to be annexed to the Cape Colony (which would imply extending over it the authority of the Colonial laws, which are utterly unsuited to such a state of society), but was to be governed by British military officers, with the assistance of the Chiefs themselves, whose authority was to be supported as far as possible. For the maintenance of British power a few commanding posts were to be garrisoned; and it was suggested that Kafir troops should be enrolled under European officers, and employed in the western districts of the Colony, where they would serve both as hostages for the good conduct of their relations, and, by relieving the Hottentot regiments, would set the latter free from service in Kafraria. Security for person and property being thus maintained, every endeavour was to be made, with the assistance of the Missionaries, to diffuse a knowledge of religion and the arts of civilized life. As soon as the new system of government was organized, means were to be taken for raising a revenue in the territory, sufficient to defray the very moderate expenses of the kind of government which was contemplated. It was pointed out, that it was right to call upon the Kafirs to provide for the expense of their own government, not only for the purpose of preventing Kafraria from being a burden either on this Country or on the Cape, but also because this demand upon them would act as a stimulus to industry.

The above is a short summary of the most important instructions contained in a Despatch in which our views were very fully explained*. It will be seen

* See page 1 of Papers relating to the Kafir Tribes, presented to Parliament in February, 1848; see also the Despatch to Sir Harry

that the principle on which we proposed to act was that of endeavouring to protect the Colonists from the depredations and constantly recurring wars with their savage neighbours, by civilizing and reclaiming the Kafir tribes. There was no reason to regard this object as unattainable. The first step towards it must be the maintenance of order, and security for persons and property, which it was conceived might be accomplished by the establishment of military posts, and the appointment of British officers authorized to administer justice both to Kafirs and Colonists, and to enforce the prompt punishment of all wrongs which either might inflict on the other. If this first step could be attained, and a sense of security created in Kafraria, it was not doubted that trade, with its civilizing influences, would quickly spring up, and that the Kafirs would gradually acquire the tastes and habits of the Europeans with whom they would be brought in contact; while, by the efforts of the Missionaries and the measures of the Government, instruction in religion and in the knowledge and arts of civilized life would be diffused, so that the rising generation would grow up with a very different character from that of their parents. In accordance with these views, and with the instructions he had received, the Governor, by a Proclamation dated the 23rd of December, 1847*,

Smith, of December 10, 1847, in which, with reference to Natal, the general system of governing barbarous tribes is more fully entered into. (Papers relating to Natal, presented July, 1848, p. 137.)

* See Papers of July, 1848, pp. 24, 39.

declared that the territory between the Keiskamma and the Kei was taken possession of on behalf of the Crown, by the name of British Kafraria, and he immediately proceeded to organize the government of the district on the principles I have described. Some additional territory was also included within the boundaries of the Colony.

The policy thus adopted was, in fact, precisely the same as that which has been followed with so much success in New Zealand ; and although no doubt there are some important points of difference in the character of the natives of New Zealand and of the Kafirs, yet, in the main, human nature is everywhere the same, and the latter are far less completely barbarous than the former were forty or fifty years ago, since they are a pastoral, and to a considerable extent also an agricultural people, and have never, so far as I am aware, been addicted to cannibalism, which prevailed so extensively among the New Zealanders. It is the same policy which has also been successfully pursued with some of the wild predatory tribes of India, of which an interesting account will be found in the evidence of Colonel Ovans, before the Committee of the House of Commons on the Kafir tribes in 1851. This policy is likewise supported by the concurrent opinion of Sir Benjamin D'Urban, Sir George Napier, Sir Henry Pottinger, and Sir Harry Smith, who have all expressed their conviction that there is no other, by which the inhabitants of the Colony can be effectually protected. The opinion of all these Officers, from their great ability and experience, is entitled to the highest consideration; and it is particularly worthy of remark, that Sir George Napier states that, when he assumed the Government of the Cape, he held a different opinion, and considered Sir Benjamin D'Urban to have taken an erroneous view of the subject, but that experience convinced him that he had himself been mistaken, and that Sir Benjamin D'Urban had been right*.

For nearly three years the policy thus adopted appeared to have been attended with the most gratifying success. In the papers laid before Parliament, there will be found a series of Reports on the state of British Kafraria, under the system of administration

---

* See the evidence of Sir George Napier before the Committee of 1851 on the Kafir tribes. See also Sir Henry Pottinger's despatches in the Papers presented to Parliament in February, 1848, and especially his letter to Sir George Berkeley of the 27th of March, 1847, enclosed in his despatch No. 37, of the 14th of April, 1847. In that letter (p. 73) he says :—" Beyond the Buffalo, as far as the Kei, I intend to place the whole country under the protection of the Queen of England, under the name of British Kafraria. In that tract all the Kafir chiefs and tribes would reside, who chose to place themselves under Her Majesty's protection. They would be allowed to retain whatever may be found good and desirable of their own laws and customs, whilst all objectionable portions would be peremptorily abolished, and British political agents would be appointed to reside amongst them, to assist the chiefs in administering justice and settling disputes; to guide and aid the whole mass of the population in its slow (but it is to be hoped eventual) progress towards civilization; and to narrowly watch the proceedings of each chief and tribe, so that if any might be disposed to break the peace or disturb the desired tranquillity, they should be at the instant seized, or, if necessary, attacked and crushed."

which had been adopted, all showing that, up to the
close of 1850, improvement was going on as steadily
and rapidly as could possibly have been expected,
while the frontier Colonists were in the enjoyment of
a security and an exemption from plunder which they
had never before known. There were, in short, the
strongest grounds for hoping that, if this state of
things could be maintained but for a very few years
longer, the peace of the Colony might be considered
as having been permanently and securely established.
Unfortunately these hopes were dashed to the ground,
by the unlooked-for and calamitous war which again
broke out in the month of December, 1850. Before
however I proceed to speak of that most unfortunate
event, there are some occurrences of an earlier date
which I must notice.

As soon as Sir Harry Smith had taken the measures which were immediately required on the termination of the war, for settling the affairs of Kafraria, his
attention was called to the condition of the northern
frontier and to the settlement of Natal, and he undertook a toilsome journey beyond the Orange River and
thence to Natal. In February, 1848, he reported the
result of his personal examination of the territory north
of the Orange River. He described it as being occupied by a large number of emigrant farmers from the
Cape, who were living in the midst of various native
tribes, and were suffering much from the want of any
settled government and of the security which such a
government could alone afford. He stated that these

people were so sensible of the evils arising from this state of things, that they were most anxious for the regular establishment among them of British authority, which had already been virtually extended over this district by the treaties and arrangements made by Sir Peregrine Maitland in 1845. This feeling was, he said, shared by the native Chiefs, who felt that, from their mutual jealousies and the position in which they were placed, with respect to the persons of European race who had settled among them, nothing but the establishment of the paramount power of the British Crown could maintain peace and good order in the country. In these circumstances Sir Harry Smith reported, that he had thought it necessary to proclaim the sovereignty of the Queen, over the territory between the Orange and Vaal Rivers, explaining that his object in doing so was only to exercise so much authority, as might be necessary to preserve peace among the inhabitants of various races and among the different tribes, and to enable the natives and the emigrant farmers respectively to manage their own affairs*.

The answer returned to the Despatch in which the Governor reported the course he had taken, referred him to previous declarations of the determination of Her Majesty's Government, to encourage no extension of the British dominions in Africa; but it proceeded to express a sense of the importance of allowing a free development of his plans, and a readiness to believe,

* See Sir H. Smith's Despatch of Feb. 3, 1848, in the Papers relating to the Kafir tribes presented to Parliament in July,1848, p. 59.

on his authority, the necessity of departing from our general line of policy in this instance, by the establishment of British supremacy in the territory in question. He was told that "the tendency of these measures [those he had reported his having adopted], if duly executed, will be to give somewhat more regularity and greater strength to that rude system of government which has grown up of itself among these people from the necessity of their position, and to provide them the assistance which they really require, for the purpose chiefly of settling their disputes among themselves, by the interposition of an authority to which all the different races of men, whom circumstances have brought into such singular relations with each other, look up with respect. But it is essential that the management of their own concerns, with the duty of providing for their defence, and for the payment of the expense of that system of government which is established among them, should be thrown entirely on the emigrant Boers and the native tribes among whom they are settled."

With these views, and on these conditions, the Governor was informed that we should be prepared to sanction the assumption of this territory, when we should have ascertained, what should be the proper steps to take, in order to give legal validity to his proceedings, and when he should have supplied some further information which was called for[*].

* See Despatch to Sir Harry Smith of June 21, 1848, p. 67 of the above Papers.

In the August following the proclamation of sovereignty, some of the Boers revolted, but the Governor
promptly assembled a small force on the Orange River,
made himself an exceedingly rapid journey from Cape
Town to meet it, and after a sharp skirmish put an
end to this revolt, compelling those who had been
engaged in it to defray the expense incurred in its
suppression, by fines which he imposed upon them.
Subsequently, when the information called for from
the Governor had been obtained, Her Majesty was
advised to refer the consideration of the measures
which should be adopted with reference to the Orange
River Sovereignty to the Board of Trade.   As some
legal questions of great nicety arose upon the subject,
much advantage was derived from having it considered
by this Committee of the Privy Council, to which, as
I have mentioned in a former Letter, Lord Campbell,
Sir Edward Ryan, and Sir James Stephen had been
added, for the purpose of enabling it the better to deal
with Colonial questions which might be referred to it
by Her Majesty.   The Committee finally agreed upon
a Report, which was laid before the Queen in Council
and approved, in which the grounds for permitting
British authority to be established in the Orange
River Sovereignty, and the steps which ought to be
taken for that purpose, are fully explained; it will be
found among the Papers relating to the assumption
of sovereignty over the territory in question, which
were presented to Parliament on the 17th of May,
1851.

In the year 1849 the Cape of Good Hope was greatly disturbed by the resistance made by the Colonists to the reception of some convicts who had been sent there. The excitement which this affair created was very great, and I think the surest way of avoiding any error in giving an account of it, will be to quote three Despatches which were laid before Parliament*, explaining the course that had been pursued. I will only premise that, when the first of these Despatches was written, though no report of what had occurred had been received from the Governor, intelligence had reached me from other quarters that so violent a resistance had been made by the Colonists to the landing of a body of convicts, sent from Bermuda under the circumstances detailed in my Despatch, that the Governor had thought it necessary to yield to it, and had detained these men on board the vessel which brought them, until he could receive the instructions of Her Majesty's Government. In resisting the reception of the convicts from Bermuda, the Colonists had raised an equally violent outcry against orders which had been issued for sending military convicts from certain places to the Cape, as if this formed part of the same arrangement, though in truth it was a perfectly distinct measure, which it became necessary to explain in the second of the following Despatches, which I insert entire.

* See Papers relative to the reception of convicts at the Cape of Good Hope, presented to Parliament by Command, January 31, 1850.

Earl Grey to Governor Sir Harry Smith, Bart.

"*Downing Street, November* 30, 1849.

" SIR,

" I have hitherto deferred replying to your despatches, No. 106, of the 29th of June, and No. 123, of the 24th of July, which reached me nearly together in the middle of the month of September, because I had every reason to believe that they must be almost immediately followed by further despatches from you, which might probably convey to me intelligence of a considerable change in the aspect of affairs in the Colony. My despatch of the 18th of April, announcing the determination of Her Majesty's Government to abstain from sending any more convicts to the Cape, which might have been expected to reach you even earlier than the date at which you wrote, and could hardly fail to do so very soon afterwards, was calculated, as I trusted, to calm the excitement which had been created; while I hoped that a similar effect would be produced, when it was found, on the arrival of the expected ship with convicts from Bermuda (which had been heard of at Pernambuco, as having reached that port, and again proceeded on her voyage), that the convicts so sent, who were not to be followed by any more, were of a very different description from the criminals usually sent to a penal Colony. Hence, believing that a very short delay would be occasioned by waiting for further intelligence from you, I considered it better to incur this delay, than to send you immediate instructions, which that intelligence might show to be no longer well adapted to an altered state of affairs.

" But I now find, by the usual list you have forwarded of despatches received by you, that mine of the 18th of April, though it has not been answered, had reached you some time before the date of the last advices. I learn also, from the newspapers published in the Colony, that the Neptune, with the convicts from Bermuda, had arrived, but that the convicts on board had not been permitted to land, being detained on board in Simon's Bay, as it is stated, till further instructions are received from myself; and that the excitement which has been created, far from having subsided, had appeared greatly to have increased. I am further informed, by a communication I have received from the Admiralty, of the attempt which had been made to prevent any description of supplies from being furnished for Her Majesty's service, naval, military, or civil, with the view of enforcing the departure of the Neptune, with the convicts; but though I have despatches from you on other subjects up to five days after the arrival of the Neptune, I have none containing any information of the arrival of the Neptune, as to what had then occurred on this subject, or as to the measures which you might have in contemplation. In these circumstances I can no longer postpone transmitting to you instructions for your guidance: and in doing so it will be necessary that I should, in the first place, briefly review the past course of proceedings upon this subject, and explain what have been the grounds on which Her Majesty's Government have acted in the various measures which have been adopted.

" I need hardly remind you, that in the circular despatch which I addressed to the Governors of different Colonies to which it appeared to me that convicts, when they became entitled to tickets-of-leave, might be sent with advantage, I did not contemplate that this measure should be adopted with respect to Colonies which had not originally been established as Penal Colonies, and in which it should appear that the inhabitants were opposed to it. But about the time when this circular was written, a very serious difficulty arose as to the disposal of certain Irish convicts, who had been transported to Bermuda, for offences committed during the pressure of the famine in Ireland occasioned by the failure of the potatoes. It was of urgent importance to remove some of these men from Bermuda, as it was found that they were entirely unsuited to undergo the discipline and labour which are there enforced. It was necessary therefore that they should be removed; but at that time the state of things was such in Van Diemen's Land, from the very large number of convicts who had been sent there in the years preceding 1846, that there was no prospect that if sent to that Colony with tickets-of-leave, they would have been able to find employment, and to maintain themselves by their labour.

" It was also highly desirable, considering the character of these convicts, that they should not be placed where they would be forced to mix with ordinary criminals. These men were in general peasants, who, under the pressure of extreme want, had committed depredations, which, though they could not be passed over without punishment, yet implied comparatively little moral degradation. This circumstance of their being of so different a class from ordinary criminals, while it afforded a strong reason against sending them to a Colony where they could mix with the latter, seemed also to remove all just grounds for objecting to their reception in the Colonies to which convicts are not usually sent. I remembered that the agricultural labourers who were transported to New South Wales at the beginning of 1831, for the riots of the previous winter, had proved a most valuable accession to the labouring population of that Colony, and I believed that the Irish convicts who had in like manner been betrayed by special circumstances into crimes which they had not been in the habit of committing, or had been convicted of political or agrarian offences, which out of Ireland they would have no temptation to repeat, might be removed to a Colony where there exists a great want of labour, and where they would not be exposed to the influence of bad associates, with great advantage, not only themselves, but to the Colony; and I did not conceive it to be possible that, even if the inhabitants of the Cape should entertain a fixed objection to the reception of convicts of an ordinary description and as a general practice, there could be any such objection to receiving, in that vast territory, between two and three hundred convicts of this peculiar description, when Her Majesty's Government would thus be relieved from a difficulty of a very serious kind.

" Under this impression, I recommended that the convicts in question (to whom were afterwards added some others specially recommended for indulgence, on account of their peculiar good conduct, or length of detention without committing any fault) should be removed to the Cape, without waiting till your answer to my circular despatch could be received, believing that in doing so I was not departing in any degree from the spirit of that circular, which referred to the adoption of a permanent system. The letter indeed in which I informed you of the special measure intended to meet the immediate emergency, bore the same date as the circular, and was forwarded by the same opportunity. With the information now before me, I greatly lament that this step should have been taken. Had I been aware how strong was the feeling which existed at the Cape on this subject, I should not have advised the measure which was adopted; but I confess I fell into the error of supposing that, whatever might be the objection felt to receiving convicts as an ordinary practice (an objection which I readily admit to be founded on feelings that are entitled to respect), there would still be amongst the inhabitants of the Cape so much regard for the general interest of the British Nation, to which they had just been indebted for such truly generous assistance, and also so much of common humanity towards the unfortunate men as to whom the difficulty had arisen, that it might safely be calculated that they at least would be received without opposition. This is an error which I acknowledge, and which I greatly lament.

" In the meantime, long after the orders for the removal of these convicts from Bermuda to the Cape had been given, I received from you the first intimation of the very strong feeling which existed on this subject amongst the inhabitants of the Cape. I received this intelligence with much regret, believing, as I still believe, that in refusing to receive, in very moderate numbers, convicts whose conduct under a preliminary system of punishment has been such as to entitle them to the indulgence of tickets-of-leave, and whose best chance of being reformed consists in their being dispersed as widely as possible, the inhabitants of the Cape were declining the share of the common burdens of the Empire, which they might fairly be called upon to undertake. Still, when the strength of the feeling which existed was fully understood, no time was lost by Her Majesty's Government in making a public announcement in the House of Commons, that no more convicts would be sent to that Colony; and in my despatch of April the 18th I formally communicated to you this determination. At this time however there was nothing in the information which had reached me, which led me at all to suppose that this determination to abandon the general plan of sending convicts holding tickets-of-leave to the Cape, would not be sufficient to calm the excitement which had been created, or that so violent an opposition would be made to the reception of the comparatively small number who were already on their way thither. Till a much later period I had every reason to entertain this opinion. Your despatch of the 24th of May, which reached me on the 13th of August, was directed entirely against the proposal so inaccurately described as one for making the Cape a penal Colony; and indeed implied (so at least I understood it) that there would be by no means the same sort of objection in your opinion to sending to the Cape with tickets-of-leave (as a special measure, and one not to be repeated) the particular convicts who had been actually sent there. Accordingly I answered these despatches by referring you to that in which I had announced the determination of Her Majesty's Government to defer to the wishes expressed by the Colonists, by abstaining from sending any more convicts, and I fully believed that the instructions I had transmitted to you on the 2nd of July would suffice for your guidance as to the Bermuda convicts.

" Your despatch of the 29th of June, which was received in this office on the 14th of September, contained the first intimation which reached me of the violence of the opposition which was likely to be made to the reception of even the convicts sent in the Neptune; and this despatch showed that at its date you still contemplated receiving these convicts on shore, and providing for their reception until further instructions could be received, apparently without anticipating any difficulty in doing so. Three days later, that is, on the 17th of September, your despatch of the 24th of July, No. 123, was received, from which I learnt to what a height the excitement had risen; and that, in consequence of the extraordinary proceedings which had taken place, you had most unadvisedly, as I think, publicly announced your determination not to permit the landing of the convicts hourly expected by the Neptune.

"I have already stated that I did not immediately answer this despatch, because I was in daily expectation that I should receive from you further intelligence, which might materially alter the nature of the instructions it might be proper to give. But, further, I considered it to be quite impossible that any instructions which could be then transmitted to you, could be of any assistance to you in meeting the immediate difficulty of disposing of the Bermuda convicts. They had for three or four weeks been hourly expected to arrive at the Cape, when you wrote to me (two months before) the despatch I had just received. When they left Bermuda, these men had already suffered in health from confinement in the hulks; and it was known that when they were at Pernambuco, though their health had improved, the ship was still sickly. I knew that it must also have been obvious to you, from my despatch of the 2nd July (which was likely to reach you as soon as yours of the 24th of the same month had come into my hands), that when that despatch was written I entertained no doubt that the convicts would be landed; and you must have known that in your own correspondence, up to the time of your writing the despatch of the 24th of July, there was nothing which could lead me to form a different opinion, or to call for additional instructions. Hence I concluded that when this vessel arrived, and when you learned, as you were sure to do from the commander and from the surgeon, the condition of those on board, it must have been utterly impossible that you could fail to adopt some course or other for the immediate relief of these unfortunate men.

Hence I regarded it as highly inexpedient that I should send out instructions as to the disposal of these convicts, when it appeared certain that those instructions must arrive far too late for your guidance, and might probably be at variance with the determination which in the emergency you had adopted, and of which I should, probably in a few days, be apprised.

" It did not even occur to me as possible that you could take the course of detaining these people on board the Neptune until you could receive further instructions, since this would involve the probability of their being so detained for nearly four months, the shortest time in which you could calculate on an answer to your despatch. I felt the more confident that, in one way or another, the question as to how these persons were in the first instance to be disposed of, must have been determined long before you could hear from me, because I could not believe that, however strong might be the feeling of the Colonists against the Government for the measures which had been adopted, they would visit those measures on the heads of these unfortunate men, whose lives might be endangered by such protracted confinement.

" After this brief review of what has taken place, reserving for another despatch all that relates to military convicts, I now proceed to give you the instructions which it appears are still necessary as to the manner in which the convicts on board the Neptune are to be disposed of. You will take measures for sending them to Van Diemen's Land as soon you receive from me the necessary powers, which will be forwarded to you by the earliest opportunity ; and you will at the same time inform them that, in consideration of what they have undergone, and of the disappointment of the expectations they were encouraged to entertain when they left Bermuda, Her Majesty will be advised to grant conditional pardons on their arrival in Van Diemen's Land, to those who shall not by misconduct have disqualified themselves for that indulgence. The case of the prisoner Mitchell, which is quite distinct from that of all the others, is reserved for separate consideration, and instructions will be sent respecting him to the Lieutenant-Governor of Van Diemen's Land.

" I have only further to add, for your information, that Her Majesty will be advised immediately to revoke the Order in Council by which the sending of convicts to the Cape is rendered legal. I forbear to express my opinion either on the extraordinary proceedings of the inhabitants of the Cape, or upon your own conduct: on the former, because I am unwilling to use the terms which would alone adequately describe what I think of their proceedings; on your own conduct, because I have not yet received your explanation of the grounds upon which you acted, and because I should be unwilling to pass any judgement, prematurely, upon your course in circumstances of undoubtedly great and unprecedented difficulty.

" You will publish this and my other Despatch, No. 39, Military, of this date, in the Gazette, for the information of the inhabitants of the Cape.

" I have, etc.,

" *Lieut.-Gen. Sir H. G. Smith, Bt.,*   (Signed)   GREY.
    " *etc., etc., etc.*"

Earl Grey to Governor Sir Harry G. Smith, Bart.

" *Downing-street, November* 30, 1849.

  " SIR,—

" I have received your despatch of the 12th June, marked ' Military, separate,' which I have read with considerable surprise, as it seems to imply a forgetfulness of what has already passed on this subject, which I find it difficult to account for. I have to remind you, that the arrangement for sending military convicts, immediately on receiving sentence, to the convict establishment at the Cape, is one totally distinct from, and having different objects from, that which was proposed with respect to sending ordinary convicts to the same Colony with tickets-of-leave. It was intended that the latter should become absorbed in the general population of the Colony, and they were to be sent by the authority of an Order in Council which, in another despatch of this date, I have informed you that Her Majesty will be advised to revoke, and which made the Cape one of the places to which offenders sentenced to transportation might be sent.

" Soldiers sentenced to transportation are, on the contrary, sent under the authority of the Mutiny Act, and are placed on their arrival in the existing penal establishment of the Cape of Good Hope, where the whole cost of their maintenance is defrayed by this Country, and where they are kept quite apart from the population. It was considered expedient to send soldiers, sentenced by Courts-martial, from certain stations to the Cape (as from others they are sent home or to Van Diemen's Land), partly because this was the most convenient arrangement with a view to existing means of communication, partly because it is of importance that military convicts should be as much as possible divided, and not sent in large numbers to any one place.

" I have further to remind you, that the arrangement for sending soldiers to the Cape has not been recently introduced. My despatch stating that military convicts were to be sent there from the Mauritius, was dated so long ago as the 10th September, 1847; and on the 28th September, 1848, the same arrangement, you were informed, would be adopted with regard to soldiers sentenced by Court-martial in Hongkong. Both these despatches were received and acknowledged without even a hint that there could be any objection to the arrangement.

" Nor is this all. Throughout the correspondence which has taken place, the opinion has been expressed by yourself, as well as by preceding Governors of the Cape, that there existed no objection on the part of the inhabitants to the employment of convicts there so long as they were kept in custody. I have to refer you to Sir Peregrine Maitland's Despatches of the 10th and 23rd of September, 1846*, and to your own of the 8th of May, 1848†, in which you suggested that no fewer than 600 convicts should be sent to the Colony, to be employed in the construction of a breakwater.

" It is true that in these despatches the ultimate removal of the convicts from the Cape was contemplated; but there is nothing in the order for sending military convicts for punishment to the Cape, which prevents their being also removed when their sentences approach completion. Indeed, on referring to my despatch of the 10th of September‡, you will perceive that their removal before the termination of their punishment was what was originally intended; and if the object of your despatch of the 12th of June had been to claim, on the part of the Colonists, that this should be the course pursued, there would have been no difficulty in complying with it. In the meantime no inconvenience could possibly arise from receiving and re-

* Pages 16 and 17 of House of Commons Papers : Cape Transportation, No. 217, 1849.

† Ibid., p. 19.   ‡ Ibid., page 38.

taining them in custody in the convict establishment at the Cape.   By the Report which I have just received on the convict establishment of the Colony (in your despatch, No. 167*, of the 6th of September last), it appears that it is quite equal to receiving for punishment the moderate number of military convicts likely to be sent under the orders now in force.

"You will perceive from the enclosed return, which I have obtained from the Adjutant-General's Office, that the number to be so sent in the year would not, according to the average of the last five years, exceed twenty-five. I have not therefore thought it necessary to revoke the instructions which have been given for sending soldiers sentenced for military offences to transportation to the Cape from certain stations.   But an arrangement will be made, on which you shall receive further instructions hereafter, for removing these men, when they become entitled to their release from punishment, to some other place ; and I have also to authorize you, if you should find that there is likely to be opposition to the reception of military convicts even on these terms, to forward to this Country any who may arrive at the Cape.

"Though such opposition would be entirely inconsistent with all that has till now been said on the part of the Colonists, and though it would be no less unreasonable that they should expect the protection of the British army, and refuse to afford the smallest assistance towards an arrangement which has in view the maintenance of the discipline of that army, Her Majesty's Government do not think that the object of disposing of so small a number of convicts is

* See Papers relative to the Employment on Roads of Colonial Convicts at the Cape.

of sufficient importance to make it worth while to insist on the point.

"I have, etc.,

"*Lieut.-Gen. Sir H. G. Smith, Bt.,*   (Signed)   GREY.
   " *etc., etc., etc.*"

Enclosure.

"Return of the Number of European Soldiers belonging to Her Majesty's Army who have been transported in each of the last Five Years from the East Indies, the Mauritius, Ceylon, and Hongkong, specifying, so far as practicable, the place to which they were transported.

STATIONS.	Number of Men Transported.					Total.
	1844.	1845.	1846.	1847.	1848.	
East Indies . .	28	15	17	49	13	122
Mauritius . . .	5	...	...	...	...	5
Ceylon	...	...	...	...	...	...
Hongkong . .	1	...	...	...	...	1
Total . . .	34	15	17	49	13	128

"NOTE.—There are no records in the Adjutant-General's Office which furnish the information required as to the places to which these men were transported.

"*Adjutant-General's Office,*   (Signed)   J. MACDONALD,
  " *October* 30, 1849.   *Adjutant-General.*"

Earl Grey to Governor Sir Harry G. Smith, Bart.

"*Downing-street, December* 5, 1849.
  "SIR,

"I have to acknowledge the receipt of your despatch No. 185, of the 30th of September last, reporting the arrival of the Neptune with the convicts shipped in that vessel at Bermuda. This despatch, with the able minute of the Executive Council which it encloses, affords an explanation, which I am happy to inform you has appeared to Her Majesty's Government to be satisfactory, as to the reasons by which you were guided in the decision to which you came respecting the disposal of this party of convicts; and I have to signify to you Her Majesty's approval of the course which you felt it necessary to adopt. It is gratifying to me to be able to convey to you this announcement, for I am very sensible of the trying and anxious nature of the position in which, by the violent proceedings adopted at the Cape, you have found yourself placed.

" I have also to express my approval of the manner in which, in your published communication to the Chairman of the Public Meeting held at Cape Town, you pointed out to the Colonists the dangerous tendency of the course on which they had entered, and the objectionable nature of the principles which it involved.

" Her Majesty's Government have learned with great regret the decease of Mr. Deas, the surgeon-superintendent of the convicts by the Neptune. It is indeed to be deplored, that after having won the confidence and gratitude of the unfortunate men entrusted to his care, and also earned the approval of your inspecting officer for the manner in which he brought them out, this meritorious officer should, almost at the moment of arrival, have fallen a victim to the feelings of pain and surprise occasioned by the refusal of the inhabitants of the Cape to allow his people the refreshments indispensable to the preservation of their health.

" I have, etc.,

" (Signed)   GREY.

" *Lieut.-Gen. Sir H. G. Smith, Bt.,*
     " *etc., etc., etc.*"

Having quoted these Despatches, which state the facts, I forbear from describing the violent proceedings adopted on this occasion by the party which took the lead in opposing the admission of these convicts into the Colony. I was obliged to enter fully into this subject in the House of Lords* (where none even of the Peers in opposition to your Government said a word in excuse of the conduct of the persons to whom I refer), and I do not wish again to enter upon what must be an irritating topic. I will only say, that I think the authors of the resistance to the Government must now repent their own success. If their measures did not greatly contribute (as I firmly believe they did) to bring upon the Colony the calamity of another Kafir war, at all events there can be no doubt that when that war broke out, it would have been well for the frontier farmers if these 250 convicts had been distributed among them as servants (as would have been the case had they been landed), instead of an equal number of the Kafir servants, who immediately deserted and, it is believed, in some cases betrayed them to the enemy. It was one of the considerations which led to sending this body of convicts to the Colony, that such an increase in the number of European servants employed by the Settlers would have contributed not a little to their advantage and security.

Another subject, which during the last three years has given rise to much angry discussion at the Cape,

* See Hansard, vol. cxvii.

is the question as to the grant of Representative Institutions to the Colony. So long since as the year 1842, a petition from the inhabitants of Cape Town, praying for a Representative Assembly, had been transmitted to Lord Derby, who was then Secretary of State, by Sir George Napier, the Governor, who recommended a compliance with the wishes of the petitioners. Lord Derby, without absolutely rejecting this application, pointed out the many and serious difficulties which stood in the way of the satisfactory establishment of representative institutions in this Colony, in consequence of its state of society and peculiar local circumstances; and he desired the Governor to report his opinion as to the means which could be most advantageously adopted for surmounting these difficulties, if he continued to think that the change in the form of government he had recommended ought to be accomplished.

When we came into office, I found that there was still a strong desire on the part of the Colonists for a Representative Government, and that no answer had been received to Lord Derby's despatch* to which I have referred. Accordingly, when Sir Henry Pottinger was appointed Governor, his attention was called to the subject, and he was directed to report upon it. He did not hold the office of Governor long enough to act upon these instructions, to which of course he

---

* This Despatch will be found in the Papers relative to the Establishment of Representative Government at the Cape of Good Hope, presented by Command, February 5, 1850, p. 89.

was not expected to attend, while the war which he found in progress should be going on. When the war was at an end, and the most pressing of the subjects which afterwards required the Governor's attention had been disposed of, Sir Harry Smith applied himself, with the assistance of his Executive Council and the Judges, to the consideration of the important and difficult question on which a report had been called for.

The result of this deliberation was, that Sir Harry Smith, in a despatch dated the 29th of July, 1848*, expressed his strong opinion, confirmed by that of all the gentlemen he had consulted, that the time was come when Representative Institutions ought to be extended to the Colony. The difficulties and dangers of the change were not concealed in some of the very able Minutes drawn up by his advisers and enclosed in his Despatch; but although the experiment was admitted to be a bold one, there was a general concurrence of opinion that it was one which must be made. When this Despatch and its enclosures were received, we took some time to consider the subject, which appeared to us full of difficulty; but we finally came to the conclusion that the advice of the Governor must be followed. Indeed it was scarcely possible to do otherwise, as we learned that the wish of the Colonists for a change in the form of their government was so strong, that Sir Harry Smith had

* See page 3 of the above Papers.

considered it necessary to endeavour to allay the excitement which had been created by publicly stating, in answer to one of the addresses presented to him on the subject, that he had reported to Her Majesty's Government his opinion that the desired change ought to be conceded, and might be so without inconvenience.

The publication of this answer in the Colonial newspapers, together with the feeling which previously existed, would have rendered it hardly practicable to refuse what was asked, even if the objections to granting it had appeared stronger than they actually did. Accordingly Sir Harry Smith was informed that Her Majesty's Government had come to the conclusion, that a Representative Constitution must be granted to the Cape, but that the precise mode in which it was to be framed would require much consideration. In order to arrive at a satisfactory decision on this point, the same course was adopted which in a former Letter I have mentioned as having been followed with regard to the Australian Colonies, and the subject was referred to the Committee of Privy Council for Trade and Foreign Plantations.

A Report was made by this Committee, explaining the manner in which they advised, that the promise to grant representative institutions to the Cape should be fulfilled; and this Report having been approved by Her Majesty in Council, on the 30th of January, 1850, the necessary steps were taken to give effect to its recommendations. The Committee of Council recommended* that the leading provisions of the proposed Constitution should be embodied in Letters Patent, empowering the Governor to summon the Parliament, which was to be created as soon as the necessary arrangements for that purpose should be completed, and authorizing him, with the assistance of the existing Legislative Council, to settle by an ordinance (which was not to take effect until it had been approved, and, if necessary, amended by Her Majesty in Council) all those matters on which it was impossible to come to a satisfactory conclusion, without more minute local information than was accessible in England. The number of Members of which each Legislative body should consist, the franchise of the electors by whom they were to be returned, and the mode of dividing the Colony into districts for the purpose of the elections, were the most important points left to the decision of the existing Legislature. The powers of that Legislature were to be continued, and it was to perform its usual functions, until the writs for the election of the first Parliament for the Colony should issue.

Although the Anti-Convict agitation had occurred while this matter was under deliberation, and it was felt that the effects of this agitation must add materially to the difficulties, which were at all events to have been anticipated, in bringing the new form of

* The Report of the Committee will be found at length in the Appendix (C) to this Volume.

Government into operation, what had taken place was not held to afford any sufficient reason against proceeding with the intended change. Accordingly, on the 31st of January, 1850, the Order in Council approving the Report of the Committee was transmitted to Sir Harry Smith, in a Despatch, directing him immediately to collect the requisite information, and to make the necessary preparations for submitting to the Legislative Council the ordinances it would be called upon to pass, as soon as the Letters Patent, giving it authority to do so, should reach him. These Letters Patent were forwarded to the Governor on the 29th of May following.

When the Despatch of the 31st of January, 1850, was received by Sir Harry Smith, he found that the first step it was necessary for him to take, was to complete the Legislative Council, which had remained in abeyance since the resignation of some of its members, during the agitation on the subject of the convicts who had reached the Colony. For the purpose of filling up the Legislative Council, the Governor issued a public notice on the 6th of May, 1850, calling upon the various Municipalities and District Road Boards, to furnish him with lists of five persons whom they might think proper to recommend for the appointment of Legislative Councillors, expressing his intention of filling up the vacancies from the lists so sent to him.

This was an unusual step, since the right of appointing Legislative Councillors rested with the Crown, and the Governor was only empowered by his commission to make provisional appointments on his own judgement until the pleasure of the Crown could be known, while the effect of the measure he had taken, was to render the appointments virtually elective. It was intended as a conciliatory act towards those who, during the Anti-Convict agitation, had been opposed to the Government, and led to the selection from that party of four out of the five Legislative Councillors that were appointed. The result showed how little gratitude the Governor met with, from those whose wishes he thus endeavoured to meet. When the Legislative Council assembled, it proceeded to consider how the ordinances for completing the Constitution should be framed; but little progress had been made in its deliberations, when they were interrupted by the resignation of four of the five newly appointed Legislative Councillors. The ground of quarrel taken by these gentlemen was, that the Legislative Council proposed undertaking other business, instead of confining itself exclusively to passing the ordinances required to bring the new Constitution into operation. If this was the real as well the declared reason for their resignation, it is difficult to understand why the four Members who now retired had ever accepted seats in the Legislative Council; since it was well known from the first that it was to transact the ordinary business of the Colony till the new Parliament could meet. In the notice of the Governor, relating to his intended appointment of Legislative

Councillors, he had published the Despatch in which the report of the Committee of Privy Council was transmitted to him, and these documents distinctly stated that the existing Legislative Council was to continue in the exercise of all its usual functions, until the issue of the writs for the election of the first Parliament of the Colony.

On the resignation of the four Members, the Governor did not think it expedient to attempt filling up the vacancies thus created, or proceeding with the consideration of the ordinances*. Instead of this, he appointed the remaining Members of the Legislative Council a Commission to prepare the draft of Orders in Council, which he recommended should be passed in this Country, to establish the proposed Representative Constitution, and by a public notice in the Gazette he invited communications on the subject from all classes of the community.

The course thus taken by the Governor did not meet with our approbation; and Despatches were addressed to him (which I think it right to give at length in the Appendix†), explaining fully our views upon the subject, and our reasons for considering it necessary to adhere to the mode of proceeding originally determined upon, by requiring that ordinances should be passed by the Legislature of the Colony to provide for bringing the proposed Constitution into

* See his Despatch of October 2nd, 1852, in the further Papers presented May 19th, 1851, p. 18.

† See Appendix (D) to this Volume.

operation. Before these Despatches reached the Colony the war with the Kafirs had broken out, and the further consideration of the subject by the local Legislature was unavoidably delayed. Subsequently, after some further correspondence, to which it is unnecessary more particularly to refer, the vacant seats in the Legislative Council were again filled up by the Governor; and on the 14th of September, 1851*, to assist him in completing the arrangement for effecting the desired change in the Constitution, two draft Ordinances were transmitted to him, for the purpose of being laid before the Legislative Council. The Despatch enclosing these drafts had been acknowledged †, but no final proceedings had been taken with regard to them, when we retired from Office. I abstain from any remarks on what I learn by the newspapers, and by the proceedings in Parliament, to have since taken place. I have only to add, on the subject of the Constitution of the Cape, that Sir Andries Stockenstrom and Mr. Fairbairn, two of the Members of the Legislative Council who resigned their seats in the manner I have described, and who afterwards came over to this Country to press their own views on Parliament and the Government, signed, on the 2nd of December, 1851, a petition to the Queen, praying that the Constitution, as embodied in the Letters Patent and the draft Ordinances, might be brought into immediate operation. The Constitution they thus

---

* See further Papers, presented February 3, 1852, p. 73.
† See the above Papers, pp. 32, 37.

prayed for was the very one, without the slightest alteration, which might have been established many months before, but for their own opposition in September, 1850, to the measures necessary for giving effect to it *.

There can, I think, be no doubt that the bitter opposition made to the Government on the two subjects I have mentioned, by creating in the minds of the Kafirs a belief that the Government would not be able to command the undivided and hearty support of the White inhabitants of the Colony, was one, and not the least powerful, of the various causes which led to the breaking out of the war at the close of 1850. The first appearance of any symptoms of approaching disturbance was reported by Sir Harry Smith, on the 14th of October, 1850, when he stated that, in consequence of accounts which had reached him from Kafraria, he was about to proceed there†, though he attached no importance whatever to the excitement which had arisen.

In a despatch, dated the 21st of October, from King William's Town, he informed me that the reports he had received on his arrival at that place " were of the most satisfactory nature‡," and that I "need be under no apprehension of an outbreak." Ten days later, he reported that he had found it neces-

* See Papers of February 3, 1852, pp. 49, 98.

† Papers relating to Kafir Tribes, presented March 20, 1851, p. 16.

‡ Page 28.

sary to depose the Chief Sandilli, but he expressed the utmost confidence as to the success of this measure, and the absence of the slightest cause for alarm. On the 26th of November Sir Harry Smith reported his return to the seat of Government, having left British Kafraria " in a state of perfect tranquillity * ;" but he added that there continued to be much apprehension of an approaching war among the frontier farmers, which he had endeavoured to dispel by a proclamation issued at Graham's Town (where he had remained ten days on his return from Kafraria), in which he assured the inhabitants there was no danger of their being attacked.

On the 5th of December however he reported that he had learned by fresh accounts, that his confident expectations of the maintenance of tranquillity had not been realized, and that he was on the point of again proceeding to Kafraria at the head of an additional body of troops. On his reaching King William's Town he reported that his arrival, with the troops he had brought with him, and the measures he had adopted, would, as he confidently anticipated, prevent any serious disturbance. This confidence he continued to express in the strongest manner up to the 22nd of December†. Two days later an attack was made upon a patrol, under Colonel Mackinnon, which caused a heavy loss to the force under his command, and which proved to be the signal of a general rising throughout Kafraria; fortunately the Chief Pato, and

* Page 45.   † Pages 58–64.

the tribes under his influence, who had been formidable enemies in the last war, remained faithful, and have continued so up to the present time.

Soon after the commencement of the war it was rendered much more formidable by the revolt of many of the Hottentots within the Colony, especially those of the Kat River Settlement, which was afterwards followed by the desertion to the enemy, of a large number of men of the Cape Mounted Rifle regiment. To these defections the long continuance and severity of the contest must be mainly attributed. It is not probable that the rebel Kafirs by themselves could long have resisted the force under Sir Harry Smith; but these defections not only deprived him of a considerable amount of force, of the description best suited to the peculiar nature of the war and of the country in which it was carried on, but they also gave to the Kafirs that which they most wanted, allies capable of teaching them how to act with most effect against the British troops. The deserters from the Mounted Rifles are believed to have directed the operations of the enemy, on some of the occasions on which we experienced the most loss; and, if I am not misinformed, the death of several of the brave officers who have fallen during the war has been occasioned by the skill as marksmen, acquired by these men in our service.

A careful perusal of the Papers laid before Parliament will, I think, lead others to the same conclusion at which I have myself arrived, that a too anxious, though most humane, desire on the part of the Governor to abstain from measures of severity, had a very unfortunate effect in preventing a check from being given in the first instance to the rebellious disposition which showed itself among the Hottentots. On referring to the Governor's Despatch of the 4th of July, 1851*, and its enclosures, it will be seen that none of the rebels who have been the means of causing the death of so many of Her Majesty's faithful subjects and gallant troops have suffered capital punishment; that even men who, it is stated in the Minute of the Executive Council enclosed in the above Despatch, had been proved to have been " present, aiding, and abetting, when loyal and unoffending subjects were shot dead†," were allowed to escape with the sentence of transportation.

It cannot fail to be observed, that the opinion of the Executive Council, that the sentence of death passed upon these men must be remitted, is founded mainly upon the late period at which the question was brought under their consideration, and on the fact that so large a number of persons equally guilty had already been, not merely pardoned, but allowed to enter the Queen's service in the levies that had been raised. No doubt the advice of the Executive Council was the only advice that could be given in the circumstances stated; but it is to my mind equally clear that the impunity, or at least compara-

* Papers, February 3, 1852, p. 72.　　　† Page 74.

tive impunity, of those who had been proved guilty of the murder of Her Majesty's loyal subjects, was calculated to do infinite mischief, and that if a more prompt example had been made of the most guilty, the contagion of rebellion would not have spread so far.

One man, named Botha, among those allowed thus to escape, was the son of a Kat River Field Cornet, that is, of a man in a situation of some trust and authority, who is believed to have plotted the outbreak with the Chief Sandilli. Botha, the son, was taken fighting in Fort Beaufort when that place was attacked by the first Hottentot rebels, and by the Kafir Chief Hermanus, who was killed there. Sir Harry Smith says in his Despatch, he would have ordered this man Botha to be immediately tried and executed, if he had been on the spot when he was taken. The attack on Fort Beaufort, and the capture of Botha, took place so early as the 7th of January, 1851, that is, within a fortnight of the commencement of the war; very few indeed of the Hottentots were then engaged in the rebellion, and, in all human probability, an immediate and severe example, made by the execution of the first culprits, would have prevented many even of those who had a guilty knowledge of the intended rebellion, but were committed by no open acts, from going further, and would almost certainly have deterred those who were still really innocent, from joining the rebels.

It is difficult to collect from the correspondence,

why Sir Harry Smith's absence from Fort Beaufort prevented the immediate trial and execution of Botha and those taken with him in arms, in accordance with the intention declared in the proclamation issued by the Governor, on the 10th of January, 1851. As far as I can understand the matter, the delay seems to have arisen from a desire to conform rigidly to the law, and to avoid the exercise of any power not strictly legal. No doubt the immediate trial and execution of these rebels by courts-martial would not have been warranted by any law; the only courts-martial which exercise strictly legal powers are those constituted under the Mutiny Act, and these can take cognizance only of offences against that Act, committed by persons in the military service of the Crown. The proclamation of what is called martial-law in time of rebellion, confers no legal powers on the officers in command of the troops; it is really nothing more than a declaration that, in consequence of urgent danger, all law is for the time suspended, and that those officers will take upon themselves, without reference to the extent of their legal power, to do what is necessary for the public safety.

Thus when Captain Laye, in New Zealand, caused the four men convicted by a court-martial of the murder of Mrs. Gilfillan and her children, to be hanged in forty-eight hours,—when Colonel Drought, and the officers acting under his orders, tried and executed the rebels in Ceylon,—though by so doing I believe they only fulfilled their duty, and averted

great misfortunes, still they did that which was un-
warranted by any law, and which required to be subsequently covered by measures of legislation, passed
to indemnify those who had acted under the proclamation of martial-law. In like manner, if Botha and
his guilty associates had been tried as soon as they
were taken, and had been executed with the least
possible delay, their punishment would not have been
technically legal, but it would have been not the less
just, or the less calculated to prevent in the end a
much greater destruction of human life.

Still I cannot be surprised, that Sir Harry Smith
should have hesitated to take upon himself the same
responsibility that Lord Torrington had done, and that
he should have been anxious to proceed with strict
and technical regularity, though this, amidst the turmoil of war, necessarily occasioned so much delay, as
ultimately to lead to the escape of the guilty, and to
all the unfortunate consequences which followed from
their impunity. The nature of the attacks to which
Lord Torrington and Sir Henry Ward had exposed
themselves by the course they pursued, and the countenance given to those attacks, could hardly fail to
deter another Governor from adopting a similar course
in circumstances of the same kind. If the undue
lenity shown to the Hottentot rebels, in the beginning
of the war, really produced the bad effects which I
am persuaded it did, the responsibility for this unfortunate error rests far more with others than with
Sir Harry Smith.

As soon as the intelligence of the breaking out of the war reached us, although it was not accompanied by an application for more troops from the Governor, we immediately gave directions for sending reinforcements to the Cape, which were subsequently increased, as further accounts showed the contest to be of a more serious character than we were in the first instance led to apprehend, and more especially when we were informed of the defection of so large a proportion of the Cape Mounted Rifles. This last circumstance, coupled with the spirit of disaffection shown by many of the coloured inhabitants of the Colony, and the unfriendly feeling toward the Government of some of the most powerful native Tribes, and of the emigrant farmers in the Orange River Sovereignty and the adjacent territory, rendered it, as we thought, necessary to afford to the Governor additional assistance of another kind.

It appeared to us that there must be some causes in operation which had not yet been ascertained, to account for the existence of the discontent which was described as prevailing so generally among the coloured inhabitants of the Colony; and we considered it to be of the greatest importance that these causes should be carefully investigated, in order that they might if possible be removed. The state of things in the Orange River Sovereignty gave us great alarm. The British Resident in that district appeared to have been drawn into a position, very different from that which we had been led to anticipate that he would maintain, when the assumption of sovereignty was sanctioned; and there seemed to be great danger that, in addition to the difficulties of the war in British Kafraria, we might find ourselves entangled in another war on the northern frontier. At the same time, any attempt to retire, under the apparent pressure of danger, even from a position which ought never to have been taken up, by creating an impression of our weakness, might increase our peril, since most of the powerful Tribes with which we had been brought into contact would probably, while they respected our power, continue to profess at least to be our friends, but would not be slow to attack us if they believed that we were no longer able to defend ourselves and to punish our assailants. If the small British force in the Sovereignty were hastily withdrawn, it was not unlikely that it might be followed into the Colony by the powerful tribes in that district, and that there might be a general rising against us, of all the coloured inhabitants of Southern Africa.

Hence it was of the utmost importance that no false step should be made on the northern frontier. It was to be inferred also, as well from the despatches of Sir Harry Smith as from those of his predecessors, that the difficulty of maintaining peace and order on this frontier arose in a great degree from the disputes with regard to the occupation of land, so constantly occurring among pastoral tribes, and that if the means of settling such disputes satisfactorily could be provided, the principal cause of disturbance would be removed. But it was obvious that the Governor must be so fully occupied in conducting the war, and the general business of the Colony, as to be totally unable to devote his personal attention either to an inquiry into the causes of the discontent of the coloured classes within the Colony, or to unravelling the complicated maze of the affairs of the northern frontier. The latter especially was a matter of not less difficulty than importance, from the extreme complexity of the conflicting claims and interests to be judged of and dealt with, and on the proper management of which it depended, whether the moral power and ascendency of the British Authorities should be maintained, or whether we should become involved in fresh hostilities, which would interfere with the vigorous prosecution of the war already raging.

For these reasons we thought it expedient that two Assistant Commissioners should be appointed, to act under Sir Harry Smith in his office of High Commissioner for the settlement of the affairs of the Border Tribes. Major Hogge and Mr. Owen were the gentlemen selected for the appointment, for which they possessed the great advantage of being well acquainted with the Colony and with the native Tribes ; while at the same time, as they had both left the Cape, and did not, in consequence of being appointed to the office they accepted, intend to remain there for more than a short time, they were less likely than any of the permanent residents, to have their judgement biassed by those party and personal animosities which are unfortunately too prevalent among the latter. Major Hogge, who had gone to the Cape as a Captain of the 7th Dragoon Guards, had in the former war served as Superintendent-General of native levies, and, by the great influence he possessed with the coloured classes and the confidence they reposed in him, he was enabled to raise a very considerable force, and to contribute most materially to the successful termination of the war. Mr. Owen had served with him, and afterwards had been at the head of a division of Kafir police, which situation he resigned for the purpose of returning to England. Both Sir Henry Pottinger and Sir Harry Smith had expressed a high opinion of the value of their services.

I cannot mention these appointments without saying, how deeply I was grieved by the intelligence of the death of Major Hogge, which reached this country in the month of August last. I had felt myself personally much indebted to both these gentlemen, for having accepted the office they undertook. I knew that they had done so, in compliance with my very earnest and strongly expressed wishes, at a great sacrifice of private comfort and convenience, solely from a sense of public duty, and a belief that they had it in their power to afford useful assistance to the Government, in the critical state of Southern Africa. I had seen much of them previously to their departure, I had derived great assistance from the valuable information they were able to give me, and I had formed a very high opinion of their judgement and

ability.   I had watched with interest their progress in
the Colony, of which, even after I left Office, I had the
means, from unofficial sources, of knowing something;
and I had observed with satisfaction, that the value
of their services had fully answered the expectations I
had formed.   It was therefore with much sorrow that
I received, through the newspapers, the unexpected
and afflicting intelligence of the death of Major Hogge.
I deeply deplored the loss thus sustained not only by
his family and his friends, but by his Country (for it
is not too much to say that a man of his ability and
of his character is a loss to his Country), while it could
not but occur to me as a painful reflection, that the
breaking up of his happy family circle had been occasioned, by his undertaking a duty which I had pressed
upon his acceptance.

I trust it may be some consolation to those who
must most feel his loss, to know that, short as was
the time he had been at the Cape, it was long
enough to enable him to perform a public service
of the very highest importance.   Though the information I possess is very imperfect, and derived in
great part from the local newspapers, still it is sufficient to satisfy me, that the prevention of a new war
in the Orange River Sovereignty, at a time when it
must have led to the most calamitous consequences,
is mainly owing to his exertions, and to the sound
judgement he showed in circumstances of no ordinary
difficulty ; and I believe almost the last act of his life
was to conclude an arrangement, calculated to secure

the peace of that part of Africa.   Such seems to be the
opinion generally entertained by the inhabitants, who
have good reason to respect his memory, as that of
one to whom they are deeply indebted.   I trust that
his untimely death may not lead to the disturbance
of the peace he had established and the arrangements
he had made.   As I know that you were, like myself,
well acquainted with Major Hogge, and that you appreciated his merits, I am sure you will not think that
I have digressed too far from the subject immediately
before me, in thus expressing my feelings with respect
to him.

I will not attempt to give any account of the events
of the war, which are sufficiently known, to render it
needless for me to enter into so painful a topic.   I
must however express my great admiration of the
general conduct of the troops during this protracted
struggle, in which their gallantry, their discipline, and
their cheerful endurance of extreme fatigue have been
entitled to the greatest praise ; and it is not without
reluctance that I abstain from mentioning the names
of some officers who appear to me particularly to have
distinguished themselves, from the apprehension that
my doing so might appear invidious towards others.   I
must also express the satisfaction with which I learn,
from the newspapers, that at length the war may be
considered virtually at an end, and the enemy completely subdued, which has, I understand, been effected
without any additional troops having been sent out, or
any change in the arrangements which we had made,

and the instructions we had given previously to our retirement from Office. The present war will have been concluded by the measures we had directed, in about the same number of months from its commencement as it took to finish the war we found raging when your Administration was formed.

Having referred to the arrangements we had made before we retired from office, I cannot avoid mentioning that these arrangements included the recall of Sir Harry Smith. But I will only say on this subject, that it was with the greatest reluctance we came to the conclusion that it was necessary to submit to the Queen the advice we did. It was most painful to our feelings to do so, but on a question of this kind we were not at liberty to consult our private feelings. This was fully understood by Sir Harry Smith himself, of whose most handsome and honourable conduct I cannot too strongly express my sense. He has shown no resentment against us for what we did, but has fairly given us credit for having been guided only by considerations of public duty. I feel individually very deeply indebted to him, for the kindness with which he has acted towards me since his return, and for the readiness he has shown to believe, that no want of regard for him on my part is implied by the painful measure which was taken, and of which, though it was approved by you and by our colleagues, the chief responsibility necessarily rests with myself.

I cannot leave the subject of the Kafir war, without making some further observations on the policy which has been adopted, and on that which may be followed in future. It is impossible not to perceive, that a general feeling exists in this Country, that the Colony is not worth the sacrifices it imposes upon us, and that it was a grievous error to get entangled in a situation in which such sacrifices are required. With a third costly and troublesome war, hardly yet finished, less than twenty years after the commencement of the first, it certainly is not surprising that such a feeling should exist. Few persons would probably dissent from the opinion, that it would be far better for this Country if the British territory in South Africa were confined to Cape Town and to Simon's Bay. But however burdensome the Nation may find the possession of its African dominions, it does not follow that it can now cast them off, consistently with its honour or its duty. It has incurred responsibilities, by the measures of former years, which cannot be so lightly thrown aside.

If from the moment of the conquest of the Cape from the Dutch, the British Government had resolutely adhered to the policy of preventing any advance of the then Colonial frontier, and of limiting, instead of increasing, the extent of territory that was occupied by British subjects, I believe it would not have been impossible (though certainly it would have been very difficult) by judicious measures to have accomplished this object.

But a very different policy was pursued, and in the year 1819 more especially, a measure was adopted to which a great part of the difficulties which have since arisen may be traced. In that year the Chancellor of the Exchequer proposed to the House of Commons that a grant of £50,000 should be made, to enable the Government to assist unemployed workmen in this Country in removing to one of our Colonies; and, in doing so, he stated that the south-eastern coast of Africa had been selected as the place where this experiment was to be tried, in consequence of the natural advantages it was supposed to possess. The grant was made with the general concurrence of all parties; even Mr. Hume, with all his love of economy, expressing only regret that Ministers had not gone further, and saying that, from the excellent climate of the Cape and the fertility of the soil, the greatest advantages could not fail to result from the proposed Settlement. Accordingly about five thousand emigrants from this Country were sent to the Cape, and established in the district of Albany, at an expense of more than £120,000*.

These Settlers were thus sent out by the express act of the Government, with the cordial approbation

---

* The following were the charges incurred:—

By the Navy and Victualling Boards, for conveying and victualling Settlers	£86,760
Rations issued in the Colony	19,833
Public Buildings	15,925
	£122,518

(See Accounts laid before the House of Commons in 1821, and the extracts printed for Parliament, from the Report of Commissioners of Inquiry at the Cape of Good Hope, of May 25, 1825.)

of Parliament, to inhabit a territory immediately adjoining that occupied by numerous tribes of warlike savages, to whom their property was sure speedily to become as irresistible an object of attraction, as, little more than two centuries ago, the cattle of the inhabitants of the county in which I am now writing (Northumberland) used to be to the Moss-trooper across the Scottish Border. Indeed the Tribes of Southern Africa seem to regard cattle-stealing much in the same light that it was considered by those Border freebooters, whose exploits form the subject of the ballads collected by Sir Walter Scott; and, instead of looking upon it as a crime, or something to be ashamed of, they view it as the natural and most honourable pursuit for brave men to follow. With such neighbours close to them, the Albany Settlers were also established by the Government of the day, in such a manner as to render the protection of their property peculiarly difficult. Instead of being collected together in villages, so as to have been able to combine with facility for their common defence, they were scattered over the country, each family on its separate farm; and, as the grants of land were large, the extent of territory thus occupied, and requiring to be guarded, became very large in proportion to the population. The natural consequence was, that almost as soon as they were fairly established on their land, and had acquired some property in cattle, they began to suffer from the depredations of the Kafirs; and as early as 1822 this came to be a subject of bitter complaint. From that time to this, these de-predations have continued, with but few and short intervals; and on three occasions in the last twenty years they have led to fierce and desolating wars, for all these wars have arisen directly or indirectly from the desire of plunder on the part of the Kafirs.

Such being the origin of the obligation, which this Country has hitherto acknowledged, to protect the Cape frontier, it can hardly be at once assumed that, because the responsibility is become very burden-some, we are entitled to throw it off and leave the Settlers to shift for themselves as best they can. Notwithstanding all the difficulties and dangers with which they have had to contend, the comparatively small number of the original emigrants is now largely increased; and the European population of the eastern districts was ascertained, by the Census of 1849, to exceed 34,000*, while the property they have accumu-lated by their industry was estimated by Sir Henry Young, in 1848, at considerably more than four millions and a half †. Can British subjects possess-ing this amount of property, having been placed by the Government and Parliament in a situation of so much danger, be now abandoned to the mercy of their barbarous neighbours? No doubt they ought to be called upon to exert themselves for their own defence; no doubt they ought not to be allowed

---

* See House of Commons Sessional Paper of 1852, No. 124.

† See Sir H. Young's evidence before the Committee of the House of Lords on emigration from Ireland.

indefinitely to extend the area over which they are to spread, with the expectation of being guarded by us, and those who choose to occupy land beyond the authorized boundaries of the Colony, must do so at their own risk. But it does not appear to me that, within the limits of the territory which has been acquired by the Crown, and where subjects of the Crown have been established as Settlers by means of a Parliamentary grant, they can, without great disgrace to the Country, be refused the military aid which is necessary for their protection.

But it is said, let them manage their own affairs, and they will easily protect themselves; they are not less able to do so than the Settlers in the western parts of the United States. Nothing can be more fallacious than such an argument. The North American Indians are for the most part tribes of hunters; their numbers therefore are necessarily very small in comparison to the territory they occupy, and the force which any Indian Chief can bring into the field is far less numerous, as well as infinitely less formidable in character, than that of the Kafirs, which includes both cavalry and infantry. The Settlers in the Western States of the Union are also generally engaged in the cultivation of corn, and consequently occupy the territory in a manner which enables them to defend themselves and their property more easily than if their chief dependence was on their flocks and herds, like that of the farmers of Southern Africa. It appears likewise that in some parts of the Union, the support of the troops of the General Government is indispensable to the Settlers, and, among other places, on the borders of California and of Texas, this aid is afforded to them.

I do not however dispute its being likely that in the end, if left to themselves, the superior intelligence and civilization of the European inhabitants of Southern Africa would prevail against their barbarous neighbours; but it would only be by waging against them a war of extermination, to which they would be driven in self-defence, and in which they would suffer as well as inflict infinite misery, before it was brought to what would probably be its close. The United States, which are quoted as an example for our guidance, seem to me in this matter rather to afford us a warning. For my own part I confess I should grieve to think that the ultimate occupation of Southern Africa by a civilized population was only to be accomplished, like that of North America, by the gradual destruction of the native races, before the advancing tide of a White occupation of the soil. I believe that, instead of this, the civilization of the Black, and the ultimate amalgamation of the two races, is not impracticable, if the superior power of this Country is wisely and generously used to enforce on both sides a respect for each other's rights, and to foster all those germs of improvement which are already showing themselves among the aboriginal population. I can see no reason why, what has already been so far accomplished in New Zealand, should not be so likewise in Africa. Nor do I think that a Christian Nation would be justified, in throwing off the responsibility which Providence has cast on the British Government, by the power placed in its hands in this part of Africa, and in deliberately, and with open eyes, incurring the fearful consequences which must arise, from leaving the Settlers and the Kafirs to struggle for possession of the soil.

I must add, that looking to the success for nearly three years of the measures adopted in British Kafraria, after the termination of the last war, I see no reason for doubting (in spite of subsequent disasters) that without any heavy expense the Kafirs might be so governed as to maintain peace and order amongst them until civilization could fairly take root. I believe (and the experience gained in Natal confirms my opinion) that the policy adopted with this view was right in itself, though, from errors in its execution, it has failed for a time. I think I can see what those errors were, and, from the experience which has been gained, they might be avoided in future. In so difficult an enterprise as that of endeavouring to reclaim and civilize a barbarous people, it is only natural that there should be mistakes at first; nor ought partial failures in the beginning, to discourage us from persevering in attempts which have so high and noble an object. Before I quit the subject of the Kafir war, I must quote the opinion of one whose position and personal character combine to make him a high authority on the subject. The Bishop of Cape Town concludes his interesting journal of one of his Visitation tours, which was published some time ago, with the following observations :—

" I feel it right to express here my firm conviction, that neither the present Kafir war, nor the rebellion of the Hottentots, has been brought about by any oppression on the part of the Government of this Country. There are features in our border policy of which I cannot approve; but our government of British Kafraria has been wise, just, and humane. We have, it is true, held military possession of the country; it was essential to our own safety that we should; but we have not interfered with the government of the Chiefs more than was absolutely necessary; and when we have interfered, it has been to protect the oppressed. The real causes which have led to the present war with the Kafirs are, 1st, that, under the system which was established, the Chiefs' power was gradually fading away; 2nd, cattle-stealing was put a stop to by a very efficient police; 3rd, the distress consequent upon the severe drought of last year; and 4th, a knowledge of our internal divisions, and the alienation of feeling between the white and coloured races, and between the English and the Dutch. For the Hottentot rebellion there is no excuse whatever. The rebels of the Kat River had had one of the finest parts of the country given to them to live on; Government dealt most liberally with them. Sobriety and industry would have

enabled them to take their place among the landed
proprietors of the country. That the white man has
failed in his duty to the coloured races in South
Africa, the Christian to the heathen, I do not deny;
I feel it to be a great reproach. But whatever may
be the amount of his shortcoming in this respect, it
would be a grievous wrong to assign it as a justification of the rebellion which has spread over so large a
portion of the eastern province."

I am persuaded that in this passage the Bishop has
taken a most accurate view of the subject. I have no
doubt that, with regard to the Kafirs, all the causes
he mentions contributed to produce the outbreak
which so unfortunately occurred; and I think it may
be worth while to insert in the Appendix a despatch*
which, on receiving Sir Harry Smith's report that the
first alarm had passed away, I addressed to him, for
the purpose of pointing out the steps which might be
taken to conciliate the Chiefs, without whose assistance, I believe with Sir Henry Pottinger, that it will
be very difficult, if not impossible, to govern such a
population, and whose enmity must be a source of
extreme danger, so long as the feeling of clanship is
as strong as it now is among these Tribes.

What I have thought it necessary to say of the
Cape has extended to so much length, that I must
confine myself to a very slight notice of the affairs of

---

* See, in the Appendix (E), Despatch to Sir H. Smith of January
7, 1851.

the dependent Settlement of Natal, though there is much that is interesting in its history during the last six years. Within that period provision has been made by a revenue, raised within the Settlement, for all the expenses of its civil government, which had previously been met in great part by advances from the Treasury of the Cape of Good Hope and from the Military Chest*. These advances have been repaid, and the civil administration of Natal has been carried on, without our having been compelled to apply to Parliament for pecuniary assistance, which, I must be permitted to say, is a circumstance not a little out of the usual course, as well as highly satisfactory, considering how short a time it is since the territory was taken possession of, and how little progress had been made, in 1846, in organizing a Government capable of maintaining itself. In the last six years the troublesome and perplexing questions relating to land, which had arisen from the measures previously adopted, have also been settled, and a very considerable number of emigrants from this Country have been sent to Natal.

A part of the revenue, by which the necessary expenditure of the Colony has been defrayed, has been raised by a direct tax of seven shillings a-year imposed upon each native hut, from which source an income

* See, in the Papers relating to Natal presented in 1850 and 1851, Sir Harry Smith's despatches of September 12, 24, 1849, and of April 15, 1851, with their enclosures.

of nearly £9000 was derived in the first year of its being levied, and which has since, I believe, been still more productive*. I would particularly call your attention to the imposition of this tax, as a measure of very much greater importance than it would appear to be from the mere amount of the revenue realized by it, though this was far from being of slight moment to such an infant Colony. The tax derived its chief importance, from its forming an essential part of a general scheme of policy for the civilization and improvement of the native inhabitants of Natal, of whom it is proper therefore that I should give a short account.

Very few indeed of these people belong to tribes which inhabited the territory now included in the Colony of Natal even fifty years ago†; the population which then existed there having been almost entirely exterminated or driven away, in the bloody wars, of which this part of Africa has been the scene. The present native inhabitants of the Settlement, who are estimated at not less than 100,000, consist for the most part of broken tribes or individuals who have fled from the tyranny of the more powerful Chiefs of that part of Africa, and have sought shelter in the British dominions. They are of a Kafir race, and speak a dialect of the same language as the tribes with whom we have been at war on the Cape frontier;

---

* See in the above Papers Sir Harry Smith's despatches of July 31, August 31, and September 12, 1849 ; of February 26 and October 30, 1850 ; and of April 15, 1851.

† See Natal Papers of August, 1850, p. 45.

they are probably even more uncivilized than the latter but, like them, are a pastoral people, and possess a considerable number of cattle.

Such being the native population of Natal, it is obvious that, if they were allowed to continue uncivilized and unimproved, adhering to the barbarous customs of their ancestors, while living in the midst of the European Settlers, they could not fail to prove an intolerable nuisance to the latter. They would become a source of danger, which would daily grow more serious, as by natural increase and fresh immigrations their numbers augmented, beyond what the lands, that could without inconvenience be assigned to them, would be sufficient to support, when occupied after the manner of savages. On the other hand, if they could gradually be brought under the influence of religion and of education, and could be made to exchange their barbarous habits for those of civilized life, the presence of these people would be the greatest possible advantage to the Colonists, by affording them a supply of labour, which is urgently required, and which alone is wanting to render a territory possessing remarkable natural advantages productive. With the habits of civilized life, these people would also naturally acquire the wants and the tastes belonging to it, and would thus create a demand for articles of European manufacture which would increase both the trade and revenue of the Colony.

The improvement of the native inhabitants being of this vital importance, the measures proposed for effecting it were founded upon precisely the same principles which I have already fully explained in speaking of the Negro population of the West Indies. For the reasons I have there stated, the levy of a direct tax upon these people was considered an indispensable part of the system to be pursued, as well with the view of creating a motive for exertion, as with that of raising the pecuniary means, which could hardly otherwise have been found, for the payment of magistrates, and for providing the requisite establishment for the management of so large a population. It was obviously just, that the inhabitants of the surrounding districts, who have flocked into the British territory (sometimes from very great distances) for the sake of the protection they enjoy there, should be required to defray the expenses it was necessary to incur, in order to render it possible to grant them the protection they desired, without injury to the Colony. The justice of this was felt by themselves, and they consequently paid the tax (which they were allowed to do, when they preferred it, in cattle instead of in money) with readiness and goodwill.

For a full exposition of the further measures which were contemplated for the improvement of the native population of Natal, I must refer you to a despatch which I addressed to Sir Harry Smith* on the 30th

* The instructions contained in this Despatch were modified in some particulars by a later one; but as the last has not yet been laid before Parliament, I am unable to quote it. See Appendix (F) to this Volume.

of November, 1849, which I insert in the Appendix.
I will only add, upon this interesting subject, that
though the results aimed at by our policy can only
be very slowly and gradually attained, and though,
from the necessity of proceeding with extreme caution, in the introduction of changes affecting so large
and so barbarous a population, the measures we proposed have as yet been brought only very partially
into operation, it is satisfactory to know that they
have already so far succeeded as to prevent the war,
which has so long raged in British Kafraria and on
the Cape frontier, from extending into Natal. In
that Settlement the war, which has been raging at
so small a distance, has had no bad effect beyond that
of creating some temporary alarm, the native inhabitants having continued to pay a ready and cheerful
obedience to the Government, and good order and
security having never ceased to be maintained. If
these blessings of peace and order can be preserved,
I feel persuaded that, under their shelter, every other
improvement will gradually grow up ; and I trust I
am not too sanguine in believing that, although, for
many years to come, the affairs of Natal will require
to be watched with the most anxious attention, to
guard against the various abuses and dangers which,
in such a state of society, are likely from time to time
to arise, still, before your Administration was broken
up, the first and most difficult steps had been accomplished, in the adoption of a policy which, if duly

followed up, will ultimately lead to the civilization of the native inhabitants and the prosperity of the Colony.

December 16, 1852.

LETTER XIII.

HONGKONG.—LABUAN.—FALKLAND ISLANDS.—WEST
COAST OF AFRICA.—MALTA.—CONCLUDING OBSER-
VATIONS.

My dear Lord John,

I have now gone through all the Colonies of
which the affairs require to be noticed at any length;
those which remain to be mentioned are chiefly valuable from serving as factories and trading-stations,
or as naval and military posts, and may be dismissed
much more briefly.

The first I will mention is Hongkong. The chief
subject we had to consider with respect to this Island
was that of the very heavy expense which it occasioned to the Country. If the exceedingly large
amount of that expense, and the limited use of which
the place has proved to our commerce, could have
been foreseen, it may well be doubted whether it
would have been thought worth while that it should
be taken possession of. This had however been done
long prior to the formation of your Administration;

and it only remained for us to endeavour to reduce the expense of the establishment, which had been formed on a scale suited to the supposed importance of Hongkong, at a time when it was confidently anticipated that it would become the great emporium of the Chinese trade. In 1846 it was already obvious that this would not be the case, and that the greater part of our commerce with China would be carried on in the ports of that country to which our merchants are admitted. The reduction of the establishment of a Colony, which has originally been formed on too large and costly a scale, must always, for obvious reasons, be a work of much difficulty; but I trust that, without the slightest injustice, or even harshness to any individual, and with no sacrifice except that of our own patronage, we succeeded in effecting a satisfactory reduction of the large expenditure of the Country at Hongkong.

By a despatch from the Governor, Sir Samuel Bonham, which was printed with the miscellaneous estimates laid before Parliament in the year 1851, it is shown that the vote required for the service of this Colony, which had been £49,000 in 1845 and £36,900 in 1846, has since been progressively reduced to £15,500 in 1851. A considerable part of this reduction is due to the diminished expenditure on public works; but the Governor shows, in the despatch to which I refer, that, excluding the charge for public works in both years, the estimated expenditure of the Colony for 1851 was £5068 less than that of 1848, when he assumed the government of the Colony, and his predecessor, Sir John Davis, reported in 1847 that he had previously effected permanent retrenchments, in salaries alone, to the amount of £2800 a-year*. There was a further reduction in the estimate voted in the last Session, but this consists principally in a transfer of half the Governor's salary to the estimate for consular services. The military expenditure at Hongkong has also been largely reduced : in 1847 it amounted to £115,149 ; in 1851 it was only £51,895†. This reduction is owing, partly to the completion of military works and buildings, and to the determination not to undertake others that had been projected, partly to a considerable diminution of the Garrison. I have only to add, with regard to Hongkong, that its trade and importance appear to be increasing, and that it is generally in a satisfactory condition.

Another trading port which we possess in the Eastern Seas is that of Labuan. On our accession to Office we found that memorials, earnestly praying that it might be occupied, with a view to opening a commercial intercourse with the large and imperfectly known Island of Borneo, had been addressed to the Government from more than one quarter, and especially by the Chamber of Commerce of Manchester, and by the merchants of both London and Glasgow.

* See Sir John Davis's Despatch of March 13, 1847. (Blue Book Reports presented in 1847.)

† See Blue Book Reports presented in 1848 and 1852.

We were of opinion that the reasons urged for this step were sufficient to make it proper to adopt it, and accordingly arrangements were made for taking possession of Labuan (which had been previously ceded to this Country) as a British Colony.   Sir James Brooke, so well known for his philanthropic and enterprising attempts to introduce civilization into Borneo, was appointed Governor of Labuan, and at the same time Consul in Borneo.

Hitherto the advantage derived from the formation of this Settlement has not been so great as was anticipated; partly, as it appears, because piracy still prevails on the coast of Borneo, enough to check the native trade; partly because the coal which exists in the Island, and which afforded one of the principal reasons for taking possession of it, has not yet been worked to the extent which was expected; the Company, to which a portion of the coal-field was let, not having hitherto carried on its operations with sufficient energy to supply even the present demand*. This last obstacle to the progress of the Colony will probably be removed, either by the transfer of the business of the Company into different hands, or by other persons obtaining a lease of another portion of the coal-field.   From the rapidly increasing demand for coals for steam-navigation in the Eastern Seas, I had hoped that before we left Office an application for another part of the coal-field, which is still in the hands of the Crown, might have been made; but

* See Blue Book Report presented to Parliament in 1852.

none had then been received; it is not however probable that so favourable an opening for enterprise will long be neglected. There appears to be some reason to believe that a commercial intercourse between Labuan and Borneo is at length beginning, which may by degrees be extended.

There is another small Establishment, which was formed for the convenience of our commerce in a different part of the world, which I must not pass entirely unnoticed. I refer to the Falkland Islands, which have long been claimed as belonging to the British Crown, but of which no use had been made, until it was determined to occupy them, when you held the office of Secretary of State for the Colonies. The object of doing so was to create a small Settlement where passing ships might refit and obtain supplies, for which these Islands, notwithstanding the inclemency of their climate, were considered to be peculiarly well adapted, from their possessing admirable harbours, and lying directly in the track of vessels returning to this Country from Australia or the Pacific by Cape Horn. They also afforded considerable resources in the herds of wild cattle which are to be found upon them. These cattle, being the property of the Crown, were sold to Mr. Lafone, an enterprising merchant, engaged in the commerce of the River Plate; and a considerable sum of money, to be paid in instalments, was thus placed at the disposal of the Government for the improvement of the Islands.

During the five years and a half of your Administration, few measures of importance were adopted with reference to the Falkland Islands. A portion of the money paid by Mr. Lafone for the wild cattle, was expended in sending out a small party of military pensioners, (who have not proved by any means such good settlers as those sent to New Zealand); and an arrangement was concluded by which a regular communication will be established between this Country and the Falkland Islands, by means of a small vessel plying between these Islands and Monte Video, where it will meet the mail-steamer from England every alternate month. A charter has also been granted to a Company formed by Mr. Lafone, to which he has transferred the undertaking, which was previously entirely in his own hands, and he has thus obtained the assistance of additional capital for the enterprise in which he has embarked.

Hitherto this Settlement has not advanced rapidly; probably it could hardly have been expected to do so, unless a larger expenditure had been incurred than was considered advisable, in carrying out and establishing emigrants there; but it seems now to have taken root, and will, I trust, do well hereafter. Already, from the growing up of some little trade, and from land having been brought into cultivation, it has been found possible, in the last four years, to discontinue the issue of rations from the Government stores to the inhabitants, who can now purchase for themselves what they require. Those of the working-class can find ample employment at good wages, and ships which call there can depend upon obtaining the most necessary supplies. The advantages offered by this place of call on the long voyage home, are beginning to be known, so that each year more vessels are stopping there on their way; and, from the great increase of the trade with Australia and California, it is probable that the Port of Stanley (the name of the Settlement) will be more and more resorted to. I am informed that a ship wanting water or provisions, in the run home from Cape Horn, may save not less than from ten days to a fortnight, by calling at Stanley instead of Buenos Ayres or Rio de Janeiro, besides having no port charges to pay. In proportion as more vessels call for supplies, these will be furnished more abundantly and better, since private enterprise will be sure to meet the demand, which the greater resort of shipping to the port will create. It is to be hoped also that the means of refitting ships that have suffered in the stormy passage round Cape Horn, which already exist to some extent, will be increased in the same manner, and that a plan of establishing there a patent slip, which was at one time under consideration, with a view to its being undertaken by the Government, will be taken up as a private speculation.

But by far the most important of the British possessions held chiefly for commercial objects are those on the coast of Africa. It is painful to think that our oldest establishments in that part of the world are the forts originally occupied as slave-factories. I trust that the Nation is making the best reparation it can for its sins against Africa, by now maintaining these same forts as the most effectual check that can be put on the infamous traffic in slaves, which they were in former times intended to promote, and as centres from which legitimate trade, carrying with it civilization and the light of Christianity, may be spread through a large part of that great continent. Of the British possessions in Western Africa, the forts on the Gold Coast are those which seem to be producing the most effect, in the improvement and civilization of the hitherto barbarous inhabitants of Africa.

The position which is there occupied by this Country is very singular and anomalous. The British territory, properly so called, is confined to the forts, and the distance of a cannon-shot around them. Beyond this circle no dominion is claimed on behalf of the Crown ; but British influence and authority extend over an area of not less than 8000 square miles, constituting the territories of various native Chiefs, and inhabited by a population estimated at 400,000 souls at least*. Justice is administered to this large population, by their own consent and under the sanction of an Act of Parliament, by British magistrates. The principal of these magistrates is an officer who bears the somewhat strange title of the Judicial Assessor †,

---

* See Blue Book Report presented to Parliament in 1852.

† Nominally this officer is appointed as an assessor or assistant to the native Sovereigns or Chiefs in the countries adjacent to Her Majesty's forts and settlements on the Gold Coast. (See Blue Book Report presented in 1850.)

who sits principally at Cape Coast Castle, and exercises a superintendence over the proceedings of the magistrates who sit at the other forts. The population of the country under British influence and protection, bring their various disputes for decision before these magistrates, on whom the singular duty is imposed, of enforcing the rude laws and customs of so uncivilized a people, qualified only by those plain and universal principles of justice, which even the most ignorant races understand when explained to them.

It is an inevitable consequence of this system, that the British Authorities must tolerate much of which they do not approve. For instance, the custom of domestic slavery is too firmly established to be suddenly altered : it has been necessary to recognize its existence, and to be content with prohibiting the sale of a slave out of the country which is under British protection, and to enforce limits to the authority of the masters by taking cognizance of and punishing their ill-usage of their slaves. No other course can be taken, because our authority rests entirely on the moral ascendency of those who exercise it, and on the willing obedience of the population. The physical force at the command of the Governor consists of a mere handful of troops, generally not more than two or three companies of a West India regiment, which of course would be powerless amidst such a population, unless their obedience were voluntary. So entirely does the Governor of Cape Coast Castle depend for

the maintenance of his authority on the support of the
people themselves, that in the only case in which I
remember a recourse to arms to have been necessary,
Sir William Winniett, with only a very few Europeans
to assist him, conducted an expedition of about 5000
natives, against the Chief of Appolonia, whose extreme
tyranny, cruelty, and contempt of British authority
called for severe chastisement.   The tyrant was de-
posed and captured by this force, and the expenses of
the expedition were defrayed from his ill-gotten trea-
sures, of which he was deprived.

It is obvious that, such being the system which
prevails, it would be in the highest degree impolitic
to enforce at once all the laws we should think right,
and violently to abrogate all we disapprove, without
reference to the feelings of the people.   The attempt
to do so would undoubtedly provoke resistance to
our authority, and we should have neither the right
nor the means to enforce it.   Those who now willingly
obey the Governor and the magistrates appointed by
the Queen, within the limits sanctioned by opinion, are
not British subjects, and the attempt to reduce them
to the entire obedience, which as such, might be required from them, and to compel them by force to
submit to laws which they cannot be induced willingly to accept, would render it necessary to employ
a very large body of troops at an enormous expense,
and would after all probably fail.   By the system now
pursued, on the contrary, at a very small cost compared to the importance of the object to be attained,

a great amount of immediate good is effected, and the sure foundations are laid for much greater good being accomplished hereafter.

Already wars between the various Chiefs in the territory under our influence, have been completely put an end to, by the practice which has been established of bringing their quarrels and disputes to our magistrates for adjudication; and even the most powerful Chief, who should refuse to submit to the decision pronounced (so long as the decisions of the English magistrates are looked up to as they now are), would be crushed by a general combination against him. Thus for several years internal wars have ceased; and the dread of British power, and the knowledge that the united strength of all the Chiefs in the district we protect, directed by British officers and supported by a small disciplined force, would be promptly exerted to punish aggression upon any part of this territory, has been sufficient to restrain even the most powerful of the surrounding tribes or nations from attempting to injure those who acknowledge our authority. The Gold Coast has thus for several years enjoyed an exemption from war, whether external or intestine, while at the same time there has been a slow but constant mitigation of the oppression to which the bulk of the population of Africa is subject from their rulers.

The public administration of justice by the British magistrates, whose practice it is to explain the grounds of their decisions, has been a powerful instrument of improvement, by preventing the infliction of the barbarous punishments formerly in use, and by gradually diffusing more correct notions as to right and wrong, and as to what actions constitute offences which ought to be punished. It is only so lately as since the year 1849 that the important principle has been recognized that punishments ought not to be inflicted on persons accused of witchcraft, and that outrages committed upon those who have not conformed to the rules of the degrading superstition of the " Fetish" are to be regarded as giving the sufferers the like claim to redress as the same outrages committed under any other circumstances*. Those who are acquainted with African manners will easily see that the recognition of these rules at once puts an end to the most fertile source of oppression, and the most common pretence for the plunder, by the priests and chiefs, of those who have gained some little property by their industry.

By these means the security of life and property may be said to have been within a few years almost completely established; and this first great step towards improvement having been gained, the natural consequence is that trade and industry are daily increasing, and education and Missionary labours are successfully carried on under the shelter of the peace and order which are maintained. I anticipate that improvement will now proceed at a rate constantly accelerated; since a generation, many of whom have

* See Blue Book Report presented in 1850.

had the advantage of education in the Government or Missionary schools, have now risen to manhood, and are becoming the means of diffusing amongst their countrymen more or less of that instruction which they have themselves received. It is also a most important circumstance, as regards the prospects of future improvement, that the advantage of combining industrial with intellectual and religious instruction is now recognized by the Wesleyan Missionary body in this part of Africa. An exceedingly interesting report upon this subject by Mr. Freeman, the excellent and enlightened Missionary of the Wesleyan Society, will be found attached to the last general Report upon the condition of the Colony, which has been laid before Parliament. Mr. Freeman has pointed out with much clearness and ability the importance of the instruction of the people in agriculture, with a view to their civilization and moral improvement; and the experiments conducted under his direction prove beyond all doubt the remarkable fertility of the soil, and the ease with which many valuable productions of tropical climates can be raised there. Indeed the country seems so well adapted for producing various articles which are always sure to sell well in the markets of Europe, that, as security is now completely established and there appears to be no dearth of labour, this part of Africa seems to afford a very promising field for the application of English capital.

In the state of things I have described, it is, I think, obvious that the right policy for the Government to adopt, was to maintain the general system, which is working so well, and at the same time to take every opportunity of introducing improvements as fast as this could safely be done.   Such is the view which was acted upon, during the period of which I am treating in these Letters; and, without any great or sudden change having been made, various measures have been taken from time to time to promote the progress of improvement.   Of these not the least important is that to which I have just referred, as having put a stop to the infliction of punishment or violence, upon those who are accused of witchcraft, or who have broken the superstitious rules of the Fetish.   Though made under the guise of a decision of the Judicial Assessor, this is in truth the enactment of a new law, directed against one of the greatest evils under which the people of Africa laboured; and their acquiescence in the establishment of this law may be said, without exaggeration, both to afford a striking proof of their having already made a great step onwards in civilization, and also to have removed one of the most formidable obstacles to their future advance.   In like manner, by other decisions of the Judicial Assessor, the laws and customs which they recognize, are gradually and silently brought more into harmony with justice, and with the feelings and opinions of Christian nations.

This progressive improvement of the laws under which the people live, has been assisted by the establishment of a Legislative Council, with the concurrence of which the Governor can pass laws for the portion of territory which belongs to the Crown. Cape Coast Castle and the other British forts in its vicinity had latterly been considered a kind of dependency of Sierra Leone, and had been governed by an officer of no higher rank than that of Lieutenant-Governor, who possessed no legislative power whatever. This appeared to me an inconvenient arrangement, and accordingly the Queen was advised to grant to the late Sir William Winniett a commission as Governor, by which he was authorized, with the assistance of a Legislative Council, to pass ordinances for the British territory thus erected into a distinct Colony. It is true that these ordinances have, in strictness, the force of law only within the very limited space surrounding each fort, which is under the dominion of the Crown; but there can be little doubt that, in the state of society which I have endeavoured to describe, laws suited to its growing wants, when passed by the Governor of Cape Coast Castle, will practically be accepted as valid throughout the district which acknowledges our influence, though they are not legally binding beyond the reach of a cannon-shot from the walls of the forts. By a more recent arrangement, of which I shall have to speak before I close this Letter, this extension of the authority of such laws will be rendered easier.

We were also enabled during your Administration to do much towards consolidating the power and influence of this Country on the Gold Coast, by the acquisition of the Danish Forts, which are in close proximity to those previously belonging to us. The Government of Denmark, feeling that the maintenance of an establishment on the African coast was too heavy a burden for that kingdom, but being at the same time anxious that its forts should only pass into the hands of a Power by which they would certainly be used not to encourage, but as much as possible to check, the Slave-trade, very handsomely offered to cede these possessions to the Queen, in return for the payment of the value, at a very moderate estimate, of the guns and other property which were to be made over to us. Accordingly it was settled that the cession should be made on the purchase of the property in question, for the sum of £10,000, being completed, and we obtained from Parliament a grant by which this arrangement was carried into effect[*].

In connection with the acquisition of the Danish Forts it was determined that, instead of employing as heretofore, a part of one of the West India regiments on the Gold Coast, a local corps should be raised, to garrison the forts and supply the small military force necessary for the support of the authority of the Government. It was represented to me, both by the Governor and the merchants, that as the duties performed by the troops on this coast partake much of the nature of those of a police force, for the proper discharge of which an acquaint-

[*] See the Correspondence printed with the Miscellaneous Estimates, laid before Parliament in 1851.

ance with the people is necessary, the arrangement by which the forts had hitherto been garrisoned by detachments from the West India regiments, which it is necessary to relieve at short intervals, was not a convenient one, and that it would be much better that a local corps should be raised for the purpose. It was also stated that, while the Natives of this part of Africa cannot be prevailed upon to enlist in a West India regiment, with a prospect of being required to leave their own country, when the detachment they have joined may be moved to another station, there would be no difficulty in obtaining a very good class of recruits for a local corps. Such were the grounds on which it was decided that a force of this kind should be formed. It was further determined, that the men raised for it should not be confined entirely to military duties, but should receive as much as possible the same sort of instruction which is given in this country to the invaluable corps of Sappers and Miners, and that they should be employed in the various works required for keeping the forts in order, and also in making and repairing roads.

Sir William Winniett had already done a good deal, with comparatively small means, toward opening paths or roads on some of the most important lines of communication, and the Natives themselves were beginning to be sensible of the advantage to be derived from them. I attached the highest importance to this plan, of making the corps which was to be raised, act both as pioneers and as soldiers. The measure promised to afford the means of constructing, at a very moderate cost, roads, which are in all countries among the most efficient instruments of civilization, with the further advantage that the men composing the force would receive the very best industrial education that could be given to them, and, as they were only to be enlisted for five years, this education would be given, in the course of no very long time, to a considerable number of the Natives of the coast. At my request, a selection of officers and non-commissioned officers for the new corps was made by the Commander-in-Chief with a view to these objects.

These measures however fell far short of what it was desirable to accomplish for the improvement of this part of Africa. The extension of roads and of schools much beyond what could be accomplished by the means at present available, the employment of a greater number of magistrates for the more perfect administration of justice, and the establishment of hospitals and dispensaries for the relief of the sick, would have been attended with obvious and great advantage. But these objects could not be attained without a large increase of expense, and Parliament has always shown what I consider a well-founded reluctance to increase its votes for purposes of this description. It does not appear to me that the people of this Country, ought to be called upon to pay for the cost of extensive schemes of internal improvement in Africa. Experience shows that, if the Government of the day is allowed to draw at its discretion upon Parliamentary grants for such schemes, they are too apt to be prosecuted without a due regard to economy, or to that caution which is necessary for their ultimate success. I have always believed that if Parliament had originally been less liberal in its pecuniary assistance, the philanthropic objects contemplated in the formation of the Colony of Sierra Leone would probably have been more perfectly attained. Parliament is, I think, right, to be very sparing in its grants for purposes of this kind, not merely for the sake of avoiding undue demands upon the people of this Country, but also because the surest test of the soundness of measures for the improvement of an uncivilized people, is that they should be self-supporting; and great advantage arises from throwing those who are to carry plans of this kind into effect upon their own resources. The people also, for whose benefit such measures are attempted, are rendered more sensible of their value when the pecuniary means required for their adoption are furnished by themselves.

For these reasons, I considered myself bound to adhere to the rule of not proposing to my colleagues, that Parliament should be asked to increase the usual grants for the civil establishments on the West Coast of Africa; and though I was most anxious for the adoption of measures of improvement, which could not be accomplished without considerable expense, I thought it right, in this part of the African continent as well as in Natal, to proceed with these measures only, as their cost could be provided for by means of local resources.   Hence it was an object of great importance to raise a revenue in the country itself; and two modes of doing so suggested themselves: one was the imposition of very moderate duties on the import of certain articles, and particularly spirits; the other was, to induce the people of the protected territory to consent to the imposition of some sort of direct taxation, for objects of which the benefit could be clearly explained to them.

The first of these resources could not be made available, in consequence of the refusal of the Dutch Government to concur in the imposition of any new duties of the kind proposed.   The kingdom of Holland possesses forts on this coast close to our own, through which a part of the trade of the district is carried on; it is obvious therefore that, unless goods imported to these places should be subject to the same burden, the imposition of duties on goods imported through the British forts, would have no other effect but that of driving the trade away from the latter, to places where no such charges on importation would be made.   It was consequently necessary to look to some kind of direct taxation, as the only mode of raising the revenue which was required, and as being also one which, for the reasons I have so fully stated in former Letters, possessed some special advantages. But the difficulty was how to impose any such taxation, in the absence of any regularly constituted government for the whole territory. It clearly could only be done by the general consent of the chiefs and people; and I had many conversations with Sir William Winniett, the last time he was in England upon leave of absence, and after his death with his successor Major Hill, as to the most likely means of obtaining this general assent. The subject was not one which admitted of precise instructions being given to the Governor as to the measures he should take; these it was necessary to leave to be determined by his own judgement on the spot, after having explained the object in view and made the suggestions which occurred to me.

The premature and lamented death of Sir William Winniett prevented him from taking any steps of importance, in furtherance of the design of which the execution had been entrusted to him; but I have learned with great satisfaction since we retired from Office, that his successor, Major Hill, has given proof both of the ability which I did not doubt that he possessed, and of how well he had entered into the policy on which he had been instructed to act, by inducing the Chiefs of the Gold Coast to agree to the imposition of such a tax as I had contemplated. Knowing the deep interest I take in the subject, Major Hill was good enough to write me a private letter after he had received an account of the change of Government in February last, in which he informed me that he had succeeded in inducing the Chiefs and people throughout the countries under British protection, to agree to a poll-tax of one shilling per head for each man, woman, and child, by which he calculates that a revenue of £20,000 a year will be obtained, to be expended in extending the judicial system, educating the children, offording increased medical aid to the population, opening and improving the internal communications, and other measures of utility. Considering that the whole annual income derived from the votes of Parliament and from all other sources, applicable to measures of improvement and the expenses of the civil government, has hitherto fallen short of £6000, it is obvious that the adoption of a measure by which the funds available for these purposes will be so largely increased, is calculated to accelerate very much the march of improvement. I cannot but regard with great satisfaction the success which, in three different countries so widely removed from each other as Ceylon, Natal, and the Gold Coast, has thus far attended the experiment of imposing direct taxation on an uncivilized population, with a view to their improvement. The experiment is a novel one in modern Colonial administration, and is the practical realization of views which I was led to form more than twenty years ago when Under-Secretary of State, and on which at that time I earnestly, but in vain, recommended that the measure for the abolition of slavery should be founded.

But even the imposition of the tax I have mentioned is of less importance, and less full of promise for the future, than the steps which have been taken in order to obtain an authority for its collection, which should be regarded by the people as binding upon them. For this purpose, and with a view to future legislation, the Governor thought it advisable to form the native Chiefs, with his Council and himself, into a Legislative Assembly, reserving the power to the Governor to assemble, prorogue, and dissolve this meeting at pleasure. On the 19th of April last, Major Hill had a general meeting of the Kings and Chiefs of the protected territory at Cape Coast Castle, when they unanimously agreed to resolutions by which the authority of the new Assembly was recognized and its constitution settled.

I have had no hesitation in thus stating the substance of the information I have received from Major Hill, for, though it was conveyed to me in a private letter, the proceedings he describes were essentially of a public character, and necessarily known to every person on the coast. I must add that I am much gratified by learning, that a design which I had so long entertained, and in effecting which there were so many difficulties, has been thus successfully accomplished by Major Hill. I am persuaded I do not overrate the importance of the establishment of this rude Negro Parliament, when I say, that I believe it has converted a number of barbarous tribes, possessing nothing which deserves the name of a government, into a nation, with a regularly organized authority, and institutions simple and unpretending, but suited to the actual state of society, and containing within themselves all that is necessary for their future development, so that they may meet the growing wants of an advancing civilization. I trust that those whose duty it may be to watch over the future progress of the nation, which has thus, as I may say, been created, will endeavour to guard it carefully from the dangers to which it will be exposed, either by an attempt on the one hand to force too rapidly into existence, before the people's minds are prepared for them, the more regular government and more perfect laws of civilized nations, or by neglecting, on the other hand, to proceed steadily but cautiously with those many social and legal reforms which must be successively adopted, before the traces of recent barbarism and its evils can be got rid of.

The true policy I believe to be that, which for the five years and a half of your Administration was pursued,—namely, to keep constantly in sight the formation of a regular government on the European model, and the establishment of a civilized polity, as the goal ultimately to be attained; but, in the endeavour to arrive at it, taking care that each successive step shall appear to the people themselves as nothing more than the natural mode of providing for some want, or remedying some evil, which they practically feel at the moment. It is thus in fact that our own institutions and laws have grown up, as well as those which have been most permanent and most successful among other nations. Thus, in adopting the measure to which I have adverted on the Gold Coast, wants of which the people were sensible, and to meet which funds were required, have by judicious management led them to concur not only in the imposition of a tax, but in the creation of a Legislature possessing the authority to make other laws, as from time to time they are perceived to be necessary. The real interest of this Country is gradually to train the inhabitants of this part of Africa in the arts of civilization and government, until they shall grow into a nation capable of protecting themselves and of managing their own affairs, so that the interference and assistance of the British Authorities may by degrees be less and less required. Orderly and civilized communities cannot grow up in a country capable of yielding such valuable productions, without our carrying on with them a large and mutually advantageous trade; but in a climate so uncongenial to European constitutions, it is not desirable that the maintenance of order and the progress of civilization should continue to depend on the exercise of authority by white men, or that the duty of governing and protecting the inhabitants of Western Africa should be thrown upon this Country longer than can be avoided.

The British Settlement on the Gambia differs considerably in its character from those on the Gold Coast. The Governor of the former does not exercise any authority over the surrounding population, such as that which I have described as having been established at Cape Coast Castle. But, on the other hand, Bathurst on the Gambia is the trading-port of a navigable river, affording means of intercourse with the interior of Africa to a distance of several hundred miles. To the trade of this noble river comparative security has been given by the small British force at Bathurst and Macarthy's Island, with the assistance of a steamer, which has for several years been placed at the disposal of the local Government. This comparative security has produced its usual effect, in giving encouragement to trade and industry, among the inhabitants of the countries through which the Gambia flows. A satisfactory account of the improvement which is going on in these countries will be found in the very interesting final Report* of the late Governor, Mr. Macdonnell, who, after having administered the affairs of this Colony with great judgement and energy for between four and five years, seemed to me well entitled to the reward of being removed to a less unhealthy climate, and was therefore, on my advice, on the eve of my retirement from office, appointed Lieutenant-Governor of St. Vincent.

One of the most remarkable and encouraging circumstances mentioned by Governor Macdonnell is, that the population of this part of Africa has shown a far greater disposition to engage in agriculture with perseverance and industry, than seems to have been evinced anywhere else on that continent. The Go-

* See Blue Book Reports presented in 1852.

vernor states that ground-nuts, which are the principal article of export from the Gambia, are raised chiefly by the natives of countries far in the interior, who come down for two or three years to the lower part of the river, where they hire land from the various Chiefs on its banks, for the cultivation of the plant which produces these nuts; and having thus by their industry earned the means of purchasing the European goods it is their object to obtain, they carry them back with them to their own country. It is obvious that a trade so conducted, must have a powerful effect in carrying some knowledge of civilized life and manners far into the interior of Africa.

So rapidly has this branch of industry grown up to its present importance, that the quantity of ground-nuts raised in the countries bordering on the Gambia, and exported from Bathurst, was no more than 47 tons in 1837, while in 1851 the quantity exported (including 1000 tons sent from the French factory of Albreda) had risen to 12,094 tons, valued at £145,133. The Governor points out, that nothing but a market, affording a fair and steady profit for the produce of agricultural labour, seems to be wanting, in order to ensure an almost indefinite increase in the exports from the Gambia, which of course would lead to a corresponding augmentation of the consumption of articles of European manufacture. A steady demand for the produce of their industry would, he says, cause the Natives from the interior to flock to the Gambia in increased numbers; as the experience of past years shows, that the number of additional labourers who annually migrate from the interior to Bathurst and the surrounding territories, has always been proportioned to the demand for the produce of labour.

This being the case, the Governor seems justified in his conclusion, that cotton might be grown largely and successfully on the banks of the Gambia. All that is required for this purpose, is a steady demand and some little instruction and encouragement to be given, in the first instance, to those who may be willing to undertake the cultivation. Cotton being longer in coming to maturity than ground-nuts, the latter are naturally preferred by those who are ignorant of the advantages presented by the former; but if, as there seems reason to believe, the value of cotton would be amply remunerative, for the time and labour expended on its cultivation, it can hardly be doubted that the population, which is now found to be ready to cultivate ground-nuts to the extent of the demand, might, by judicious management, be led to cultivate cotton also. The cotton-plant is known to thrive admirably in this part of Africa, and land fit for its cultivation is to be had in abundance. The establishment of this as a regular branch of industry in Africa, would, in my opinion, be at once the most certain means of civilizing its inhabitants, and one of the greatest boons which could be conferred upon this country. There is no article of production to which the labour of the Africans could be so advantageously applied, because there is none of which it is so impossible that the supply should exceed the demand ; and to this Country it is of vital importance to multiply as much as possible the sources of our supply of cotton, since from the very large part of our population who are now directly or indirectly dependent upon its manufacture, a short crop of cotton in the United States is become to us almost as great a national calamity as a deficient harvest at home.

I have therefore always taken a deep interest in the attempt to extend the cultivation of cotton in Africa, and I should have wished measures to be adopted to promote it by your Administration, had I not been persuaded that, as a general rule, the direct interference of a Government to encourage any branch of industry is injurious. To open out new sources of production ought to be left to private enterprise, which a Government should only endeavour indirectly to assist, by maintaining security, and by diffusing information calculated to direct public attention to any unexplored but promising fields for industry which may exist. In this way we did all we could to encourage the growth of cotton in Africa. The Governors of our Settlements were directed to lose no opportunity of pointing out to the chiefs and traders with whom they were brought into contact, the advantages which might be derived from it ; and in my personal communications with the leading merchants, I availed myself of all suitable occasions for making similar suggestions. I hope this may have in some degree contributed towards rousing that greater attention, which, I trust,

is now beginning to be shown to this important subject in all our Settlements in Western Africa; and
that our merchants will now seriously take up a
business which, if pursued with energy and judgement, affords, I believe, an unusual prospect of producing at once great public advantages, and large
gains to those by whose enterprise such a branch of
industry may be established.

Sierra Leone is the most considerable of the British
Possessions on the west coast of Africa, in respect of
the number of British subjects (in the strict sense of
the word) by whom it is inhabited. But comparing
its actual condition with the length of time that has
elapsed since the Colony was established, and with
the very large amount of the expenditure which for
many years was incurred there by this Country, I
fear it must be admitted to have disappointed the
expectations of its philanthropic founders. Its comparative want of success would not, I think, be difficult to explain, if this were a fitting occasion for
pointing out the faults, which seem to me to have
been committed, in its early management; but as
this topic does not come within the circle of those
with which I am engaged, I will merely repeat the
expression of my opinion, that the too great readiness
of Parliament in meeting the demands made upon its
liberality, on account of this Colony in its earlier days,
had an opposite effect on its real prosperity from
that which was expected. For a good many years,
however, the expenditure of this Country at Sierra

Leone has been brought within moderate bounds. The Parliamentary grant for the civil establishment for 1851 was only £4465, exclusive of the cost of the Liberated African Department, amounting to £3545, —a charge arising from the measures adopted for the suppression of the Slave-trade.

During your Administration the chief subject connected with Sierra Leone, that required our attention, was the state of its finances; at one time they were in an exceedingly unsatisfactory condition, nor was it without much trouble that they were restored to order. In connection with them I ought to mention, that here also the experiment of direct taxation upon an uncivilized population has been tried, in the form of a house and land tax; but there was so much delay on the part of the local Government, in passing the ordinance for this purpose, and in amending that originally passed, which was in the first instance very defective, that the law, as finally adopted, did not come into operation until the 1st of January, 1852; and I have no information as to its effects, except that, in the Governor's Annual Report, dated the 26th of June last, I observe it to be stated, that this tax " has been prolific beyond his most sanguine expectations, and promises to be a most fruitful source of revenue."

Before I pass from the subject of our Settlements in Western Africa, I will only say of them generally, that their actual condition seems to be such as to warrant the belief, that this Country is destined at length to see the fruit of the persevering efforts it has so long made to render these Settlements the means of diffusing Christianity, civilization, and commerce among the degraded inhabitants of that great continent. The first and really difficult steps, toward the accomplishment of this high and worthy object, have been gained, and there now remain no apparent obstacles of any magnitude, to the progress of improvement, which, by the favour of Providence, may henceforth be reasonably expected to proceed at a rate becoming continually faster, as each successive advance which is effected renders the next more easy. Nothing will, I believe, more powerfully contribute to this result than the establishment of the line of steam communication which has been lately opened between this Country and the various British Possessions and principal trading-ports on the west coast of Africa*. This arrangement, for which the contract had been concluded just before we left Office, is calculated, in my opinion, to contribute more than any other measure that could have been adopted, to the extension of African commerce and of African civilization.

The British Possessions in the Mediterranean (a-

---

* I take this opportunity of observing, that I have not noticed in the preceding Letters various measures which were adopted during your Administration for the extension of steam communication with our Colonies. I have abstained from doing so, because this branch of business is not conducted under the direction of the Secretary of State for the Colonies, but under that of the Treasury and Admiralty.

mong which, I have already observed that the Ionian Islands are not properly to be included) consist of the two important naval and military stations of Gibraltar and Malta. It does not enter into my plan to advert to what relates to them as such; but Malta, besides being a garrison and naval station, also contains a considerable and increasing population; its civil government is therefore a subject of importance.

When your Administration was formed, much uneasiness and dissatisfaction, if not positive discontent, prevailed among the inhabitants of Malta. It appeared to us, that one step towards the correction of this state of things would be to entrust the civil government to a person who, not being burdened with the command of the troops, might have more leisure to look closely into the state of its civil affairs, and ascertain what improvements were required in their management. Accordingly, on the resignation of Sir Patrick Stuart, I recommended Mr. More O'Ferrall to the Queen, for the appointment of Governor of Malta, for which he appeared to be well qualified, by his experience in Parliament and in the important offices he had held in the Government of this Country. The appointment of a Civil Governor, and the choice of Mr. More O'Ferrall for the office, answered their intended object, and gave so much satisfaction to the Maltese, that when he found it necessary to resign the government of the Island, after having held it between three and four years, a petition, very numerously and most respectably signed, was addressed to the Queen, praying that his resignation might not be accepted. Mr. More O'Ferrall had well deserved this somewhat unusual mark of approbation from the Maltese. Although his administration was comparatively short, many valuable measures of reform were carried by him or with his assistance.

Of these, one of the most important was a change in the form of the Government, by which the Legislature was made partly elective. Although it has always been considered (as I think justly) that, in so important a garrison, the Crown ought to keep very extensive powers, so that in any time of danger its servants may have ample authority to adopt any measures of precaution which may be necessary, it was thought highly desirable to introduce the principle of representation in a modified form into the Government. Accordingly, after a good deal of correspondence with Mr. More O'Ferrall, a measure was arranged, by which we thought that this might be accomplished in a manner free from danger; and the Queen was advised to grant a commission to the Governor, by which a change in the constitution of the Government was effected, which seems to have given complete satisfaction to the great majority of the Maltese, and has hitherto worked exceedingly well.

During the administration of Mr. More O'Ferrall, various other useful measures were adopted. Arrangements were made for improving the system of public education and of prison discipline. In the former, the system of National Education in Ireland was selected as a model for imitation; and in building a new prison and making rules for its management, the example of this Country in the improved modern prisons was also followed. The persons to whom the task of introducing these improvements was entrusted, were in both cases sent to this Country in order that they might make themselves acquainted by personal examination with the arrangements they were to follow. The police was also improved and increased; and the periods of quarantine on ships coming from suspected places were materially reduced; the Governor stating that he would have gone further in getting rid of this mischievous obstruction to the trade and mutual intercourse of the countries washed by the Mediterranean Sea, had he not found that the prejudices of the people on the subject were so strong that he could not have done more without creating much alarm and dissatisfaction*. Great additional facilities were likewise given to trade, by the construction of bonding stores, and particularly by a large increase in the means of storing corn and oil, of which Malta is becoming an important mart.

Various public works were also undertaken and executed, which, with the other measures of improvement I have mentioned, necessarily occasioned a con-

* See Blue Book Reports.

siderable expenditure. For this however Mr. More
O'Ferrall was able to provide without the imposition
of any new taxes; the public income was only increased
by the growing productiveness of the old taxes, and
by an augmentation of about £4000 a-year in the
rents of Crown property, which was brought about
by a new valuation, a measure of obvious justice and
propriety. It was mainly by the exercise of a strict
and judicious economy, that Mr. More O'Ferrall was
able to accomplish so much without any further increase of the public income than that derived from
the sources I have mentioned. The various public
establishments were carefully revised, offices that could
be dispensed with were abolished or consolidated
with others, and, above all, a complete reform was
effected in the mode of relief to the sick and destitute.
A system of affording such relief had grown up, par-
taking somewhat of the character of that which formerly prevailed in the southern counties of England,
and having the same demoralizing tendencies. This
evil, which was becoming serious, Mr. More O'Ferrall
effectually corrected by similar means to those which
have been had recourse to in this Country,—namely,
by providing for the grant of relief to the sick and
destitute who require it, chiefly by admitting them to
well regulated hospitals and workhouses. The pecuniary saving is by no means the most important part
of the good effected by this reform. The result of
the various measures I have thus slightly adverted to

has been that Malta has greatly prospered during the last few years, and is now, I believe, in a far more flourishing condition than at any former period.

I have now completed the review which I undertook of the affairs of the British Colonies from 1846 to 1852. I am aware that I have very imperfectly executed this task, the difficulty of which has proved greater than I had anticipated, and has been increased by the rules I have thought it right to observe as to the sources of information of which I was at liberty to avail myself, and as to the reserve which ought to be maintained in writing upon such subjects as those with which I have had to deal. The information I have used is only that which is accessible to the public, and for the most part it has been drawn from the voluminous Papers which have been laid before Parliament, and the records of its proceedings, or from those of the Colonial Legislatures; but I have also to some extent availed myself both of our own and of the Colonial newspapers, though of course I have not placed the same reliance upon them as upon official documents. Of the latter, I have thought it my duty carefully to abstain from referring to any which have not in some way or other been made public. In like manner, I have refrained from giving any account of the reasons which led to the adoption of various measures by the Government, except when these have been stated either in the debates in Parliament or in public documents, or when they are clearly shown by the measures themselves. Of my own individual opinions, and of the considerations which weighed most with myself, I have felt justified in speaking somewhat more freely.

My adherence to the rule I have laid down, with respect to the information I was to use, has debarred me from entering as fully as I could have wished into some matters of importance ; and still greater restraint has been imposed upon me, by my determination not to say anything or to urge any arguments which could have a tendency, so far as I can judge, to create any real public inconvenience. I do not mean that the caution I have observed has been carried so far as to prevent its being probable that what I have said may revive the recollection of some angry discussions, and that arguments which I have used may perhaps give offence to some persons ; but within certain limits I cannot for my own part see any objection to this : it is only by free discussion that truth can be elicited, and the most important public principles established. A retrospect of public affairs, necessarily implies that the conduct of those who have taken part in them should be made the subject of comment, which cannot always be of a favourable character; and it is for the general interest, that these matters should be canvassed without unnecessary restraint. It tends to keep up a due sense of their responsibility in the minds of those who are engaged in the exciting scenes of political life,

that they should know that all they may do is liable
to be reviewed and discussed when time and the results of their acts shall have thrown a light on their
real character. I make no apology therefore for having
spoken freely of men and things, and I trust I have
said nothing calculated to excite animosities or em-
bitter controversies of a dangerous character. It certainly has been my most anxious desire to avoid doing
so; and whenever it has appeared to me that injury
could be occasioned to public interests by touching
on matters to which, in defence of our measures, it
would have been desirable to advert, I have never
hesitated to leave our vindication incomplete, rather
than risk any damage to the Public. If I am not mistaken, you will easily detect more than one omission
in these Letters, which has been dictated by this
motive for reserve.

I trust however that the result of my review of
Colonial affairs will not appear upon the whole unsatisfactory to those who will impartially consider the
subject and the difficulties with which we have had
to struggle. No doubt during the five years and a
half of your government, while these affairs were under
my immediate superintendence, mistakes were committed. Looking back, with the advantage of the
experience we have gained, and judging of our measures by their results, I can see many things which
might have been better done than they were. Knowing what the pressure of public business is in this
Country, the degree to which the attention of those

who conduct it cannot fail to be distracted by the
variety of different subjects which must day by day
be considered and dealt with, the important decisions
which must be come to with little time for deliberation, and often with a great difficulty in obtaining
correct information,—he must indeed be a sanguine
man who can expect, that any of the great departments of the State can ever be conducted without
many and serious mistakes being committed ; and
perhaps there is no department of the Government
where there is the same difficulty in avoiding such
mistakes as in that of the Colonies.

But while I freely admit that errors have been
committed, I am prepared to maintain that, in the
administration of the Colonies during the years of
which I have been speaking, those views of Colonial
policy which in my first Letter I have endeavoured to
explain, and of the correctness of which I am more
than ever satisfied, have been steadily and consistently
acted upon to the best of our judgement; every measure taken by us was decided upon with a strict regard to the principles which governed our whole policy,
and, what is more, every appointment was guided by
a consideration of fitness for the public service.

Let me add, with regard to the results of our policy,
—for after all it must be judged by its fruits,—that,
taking our Colonial Empire as a whole, I greatly
doubt whether any other period of equal length can
be pointed out in our history in which that Empire
has prospered so much, and has made such large

strides towards future greatness, as during the years of which I have been speaking. There has certainly been no similar period during which, in spite of all the difficulties that have been encountered, the advance has been greater. The facts and statistics which I have quoted, from official documents, enable me to make this assertion without fear of contradiction. With the single exception of the Cape, where we left, as we found, a distressing war going on, profound peace and internal tranquillity prevailed throughout the whole of our extensive Colonial Empire at the time of our quitting Office. A commercial revolution deeply affecting the interests of many of our most important Colonies has been safely passed through, not it is true without much distress and loss to individuals, which I deeply lament, but with great advantage to the permanent welfare of these Colonies and of the Mother-country; and, except where our measures have been thwarted by the opposition to the new commercial policy, the difficulties inseparable from so great a change have been nearly surmounted. Various important and difficult questions, touching both the internal government of the Colonies and their relations with the Mother-country, have been happily settled; and in almost all the Colonies a great reduction of the charges they impose on the British Treasury has been effected, and principles have been established, and rules laid down, which, if they shall continue to be acted upon, must lead to still larger and early reductions of our expenditure. The burden of taxation has also been diminished, and the state of the finances at the same time improved, in the Colonies where the most direct authority is exercised by the Crown. Finally, while the principle of leaving to the Colonists the management of their own affairs has been carried further than at any former period, this has been accomplished without disturbing any of the ancient landmarks which define the limits of the powers vested respectively in the Crown, the Imperial Parliament, and the Colonial Legislatures. I may be deceived, but to this maintenance of the long-established boundaries of these different authorities I attach the highest importance. If, in deference to the popular doctrines of the day, an attempt had been made, or should hereafter be so, to meet the natural desire of the most advanced of our Colonies to be exempted from undue interference on the part of the Imperial Government in their internal affairs,—not by a judiciously sparing exercise of what are still the acknowledged powers of the Crown and of Parliament, but by a formal surrender of the powers themselves,—I entertain a strong persuasion that such concessions, far from tending to avert future difficulties and disputes between the Parent State and her Dependencies, would have the very opposite effect, and would be too likely to lead to frequent and dangerous contests of authority, and ultimately, by a few short and easy steps, to the severance of the tie which unites the fairest portions of our Colonial Empire to the British Crown. I know that some of those who advocate the changes to which I allude are prepared for this result, if they do not regard its probability as an additional recommendation of the measures they propose; but I earnestly trust that such is not the view of this great question which is destined to gain acceptance with Parliament and with the Public. For my own part,—though, with the consequences of the American Revolution before my eyes, I certainly am not prepared to say that the loss of our Colonial Empire must necessarily be fatal to our national greatness and prosperity,—still I should regard such an event as a grievous calamity, and as lowering by many steps the rank of this Country among the nations of the world. You, I am persuaded, will concur with me in this opinion, and will feel no less strongly than myself the desire that the great British Empire may to a long futurity be held together, and preserve its station among the principal Powers of the earth.

Yours very truly,
GREY.

December 27, 1852.

POSTSCRIPT.

I must add one or two additional observations on the subject of my Eighth Letter, in consequence of the determination you have announced, on the part of the new Government, to discontinue altogether the removal of convicts to the Australian Colonies as soon as the ships now chartered shall have been despatched. I confess I heard this announcement with much surprise and alarm. This alarm has not been diminished by the Duke of Newcastle's subsequent explanation, that transportation to Western Australia is still to be continued upon a small scale, and for a short time ; but that, on the other hand, its cessation to Van Diemen's Land is to be absolute and immediate, and that not even any ship already chartered is to be sent there. The intention of the late Government to stop transportation to Van Diemen's Land did not surprise me. Judging from the information before the public, I did not approve of that course ; but there may probably have been reasons for it of which I am not aware, and, upon the whole, little harm might have been done by the measure, if carried into execution with due time for preparation, and in a proper manner. It would indeed,

I am persuaded, have inflicted a heavy blow on the rising prosperity of Van Diemen's Land; but if so, the inhabitants of that Colony would have had only themselves to blame for it.   On the other hand, the lesson which would have been thus gained would not have been without its value, while, by incurring some additional expense, and not making the change too suddenly, it would have been practicable to find the means of disposing elsewhere of the convicts who would otherwise have gone to Van Diemen's Land.

These precautions, if I rightly understood the intimation conveyed in Her Majesty's Speech from the Throne, and the subsequent explanations of Sir John Pakington, were not to have been neglected, and it was intended that time should be taken for preparing and completing the intended new arrangements before those now in force were discontinued.   But we are now told that the removal of convicts to Van Diemen's Land is to cease at once, and that it is not to be continued for more than a short time to any of the Australian Colonies.   This involves an entire change in the present system of secondary punishment; and I am altogether at a loss to understand how the new arrangements which will in consequence be necessary can be matured with due care and deliberation, and how they can be submitted to the judgement of Parliament in the very short time that will be allowed for the purpose.   What is to become of the large number of convicts now undergoing their preliminary punishment, and to whom an express promise has been made that

by good conduct they would obtain tickets-of-leave in
the Colonies at an early period? There cannot be less,
I apprehend, than from two to three hundred men
monthly becoming entitled to this boon for the next
two years, and it will be a difficult question to determine what is to be done with them.   Faith cannot, of
course, be broken with these men by detaining them
at Portland, or any other of our penal establishments,
beyond the time at which they have a right, under
the regulations printed for their information, to look
for their release from the forced labour there imposed
upon them.   But if the Australian Colonies are to be
closed against them, I am not aware of any other place
to which they can be sent; and I am quite certain
there is no part of the British dominions in which it
is possible to make arrangements for receiving them
with tickets-of-leave in the time within which some
mode of disposing of them must be discovered.   To
send them abroad as exiles would probably be equally
difficult, and would be merely recurring to our original plan, which was given up because it was found
not to answer.

Are they then, as a substitute for the tickets-of-
leave they have been promised in the Colonies, to be
allowed their discharge in this Country? and is the ultimate removal from their native country, of criminals
sentenced to transportation, to cease in future to be an
essential part of their punishment?   If this is what is
intended, I am compelled to express my opinion, that
so momentous a change in what has been our policy

for near two hundred years, ought not to have been decided upon without the previous concurrence of Parliament. So far as it has yet been expressed, the judgement of Parliament has been decidedly adverse to doing away with the punishment of transportation. I have mentioned in my Eighth Letter the opinion expressed in 1847 by the Committee of the House of Lords, after examining the judges and many persons of great experience in the administration of our criminal law. I have also mentioned that, in 1841, an address to the Crown was voted by the House of Commons against the Government of that day, objecting to the detention in this Country of convicts sentenced to transportation. None of the motions made during your own Administration, for obtaining a contrary opinion from the same House, obtained any considerable support. Looking further back, even the Committee which, in 1838, condemned the former system of transportation, did not fail to recognize the advantage, if not the necessity, of the ultimate removal of convicts from our shores.

Such has been the judgement hitherto pronounced by Parliament on this subject; and I am persuaded that there is not a magistrate who has any experience of the administration of the criminal law, especially in the rural districts, who will not express a strong opinion as to the great advantage of not allowing men who have been convicted of serious crimes to return to their former homes. In country villages the occasional return of such men is almost invariably attended with bad effects. They cannot, for the reasons which have been so often explained, find the means of maintaining themselves honestly. They are driven to resume their former bad habits; and in the spirit of bravado which is so general among criminals, they make light of the punishment they have undergone, and thus destroy the wholesome terror of the law in the minds of the least steady of the young men of their neighbourhood, whom they instruct in all the arts and practices of criminals.

If this happens now, when only a small percentage of criminals sentenced to transportation ever return to their homes, what will be the consequence when some two or three thousand men, who under the existing system would be permanently removed from the United Kingdom, are to be annually turned loose on society?

It is with sincere regret that I make these remarks upon one of the first measures announced by an Administration which I am exceedingly anxious to support, so far as my duty will permit me; but I consider so great a public interest to be involved in this question, that I could not with propriety abstain from declaring the opinion I entertain upon it, when the publication of these volumes affords me an opportunity of doing so.

G.

February 22, 1853.

APPENDIX.

A.

Copy of a Despatch from Governor Sir C. A. Fitzroy to Earl Grey.

" *Government House, Sydney, June* 18, 1851.

" My Lord,

" At the request of the Legislative Council of this Colony, I have the honour to forward an Address embodying a declaration and remonstrance against the New Constitution Act, 13 & 14 Vict., chap. 59.

" I have, etc.,

" C. A. Fitzroy."

" *Enclosure.*

" To his Excellency Sir Charles Augustus Fitzroy, Knight Companion of the Royal Hanoverian Guelphic Order, Captain-General and Governor-in-Chief of the territory of New South Wales and its dependencies, and Vice-Admiral of the same, etc., etc., etc.

" May it please your Excellency,—

" We, Her Majesty's most dutiful and loyal subjects the Members of the Legislative Council of New South Wales, in Council assembled, beg respectfully to forward to your Excellency, for transmission to the Right Honourable the Secretary of State for the Colonies, the following declaration and remonstrance against the New Constitution Act, 13 & 14 Vict., chap. 59, this day appointed by the Council.

" We, the Legislative Council of New South Wales, in Council assembled, feel it to be a duty which we owe to ourselves, to our constituents, and to posterity, before we

give place to the New Legislature established by the 13 &
14 Vict., chap. 59, to record our deep disappointment and
dissatisfaction at the Constitution conferred by that Act on
this Colony. After the reiterated reports, resolutions, addresses, and petitions which have proceeded from us during
the whole course of our Legislative career, against the
schedules appended to the 5 & 6 Vict., chap. 76, and the
appropriations of our ordinary revenue under the sole authority of Parliament, against the administration of our
waste lands and our territorial revenue thence arising,
against the withholding of the Customs department from
our control, against the dispensation of the patronage of
the Colony at dictation of the Minister for the Colonies,
and against the veto reserved and exercised by the same
Minister, in the name of the Crown, in matters of local
Legislation, we feel that we had a right to expect that these
undoubted grievances would have been redressed by the 13
& 14 Vict., chap. 59, or that power to redress them would
have been conferred on the constituent bodies thereby created, with the avowed intention of establishing an authority
more competent than Parliament itself to frame suitable
Constitutions for the whole group of the Australian Colonies. These our reasonable expectations have been utterly
frustrated. The schedules, instead of being abolished, have
been increased. The powers of altering the appropriations
in these schedules, conferred on the Colonial Legislature by
this new Act, limited as these powers are, have been in
effect nullified by the subsequent instructions of the Colonial Minister*. The exploded fallacies of the Wakefield

* The following are the instructions adverted to; it will be seen
how little they justify this assertion of the Legislative Council.
" The effect of Sections 13, 17, and 18, is to give the Legislature a
considerably increased control over that part of the Colonial expenditure now charged on what is called the Civil List. The Le-

theory are still clung to; the pernicious Land Sales Act (5 & 6 Vict., chap. 36) is still enforced, and thousands of our fellow-subjects (in consequence of the undue price put by that mischievous and impolitic enactment upon our waste

gislatures will have the power to alter, by Acts passed for that purpose, all or any of the sums specified in the Schedules. In the case of these alterations affecting the salary of the Governor or the appropriation for public worship, it is required by the present Act of Parliament that the Colonial Acts should be reserved for the signification of Her Majesty's pleasure.

*   *   *   *

"It has been deemed right by Parliament, in order more completely to maintain the independence of the Judges of the Supreme Court, to provide that no diminution of Judicial salaries, by Colonial enactments, shall affect Judges appointed previously to the passing of such enactment.

"All other salaries, except those of the Governor and Judges, are placed by Parliament under the ordinary control of the Legislature. With regard to the mode of exercising this control, you will however observe that reductions of fixed establishments, or of any expenditure provided for by permanent laws, can only be effected by Acts of the Legislature, which of course require the assent of the Crown, signified by yourself, and confirmed by Her Majesty; but I wish you distinctly to understand, that there is no desire on the part of Her Majesty's Government to prevent prospective reductions of charges which, in the opinion of the Colonists, will safely admit of being diminished. The interests of existing office-holders must be protected, because they accepted those offices with expectations which cannot justly be disappointed. But, subject to these interests, there is no objection to the Legislature fixing whatever scale of emoluments they may think fit for public servants to be hereafter appointed. I should, for my own part, consider it highly injudicious to reduce the salary of an office, so as to render it no longer an object of ambition to men of ability and respectable station. But this is a matter in which the interests of the Colonists only are involved, as they will be the sufferers from any failure to provide adequate remuneration for those by whom the public service is carried on; the determination therefore of what is sufficient must be left to the lands, in defiance of the precedents of the United States, of Canada and the other North American Colonies, and even of the neighbouring Colony of the Cape of Good Hope) are annually diverted from our shores, and thus forced, against their will, to seek a home for themselves and their children in the backwoods of America. Nor is this all. Our territorial revenue, diminished as it is by this most mistaken policy, is in a great measure confined to the introduction among us of people unsuited to our wants, and in many instances the outpourings of the poorhouses and unions of the United Kingdom, instead of being applied in directing to this Colony a stream of vigorous and efficient labour, calculated to elevate the character of our industrial population. The bestowal of office among us, with but partial exception, is still exercised by or at the nomination of the Colonial Minister, and without any re-

Legislatures, with whom will rest the responsibility for the judicious exercise of the power.

" I consider it however absolutely essential that, whatever may be the rate of payment, the salaries of all the principal officers of the Government should, for the reasons stated in the Report of the Committee of the Privy Council, be permanently granted; that is, not voted from year to year, but provided for in the same manner as charges on the Consolidated Fund in this country, by Acts, and therefore only susceptible of alteration by Acts of the Legislature passed in the ordinary manner, with the consent of the Crown. You will therefore understand that you are not at liberty to give the assent of the Crown to any Act which may be passed, reducing the salaries of those who are now in the public service, or rendering dependent on annual votes any of the charges now provided for by permanent appropriation. Any Acts of this sort you will reserve for the signication of Her Majesty's pleasure, unless you consider them so manifestly objectionable as to call for their rejection. Subject to this restriction you are authorized to exercise your own judgement in giving or withholding your assent from Acts for the reduction of the fixed charges on the Colonial revenue."

ference to the just claims of the Colonists, as if the Colony itself were but the fief of that Minister. The salaries of the officers of the customs, and all other departments of Government included in the schedules, are placed beyond our control; and the only result of this new enactment, introduced into Parliament by the Prime Minister himself with the declared intention of conferring upon us enlarged powers of self-government, and treating us at last as an integral portion of the Empire, is that all the material powers exercised for centuries by the House of Commons are still withheld from us; that our loyalty, and desire for the maintenance of order and good government, are so far distrusted that we are not permitted to vote our own Civil List, lest it might prove inadequate to the requirements of the public service; that our waste lands and our territorial revenue, for which Her Majesty is but a trustee, instead of being spontaneously surrendered, as the equivalent for such Civil List, is still reserved, to the great detriment of all classes of Her Majesty's subjects, in order to swell the patronage and power of the Ministers of the Crown; that whilst, in defiance of the Declaratory Act (18 George III., chap. 12, sect. 1), which has hitherto been considered the Magna Charta of the representative rights of all the British plantations, a large amount of our public revenue is thus levied and appropriated by the authority of Parliament, we have not even the consolation of seeing that portion of it which is applied to the payment of the salaries of our public officers distributed, as it ought to be, among the settled inhabitants; and that, as a fit climax to this system of misrule, we are not allowed to exercise the most ordinary legislation which is not subject to the veto of the Colonial Minister.

" Thus circumstanced, we feel that, on the eve of the

dissolution of this Council, and as the closing act of our legislative existence, no other course is open to us but to enter on our own journals our declaration, protest, and remonstrance, as well against the Act of Parliament itself (13 & 14 Vict., chap. 59) as against the instructions of the Minister by which the small power of retrenchment that Act confers on the Colonial Legislature has been thus overridden, and to bequeath the redress of the grievances which we have been unable to effect by constitutional means to the Legislative Council by which we are about to be succeeded.

" We, the Legislative Council of New South Wales, do accordingly hereby solemnly protest, insist, and declare as follows :—

" 1st. That the Imperial Parliament has not, nor of right ought to have, any power to tax the people of this Colony, or to appropriate any of the moneys levied by authority of the Colonial Legislature ; that this power can only be lawfully exercised by the Colonial Legislature ; and that the Imperial Parliament has solemnly disclaimed this power by 18 Geo. III., chap. 12, sect. 1, which Act remains unrepealed.

" 2nd. That the revenue arising from the public lands, derived as it is ' mainly ' from the value imparted to them by the labour and capital of the people of this Colony, is as much their property as the ordinary revenue, and ought therefore to be subject only to the like control and appropriation.

" 3rd. That the Customs and all other departments should be subject to the direct supervision and control of the Colonial Legislature, which should have the appropriation of the gross revenues of the Colony, from whatever source arising, and, as a necessary incident to this authority, the regulation of the salaries of all Colonial officers.

" 4th. That offices of trust and emolument should be conferred only on the settled inhabitants, the office of Governor alone excepted; that this officer should be appointed and paid by the Crown; and that the whole patronage of the Colony should be vested in him and the Executive Council, unfettered by instructions from the Minister for the Colonies.

" 5th. That plenary powers of legislation should be conferred upon and exercised by the Colonial Legislature for the time being, and that no Bills should be reserved for the signification of Her Majesty's pleasure, unless they affect the prerogatives of the Crown, or the general interests of the Empire.

" Solemnly protesting against these wrongs, and declaring and insisting upon these our undoubted rights, we leave the redress of the one and the assertion of the other to the people whom we represent, and the Legislature which shall follow us.

" (Signed)   CHARLES NICHOLSON,

Speaker.

" *Legislative Council Chamber, Sydney,*
   " *May* 1, 1851."

Copy of a Despatch from Earl Grey to Sir C. A. Fitzroy.

" *Downing-street, January* 23, 1852.

  " SIR,

" I have to acknowledge your Despatch, No. 105, of the 18th of June last, enclosing an address from the late Legislative Council of New South Wales, embodying a declaration and remonstrance against the Constitutional Act,

13th and 14th Vict., chap. 59. The same document had reached me a short time before, with a letter from the Speaker of the Council.

" It cannot be otherwise than a subject of regret to me, that the Council should have entertained so much objection to different provisions of that measure, and should have thought it necessary to declare those objections in this formal shape before separating for the last time. But I must be permitted to doubt whether this remonstrance accurately expresses the feeling of the community.

" For it is certain that Her Majesty's Government, in framing this measure, took as much pains as was in their power to make themselves acquainted with and to consult the feelings as well as wants of the Colonists, and had every reason to believe that they had succeeded in doing so; for the Report of the Committee of Privy Council, which was closely followed in the Bill they submitted to Parliament, was received in New South Wales with very general expressions of satisfaction.

" In the Port Philip district, which was chiefly affected by the proposed Bill, that satisfaction was expressed in the strongest manner: and in the remainder of the Colony likewise public opinion, from such evidence as could be collected here, appeared decidedly favourable to it. I do not mean to say that there were not differences of opinion as to some of the proposed provisions. Such differences are unavoidable on political subjects of great interest, but assuredly there was no token of that deep disappointment and dissatisfaction which the Council now expresses.

" The Act, therefore, which embodies the recommendations of that Report thus favourably received, from which it only slightly varies, and not, I believe, in any of those particulars to which the objections now taken by the Council relate, can hardly be supposed to be unacceptable to the Colonists. If indeed the institutions created by it had been tried and found insufficient—if any of its provisions had been found oppressive or impracticable,—then it would be perfectly natural that those whose anticipations had been favourable should profess themselves disappointed. But it had not been tried at all; and I am therefore entitled rather to suppose that this declaration of the Legislative Council does not, as I have said, accurately represent public feeling, than that public feeling has thus changed without a motive.

" I feel however that too much weight is due to the authority of that body, which has now separated for the last time, after conducting the legislative affairs of the Colony down to the period of its separation, to admit of my receiving a remonstrance from them condemning so strongly what has been done by Her Majesty's Government, or rather by the Imperial Parliament, without recording fully the grounds on which I think myself entitled to deny the justice of their objections to the measure which has called forth their censure.

" And for this purpose I must repeat the declaration which Her Majesty's Government had frequent occasion to make when the Act was in contemplation, namely, that it did not purpose or profess to make a new constitution for New South Wales. Its primary object (as regarded that Colony) was the separation of Port Philip. Its further object was to accommodate the existing constitution to that separation. The changes made in that constitution were for the most part inconsiderable, and their effect was only to extend, in no one instance to curtail, existing rights. But there was one fundamental alteration, namely that it gave (subject to certain conditions) to the two Legislatures the power which the former united one did not possess, of amending and altering, almost to the fullest extent, their own institutions. This, and this only, was the great constitutional change effected by the Act; and no allegation has as yet reached me that the powers thus conferred on the Legislature are likely to prove in any degree inadequate to the purposes of good government and progressive improvement.

" I must therefore regard the remonstrance, except in some points of detail, rather as a protest against the principles on which the Australian Provinces have hitherto been governed, and against some laws affecting those Colonies, which Parliament has thought fit to maintain, than against this particular Act.

" With regard to the schedules of expenditure, it is obvious on the face of the Act, that the powers of the new Legislatures over them will be considerably more extensive than those possessed by the old one. I am not aware to what particular expression of mine the Legislative Council refer, when they say these powers have been nullified by the subsequent instructions of the Colonial Minister. I stated in my despatch transmitting the Act, that it was essential that existing interests should be protected. To this I cannot suppose that the Legislative Council entertain any objection. The declaration was made out of regard to the natural apprehensions of those who were to be rendered more dependent on the votes of the Legislature than heretofore, and not from any expectation so injurious to the Legislature as that such a restriction would be distasteful. I referred further to the opinion of the Committee of the Privy Council, that the salaries of the principal officers ought to be permanently granted; and if this is the restriction complained of, I cannot do otherwise than repeat my agreement in that opinion. It was the conviction that the maintenance of this principle is very essential to the success of constitutional government at its outset, and not any wish to secure particular sums for particular services, which mainly induced Parliament to preserve this portion of the former constitution of New South Wales, subject to the increased power of alteration conferred on the Legislature.

" The Legislative Council, if I understand them rightly, allege that the maintenance of these schedules involves a violation of the declaratory Act, 18 George III., chap. 12; an objection which, as far as I am aware, is for the first time urged against them. It might be sufficient to answer, that the Act in question refers in terms only to the imposition of taxes by the Imperial Legislature, and the appropriation of the produce of taxes so imposed. But it is more important to observe that the Act of George III. neither declares, nor was intended to declare, anything beyond the renunciation by Parliament of any right to interfere with chartered Provincial Legislatures. The constitution of New South Wales is itself created by Act of Parliament superseding that form of government which, under the peculiar circumstances of the Colony, it had been thought necessary to maintain until ten years ago; and Parliament, in creating such a constitution, had an unquestionable right to annex to the grant such conditions as it might think expedient.

" The administration of the waste lands is a subject which I should have preferred to consider independently of the Constitutional Act, with which it does not appear to me to have any very close connection; but as the Legislative Council have thought it right to introduce this topic into their remonstrance, I cannot do otherwise than advert to what they have urged. And in doing so, it is my duty not to withhold the expression of my decided dissent from the doctrine that the waste lands in New South Wales, or the revenue derived from them, are in any reasonable sense the exclusive property of its inhabitants, or that their representatives ought to have as of right the control and disposal of that revenue.

" The waste lands of the vast Colonial possessions of the British Empire are held by the Crown as Trustee for the inhabitants of that Empire at large, and not for the inhabitants of the particular Provinces divided by arbitrary geographical limits in which any such waste lands happen to be situated. Otherwise this consequence would follow, that the first inhabitants of any of these vast Provinces (if possessing those representative institutions which arise as of right in ordinary British Colonies) are indefeasibly entitled to administer all the lands and land-revenue of the great unexplored tract called a province, of which they may occupy an extremity, wholly without regard to the nation which has founded the settlement, perhaps at great expense, in order to serve as a home for her own emigrants and a market for her own industry.

" For the right thus defined and claimed by the Legislative Council, if their expressions were to be strictly taken, would belong as fully to the 4000 inhabitants of Western Australia as to the 200,000 of New South Wales; nay, would have equally belonged to the first few families which settled in a corner of New Zealand, and would entitle each small community, from the first day of its planting, to the ownership of tracts sufficient to maintain empires.

" When and on what conditions it may be desirable to transfer the control of the waste lands of a Colony to its local Legislature, is in my belief a question of expediency and not of right : of expediency respectively both to the local community and to the people of the Empire at large, whose claims require joint consideration of mutual adjustment. And I consider that of the Australian waste lands, —lands to which I must add that their present value has been mainly given through the expenditure incurred by this country in founding, maintaining, and defending the several settlements,—to be for the present wisely as well as rightfully vested in the general Government, under the strict rules imposed by Parliament.

" But while such are my views as to the right under which this revenue is administered, I willingly acknowledge that it is one most essential duty of those who administer it, to regard in an especial manner the interests of those who have established themselves on the spot, and whose purchases afford the fund to be so disposed of; and I believe this object to be attained in a high degree by the existing arrangement.

" It will be remembered that the Waste Lands Act, now termed ' pernicious,' was adopted on the recommendation of a Committee of the House of Commons, by which the whole subject was investigated with the utmost care. The object of this Act was to give permanence and more complete effect to a course of policy regarding those lands, which had been already adopted to some extent in the beginning of 1831 by the Executive Government. From the adoption of that policy may be dated the extraordinary, and I believe, unparalleled advance which the Colony has made in wealth and prosperity.

" Such being the circumstances under which Parliament has thought fit to entrust to the Crown the expenditure of the territorial revenue in the Australian Colonies, with the obligation of applying not less than one-half of the net receipts from the sale of land to emigration from the United Kingdom, it is to me a subject equally of surprise and regret that the Council should have seen reason to express the opinion, that the duty thus imposed on the advisers of the Crown has been so ill performed as to warrant the assertion, that the use of the territorial revenue had been in great measure confined to the introduction of people unsuited to the wants of the Colony, and in many instances the outpourings of the poor-houses and unions of the United Kingdom. The view thus communicated to me is certainly inconsistent with the detailed information which has been furnished respecting the successive emigrant ships as they reached Australia, and with the general opinions previously transmitted from all the Colonies to which emigrants have been sent.

" Emigration to New South Wales by means of public funds having been resumed in the year 1847, no fewer than 31,400 persons had been sent out to this one Colony since that time by the Emigration Commissioners at the date when they made their last annual Report, on the 2nd of May, 1851; and any one who consults the detailed reports which have been made respecting these emigrants on their reaching the Colony, and which are republished in the annual reports of the Emigration Commissioners, may easily see how small, amidst this great multitude, is the proportion of persons of whom there has been any serious complaint. Nor have there been wanting general testimonials of a gratifying nature to the satisfaction felt with the character of the emigrants selected and sent out by the Emigration Commissioners.

" The only part of this emigration against which any decidedly unfavourable opinion was expressed, was that which was called 'Assisted Emigration.' But this mode of promoting emigration was adopted, contrary to my own opinion and that of the Emigration Commissioners, in deference to the urgent representations of gentlemen who were supposed to enjoy the confidence of the Colonists, and more especially of one to whom the Legislative Council had granted a salary for his services as agent for the Colony, and who was therefore entitled to be listened to with attention when he urged on its behalf that the plan to which I have adverted should be adopted. For this reason, and because in carrying on a service of so comprehensive a character, and comparatively so recent an origin, as emigration, I have always thought it right not to refuse a fair trial to any reasonable project, advocated by gentlemen interested in the supply of labour to the Colony, I gave directions to the Emigration Commissioners to try, as an experiment, and with great caution, the plan of what has been called Assisted Emigration. At Sydney (at Melbourne a different opinion was entertained) the experiment was considered to have failed, and it was therefore immediately discontinued.

" But setting aside this experimental measure, I am fully justified in asserting, that all the reports as to the emigrants made at the time of their arrival tend to establish the conclusion, that the arduous undertaking of collecting and conveying to Australia so large a body of people from all parts of the United Kingdom has been conducted in a manner highly advantageous to the Colony, and creditable to the Board by which it was conducted. I must add, that the reports which support this conclusion were made by persons who have shown themselves vigilant in detecting, and prompt in exposing, those cases of abuse which it was impossible to expect should not occasionally occur in conducting emigration on so large a scale; nor can there be any doubt that these reports expressed what was the general opinion of the settlers at the time.

" The Council further declare, that the Customs and all other departments should be subject to the direct supervision and control of the Colonial Legislature, which should have the appropriation of the gross revenues of the Colony from whatever source arising.

" I have no wish to controvert the assertion that the Colonial Legislature ought to be enabled to exercise a superintendence, and in one sense a control, over the administration of the Customs, as of other departments of the public service; but I have to point out that the power to exercise a superintendence over the Customs department has already been in effect conferred upon the Legislative Council by my circular despatch of the 8th of August, 1850, which the Legislative Council, in framing the remonstrance, seem to have entirely overlooked. By that despatch the management of the Customs department, which had formerly been retained in their own hands by the Lords Commissioners of the Treasury (as was necessary while the former Navigation Laws were in force), has been entrusted to the local Government, subject to the same conditions as other branches of the public service. That Government has ever shown a perfect readiness to communicate to the Legislative Council the most ample information as to the manner in which the administration is conducted; and thus the people of New South Wales, through their representatives, possess the same power with their fellow-subjects at home of interfering to correct any abuse or mismanagement which may occur in the conduct of their affairs, by advice or remonstrance addressed to the Crown, or the Governor by whom the Crown is represented. No more direct control than this over the Customs depart-

ment could be given to the Legislative Council of New
South Wales, without violating those important constitutional principles as to the strict separation of the executive
from legislative functions, which in this country it has
always been considered expedient to maintain.

" With regard to the claim that the gross instead of the
nett revenue derived from customs should be placed at the
disposal of the Legislature, I have to observe, that in this
respect the law of New South Wales is precisely the same
with that which has always existed in this country, where
the Crown has always had the power of paying, out of the
gross revenue, the expenses of collection, and the salaries
of the officers employed in it. I believe this practice to be
that best calculated to ensure an efficient performance of
this important branch of the public business; and, coupled
with the rule that full information as to the details of the
expenditure incurred shall, when called for, be laid before
the Legislatures, it affords also, in my judgement, ample
security against abuse. At all events, it can hardly be
considered that there is any grievance to be complained of
in this matter, when the Legislative Council is placed with
regard to it precisely on the same footing with the Imperial
Parliament.

" On the subject of official appointments, it is impossible
for Her Majesty's Government to recognize, on the part of
the inhabitants of New South Wales, any monopoly of a
right to such situations, so as to preclude them from being
bestowed on others of Her Majesty's subjects. The inhabitants of New South Wales are not considered disqualified
from receiving similar appointments either in other colonies or at home: nor would anything be more injurious to
the general interests of the British Empire, than to lay down
a rule by which it should be broken up into a number of

small communities, the members of each of which should be considered as only admissible to employment in that to which they more immediately belonged.

" But while the principle of regarding all Her Majesty's subjects as admissible to office in New South Wales cannot be abandoned, there has assuredly been no practical grievance inflicted in this respect on the inhabitants of the Colony, since for several years past public employments there have, with scarcely an exception, been filled by persons selected by the Governor, whose nominations have been almost invariably approved by the Secretary of State; and I consider it of great importance to the interests of the Colony, as tending to secure a good selection of persons for such employments, that the existing rule should be maintained, by which the Governor is required to report his appointments, and receive Her Majesty's confirmation of them, if they are to offices exceeding a certain value.

" With regard to the last clause of the protest, which claims what are termed plenary powers for the local Legislature, it is scarcely necessary to remark, that although the Council naturally confine their declaration to the case of the province which they have represented, it is impossible for me to notice it in answer, except as applying generally to the colonial possessions of the British Crown. For the constitutional rule or principle, against which protest is here made, is equally in force in every Colony, from the comparatively old and numerous communities in North America down to the smallest settlement enjoying a separate Legislature. It could scarcely be altered in one Colony without a general change of system, and the introduction of so vast a change would require far more practical and pressing grounds to justify it than what I must term a theoretical preference of some different and untried scheme.

" It is not denied that the Governor of a Colony, as representing the Crown, must necessarily be a party to all legislation; and there would be obvious objections to placing in the hands of even the ablest Governor the power of binding the Crown by his acceptance of Acts in necessary ignorance of the views which the Crown, through its advisers, charged with the superintendence of the general interests of the Empire, may entertain. This I believe to be the main ground on which this power has been generally retained and exercised by the Crown, from the earliest periods of Colonial history; nor does it seem to me that it could be abandoned with safety to the permanence of the connection between the Mother-country and her Colonies.

" I am satisfied, at all events, that they are doing little service to the cause of good government who urge the adoption of a change of such magnitude as this, unless they are prepared with a well-considered substitute for the system which they propose to abandon. I am aware of no substitute having been prepared which, in my opinion, answers this description. The only one which I have seen suggested, and to which I believe the Legislative Council to refer, though I am not certain of their meaning, is this, that subjects of legislation should be divided into local and Imperial; that on the former the Governor should give or withhold the Royal assent, without further confirmation from the Crown; that on the latter, the local Legislature should have no power at all; its acts, or any portions of them, affecting these subjects being absolutely null and void; and the heads so reserved are of course numerous, including amongst others the very extensive one of the prerogative of the Crown.

" I am unwilling to enter on a subject merely controversial, and which is not fully placed before me with the arguments of those who advocate the innovation. But I cannot refrain from observing on the practical inconvenience which would seem necessarily to attend a system under which large subjects, and many of them very difficult to define, would be absolutely withdrawn from the power of the local Legislature ; so that they would be at once unable to legislate at all on many matters on which it is most desirable that they should legislate, subject to the control of the Crown, and at the same time under constant uncertainty whether Acts passed with strictly constitutional intentions might not be invalid through some inadvertent infringement of the limits of their authority,—limits which could ultimately only be defined and preserved through the uncertain process of judicial interposition in courts of law. I say nothing of the extreme difficulty of constituting a tribunal fit to judge of the validity of such Acts, or the certainty that its decisions would soon be felt as far greater hardships than the refusal of the Crown through its Ministers to allow an Act, which refusal further consideration may at all times change or modify.

" If indeed this power of the Crown were complained of as practically a grievance, the representations of the Council would have great additional weight. But no such complaint appears to be made, nor do I see how it could be. From the information afforded by the records of this Office, it seems that not more than seven Acts of the Legislature of New South Wales have been disallowed since the commencement of representative institutions, and about the same number returned for the insertion of amendments before Her Majesty's confirmation could be given ; and of the trifling number thus interfered with, nearly all were in the first three Sessions, when the experiment was new, several were obviously such Acts as the local Legislature, under the purposed division of subjects to which I have above adverted, would have had no right to pass at all.

" On the other hand, a very slight examination of the Acts, more than two hundred in number, which have received the Royal confirmation, will probably show that many of them would have been either wholly or partially in excess of like powers of the Legislature, and absolutely void, if such a division of authorities had existed. And this shows the practical convenience of the law as it now stands; for the Council of New South Wales has legislated, and will continue to legislate, without hindrance, on many subjects either of Imperial cognizance, or touching the prerogative, to the great advantage of the community; because the interests of the Crown and the Empire are sufficiently guarded by the power of disallowance possessed by the Crown, rarely as it is found necessary to exercise it.

" I have thus explained to you the views of Her Majesty's Government on all the principal heads of the declaration of the late Legislative Council; and I trust that, however this explanation may be received by those who, as members of that body, adopted the declaration, their constituents will be more disposed to weigh the considerations here advanced, and to endeavour to the best of their power to mitigate the opposition of opinions, and conciliate jarring interests, than to adopt, without demur, the sweeping conclusions which that declaration advocates.

" At all events I feel certain, that on reflection they will acquit Her Majesty's Government of any intention to inflict on them a system of misrule and oppression. We have had the interests of the local community and of the Empire, which, rightly considered, are the same, solely in view; and to attribute to us other motives, would be as unjust as it would be on my part to impute the language of this

declaration, because I do not agree in it, to a spirit of faction or resentment. Whatever may be the censure in which
the late Council may have thought fit to indulge towards
myself, I cannot be guilty of such injustice towards them.
Amidst the deep satisfaction with which I have watched of
late years the extraordinary progress of New South Wales,
in nearly all that constitutes the social and material welfare of a community, I have never ceased to appreciate the
manner in which its Legislature has contributed to that
advance by the zealous and constant discharge of its duty
to its constituents; and it is my sincere hope that the now
separate Legislatures, using with their best abilities the
powers which the Act now under discussion has conferred
on them, will follow in that course of improvement which
their predecessors have marked out for them.

" I have, etc.,

(Signed) " GREY."

B.

Extract from Speech of Earl Grey in the House of Lords,
June, 1852, on Second Reading of New Zealand Bill.

" EARL GREY said, that before adverting to the important
political questions arising out of the Bill now under their
Lordships' consideration, he thought it right to notice what
had fallen from the noble Duke on the clauses having reference to the claims of the New Zealand Company. He
certainly regretted that it was necessary to lay upon this
rising Colony a charge such as that which was proposed by
this Bill; but at the same time it was right that Parliament should do justice to the parties by whose exertions

and personal sacrifices the Colony had been created—without whom, in fact, there would be no Colony of New Zealand at all. Persons now found great fault with the New Zealand Company, and though he had never been a great admirer of that body, he must say that he thought the run now made against that Company was not less unjust and unmerited than the exaggerated credit which had been given them in the first instance. He had no doubt that the Company had been actuated throughout by the best motives; and, as evidence of their good intentions, he would remind their Lordships that the Directors had sacrificed large sums of their own money in the establishment of the Colony, for the repayment of which they had only the remote and distant prospect that was afforded by the arrangement proposed by this Bill. The fault to be found with the New Zealand Company was not that they committed any of the offences which the noble Duke imputed to them.

" The DUKE OF NEWCASTLE : No, no !

" EARL GREY : The noble Duke disclaimed the intention of imputing any offence to them, but the statement of the noble Duke implied it. Their real fault was, that they had shown themselves deficient in worldly wisdom and prudence, in too readily adopting for their guide a very clever projector, whose talents could not be denied, but whose cleverness was not accompanied by other qualities quite as necessary to make him a safe and trustworthy guide. They did not display that judgement that might have been expected from them in conducting the great enterprise into which they had somewhat rashly entered. Perhaps that was the necessary consequence of the constitution of such a body; for unless some person took the lead, and became manager, he believed a company of which the affairs were conducted

by a Board of Directors without check or control was not
likely to deal satisfactorily with matters of this kind. That
the New Zealand Company had not succeeded was not very
much to be wondered at, because the necessary expenses of
founding new colonies in distant parts of the world were so
great, that measures of this kind would never answer as a
pecuniary speculation. Schemes of this kind had always
been exceedingly attractive; but from the enterprises of
the early adventurers who founded some of the present
United States down to the present time, the result had invariably been the same; and however successful some of
their attempts had been in creating flourishing colonies,
they had uniformly proved ruinous as pecuniary specula-
tions to the projectors. He was told that the Company
with which his noble friend (Lord Lyttelton) near him was
connected (the Canterbury Settlement), had within the last
few days undergone the common lot of those schemes, and
was obliged to acknowledge itself insolvent. Those who
had attended to such matters must be well aware, that it
was not one of the smallest difficulties of the Colonial Department to deal with the many proposals for the formation
of new colonies. Sanguine projectors were continually putting forward schemes by which they confidently asserted
that, without risk or expense to the public, valuable colonies might be established. Unfortunately the performance
of such promises could not be ensured. Though projectors
could found colonies, it was beyond their power to prevent
their becoming a burden upon the country. In these days,
if a body of Englishmen, sent out to a distant land, were
exposed to the danger of starvation or destruction by
savages, no Government or Parliament could allow such
calamities to happen, or leave the settlers to their fate,
because they had been sent out under an assurance that

the Colony would be self-supporting. Neither could the Government allow that a band of persons should place themselves on any piece of ground they selected, and without mercy shoot out of their way any of the native inhabitants that might oppose them. Hence it was absolutely necessary that the Government should exercise some control over the formation of new settlements, though there were many obvious reasons why this control should not be carried further than was absolutely required. He could best explain what he thought the proper course to be taken in such cases, by stating what had been done while he had the honour of holding the office of Secretary of State. When the establishment of the Canterbury Settlement was projected, he was told that a large sum of money would be provided by the projectors, and that they were ready to undertake the scheme at their own risk; and it was urged that the mere sanction of the Government, which was all that was asked, ought not to be withheld. He agreed that it ought not to be so. He did not fail very strongly to express his opinion to the projectors: he stated, that although the plan might possibly lead ultimately to the formation of a flourishing community, the result would greatly disappoint their expectations in a pecuniary point of view; that it was quite impossible that such a measure should go on with the large price they proposed to ask for land, making promises to the purchasers which they could not perform, and that they would involve themselves in losses, liabilities and difficulties without end. But he also stated at the time to the projectors, that, provided nothing was done which could in any way delude the public as to the real state of the case—if proper precautions were taken, and regulations were adopted to ensure the safety of the Colonists, and guard against abuse—if he were satisfied that adequate securities were provided upon these points, and against any expense being brought upon the public—he should not consider it his duty on the part of the Government to make any objection to the scheme being undertaken at their own risk by that Company. This had appeared to him the proper course to be adopted, because though he felt convinced the scheme would disappoint the expectations of the founders, and that great individual losses might be sustained, still he had no doubt that a settlement would be formed which in the end would become a great and flourishing community, destined to spread the British name and the British language through a large extent of valuable territory; and he considered it no part of the duty of the Government, if these public advantages were to be obtained, to enforce on the projectors greater prudence in regard to their own individual interests. The result, it now seemed, had been precisely what he anticipated : a settlement which would, no doubt, become a very flourishing one had been founded, but great loss had, he understood, been sustained by the projectors; but no claim on the Government, by the Canterbury Association, was likely to arise from the failure of that project, for the relations between the Association and the Government were clearly defined in the first instance : they had not been allowed to enter upon the undertaking at all until they had satisfied the Government that the public interests at stake had been provided for; and care had been taken that, when they were allowed to proceed, no difficulty should be thrown in their way, so that they had not any grounds for saying that their failure—if failure it be—was in any way attributable to the conduct of Government or of Parliament, and therefore were entitled to ask for no pecuniary relief. If the same course had been taken with respect to the New Zealand Company, and it were in the same position, the same remark would be applicable to them; but the circumstances were different, because in the first instance that Company had been permitted to enter upon its undertaking without the sanction of the Government, and without proper securities having been provided, and because afterwards having been permitted to send out the first settlers in a very irregular manner, their operations had been thwarted by the Government. Partly by measures adopted by the local authorities, partly by measures adopted by the Government at home, the Company was prevented from having such a chance of success as they otherwise would have had,—a fact that was clearly shown by the investigation of the Committee to whom the question had been referred. These circumstances were held to give a claim to the New Zealand Company, and though the project might have failed if they had never occurred, they undoubtedly left the projectors without the chance of success to which they were entitled, and it clearly appeared to him that it was the duty of the Government and of Parliament to place them in the situation they would have been in if they had no such grounds of complaint. The noble Earl opposite (the Earl of Derby), when Secretary of State for the Colonies, felt these claims so much, that before he left office he had made arrangements for in some degree assisting the New Zealand Company by means of a loan of money. When he (Earl Grey) came into office, he found the Company complaining that what had been done for them was very far from making up for the injury they had sustained by previous measures, and by the great delay they experienced in getting possession of the land. He felt that there was force in that complaint; that they were entitled to some further compensation, and that something

more should be done to enable them to try fairly the scheme
to carry out which they were originally formed.   Accordingly, the Government having settled what was the largest
amount of money that Parliament should be recommended
to advance, the matter was placed in the hands of his lamented friend the late Mr. Charles Buller, to consider what
was the best arrangement, under existing circumstances, to
enable the Company, with such assistance, fairly and fully
to try whether their scheme was one capable of being successfully worked.   A plan was accordingly prepared with
great care by Mr. Buller, to whom, in concert with the
New Zealand Company, it was entirely left to make what
in his judgement was the best arrangement, subject only to
two conditions, on which he (Earl Grey) specially guarded
himself, namely, that the pecuniary assistance should not
exceed a certain sum, and that the arrangement was to be
a conclusive measure, and a discharge in full of all possible
claims on the part of the New Zealand Company, whether
it should succeed or fail.   After much consideration, Mr.
Charles Buller prepared the drafts of letters between the
Colonial Office and the Directors of the Company, in which
were embodied the terms of the arrangement he proposed.
These terms were assented to by the Government and the
Company : the letters on both sides were written from Mr.
Buller's drafts.   The Bill of 1847 was prepared to carry
into effect the arrangement, and ultimately it received the
assent of Parliament.   Such had been the circumstances
under which the grant of additional aid, and of very large
powers to the New Zealand Company, had been recommended by the late Government, and sanctioned by Parliament. With regard to the manner in which the arrangement thus sanctioned had been carried into effect, it had
appeared to him that there was one clear rule to be fol-

lowed, namely, that the Company should receive every possible support from the Government in working out the plan; and, it being part of the arrangement that a Commissioner should be appointed by the Government, to watch over the proceedings of the Company, his (Earl Grey's) instructions to that Commissioner were not to interfere further than was necessary for the strict protection of the public interests, and for the purpose of seeing that the British Treasury and the Colony were not involved in larger or heavier liabilities than intended when the Act passed. The Commissioner was directed by no means to exercise the power he possessed of putting a veto on any act of the Company, in every case in which their measures might appear to him injudicious; the principle of the Act of Parliament was to invest the Company with the power and the responsibility of conducting a great experiment in colonization; and the only way in which this experiment could be fairly tried was to leave them free and unfettered to act upon their own judgement, except in cases in which interference was clearly necessary for the protection of the public interest. At the end of the period named by the Company as that in which the experiment might be fairly tried, they found that, notwithstanding the large pecuniary assistance they had received, they could not go on; and they claimed under the terms agreed on, to be relieved from the debt due to the Government, and they claimed also a certain sum to be obtained from the sale of lands in New Zealand. He was astonished to hear the noble Duke draw a distinction between the legal and moral right of the New Zealand Company to the ultimate payment of the money due to them and charged on the land fund, and deny their moral claim to more than they could obtain under a strict technical construction of the Act of Parliament. It seemed to

him, that whatever might be the strict construction of the
Act of Parliament, the Government and Parliament in dealing with the Company were bound to act in the same
manner as one honourable man would deal with another in
a transaction in private affairs, and ought to carry fairly into
effect the obvious intention of the agreement.   Looking at
the subject in this light, he thought it was impossible to
say that the New Zealand Company had no claim whatever.   Their Lordships should recollect that the whole
capital of the New Zealand Company had been applied
in creating this colony, and giving value to those lands,
the sale of which was to produce the fund which they
calculated upon for the ultimate repayment of those advances, and he repeated that that was a claim which they
could not honourably decline to recognize.   It was true
that the Act of Parliament pointed out no specific portion of the lands that was to be applied for the support
of emigration, and therefore under the letter of the law
the Crown might no doubt apply so large a proportion
of the fund to emigration that the claim of the Company
would be practically defeated; but this would be inconsistent with good faith; the proportion of the proceeds of
the land sales applied to emigration had been left undeter-
mined, and it was considered that it was the interest both
of the Company and of the Colony, if the debt was ultimately to be paid, so to divide the whole receipts between
the promotion of emigration and the payment of the Company as to leave as large a sum as possible for the former
without neglecting the latter object, because by that means
the demand for land would be increased, and the debt of
the Company would be thereby extinguished.   The Act of
Parliament contemplated obviously the ultimate payment
of the debt, and it was the interest of the Company and

of Parliament that it should be discharged as speedily as possible, by the best possible administration of the lands. The noble Duke said the Company asked for inquiry, and that, pending that inquiry, Parliament ought not to deal with the subject. If by passing the Bill now before the House without the clauses relating to the Company, their position would be unaltered, he should concur in the opinion that Parliament had better not at present deal with this part of the question; but as it was clear that to pass this Bill, omitting the clauses, would alter the position of the Company greatly to their injury, he thought the clauses ought to be retained, though he entirely agreed that inquiry into this matter was right and proper, and he trusted that in another Session the House of Commons would institute a searching investigation respecting it. It was his desire that the inquiry should be conducted on the strictest principles—that every letter, public and private, in connection with the case, should be laid before the Committee, so that the subject should be fairly investigated and reported on by a competent and impartial tribunal. Although he was far from being prepared to defend all the proceedings of the Company, for he would admit that they had frequently acted with imprudence, still he was happy to be able to state that, having investigated the entire case, he had come to the conclusion at which he anticipated the Committee also would arrive—that there had been throughout all these complicated transactions nothing to reflect on the honour, the probity, or the good faith of the gentlemen who had conducted the affairs of the Company. If there were to be an inquiry, it would be inexpedient to enter prematurely into a review of the entire question, in order to convince their Lordships that there was no ground for the charges that had been brought against the Company.

Indeed it would be impossible to do so without having the papers before them which were not yet on their Lordships' table. But without going into the whole case, there were two charges brought against the Company of so serious a nature, and which had been stated with so much confidence, that he must make some observations upon them, especially as an endeavour was made to implicate him in them. These clauses related, first, to an alleged misappropriation of the public funds; and, secondly, to the sending out of certain legal opinions. Now, he must say with regard to the first, that no misapplication of public money could possibly have taken place without the sanction of one or other of the gentlemen who had in succession held the office of the Crown Commissioner; and he had such perfect confidence in both those gentlemen, that he was no less convinced that no money could have been misapplied from the sums appropriated with their sanction, than he should have been had he been personally cognizant of the manner in which every shilling had been expended. The first Commissioner had become involved in disputes with the Company, which ended in his removal; and it was absurd to suppose that he could have allowed them to misappropriate the public money. He was succeeded by a gentleman in whose honour he (Earl Grey) felt no less confidence than in that of Mr. Cowell; while he had greater reliance on his judgement, his discretion, and temper. The instructions he had given to these gentlemen were, that they should not interfere in the application of public money except in cases of abuse, and that he believed to have been the right and proper mode of carrying into effect the arrangement sanctioned by Parliament, for the reason he had already explained. The second charge was, that the New Zealand Company having in a question between themselves and a body of their settlers obtained two opinions from eminent counsel, one adverse and the other in favour of their own view of the subject, had transmitted the latter as if it were the only one to the Colony, and had thus unfairly obtained the assent of the settlers to an arrangement unfavourable to them. Now it would be manifestly absurd were he to enter into the entire history of the complicated transactions to which these opinions related; but he would merely say that in 1849 papers were laid before Parliament, were given to the world, and were sent to the Colonies, in which there was a despatch mentioning the fact that an opinion adverse to the Company had been given by an eminent counsel. It was therefore evident, that the circumstance of an opinion of that sort having been given had been known to all the world for three years, and yet during that time no attempt had been made to unsettle the arrangement made, and now insinuated to have been unduly influenced by the withholding of that opinion. The question raised was, whether the settlement between the New Zealand Company and the Nelson settlers was a fair one, and he believed it was a most advantageous conclusion of affairs for the settlers; and as the existence of the opinion had been publicly known for three years, he said, let the investigation take place by all means; let it be conducted on the most rigorous principles, but in the meantime let the bargain be adhered to, and in justice to the Company let the arrangements suggested by Her Majesty's Government be sanctioned by their Lordships. He would ask what had rendered the land of New Zealand more valuable than the land in New Guinea or other countries uninhabited by civilized men. It was because the Government, Parliament, and the New Zealand Company, had expended large sums in establishing settlers in the former—it was this, and this only, which had given value to the land there; and therefore it was not unreasonable to say that the Company, having received no return for its expenditure during many years (and it was probable it would receive nothing for many more), should have a claim on the land of which the value had been thus enhanced by their means. He thought however that a clause should be inserted in the Bill, that any future claims under the Act of 1847 should be defrayed out of the Colonial funds by the Government of New Zealand, and that none should be in future paid by the Imperial Government. These claims should no longer be on the British Treasury and nation."

C.

Copy of a Despatch from Earl Grey to Governor Sir H. G. Smith, Bart., G.C.B.

"*Downing-street, January* 31, 1850.

" Sir,

" I have now to transmit to you the Report of the Committee of the Board of Trade and Plantations, to which Her Majesty has been pleased to refer the subject of the proposed establishment of a Representative Legislature in the Colony of the Cape of Good Hope.

" This Report so clearly lays down the outlines of those institutions which it is proposed to establish in the Colony, and so fully points out the general reasons which have induced the Committee to adopt its conclusions, both in those instances in which they concur with, and those in which they differ from, the views so ably expressed in the several minutes and papers which I have received from you, that all comment on it from myself is rendered unnecessary.

"You will observe that the recommendation of the Committee is, that the main and leading features of the Constitution to be granted to the Colony should be laid down in Letters Patent. It will be my duty to proceed immediately to cause the necessary instrument for this purpose to be prepared; but it also directs that all the subordinate arrangements should be made by Ordinance in the Colony.

"You will, therefore, on the receipt of this despatch, immediately proceed to cause the necessary information to be collected, and whatever other preliminary work may require to be done, performed, with a view to the preparation of these Ordinances. The various details of the machinery of elections, the definition of the franchise of the electors both for the Assembly and the Legislative Council, and many other particulars, which will readily occur to you, are all subjects on which the necessary provisions will be made by Ordinance, and not by Letters Patent, and as to which, therefore, you may, with a view to expedition, prepare at once the matter to be embodied in the Ordinance, without waiting for the arrival of the Letters Patent themselves, though of course, until they reach you, the subject cannot be brought under the consideration of the Legislative Council.

"I have, etc.,

"(Signed)   GREY."

" *Lieut.-Governor Sir H. G. Smith,*
        " *etc., etc., etc.*"

Enclosure.

At the Court at Windsor, the 30th day of January, 1850.

Present—THE QUEEN'S MOST EXCELLENT MAJESTY IN
COUNCIL.

" WHEREAS there was this day read at the Board a Report of the Right Honourable the Lords of the Committee in Council, appointed for the consideration of all matters relating to Trade and Foreign Plantations, dated the 19th instant, in the words following, viz. :—

" Your Majesty having been pleased by your Order in Council of January 31, 1849, to refer to this Committee various papers relating to the proposed establishment of a Representative Legislature in the Colony of the Cape of Good Hope, in order that we might consider the same and report to Your Majesty our opinion as to the measures it would be advisable to adopt ; we have now, in obedience to Your Majesty's commands, humbly to submit to Your Majesty the following Report of the results of our deliberations.

" In laying before Your Majesty the conclusions to which we have come, we think it right, in the first place, to observe, that we have assumed the question referred to us to be, not whether it may be expedient to grant Representative Institutions to the Colony of the Cape of Good Hope, but rather what may be the particular form of Representative Constitution which may be taken for the purpose of carrying into effect the changes in its existing Constitution, which we may decide upon recommending. The former question appeared to us to have been already practically decided by the Despatch which, on Feb. 12, 1849, No. 276, was addressed by the Secretary of State for the Colonial Department to the Governor of the Cape of Good Hope, and in which that officer was informed that Your Majesty's Servants would be prepared to advise Your Majesty to adopt the recommendation of the Governor, that a Representative Legislature should be established in this Colony, reserving for further and more mature consideration the question as to the manner in which this object should be effected. This last question, which is that which we understand to have been referred to us, we have found to be one of equal difficulty and importance. While we fully recognize the necessity of a change in the existing form of Government at the Cape, and the expediency of granting to its inhabitants the benefit of a Constitution founded on the principle of representation, we have found in the peculiar circumstances of the Colony very serious obstacles to the establishment of any such system of Government, of which the satisfactory operation can be anticipated with any confidence; and we are bound to express our fear, that we have failed in discovering any mode of proceeding which we can recommend, as being free from grave objections; we shall therefore only be able to point out that to which it appears to us that there are the fewest, and of which upon that ground we are prepared to advise the adoption.

" The difficulties which must be encountered in any attempt to establish a representative Government in the Colony of the Cape of Good Hope, have been explained in a Despatch (forming part of the papers referred to us) which on the 15th of April, 1842, Lord Stanley, who then held the seals of the Colonial Department, addressed to Governor Sir George Napier. Referring to this Despatch for a fuller statement of his Lordship's views, we may observe that the most serious difficulties he anticipated in the satisfactory working of a Representative Legislature in this Colony, were first, those which he thought were likely to arise from

the great distance of many of the districts of the Colony
from the capital, which was calculated to prevent those remote parts of the country from having their due weight in
a Legislature meeting at Cape Town; and secondly, those
which would be occasioned by the circumstance that the
population of the Colony was composed of various races,
widely differing from each other in character, and in the
progress they have made in civilization.

"In the able papers forming the enclosures of the Despatch of the present Governor of the Cape, dated July 29th,
1848, the questions are very fully discussed—whether these
difficulties are likely so to affect the working of representative institutions, as to be a valid objection to their being
granted; and whether, if they are to be granted, it is
expedient either to divide the Colony into two or more districts, having separate Legislatures, or to remove the place
of meeting of a single Legislature to some more central
situation than that of Cape Town.

"After an elaborate examination of these questions in
all their bearings, the Judges and the members of the Executive Council of the Colony have concurred in expressing their opinion, that a Legislature in which the inhabitants of the Colony are represented ought to be created;
that there ought to be but one such Legislature for the
whole Colony, and that Cape Town should continue as at
present to be the seat of the Government.

"We are not disposed to dissent from these practical
conclusions, because, upon the whole, we think that it has
been shown that still greater inconvenience would result
from any other course that could be adopted; but we regret our inability to express our opinion that, in the practical working of a representative constitution at the Cape,
the geographical difficulties anticipated by Lord Stanley

will not be experienced to a very serious degree. The formidable distance which separates much of the wide territory included within the Colony from the seat of Government, must, we apprehend, greatly affect the value, to the inhabitants of the remoter districts, of the privilege of choosing their own representatives, more especially when the imperfection of the existing means of communication (greatly as these have of late been improved) is considered; and the fact that there are few, if any, of the residents in these districts who possess wealth and leisure enough to enable them, if chosen members of the Legislature, to reside for any considerable time in each year in the capital, for the discharge of their senatorial duties, without extreme inconvenience. We have not long since, in reporting to Your Majesty on the changes proposed in the constitution of the Australian Colonies, had occasion to point out how intolerable a grievance it had been felt by the inhabitants of the district of Port Philip to be placed under the authority of a Legislature meeting at Sydney, and to be called upon to elect members of that body. We regarded this grievance as so real, that we had no hesitation in recommending that the district in question should be erected into a distinct Government as the province of Victoria.

" We can hardly doubt that the residents in the eastern and northern portions of the Cape territory, will experience similar inconvenience to that which has been felt by the inhabitants of Port Philip; and we are only withheld from advising that the Colony should be divided by the circumstance, that it appears to be the decided opinion of those whose local knowledge gives them better means of forming a sound judgement than ourselves, that the means do not exist of forming two separate Legislatures with advantage; and also by the consideration, that hereafter,

if the population of the eastern district should be largely
increased, the division may be at any time effected, if in
the opinion of the Representative Legislature, which may
in the first instance be created for the whole Colony, this
division should become desirable.

" We would submit to Your Majesty that, in order to
mitigate as much as may be possible the inconvenience to
which the inhabitants of the eastern district will unavoidably be subjected, it would be proper that the members of
the Legislature should receive a pecuniary allowance sufficient to cover the expense to which they will be put on
their journey, and by their residence at a distance from
their homes ; and also that arrangements should be made
restricting the annual sessions of the Legislature to as short
a period as may be practicable.   With a view to the latter
object, we are of opinion that as large a share as possible
of business should be intrusted to the municipal and other
local bodies which already exist, and that no opportunity
should be lost of improving the organization of these bodies
and extending their functions, leaving to the General Legislature only that class of business which, in the strictest
sense of the words, is of common interest to the whole
Colony.   With the same object, we would further recommend that the amount of the allowance to be made to
members for their attendance should not be made to depend
upon the length of the session, but should be of a fixed
amount, to be paid only when the business of the session
should be completed.

" With regard to the difficulties which were considered
by Lord Stanley as being likely to arise in the working
of a representative Government, from the circumstance
that the population of the Colony is composed of various
races differing from each other in language, in character,

and in the progress they have made in civilization, we are
willing to hope that they may be found less serious in
practice than his Lordship anticipated; and we trust that
the fact mentioned by Mr. Montagu, the Colonial Secretary, in his minute of the 10th of April, 1848, that the
coloured inhabitants have taken part, without objection, in
the Municipal Government of Cape Town, both as electors
and as representatives, may be accepted as a proof that
they will also be able to take their fair share in the exercise
of those powers which will be entrusted to the people by the
creation of a representative Legislature. At the same time
we are bound to observe that there is a great difference
between the coloured inhabitants of Cape Town, who are
in general removed by at least three or four generations
from the untutored natives of Africa, as they existed before
they were brought into contact with European civilization,
and the rude and ignorant beings, some of them still but
little, if at all, raised above the condition of their original
barbarism, who are to be found in other districts of the
Colony, and in some, constitute a very considerable portion
of its inhabitants. We think it will be indispensable that
arrangements should be made for securing the effective
protection of the Crown for this population of African race,
as they cannot themselves exercise any considerable share
of that popular power which will be created by the establishment of a representative Legislature. We shall, in a
subsequent portion of our Report, have occasion to return
to this subject.

" Should Your Majesty be pleased to adopt our advice
by sanctioning the creation of a General Legislature for
the whole Colony, in which its inhabitants should be represented, the next question to be determined will be, shall
that Legislature consist of a single deliberate body on the

principle of the Legislative Council of New South Wales, which, with the Governor, should exercise the powers of legislation; or will it be better that the old Colonial system should be adopted of a Legislature of three estates, consisting of the Governor, a Legislative Council, and a Representative Assembly? We have no hesitation in giving it as our opinion that the latter should be preferred. In our Report upon the Australian Colonies we have fully explained our reasons for considering it better, in cases in which a regard for existing arrangements does not prescribe a different course, that two deliberate bodies should be required to co-operate in the task of legislation; and we find that the principle which we had thus recommended, as that which ought generally to be followed in the constitution of a Colonial Legislature, has also been pointed out as the one most suitable to the special circumstances of the Cape by the Governor and the majority of his advisers on this subject. We therefore beg leave humbly to submit to Your Majesty our recommendation, that the Legislature of the Cape of Good Hope should consist of three estates, as in the older British Colonies; though, for reasons which we shall almost immediately proceed to state, we do not advise that the Legislative Council should be constituted upon the model which has hitherto been generally followed.

" Previously however to explaining our views with reference to the composition of the Legislative Council, it will be convenient that we should advert to the much less difficult question which relates to the constitution of the Assembly. We are of opinion that this body should be elected by voters whose qualification should be that recommended by Mr. Montagu; that is to say, that in the towns and villages in which Municipal Boards have been created the franchise should be the same with the existing municipal franchise; and that in the electoral districts, in which Municipal Boards have not been constituted, the right of voting should be conferred on all those whose property has been assessed for the expense of the roads. This franchise possesses the great advantage of extreme simplicity, and of introducing as little novelty as possible.

" Closely connected with the question as to the electoral franchise, is that respecting the qualification for members of the Assembly. In the Minutes transmitted by Sir H. Smith different proposals are made upon this head ; but we confess that we do not find any reasons to be advanced for narrowing the choice of the electors, which appear to us sufficient to establish the necessity of doing so; and believing that if the electors should not prove trustworthy, but should be inclined to make a bad use of their franchise, no qualification which may be required for members, whether it be the possession of property or belonging to a liberal profession, would prevent the choice of representatives who would express the sentiments of their constituents, we would recommend that no person entitled to the elective franchise should be excluded from sitting as a member of the Assembly. At the same time we think it would be expedient that, in making the arrangements which would be necessary for the introduction of the proposed change in the constitution of the Colony, the existing Legislative Council should be empowered to establish a qualification for members of the Assembly, if it should judge this to be expedient for local reasons of which we are not aware.

" With regard to the number of members of which the Assembly should consist, and to the principle upon which the division of the Colony into electoral districts should be made, we are disposed generally to concur with Mr. Montagu, the Colonial Secretary. We consider it to be an important and valuable suggestion that the towns and the rural districts should be separately represented in the manner recommended by Mr. Montagu; we do not however concur with him in thinking that it would be expedient altogether to reject the principle of making some allowance for the extent as well as the population of a district, in determining its share of the representation, on the plan which is adverted to in the Despatch of Lord Stanley we have already quoted, as having been in some cases adopted in North America. No doubt if that principle were carried to the extent which has been supposed by Mr. Montagu, in the case he has 'put in illustration of its probable operation, it would lead to very inconvenient results; but we apprehend that this has never been contemplated; and on the other hand, if the inhabitants of Cape Town, who are said to constitute one-fifth of the whole population of the Colony, were on that account to return so many as a fifth of the members of the Assembly, there can be no doubt that the power of joint and combined action which they would enjoy from their residing within so limited a space, and with such facilities for communicating with each other, would give them far more than a proportionate weight in the Legislature, with the same number of inhabitants scattered over a wide extent of territory, and that the more remote and thinly peópled districts would be deprived of that share of influence which in fairness they ought to possess. Hence we would recommend that a rule should be adopted, by which the strict numerical proportion between the number of the population and that of the members they should be entitled to return, should be somewhat qualified in favour of the more thinly-peopled districts.

" The last point which it is necessary that we should here notice with reference to the constitution of the Assembly, is the period for which it should be elected. Upon this question we are disposed rather to concur with the Attorney-General than with the Colonial Secretary; and we should recommend that the Assembly should be elected for five years, unless sooner dissolved by the Governor acting on behalf of the Crown. We are of opinion that, in a territory of such great extent, frequent elections would prove a very serious inconvenience, and that a sufficiently close connection would be maintained between the representatives and their constituents by parliaments of five years' duration.

" The question as to how the Legislative Council ought to be constituted, which we will now proceed to consider, is one of much greater difficulty. It is on all hands admitted, that it is highly desirable that there should be a second branch of the Legislature less easily swayed by the popular feeling of the moment than the Representative Assembly, and capable of acting as a check and counterpoise to that body, in order to guard against hasty legislalation without requiring the too frequent interference of the Governor or of the Crown. But in order to perform these functions with effect, it is necessary that the Legislative Council should be a body of real weight and influence, commanding the respect and confidence of the public. To create such a body is obviously a problem of no easy solution. If the ordinary Colonial Constitution be taken as the example to be followed, the Council ought to be composed of a moderate number of persons (including some holding offices in the public service) nominated by the Crown, and holding their seats (practically at least) for life. This is the description of Legislative Council of which the majority of Sir Harry Smith's advisers have recommended the adoption; but after very careful consideration of the subject, and of the arguments they have advanced in favour of the conclusion to which they have come, we have not been able to concur in it. In stating their reasons for advising that a Representative Legislature should be established in the Colony of the Cape of Good Hope, the very able and experienced servants of the Crown who were consulted by the Governor, have unanimously expressed the strongest opinion that the existing Legislative Council does not command the confidence of the inhabitants of the Colony, and has little influence on public opinion. But the composition of the existing Legislative Council is practically the same with that which is recommended for the body, which, under the same designation, is proposed to be joined with a Representative Assembly in the work of legislation; it consists of official members and of members not holding any office in the public service, who owe their seats to the nomination of the Crown. We cannot believe that the character of this body would be essentially altered by increasing the proportion of unofficial to official members, or by making the life-tenure of their seats to depend, not on a usage which is practically almost invariably followed, but on the law; nor have we any reason to believe that it would be in the power of the Governors of the Colony in time to come, to make a more careful and judicious selection of members to be appointed to the Council, than that which has been made by their predecessors. On the contrary, we are persuaded that, after the establishment of a Representative Assembly, that body will have so much more real authority than a Council nominated by the Crown, that seats in the former will be a greater object of ambition than those in the latter, and it will thus become impossible to obtain the services in the Legislative Council of gentlemen of as much weight and influence with their fellow-citizens as those who have been heretofore appointed.

"The inference, we think, is irresistible, that a body, which even while it exercises the whole power of legislation has little hold over public opinion, will cease to have any real weight or influence when it comes to be overshadowed by so substantial a power as that of an Assembly elected by the people. Hence we concur with the Chief Justice of the Colony in believing, that if it is desired to give to the Legislative Council strength to act in any degree as a balance to the Assembly, the elective principle must enter into its composition. We are fully aware of the importance of such a departure from all former precedents; but the considerations by which the innovation is recommended are, in our judgement, of too much weight to be disregarded.

"We recommend, therefore, that the members of the Legislative Council should be elected, but by a different body of electors from those by whom the members of the Assembly are to be chosen, and for a longer term. We would propose that the Council, unless sooner dissolved, should be chosen for ten years; that is to say, for a term equal to twice that for which we have proposed that the Assembly should be elected, and that it should be renewed not all at once, but by half of the members being subject to re-election at the end of every five years. In the first instance the members who had been elected by the smallest number of votes should be those to go out of the Council at the end of five years. At the subsequent periodical renewals of the Council the members to go out would of course be those who had served their full term.

"With regard to the franchise, in right of which persons

should be entitled to vote in the election of members of the Legislative Council, we are of opinion that if a property qualification is taken at all, it ought to be one considerably higher than that which is required to give the right of voting in elections for the Assembly. It must not be forgotten that hitherto it has been the practice in the British Colonies, that the members of the Legislative Council should be nominated by the Crown; and in proposing that they should be elected, we are aware that we are advising a measure which will add not a little to the power of the popular element in the Constitution; hence we are of opinion that it will be only a proper precaution to require that the electors by whom its members shall be chosen shall be of a higher station in society, than will be necessarily possessed by those who will be the constituents of the House of Assembly. Unless this is provided for, the Constitution will want, as it appears to us, that due balance which it ought to have.

" It is not in our power, from the information within our reach, to form a judgement as to what ought to be the amount of property which should give the right of voting in the election of members of the Legislative Council, and we would recommend that this question should be left to be decided (subject to Your Majesty's approbation) by the existing Colonial Legislature; but we would at the same time suggest, as a question well deserving the consideration of that body, whether it might not be a better arrangement to adopt a franchise of a different kind, and to confer the right of voting in the election of members of the Legislative Council on those who had been called either by the choice of the Crown or of their fellow-citizens to fill certain situations of trust and responsibility. It is an advantage, with a view to the adoption of a franchise founded on this

principle, that there are a considerable number of situations of trust connected with the local administration of
the Colony, the fact of having been appointed to which
might fairly be taken as a proof that the holders had
been considered entitled to confidence, either by the
Crown or by their fellow-citizens. In the rural districts
the Justices of the Peace and Field Cornets are generally
selected by the Governor on account of the estimation
in which they are held, and their reputation as men of
worth, intelligence, and activity. In the municipalities
it is fair to presume that the Commissioners and Ward-
masters are chosen by those whose affairs they are trusted
to administer on similar grounds. It appears to us probable that a body of electors having great claims on the public confidence might be formed from the persons who were
either actually the holders, or had formerly for a certain
length of time held such situations as those we have just
mentioned, to whom might hereafter be added those who
for a whole Parliament had sat in the Assembly as representatives of the people. It is impossible, without more
accurate local information than we possess, to point out
precisely what should be the situations from holding which
the right of voting in the election of members of the
Legislative Council should be derived. This is a question
which will require careful investigation on the spot; we
will only remark that, in our opinion, the principle to be
observed in making the decision should be, to take care
that the rural and urban communities had each their due
weight in the constituent body to be thus formed.

"The adoption of either such a franchise as that
which we have now suggested, or of one resting on a high
property qualification, which would prevent the electors
of the Legislative Council from forming a very numerous

body, would render it difficult to divide the Colony into districts for the purpose of these elections ; and we are also of opinion that, even if this difficulty did not exist, it would be better that the members of the Legislative Council should be chosen for the whole Colony than only for particular districts, since it would thus be more probable that the preference would be given to men of the highest reputation, rather than those of mere local influence. We therefore recommend that in electing the members of the Legislative Council, the electors in all parts of the Colony should send in writing certified declarations of the names of the candidates for whom they intended to vote, to the seat of Government, and that these declarations should there be publicly examined, and the result proclaimed.

" The adoption of this proposal would render it further necessary, to provide against the risk of having the Legislative Council composed exclusively of persons of the same political opinions. It is the invariable tendency of free governments to lead to the formation of political parties ; and we believe that much of the usefulness of deliberative bodies exercising the power of legislation, depends upon their being so constituted as not entirely to exclude any of the parties into which the community is divided. In a popular Assembly, chosen by electoral districts of limited size, it is found that the various local influences which prevail, and the diversities of opinion and of interest which exist between different bodies of constituents, are in general sufficient, practically to secure a fair representation of every political party; but it is obvious that this would not be the case in a Legislative Council chosen by one election for the whole Colony, and that if it is desired that the body should not be a representation of a single interest and a single class of opinions, some means must be adopted to guard against its falling entirely into the hands of the dominant party. With this view we would recommend that, in the election of the Council, each elector should have as many votes as there might be members to be chosen, and should be entitled either to give all these votes to a single candidate, or to divide them amongst different candidates at his pleasure ; that is to say, that if ten or five members of the Legislative Council had to be elected, each voter should have a right either to give ten or five votes to any one candidate, or to distribute them amongst several. By this arrangement, a monopoly of power in the Legislative Council by any one party, or any one district of the Colony, would be prevented, since a minority of the electors, by giving all their votes to a single candidate, would be enabled to secure his return.

" We observe, from the papers before us, that it appears to be supposed that the Colony could not conveniently furnish more than ten unofficial members of the Legislative Council appointed by the Crown ; we conclude that it would be equally difficult to find any large number of elective members who could serve without serious inconvenience to themselves, and who would be fit for this important trust ; we would therefore advise that for the present this should be the number of the Council. Although it would be a smaller body than would in some respects be desirable, we are of opinion that a Legislative Council of ten members would be sufficient in the first instance ; and as the Colony advances in wealth and population, the number might be increased.

" We have said that we recommend that the Legislative Councillors should be elected for ten years, half the body going out (but being eligible for re-election) every five years, provided the Council were not sooner dissolved.

Upon this subject we would remark, that it appears to us, that in order to guard against the possible contingency of an irreconcileable difference between the two branches of the Legislature, the Governor should be invested with the power of dissolving the Legislative Council if he should find it necessary to do so. We are however of opinion, that it would be right to provide that the Legislative Council should not be dissolved unless the Assembly were dissolved at the same time; but that the Assembly might be dissolved in the usual manner, without requiring that the Legislative Council should be so likewise. After a dissolution, as well as on the first election of the Legislative Council, the five members chosen by the smallest number of votes, would have to go out at the end of five years, in order that the periodical renewal of that body, by one-half at a time, might afterwards proceed with regularity. With the same object it would be necessary to provide that vacancies occasioned by the death or resignation of members, should be filled by new members elected only for the remaining term, for which those whom they succeeded would have sat.

" In so limited a body it would be necessary to require the regular attendance of all the members; we therefore recommend that any member who should be absent from more than half the meetings of the Legislative Council in any of its sessions, without the special leave of the Council, should be considered to have resigned his seat, and that it should be declared vacant accordingly.

" To this Legislative Council we should not propose to add any official members, with the exception of the Chief Justice, who might we think with great advantage be made its *ex-officio* Speaker. His high and dignified position would eminently qualify him for filling this situation, and we think it would be exceedingly useful to the Council, in considering many of the questions which would come before it, to have the benefit of the advice and assistance of the first legal authority in the Colony. With this single exception, we are decidedly of opinion that it would be highly inexpedient to add official members to the Legislative Council, since such an addition would necessarily detract something from that character of independence which we are anxious to secure for that body.

" If, however, this recommendation should be approved by Your Majesty, we think that its adoption would render it expedient to confer upon the Governor the same power which has been given to the Governor of New South Wales, of returning, with amendments, for the consideration of the other branches of the Legislature, Bills which are tendered to him for his assent on behalf of the Crown. The Legislative Council, as it is constituted in some of the older Colonies, can sometimes be made use of with advantage by the Governor, to relieve himself from the embarrassing necessity of either accepting Bills containing objectionable provisions, or rejecting on account of such provisions, measures which are in other respects highly useful and even necessary. If the Governor is deprived of a preponderating influence in the Legislative Council, we are of opinion that he should be enabled to amend Bills which may be presented to him in the manner we have suggested. For all really useful objects this power would be of far more service than the influence in the Legislative Council, of which he would be deprived.

" The elective character we have proposed to give to the Legislative Council would also, we think, render it expedient to vary in another respect the ordinary rules for the transaction of the public business in a Legislature composed of three estates ; and we would recommend that it should be expressly provided that the Legislative Council should be entitled to amend, if it should so think fit, money Bills sent up to it from the Assembly, by either increasing or diminishing the amount of the taxation to be imposed, or of the appropriations of revenue to be made by the Bills proposed to it. These amendments would, of course, like any others, require the concurrence of the Assembly, before the Bills in which they were introduced would be presented for the assent of the Governor.

" Having thus fully explained our views as to what we think would be the best constitution of the Legislature for the Cape of Good Hope, we have now humbly to submit to Your Majesty some further observations on points which we consider to be of importance with, reference to the successful working of the system of government which it is proposed to establish.

" It has been suggested in most of the Minutes inclosed in Sir H. Smith's Despatch, that the principal officers of the Colonial Government should be at liberty to become members of the Assembly by election. We cannot concur in this recommendation, which is contrary to what has been the usual practice of Colonial Governments. It is true that of late years in the North American Colonies, what was formerly the general usage has been departed from, and that some of the principal offices of the Government are now held by members of the Legislature ; but this change of practice has been coupled with the establishment of what has been termed ' responsible,' but what would more correctly be described as ' parliamentary,' or ' party government,' the essence of which is that the offices of the Colonial Government which are conferred on members of the Legislature, are to be held by them only while they continue to be supported by a majority of the

House of Assembly. This system of administration we regard as altogether unsuited to the present circumstances of the Cape Colony, because we believe it to be one which can never work with advantage except in countries which have made such progress in wealth and population that there are to be found in them a considerable number of persons who can devote a large proportion of their time to public affairs.

" When this system has not been established, the principal officers of the Executive Government have almost invariably, by their exclusion from seats in the popular assemblies, been withdrawn from the party contests in which they would otherwise have been involved.

" It is suggested that without the assistance to be derived from the members of the colonial administration, the Assembly would experience considerable difficulty in dealing with the various subjects which must come under its consideration. We do not think that the experience of other Colonies warrants any such apprehension ; but if it is true that from peculiar circumstances this difficulty is likely to be felt at the Cape, we see no objection to providing that the Colonial Secretary, the Attorney-General, and the Treasurer, should have the privilege of taking part in the discussions of both branches of the Legislature, so far as might be necessary for the explanation of any measures proposed by the Government, but without being entitled to vote.

" It is strongly recommended by more than one of the Governor's advisers, that the last estimate for the fixed expenditure of the Colony should continue in force until the new one is voted. This recommendation is founded on the same principle (though the mode of applying it is different) with that contained in the following passage of the Report which we had the honour of submitting to Your Majesty on the Constitutions of the Australian Colonies :—

" ' Passing to the subject of a Civil List, we have to observe, that the very large proportion of the revenue of New South Wales, at present withdrawn from the control of the Legislature by the permanent appropriation of Parliament, has been a continual subject of complaint and remonstrance in the Colony since the passing of the Constitutional Act of 1842; and we cannot conceal our opinion that these complaints are not without some foundation. It appears to us hardly consistent with the full adoption of the principles of representative Government, that as to a large part of the public expenditure of the Colony the Legislature should be deprived of all authority ; nor does there appear to us to be any real occasion for imposing a restriction upon the powers of that body, which manifests so much jealousy as to the manner in which those powers may be exercised. The expenditure thus provided for is all incurred for services in which the Colonists alone are interested. The Colonists themselves are mainly concerned in the proper and efficient performance of those services ; and it appears to us that they ought to possess, through their representatives, the power of making such changes from time to time in the public establishments as circumstances may require. But while we are of opinion that there is no sufficient reason for refusing to the Legislatures of the Colonies a control over the whole of their expenditure, we also think that great inconvenience and very serious evils might be expected to arise, from leaving the whole of the public establishments to be provided for by annual vote. In this country Your Majesty's Civil List is settled upon Your Majesty for life, and, in addition to this, Parliament has thought fit to provide, by a permanent charge on the Consolidated Fund, for a very considerable part of the establishments kept up for the public service, including the whole of those of a judicial character, leaving to be defrayed by annual votes those charges only which have been regarded as requiring the more frequent revision of the Legislature. The reasons which have induced the British Parliament in this manner to withdraw various heads of expenditure from annual discussion, and to make provision for them in a manner which can only be altered by an Act of the whole Legislature, apply, as we apprehend, with much increased force in favour of adopting a similar policy in the Colonies. It is not to be denied that in these smaller societies, party spirit is apt to run still higher than amongst ourselves, and that questions respecting the remuneration of public servants are occasionally discussed rather with reference to personal feelings than to a calm consideration of the real interest of the community. We believe also that true economy is promoted, by giving to those who are employed in the public service some reasonable assurance for the permanence of their official incomes. It is thus only that efficient service can be secured in return for a moderate remuneration. With these views the arrangement which we should recommend is, that Parliament should, in the first instance, charge upon the revenues of the several Colonies, an amount sufficient to defray the expense of those services which it would be inexpedient to leave to be provided for by annual votes of the respective Legislatures, leaving however to those Legislatures full power to alter this appropriation by laws to be passed in the usual form. It would remain for Your Majesty to determine what instructions should be given to the Governors of these Colonies, as to their assenting on behalf of the Crown to any laws which might be tendered to them by

the Legislatures, for repealing or altering any of the charges
created by Parliament on the revenues of the respective
Colonies. We conceive that it might be advisable, by such
instructions, to restrain the Governors from assenting to
acts making any alterations in the salaries of their own
offices, or of those of the judges and some others of the
public servants, unless these acts contained clauses suspending their operation, until they should be confirmed by
Your Majesty's immediate authority. It appears to us
that this course ought to be adopted, because we consider
that the salaries of the principal officers of the Colonial
governments ought not to be changed without Your Majesty's direct concurrence; and because the present holders
of some of the offices of lower rank have received their appointments, under circumstances which give them a strong
claim to the protection which would be thus afforded to
them. Men who have abandoned other prospects for the
purpose of accepting Colonial employment, which they had
reason to expect would be permanent, and who have since
faithfully discharged their duties, must be regarded as
having claims which rest upon the grounds of public faith,
and on contracts, which on their side have hitherto been
strictly fulfilled, to retain their present salaries, so long as
they shall conduct themselves properly, or to receive adequate compensation for their loss. We doubt not that
such claims would be respected by the local Legislatures,
whatever reductions they might see fit to make in other
cases; but we think that Your Majesty ought to secure
them even from the risk of a hasty and ill-considered decision to their prejudice, occasioned by some temporary excitement; subject to these qualifications, we are of opinion
that complete control over the Colonial expenditure ought
to be given to the respective Legislatures.'

" We are of opinion that the mode of proceeding here recommended, is that which it is preferable to adopt in making the arrangements for the future government of the Cape, and we would strongly advise that the fixed establishments should be provided for by a permanent appropriation, in the same manner with that portion of the civil establishment of this country which is charged upon the Consolidated Fund.

" The concurrence of the three branches of the Legislature would thus be necessary for any alterations in this appropriation, but we beg leave to explain, that we are far from intending that by this arrangement the Assembly should be debarred from the power of making reductions, even though they might be injudicious, in the amount of the expenditure provided for by their constituents. On the contrary, we should hold it to be highly inexpedient that the power which we have advised that Your Majesty should retain, should be practically exercised to check any retrenchments proposed by the Assembly with a *bonâ fide* view to the reduction of expenditure, and with a due regard to the claims of individuals on the public faith. There are but two exceptions which we are aware of, which it would be necessary to make, and these regard the salary of the Governor and the appropriations which are now made from the Colonial revenue for the maintenance of the establishments required for the preservation of order, and the spread of civilization amongst the border tribes.

" With regard to the Governor's salary, we think it necessary that it should be secured against injudicious reduction, because we consider it to be of vital importance that the salaries attached to the principal colonial governments should be sufficient to form an inducement for the acceptance of these offices to men occupying a high position at home, and who have been here accustomed to take a leading part in public affairs. We are persuaded that the maintenance, in a manner satisfactory to both parties, of the connection between the Mother-country and those British Colonies which are rapidly advancing from the condition of infant communities, during their progress in population, in wealth, and in the exercise of the powers of self-government, will mainly depend upon the office of Governor being in all cases placed in the ablest hands that can be found.

" With regard to the appropriation we have proposed from the Colonial revenue, for objects connected with the policy to be followed towards the border tribes, we have to observe, that we consider, that to place the appropriation of sufficient funds for these purposes beyond the control of the Assembly, is absolutely necessary, in justice to Your Majesty's subjects at home who are interested in the maintenance of tranquillity, and to the native tribes who will not be represented in the Assembly, and yet are large contributors to the revenue from which this appropriation is to be made, since the various goods which they are beginning to consume in very considerable quantities, are subject to duties for the benefit of the Colonial Treasury.

" In connection with this part of the subject before us, we have to remark that we should not recommend that the authority of the proposed Legislature should be extended either over the districts known as the Orange River Sovereignty and British Kafraria, or over the Settlement of Natal. For the latter a separate Legislature has been already created; and with regard to the two former we shall have the honour of submitting to Your Majesty a distinct report.

" We have now gone through all the points which have

appeared to us to require attention with reference to the proposed change in the form of government at present in existence at the Cape of Good Hope. It only remains that we should very briefly explain the practical steps by which we are of opinion that this change may most conveniently be carried into effect.

" In the recommendations which we have humbly submitted to Your Majesty, we have suggested various arrangements, of which it would be impossible that the details should be determined in this country, since for this purpose accurate local knowledge, which is here unattainable, would be required.

" Hence, we would submit, that the most convenient course which could be adopted would be that Your Majesty should, by letters patent, authorize the Governor to summon a Legislature of the kind we have endeavoured to describe, as soon as Ordinances for regulating all the details of the arrangement should have been passed by the existing Legislative Council, and should have been confirmed by Your Majesty.

" We would recommend that in the letters patent to be issued for this purpose, the main and leading provisions of the Constitution to be granted to the Colony should alone be laid down, and that power should be given to the existing Legislative Council to pass Ordinances, subject to Your Majesty's approbation, for regulating all the subordinate arrangements, of which we are of opinion that as large a share as possible should be thus left to be determined on the spot.

" We would however humbly advise that Your Majesty would distinctly reserve to yourself the power of amending by Orders to be made in your Privy Council, the Ordinances which, in pursuance of the above recommendation, may be passed in the Colony.

" We are aware that some delay will necessarily be occasioned in effecting the intended change by the adoption of this mode of proceeding; but in creating representative institutions, and in deciding upon the form of government under which the Colony is in future to be placed, and which must exercise so powerful an influence in promoting or retarding its future progress in prosperity, the delay of a few months in carrying the change into effect, is so utterly immaterial compared to the importance of taking every possible precaution for guarding against the danger of error, that we feel it to be our duty to express to Your Majesty our strong opinion that the course we have suggested is the only one which can with prudence be adopted.

" Her Majesty having taken the said Report into consideration, was pleased, by and with the advice of Her Privy Council, to approve thereof.

" (Signed)   Wm. L. Bathurst."

D.

Copy of a Despatch from Earl Grey to Governor Sir H. G. Smith, Bart.

" *Downing-street, December* 10, 1850.

" Sir,

" I have had the honour of receiving your Despatch, No. 138, of the 24th of September, in which you inform me that, by the resignation of four members of the Legislative Council, that body had been interrupted in considering the measures required for giving effect to Her Majesty's letters patent of the 23rd of May last, by which provision was made for establishing a Representative Constitution in the Colony of the Cape of Good Hope. Though I have not yet received from you any official account of your subsequent proceedings, and of the state of affairs in the Colony, I am likewise made acquainted with what had occurred up to the 3rd of October, by the Government *Gazettes*, and some of the colonial newspapers, which you have transmitted to me, from which I learn that you had regarded the Legislative Council as having been rendered incapable, by the retirement of the four members who had left it, of continuing its sittings with a view to the passing of the Ordinances contemplated by the letters patent for the completion of the Constitution; and that, in order to enable Her Majesty to provide by other means for that object, you intended to send to me a report from the remaining members of the Legislative Council, acting as a board of Commissioners, on the measures which ought to be adopted.

"It is a great disadvantage to me to be under the necessity of expressing to you the opinion of Her Majesty's Government upon transactions of so much importance, in the absence of that fuller information as to your views and intentions, which you state in the Despatch now before me, that you meant in a few days to furnish; but as your sudden summons to the frontier by the intelligence of apprehended disturbances in Kafraria, which I presume to have prevented you from writing again on this subject as early as you had proposed, may probably compel you to defer doing so for some time longer, I am unwilling to lose the opportunity of communicating with you afforded by the departure of the first of the steam-packets by which monthly mails are now to be forwarded to the Colony; and though, in the absence of the further information I expect from you, it is out of my power to convey to you positive instructions as to the course you are to adopt, it may obviate some delay in bringing about the intended establishment of a Representative Government in the Colony if I now make known to you the judgement which Her Majesty's Government have formed upon the subject, from the information at present in our possession.

" In order to render more clearly intelligible what I shall have to say upon the recent transactions, it will be convenient that I should in the first instance shortly refer to some of the previous proceedings respecting the proposed change in the form of government now existing at the Cape. You will no doubt recollect that, having received your Despatch of the 29th* of July, 1848, expressing your opinion that the time was now come when the Colony might properly receive representative institutions, and transmitting to me the minutes drawn up at your desire by the chief officers of your Government in explanation of their views as to the manner in which this change might be effected, I advised Her Majesty to refer these papers for the consideration of a Committee of her Privy Council. That Committee, after very mature deliberation, presented to the Queen a report which Her Majesty was pleased to approve, stating very fully their views as to the manner in which it would be proper to constitute a representative Legislature for the Cape of Good Hope. In this report it was pointed out by the Committee, that while they were able from the information before them to form an opinion as to the general nature of the form of government which it would be expedient to establish in the Colony, it was impossible, from the

* *Vide* Correspondence relative to the establishment of a Representative Assembly at the Cape, presented to Parliament by Her Majesty's Command, 5th February, 1850, page 3.

want of statistical information, and of a sufficiently accurate knowledge of various local circumstances, that the details of any measure for carrying their views into effect should be arranged in this country; and they accordingly recommended that letters patent should be issued, by which the main and leading provisions of the Constitution to be granted to the Colony should be determined, while the duty should be imposed upon the existing local Legislature, of filling up the outline so traced out, and settling by Ordinances which were to be passed, subject to Her Majesty's confirmation, the various details which would require to be provided for, before the new institutions could be brought into operation.

" In my Despatch of the 31st of January of the present year* I forwarded to you a copy of this Report, at the same time instructing you immediately to take such steps, by collecting information and considering the various points referred to you, as might enable you with the least possible delay, on the receipt of the letters patent, to propose to the Legislative Council the Ordinances which it was requisite to pass. The letters patent were prepared, and as soon as they were completed by going through the proper legal formalities, they were transmitted to you in my Despatch of the 29th of May†. When the first of these Despatches reached you, the Legislative Council still remained incomplete, in consequence of the resignation of their seats in it by all the unofficial members except one, in July, 1849. You informed me by your Despatch of the 17th of May,

---

* *Vide* Correspondence relative to the establishment of a Representative Assembly at the Cape of Good Hope, presented to Parliament by Her Majesty's Command, 5th February, 1850, page 100.

† *Vide* Further Correspondence presented to Parliament by Her Majesty's Command, 28th June, 1850, page 3.

that you intended to fill the vacant seats, by calling upon the various Municipalities and District Road Boards throughout the Colony, to furnish you with the names of the persons whom they might wish to have appointed, selecting for appointment from among those so recommended to you 'the five gentlemen willing to serve who should appear best entitled to the confidence of the several classes and districts composing the entire Colony.' On the 14th of August you reported to me, that, in accordance with your intention thus expressed, you had provisionally appointed to the vacant seats in the Legislative Council the five gentlemen whom you regarded as entitled, under the terms of your notice, to be selected from those whose names had been returned to you.

"Though the step you had thus taken was one of a very unusual character, and in strictness you had no authority to divest yourself of the responsibility imposed upon you by your commission and instructions, of selecting upon your own judgement the persons to be provisionally appointed to fill vacancies in the Legislative Council; and though it was certainly a very irregular proceeding that you should have taken upon yourself to give to that body, which had hitherto been nominated by Her Majesty's authority, a representative character, by calling upon the Colonists to elect and recommend to you the persons to be appointed; still, having regard to all the circumstances of the case, I did not disapprove of the course you had adopted, and of your having endeavoured to obtain the assistance of persons having the confidence of the inhabitants of the Cape in deciding upon the measures which should be taken, in order to give effect to Her Majesty's gracious intention of conferring upon them representative institutions.

"The result however of the mode of proceeding you

adopted has not answered your expectation; and I learn by your present Despatch, that four out of five persons whom you had thus provisionally nominated members of the Legislative Council have resigned their seats, before any real business had been done. From a statement published by these gentlemen of their reasons for having thus acted, it appears they have resigned their seats in the Legislative Council because a majority of that body differed from them as to the propriety of the Legislative Council's proceeding with any other business, except that of framing and passing the Ordinance which is required to give effect to the letters patent of the 23rd of May*. If these gentlemen entertained the opinion that no other business but that of settling the Constitution of the future Legislature could properly be undertaken by that which now exists, I am at a loss to understand why this objection was not raised at an earlier period, or indeed why it was that they accepted at all the seats which you offered to them in the Legislative Council. In Her Majesty's letters patent which were published by you for general information, it is distinctly provided that the existing Legislature should continue in the exercise of all its functions, until the first writs should be issued for the election of the new Parliament, which is to be summoned as soon as the necessary arrangements for that purpose can be completed. It was with a full knowledge of this provision of the letters patent that the members who have now retired accepted their seats in the Legislative Council, and were sworn in, as I believe is the usual practice, faithfully to perform the duties of the trust they had accepted. Nor does any objection to the transaction

* *Vide* Further Papers relative to Representative Assembly at the Cape of Good Hope, presented by Her Majesty's Command, June 28, 1850, p. 3.

of ordinary business appear to have been suggested by the
gentlemen by whom it was afterwards advanced, either at
the first meeting of the Legislative Council, when you laid
before it a Minute clearly implying that some other subjects besides the Ordinance for regulating the election of
the new Parliament would be brought before it, or when
you laid on the table your Minutes of the 10th of September, pointing out various important topics which required its attention.

" It seems clear, therefore, that the objection which was
raised to the transaction of any business by the Legislative
Council, except that which formed the special and most
important object of its meeting, had not occurred even to
the gentlemen who have put it forward as the ground for
their resignation of their seats, only a few days previously ;
and I must add that, upon attentively considering the proceedings which ensued when this objection was urged, they
seem to me clearly to prove that it was not one upon which
there was any real ground for insisting.   I find that after
the resolution moved by Sir A. Stockenstrom had been
rejected by a majority of the Council, another was moved
by the Attorney-General, for the purpose of clearly mark-
ing what were the views of the majority, in which it was
stated, ' that in the opinion of the Council it is indispensably necessary that the consideration of the annual estimates should be proceeded with, and that, with regard to
all other matters, their being taken into consideration should
depend upon their peculiar nature, as admitting or not
admitting of delay.'   The terms of this resolution (which
was carried by the same majority of 8 to 4, which had
rejected that of Sir A. Stockenstrom) describe precisely
that line of conduct which I consider it to have been the
duty of the Legislative Council to have adopted.

" It was clearly desirable that the important business for which the Legislature had been principally summoned should be proceeded with as expeditiously as was consistent with due deliberation ; and that all matters which would admit of being postponed without serious inconvenience, should be left to the consideration of the new Parliament which was shortly to be assembled ; but, on the other hand, there can be no subject on which mature deliberation is more obviously necessary, than that of the various arrangements to be made in establishing a representative system of government. It would therefore have been in the highest degree improper that an Ordinance to be passed for this purpose should be hurried through the Legislature ; and as by the terms of the letters patent it would not, when passed, come into force until it had been submitted to and confirmed by Her Majesty, it was impossible that, while this measure was in progress, all the ordinary business of the Colony should be suspended ; consequently, the resolution of the Attorney-General, which confined the business to be transacted to the consideration of the annual estimates, and of matters too urgent to admit of delay, was in strict comformity with the terms of the letters latent and with the views of Her Majesty's Government.

" Nor is this all. In considering these transactions it must be borne in mind that, up to a very recent period, it had been the general opinion of those whose duty it had been to consider the subject, that the state of society in the extensive territory included within the boundaries of the Cape Colony, was not yet such as to render it expedient that any form of representative Legislature should be created in this part of the British dominions, or that the Crown should divest itself of any portion of the power both executive and legislative which it has hitherto exercised there without any limitation, except that of the responsibility of the advisers of the Crown to the Imperial Parliament. Yet, though this had been the opinion hitherto entertained, Her Majesty had now been advised, and had been graciously pleased to approve of that advice, freely to concede to the inhabitants of the Cape, representative government in its most complete form, granting to them the right, which is not at present enjoyed by any other British Colony, of electing not only the members of the House of Assembly, but those also of the second branch of the Legislature, who are everywhere else nominated by the Crown. Further still. By the Act of the Governor, which had not been disapproved by Her Majesty's Government, even before the arrangements for calling together the new Parliament could be completed, the inhabitants of the Colony had been practically allowed to select a large proportion of the members of the Legislature, hitherto named, without any popular influence whatever, by the sole authority of the Crown. Yet, because under these circumstances a majority of the Legislative Council refused to act in direct opposition to the very authority by which they had been entrusted with the powers committed to them, and determined that they would proceed with that ordinary business which it was necessary to transact to prevent the affairs of the Colony from falling into confusion, four out of five members of the Legislative Council appointed by you on the recommendation of the inhabitants have thought fit to resign their seats in that body, and thus to interrupt the progress of the measure by which the power of legislation was for the future to have been made over to a Parliament elected by the people, instead of being exercised by the Crown through its nominees.

" If the result of this proceeding on their part should be to postpone for some months the time when the Colonists shall enter upon the enjoyment of those privileges, which have been so freely and ungrudgingly offered to them by the Crown, her Majesty's servants feel that the responsibility for the delay will rest not with them, but with those who have met in so different a spirit from that in which it was tendered, the boon which was held out for their acceptance. We have been earnestly desirous that a representative Legislature should be established as soon as possible at the Cape, but the accomplishment of this object has been thwarted for a time (I trust only for a time) by those who have misused the confidence placed in them by the inhabitants of the Colony.

" With regard to the course taken by yourself in consequence of the difficulty in which you were placed by the resignation of the four members who retired from the Legislative Council, I cannot convey to you the final judgement of Her Majesty's Government in the absence of the fuller information which I am led to expect; but I must not conceal from you that I am altogether unable to understand, from that which has already reached me, your reasons for having considered it necessary to interrupt the sittings of the Legislative Council on account of the resignation of four of its members. What was the obstacle to your making new appointments, or proceeding with the remaining members to consider and to pass the Ordinance for completing the Constitution—though it seems to have been considered insurmountable by your Executive Council as well as by yourself—I am entirely at a loss to conjecture; and you have not explained this, either in your Despatch or in the announcement of your intentions published in the Government Gazette. When on a previous occasion, in July, 1849, you reported to me that the Legislative Council had been virtually dissolved by the resignation of some of its members, I inferred that the same intimidation which had prevented a gentleman, whom you had provisionally appointed to fill one of the vacancies so created, from retaining the seat which he had accepted, had been successfully exerted to prevent your collecting a quorum of the Legislative Council legally competent to act.   Assuming this to have been the case, and having regard to the very peculiar difficulties of your position at that time, I abstained from expressing any disapprobation of your course in allowing the functions of the Legislative Council to be suspended, though even then I was very far from being satisfied that a more decided line of conduct would not have been the right one.

" But in the present case the reasons, such as they were, that led you to acquiesce in having the functions of the Legislative Council placed in abeyance in 1849, certainly did not exist.   In addition to the five official members, two of the unofficial members were willing to continue their services, and have placed upon record, in a very able paper, the reasons which led them to concur with their official colleagues in the vote for proceeding with the general business of the Colony.   As six Members form a quorum of the Legislative Council legally competent to act, I cannot see therefore why its sittings should have been interrupted, even assuming—which is not stated—that you found it impossible to make any satisfactory arrangement for filling up the vacant seats by fresh nominations.   No intimidation is alleged to have been attempted ; but if it had been so, as I gather from your Despatch that the obstruction to your proceedings was mainly the work of a party at Cape Town, there would have been an obvious and easy mode of defeating such an attempt, by removing the place of meeting to Graham's Town, and filling up the vacant seats by appointing to them gentlemen resident in that division of the Colony.

" For your further proceedings I find it still more difficult to account. It appears, from the Government Gazettes which you have transmitted to me, that, having suspended the sittings of the Legislative Council as such, you formed the remaining members of it into a Board of Commissioners, whom you instructed to report to you their views with regard to the Constitution which ought to be established in the Colony; and having obtained from them a report, you caused it to be published for general information, at the same time inviting all persons who might either approve or dissent from the conclusions of the Commissioners to communicate their opinions to you in Petitions, which you undertook to forward to the Secretary of State. These proceedings are regarded by Her Majesty's Government as objectionable and injudicious, and calculated to create and to keep up a most mischievous agitation on the subject of the future Constitution of the Colony.

" Such is the view adopted by Her Majesty's Government of the recent transactions at the Cape, from the information now before us : and although, as I have said, this view is on certain points liable to be altered by the further explanations I may receive from you, and I am not therefore able to give you final and positive instructions as to the course which you are now to adopt, yet, as it may obviate considerable delay in a case where delay may be very injurious, I will now proceed at once to give you such directions as to the line of conduct which you are to pursue, as would be required on the assumption that your future Despatches will contain nothing to alter the judgement which has been formed by Her Majesty's Government on those already received ; at the same time informing you that these instructions are only given conditionally, and are not to be acted upon if you should be aware that there is anything in your Despatches, of a date subsequent to those which have already reached me, which is calculated to change the views which have been formed from these.

" Judging, then, of the case as it now appears to me, I am not prepared to advise Her Majesty, in consequence of the proceedings which have taken place at the Cape, to alter the mode of proceeding in establishing Representative Institutions in the Colony, which havebeen adopted on mature deliberation, and for that purpose to revoke the letters patent under the Great Seal of the United Kingdom which have been transmitted to you.   Hence, as these letters patent require that Ordinances should be passed by the existing Legislative Council, to regulate the various matters connected with the proposed change in the Constitution, it will be your duty to call upon that body to consider and pass such Ordinances accordingly. These Ordinances, when passed, it will be necessary for you to transmit to me for Her Majesty's approval, before they can come into operation; and, in the meantime, you will have to call upon the existing Legislative Council to provide for the public service by voting the Estimates for the year, and also to sanction the expenditure which you have thought yourself compelled to incur without having obtained for it the usual Legislative authority.   Such other subjects as may be urgent you will also call upon the existing Legislature to deal with, in such manner as the interest of the Colony may require, but all important questions which can, without serious public inconvenience, be reserved for the consideration of the new Parliament, undoubtedly ought to be so.

" With regard to the manner in which the new Parliament is to be constituted, so wide a discretion has been left to the existing Legislative Council, that I am aware of only one particular in which the arrangements proposed by the remaining members of that body, in the Report they agreed to as Commissioners, might not have been provided for by the Ordinances which you were empowered to pass. The letters patent require that the Chief Justice shall be *ex officio* Speaker of the Legislative Council which is to constitute the second branch of the new Parliament, and to this the Commissioners object, on the ground that the Chief Justice ought not to mix in Colonial politics, and that his duties as a member of the Legislative Council would be inconsistent with his judicial character. I cannot agree with the Commissioners in this opinion. In this country, not only does the Lord Chancellor preside, but it has also long been customary for persons holding other high judicial offices to sit in the House of Lords, and without inconveniently mixing themselves in party contests, or compromising their judicial character, to afford the most valuable assistance to that branch of the Legislature in the discharge of its duties. I see no reason to doubt that the Chief Justice of the Cape of Good Hope might equally, as Speaker of the Legislative Council, maintain a dignified neutrality in party contests, and at the same time, from his legal knowledge and experience, be enabled to give on many occasions very useful advice and information to the Body over which he presided.

" For these reasons I differ from the Commissioners upon the point in question; and though it is not in itself of very great importance, or one upon which I think there would be any occasion for refusing to consent to an alteration in the measure as originally proposed, which should appear to be generally desired by the inhabitants of the

Cape, I am not prepared at this moment to advise Her Majesty to make any change in the letters patent which have been transmitted to you. After what has occurred, I consider it to be indispensable that in the first instance the authority of the Crown should be maintained, by carrying into effect the grant of Representative Institutions to the Cape, in the manner which Her Majesty has prescribed. Hereafter, when a freely elected Parliament shall have met, any proposals for amending these institutions which may emanate from its authority, and which may be submitted to Her Majesty in a becoming manner, would no doubt be favourably received, and would meet with the utmost consideration. And I am the more disposed to regard any immediate change of the letters patent as inexpedient, because the frequent alterations in instruments of such high authority as Charters or Letters-patent under the the Great Seal of the United Kingdom are manifestly inconvenient; and the probability is that this is not the only change in the proposed arrangement which will be suggested by experience when the new Parliament shall have been brought into operation.

" You will doubtless recollect that the Committee of Her Majesty's Privy Council, of which the Report has been transmitted to you, did not come to the conclusion that one Legislature only should be established for the whole Colony without much hesitation, and chiefly in deference to the strongly expressed and unanimous opinion of the Judges and Officers of your Government, whose minutes on the proposed establishment of Representative Government you transmitted to me. Against the concurrent opinion of gentlemen possessing so much local knowledge, as well as experience and ability, it was not considered expedient by the Committee to recommend a division of the

Colony; but in abstaining from doing so, they pointed out the inconvenience which was to be expected from the opposite arrangement, and the probability that it would require hereafter to be reconsidered. I find that the reasons for anticipating such a necessity, are now even stronger than they then were, and it is impossible to read the statement which the two members of the Legislative Council, who may be considered as representing the Eastern division of the Colony, have published in the Government Gazette of the 3rd of October, of their objections to allowing the whole power of Legislation for the entire Colony to be exercised by a Legislature sitting at Cape Town, without being compelled to recognize the force of these objections. Hence, though the difficulty of dividing the Colony, and at the same time providing for the co-operation of the two divisions upon matters which are of common interest, would be great, the subject is one which will, I think, require to be considered, when, after the new Parliament has been brought into operation, it can be dealt with on the spot by persons possessing accurate local knowledge, and entitled to the confidence of the people as their representatives.

" Except with regard to the exclusion of the Chief Justice from the Legislative Council, there is nothing recommended by the remaining members of that body which, so far as I am aware, might not have been lawfully introduced into the Ordinances they were called upon to pass. But, on some points, the deviations they propose from the arrangements recommended by the Committee of Privy Council appear to me to be injudicious, and on one I certainly could not advise Her Majesty to sanction the desired departure from these arrangements. I refer to the opinion expressed by the members of the Legislative Council against

any limitation of the power of the new Legislature over
the whole expenditure of the Colony. Upon this subject
it does not appear to me that the members of the Legislative Council have quite clearly understood the recommendation of the Committee of Privy Council. That Committee, in their report, have not advised that there should
be any portion of the Colonial expenditure exempt from
liability to revision by the authority of the Legislature. In
general, on the first establishment of Representative Government in a Colony, it has been considered expedient to
reserve a Civil List, over which the Legislature should have
either no power, or an authority limited by very strict conditions. Such was the course pursued by Parliament in
the New South Wales Act of 1842, and in the Act for the
Union of the two provinces of Upper and Lower Canada in
1840. But this was not proposed with regard to the Cape
of Good Hope; all that was recommended with reference
to that Colony was, that the fixed establishment should
be provided for by permanent laws, precisely in the same
manner as a very large proportion of the civil expenditure
of this country is charged on the Consolidated Fund by
permanent Acts of Parliament, which can only be altered
with the concurrence of all branches of the Legislature.

" This arrangement was recommended on the ground
that it would be highly inexpedient, more especially on the
first establishment of representative institutions in a Colony
which has not hitherto possessed them, that the various
items of expenditure of the fixed establishment should become the subject of annual discussion in voting the estimates; but it was distinctly explained, that it was by no
means intended that the power thus vested in the Crown
should be used to resist any fair and legitimate reductions
of expenditure which might be proposed by the Legisla-

ture. The same principle was introduced by Her Majesty's Government into the Bill for the better government of the Australian Colonies, which was submitted to Parliament during the last Session, and, having obtained the sanction of Parliament, is now embodied in the Act which has been passed.

" In transmitting that Act to the Governors of those Colonies, I have explained in the following terms the views of Her Majesty's Government with regard to the manner in which the power reserved to the Crown on this subject ought to be employed.

" ' All other salaries, except those of the Governor and Judges, are placed by Parliament under the ordinary control of the Legislature. With regard to the mode of exercising this control, you will however observe that reductions of fixed establishments, or of any expenditure provided for by permanent laws, can only be effected by Acts of the Legislature, which of course require the assent of the Crown, signified by yourself, and confirmed by Her Majesty ; but I wish you distinctly to understand, that there is no desire on the part of Her Majesty's Government to prevent prospective reductions of charges which, in the opinion of the Colonists, will safely admit of being diminished. The interests of existing office-holders must be protected, because they accepted those offices with expectations which cannot justly be disappointed. But subject to these interests, there is no objection to the Legislature fixing whatever scale of emoluments they may think fit for public servants to be hereafter appointed. I should, for my own part, consider it highly injudicious to reduce the salary of an office, so as to render it no longer an object of ambition to men of ability and of respectable station, but this is a matter in which the interests of the Colonists only are involved, as they will be the sufferers from any failure to provide adequate remuneration for those by whom the public service is carried on; the determination therefore of what is sufficient must be left to the Legislatures, with whom will rest the responsibility for the judicious exercise of the power.

" 'I consider it however absolutely essential that, whatever may be the rate of payment, the salaries of all the principal officers of the Government should, for the reasons stated in the Report of the Committee of the Privy Council, be permanently granted, that is, not voted from year to year, but provided for in the same manner as charges on the Consolidated Fund in this country by Acts, and therefore only susceptible of alteration by Acts of the Legislature, passed in the ordinary manner, with the consent of the Crown. You will therefore understand, that you are not at liberty to give the assent of the Crown to any Act which may be passed, reducing the salaries of those who are now in the public service, or rendering dependent on annual votes any of the charges now provided for by permanent appropriations. Any Acts of this sort you will reserve for the signification of Her Majesty's pleasure, unless you consider them so manifestly objectionable as to call for their rejection. Subject to this restriction, you are authorized to exercise your own judgement in giving or withholding your assent from Acts for the reduction of the fixed charges on the Colonial revenue.'

" Being firmly convinced that there can be no just ground of objection on the part of the Colonists, to the retention by the Crown of the power in question, with a view to its being thus exercised, believing it to be one which is absolutely essential for the safe working of Representative Government on its first introduction, and seeing that this conclusion has been deliberately sanctioned by Parliament during the last Session, I have to inform you that I cannot advise Her Majesty to give her sanction to any Ordinances which may be passed by the Legislative Council of the Cape for the purpose of introducing Representative Government, unless they include that permanent provision for the fixed charges of the Civil Government which has been recommended by the Committee of Privy Council; nor will you omit to observe that, among the charges which must thus be provided for, are those which are necessary for maintaining the existing arrangements with regard to the Border Tribes.

" None of the other points on which the members of the Legislative Council have proposed to deviate from the recommendations of the Committee of Privy Council, are so material as that which I have just noticed; and as Her Majesty has reserved to herself, by the letters patent, full power to amend any Ordinances which may be passed under their authority, it is not necessary that I should enter at length into these. I may however observe, that I think it would be highly injudicious, to allow the remuneration of the members of the Legislature to depend on the number of days it may have sat, since experience, I believe, fully confirms what it might have been concluded beforehand would be the objection to this arrangement, namely, that it has a tendency to encourage an unprofitable waste both of time and of the public money. I am also of opinion, that the mode proposed for regulating the election of the members of the Legislative Council is one much less likely to answer, than that suggested by the Committee of Privy Council, and will not be equally certain to secure their fair share of influence, to any party supported by a large minority of the electors; this is a consideration which is of great importance, especially with reference to the interests of the eastern division of the province.

"I purposely omit noticing some other points of less moment, and I have now only in conclusion to observe, that if you shall judge that there is nothing in the Despatches which you may have addressed to me after those which I have already received, which is calculated materially to alter the view which Her Majesty's Government now take of the transactions recently reported to us, you will consider the instructions contained in this Despatch as those upon which you are to act, and you will accordingly forthwith call together your Legislative Council in order to pass the Ordinances that are required from it; and I trust it is scarcely necessary to add, that Her Majesty expects that you will not fail, by the firm exercise of the ample power with which you are invested, to defeat all attempts (should any such be made, which I trust will not be the case) to thwart you in the execution of the duty assigned to you. If, on the contrary, you are convinced that there are circumstances and considerations which had not been under the notice of Her Majesty's Government when these instructions were framed, and which render them inapplicable, you will then be at liberty to wait for further directions; but you will, I am persuaded, understand the necessity of being very sure of the sufficiency of the grounds on which you act, if the last should be the course which you adopt.

"I have, etc.,

"(Signed) GREY.

"*Governor Sir H. G. Smith, Bart., etc.*"

E.

Copy of a Despatch from Earl Grey to Governor Sir H. G. Smith, Bart.

"*Downing-street, January 7*, 1851.

" SIR,

" I have already acknowledged Mr. Montagu's letter to Mr. Hawes, of the 24th of October, and I have expressed the satisfaction with which I have learned from the further letters from Colonel Mackinnon, which were enclosed in it, that all the uneasiness with respect to the tranquillity of British Kafraria had ceased.

" It is not enough, however, that this alarm should have passed away. Its occurrence points out the necessity of endeavouring to ascertain and to remove the causes of that discontent on the part of the chiefs, which seems to have been its origin. Though the statements furnished to you by Colonel Mackinnon afford satisfactory evidence that this feeling did not exist amongst the Kafir population generally, and that, owing to their experience of the beneficial effects of British rule in Kafraria, the great majority of these people showed little or no inclination to support the chiefs in any attempt to throw off subjection to British control, still it would be unsafe to presume that if the chiefs should continue to be dissatisfied with the state of things which has arisen, their followers may not hereafter be induced by their influence to join in an attempt to effect a change by violence. It is also certain that the relaxation which is now taking place of the ancient ties of dependence which bound the people to their chiefs, is attended with considerable inconvenience in other respects, besides its being calculated to create a discontent on the part of the latter, which is natural at all events, if not well founded.

" The difficulties now experienced in British Kafraria appear to be of the same character with those which are very generally found to arise from similar causes in a particular stage of the progress of barbarous tribes, when brought under the authority of a civilized power. The first effect of establishing such an authority is to put a stop to the injustice and tyranny almost universally exercised over savages by their chiefs, by enabling the population to appeal to the Government for protection against the wrongs which they may suffer. But it unfortunately happens that it is impossible to protect the people from acts of violence and injustice on the part of the chiefs, without gradually breaking down the authority of the latter for all purposes, and depriving them of the means of maintaining that social position in their tribes to which they have been accustomed.

" It is obvious that the effect of thus breaking down the authority of the chiefs, and lowering their social position, must be not only to create discontent among them, but also to impose upon the British Government the task of supplying the place of that authority which it has superseded in maintaining internal order among the tribes, and settling the various disputes amongst individuals which must inevitably arise. But this is a task which the British Government possesses no adequate means of efficiently performing, and I consider, therefore, that it is the wiser policy, instead of destroying whatever of social organization has hitherto existed among the savage tribes now brought under our control, to endeavour to maintain as much of it as possible, correcting the abuses and supplying the defects of the system. You will recollect that this is the policy which I directed you to pursue with regard to Natal in my Despatch

of the 10th December, 1847, and having recently had occasion to enter more fully into the subject in a Despatch
addressed to the Governor of the British Ports on the Gold
Coast, I cannot more clearly explain my views to you than
in the words I have used in writing to Sir W. Winniett,
which convey instructions not less applicable to Kafraria
than to Western Africa :—

" 'If I am correctly informed as to the state of society
which existed in this part of Africa before it was modified
by the influence of British power, the chiefs were enabled
to maintain their station and to live in the manner considered suitable to their rank, by means of exactions of a
very arbitrary character, and by the forced and gratuitous
services of their people. These sources of income could
not but fail with the establishment of a more regular system
of government, and it would be good policy to prevent the
discontent which this is calculated to excite in the chiefs,
and to give them a substantial interest in the maintenance
of the Protectorate, by allowing them, as a substitute for
what they have lost, salaries or emoluments sufficient for
their support in a style of living fully equal to that to which
they have been accustomed, the duty being imposed upon
them, in return, of acting as the executive officers of the
Government, in maintaining order and carrying the law
into effect.

" ' Great care should be taken to make the performance
of these duties the condition on which the proposed payments should be made, lest they should reduce those who
might receive them to the character of idle dependants on
the Government.

" 'I have said that the condition on which the chiefs
should receive these salaries ought to be that of maintaining the general regulations which may be established, and

enforcing order in their several districts. For this purpose they should have the assistance of a certain number of the inhabitants of each district, who (if this slight distinction were likely to afford any encouragement to their exertions) might be enrolled as constables, receiving some small annual fee for their trouble.

" ' The chiefs should not have the power of inflicting punishments for offences by their own authority; but should be required to bring the offenders to be dealt with by the nearest magistrate.

" ' To provide the funds necessary for making these payments, and meeting some other expenses for which provision will, I think, be required, it appears to be most advisable to have recourse to taxes on lands and houses, or perhaps to a poll-tax.

" ' The most convenient form of imposing a land-tax in a rude state of society, I believe to be that of requiring from all who cultivate the soil a tithe or some other fixed proportion of the produce, as their contribution towards the public expenditure. This is the mode of raising a revenue for public purposes, which seems to have been the first adopted by mankind in the earliest stages of civilization, and to have prevailed generally among all nations in the remotest periods of which we know anything from history, while in Asia it continues to the present day to be almost universal. It is also a mode of taxation which, in an early stage of civilization, when money is scarce, and when little capital has been invested in land, seems to be the least burdensome that can be had recourse to, though in a more advanced state of society it is the reverse. I am of opinion that the circumstances of the Gold Coast at the present moment, are precisely those in which the levy of tithes of the produce of the soil would afford the easiest and best means of raising from the people the means of providing for the expenditure which is necessary, in order to supply that want of a more effective system of administration which in the progress of improvement is beginning to be felt.

" ' The levy of tithes would have this further convenience, that they might be received by the chiefs, to whom they would perhaps afford a more suitable equivalent for their former exactions than a money payment, and from the tithes so received by them they might be required to remunerate the persons, whose employment, under the name of constables, to assist in enforcing the law I have already suggested.

" ' I should not, however, consider the imposition of tithes as expedient or even safe, unless it were guarded by giving to the cultivator a right of commuting the payment of tithes in kind for a money payment at a very low rate in proportion to the extent of land in cultivation. By giving the cultivator this right from the first, the danger of checking industry and improvement might be averted, while the facility of obtaining contributions in the first instance from men in a very barbarous condition, and among whom money is very scarce, would be retained.

" ' If the levy of tithes did not, after adequately paying the chiefs and their followers, afford a sufficient surplus for other necessary expenses, it might be expedient also to impose a house-tax, which ought to be very moderate in amount, and should be graduated on the principle of requiring all permanent inhabitants to pay something, while dwellings of greater value than the ordinary ones (if such there be) should be assessed at a somewhat higher rate. I believe that very moderate taxes of this description would act, for obvious reasons, rather as an encouragement to industry than the reverse, and that if it were explained to the population that these taxes were a substitute for the arbitrary exactions to which they were formerly subject, and also intended to promote objects in which they are greatly interested, they would be cheerfully submitted to.'

" I have, etc.

" (Signed)   GREY."

" *Governor Sir H. G. Smith, Bart.,*
    " *etc., etc., etc.*"

F.

Copy of a Despatch from Earl Grey to ·Governor Sir H. G. Smith, Bart.

"*Downing-street, November* 30, 1849.

" SIR,

" I have received your Despatches, Nos. 117 and 137, of the 17th and 31st of July, forwarding copies of a correspondence between yourself and the Lieut.-Governor of Natal, to the location of the natives in that district, and the collection of a revenue from by a Capitation Tax or Quitrent, and reporting that, under the circumstances represented to you by the local authorities at Natal, you had authorized the non-issue of the Proclamation recognizing native laws in the district, which was required by the Royal Instructions to the Lieutenant-Governor accompanying the letters patent establishing Legislative Council there.

" I have to convey to you my approval of your having authorized the suspension of the Proclamation, and I have now advised Her Majesty, for the reasons of policy assigned by the local authorities (without considering the question as to the supposed contradiction between the instruction and the Ordinance of 1845), to issue an additional instruction, revoking the clause of the Royal instructions relating to that subject.

" I have read, with great interest, the very able letters of Mr. Shepstone, the Diplomatic Agent, respecting the government of the native tribes : his views are, substantially, in accordance with my own, and I agree with him in thinking that the present state of Natal and of the Black population which has flocked there for our protection, affords a noble opportunity for the diffusion of Christianity and civilization, which it would be a disgrace to this Country to neglect.

" When I -was called upon, in 1846, to decide whether it was expedient to retain Natal as a British Colony, I stated my conviction that the withdrawal of British authority from the district would be followed by the speedy destruction of the Black population which had taken shelter there ; while, on the other hand, by taking proper measures for their control and protection under the Government, they might rapidly advance in civilization, and their improvement would exercise an important and beneficial influence to a great distance in the interior of Africa.

" These were the main objects to which I looked in the retention of Natal as a British Colony, not doubting that if these could be attained other advantages would follow in their train.

" I am fully sensible that the government of this large population, said to amount to upwards of 100,000 souls, is a task of extreme difficulty and of no small danger, but it is a task from which we cannot now shrink, as its abandonment could only be effected by means which would be revolting to humanity. It is gratifying, therefore, to learn, by the reports from the Local Government, that this large body of natives is not only amenable to British control, but generally desirous of it, and that Mr. Shepstone has obtained an ascendency over them, by his personal influence and by the energy and ability which he has shown in managing them.

" I am confident that, if proper means are taken to stimulate these people to exertion, and to direct their efforts, they may be made, without charge to this Country, to supply all that is necessary for their improvement; and that, by levying moderate taxes, sufficient means will be found of forming and conducting a Government for them.

" I am confirmed in this view by the success which you state has attended your measures for collecting quit-rents in the Fingoe locations, in the district of Victoria; and I approve, as a provisional measure, of the tax of 7s. a-year per hut, which the Natal Government have lately imposed on the natives. This tax will not be sufficient to meet all the expenses for which provision requires to be made ; but as the success of this policy entirely depends on the prudence with which such measures are enforced, the Local Government have, perhaps, acted wisely for the present in not fixing a higher rate. It may be regretted that some such tax was not imposed at an earlier date, as the rate might have been gradually increased, and by this time a revenue of some importance might have been raised.

" With reference to this subject of the taxation of the natives, I have been led by Mr. Shepstone's representations to consider, whether an important change in the mode of levying it might not be introduced with advantage, at least with regard to a large proportion of the native population. I understand Mr. Shepstone to state, that this native population consists at present of two classes,—of tribes settled in the district and living under their chiefs according to their usual form of government, and, in addition, of a very large number of families which have been compelled to take up their abode within the district by stress of war and other calamities, some of which have joined themselves to tribes, while others are not strictly dependent on any chief.

" With respect, at all events, to the first of these classes, namely, the tribes, it is possible that taxation may be more easily and justly levied in the shape of a tribute as due from the tribe, than of taxes as due from individuals. It is often the case with similar tribes (whether this is the case in Natal or not, is a point which I recommend to your investigation), that the individuals, at least of the lower classes within the tribe, possess, according to their notions, little or no property on which a tax could be levied, and that their land, crops, and cattle are regarded as appertaining to the tribe in general, so that each individual has only his customary share in the enjoyment of the produce. Now, in such instances it may well be worth investigation, whether the tax on persons might not be, as before said, commuted to a tribute, imposed on the tribe, for which the chiefs should be the responsible parties, and the property of the tribe the responsible fund. Any extortion or malversation on the part of the chiefs might be corrected by that general superintendence, which, according to the scheme I am now considering, is to be left to the Colonial Government, over the Native authorities.

" These chiefs, as I have termed them, to whom the administration of the native villages or communities and the levying of the tribute is thus entrusted, might be either such as are already recognized according to the native usage, whether hereditary or otherwise, or, where these fail, they might be appointed by the Colonial Government : ultimately, perhaps, they might be persons chosen by each community and approved of by the Government, which would be a first step towards admitting these people to a share in the management of their own affairs. If it were possible in this manner to appoint or to provide for the election of chiefs, the scheme of taxation or tribute, which I am now describing, might be extended, not to the tribes only, but to the natives generally.

" And the reducing of the taxes in this manner to simple assessments on land and cattle would have the further advantage of rendering it possible, ultimately, to establish one uniform system of taxation for natives and Europeans. Further : if the country were divided into districts, and each district charged with an assessment proportioned to the extent of occupied land and the number of stock pastured upon it, this natural advantage would be obtained, that all land on which no assessment was paid would be regarded as belonging to the Crown ; and thus the effect of those profuse grants, which there is reason to apprehend have been made, would be in part corrected.

" I consider it however of the highest importance that whatever is collected in this manner should be locally expended. Each district should be required to maintain a policeman or constable, with assistants if necessary : to provide sufficient roads ; to support a school and a dispensary or hospital, where every inhabitant should have the right to be treated gratuitously. This last I regard as an object of peculiar importance, as the experience of New

Zealand proves how greatly the establishment of public hospitals contributes to the improvement of an uncivilized race. It is obvious that all these expenses cannot be provided for at once: but by applying whatever revenue is collected by direct taxation to objects of local interest, the imposition of this burden would be rendered less unpalatable, while the general Government, being relieved from these charges, would probably find the revenue from indirect taxation sufficient to meet its necessary expenditure. To carry this system into effect, it would be necessary that there should be in each district an authority of a municipal character, but of course, in the first instance, of the simplest kind; and to this authority, under the superintendence of the Government, would be committed the duty of gradually creating these establishments.

" In the districts inhabited by Whites, this authority might, at first, consist only of a Mayor or Field Cornet (with perhaps an assessor or two), who should be allowed some very small annual salary for his trouble from the local taxes collected as above mentioned. It should be his duty with the assistance of his assessors (who would gradually grow into a District Council), to apportion the assessment among the inhabitants of the district.

" In the locations occupied by native tribes, a system of the same description, but adapted to their usages, might be introduced; and one great advantage of it would be, that the chiefs might act as the municipal officers, and might bear the same titles. This would be a step towards their gradual assimilation in sentiments and habits to the Whites, whose official designations they would thus enjoy. And the chiefs, if thus employed, as may perhaps be advisable, in the collection of any part of the local taxes, might be allowed a percentage on the amount so collected.

" I have in former Despatches stated my opinion, assuming that there is an assessment on cotton or land payable by natives as well as by Europeans, that the tax on cattle should be rated higher, in order to discourage the exclusive desire to possess that kind of property; that if the natives cannot pay their taxes in money, which they should be encouraged to do, they should be required to pay in labour or in kind, both being so rated as to make money payments preferable. To these might be added some very small poll-tax, if a poll-tax should be considered preferable to the general tribute payable by the tribe, which I have above suggested.

" The Commissioners reckoned that, in a location of 10,000 natives, 7000 would be of a taxable age, and that a poll-tax therefore of 3s. would produce £1050; but supposing a quit-rent likewise of £1, as in the case of the Fingoes, in Victoria, to be levied on half that number, there would be a further income of £3500, which alone would be sufficient to defray the ordinary expenses of management; and I, of course, assume that the amount, whether levied wholly by a poll-tax and quit-rent, or wholly or partly in the form of such a tribute as I have above suggested, would be the same.

" The taxes raised in each location (which should be levied quarterly or in advance) must, as I have said, be kept for local objects, and applied to the payment of the expenses of that particular location. It will be for the local Government to determine whether the chiefs should be made to assist in managing the expenditure, by entrusting to them this duty. Whenever they are qualified to perform it, the rudiments of municipal institutions would thus be created among them.

" The labour of the natives, when given in lieu of taxes,

might be applied to the formation of roads, and in the construction, in each location, of at least one village, built after the manner of Europeans, and of a market-place. This would enable the local Government to carry into effect the suggestions of Dr. Adams, the American Missionary, that a mission village should be established at each station, where those most advanced and desirous of benefiting by the privileges of the station may be encouraged to locate themselves. The Rev. Mr. Allison states, in a letter to the Lieutenant-Governor, that the natives under his care had built a village, after the manner of Europeans, thirty miles to the south of Pieter Maritzburg; and the Surveyor-General reports, that the sandstone, in the vicinity of that town, is an excellent building stone, and can be obtained in large masses; with these facilities, I should hope that the natives may be usefully employed.

" If the payment of taxes is made in kind, means will be afforded of giving rations to a native police, the expenses of which might be defrayed almost entirely by these means. I consider the extension of the native police as most important; and, indeed, as the first step towards the maintenance of order in the several locations.

" With respect to the whole of these connected suggestions as to taxation, but especially to that part of them which relates to the assessment of tribes, instead of individuals, towards this necessary local taxation, you will understand me to be anxious to prescribe rules only insofar as persons thoroughly acquainted with the natives and their usages, and especially Mr. Shepstone, the Superintendent, may, from their own experience and judgement, be satisfied that they are practicable. My object is to point out, for your guidance, those objects which appear to me most desirable and most advantageous on general principles, if they suit those peculiar circumstances of time and place, as to which I must place reliance on your opinion, and that of your ablest advisers.

" But before any taxes can be effectually enforced, it will be necessary that a registry should be made of the natives belonging to each location, and this cannot be done until permanent locations have been assigned to them. I regret that so much delay has occurred in taking this important step; but I am aware that difficulties have arisen from the undefined claims of the Boers throughout the district.

" One of the proposals made, in order apparently to meet these difficulties, is to establish a very limited number of locations, with a reduced territory for each, and to remove the rest of the natives beyond the Colonial boundary, still maintaining a control over them in the event of the chief, Faku, giving his consent to their settling on lands claimed by him. I cannot sanction a proposal to which there are so many objections. I am of opinion that permanent locations of sufficient extent should be established within the Colony; and that, in selecting the sites of these locations, sufficient intervals should be left between each of them for the spread of White settlements; each European emigrant would thus have it in his power to draw supplies of labour from the location in his more immediate proximity. I conceive that it would be no objection to this mode of proceeding, that it would be difficult or impossible to assign to the natives such locations of an extent sufficient for their support as a pastoral people, or at least as a people depending mainly for support on their flocks and herds. I regard it, on the contrary, as desirable that these people should be placed in circumstances in which they should find regular industry necessary for their subsistence.

" I am aware that in these latter recommendations, I am differing from yourself, and from some of the local authorities at Natal; but if the policy of isolating the natives should be adopted, it would too probably end, sooner or later, in their expulsion or extermination, when the European inhabitants should increase in numbers so as to require additional space. No Government would be strong enough to save them from this fate; and the experience of North America and Australia shows what is the result of endeavouring thus to isolate the barbarous tribes occupying lands which are to be settled by civilized men, while the opposite policy, pursued by the Government of New Zealand, holds out the hope at least of a result more consonant with feelings of humanity. The separation of the races is no doubt the policy which, in the first instance, presents the fewest difficulties and dangers, but it is necessary to look to the ultimate consequences of what is done.

" It is of the greatest importance that the locations of the natives should be most accurately defined, and their villages so arranged at different points of these locations, that they may be, as nearly as possible, equidistant from the settlements of the Europeans, so that, in course of time, the two races may, by their mutual wants, become amalgamated. Every encouragement should also be afforded to the younger natives to become servants in the families of the European settlers. In this intercourse, which would gradually become closer, the natives would derive benefit from example and instruction, which they could not otherwise obtain, while, on the other hand, the Government may avail themselves of the assistance of the Europeans, settled in the vicinity of the locations, in managing their local expenditure.

" I have fully explained, in another Despatch, my views

respecting the land claims of the Boers; but I must here remind you (as the subject is so closely connected with that now under consideration) that the late Governor West represented that the farms claimed by them were scattered, at wide intervals, over an extensive territory in such a manner, that the local Government scarcely knew what lands were to be considered as having absolutely reverted to the disposal of the Crown, while no sensible increase of the White population within the district had yet taken place; and a small number only of the Boers had taken possession of their farms in the division of Klip river.

" The effect therefore of keeping open these undefined claims, is to preclude the Crown from disposing of large tracts of land, suitable either for European emigrants or for the location of natives, and this is a serious evil which must be remedied. I cannot entertain a doubt that the extent and capabilities of Natal are amply sufficient, after satisfying the just claims of the Boers, to support large bodies of emigrants from this country, as well as the native population now settled there. It would appear, from the report of the Surveyor-General, that the area of the district is probably not less than 16,000 square miles,—that it is everywhere covered with vegetation,—that water abounds in every part,—and that the soil is, in all cases, well adapted for cultivation. And, in your proclamation of the 10th of February, 1848, you state, that in this vast district, there is space for a population of two millions.

" The officer administering the Government of Natal should therefore be instructed to take steps for immediately assigning, as above stated, to the several tribes, permanent locations of sufficient extent, and in sites to be selected on the principle which I have stated, of intermixing them with White settlements. When this has been done, a registry should be made of the natives in each location with as little delay as possible. The expense of making such a registry, with the assistance of the chiefs or other superior natives, cannot be very great, and the means of defraying it may be derived from the tax of 7s., which has already been imposed on each hut in the several kraals. I consider this measure as absolutely necessary with a view to regulating the taxation of the natives.

" With respect to the government of the locations, Mr. Shepstone remarks that, practically, the line of policy that has been pursued towards the natives is in accordance with the 8th clause of the Royal Instructions, with the exception that the former absolutism and supremacy of the chiefs are transferred to the Supreme Government; for that, in his capacity of diplomatic agent, he had administered to the natives, on behalf the Government, their own laws, through their chiefs where native agency existed, and directly where it did not; this ought clearly, for the present, to continue.

" But it is pointed out by Mr. Shepstone, that this system has been practically adopted without any proper legal authority, and that a very serious responsibility has thus been incurred by those by whom the management of the natives on this principle has been undertaken. It is important that this deficiency of authority should, as soon as possible, be supplied. With this view the proper course will be to propose to the Legislative Council of Natal the passing of an Ordinance qualifying the effect of the Ordinance of 1845, which, as Mr. Cloete points out, establishes the Roman-Dutch law in and for the district of Natal, by maintaining, as far as this can safely be done, the native habits and usages, either within certain defined local limits, or else in all transactions of the natives with each other.

In such an Ordinance the right of amending laws thus maintained in force, as from time to time may appear necessary or desirable, should, of course, be reserved.

" Any native who may have quitted his location to reside elsewhere as a farmer, labourer, or otherwise, would become amenable to the general law of the district; but he should not be allowed to leave the location without a pass, and I concur in Mr. Cloete's suggestion, that each adult male should be distinguished by a plate or medal, with the number of the station to which they may belong. Every encouragement should be given to the natives to clothe themselves, especially when resorting to the villages or markets, or when appearing before any Government officer : a common Jersey frock or shirt might suffice, and could be supplied at a very small cost. As soon as it can safely be done, a small fine should be imposed on those who should appear without such clothing in any of the towns or villages inhabited by Europeans.

" When you recently proclaimed Her Majesty's sovereignty over the tribes between the Orange and Vaal rivers, in which territory there existed both a population of emigrant Boers, and also of native tribes, you found it necessary to frame regulations similar to those which Mr. Shepstone considers requisite, in order to establish native usages in native locations, and Roman-Dutch law in the lands occupied by the Boers. Though these arrangements and the declaration of Her Majesty's sovereignty over this district have not yet been confirmed, I have furnished Mr. Pine, who is proceeding to undertake the administration of Natal as Lieut.-Governor, with a copy of the regulations, because he may find them serviceable by way of precedent and comparison. I must however call your attention to one point of comparison which is of some importance.

Mr. Shepstone's view is, that the laws of the natives should be administered by the Government 'through the agency of hereditary chiefs, and such other persons as it may be fit to appoint.' Whether Mr. Cloete concurs with him as to this, I do not exactly collect. By your regulations (Clause 13) you will observe, that natives, in their own locations, are to be governed by their own usages, subject only to the right of interference by the British Resident. Perhaps this regulation practically attains the same end with that suggested by Mr. Shepstone, although the wording is slightly different. And, if so, yours appears to me preferable, because it is better that the British Government should appear in the character of controller and rectifier of native usages, than of their actual administrator through chiefs as agents.

"I have stated to you in former Despatches my views in regard to the co-operation of the Missionaries in the improvement of the natives and the establishment of schools. I now only revert to the subject in order to state, that I attach the greatest importance to the principle of making these schools of an industrial character.

"Mr. Allison's account of the progress of his mission is highly interesting, and the local Government might apply to him to furnish native teachers for the locations. One or two agricultural instructors, European or native, might be employed to perambulate the locations, and to give practical instructions to the men working in the field; the women should be taught some employment at home, which would probably tend to their being gradually relieved from that heavy share of out-of-door labour which now falls upon them instead of on the men.

"The establishment of native dispensaries and hospitals, as I have already stated, would be highly useful and beneficial, the latter containing wards to serve as workhouses and houses of correction, to which vagrants and persons sentenced to short periods of confinement for petty offences might be committed.

"I would remark, in conclusion, that the Report of the Commissioners for locating the natives in 1847, the later Reports on the same subject by Mr. Cloete and Mr. Shepstone, and the regulations for the management of the Fingoes in Victoria, are so ably drawn up, and are substantially so entirely in accordance with my own views, that it is unnecessary for me to enter into any further details of the measures necessary for bringing the rude tribes in Natal into the condition of civilized communities; and I confidently trust that by the means which have been pointed out, and by the energy of the local Government, this great change may eventually be accomplished, and that, in course of time, its influence may be felt far and wide in the interior of Africa.

"I have, etc.,

"*Governor Sir H. G. Smith,*   (Signed)   GREY.
    "*etc., etc., etc.*"

THE END.